CANON LAW SOCIETY OF AMERICA

PROCEEDINGS OF THE SEVENTY-SIXTH ANNUAL CONVENTION

St. Louis, Misssouri
October 13-16, 2014

Canon Law Society of America

ISBN 978-1-932208-39-9
ISSN 0277-9889
SAN 237-6296

The Canon Law Society of America's programs and publications are designed solely to help canonists maintain their professional competence. In dealing with specific canonical matters, the canonist using Canon Law Society of America (CLSA) publications or orally conveyed information should also research original sources of authority.

The views and opinions expressed in this publication are those of the individual authors and do not represent the views of the CLSA, its Board of Governors, staff or members. The CLSA does not endorse the views or opinions expressed by the individual authors. The publisher and authors specifically disclaim any liability, loss or risk, personal or otherwise, which is incurred as consequence, directly or indirectly, of the use, reliance, or application of any of the contents of this publication.

Unless otherwise noted, all canons quoted are from the *Code of Canon Law, Latin-English Edition* (Washington, DC: Canon Law Society of America, 2012) and the *Code of Canons of the Eastern Churches, Latin-English Edition* (Washington, DC: Canon Law Society of America, 2002).

Printed in the United States of America.

Canon Law Society of America
Office of the Executive Coordinator
3025 Fourth Street, NE
The Hecker Center, Suite 111
Washington, DC 20017-1102

Table of Contents

FOREWORD

The Canon Law Society of America (CLSA) is pleased to present the Proceedings of the seventy-sixth annual convention held in St. Louis, Missouri, October 13-16, 2014. The CLSA annually publishes for its members, and others in the canonical community, the major addresses, seminars and reports presented at the annual meeting.

We are grateful to the presenters who provided their final texts in a timely fashion. Texts have been edited for consistency in conformity with the CLSA Style Sheet and Publication Guidelines including capitalization, use of footnotes, gender-inclusive language, and citation of canons. Included in this edition of *CLSA Proceedings* are the Tribunal Statistics collected from participating (arch) dioceses and (arch)eparchies along with a listing of the participants who attended the convention in St. Louis.

The CLSA, established on November 12, 1939 as a professional association dedicated to the promotion of both the study and the application of canon law in the Catholic Church today, numbers over 1,400 members who reside in the United States and 37 other counties. *CLSA Proceedings 76* (2014) should take its place among previous volumes as a professional resource. Additional copies of this volume may be purchased from the CLSA website: www.clsa.org.

For information on how to become a member of the CLSA, please visit the CLSA website (www.clsa.org) or contact the Office of the Executive Coordinator.

Reverend Roger H. Keeler
Executive Coordinator
Canon Law Society of America
3025 Fourth Street, NE
The Hecker Center, Suite 111
Washington, DC 20017-1102

Keynote Address

Christian Unity Fifty Years After Vatican II

Most Rev. Brian Farrell, LC, STD

Introduction

FIFTY YEARS ON A METAPHORICAL PLANE JOURNEY

Cardinal Koch, President of the Pontifical Council for promoting Christian Unity, has compared fifty years of ecumenism to an airplane journey: lots of preparation, then an ever faster race down the runway, and a powerful takeoff. After a while the plane reaches its cruising height and the journey settles into its routine. At that point you might even think the plane is not moving or moving very slowly. But you trust that the crew will eventually get you to your destination. The ecumenical journey is at that point today. Many people feel that not much is being achieved, no new ground is being broken, but we go forward trusting that the pilot, the Holy Spirit who has begun this journey with the Church, will bring it to fulfilment, in his way and in his time. Ecumenism is a question of faith; and faith demands hope.

The Council's Decree on Ecumenism needs to be seen in its wider context. There has never been a time when saintly figures and wise scholars were not concerned with the question of Church unity; but the twentieth century brought a new widespread awareness of the scandal of division among Christians. In the last century two major events occurred which had incalculable consequences for the search for Christian unity: the foundation of the World Council of Churches (WCC) in 1948 and the Second Vatican Council in the 1960's. Through and with the Council, Pope John XXIII and Pope Paul VI launched the Catholic Church *irrevocably* on the path of dialogue with the world in which the Church lives: with all men and women of good will (see *Gaudium et Spes* and other documents), with all religious traditions (see *Nostra Aetate*, *Ad Gentes*), and especially with all Christ's followers (*Lumen Gentium, Orientalium Ecclesiarum, Unitatis Redintegratio*). In this way the great figures of the Council saved our Church from a dangerous fate in-waiting: the danger of living in a walled fortress, in an ever diminishing Catholic ghetto, easily expelled from the public square by the dominant culture of the day.

Unitatis Redintegratio is a lasting jewel from the Council's treasury, having a continuing transforming effect on the Catholic Church's relationship to other Churches and Communions. The Decree on Ecumenism took account of the WCC's vision of the ecumenical movement as it was formulated in the New Delhi Assembly of 1961. It did not advocate a new, separate, Catholic ecumenism but recognized that the already existing movement, which had begun outside the Catholic Church, was itself "fostered by the grace of the Holy Spirit" (*UR*,1). In this way the Council brought the Catholic Church decisively into the search for Christian unity that was already stirring the consciences of Christians in many Churches and Communions.

The ecumenical journey of the last fifty years has enabled Catholics to understand better who we are as Church. By engaging in serious study and discussion with our ecumenical partners we understand better the strengths and weaknesses in our own Church. We give thanks to God for all that we are as Catholics, but we also realize how imperfect we are, not just in the life of fellowship with God through grace, but even in our institutional realization of Christ's intentions for his Church. And this is an indispensable principle and attitude of ecumenical dialogue: if we have nothing to learn, we have nothing to offer.

At this point I should say what I intend to do in this conversation. I am not so much a scholar of ecumenism as a practitioner, so I will try to tell you, from my experience, how things were fifty years ago, how they are today, and where is there hope of a better future.

I. The way we were: Cappello, Congar and Maximos IV Saigh

To understand where we are, we need to know where we are coming from. We Catholics did not always recognize that we had much in common with other Christians. Most of the bishops who arrived in Rome for the Council in 1962 held very definite views on Catholic *exclusivism*. So, we need to recognize the enormity of the change of perspective that the Council achieved. One example of that change, regarding the admission of other Christians to Catholic sacraments: how did we move from the "haud licitum est" of canon 731 of the 1917 code to canon 844 of the present code, based on *UR* 8: "Witness to the unity of the Church very generally forbids common worship, but the grace to be had from it sometimes commends this practice"?

A new way of looking at other Christians took shape in the consciousness of the Council, which I will try to crystallize in three brief quotations:

1. In 1961, when preparations for the Council were reaching a feverish point in Rome, with a host of commissions studying the vast material coming from the observations of the world's bishops, universities, theological faculties and the Roman Curia, the Gregorian university held a routine editorial presentation of the umpteenth edition of Father Felice Cappello's well-known manual, the *Tractatus canonico-moralis de Sacramentis*. Probably very few people noticed, except the poor students

who had to buy the book and study it! Generations of priests and bishops had studied that manual, and based their approach to non-Catholic Christians on it and on similar writings. So, what did Cappello have to say? He said that heretics (read Protestants) and schismatics (read Orthodox) even if they are good people and properly disposed, cannot be admitted to the Eucharist and to the other sacraments "because in no way do they belong to the Church." This was the prevailing view. If you did not belong, the Church had nothing to share with you.

2. Move on to the next year, 1962, the first session of the Council, a time of an open clash of ideas. For Friday, November 30, in Yves Congar's *Diary of the Council,* we read that that very morning he had a rather testy meeting with Cardinal Ottaviani. He writes: "I realize that I am once more and always under suspicion. This will not stop me from working. They don't like my work because, and they know it, it aims at re-circulating certain ideas that for four hundred years, but especially in the last hundred, they have tried in every way to eliminate. But this is my vocation and my service, in the name of the Gospel and of Tradition."

   But what are the ideas that Congar is talking about?

3. A year later, in 1963, during the second session of the Council, *Lumen Gentium* was discussed at length and then the Bishops moved on to the draft of *UR*. At a certain point the Melchite Patriarch, Maximos IV Saigh, stood up to say: "In the name of many other Eastern bishops, we especially wish to express publicly our joy – and, we are certain, the joy of our Orthodox brethren – to finally see a first presence, as yet timid, but frank and official, of a true theology of the Church, which has never ceased to be that of the whole Eastern tradition: the Church is above all a mystery of communion: the communion of the Father and of the Son and of the Holy Spirit, that flows from the resurrection of Christ and is endlessly spread to all the members of the new people of God by the life-giving Spirit through the Divine Liturgy" (*Acta Synodalia Sacrosancti Concilii Oecumenici Vaticani II*, II/5, 543).

A communion flowing from the intimate life of the Trinity; not a 'perfect society' modeled on Roman law. Commentators at the time saw this development in Catholic ecclesiology as a moving beyond the juridical ecclesiology of the Counter-reformation and a return to a more traditional, patristic, sacramentally-based ecclesiology.[1] The miracle that produced *Lumen Gentium* and *Unitatis Redintegratio* is that in three short years the whole body of the bishops moved from Cappello's "they are simply outside the Church" to the recognition that in the "communio sanctorum" – communion in what is holy – the Spirit of Christ is operative in the Churches and Communities not in full communion with

1 Cf. R. Aubert, *Irènikon*, 37 (1964) 365.

the Catholic Church, which "have by no means been deprived of significance and importance in the mystery of salvation."[2] It is not that outside the Catholic Church there is an ecclesial wasteland. All the baptized in their communities have, to some degree, a real sharing in the "elements or endowments which together go to build up and give life to the Church itself."[3] This understructure of our Catholic commitment to ecumenism may seem like a 'given' to us now, to be taken for granted, but fifty years ago it appeared as an almost revolutionary breakthrough. Looking at other Christians, the first thing we are now expected to see is not our division and separation, but the communion of all rooted in our common baptism into Christ. Only in that fundamental communion can we then speak about our differences. As a result, Catholics had to find a new language and a new relationship to those Christians who are not in full communion with the Catholic Church. That was the vision and excitement of the preparations and take-off of Cardinal Koch's metaphorical ecumenical plane journey.

II. So, how far have we come since then?

Today grass-roots ecumenism is everywhere, in parishes and dioceses. But that is not my theme; I can best speak to you about the search for Christian unity from the perspective of the Pontifical Council for promoting Christian Unity. The view from via della Conciliazione is general, global, international.

The Pontifical Council for promoting Christian Unity

The PCPCU has two distinct and independent sections: Eastern and Western. The Western section deals with the Communities that have separated from the Latin Church in the second millennium. The Eastern section deals with the Churches of the first millennium – the Eastern Orthodox Churches of the Byzantine, Slav and Syrian traditions; the Oriental Orthodox Churches: Armenian, Coptic, Ethiopian, Syriac and Malankara Churches, and the small but resilient Assyrian Church of the East. Events in North Africa and the Middle East have recently brought these ancient Christian Churches into the limelight, unfortunately for the wrong reason: their people are the victims of terrible suffering and persecution.

The Oriental-Orthodox

Between 1980 and 1990, Pope St. John Paul II was able to sign various Common Declarations with Heads of the Oriental Orthodox Churches that basically settled the Christological controversies going back to the Council of Chalcedon (451 A.D.), and, in the case of the Assyrian Church, to the Council of Ephesus (381 A.D.). With some of these Churches we have agreements permitting a certain degree of intercommunion. This is especially important in the Middle East

2 *UR*, no. 4.

3 Ibid.

where Catholics and Orthodox often live side by side in the same family or same village.

In 2003, the bilateral dialogues with these Churches became a dialogue between the Catholic Church and the Oriental Orthodox Churches all together as a family of Churches. This new phase of dialogue is proceeding with promising results. The Commission has produced a document called: "*Nature, Constitution and Mission of the Church,*" now awaiting a response from the various Church authorities. It is inspiring to think that with these Churches of apostolic origin, after a separation of 1,500 years, we have the same doctrines and the same basic ecclesial structure, and that these Churches are now fully part of the movement towards the restoration of unity. Progress can only be slow, given the huge differences in culture and mentality. But in the last two years the pace of *rapproachment* has quickened, under new, more open and better educated Patriarchs in various of these Churches.

The Eastern Orthodox

As you well know, the break between Constantinople and Rome was at heart a breakdown of trust, the result of a long process of differentiation and mutual alienation. What has been happening since Pope Paul VI and Patriarch Athenagoras met in Jerusalem in 1964, exactly fifty years ago, is a process in the opposite direction: a journey of reconciliation and healing of memories. The journey had a hugely symbolic start on the second-last day of the Council in the banishment from the Churches' memory of the mutual excommunications of 1054. It continues in the mutual visits, the ongoing correspondence, the many forms of international and local cooperation between Catholics and Orthodox, to the point that Pope Benedict in a public Angelus prayer (June 29, 2007) could state that with the Orthodox Churches we are already in almost complete communion.

So what are the differences that still keep us apart? After thirty-five years of very substantial theological dialogue we have reached the heart of the matter: the question of the primacy of the Bishop of Rome over the universal Church. This has been the theme of the dialogue since 2006, in two phases:

1. A first phase ended with the 'Ravenna document' (2007) entitled: "Ecclesiological and Canonical Consequences of the Sacramental Nature of the Church: Ecclesial Communion, Conciliarity and Authority." For the first time, Catholics and Orthodox **together** agreed that there are three levels in the ontological structure of the Church: local, intermediate or regional, and universal. At each level there must be synodality and primacy: no primacy without a synod, no synod without its primate. At the universal level the *Protos* is the bishop of Rome according to the ancient *taxis* (order) of the Churches.

> 41. Both sides agree that this canonical *taxis* was recognised by all in the era of the undivided Church. Further, they agree that Rome, as the Church that "presides in love" according to the phrase of St Ignatius of Antioch (To the Romans, Prologue), occupied the first place in the *taxis*, and that the bishop of Rome was therefore the *protos* among the patriarchs. They disagree, however, on the interpretation of the historical evidence from this era regarding the prerogatives of the bishop of Rome as *protos*, a matter that was already understood in different ways in the first millennium.

On the one hand, this was a huge and unexpected achievement; but on the other hand, the most difficult of all questions landed on the ecumenical agenda: what authority would the Bishop of Rome as the "first bishop" have in a reunited Church, and how would that authority be exercised?

2. This question became the subject of the current phase of dialogue: the "Role of the Bishop of Rome in the Communion of the Church in the First Millennium." The idea being that the next, future, phase would deal with the Second Millennium, when the Churches fell out of communion and the West underwent an ecclesiological and canonical development which the East has not known. The Orthodox world also changed significantly in the second millennium, going from the original four patriarchates to the present fourteen autocephalous churches, which have adopted various models of primacy and synodality. All of this will need to be examined.

The current difficult phase has already lasted seven years, and after various attempts, and failures, we are still trying to write an agreed working text. The latest meeting of the Commission, in Amman, Jordan, in September 2014, rejected the draft document on primacy and synodality which it was supposed to discuss. It then set out to write a new document, which in turn was rejected. The hope is now that a new working document can be prepared, to be discussed and approved by the Coordinating Committee, and then presented to the next Plenary session of the Commission, maybe not till 2017.

Frankly, we need a bit of a miracle if the theological dialogue is to overcome the present impasse. Our Pontifical Council will continue to promote the foundational theological studies needed to offset the Orthodox fear of a universal primacy that should not be measured in terms of subordination, but of spiritual and ecclesial *koinonia* and solidarity.

DIALOGUE IN THE WEST

The historical Protestant Churches

Fifty years of bilateral dialogues with the Anglican and mainline Protestant Churches have shown that, to a large degree, we still share the fundamentals of the faith as handed on by the Apostles and guaranteed by Scripture and Tradition. At the same time, the dialogues have deepened our understanding of the essence of our divergence: that we do not agree on what it means to 'be church.' Different ecclesiologies necessarily lead to different conceptions of Church unity, and therefore to different notions of the ecumenical goal itself.

The dialogues set out to lead us beyond the controversies of the sixteenth century, and have been partially successful in that. The highpoint was the signing of the "Joint Declaration on the Doctrine of Justification" with the Lutheran World Federation in 1999, and agreed to by the World Methodist Conference in 2006. In "Harvesting the Fruits," Cardinal Kasper presents a thorough examination of over forty years of dialogue with Anglicans, Lutherans, Reformed and Methodists, and shows that important *convergence*, but not full *consensus*, has been reached as regards the relationship between Scripture and Tradition, the sacramental nature of the Church, apostolic succession, ministry, and the Eucharist. But in the meantime new sources of disagreement have emerged: in ethical and moral matters, life-issues, marriage and the family, human sexuality and bioethics. Clearly these are not just secondary matters. They define one's anthropological and social project; and are therefore deeply church-dividing.

Underlying this recent development is a new hermeneutic of the Scriptures: the idea being that the biblical word is so conditioned by its historical, social context, that it must be continually 'contextualized' anew and re-interpreted in every changing set of circumstances. At the same time, as some Protestant commentators point out, a monumental theological poverty stands behind much moral decision-making. As one writer puts it, the thinking is this: "God is love pure and simple. Thus, one is to see in Christ's death no judgment upon the human condition. Rather one is to see an affirmation of creation and the persons we are. The mission of the Church is to see that those who have been excluded are included." He concludes: "This isn't an ethical divide about rightness or wrongness ... It's a theological chasm – one that separates those who hold a theology of divine acceptance from those who hold a theology of divine redemption."[4]

The practical result is that changes in belief and practice within communities are not made after prolonged investigation and theological debate, but by so-called "prophetic actions," which are generally driven by the idea of 'radical inclusion': every shade of belief, every life-style should be represented in the church body. This leads to tension and polarization in communities, and so the

4 Philip Turner, "An Unworkable Theology" in *First Things*, June/July 2005, pp. 10-12.

churches give up the attempt to act as a unified body or to discipline their membership. The idea of 'local options' takes root. So there is new fragmentation, leading to a new alignment between more traditional or confessional congregations and those that more fully adopt the utilitarian and secularizing tendencies of the dominant cultural model.

This poses a certain dilemma for Catholic ecumenism at the global level: How do we continue to dialogue with the various World Communions, when dissenting groups within them knock on our door, seeking recognition of what they believe to be their greater degree of communion with the Catholic Church? A case in point is what happened in the creation of the Ordinariate for Catholic Anglicans. It is important to remember that the idea of the Ordinariate originated with Anglicans who were no longer at ease with changes in their own Communion, who asked to become Catholic yet hold on to important parts of their Anglican patrimony. Something analogous is stirring among certain Lutherans, especially in Scandinavia and the Baltic countries, but because of deeper differences about the nature of the Church and ministry, it is very difficult to imagine that a similar Ordinariate could be established.

One bright light along the way is the recent agreed document between Catholics and Lutherans, "From Conflict to Communion," an attempt, for the first time, to prepare Catholics and Lutherans to commemorate **together** the five hundredth anniversary of the Reformation in 2017. Every previous centenary saw, on the Lutheran side, a glorification of the figure of Martin Luther and of the Reformation as a liberation from Catholic 'exaggeration'; and, in response, a counter-attack by Catholic apologists. "From Conflict to Communion" presents a shared reading of Luther's intentions and Reformation history, with the controversial points being examined not only in their sixteenth century drama, but in the light of the achievements of fifty years of ecumenical dialogue. So, while there is a growing together in life and collaboration with the mainline Reformation churches, the goal of visible communion has receded into an unknown future.

The Charismatic Churches

Perhaps one of the more significant ecumenical novelties brought in by Pope Francis is his personal interest in Evangelicals, Charismatics and Pentecostals – who now number between 400 and 600 million around the world – making them the second largest Christian presence after Catholicism. There is no center, no binding structure: the common denominator is *personal and collective experience* of the action of the Holy Spirit, manifested in interior certainty of salvation, and external signs and words of spiritual conviction, and leading to a radical change in one's behavior. We Catholics can be greatly perplexed by their lack of ecclesial and ecclesiological consistency, but we must recognize their genuine faith and Christian missionary vitality.

The PCPCU has three formal conversations in course with this Evangelical-Pentecostal-Charismatic reality, having the purpose of understanding each other's identity, doctrinal positions and interpretation of the Christian life:

1. A long-standing dialogue with some classical Pentecostals, which has produced a number of interesting reports;

2. An ongoing yearly consultation with the Evangelical World Alliance, whose website describes it as a network of churches in 129 countries and over 100 international organizations joining together to give a world-wide identity, voice and platform to more than 600 million evangelical Christians;

3. A series of conversations with a group of leaders of what used to be called 'non-denominational churches' (including not a few mega-churches), but which now prefer to be called Charismatic Churches.

Catholics, including much of the hierarchy, often see these groups as not really Christian, as sects, or in any case as aggressively targeting the faithful. There is of course much of that, but the Church's response cannot be just to say no to five or six hundred million Christians. A proper pastoral response is called for. The PCPCU has in the past organized seminars for bishops and others active in ecumenism: twice in Latin America, twice in Africa, and twice in Asia. Interestingly, in each case, the participants reached the conclusion that the first priority was a community-wide examination of conscience as to why so many Catholics leave our own Church to join these groups. Not, what is wrong with Pentecostals and Evangelicals, but what is wrong with us, in our parishes, schools and universities? What liturgical, catechetical, pastoral and spiritual efforts are needed to meet the challenge?

In summary, among the Communions related in one way or another with the Reformation there is no headlong march into corporate unity. Ecumenical efforts and theological dialogues will be with us for the long term. The challenge for the next few years is to keep ecumenism from falling into a routine, into the niceties of good-neighbourliness, without bite!

III. So, is there Hope for the Future?

In speaking about the future of ecumenism to an audience of canon lawyers I realize that I have to try to be precise and practical. You have a reputation of not being into wishful thinking!

In a recent consultation, in which our Council took part with the WCC, it was agreed that:

> ... the churches have entered into the 21st century with the awareness that the differences between them have surfaced in new ways ... that the goal of full visible unity is being eclipsed by a return to institutional concerns, the defense of denominational identity and a return to fundamentalism ... ecumenism seems to have moved from the prophetic edge to a 'comfortable center.'

Where is it possible to discover this 'prophetic edge' in the Catholic Church that might facilitate real growth in communion with other Christians? Where is there a pushing against the way things are in order to forge something better? Surely, if we read Pope Francis' *Evangelii Gaudium* with attention, we will conclude that he has that gift, in the sense given it by the American Biblist Walter Brueggemann: the task of prophetic ministry is to nurture, nourish and evoke a consciousness and perception alternative to the consciousness and perception of the dominant culture.[5] Pope Francis wants a more authentic Church. He is not afraid to call for radical reform, but with genuine discernment. Just read *EG* 43:

> The Church can also come to see that certain customs not directly connected to the heart of the Gospel, even some which have deep historical roots, are no longer properly understood and appreciated. Some of these customs may be beautiful, but they no longer serve as means of communicating the Gospel. We should not be afraid to re-examine them ... the Church has rules or precepts which may have been quite effective in their time, but no longer have the same usefulness for directing and shaping people's lives.

Pope Francis has not offered a blueprint for systematic reform, at least not yet. But he has indicated some areas in which he very much wants to see reform in Church governance. Both the papacy itself and bishops' conferences are in his sights:

> Since I am called to put into practice what I ask of others, I too must think about a conversion of the papacy. It is my duty, as the Bishop of Rome, to be open to suggestions which can help make the exercise of my ministry more faithful to the meaning which Jesus Christ wished to give it and to the present needs of evangelization...[6]

And as regards Episcopal Conferences, he writes:

5 *The Prophetic Imagination*, Fortress Press, 1978, 13.

6 *EG* 32.

> The Second Vatican Council stated that, like the ancient patriarchal Churches, episcopal conferences are in a position 'to contribute in many and fruitful ways to the concrete realization of the collegial spirit.' Yet this desire has not been fully realized, since a juridical status of episcopal conferences which would see them as subjects of specific attributions, including genuine doctrinal authority, has not yet been sufficiently elaborated. Excessive centralization, rather than proving helpful, complicates the Church's life and her missionary outreach.[7]

What he envisions is a different, broader, sharing of responsibility and authority – a genuine collegiality and synodality. For this he wants Catholics to learn from the Orthodox: "To give but one example, in the dialogue with our Orthodox brothers and sisters, we Catholics have the opportunity to learn more about the meaning of episcopal collegiality and their experience of synodality."[8]

Were it possible to institute such a reform, the Church resulting from it would have to be the fullest possible implementation of *Lumen Gentium*, especially chapter 3 (on the hierarchical structure of the church and in particular on the episcopate). It would be grounded in the sacramental nature, function and mission of the local bishop as the transmitter and guarantor of the apostolic tradition (with an important role for diocesan synods, priests' councils, pastoral councils); in collegial communion with the other bishops, especially those of the same region (thus a substantive role for bishops' conferences and perhaps for metropolitan provinces); and in communion of faith and mission with the whole College, and therefore with its head, the first bishop, the Bishop of Rome (therefore a role for the Synod of Bishops and General Councils).

We already have these institutions, but are they truly collegial and synodical? What needs to be done to make them so? Technically, it would require a profound review of canonical prescriptions and approaches, and it cannot happen without a cultural *tsunami* among canon lawyers themselves. No one believes that such a reform will be easy or without opposition.

Perhaps canon lawyers should ask whether there is truth in a recent critique that suggests that canon law studies have not done all they could to incorporate the genuine ecclesiology of the Council into the legislation and its application, but have continued to be encased in the juridical positivism of the 1917 code (cf. Hervé Legrande, *Concilium*). Did the 1983 code fall short of the ecclesiological development of the Council? As one European bishop wrote recently:

---

7 Ibid.

8 *EG* 246.

> Every debate...since the Second Vatican Council, in whichever direction it was inclined to go, has had to face this ecclesiological question, that of the correct relationship between primacy and collegiality in the Catholic Church... The bond between the collegiality of the bishops and the primacy of the bishop of Rome that was manifest during the Second Vatican Council must be restored and without delay. It represents the key to a new and better approach to many of the questions facing the Church.

I am convinced that this kind of reform of the Church is the greatest source of hope for ecumenism in the twenty-first century, especially for a restoration of communion with the East. Such an enormous challenge cannot be understood or seriously faced in the spirit of the usual cultural wars. It can only be taken up by a confident, humble and prayerful Church that works at discerning the Lord's intentions, which include his prayer at the Last Supper: "that all may be one, so that the world may believe."[9]

On our metaphorical ecumenical plane journey, the pilot has just announced that we are not going to arrive on schedule; the bad weather and turbulence along the way is delaying our arrival. But "not to worry" – he tries to assure us – "we will eventually get there." Fifty years on, *UR*'s last words are both a prophecy of human failure, and a prophecy of God's ability to turn our failure into success: "the holy task of reconciling all Christians in the unity of the one and only Church of Christ transcends human energies and abilities. Its hope lies entirely in the prayer of Christ for the Church, in the love of the Father for us and in the power of the Holy Spirit" (no. 24).

9 Cf. John 17:21.

Major Address

Future Paths for the Ecumenical Movement: Canonical Considerations, Challenges, and Contributions

Prof. Dr. Myriam Wijlens, STL, JCD

The Convention Planning Committee invited me to speak about developments in the world of ecumenism that are of relevance for canon law. I will do so by first reflecting upon the following rather intriguing question: Considering that the Convention Planning Committee wanted to commemorate the 50th anniversary of the promulgation of the Dogmatic Constitution on the Church, *Lumen gentium*, the Decree on Ecumenism, *Unitatis redintegratio*, and the Decree on the Oriental Churches, *Orientalium Ecclesiarium*, would it not have been more obvious for a canon law convention to focus on the Dogmatic Constitution on the Church which provides plenty of ecclesiological topics? Or to phrase it somewhat differently: What might have motivated the Convention Planning Committee to choose the unity of the church in the sense of ecumenism and not an ecclesiological topic? Moreover, what does such a decision imply for ecclesiological topics? The decision is more than laudable as I hope to outline, but it bears a great responsibility for canon lawyers. So in the first section of this presentation I will reflect on what I will call 'unity as a hermeneutical criterion.' After that I will present three projects from the field of ecumenism that are of interest to canon lawyers. The Colloquium of Anglican and Roman Catholic Lawyers, the Peter and Paul Seminar, and the project called "Receptive Ecumenism." The latter will take a special place in this as it is drawing a lot of attention worldwide not only among professional ecumenists, but also and in particular by church leaders including the Pontifical Council for the Promotion of Christian Unity. Although the three projects are not connected I think they could benefit from each other.

The Restoration of Unity: a Hermeneutical Principle for Canon Law

On January 25, 1959, on the feast of Saint Paul, the day that marked the end of the week of prayer for Christian unity, Pope John XXIII informed the world about his intention to convoke an Ecumenical Council.[1] The purpose he said, would be to meet the spiritual demands of the present time accurately and forcefully.

1 John XXIII, Papal Allocution *Questa festiva*, *AAS* 51 (1959) 65-69. English translation: "Announcement of Ecumenical Council and Synod," *The Pope Speaks* 4 (1959) 398-401.

The whole world was taken by surprise by this initiative. At the time no one could have imagined what would come out of the council. For some the thought alone caused great anxiety as they feared loss of power and control, others were filled with hope that long desired reforms would finally take place.[2]

More than five years later on Saturday November 21, 1964, Pope Paul VI promulgated the Dogmatic Constitution on the Church, *Lumen gentium*, the Decree on Ecumenism, *Unitatis redintegratio* and the Decree on the Oriental Churches, *Orientalium Ecclesiarum*. Their promulgation marked the end of a week that would go down in history under the name "the black week" (*la settimana nera*) at Vatican II. It had begun on November 14, 1964. Such a qualification came of course not from the minority at the council who were possibly delighted by the events that had occurred. The majority, on the other hand, had seen itself confronted with basically four incidents, which later on gave many the feeling that they had approved texts severely weakened by concessions granted in order to win over a defiant minority. The four occurrences were: 1) it was announced that the vote on the Declaration on Religious Freedom would be postponed to a later session of the council; 2) the fathers had been confronted with the so-called *Nota explicative praevia* which presented a key to interpreting major ecclesiological issues in the third chapter of *Lumen gentium;* 3) nineteen *modi* had been introduced to the final text of the Decree on Ecumenism without the council having been given an occasion to discuss them, and 4) there was the papal declaration entitling Mary *Mater Ecclesiae*, a title that the Doctrinal Commission had consistently refused.[3] Despite the tensions and disappointments that these four incidents caused, the three documents found almost unanimous approval from the council fathers. Nevertheless "these four episodes stole the sense of euphoria from the majority of the Council fathers and created instead an atmosphere of suspicion and distrust."[4]

Yet, with the promulgation of these three documents important changes with regard to ecclesiology and ecumenism had taken place and a new phase of the

2 In 1950 Yves Congar published a book about reform in the church. In 1968 the second edition of the book was published in which he wrote in the foreword: "In a few short weeks John XXIII created a new climate in the church, and then came the council. This most significant breakthrough came from on high. All of a sudden, forces of renewal which had scarcely had room to breathe found ways to be expressed. The cautious suggestions for reform mentioned in my text of 1950 have been surpassed by far. What is happening right now, in as far as it is positive, is certainly in line with what I had intended, yet it goes a great deal further, well beyond what one could have hoped for in 1950." Yves Congar, *True and False Reform in the Church* (Mahwah: Paulist, 2011).

3 See the very interesting article by Luis Antonio Tagle – the current Cardinal and archbishop of Manilla (Philippines):"The 'Black Week' of Vatican II (November 14-21, 1964)" in Giuseppe Alberigo, Joseph Komonchak, eds., *History of Vatican II,* Vol. IV, *Church as Communion, Third Session and Intersession, September 1964 – September 1965* (Maryknoll: Orbis, Leuven: Peeters, 2003) 387-452.

4 Tagle, "The 'Black Week,'"p. 388.

council could begin: its reception or, to use another word, its implementation. All that the council entailed – and this is much more than can be deducted from studying the final documents only[5] – had to shape the Church not only in its being and its self understanding, but also and above all in its operations which gives expression to underlying notions.

Among the instruments that had to assist the community in facilitating such a reception are the 1983 Code of Canon Law for the Latin Church and the 1990 Code of Canons of the Eastern Churches. Pope John XXIII had already envisioned such a revision as he announced the council and said that the council would lead to the "desired and long awaited modernization of the Code of Canon Law, which is expected to accompany and to crown these events [i.e., the Synod for Rome and Vatican II]."[6] Pope John Paul II, while promulgating the Code of Canon Law spoke about a translation of the conciliar doctrine into canonical structures. The canonical norms thus published after the council have had and still have as its main purpose facilitating the reception of the doctrine of Vatican II.

In 2012 the Board of Governors of the CLSA approved the proposal from the Convention Planning Committee that the theme of the 2014 convention was going to be "The Unity of the Church: Challenges and Prospects." The theme was chosen to commemorate the 50th anniversary of the approval by the council, and the promulgation by Pope Paul VI, of the three aforementioned documents. At first someone might be a bit surprised that in commemorating these three documents the focus is on the unity of the church and, more specifically, on the ecumenical aspect of unity. People might have expected that on such an occasion canon lawyers would focus in particular on ecclesiological themes arising in particular from *Lumen gentium*. Although such an expectation is understandable, the decision by the Convention Planning Committee and the Board of Governors reveals a deeper understanding and appreciation of the council's doctrine, intention and its nature.

5 In earlier studies I reflected about the hermeneutics of Vatican II and the consequences for canon law in Myriam Wijlens, "Zur Verhältnisbestimmung von Konzil und nachkonziliarer Rechtsordnung: Eine theologisch-kanonistische Reflexion," in Peter Hünermann, e.a. (eds.), *Das Zweite Vatikanische Konzil und die Zeichen der Zeit Heute* (Freiburg i.Br.: Herder, 2006) 331-339; *Idem*, "Die Konzilshermeneutik und das Kirchenrecht," Dominikus Meier, e.a. (eds.), *Rezeption des Zweiten Vatikanischen Konzils in Theologie und Kirchenrecht heute, Festschrift für Klaus Lüdicke zur Vollendung seines 65. Lebensjahres,* Beihefte zum MKCIC, Nr. 55 (Essen: Ludgerus, 2008) 711-729; Idem, "Die Verbindlichkeit des Zweiten Vatikanischen Konzils: eine kirchenrechtliche Betrachtung," Christoph Böttigheimer (Hrsg.), *Zweites Vatikanisches Konzil. Programmatik – Rezeption – Vision.* (Freiburg i.Br.: Herder, 2014). Quaestiones disputatae, vol. 261, 37-62.

6 John XXIII, Papal allocution, *Questa festiva*, 400-401.

In taking Vatican II's commitment to the restoration of Christian unity as the theme for this convention, they lifted it in such a way that it becomes a hermeneutical key for interpreting and receiving the entire council. In doing so, they stand in line with the very intention of the council as stated by Pope John XXIII in his landmark address at the opening of the council: "The Catholic Church considers it her duty to work actively for the fulfillment of the great mystery of that unity for which Jesus Christ prayed so earnestly to his heavenly Father on the eve of his great sacrifice..."[7] The council made the intention of Pope John XXIII its own when it forcefully begins the Decree on Ecumenism with the statement: "The restoration of the unity among all Christians is one of the principal concerns of the Second Vatican Council" (*UR* 1).[8] Pope Paul VI, while promulgating the three conciliar documents, stated that *Lumen gentium* had to be interpreted in light of the Decree on Ecumenism.[9]

While promulgating the 1983 Code of Canon Law, Pope John Paul II listed four different aspects of the "newness" of the council that would also be the novelty of the code. They are:

- "The doctrine in which the Church is presented as the People of God (cf. *Lumen gentium*, no. 2), and authority as a service (cf. ibid., no. 3);

- The doctrine in which the Church is seen as a "communion," and which, therefore, determines the relations which should exist between the particular Churches and the universal Church, and between collegiality and the primacy;

- The doctrine, moreover, according to which all the members of the People of God, in the way suited to each of them, participate in the threefold office of Christ: priestly, prophetic and kingly. With this teaching there is also linked that which concerns the duties and rights of the faithful, and particularly of the laity; and finally,

7 John XXIII, Papal allocution *Gaudet Mater Ecclesia*. *AAS* 548 (1962) 786-796; English translation: "The Council – At the Threshold of a New Era: Address of Pope John XXIII at the Opening of the Council." *The Pope Speaks* 8 (1962) 207-216, here 214.

8 In another study I have extensively reflected on the meaning of this commitment to restoring Christian unity. See Myriam Wijlens, "'That all may be one...' (John 17:21). The Lord's Prayer in the Work of Canon Lawyers: A Mere Option?" *The Jurist* 65 (2005) 181-204. The study also reflects about the relevance of actions that implement the rhetoric such as the decision to invite observers of other churches to the council, the historic visit of Pope Paul VI with the Patriarch Anténagoras in Jerusalem in 1964, the mutual lifting of the excommunication of 1054.

9 Cf. Paul VI, Address on the Occasion of the Promulgation of the Dogmatic Constitution on the Church, the Decree on Ecumenism and the Decree on the Eastern Churches, *AAS* 54 (11964) 1012-1013. See also Francis A. Sullivan, "*Subsistit in*: The Significance of Vatican II's Decision to say of the Church of Christ not that it is, 'but that it subsists in' the Roman Catholic Church," *One in Christ* 22 (1986) 117.

- The Church's commitment to ecumenism."[10]

Note that Pope John Paul II refers to the first three as doctrine, but the last is identified as a "commitment (*studium*) to ecumenism." *Studium* means commitment characterized by zeal and eagerness. This is much more than just "translating" the doctrine into norms, it is an attitude of mind and heart.

In earlier studies I have argued that each of these points can be seen as a hermeneutical principle for interpreting and applying the law,[11] but I believe the unity of the Church is an overriding one for the others, or maybe it would be better to say: it is a principle that precedes the other principles. It means that no revision or reform can occur that does not see to its ecumenical impact.

Required, therefore, is a change of heart and mind which, according to the Decree on Ecumenism, is the "soul of the whole ecumenical movement" (*UR* 7-8). Conversion, which is a turn anew to the Lord Jesus Christ, however, is not just a spiritual attitude, because a conversion that has no effect in the concrete life of the faithful is no conversion at all. The Decree on Ecumenism thus states that "all [i.e., churches] are led to examine their own faithfulness to Christ's will for the Church and accordingly undertake with vigor the task of renewal and reform" (*UR* 4). Hence, the conversion should be followed by renewal and reform: *ecclesia semper reformanda.*

In 1995 Pope John Paul II not only affirms the commitment to the restoration of unity, but also qualifies it as irrevocable in his first encyclical on ecumenism *Ut unum sint.*[12] He explains that ecumenism is to penetrate, yes to permeate, the whole life of the Church. It implies a conversion that has to lead to renewal and reform. Hence it is not just a personal, but also a necessary communal conversion (*UUS* 15):

> In the teaching of the Second Vatican Council there is a clear connection between renewal, conversion and reform. The Council states that 'Christ summons the Church, as she goes her pilgrim way, to that continual reformation of which she

10 The original last part reads: "(*studium...*] *ab Ecclesia in oecumenismum impendendum,*" John Paul II, Apostolic constitution *Sacrae disciplinae leges. AAS* 75/2 (1983) xii-xiv; English translation: *Code of Canon Law: Latin-English Edition*, New English Translation (Washington, DC: Canon Law Society of America, 1988) xxx.

11 See Myriam Wijlens, "'That All May be One...' (John 17:21)" 181-204, and Idem, "The Doctrine of the People of God and Hierarchical Authority as Service in Latin Church Legislation on the Local Church," *The Jurist* 68 (2008) 328-349.

12 "At the Second Vatican Council, the Catholic Church committed herself *irrevocably* to following the path of the ecumenical venture, thus heeding the Spirit of the Lord, who teaches people to interpret carefully the 'signs of the times'." Pope John Paul II, encyclical letter *Ut unum sint, AAS* 87(1995) 921-982, English translation: *Ut unum sint*, (London; Catholic Truth Society, 1995), no. 3.

> always has a need, insofar as she is an institution of human beings here on earth. Therefore, if the influence of events or of the times has led to deficiencies…these should be appropriately rectified at the proper moment.' No Christian Community can exempt itself from this call. (*UUS* 16)

In commenting on this point Cardinal Kasper clarifies that there are two levels of ecumenism: *ad extra* and *ad intra*: "*ad extra* through ecumenical encounters, dialogues and co-operation, and ecumenism *ad intra* through reform and renewal of the Catholic Church itself. There is no ecumenism without conversion and reform (*UR* 6-9; *UUS* 15-17)."[13] According to the French theologian Hervé Legrand, such a commitment to the restoration is "not simply a matter of exposing our own treasures to others apologetically, or of teaching them a lesson. Our areas of weaknesses are also where they have their own problems, which they themselves have identified. The ecumenical task consists less in changing others than in changing ourselves, in correcting that which is within our reach and for which we are responsible."[14]

So, is the unity of the church of Christ a hermeneutical criterion? Pope John Paul II concludes: "Thus it is absolutely clear that ecumenism, the movement promoting Christian unity, *is not just some sort of 'appendix'* which is added to the Church's traditional activity. Rather, ecumenism is an organic part of her life and work, and consequently must pervade all that she is and does; it must be like the fruit borne by a healthy and flourishing tree which grows to its full stature" (*UUS* 20 – emphasis in original.)

---

13 Cardinal Walter Kasper said this while addressing the plenary of the Pontifical Council for Christian Unity held November 12-17, 2001: "Present Situation and Future of the Ecumenical Movement", see http://www.vatican.va/roman_curia/pontifical_councils/chrstuni/card-kasper-docs/rc_pc_chrstuni_doc_20011117_kasper-prolusio_en.html (accessed October 20, 2014).

14 Hervé Legrand, "The Episcopate. The Ecumenical Critique of Catholic Theology," Translated from the French by Catherine E. Clifford (unpublished paper). This is fully in line with Vatican II which urges Catholics "to make a careful and honest appraisal of whatever needs to be renewed and done in the Catholic household itself, in order that its life may bear witness more clearly and faithfully to the teachings and institutions which have been handed down from Christ through the apostles" (*UR* 4).

First analyses of the proclamations of, and actions by, Pope Francis indicate that he stands fully in line with his predecessors.[15]

A church which considers unity as a hermeneutical criterion will ask from its experts on structures – which canon lawyers are – to take on an internal disposition of making the restoration of unity a priority of one's own. The issue, therefore, does not just rest with canonical norms and institutions alone, but touches deeply and fundamentally, first and foremost, the canon lawyer or the person who interacts with the law. Required therefore is a conversion (a *metanoia*) to the unity of the church of Christ. Such a conversion does not just concern canon lawyers alone, but it has to touch and operate in the whole community. It is a task of canon lawyers to assist the community in this. All actions performed in the community should be governed by that commitment.

For canon lawyers to adopt the commitment to the restoration of the unity of the church as a hermeneutical criteria is, therefore, a consequence of what Vatican II intended and what popes ever since John XXIII accentuated. Seeing the commitment to unity as a hermeneutical criterion implies that studies and discussions about typical ecclesiological topics originating from *Lumen gentium* are seen through the lenses of that commitment. Topics include the relationship between primacy and collegiality; between the local and universal church – and related to these – the reform of the Roman Curia; the competence and authority belonging to an episcopal conference; the working of the synod of bishops; governing of a diocese by a bishop; the participation of the laity in the church, and structures facilitating the establishment of the *sensus fidelium* on a specific issue. These are topics that are not just discussed from mere ecclesiological or canonical perspectives, but also while keeping this question in mind: What will be the impact on the restoration of Christian unity?

A lecture on a topic such as "ecumenism and canon law" involves, therefore, much more – and goes far beyond – that which many would initially associate with it; namely, a reflection about mixed marriages, sharing the Eucharist with

15 Hector Scerri, "The Ecumenical Commitment of Pope Francis," *Roczniki Teologii Ekumenicznej* 60 (2013) 25-42. See also Peter DeMey, "Towards a Healthy Future of Catholicity in the Roman Catholic Church: Recommendations by Pope Francis" to be published in Dagmar Heller, Peter Szentpetery (eds.), *Catholicity under Pressure: the Ambiguous Relationship between Diversity and Unity, Proceedings of the 18th Academic Consultation of the Societas Oecumenica, Budapest, 21-26 August, 2014.* Beiheft zur Ökumenische Rundschau (Leipzig: EVA, 2015- forthcoming) and Gerard Mannion, "Pope Francis and the Ecumenical Future: Groundwork for a 'Costly Ecumenism'?" Expanded version of plenary address to the 'Hope in the Ecumenical Future' International Conference, Ripon College and Oxford University, April 2014 (manuscript made available by the author).

other Christians, baptized non-Catholics as godparents, and possibly funerals for baptized non-Catholics.[16]

Hence, the decision of the Convention Planning Committee and the Board of Governors does not imply that ecclesiological subjects arising from *Lumen gentium* and other conciliar documents are not on the agenda. On the contrary, they are! However, they are to be attended to from a specific point of view, namely, the impact they have on the unity of the Church of Christ. That implies that before canon lawyers attend to the ecclesiological issues, they pause for a moment and reflect first about the implications of the church's commitment to the restoration of the unity of Christ for canonical institutions. They scrutinize regularly whether existing canonical provisions could or should be changed for the sake of unity.[17] They interpret norms in view of building unity, and they apply the norms by beginning to phrase the situation in which the law as such needs to be applied in an ecumenically conducive way. This would apply equally for universal and particular law.

Although such a view on canon law and ecumenism is possibly not very wide spread yet, there are nevertheless groups who work on this. In my next section I will present three projects.

---

16 See in this regard my earlier publications *Sharing the Eucharist: A Theological Evaluation of the Post Conciliar Legislation.* With a foreword by Johannes Cardinal Willebrands (Lanham, MD: University Press of America, 2000) xx-397p. and "Interchurch Marriages and Pastoral Care in Sickness: A Canonical Consideration," *CLSA Proceedings 72* (Washington, DC: CLSA, 2010) 249-266. Published also in: *Proceedings Canon Law Society of Australia and New Zealand* 45 (2011) 91-108.

17 Pope Francis' remarks also applies for canonical institutions: "In her ongoing discernment, the Church can also come to see that certain customs not directly connected to the heart of the Gospel, even some which have deep historical roots, are no longer properly understood and appreciated. Some of these customs may be beautiful, but they no longer serve as means of communicating the Gospel. We should not be afraid to re-examine them. At the same time, the Church has rules or precepts which may have been quite effective in their time, but no longer have the same usefulness for directing and shaping people's lives. Saint Thomas Aquinas pointed out that the precepts which Christ and the apostles gave to the people of God 'are very few.' Citing Saint Augustine, he noted that the precepts subsequently enjoined by the Church should be insisted upon with moderation 'so as not to burden the lives of the faithful' and make our religion a form of servitude, whereas 'God's mercy has willed that we should be free.' This warning, issued many centuries ago, is most timely today. It ought to be one of the criteria to be taken into account in considering a reform of the Church and her preaching which would enable it to reach everyone." Pope Francis, Apostolic Exhortation on the Proclamation of the Gospel in Today's World, *Evangelii Gaudium*," no. 43, English Translation: http://w2.vatican.va/content/francesco/en/apost_exhortations/documents/papa-francesco_esortazione-ap_20131124_evangelii-gaudium.html (accessed October 20, 2014).

Projects on Ecumenism and Canon Law.

The first project goes by the name "Colloquium of Anglican and Roman Catholic Canon Lawyers" which has been meeting annually since 1999. The second project is entitled "The Peter and Paul Seminar." Its first meeting was in 1998. The third project is known as "Receptive Ecumenism," and it was basically launched in 2006. It would have been fascinating as well to say a few words about projects going on within other denominations, such as the project by Prof. Norman Doe from Cardiff in England, who has been working on principles of canon law common to the Anglican Communion, but I can only do so within the description of the first project.[18]

Another project worth reporting on is the one led by the Dutch reformed ecclesiologist and specialist on church law, Prof. Leo Koffeman. Koffeman was the main drafter of a church order for three uniting protestant churches in The Netherlands: one of them Reformed, one Lutheran. He has taken a great interest in challenges that arise when a church order is to be written for a body that is supra national. In November 2011, Koffeman organized a conference on this topic to which he invited among others, Norman Doe and myself to explain how our legal systems handles the tension between unity and diversity: How do you guarantee unity and diversity with the help of canonical structures?[19] Among the interesting questions related to this topic is: Who decides what is to be decided by whom with regard to which subjects?[20] Although this is of course at the end of

---

18 Norman Doe, *Canon Law in the Anglican Communion: A World Wide Perspective* (Oxford: Clarendon, 1998) and Idem, *An Anglican Covenant? Theological and Legal Considerations for a Global Debate* (Norwich: Canterbury Press, 2008), Idem, "Canon Law and Covenant in Anglicanism," in Allan J. Janssen, Leo J. Koffeman, eds., *Protestant Church Polity in Changing Contexts,* Vol. I *Ecclesiological and Historical Contributions. Proceedings of the International Conference, Utrecht, the Netherlands, 7-10 November 2011* (Münster: Lit, 2014) 169-190.

19 The studies presented at the conference are published in Allan J. Janssen, Leo J. Koffeman, eds., *Protestant Church Polity in Changing Contexts*, Vol. I (Münster: Lit, 2014).

20 When the legislator in the Catholic Church drafted the Code of Canon Law, decisions were made as to what would be left to particular law issued by a bishop or by an episcopal conference. The legislator also decided whether it would be optional for a bishop or episcopal conference to legislate on a given topic or rather be obligatory. Such decisions are deeply ecclesiological as they express and gave shape to the relationship between the local and universal Church. The decisions taken also reveal how far the legislator has internalized the principle of subsidiarity and the understanding that a diocesan bishop in virtue of his office has all the power needed to govern his diocese. Before Vatican II the bishops were granted power to dispense (model of concession), but after the council the notion of reservation was introduced: only what is needed for the preservation of the unity of the church is reserved to a higher authority. The legislator of the universal law thus not only gives expression to these notions in the Code of Canon Law, but his decisions as to what has been reserved to a higher authority could also be evaluated from an ecclesiological point of view.

the day a theological question, it nevertheless arises in the context of unity and legitimate diversity.

These different projects reveal a few communalities: they all find their origin in private initiatives. They are neither mandated by churches nor are they funded by churches. Canon lawyers and theologians began to act because they saw a need. Those involved in these projects are very often official delegates by their churches to national or international dialogues. It is interesting that these activities really all go back to the 1990's. I am not sure what the cause is for that yet. Let us attend to the three projects.

1. Colloquium of Anglican and Roman Catholic Lawyers

The first project concerns the Colloquium of Anglican and Roman Catholic Lawyers which arose in conjunction with the international dialogue between the Anglican and Roman Catholic Church, ARCIC.[21] That dialogue was founded in 1967 by Pope Paul VI and the Archbishop of Canterbury, Michael Ramsey. The work done by theologians, historians, liturgists, and scripture scholars resulted in various statements by ARCIC. Canon lawyers were not involved. In fact Roman Catholic canon law does not foresee that canon law could be an *instrument* in ecumenism. In the mid-1990's, the Ecclesiastical Law Society of the Anglican Church approached the Canon Law Society of Great Britain and Ireland to seek a form of collaboration and study of canonical matters. This resulted in establishing a lecture commemorating William Lyndwood, "perhaps the greatest pre-Reformation English canonist" a man whose work is respected by Anglicans and Catholics alike.

Why did the Anglicans seek this contact? At the time the Anglicans became increasingly aware of the relevance of canon law in their own church. There was a growing consensus within Anglicanism of what has been styled by some as the Anglican *ius commune*. The question was raised whether canon law could have a place as a fifth instrument of unity within Anglicanism?[22] This question was affirmed in 2002 and a project in which principles of canon law common to the

21 A fine description of the first ten years of the project can be found in "A Decade of Ecumenical Dialogue: A Report of the Proceedings of the Colloquium of Anglican and Roman Catholic Lawyers 1999-2009," *Ecclesiastical Law Journal* (2009) 11, 323-324. This report has been written by the members together. The description of the project in the current study is basically taken from this report.

22 The other four are: the Archbishop of Canterbury, the Lambeth Conference, the Primates' Meeting and the Anglican Consultative Council. See *Report of the Meeting of the Primates of the Anglican Communion*, Canterbury, 10-17 April 2002 para 6. Cf. http://www.anglicannews.org/news/2002/04/report-of-the-meeting-of-primates-of-the-anglican-communion.aspx (accessed October 10, 2014).

member churches of the Anglican Communion began. It is entitled: *The Principles of Canon Law Common to the Churches of the Anglican Communion.*[23]

This project was possibly also governed by the fact that for quite some time now the Anglican Communion has been facing serious challenges that have the potential of being church dividing. Among them are the ordination of women and homosexuality. What became clear was not only the need to discuss these topics, but that there was a need to ask the question: Who should decide on these topics? What on first sight might appear to be a mere ethical question turns into an ecclesiological one that can be church dividing. Hence, the question arises how a church division can be prevented. Actually, it then becomes clear that ecumenical work does not only concern the restoration of unity, but also the preservation of unity.[24] This is, in a nutshell, a request by Anglican canon lawyers seeking contact with their Roman Catholic colleagues.

In 1998 it was decided to establish a colloquium in which canon lawyers of both the Anglican and the Roman Catholic Church could discuss different topics. Methodologically they would proceed as follows: They would identify a topic and then pair canon lawyers from each denomination and invite them to write parallel papers on the given topic. The papers would be distributed before the meeting and would then be discussed thoroughly. The results are regularly published. From a methodological perspective this could be seen as doing comparative canon law. In the fifteen years that followed subjects that were discussed include: church property law, clerical discipline, initiation in the church, author-

23 "It is important to recognize the limits of this exercise. It does not, in particular, constitute a corpus of canon law applicable to any province of the Communion, let alone the Communion as a whole. Nor is it intended that it should provide the basis for a common legal system for the Communion as a whole at some stage in the future: a common legal system would be inconsistent with the 'autonomy in communion' enjoyed by the member provinces, and to adopt such a system would (in addition to giving rise to difficulties from the point of view of the unique situation prevailing in England by virtue of the General Synod's role as a legislative organ of the state) involve a fundamental change in the character of the Communion." "A Decade of Ecumenical Dialogue," 323-324. A 'principle of canon law' is "a foundational proposition or maxim of general applicability which has a strong dimension of weight, is induced from the similarities of the legal systems of churches, derives from the canonical tradition or other practices of the church, expresses a basic theological truth or ethical value, and is about, is implicit in, or underlies canon law...While the vast majority of the principles derive from similarities between the written laws of churches, some are based on unwritten assumptions, general propositions implicit in church laws." "A Decade of Ecumenical Dialogue," 290.

24 Faith and Order has thus taken up the project referred to as moral discernment. Faith and Order did not intend to solve ethical problems or even suggest how churches should decide on specific moral issues. Rather it investigates the reasons why churches arrive at different conclusions with regard to ethical questions despite possibly using the same sources. Hence, the document investigates how moral discernment takes place in different churches. See Faith and Order, *Moral Discernment in the Churches: A Study Document* (Geneva, WCC, 2013) 62.

ity in the church, ecumenical co-operation, orders and primacy, preparation for ministry, marriage, and only last year council and consent. The project on church property law raised questions concerning who owns, administers and represents property. With regard to initiation, the project compared rules and regulations on baptism of adults and children, the requirements for ministers, and the way the sacraments are administered. Issues such a godparents and registration are being studied.[25]

The intention of the projects was to discover what Anglicans and Roman Catholics have in common, what they do not share, and what is simply done in another way. By working in this way "convergences of law have been identified, differences noted and sets of shared principles developed."[26] In going over some of the reports, it would appear that the project predominantly compares law or how specific issues are organized; the theology governing the regulations is not the explicit object of study. Possibly, this is how the ecumenical dialogues on doctrinal subjects began.

Among the canon lawyers who participate in this project are Josef Fox OP, Robert Ombres OP, James Conn SJ, Michael Hilbert SJ, and Aidan McGrath OFM.

2. Peter and Paul Seminar

The second project goes by the name 'The Peter and Paul Seminar': this name was chosen as Peter is traditionally connected with the unity of the Church, while Paul is remembered as an apostle blessed with creativity. The Seminar was convoked by Ladislas Örsy in 1998 in response to the publication *Pour la Conversion des Églises* (For the Conversion of the Churches) by the Groupe des Dombes, a group of twenty Roman Catholic and twenty protestant theologians from the francophone world.[27] This document reflects upon conversion of churches in relation to identity. It determined three levels of identity: Christian,

25 The study "A Decade of Ecumenical Dialogue on Canon Law" presents a summary of the findings of the different projects. Reports on the different studies can also be found in (1999) 5 *Ecc LJ* 281, (2001) 6 *Ecc LJ* 61, (2002) 6 *Ecc LJ* 403, (2003) 7 *Ecc LJ* 225, (2005) 8 *Ecc LJ* 99, (2006) 8 *Ecc LJ* 358, (2006) 484, (2007) 9 *Ecc LJ* 321, (2008) 10 *Ecc LJ* 357.

26 "A Decade of Ecumenical Dialogue on Canon Law," 287.

27 For a description of the early phase of the Peter and Paul Seminar see Myriam Wijlens, "'Peter and Paul Seminar': A Follow up by Theologians and Canon Lawyers to the Groupe des Dombes' Publication *For the Conversion of the Churches,*" *The Jurist* 64 (2004) 6-20.

ecclesial and confessional.[28] The confessional identity refers to elements that were taken on in the course of history and that often times only emerged after the churches separated. The proposal is to identify them and possibly offer them for the sake of the unity of the church – for the healing of the broken body. While the proposal from the Groupe des Dombes is theoretical, the Peter and Paul Seminar intends to see to practical implications and consequences. It considers the question: Do the existing canonical institutions implement the doctrine as taught by Vatican II, and do they above all foster the restoration of Christian unity? If not, how can they be changed in such a way that they do while preserving the Christian and ecclesial identity? Methodologically it implies proceeding in four steps:

1. Identify the doctrine in need of support and protection by way of canonical institutions;
2. Determine the doctrine that governs the already existing institution;
3. Establish whether on the basis of the answer of the former two questions there is a need to change the current institution;
4. Propose a new structure.

Answering these questions requires the close cooperation of historians, systematic theologians and canon lawyers. Historians of dogma can help in particular to identify what has been addressed in the course of history on the doctrinal level, or what authority is to be attributed to a specific doctrine.[29] Specialists in

28 First, there is a *Christian* identity, which consists in God's initiative to make himself known to humanity through the message of his Son Jesus Christ and the gift of the Holy Spirit. The corresponding conversion is the appropriation through faith and practice of the mystery of baptism, which is grace open to mission.
Second, there is an *ecclesial* identity, which signifies that the Church is the Body of Christ where, because of the gift of the Holy Spirit, the gift of God to humanity in Jesus Christ becomes manifest. The ecclesial identity must stand in service of the Christian identity. The ecclesial conversion corresponds to this.
Third, there is a *confessional* identity which refers to many elements that exist and that emerged only after the churches separated and that were often caused by historical events that have lost their significance. The corresponding conversion consists in giving up those elements that are neither foundational nor indispensable. They could be sacrificed for the sake of unity, for the healing of the broken body of the Church of Christ. Institutional conversion consists in such a sacrifice. This, however, can be phrased positively, namely: the conversion of the churches consists in a strengthening of each one's Christian and ecclesial identity at the expense of confessional identity. It implies bringing new dynamics into the ecumenical endeavor where there is a change from the inside for the sake of the others and for the sake of the whole. Cf. Groupe des Dombes, *For the Conversion of the Churches*, No. 10-35.

29 An excellent example of this concerns the work by Piet Fransen who clarified that the anathemas issued at the council of Trent do not all carry the same weight and thus authority. Piet Fransen, *Hermeneutics of the Councils and Other Studies.* Bibliotheca Ephemeridum Theologicarum Lovaniensium. Vol. 69 (Leuven: Peeters, 1985). Another example concerns the clarification of the maximalist interpretation of Vatican I which went far beyond what the council itself had ever intended.

the history of institutions can identify what has been received from Roman law, etc.

The participants in the project are internationally recognized scholars in their own field of expertise. In 1998 the group first identified possible topics which would be in need of such a review process.[30] In a second step the Peter and Paul Seminar decided to focus on the topic of the collegiality of bishops. The papers were presented at a colloquium at Georgetown University in Washington, DC, in 2004. This project resulted in the awareness that the focus was too exclusively on the universal level of the church and that the questions that had arisen could not be answered responsibly without attending to what was subsequently called "Leadership in the Local Church."

In 2008 the faculties of Theology and Canon Law of Saint Paul University in Ottawa graciously hosted the Peter and Paul Seminar's conference on this topic. This resulted in an awareness that there was a need and that it was also possible to propose changes to the existing law, but that it might not be opportune at the time. The time did not seem to be ripe for such a proposal with far reaching changes. Pope Benedict XVI's 2005 Christmas address to the Roman Curia in which he spoke about the topic of hermeneutics of continuity, discontinuity and hermeneutics of reform[31] dominated discussions worldwide, which led to serious concerns as to where the Holy See might be going with regard to Vatican II. The intuition that the time did not seem to be right seemed to be proven in January of 2009 when Pope Benedict XVI lifted the excommunication of the four Lefebvrist' bishops. Another indication that the time was not ripe came from a tendency by Rome to control increasingly. There were heavy discussions in the English speaking world on the (imposed) translations of liturgical texts after the publication of the Instruction *Liturgiam authenticam* on the use of vernacular languages in liturgical books.[32] Moreover, the limitations posed on episcopal conferences with *Apostolos Suos*[33] could be felt. In such a context any proposal to change the law might have implied losing instead of gaining. The Peter and Paul Seminar concluded, therefore, that the mentality required to make and accept such a reform was not present. It was felt that the many canons that currently contain discretionary clauses – such as "if opportune," "in case of necessity," "in case of

30 The studies were published in *The Jurist* 59 (1999) 329-468.

31 Pope Benedict XVI, Address to the Roman Curia offering them his Christmas Greetings on December 22, 2005, http://www.vatican.va/holy_father/benedict_xvi/speeches/2005/december/documents/hf_ben_xvi_spe_20051222_roman-curia_en.html (accessed October 20, 2014).

32 Congregation for Divine Worship and the Discipline of the Sacraments, Fifth instruction "For the Right Implementation of the Constitution on the Sacred Liturgy of the Second Vatican Council: *Liturgiam authenticam*, on the use of vernacular languages in the publication of the books of the Roman Liturgy," *AAS* 93 (2001) 685-726.

33 John Paul II, Motu proprio "*Apostolos Suos,* On the Theological and Juridical Nature of Episcopal Conferences," *AAS* 90 (1998) 641-658 English translation *Origins* 28: 152-158.

urgent need," etc. – that leave important space for adaptation to the particularity of specific cases might even be eliminated.[34] The Seminar felt that there might not be the openness to enter into a conversion process leading to renewal and reform as intended by Vatican II. At the same time it was pointed out that many of the current norms do not forbid applying them with a more open mentality.

I recall a bishop from Canada who left the conference stating that only now did he see why he and parish priests should consult with the laity; not because the law foresees it, but because the law gives expression to the charisms granted by the Lord to the church for its edification. He also saw that he could invite the laity to write the *Ad limina* report with him as it would provide an opportunity to engage the diocese in dialogue about situations and challenges to be met. Such notions are not just relevant for the implementation of the doctrine of Vatican II with regard to, for example, chapter 2 of *Lumen gentium*, they are also relevant for ecumenical dialogue as it implements a certain form of synodality.[35] The Canadian bishop, furthermore, became aware that the law does not forbid inviting guests from other churches to either diocesan or parish pastoral councils! It would be another possibility of fostering bonds that already exist.

That first conclusion, however, that the time was not ripe for drafting new norms pointed to another much more fundamental issue that the Peter and Paul Seminar subsequently decided to focus on: What does it take for an institution to enter into a conversion process that leads to a continuous renewal and reform? How does one move an organization?[36] After more theoretical reflections on the subject at a conference held in Erfurt, Germany, in 2009, in which also an expert on management of large organizations participated, it was decided to do a case study. For the next round the focus was on liturgical reform in the course of history. What can be learned from the processes that went on? What was conducive in such reform processes, and how did reforms deal with those who opposed it? The focus of the research was not on liturgy as such, but on the reform processes that concern liturgy.

With the exception of the last round on liturgy, all study projects of the Peter and Paul Seminar have been published in *The Jurist*. As co-moderator of the

34 Such clauses would be: "except for grave reasons" (e.g. c. 193 §1), "in accord with his own prudent judgment" (e.g. c. 468), "as he determines it opportune" (e.g. c. 344, 1°), etc.

35 An example of the relevance of synodality on all levels of the church is expressed in the so called Ravenna Document issued by the Joint International Commission for the Theological Dialogue between the Roman Catholic Church and the Orthodox Church, Ecclesiological and Canonical Consequences of the Sacramental Nature of the Church: Ecclesial Communion, Conciliarity and Authority, Ravenna, 13 October 2007. Cf. http://www.vatican.va/roman_curia/pontifical_councils/chrstuni/ch_orthodox_docs/rc_pc_chrstuni_doc_20071013_documento-ravenna_en.html (accessed October 20, 2014).

36 Considering the reforms that pope Francis tries to bring to the church, this question is of extreme relevance.

Peter and Paul Seminar, I would like to use this opportunity to express a word of gratitude to Msgr. Thomas Green who, as a member of the Peter and Paul Seminar, and as editor of *The Jurist* has done a tremendous service to the project by editing and translating papers amounting to over a thousand pages. The studies on liturgical reform were published in *Questions liturgiques, Studies in Liturgy*.[37]

In looking back, the Peter and Paul Seminar has focused on the canonical institutions that are to implement Vatican II in all that it entails. The unity of the church has been the decisive motivation for the research. In a meeting earlier this year, in Paris, it was concluded that the studies published in 2004 and 2008 on leadership of the church are of great relevance for the developments that are currently taking place in Rome. Reading them again is highly recommended. We are currently attending to the possibility of bringing these papers to the attention of a wider public.

Canon lawyers who are members include James Coriden, Thomas Green, John Faris, Astrid Kaptijn and myself. The founder of the Seminar, Ladislas Örsy, holds an eminent position, but does not actively engage in the group. The theologians include among others Catherine Clifford, Eugene Duffy, Peter de-Mey, Gilles Routhier, Laurent Villemin, Henk Witte and Joseph Famerée. Over the years the Peter and Paul Seminar has invited guest participants to provide the knowledge and expertise that the Seminar itself does not have. Among those guests were Mathijs Lamberights, Thomas Whelan, Chad Glendinning, Massimo Fagliolo and Brian E. Daley.

In summary, the first of the three projects focuses on unity by doing a comparative study of the norms in two different churches that are currently in place. It involves canon lawyers from both churches. The project does not seem to focus too intensely on the theology governing the norms, nor does it have as its goal at this point reconciling them or arriving at a common set of norms.

The second project involves one denomination only, namely the Roman Catholic Church. It analyses the doctrinal points that are in need of support and protection by the community, and determines whether the current norms do this sufficiently in order to propose a reform in which the unity of the church is an overriding principle.

The third project focuses on learning from other denominations. It involves all denominations. Canon law only came into the picture as of 2012, when I was first invited to accept the St. Cutbeth's Research Grant at Durham University. Based on my research, I was subsequently asked to accept an honorary professorship in "Canon law and Ecumenism" at Durham University in England in order to participate on a long term basis in the project.

37 *Questions liturgiques, Studies in Liturgy* 93 (2012) 153-258 and 95 (2014) 3-155.

3. Receptive Ecumenism

In 2006 the Roman Catholic systematic theologian Dr. Paul Murray from the University of Durham in England proposed a new methodological approach to ecumenism which goes by the name "Receptive Ecumenism." From the beginning church leaders of different denominations from all over the world supported it strongly. The first major conference, held in 2006, was entitled "Receptive Ecumenism and the Call to Catholic Learning."[38] One of the most prominent speakers at this conference was Cardinal Walter Kasper.[39] The second conference was once held again in Durham in 2009 and was called "Receptive Ecumenism and the Call to Ecclesial Learning."[40] The third one was held at Fairfield University in Fairfield, CT, in June 2014, and was entitled "Receptive Ecumenism in International Perspective: Contextual Ecclesial Learning." In these conferences people from different denominations and relevant ecumenical organizations such as the World Council of Churches and Faith & Order participated. The project is now such that a wide range of churches are actively engaged.

The proposed method of Receptive Ecumenism is considered to be so promising that it has been adopted by the current bi-lateral dialogue between the Roman

38 The proceedings were published in Paul D. Murray, ed., *Receptive Ecumenism and the Call to Catholic Learning: Exploring a Way for Contemporary Ecumenism* (Oxford: University Press, 2008). For a description of what "Receptive Ecumenism" is, this study very much relies on the just mentioned book and the following publications all by Paul D. Murray, "Receptive Ecumenism and Catholic Learning: Establishing the Agenda," *International Journal for the Study of the Christian Church* 7 (2007) 279-301; "Receptive Ecumenism and Ecclesial Learning. Receiving our Gifts for Our Needs," *Louvain Studies* 33 (2008) 30-45.

39 The Australian theologian Gerard Kelly writes that the Pontifical Council for the Promotion of Christian Unity saw the project as being in line with Cardinal Kasper's project *Harvesting the Fruits: Basic Aspects of Christian Faith in Ecumenical Dialogue* (London: Continuum, 2009). Gerard Kelly, "An Introduction to Receptive Ecumenism," paper delivered at the Ecumenical Consultation on Receptive Ecumenism hosted by the Archdiocese of Melbourne at the Treacy Centre, Parkville (Melbourne) August 19, 2011.

40 Paul Murray intends to publish the presentations of the conference as Paul D. Murray, ed., *Receptive Ecumenism and Ecclesial Learning: Learning to Be Church Together.*

Catholic Church and the Anglican Church (ARCIC III),[41] and it is playing an important role in the official so called "conversation" between the Roman Catholic Church and the Community of Protestant Churches in Europe, that is, those churches that are in a fellowship based on the Leuenberg Agreement of 1973.[42]

What is Receptive Ecumenism? Receptive Ecumenism is about showing 'wounded hands,' recognizing deficiencies, and acknowledging areas for growth within one's own tradition leading to a willingness to ask what can and must be learned, with dynamic integrity, from the dialogue partner. It is a receptive *ecclesial* learning and receiving in humility in order to grow and be enriched oneself.[43] It is an ecumenical learning that implies enrichment rather than diminishment of identity. Engaging in Receptive Ecumenism thus requires a programmatic shift from asking: What do our dialogue partners need to learn from us?, to asking: What do *we* need to learn and *what* can we learn from our dialogue partners?[44] Murray refers to the famous phrase by John F. Kennedy: "Do not ask what your country can do for you, but ask what you can do for your country." It hints at the understanding that you cannot change others, only yourself; but "changing yourself will open up new possibilities and might in turn lead to changes in others."[45] Hence the question is not any longer: How can they become more like us so that division might be eased? But instead the question should be: How might *we* become more like them in diverse particular ways so that any specific difficul-

41 On May 27, 2011 a communiqué about ARCIC III was issued which stated: "In considering the method that ARCIC III will use, the Commission was particularly helped by the approach of 'receptive ecumenism,' which seeks to make ecumenical progress by learning from our partner, rather than simply asking our partner to learn from us. Receptive ecumenism is more about self-examination and inner conversion than convincing the other; Anglicans and Roman Catholics can help each other grow in faith, life and witness to Christ if they are open to being transformed by God's grace mediated through each other. ARCIC is committed to modeling the receptive ecumenism it advocates. It intends to find ways to consult with the members of its churches at many levels as its work matures." See http://iarccum.org/doc/?d=39 (accessed December 9, 2014). See also Paul Murray, "ARCIC II: Recognizing the Need for an Ecumenical Gear-Change," *One in Christ* 45 (2011) 200-211.

42 "The CPCE [=Community of Protestant Churches in Europe] is the umbrella organisation of the protestant churches. 94 Lutheran, Methodist, Reformed and United Churches from over thirty countries in Europe and South America belong to it. With that the CPCE represents altogether around 50 million Protestants. The CPCE exists thanks to the Leuenberg Agreement of 1973. It concluded: churches are allowed to be different because they appeal to the Gospel as their common basis. That sounds simple, but has far-reaching consequences: since then a Lutheran minister can preach from a reformed pulpit or a French minister lead a congregation in Germany." http://www.leuenberg.net/node/873 (accessed October 2, 2014).

43 Paul D. Murray & Andrea L. Murray, "The Roots, Range and Reach of Receptive Ecumenism," In Clive Barrett (ed.) *The Process of Unity: Reflections on Ecumenism* (London: DLT, 2012) 81.

44 Murray, "Receptive Ecumenism and Ecclesial Learning," *Louvain Studies* 33 (2008) 33.

45 Ibid., 32.

ties we experience in our own thought and practice might be eased? The idea is, therefore, not to get the best China tea service out, but to show how wounded we are ourselves, and how much we are in need of healing and indeed conversion. Hence, Receptive Ecumenism is not about the "best China," but about the 'wounded hands.'[46]

The presumption behind this thinking is that if all would act in this way, change would occur and all would become a bit more like the others. "In accordance with this, the idea is for each of the Christian traditions, singly and jointly, to become more, not less, than they currently are by recognizing their own respective sticking points and correlatively learning from, and receiving from, each other's particular gifts."[47]

Of course the key aspect in this whole process is the capacity of each and every tradition to learn: it is not just learning by individuals, but it is a learning process that takes place on a communal, indeed, ecclesial level. Required, therefore, is not only a conversion to such an attitude and openness on an individual level, but also and in particular on an ecclesial level. The ecclesial level has an institutional dimension. It is here that canon law comes in, as will be outlined below. Before doing so, it is necessary to point to two major assumptions behind the project.

1. The significance of the call to organic structural unity

   Once it became clear that visible unity is not as easy to achieve as many had hoped, there was a tendency to focus more on collaboration in practical matters of service and mission and less on dialogues concerning doctrinal and ecclesiological issues. Hence, for many, unity is not a reachable goal in the near future any longer. Receptive Ecumenism recognizes this phenomenon, but resists it. It sees the eschatological reality of the unity as being of relevance to the present. So the point is "to live now oriented upon this promise and calling, disposed to the challenge of conversion that it entails and open to the possibilities of greater flourishing that it represents."[48] Receptive Ecumenism thus opens into a space of real ecclesial learning.

2. Receptive Ecumenism is a Transformative Praxis

   It is important to recall that Christianity is not a belief system, but a practice of discipleship. Applied to the church, this implies that she is not

46 Paul Murray, "Recent Initiatives in Receptive Ecumenism at Durham University, UT and their Relationship to the Work of the Faith and Order Commission," p. 2 (unpublished manuscript made available by author).

47 Murray, "Receptive Ecumenism and Ecclesial Learning," *Louvain Studies* 33 (2008) 33.

48 Ibid., 36.

just a concept, but a life-world – a living breathing organizational reality. For Receptive Ecumenism this implies that "ecclesial learning is not simply theoretical, or purely doctrinal in character." A key assumption for this is that Receptive Ecumenism cannot imply only asking what we can learn from each other; it must go beyond that and ask: What *prevents* Christian churches from learning actually taking place? "What are the organizational, psychological, sociological and cultural bars to effective receptive learning taking place and how might these debilitating factors best be negotiated and navigated?"[49] One could easily add to this: How do canonical structures impede or frustrate ecclesial learning? Does the Catholic Church even have structures that facilitate learning? Are people (sometimes) hiding behind canonical norms pretending any other action is not allowed or possible? Are canonical norms at times granted more weight than they have from a doctrinal point of view? Receptive Ecumenism invites attention to these and related questions. It is therefore to be seen as a transformative process. Such a transformative process requires the cooperation of many different disciplines such as theology, psychology, and yes, even canon law. My own contribution in this project focuses on discovering possibilities for canonical institutions to facilitate ecclesial learning and investigating how what has been learned can have an impact on existing institutions.

Before attending to this, the question might be raised whether there is anything new to Receptive Ecumenism?[50] The newness of Receptive Ecumenism consists, according to Paul Murray, in the way "in which it takes this admirable disposition and accords a strategic, programmatic priority to it in the hope of releasing its potential and shaping influence in ways previously not achieved."[51] The point is thus not just listening to a doctrine with the primary purpose of finding middle ground between traditions, but to ask how we can be enriched within ourselves. It is a learning *in face of* and *across* continuing difference to arrive at an enriched standpoint. The enrichment has everything to do with moving beyond the theoretical results that came out of the dialogues into building on the theoretical outcomes and looking for concrete expressions in each other's own church.

Projects on the local level

To test the proposed method a project has been set out in which nine major Christian denominational groups in the northeast of England participate. It will

49 Ibid., 37.

50 Indeed this question is being asked by Paul Murray himself as he reflects on the vision of Paul Couturier, recent ecumenical dialogues, and above all on the invitation expressed by Pope John Paul II in *Ut unum sint*, when he asked theologians and leaders of other churches to help him reimagining the petrine ministry in such a way that it is open to a new situation. John Paul II, Encyclical letter *Ut unum sint*, nos. 94-95.

51 Murray, "Receptive Ecumenism," 39.

last about three to four years. The purpose is "to examine how respective difficulties and sticking points in the organizational cultures, structures, and processes of each of the participant church traditions, from regional to congregational levels, might fruitfully be addressed by learning from, or receiving, examples of 'best practice' in the other traditions. The practical and organizational act here as portals into the theological rather than the other way around: asking first how the specific difficulties and limitations of one tradition might be tended to by learning and receiving from what is strong in the others and then subjecting these possibilities to rigorous ecclesiological testing against the terms of the relevant host tradition."[52]

The project is divided in three areas:

- Governance and Finance: the focus is here on financial administration and pastoral strategy: How are the churches organized and administered? How do, for example, budget plans and strategy relate?

- Learning and Formation: What are the structures and processes that promote the transmission of Christian identity, faith and mission? What kind of identity impedes learning?

- Leadership and ministry: e.g. How do churches respond to a decline in ministers and clergy; How do they nurture active congregations? What kind of strategies are developed?

It is hoped that by taking stock the churches learn first of all about their own ways: How do they act? From a canonical perspective this learning goes far beyond writing down the norms. An analysis is made of how the church in a specific field operates. Such actions might be in agreement with the norms, they might also be beyond the law (*praeter ius*) or even against the law. Furthermore, an awareness might occur that the way the church operates is in agreement with the law, but there might be other ways of doing things. Thus, for example, the issue of transmitting the faith to youth is an object of the project. The investigation attends to the question: Who makes decisions about the content and form of youth ministry in the respective churches? What institutions are involved in this? In the Roman Catholic Church this could be the diocesan pastoral council and/or the presbyteral council or maybe the diocesan bishop with his vicar for youth ministry. Are young people themselves involved in the decision making process? How and when? Are the existing institutions used? How are they used? What is on the agenda of the presbyteral and diocesan pastoral council, and who decides the agenda? The different operations will reveal certain theological premises of which a church might not even be aware. Comparing the modalities of different

52 Paul Murray, "Introducing Receptive Ecumenism," *The Ecumenist* 51 (2014) vol. 2, 6.

churches could help each and every church to step back and ask whether one could benefit from the other churches' way or enhance one's own way of operating. The practices that are in place in different churches might have developed based on different or similar theological notions.

Ecumenical engagement will thus be very different from the dialogues as they were engaged till now. The project is very practical and organizational. Because canon lawyers are very familiar with the three areas outlined above, the project should not only be appealing to canon lawyers, but in fact canon lawyers are indispensible for the success of the project. Their task clearly exists in analyzing the actual actions together with outlining alternative methods of operating which, in a first stage, would still be in accordance with the existing laws. In a second stage, canon lawyers could provide (to the legislator) alternative modalities that would be in agreement with Catholic theology, but that would differ from the current existing institutions. It is exactly here that the three projects of the Colloquium of Anglican and Roman Catholic Canon lawyers, the Peter and Paul Seminar, and Receptive Ecumenism meet and can benefit from each other. The proposal of the Groupe des Dombes to distinguish the confessional identity from the ecclesial and Christian identity could serve as a criterion for what can be received in the context of Receptive Ecumenism and what would not serve as the theological basis.

It is quite remarkable that there are nine denominations participating in the Receptive Ecumenism "field" project in Northern England. They are all willing to put their cards on the table, so to speak, as they have all agreed to make their internal data available to each other.

This project is accompanied by a team of experts from the fields of theology, sociology, finances, ecumenism and anthropology of religion. To bring in such expertise might have the drawback that receptive ecumenical learning occurs more among the experts rather than the people on the ground. Hence it is hoped for that "a series of self-initiated self-help projects where church members in a diverse range of contexts ask themselves where the specific difficulties in their own tradition lie and how they might be fruitfully learn in these regards, with appropriate testing, from other traditions."[53]

Projects on the universal level

Whereas the above projects are within a Roman Catholic perspective on the local level, it is not difficult to imagine projects on the universal level. A few can be envisioned.

There is the project on the *petrine ministry*. In his famous encyclical on ecumenism *Ut unum sint* published in 1995, Pope John Paul II writes:

53 Ibid., 6.

> As Bishop of Rome I am fully aware ... that Christ ardently desires the full and visible communion of all those Communities in which, by virtue of God's faithfulness, his Spirit dwells. I am convinced that I have a particular responsibility in this regard, above all in acknowledging the ecumenical aspirations of the majority of the Christian Communities and in heeding the request made of me to find a way of exercising the primacy which, while in no way renouncing what is essential to its mission, is nonetheless open to a new situation ... When addressing the Ecumenical Patriarch, His Holiness Dimitrios I, I acknowledged my awareness that 'for a great variety of reasons, and against the will of all concerned, what should have been a service sometimes manifested itself in a very different light. [Here Pope John Paul II reveals the 'wounded hands' - MW]. But...it is out of a desire to obey the will of Christ truly that I recognize that as Bishop of Rome I am called to exercise that ministry...I insistently pray the Holy Spirit to shine his light upon us, enlightening all the Pastors and theologians of our Churches, that we may seek – together, of course – the forms in which this ministry may accomplish a service of love recognized by all concerned.' This is an immense task, which we cannot refuse and which I cannot carry out by myself. Could not the real but imperfect communion existing between us persuade Church leaders and their theologians to engage with me in a patient and fraternal dialogue on this subject, a dialogue in which, leaving useless controversies behind, we could listen to one another, keeping before us only the will of Christ for his Church and allowing ourselves to be deeply moved by his plea 'that they may all be one ... so that the world may believe that you have sent me' (Jn 17:21)?[54]

In this text the Pope thus acknowledges the need for growth and change – he shows the 'wounded hands' – and then asks for help from others, thus taking on a learning attitude.

This invitation by Pope John Paul II led to numerous reactions by different churches.[55] One project resulting from this is the study by the Group of Farfa Sabina on the petrine ministry: a group of seven Lutherans invited seven Roman Catholic theologians to reflect with them about the petrine ministry and explain

54 John Paul II, *Ut unum sint*, nos. 95-96.

55 Several responses to the invitation by Pope John Paul II were published in James Puglisi, ed., *Petrine Ministry and the Unity of the Church: Toward a Patient and Fraternal Dialogue* (Collegeville, MN: Liturgical Press, 2002).

to them how Vatican I was to be understood.[56] The Catholic members accepted the invitation. They first explained what the context of Vatican I had been, then how the texts had developed and what had been intended. This was followed by the acknowledgement that in the reception of Vatican I, unfortunately, a maximalistic interpretation had occurred which had not been intended by the council fathers, but that had characterized the post-Vatican I period. In a next step they clarified that the doctrine of Vatican I had been adopted in Vatican II, but that Vatican II's doctrine on the collegiality of bishops now provides the context in which the doctrine on the primacy needs to be interpreted. They thus affirmed that Vatican II provides the hermeneutical criterion for understanding Vatican I: the primacy is to be understood in conjunction with collegiality. When the Group of Farfa Sabina finally came to interpreting the current norms in the Code of Canon Law on the papacy – in particular c. 333 on the primacy of jurisdiction, and c. 749 on papal infallibility – it was pointed out that it is necessary to consider the whole hermeneutical discussion on Vatican II and its impact on Vatican I for interpreting these norms.

This procedure and perspective opened a window for both sides. It led to a very open discussion in which the Lutherans could investigate what Martin Luther had really intended when he discussed the papacy revealing that – not unlike the one-sided reception of Vatican I – his understanding had also been received in a biased fashion. Here a correction was needed as well. He had not rejected the petrine ministry as such, but had rejected it under certain circumstances.

The working method and the content discussed by the Group of Farfa Sabina required an upright willingness to acknowledge on both sides that things had gone wrong in reception and that certainly in that area there was – and is – a need for correction. From there the Group outlined a pathway for the future and identified steps that each church has to undertake.

---

56 Group of Farfa Sabina, *Communion of Churches and Petrine Ministry; Lutheran-Catholic Convergences* (Grand Rapids, MI: Eerdmans, 2014). This document was preceded by a study about the petrine ministry by members of different denominations who gathered in 2003 and 2004: James Puglisi, ed., *How Can the Petrine Ministry Be a Service to the Unity of the Universal Church?* (Grand Rapids, MI: Eerdmans, 2010). That study led to the formation of a group of seven Lutheran and seven Catholic scholars who met over a period of five years (2005-2009) in a monastery in the hills just outside Rome in Farfa Sabina (hence the name of the group). Members of the group were, from Catholic side: James Puglisi (Catholic convener), Johannes Brosseder, Hervé Legrand, Hermann Josef Pottmeyer, and myself, and from Lutheran side there were among others Peder Norgaard Hoyen (Lutheran convener), André Birmelé, Theodor Dieter and Harding Meyer. The German version was originally published in 2010 and is entitled: Gruppe von Farfa Sabina, *Gemeinschaft der Kirchen und Petrusamt: Lutherisch-Katholische Annäherungen* (Leipzig: EVA, 2 rev., 2014).

The study was first published in the German speaking world where it was received very well and in particular by Lutherans.[57] The English version is scheduled for publication at Christmas 2014.

A second area in which Receptive Ecumenism could be beneficial would be the *role and tasks of the laity* in the church. The very fine workshop presented at this Convention by Dr. Asselin from Saint Paul University in Ottawa on the laity,[58] made me think again that the appreciation of the laity by the Second Vatican Council relates to the rediscovery of the meaning of baptism. The theology of the participation in the threefold ministry of Christ is deeply connected to Calvinistic theology.[59] The churches originating from the Reformation also currently experience the need for a reflection upon the relationship between the common priesthood and ordained ministry in their own church. The reasons lie with the lack of ordained ministers and are related to the increased involvement of non-ordained in their church. The Roman Catholic Church also experiences an increased need to reflect on the relationship between the ordained and non-ordained with regard to ministry. There are theological questions pertaining to laity who lead a parish (c. 517 §2), assist at weddings (c. 1112 §1), baptize (c. 861 §2) and preach (c. 766). Despite the fact that both traditions hold different views on ordination, it might nevertheless be worthwhile to engage in a dialogue with each other on these topics. Not only could we learn from each other, but we might then also be walking on pathways that could lead toward each other as well.

A third area concerns the topic of the *sensus fidelium*. Vatican II affirmed the doctrine in the second chapter of *Lumen gentium* when dealing with the *munus docendi* of the whole church (*LG* 12). The text reads:

> The universal body of the faithful who have received the anointing of the holy one (see Jn 2: 20, 27), cannot be mistaken in belief (*in credendo falli nequit*). It displays (*manifestat*)[60]

57 See e.g. the reaction by the Lutheran Bishop Friedrich Weber, "Stellungnahme zu den Ergebnissen des Studienprojektes der Lutherisch-katholischen Gruppe von Farfa Sabina uber „Die Gemeinschaft der Kirche und das Petrusamt" während des Symposions am 20.02.2011 im Coelicum der katholisch-theologischen Fakultät der Universität Erfurt. Cf. http://www.landeskirche-braunschweig.de/uploads/tx_mitdownload/Vortrag_Erfurt_Farfa_Sabina_2_2011.pdf (accessed October 30, 2014).

58 Anne Asselin, "Lay People as 'Protagonists in the Church': Pathways for the Future," in *Proceedings of the Seventh-Sixth Annual Convention* (Washington, DC: CLSA, 2015), pp. 119-136.

59 See e.g. Ludwig Schick, *Das dreifache Amt Christi und der Kirche : zur Entstehung und Entwicklung der Trilogien* Europäischen Hochschulschriften, vol. 23 (Frankfurt a.M.: Peter Lang, 1982).

60 In an earlier draft the text used the word *exercet*. Francisco Gil Hellín, *Concilii Vaticani II Synopsis in ordinem redigens schemata cum relationibus necnon partum orations atque animadversions, Constitutio Dogmatica De Ecclesia Lumen gentium* (Vatican: Libereria editrice, 1995) 98.

> this particular quality through a supernatural sense of the faith (*sensus fidei*) in the whole people when 'from the bishop to the last of the faithful laity' it expresses the consent of all in matters of faith and morals. Through this sense of faith which is aroused and sustained by the Spirit of truth, the people of God, under the guidance of the sacred magisterium to which it is faithfully obedient (*obsequens*),[61] receives no longer the words of human beings but truly the word of God (see 1 Thess 2:13).

The *relatio* explained that by *sensus fidei* the church understands a kind of capacity (*facultas*) of the *entire* Church, "through which it grasps in faith the transmitted revelation, so that it can distinguish between truth and error in matters of belief."[62] It should be noted though that the text does add that this all happens under the guidance of the magisterium (*sub ductu magisterii*).

The doctrine of the *sensus fidelium* in the second chapter of *Lumen gentium* (*LG* 12) was not really reconciled with the hitherto model of understanding revelation which can be found in the third chapter of *Lumen gentium* which sees revelation as a set of truths to be proclaimed by the magisterium and to be received by the other faithful.[63] After the council ended, structures should have been developed to assist the church in ascertaining the *sensus fidei* or *sensus fidelium*, but neither the Code of Canon Law nor other legal documents issued for the uni-

61 The word *obsequium* is a relatively new word in the history of the church. It is not to be equated with *oebedientia* which could be translated with obedience; *obsequium* refers more to respect. Ladislas Örsy sees *obsequium* as a seminal locution: a word which deepest meaning must still unfold itself in times to come. Cf. Ladislas Örsy, *The Church: Learning and Teaching. Magisterium, Assent, Dissent, Academic Freedom* (Wilmington, DE: Glazier, 1987) 82-89.

62 The relatio stated that the text "agit de obiectiva analysi sensus fidei: est scilicet quasi facultas *totius* Ecclesiae, qua ipsa in fide perspicit Revelationem traditam, discernens inter verum et falsum in rebus fidei, ac simul penitius in eam intrat eamque plenius in vita applicat." *AS* III/I, 199 (Emphasis in original). See for the subsequent thoughts also Miguel M. Garijo-Guembe, *Communion of the Saints: Foundation, Nature, and Structure of the Church* (Collegeville, MN: Liturgical Press, 1994) 136.

63 The International Theological Commission published in 2014 the document: Sensus fidei in the Life of the Church. Cf. http://www.vatican.va/roman_curia/congregations/cfaith/cti_documents/rc_cti_20140610_sensus-fidei_en.html (accessed October 30, 2014). This document also remains on the level of doctrine and does not provide for structures that could assist the community in ascertaining the sensus fidei. The Australian fundamental theologian Ormond Rush has done serious study of the sensus fidelium. See e.g. his book, *The Eyes of Faith: The Sense of the Faithful and the Church's Reception of Revelation* (Washington, D.C.: The Catholic University of America Press, 2009). John J. Burkhard has published several articles in which he gives an overview of many publications on the subject: "Sensus fidei: Theological Reflection since Vatican II, I. 1965-1984," *The Heythrop Journal* 34 (1993) 41-59; Idem "Sensus fidei: Recent theological Reflection (1990-2001) Part II," *The Heythrop Journal* 47 (2006) 38-54.

versal church provided for it.[64] It was thus somewhat of a surprise when in preparation for the Extraordinary Synod on the Family to be held in October 2014, at the end of 2012 a questionnaire was sent out to the bishops suggesting that all the faithful be asked to respond. Although the questionnaire itself did not seem to be perfect, and possibly did not fulfill professional criteria for conducting such a survey – as it could not really secure a true reflection of what the faithful believe – nevertheless, it was a major shift in the operation of the church as the faith of all was to be ascertained. Yet, there would seem to be space for serious improvement in the method. It is here that Receptive Ecumenism might come in: after acknowledging that we as Catholics are not really skilled in ascertaining the faith of all (showing the 'wounded hands'), we might turn to other churches asking how they engage in dialogue with each other about what their faith really is. Could they help us? Moreover, if the *sensus fidei* finds it roots in baptism, what does this imply for the need to listen to the faith of other churches with regard to marriage and the family? Can their belief in establishing the *sensus fidelium* be left out a priori? How does the existing communion – albeit a communion *non plena* – work out here?[65]

Pope Francis spoke about learning and receiving from others in his Apostolic Exhortation *Evangelii Gaudium* of November 24, 2013 when he wrote:

> How many important things unite us! If we really believe in the abundantly free working of the Hoy Spirit we can learn so much from one another! It is not just about better informed about others, but rather good reaping what the Spirit has sown in them, which is also meant to be a gift for us. To give but one example, in the dialogue with our Orthodox brothers and sisters, we Catholics have the opportunity to learn more about the meaning of episcopal collegiality and their experience of synodality. Through an exchange of gifts, the Spirit can lead us ever more fully into truth and goodness.[66]

---

64 Cf. Myriam Wijlens, "S*ensus fidelium* – Authority: Protecting and Promoting the Ecclesiology of Vatican II with the Assistance of Institutions?" in Victor George D'Souza, ed., *In the Service of Truth and Justice: Festschrift in Honour of Prof. Augustine Mendonca*, (Bangalore, St. Peter's Pontifical Institute: 2008) 425-448. Also published in: Peter De Mey, Pieter De Witte, Gerard Mannion, eds., *Believing in Community: Ecumenical Reflections on the Church*. Bibliotheca Ephemeridum Theologicarum Lovaniensum 261 (Louvain: Peeters, 2013) 207-228.

65 Myriam Wijlens, "*Sensus fidei fidelium* and Receptive Ecumenism: Canonical Considerations," Lecture given at the Conference on Receptive Ecumenism III. Fairfield Connecticut, June 9-12, 2014 (publication forthcoming).

66 Pope Francis, Apostolic Exhortation *Evangelii Gaudium* (November 24, 2013) 246. Cf. http://w2.vatican.va/content/francesco/en/apost_exhortations/documents/papa-francesco_esortazione-ap_20131124_evangelii-gaudium.html (accessed October 30, 2014)

Do other churches also turn to the Catholic Church and show their 'wounded hands'? Recently a Greek orthodox professor asked Catholic colleagues about the role of theologians at Vatican II. He raised the question because the Orthodox Church is scheduled to convene in the Holy and Great Synod in 2016. He asked about the role, task and authority of theologians in Vatican II and in other synods. He showed his 'wounded hands' when he said that in his church there is not much experience of professional theologians and bishops working together. Of course a Roman Catholic response to such a question show our own 'wounded hands,' as the relationship between bishops and theologians might have been great during Vatican II – here Roman Catholics could offer the finest 'China tea service' – but it deteriorated after the council rather rapidly. Maybe there is a need for learning together.

It would not be difficult to continue the list of areas where mutual learning and growth might, and could, take place. All these topics deal with ecclesiologial issues, and yet, they have a tremendous impact on the unity of the church. Ecclesial learning for the sake of unity could be a method to move forward.

Pope Francis spoke in favour of the method of Receptive Ecumenism during the Week of Prayer for Christian Unity in January 2014:

> It is good to acknowledge the grace with which God blesses us and, even more so, to find in other Christians something of which we are in need, something that we can receive as a gift from our brothers and our sisters. The Canadian group that prepared the prayers for this Week of Prayer has not invited the communities to think about what they can give their Christian neighbours, but has exhorted them to meet to understand what all can receive from time to time from the others. This requires something more. It requires much prayer, humility, reflection and constant conversion. Let us go forward on this path, praying for the unity of Christians, so that this scandal may cease and be no longer with us.[67]

67 In Rome, in an address to pilgrims from the Oriental Lumen Foundation in America, Pope Francis said to them: "Every Christian pilgrimage is not only a geographical journey, but also and above all an opportunity to take a path of inner renewal taking us ever closer to Christ our Lord...These dimensions are absolutely essential to proceed along the road that leads us to reconciliation and full communion among all believers in Christ. There is no true ecumenical dialogue without openness to inner renewal and the search for greater fidelity to Christ and to His will." See *Vatican Information Service*, October 24, 2014.

Conclusion

The Convention Planning Committee chose the unity of the church to commemorate the promulgation of the three conciliar documents *Lumen gentium, Unitatis redintegratio* and *Orientalium Eccelsiarum*. They rightly perceived that unity is the hermeneutical criterion that must precede all reflections and actions in the church. Canonical structures play their own role in achieving that unity, but they can only come to life through the people who apply them. It all begins with an internal disposition to be open to conversion. This is not just a matter of individuals, but of the institution as such. Canon lawyers are to assist the institution by entering in such a conversion process leading to renewal and reform. They can do so by asking the simple question: Are these structures, is this interpretation, is this application of the law, in fact promoting church unity or is it impeding or obstructing it? If they obstruct, then the question must be raised: What can be done about it? In looking for an answer to the question, the conversion would imply being open to learning from other churches while preserving what belongs to the ecclesial and Christian identity of the church. That would then result in the Catholic Church growing to be more in who she really is. Dialogue will not lead to giving up, but to growth and enrichment.

The Convention Planning Committee had the right intuition with the subject for this Convention. It leaves the participants with the awareness to take their own responsibility seriously and play their part in responding to the prayer of the Lord that "all may be one" (Jn. 17:21). In doing so, canon lawyers could assist the community in transferring what St. Paul has said for individuals to the church as such:

> That is the one thing that would make me completely happy: There must be no competition among you, no conceit; but everybody is to be self-effacing. Always consider the other person to be better than ourselves, so that nobody thinks of his own interests first but everybody thinks of other people's interest instead (Phil 2: 2-4).

Major Address

Marriage in the Eastern and Western Churches

Chorbishop John D. Faris, JCOD

Church Breathes with Two Lungs

I have been asked to speak about the canonical institution of marriage in the Eastern and Western Churches. Such an assignment is not only broad, but also complex: certain Eastern Catholic communities are in full communion with the Church of Rome, that is, they are Catholic and observe a discipline that emerges from a discipline heavily influenced by Western canonists. We shall begin with a comparison of the laws regulating marriages in the Latin and Eastern Catholic Churches. This comparison will be followed by an examination of the teaching and practice of the Orthodox Churches regarding divorce and remarriage. Lastly, we will explore possible convergences of Catholic and Orthodox pastoral practices for divorced remarried faithful.

Marriage in the Catholic Churches[1]

In the apostolic constitution *Sacri Canones*,[2] Pope Saint John Paul II declared that it had always been the desire of the Roman Pontiffs that there be two distinct

1 A practical comparison of marriage disciplines can be found in Lorenzo Lorusso, *Eastern Catholics and Latin Pastors: Issues and Canonical Norms*, trans. John D. Faris (Washington, D.C.: Canon Law Society of America, 2013) [abbreviated Lorusso, *Eastern Catholics and Latin Pastors*] 212-263.

2 John Paul II, apostolic constitution *Sacri Canones*, 18, 18 October 1990: *AAS* 82 (1990) 1033-1044. An English translation is published in *Code of Canons of the Eastern Churches: Latin-English Edition: New English Translation* (Washington, DC: Canon Law Society of America, 2001) [abbreviated *CCEC*] xxi-xxvii.

codes,[3] one for the Latin Church[4] and another for the Eastern Catholic Churches.[5] The Legislator drew a metaphor from anatomy to describe the benefit of two distinct codes for the one Catholic Church: ". . . the Church, gathered by one Spirit, breathes, as it were, with the two lungs of East and West, and burns with the love of Christ, having one heart, as it were, with two ventricles."[6] In this context, the metaphor of the two lungs (or two ventricles of the heart—less often referred to) refers to the Western or Latin Church and the Eastern *Catholic* Churches.

The limitations of time, space – and the attention span of participants at the end of a busy convention – do not permit me to treat all aspects of Catholic marriage law, much less the history of its evolution. The approach that I shall take will be to contrast the requirements of the two codes on the presumption that the great majority of those present are familiar with marriage law as articulated in the *Codex Iuris Canonici*. In short, we are going to focus on the salient differences. While pastors and other church ministers may dismiss the canonical differences between the two codes as unimportant details, we canonists realize that non-observance of these requirements can sometimes result in invalid marriages, something any Church minister should want to avoid.

After this review of salient issues regarding marriage in both codes, we shall move to a much more interesting topic: how the Orthodox Churches deal with divorce and re-marriage. We shall then conclude with possible directions both the Catholic and Orthodox Churches can take, in hopes of a unified, more effective witness to the sanctity of marriage and pastoral response to those faithful of our Churches whose marriages have failed and are re-married.

Terminology

A cursory examination of the opening canons on the sections on marriage indicates a fundamental difference in approach. The Latin Code treats marriage as a contract: *CIC* canon 1108 § 1 speaks of "assisting at a marriage" and goes

3 See D. Faltin, "La Codificazione del Diritto Orientale," in *La Sacra Congregazione per le Chiese Orientale nel Cinquantesimo della Fondazione 1917-1967* (Rome, 1969) 127-128.

4 *Codex Iuris Canonici auctoritate Ioannis Pauli PP. II promulgatus* (Vatican City: Libreria Editrice Vaticana, 1983). English translation from *Code of Canon Law, Latin-English Edition: New English Translation* (Washington, DC: Canon Law Society of America, 2012) [abbreviated "CIC" or "Latin Code"]. English translations of canons from this code will be taken from this source unless otherwise indicated.

5 *Codex Canonum Ecclesiarum Orientalium auctoritate Ioannis Pauli PP. II promulgatus* (Vatican City: Libreria Editrice Vaticana, 1990) [abbreviated "CCEO" or "Eastern Code"]. English translation from *Code of Canons of the Eastern Churches: Latin-English Edition: New English Translation* (Washington, DC: Canon Law Society of America, 2001) [abbreviated *CCEC*]. English translations of canons from this code will be taken from this source unless otherwise indicated.

6 *CCEC*, xxiii-xxiv

further by providing that "only marriages are valid which are contracted in the presence of the local Ordinary or pastor or of the priest or deacon delegated by either of them and two witnesses." *CCEO* canon 828 § 1 speaks of "blessing the marriage" and requires that "only those marriages are valid which are celebrated with a sacred rite, in the presence of the local hierarch, local pastor, or a priest who has been given the faculty of blessing the marriage by either of them, and at least two witnesses." The distinction gives rise to significant differences in canonical arrangements.

Laws Governing Marriage

Taking into consideration the basic right of persons to marry,[7] several bodies of law govern the marriages of Catholics. The marriage of Catholics is governed by divine law, by positive (canon) law, and by civil law[8] with regard to merely civil effects.

There was a *lacuna* in Catholic Church law, which prior to 1990 lacked a provision regarding the law to be observed by a baptized non-Catholic who marries a Catholic. The Eastern Code filled the gap and provides that baptized non-Catholics are bound by the matrimonial laws of their own Church or ecclesial community or the law to which they are subject if their ecclesial community has no marriage law.[9] This same principle is applicable in adjudicating the validity of a marriage between baptized non-Catholics: the laws to which the parties were subject must be observed.[10] With regard to canonical form, if either of the parties is a member of an Eastern Church, the marriage must have been celebrated with a sacred rite.[11] This provision has no counterpart in the Latin Code, but was incorporated into an instruction to be used in Latin tribunals.[12]

Canonical Form for the Celebration of Marriage

Elements

There are several elements required for the *valid* celebration of a marriage:

1. *Presence of an ecclesiastical official*

In the Latin Church, the official person who assists at the marriage: is present, asks for an expression of consent from the consenting parties and

7 *CCEO* c. 778/*CIC* c. 1058.
8 *CCEO* c. 780 §1/*CIC* c. 1059.
9 *CCEO* c. 780.
10 *CCEO* c. 781, 1°.
11 *CCEO* c. 781, 2°.
12 Pontifical Council for Legislative Texts, *Dignitas connubii*, 25 January 2005, arts. 2 and 4.

receives it in the name of the Church.[13] Such officials are to be the local ordinary or pastor or a priest or deacon delegated by either of them.[14] The Latin Code also provides that when there is a shortage of priests and deacons the diocesan bishop can delegate lay persons to witness marriages contingent on the favorable opinion of the conference of bishops and the permission of the Holy See.[15]

In the Eastern Catholic Churches, the competent minister for the celebration of marriage is the local hierarch,[16] pastor or priest who has been given the faculty to bless the marriage.[17] The form also includes the element of a *ritus sacer*, which is described as the "intervention of a priest who assists and blesses."[18] Since the obligation to observe this form binds all Eastern Catholics,[19] even those Eastern Catholics who marry according to the Latin rite are obliged to receive the priestly blessing. Therefore, it is not possible for an Eastern Catholic to be married in the Latin Church by a deacon or lay person.

2. *Two witnesses*

Both codes require, along with an official minister of the Church, the presence of two witnesses.[20]

Marriages of Non-Catholics

The Eastern Code provides that a local hierarch can give to any Catholic priest (note that it is not restricted to Eastern Catholic priests) the faculty of blessing the marriage of Christian faithful of an Eastern non-Catholic Church under certain conditions: (1) the faithful cannot approach a priest of their own church without great difficulty; (2) the faithful freely ask for the blessing of their marriage; (3) nothing stands in the way of a valid and licit celebration of the marriage.[21]

This third requirement raises interesting issues. We have already noted above that in the celebration of marriages of baptized non-Catholics, the law proper to

13 *CIC* c. 1108 §2.
14 *CIC* cc. 1108-1111.
15 *CIC* c. 1112.
16 The patriarch and major archbishop *ipso iure* have the personal (*per se ipsum*) faculty to bless marriages everywhere provided that at least one of the parties is ascribed to the Church over which those prelates preside (*CCEO* c. 829 §3 and 152). Since the faculty is personal, the patriarch or major archbishop cannot delegate it to another. See also *CCEO* c. 830, which restricts delegation to the local hierarch or pastor.
17 *CCEO* c. 828 §1.
18 *CCEO* c. 828 §2.
19 See *CCEO* cc. 1 and 834 §1.
20 *CCEO* c. 828 §1/*CIC* c. 1108 §1.
21 *CCEO* c. 833. There is no counterpart to this canon in the Latin Code.

their Church or ecclesial community is to be observed. Therefore, the local hierarch who gives the faculty must ensure that the laws, in this case impediments which might affect the validity or liceity of a marriage, are taken into account.[22]

The matter of a prior marriage bond is a significant factor. Under the present Catholic law, if the Eastern non-Catholic was already married in the presence of a priest, the validity of the former marriage must be assessed by the competent Catholic authority before a marriage can be celebrated, notwithstanding a "Freedom to Marry" certificate issued by the Orthodox Church.

Obligation for Observance

Both the Latin Code and Eastern Code require for validity the observance of a canonical form[23] if at least one of the parties was baptized in or received into the Catholic Church; as will be seen, the elements of the form are not identical. In the case of a Catholic marrying a member of an Eastern non-Catholic Church, this requirement is only for liceity; for validity, the marriage must be celebrated with the blessing of a priest.[24]

Both codes allow for the celebration of the marriage in the presence of only two witnesses in danger of death or, outside of the danger of death, when a competent person to assist at marriage would be unavailable for a month.[25] If another priest (or deacon, in the Latin Code) is available, he is to be called upon.[26] The Eastern Code adds a stipulation that the parties of a marriage celebrated only in the presence of two witnesses should seek the nuptial blessing from a priest as soon as possible.[27]

22 One notes, for example, that in the Ethiopian Orthodox Church, the form also includes the reception of communion by both parties. "*Nella Chiesa ortodossa etiopica, il matrimonio religioso, affinché sia riconosciuto tale, deve essere celebrato solennemente in chiesa davanti al sacerdote, il quale esegue il rito sacro con la benedizione dell'anello, l'unzione degli spoi con l'olio benedetto e con l'imposizione delle corone. Elemento essenziale non è soltanto il rito della benedizione degli sposi (come nelle altre Chiese ortodosse), ma anche la comunione eucaristica degli sposi. Se questa non è ricevuta, il matrimonio, nella Chiesa etiopica, non è considerate sacramento, anche nel caso che sia stato compiuto il rito dell'incoronazione*": Giuseppe Prader, *Il matrimonio nel mondo*, 2nd updated edition (Padua: Edizioni CEDAM, 1986) 206.

23 *CCEO* c. 834 §1 and *CIC* c. 1108.

24 *CCEO* c. 834 §2 and *CIC* c. 1127. In the case of an Eastern Catholic marrying an Eastern non-Catholic, the law binding both parties requires a priestly blessing; in the case of a Latin Catholic marrying an Eastern non-Catholic, the necessity of the priestly blessing regards the Eastern non-Catholic party.

25 *CCEO* c. 832 §1/*CIC* c. 1116 §1. In a marriage celebrated in the presence of two witnesses alone, it would seem that the parties are the ministers of the sacrament – there is no other possibility.

26 *CCEO* c. 832 §2/*CIC* c. 1116 §2. The Eastern Code mentions the possibility of recourse to a non-Catholic priest.

27 *CCEO* c. 832 §3.

Dispensation from Canonical Form

A dispensation is an administrative act involving the relaxation of the obligation contained in a law, but which does not affect the juridical stability of the law itself.[28] It is possible to dispense from the observance of canonical form, but the codes differ in approaches. The Latin Code gives the local ordinary (bishop) the power to dispense from the observance of canonical form.[29] The Eastern Code, because of its concern for the priestly blessing, takes a much more rigorous approach: dispensation from the observance of canonical form is reserved to the Apostolic See or the patriarch (whose power in this matter is restricted to the historical territory of the patriarchal Church) for a most grave reason.[30] On 21 September 1991, Pope John Paul II conceded to papal representatives the faculty to grant this dispensation.[31]

There is an ambiguity regarding the dispensation / permission required when a Catholic party desires to marry a member of an Orthodox Church in the presence of an Orthodox priest. The parties are not observing the entire canonical form, that is, marrying in the presence of a canonically qualified minister, but, nevertheless, in the presence of a priest. A cautious approach would be a dispensation from canonical form for the sake of lawfulness.

Place of Celebration

The codes differ somewhat in their requirements regarding the place a marriage is to be celebrated.

The Eastern Code states that the marriage is to take place in a parish church or in another sacred space with the permission of the local hierarch or local pastor. The permission of the local hierarch is required if the marriage is to be celebrated elsewhere.[32]

The Latin Code takes into account other situations: the marriages of two Catholics or a Catholic to a baptized non-Catholic is to be celebrated in the parish church, in another church or oratory with the permission of the local ordinary or pastor, or in another suitable place with the permission of the local ordinary.[33] Unlike the Eastern Code, the Latin Code takes into account the marriage between a Catholic and a non-baptized person (not considered as a sacramental union by

28 *CCEO* c. 1536 §1/*CIC* c. 85.
29 *CIC* c. 1127 §2.
30 *CCEO* c. 835.
31 "Dispensation from the Form for the Celebration of Marriage," in *Roman Replies 1992*, ed. Kevin W. Vann and Lynn Jarrell, 48-49.
32 *CCEO* c. 838 §1.
33 *CIC* c. 1118 §§ 1-2.

the Catholic Church), which can always be celebrated in a church or other suitable place.[34]

While both codes assert that the marriages of Catholics alone or Catholics to baptized non-Catholics are to be celebrated in the *parish church*, they differ in the determination of *which parish church*. The Eastern Code provides that such a marriage is to be celebrated before the pastor of the groom "unless particular law or a just cause excuses."[35] This final clause mitigates the force of the law. The Eastern Code contains another provision not found in the Latin Code: a local hierarch or pastor licitly blesses a marriage even in a place that is exclusively that of another Church *sui iuris* (e.g., a Latin parish church) unless the hierarch of that place expressly refuses.[36]

Time of Celebration

The Eastern Code relegates the time of the celebration of marriage to the particular law of the Churches *sui iuris*.[37]

---

34 *CIC* c. 1118 §3.

35 *CCEO* c. 831 §2. In its mention of the "pastor of the groom," one would presume that the priest is functioning in his own church. The Maronite Church has enacted particular law on the matter: "The pastor of the groom is the one who in his parish normally blesses the marriage and who permits it to be contracted outside the parish. However, to contract the marriage outside the eparchy, permission must be obtained from the bishops of both eparchies concerned." ("The Particular Law of the Maronite Church in accordance with the Code of Canons of the Eastern Churches," Art. 83) The English translation is published in Charbel Bousamra, *The Particular Law of the Maronite Church. Analysis and Perspective* (Rome: EDUSC, 2010) 337-354.

36 This is a reversal of the principle articulated in *Crebrae allatae* c. 86 §1, 2° that the pastor or hierarch could assist at a marriage only within the limits of their territory. See the interpretation provided by Victor Pospishil, *The Law on Marriage* (Chicago: Universe Editions, 1962) 140-141.

37 The Maronite Church enacted particular law in this matter: "The celebration of marriage is to take place during the day except with the permission of the eparchial bishop that it be contracted at night for just reasons. Prohibited seasons are limited solely to the season of Lent, from Ash Monday until the evening of Holy Saturday" (Art. 85). The Byzantine Ruthenian Church provides: "It is recommended that marriage not take place during the Great Fast nor during the Great and Holy Week" (Canon 838 §2). The particular law of the Byzantine Ruthenian Church is published in "The Norms of Particular Law of the Byzantine Metropolitan Church *Sui Iuris* of Pittsburgh, U.S.A. (Pittsburgh, 1999).

Impediments

A diriment impediment renders a person incapable of validly marrying (*CCEO* c. 790/*CIC* c. 1073). The point of departure in the codification process was that marriage impediments would be substantially the same for both the Latin Code and the Eastern Code, but in adhering to its mandate to prepare a draft that would reflect genuine Eastern traditions, the Revision Commission was obliged to incorporate certain differences in the Eastern Code.[38] A comparison of impediments as articulated in both codes indicates that (1) some impediments are substantially identical; (2) others, while found in both codes have substantial variations; and (3) there is one impediment that is unique to the Eastern Code. We shall examine these impediments in this order.

The Latin Code restricts the authority to establish an invalidating impediment to the supreme authority (Pope/College of Bishops).[39] The Eastern Code, in recognition of the self-governing authority (i.e., *sui iuris* status) of the patriarchal/major archiepiscopal churches, provides that the synod of bishops can also create an invalidating impediment, having consulted other Catholic bishops who might have an interest in the matter as well as the Apostolic See.[40] Nevertheless, this consultation is for liceity only.

Identical Impediments

Certain impediments are substantially the same in both codes: age, [41] impotence,[42] prior bond, [43] disparity of worship, [44] sacred orders, [45] conjugicide, [46] consanguinity[47] and adoption.[48]

---

38 *Nuntia* 28 (1989) 108-109.

39 *CIC* cc. 1075-1076.

40 *CCEO* c. 792.

41 *CCEO* c. 800/*CIC* c. 1083. While the substance of the impediment is identical in both canons, there is a difference regarding a possible modification of the age requirement. In Latin Code, the conference of bishops can establish a higher age (*CIC* c. 1083 §2); in the Eastern Churches, it is within the competence of the legislative authority of the church *sui iuris* to establish a higher age (*CCEO* c. 800 §2). In both cases, the higher age affects only lawfulness of the marriage.

42 *CCEO* c. 801/*CIC* c. 1084.

43 *CCEO* c. 802/*CIC* c. 1085. *CIC* c. 1085 §1 qualifies the prior marriage by insertion of the phrase "even if it was not consummated."

44 *CCEO* c. 803/*CIC* c. 1086.

45 *CCEO* c. 804/*CIC* c. 1087.

46 *CCEO* c. 807/*CIC* c. 1090.

47 *CCEO* c. 808/*CIC* c. 1091.

48 *CCEO* c. 812/*CIC* c. 1094.

Divergent Impediments

- *Abduction.*[49] The impediment of abduction is almost identical in both codes, but it does significantly differ in determining the applicability to a victim. While the Latin Code restricts it only to women, the Eastern Code applies this impediment to both men and women.

- *Affinity.*[50] Another impediment common to both codes but containing considerable modification relates to affinity. The Latin Code invalidates marriages only with any degree of affinity in the direct line. On the other hand, the Eastern Code extends the invalidity also to the second degree of the collateral line.

- *Public Propriety.*[51] Both codes state that this impediment arises from an invalid marriage after common life has been established or from public concubinage. The Latin Code invalidates marriage in the first degree of the direct line between a man and the blood relatives of the woman and vice versa. The Eastern Code adds to the scope of this impediment an attempted marriage before a civil official or non-Catholic minister.[52]

- *Perpetual Vow of Chastity in a Religious Institute.*[53] There is a small difference in the application of this impediment in the case of hermits. This impediment does not apply to those hermits in the Latin Church that are under the authority of the diocesan bishop.

Unique Impediment

Spiritual Relationship.[54] The impediment of spiritual relationship is unique to the Eastern Code. This impediment exists between the godparents and the person baptized, and between the godparents and the parents of the person baptized. If a baptism is celebrated conditionally, this impediment does not arise unless the same sponsor is used for the second ceremony as well.

Dispensation

Dispensation from impediments is generally the same in both codes, except that the Eastern Code provides that patriarchs can dispense from the impedi-

---

49 *CCEO* c. 806/*CIC* c. 1089.
50 *CCEO* c. 809/*CIC* c. 1092.
51 *CCEO* c. 810/*CIC* c. 1093.
52 *CCEO* c. 810 §1, 3°.
53 *CCEO* c. 805/*CIC* c. 1088.
54 *CCEO* c. 811. The impediment of spiritual relationship was found in the 1917 *Codex Iuris Canonici* (c. 1079), but was not included in the 1983 Latin Code.

ments of conjugicide and public perpetual vow of chastity made in congregations of any juridical condition.[55]

Marriage Consent

The elements of marital consent are not the same in both of the codes. In conformity with *Crebrae allatae* c. 83 ("Marriage under condition cannot be celebrated."), Eastern Code canon 826 provides: "Marriage based on a condition cannot be validly celebrated." Thus, whenever a condition is placed on a marriage by an Eastern Catholic, the marriage must be considered as invalid because of a defect of consent. Such a provision conforms to genuine Eastern traditions in which a conditional marriage would be contrary to the sacred character of marriage.[56]

What is to be said regarding the validity of consent when an Eastern Catholic marries a Latin Catholic who makes a past or present condition? One interpretation is that that consent is defective because of the broad manner in which the canon is phrased; it does not say that an Eastern Catholic cannot pose a condition, but that *Matrimonium sub condicione valide celebrari non potest.*

Others who hold that the exclusion of condition affects only the consent of the Eastern Catholic party; when adjudicating the validity of a marriage involving a Latin and an Eastern Catholic, if the Latin placed a past or present condition, one would declare the marriage to be invalid or valid in consideration of the condition.

Divorce, Adjudication of Nullity or Dissolution

The Catholic Church holds a sacramental, consummated marriage to be indissoluble.[57] Before treating the adjudication of nullity or dissolution of sacramental non-consummated or non-sacramental consummated marriages, let us make some distinctions in terminology:[58]

- *Divorce* is the dissolution of a civil marriage bond by a civil government authority which frees the divorced to enter into another civil marriage. In

55 *CCEO* c. 795 §2.

56 The Latin practice of conditional marriage crept into the Armenian, Romanian and Syriac Churches in the 19th century. See Josef Prader, "De consensus matrimoniali condicionato," *Nuntia* 6 (1978) 34-41. See also *Nuntia* 15 (1982) 79-80.

57 *CCEO* c. 853/ *CIC* c. 1141.

58 This terminological distinction is one currently in use and the result of a long historical development. As one would expect, there is a great variation during various periods and among the various Churches and scholars. See Cyril Vasil and George Gallaro, "Remarriage in the Orthodox Church Challenges Catholic Church," *Studia canonica* 47 (2013) 123. The differences in terminology pose a challenge for Catholic-Orthodox dialogue.

the eyes of the Catholic Church, a civil divorce has no effect on the marriage bond. For some Orthodox Churches, a civil divorce is "sanctioned" by ecclesiastical authorities and the parties are free to marry.

- *Separation* is the termination of the spouses' common life while the marriage bond remains.

- *Declaration of nullity* is a declaration that because of a defect of form or consent, or the existence of an invalidating impediment, the marriage never existed *ab initio.*

- *Dissolution* of the marriage bond can take place in the case of a marriage that was validly celebrated but never consummated or in the cases of a non-sacramental marriage in which one or both of the parties was not baptized.

The Catholic Churches *sui iuris* regard divorce as a purely civil matter with no ecclesiastical effects.[59] There is provision in both codes for the separation of spouses.[60]

Adjudication of Nullity

Since the Catholic Church regards a sacramental, consummated, and valid marriage to be indissoluble, whenever a marriage breaks down, the only pastoral remedy in such a case for a person who desires remarriage is to ascertain if the marriage was null *ab initio* in consideration of the observation of the canonical form, the presence of any invalidating impediment, or a defect in the consent. All of us in this room are familiar with the process, which is substantially the same in the Latin and Eastern Catholic Churches.

Dissolution

The Catholic Church deems itself competent to dissolve a valid marriage between baptized parties that is "ratified," but not consummated.[61] The "Pauline Privilege" provides that the marriage of two non-baptized persons can be dissolved by the law itself in favor of the faith of the party who received baptism.[62] While not treated in the codes, another "privilege of the faith" dissolution can

---

59 The Orthodox Churches generally "ratify" a civil divorce, thereby giving the parties permission to enter into another marriage.

60 *CCEO* cc. 863-866/*CIC* cc. 1141-1154.

61 *CCEO* c. 862/*CIC* c. 1142.

62 *CCEO* cc. 854-860/*CIC* cc. 1142-149.

be given in marriages involving a baptized person and a non-baptized person.[63] Again, all of us are familiar with the basic principles of the procedures.

Orthodox Teaching and Practice on Remarriage

At the beginning of this presentation, I referred to Pope Saint John Paul II's anatomical metaphor of the Church breathing with two lungs in reference to the Catholic Churches of East and West. This same pope also applied the metaphor to the relationship of the Church of Rome (identified as *West*, but comprising both Latin and Eastern Catholic Churches) and the Church of Constantinople (the Eastern Orthodox Church), identified as *East*.

> In this perspective an expression which I have frequently employed finds its deepest meaning: the Church must breathe with her two lungs! In the first millennium of the history of Christianity, this expression refers primarily to the relationship between Byzantium and Rome.[64]

The limitations of time and space do not permit a comprehensive examination of Orthodox marriage law. Instead we shall briefly examine the teaching and practice of the Eastern Orthodox Church and the Oriental Orthodox Churches regarding divorce and remarriage.

While there have been occasions of polemical Catholic-Orthodox confrontation regarding the Orthodox practice of divorce and the concession of permission to remarry, over the years there has been a real effort on the part of Catholic scholars to understand the Orthodox position and perhaps to adopt it in the Catholic Church.[65] Nevertheless, scholars seeking a systematic and complete exposition of Orthodox doctrine on marriage, divorce and remarriage will be disappointed because, as prominent Orthodox theologian Alexander Schmemann indicates, Orthodox doctrine still lacks such a character.[66] It is almost impossible

63 Sacred Congregation for the Doctrine of the Faith, instruction *Ut notum est*, 6 December 1973. The instruction was not published in the *AAS*, but an English version is found in James I. O'Connor, ed., *Canon Law Digest* (Chicago: Canon Law Digest, 1978) 8:1177-1184.

64 John Paul II, *Ut unum sint*, 25 May 1995, n. 54: http://www.vatican.va/holy_father/john_paul_ii/encyclicals/documents/hf_jp-ii_enc_25051995_ut-unum-sint_en.html (accessed December 22, 2014).

65 "There were times when the desires to better understand the real motivation of the Orthodox Church were prevalent in the West. In many cases the West admired the Orthodox practice, and Catholic authors detected the possibility of a solution of the serious problem of the growing number of civil divorces of marriages contracted / entered religiously before the Church. See Vasil', "Remarriage," 132.

66 Alexander Schmemann, "The Indissolubility of Marriage: The Theological Tradition in the East," in *The Bond of Marriage. An Ecumenical and Interdisciplinary Study*, ed. William Basset (Notre Dame, IN: University of Notre Dame 1968) 97-112.

to arrive at clear and definite conclusions. Further, there is a great diversity of practice, with perhaps as many systems as there are ecclesiastical jurisdictions.

Let us examine two distinct, but related issues: the *teaching* of these churches regarding the indissolubility of marriage and the possibility of *remarriage* in cases where a marriage has failed.

Orthodox Teaching on Indissolubility[67]

The natural reality of marriage was transformed by Christ to a sacrament symbolizing the unity of Christ and the Church. Some Orthodox theologians hold the position that, by its very nature, marriage extends even beyond the earthly life of the parties.[68]

Christ pronounced the divine command, "Therefore what God has joined together let no one separate,"[69] and took an incontrovertible stand against divorce:

---

67 For further reading, see Jean Dauvillier and Carlo de Clercq, *Le marriage en droit canonique oriental* (Paris: Recueil Sirey, 1936); John Erickson, "Eastern Orthodox Perspectives on Divorce and Remarriage," in *Divorce and Remarriage: Religious and Psychological Perspectives,* ed. William P. Roberts, (Kansas City, MO: Sheed and Ward, 1990) 15-26; Astrid Kaptijn, "Divorce et remariage dans L'Eglise orthodoxe," *Folia Canonica* 2 (1999) 105-128; Peter L'Huillier, "The Indissolubility of Marriage in Orthodox Law and Practice," in *Catholic Divorce: The Deception of Annulments*, eds. Pierre Hégy and Joseph Martos (New York: Continuum International Publishing Group Inc., 2006) [abbreviated L'Huillier, "Indissolubility"] 108-126; Athenagoras Peckstadt, "Economia and Pastoral Guidance," *International Congress University of Leuven (18-20 April 2005)*: http://www.orthodoxresearchinstitute.org/articles/liturgics/athenagoras_remarriage.htm (accessed December 22, 2014). O. Rousseau, "Divorce and Remarriage: East and West," *Concilium* 24 (April 1967) 119-138; Vasil and Gallaro, 119-143.

68 One of the presuppositions of Orthodox teaching on marriage is explained by Meyendorff. "That marriage is a sacrament conferred upon the partners in the Body of the Church through the priest's blessing; that, as any sacrament, it pertains to the eternal life in the Kingdom of God; and that it is, therefore, not dissolved by the death of one of the partners, but creates between them – if they so wish and if 'it is given to them' (Matthew 19:11) an eternal bond": John Meyendorff, *Marriage. An Orthodox Perspective* (Crestwood, NY: St. Vladimir's Seminary Press, 1984) [abbreviated Meyendorff, *Marriage*] 54. Dr. Patrick Viscuso, during an October 2014 meeting of the North American Orthodox Catholic Consultation, indicated that this is simply a theological opinion which arose in the middle of the twentieth century, but which has no basis in the ancient canons.

The Catholic Church holds that the marriage bond ceases at the death of one of the parties (see *CCEO* c. 853 / *CIC* c. 1141). At first glance, one would be interested in an Orthodox interpretation of Mt 22:23-30.

69 Mk. 10:9.

> Anyone who divorces his wife and marries another woman commits adultery, and the man who marries a divorced woman commits adultery.[70]

> Whoever divorces his wife and marries another woman commits adultery against her; and if she herself divorces her husband and marries another man, she is committing adultery.'[71]

Such dominical statements resonate in the Pauline writings:

> For this reason a man will leave his father and mother and be united to his wife, and the two will become one flesh. This is a profound mystery – but I am talking about Christ and the Church.[72]

> To the married I give this command – not I but the Lord – that the wife should not separate from her husband (but if she does separate, let her remain unmarried or else be reconciled to her husband), and that the husband should not divorce his wife.[73]

However, in condemning the institution of divorce, the Lord made an exception that is twice referred to in the Gospel of Matthew:

> But I tell you that anyone who divorces his wife, except for sexual immorality (*porneia*), makes her the victim of adultery, and anyone who marries a divorced woman commits adultery.[74]

Much is made of this "exception clause" in the Matthean pericope, but nonetheless there is great debate regarding the meaning of the term *porneia* and the intent of the statement. Some interpret it as concession of the Lord to human weakness that would allow persons to remarry. However, another interpretation might be that Jesus is asserting that in the case of the *porneia*, the marriage has been defiled and that the guilty party *must* be sent away because future contact with such a person could result in the defilement of the other party. Moreover, the text does not indicate that the innocent party is free to marry. To construe the "exception clause" as an acknowledgement of human weakness *that would give one of the parties the right to remarry* does not find support in the text.

---

70 Lk. 16:18.

71 Mk. 10:11-12.

72 Eph. 5:31-32.

73 1 Cor. 7:10-11.

74 Mt. 5:32. See also Mt. 19:9.

In consideration of the lack of clarity of the term, the Catholic Church takes no real cognizance of the "exception clause" in its marriage discipline:

> The unchastity clauses have been the object of fierce debate among exegetes from the beginning. Many take the view that they refer not to exceptions to the indissolubility of marriage, but to invalid marital unions. Clearly, however, the Church cannot build its doctrine and practice on controversial exegetical hypotheses. She must adhere to the clear teaching of Christ.[75]

One might say that the Orthodox Church has also put aside the "exception clause." At most, Jesus indicated that there was *one exception*; over the centuries, various jurisdictions of the Orthodox Churches have articulated numerous grounds for divorce. For example, in the Russian Church, during the Synodal period (1720-1917), there was an attempt to clarify marriage law. Legislation and jurisprudence included seven grounds for divorce: adultery, dual culpability in the breaking of a previous marriage, impotence, banishment to Siberia, prolonged disappearance, apostasy, entrance into religious life by both parties.[76]

The early Church did not elaborate a detailed theory of matrimonial law. As the Church began to develop a system of matrimonial law, different approaches were adopted in the (Byzantine) East and (Roman-Germanic) West.

- In the West, St. Augustine (+430) held that the marriage bond could not be touched because of the sacrament that arose consequent to the irrevocable vows that the couple made before God. Faced with an indissoluble reality of a failed marriage, canonists were faced with the challenge to prove that the marriage never existed, that is, was invalid *ab initio*.

- In the East, Church Fathers (venerated as saints in the Catholic Church) admitted the possibility of a marriage dissolving through the misdeeds of one of the partners. St. John Chrysostom (+407) and St. Cyril of Alexandria (+444) spoke of the indissolubility of marriage, but *not absolute indissolubility*.[77] Cyril notes, "It is not a writ of divorce that dissolves marriage before God, but bad actions."[78]

---

75 Archbishop Gerhard Ludwig Müller, "Communion for the Divorced-Remarried," 24 October 2013. English translation: http://www.ewtn.com/vnews/getstory.asp?number=126992 (accessed October 5, 2014).

76 L'Huiller, "Indissolubility," 118.

77 See L'Huillier, "Indissolubility," 109.

78 *Patrologia Graeca*, 72:380: "*Ού γὰρ τὰ ρεπούδια παρα῾ Θεως λύει τὸν γάμον, αλλ' η῾ άτοποσ πράξις.*"

Resonating St. Paul (1 Cor. 7:9), the Orthodox Church regards all second marriages negatively: a successive marriage is contrary to the canonical and liturgical traditions of the Church.[79] One author explains:

> In the church's view, remarriage does not enjoy the same consideration as the first marriage. If there is a certain disfavor toward the remarriage of widowed people, there is even more so in the case of the divorced.[80]

The author refers to the remarriage of widowed people. Such a successive marriage is of no concern to Catholics, while remarriage is problematic for the Orthodox Church in case of the death of one of the spouses and is treated as a concession to human weakness.[81]

This critical attitude towards second marriages finds expression in the liturgical rites. [82] The *order of second marriage* is described as "nothing more than an expansion of the betrothal service with prayers of rejoicing replaced with penitential supplications asking for forgiveness, purification and pardon."[83] In some traditions, there is no crowning ceremony.[84]

A successive union is tolerated as a concession to human weakness (1 Cor .7:8-9). Persons in such unions were not consequently excluded from reception of Holy Communion.

Orthodox Practice Regarding Remarriage[85]

How does the Orthodox Church deal with civil divorce? In those societies with a separation of church and state, divorce is a disposition of the civil authorities without the involvement of the Church. It should be noted that for the Orthodox Church, divorce and remarriage are not intrinsically related; a divorce does not automatically confer the right to remarriage. The Church authorities regard themselves as competent to give permission for a remarriage, declaring that the former marriage to be disintegrated in fact and in law. It is interesting that there seems to be a parallel between the blessing of a marriage, i.e., the blessing of the marriage covenant of two parties that gives rise to the sacrament, and the

79 Meyendorff, *Marriage*, 54.

80 L'Huillier, "Indissolubility," 121.

81 See *The Oxford Dictionary of Byzantium,* s.v. "Remarriage," 3:1783.

82 For further reading, see Andrea Palmieri, *I rito per le seconde nozze nella Chiesa Greco-orthododossa* (Bari, Italy: Ecumenica Editrice, 2007).

83 Meyendorff, *Marriage*, 45.

84 This was reported during a discussion at the Oriental Orthodox–Roman Catholic Consultation on 3 October 2014.

85 Luigi Bressan, *Il divorzio nelle Chiese orientali* (Bologna: EDB, 1976); Dauvillier, 96-122; Patrick Viscuso, "Divorce in the Greek Orthodox Archdiocese of North and South America," *The Jurist* 50 (1990) [abbreviated Viscuso, "Divorce"] 322-341.

ecclesiastical ratification of a civil divorce, i.e., the recognition of a disintegrated marriage which permits the parties to remarry.

It is difficult to analyze the procedures for divorce in the Orthodox Church because, with the exception of application forms and miscellaneous directives documentation, it is non-existent.[86]

In the Greek Orthodox Archdiocese of North and South America, the procedure regarding the request to remarry begins – at least theoretically – with an attempt to reconcile the divorced parties. If this is of no avail, the divorced parties can together[87] petition for a divorce stating the reasons. This petition must be accompanied by the civil decree of divorce and a report by the parish priest, which includes a narrative of the events and the reasons supporting the concession of a divorce. The material is forwarded to the spiritual court which makes the decision. If the divorce is granted, the decree with the hierarch's signature is sent to the parish priest.[88]

In the Orthodox Church in America, the party who has been divorced civilly requests permission to remarry and submits the request to diocesan officials. If possible, the ecclesiastical authorities must ascertain the grounds of the divorce. The process is relatively simple if the party is the innocent party and the reasons are one of those generally accepted as reasons for divorce (e.g., adultery, impotence, prolonged disappearance, apostasy).[89]

Oral reports indicate that the procedure in the Finnish Orthodox Church follows the same path. In the Coptic Church, a penitential system is being introduced in some jurisdictions.

The current – albeit multi-form – system in the Orthodox Churches is not without its detractors. John Meyendorff suggests:

> . . . that our Church authorities stop 'giving divorces' (since the latter anyway are secured through civil courts), and rather, on the basis of a recognition, based upon the civil divorce, that marriage does not in fact exist, issue 'permissions to

86 Viscuso, in his examination of the divorce procedures in the Greek Orthodox Archdiocese, indicates that his study "is based on written and oral sources. Every effort has been made to obtain written materials that treat the submission of a petition for an ecclesiastical divorce and the procedure of the archdiocese's spiritual courts. Aside from application forms and occasional encyclicals, very little documentary material exists." Viscuso, "Divorce," 322, n. 2.

87 If both divorced parties are not submitting the petition, there must be a reasonable attempt to notify the other party of the intended petition. This party has the right to appear before the spiritual court. Viscuso, "Divorce," 324.

88 Viscuso, "Divorce," 323-325.

89 L'Huillier, "Indissolubility," 118.

> remarry.' Of course, in each particular case pastoral counseling and investigation should make sure that reconciliation is impossible; and the 'permission to remarry' should entail at least some form of penance (in conformity with each individual case) and give the right to a Church blessing according to the rite of 'second marriage.'[90]

Archbishop L'Huillier also recognizes the deficiency in this system and asks – rhetorically perhaps – if it would be beneficial for the Orthodox Church to update its laws and practices, but ends with an acceptance of the *status quo*:

> Perhaps it is preferable, despite the inconveniences involved, not to weaken the principles, while leaving a certain margin of pastoral flexibility. After all, this attitude is inspired by early Church practice before nomocanonic law was fixed. In any case it would be utopic to expect to find a solution in this domain that would be entirely satisfactory.[91]

Inter-Church Ramifications

In a society wherein faithful from different communities marry, the system of permission for successive marriages has an effect on relations with the Catholic Church.

On a national level, in 1978, the U.S. Orthodox-Catholic Theological Consultation published "An Agreed Statement on the Sanctity of Marriage"[92] which makes reference to the problem of a diversity of practice regarding failed marriages:

> However, the Orthodox Church, out of consideration of the human realities, permits divorces, after it exhausts all possible efforts to save the marriage, and tolerates remarriages in order to avoid further human tragedies. The Roman Catholic Church recognizes the dissolution of sacramental nonconsummated marriages either through solemn religious profession or by papal dispensation. To resolve the personal and pastoral issues of failed marriages which have been consummated an inquiry is often undertaken to uncover whether there exists some

90 Meyendorff, *Marriage*, 58.

91 L'Huillier, "Indissolubility," 122.

92 The statement is published in John Borelli and John H. Erickson, eds., *The Quest for Unity* (Crestwood, NY: St. Vladimir's Seminary Press and Washington, DC: United States Catholic Conference, 1996) 202-105.

initial defect in the marriage covenant which would render the marriage invalid.[93]

The Statement notes that while the Orthodox Church permits marriage as the last option, the Catholic Church, because of its position on the indissolubility of sacramental, consummated marriages, resorts to an examination of the original act of consent to ascertain if there was some defect in the consent that would vitiate the marriage *ab initio*. The Statement makes no recommendation with regard to a foreseeable or possible coalescence of these different approaches – the issue is left unaddressed.

In another ecumenical dialogue, the agreement between the Catholic Church and the Malankara Syrian Orthodox Church, widely known as the "Kerala Agreement," creates a conundrum.[94] The agreement affirms that the "intimate marital communion is divinely confirmed by Christ with the sign of unity and of indissolubility, and ordered toward the good of the spouses and the generation and education of the offspring"[95] and, further, "our two Churches accept the sacredness and indissolubility of the sacramental bond of marriage ... "[96]

However, despite this joint affirmation regarding indissolubility, the Malankara Syrian Orthodox Church allows for the separation/divorce and subsequent remarriage of the parties [97] and, therefore, does not feel the need to declare a prior marriage null in order for the parties to be canonically free to enter another marriage. [98] For Catholics, the marriage is indissoluble and its validity is to be upheld until the contrary is proven;[99] a member of the Malankara Syrian Ortho-

93 Ibid., 202.

94 Pontifical Council for Promoting Christian Unity, "Agreement between the Catholic Church and the Malankara Syrian Orthodox Church on Inter-Church Marriages," 25 June 1994: *Information Service* 84 (1993) [abbreviated "Kerala Agreement"] 159-161.

For an analysis of the problem, see Sony Kadamthodu, "Kerala Agreement on Inter-Church Marriages and Dissolution of Marriage Bond," *Iustitia* 4/1 (June 2013) [abbreviated Kadamthodu, "Kerala Agreement"] 143-160.

95 Kadamthodu, "Kerala Agreement," 159.

96 Kadamthodu, "Kerala Agreement," 160.

97 In the canonical tradition of the Malankara Syrian Orthodox Church, the separation can take two forms: "divorce" (*dulala*) and "separation" (*phesekh*). A divorce is granted only in the case of adultery from either of the parties. If granted, only the innocent party is permitted to enter into a second marriage. A separation is granted after the parties have obtained a decree of divorce from the civil court. The parties submit a petition along with the opinion of the parish priest to the diocesan bishop for consideration. After obtaining expert legal opinion, the diocesan bishop makes his decision. Kadamthodu, "Kerala Agreement," 146-147. Kadamthodu notes that there is inconsistency by the Malankara Syrian Orthodox Church in the use of the terms "separation" and "annulment." Kadamthodu, "Kerala Agreement," 147.

98 Cf. *CCEO* c. 790 §2/*CIC* c. 1073; *CCEO* c. 784/*CIC* c. 1067; and *CCEO* c. 785 §1/ *CIC* c. 1066.

99 *CCEO* c. 779; *CIC* c. 1060.

dox Church who was married can be considered free to marry only if the former union ended by death or dissolution or was declared null.

Because the canonical procedures of the Malankara Syrian Orthodox Church do not satisfy the demands of an annulment process in the Catholic Church, a set of guidelines for application of the agreement in the Catholic Church was issued along with the Agreement.[100] Number 24 of the *Guidelines* stipulates: "Any declaration of nullity of such marriages is only to be considered with the consent of the bishops concerned from both Churches."

It is important to note that a "certificate of free state" issued by an Oriental Orthodox or Orthodox authority might not make a distinction regarding nullity or divorce. The problem is that the dispositions of the Orthodox Church are not declarations of nullity, but "declarations of freedom to marry," effectively, decrees of divorce (and sometimes expressly denoted as such) based on the principle of *economy*.[101] By and large, the Orthodox Churches do not issue decrees of annulment but employ decrees of divorce.[102]

How does the Catholic Church treat intended second marriages involving a member of the Malankara Syrian Orthodox Church who has been given a decree of nullity? Certain points have already been clarified:

- The Apostolic Signatura determined that "free state certificates" issued by the Romanian Orthodox Church are insufficient in the determination of the freedom of the Orthodox party to marry since such nullity decrees

---

100 "Pastoral Guidelines on Marriages between Members of the Catholic Church and the Malankara Syrian Orthodox Church," 25 January 1994: *Information Service* 84 (1993) [abbreviated "Pastoral Guidelines," 160-161.

101 See Gefaell, "Giurisdizione," 14-15, n. 44.

102 In those countries where the institution of *Personal Statutes* exists, the possibility of an annulment, for example, on the basis of a prior bond or consanguinity does exist. See Maher Mahmassi and Ibtissam Messarra, *Statut Personnel. Textes en vigeur au Liban* (Beirut: Faculté de droit et des sciences œconomiques, 1970) 640-641. Gefaell also points out that the legal system of Greece has the institute of the declaration of invalidity, but that the factors causing the invalidity do not precisely coincide with Catholic invalidating impediments. Gefaell, "Giurisdizione," 17, n. 53.

are, in reality, divorce decrees.[103] The disposition of the Apostolic Signatura seems to be applicable also in these cases.

- In the case of an Orthodox declaration of annulment due to lack of observance of form, the Pontifical Council for Legislative Texts determined that such a declaration can be accepted by the Catholic Church.[104]

- The Apostolic Signatura in 2007 declared that if an Orthodox faithful presented him/herself for marriage, having been in a union that had not been celebrated with canonical form, the local Ordinary or the pastor with the permission of the local Ordinary can proceed in a manner analogous to that used for Catholics.[105]

What is to be done when the Orthodox Church declares a marriage null on grounds other than lack of observance of canonical form, excepting those contrary to divine law? A respected scholar, Pablo Gefaell, argues that such declarations of nullity based on Orthodox legislation not contrary to divine law cannot be ignored by the Catholic Church and should be recognized if nothing blocks

---

103 "1. Marriage between two Orthodox believers celebrated according to the rite of the Orthodox Church before an Orthodox priest must also be held valid for the Orthodox Church. 2. The declaration of nullity issued by the Orthodox Church must be considered in reality as a declaration of divorce, which has no validity for the Catholic Church. 3. As a consequence, if an Orthodox endowed with said document asks to marry a Catholic, he/she is not free to contract/enter marriage in the Catholic Church. A declaration of nullity of that marriage should be obtained through a Catholic tribunal": Apostolic Signatura, "Declaratio" (P.N. 37577/05 VAR), 20 October 2006: *Communicationes* 39 (2007) 66-67; see William Daniels, ed., *Ministerium Iustitiae: Jurisprudence of the Supreme Tribunal of the Apostolic Signatura*, Montréal: Wilson & Lafleur Limitée, 2011) 759-761.

Gefaell notes that in 1991, the Apostolic Signatura decided a declaration of nullity was simply a "religious separation." See Apostolic Signatura, (Prot. 22343/90 V.T.), 7 January 1991, in J. Llobell, "La giurisdizione della Chiesa sul matrimonio degli accattolici," in *La giurisdizione della Chiesa sul matrimonio e sulla famiglia,* ed. J. Carreras (Milan: Giuffré, 1998) 88. Cited in Gefaell, "Giurisdizione," 12, n. 34.

104 Pontifical Council for Legislative Texts, "*Adnotatio circa validitatem matrimoniorum civilium quae in Cazastania sub communistarum regimine celebrata sunt,*" 13 May 2003: *Communicationes* 35 (2003) 197-210.

105 Apostolic Signatura, Decree of 3 January 2007, P.N. 38964/06 VT. For the text and commentary, see G. P. Montini, "*La procedura di investigazione prematrimoniale è idonea alla comprovazione dello stato libero di fedeli ortodossi che hanno tentato il matrimonio civile,*" *Periodica* 97 (2008) 47-98.

such an acceptance.[106] Gefaell proposes that in cases in which there is a clear declaration of nullity by an Orthodox authority, the Catholic Church could submit the decision to a review analogous to that of an appeal tribunal (*CCEO* c. 1368/ *CIC* c. 1682) or to submit it for ordinary adjudication as a first instance case. This might be the path to take, but we need to take into account that rarely are annulments given in an Eastern Orthodox or Oriental Orthodox Church.

These statements and agreements of between the Catholic and the Orthodox Churches do not precisely address the issue of ecumenism, that is, the advancement of the reunion of Churches, but rather address pastoral approaches to marriages of members of different churches. However, the matter of successive marriages does have ecumenical ramifications.

Ecumenical Dimensions

At first glance, the issue of marriage might appear to be extraneous to the field of ecumenism. The issue has not been treated by the Joint Commission for Theological Dialogue between the Roman Catholic Church and the Orthodox Church. However, there are critical – but not necessarily unresolvable – issues to be addressed in the area of successive marriages if a reunion of Churches is to take place.

The diversity of discipline with regard to marriage was discussed at the Council of Florence (1431-1449). Pope Eugene IV challenged the Orthodox theologians regarding their practice of divorce. The Orthodox theologians begged the question, stating that it was beyond their mandate and had to be referred to the emperor. Efforts to clarify the matter with emperor John VIII Paleologus were inconclusive. On 14 July 1439, the pope queried the Orthodox bishops as to why they dissolve marriage, but the response was obfuscation: "The words that Your Beatitude have spoken are very wise and just. However, we cannot give a perfect answer to your words; besides, there are other bishops and our emperor himself: we will be able to answer perfectly only with their consent; privately, however, and on our own we can give an answer; and we will state that this is not the time to speak on this matter, although it is fair and just; after all we do not dissolve marriages except for just causes."[107] Vasil' speculates that the reasons for the

106 "*Tuttavia, bisogna tenere in conto che le decisioni giudiziarie che l'autorità ortodossa emana per i suoi fedeli hanno forza di legge per le parti coinvolte e, quindi, esse non possono essere considerate inesistenti dalla Chiesa cattolica, anzi, a mio avviso dovrebbe riconoscerle, se nulla osta in contrario*": Pablo Gefaell, "*La giurisdizione delle Chiese ortodosse per giudicare sulla validità del matrimonio del loro fedeli,*" *Ius Ecclesiae* 19 (2007) [abbreviated Gefaell, "Giurisidizione,"] 773-791. Accessed from http://www.bibliotecanonica.net/docsad/btcadb.pdf on 21 September 2014.
107 Norman Tanner, ed., *Decrees of the Ecumenical Councils* (Washington, DC: 1990) 1:550.

vague response were that the Orthodox had no intention to change their practice and did not want the issue to jeopardize the union that had been achieved.

While Pope Eugene and the Latin council fathers emphasized that a change was necessary, it is important to note that the differences were not deemed to be Church-dividing. Though the Union of Florence eventually collapsed, the breakdown was not the consequence of differences over marriage discipline. The issue was a matter of concern to the pope and his curia, but apparently not a "deal breaker."

Beginning a Conversation[108]

During the return flight to Rome from Rio de Janeiro on 28 July 2013, Pope Francis spoke to journalists about the need for a stronger pastoral approach for persons in a second marriage. The pope made a passing reference to practice of the Orthodox Churches in this matter. "The Orthodox have a different practice" and "follow the theology of 'oikonomia' (economy or stewardship), as they call it, and give a second possibility; they permit" a second marriage.[109] Because of the speaker, this passing comment has piqued the interest of Catholic canonists who seek alternative approaches for the pastoral care of the millions of remarried Catholics who cannot receive the Eucharist.

There are those among us who are disposed to adopt "whole cloth" the practice of the Orthodox Church for implementation in the Catholic Churches of West and East. To an outsider, the procedure for Orthodox divorce appears much simpler than the annulment or dissolution procedures in the Catholic Church as the Orthodox can with facility permit remarriage and admittance to the Eucharist. Let me be clear: I am not of this opinion.

With respect and love, but also in all candor, I must say that the Orthodox Church and the Catholic Church have failed woefully either in: (1) in teaching our faithful of the holiness and permanence of marriage; or (2) in providing an effective pastoral, healing response to those persons whose marriages have failed.

- In the case of the Orthodox Church, the prevailing laxity in the ratification of civil divorce decrees undercuts the teaching that marriage is indissoluble. A critic might say that the Orthodox Churches have become so indulgent that their practice overshadows and negates their teaching on

108 For further reading in this subject, see Theodore Mackin, *Divorce & Remarriage* (New York: Paulist Press, 1984).

109 "Speaking of divorce, pope speaks of Orthodox practice": http://www.catholicfreepress.org/vatican/2013/08/06/speaking-of-divorce-pope-refers-to-practice-of-orthodox-churches/ (accessed September 12, 2014).

the indissolubility of marriage. Does such a practice conform to authentic Orthodox tradition? Is it open to abuse?

- In the case of the Catholic Church, too many people are excluded from the Eucharistic table. The Catholic Church has been clear in its teaching and its practice reflects its teaching of the permanence of marriage.[110] However, is the Catholic Church effective in teaching the sanctity of marriage as tribunals dissect marriage consent in jurisprudence that is little understood by the faithful, who also lack even a basic understanding of the process and issues at stake? Has jurisprudence created an intellectual complexity regarding consent that precludes any true exchange of consent? Does the Catholic annulment process which effectively liberates the guilty party to enter into another marriage give rise to wonderment? The practice in the Catholic Church has left millions hopeless who either suffer in the bosom of the Church or seek communities that are apparently more sympathetic to their situations.

The Catholic Church and the Orthodox Church both have the responsibility to teach the sanctity and unity of marriage and to be cognizant and merciful when faced with human frailty.

Orthodox Archbishop Peter L'Huillier articulates the challenge:

> In the first place, Orthodox churches must proclaim the holiness and the unity of marriage between Christians; in the second place, the church does not think that, in the domain of marriage as in many others, it is necessary to exclude compassion systematically, as long as this pastoral tendency does not lead to official laxity. [111]

While the Orthodox Archbishop refers only to the Orthodox Church, we must confess that it is a challenge also faced by the Catholic Churches. It is essential for the Catholic Church to uphold the sanctity of marriage; one aspect of the sanctity is indissolubility. It is important for Orthodox Church *praxis* to reflect their teaching. Perhaps we can help each other to do this. We are apostolic Churches with the right to teach – even each other.[112]

---

110 The article, "Communion for the Divorced-Remarried," by Archbishop Gerhard Müller, Prefect of the Congregation for the Doctrine of the Faith, published in *L'Osservatore Romano* on 24 October 2013, succinctly summarizes the position of the modern day magisterium on the matter. English translation: http://www.ewtn.com/vnews/getstory.asp?number=126992 (accessed October 5, 2014).

111 L'Huillier, "Indissolubility," 122.

112 Ladislas Orsy, *Receiving the Council: Theological and Canonical Insights and Debates* (Collegeville, MN: Liturgical Press, 2009) 50-53.

One might formulate the *status quaestionis* as follows:

1. In the Catholic Church, there are now millions of faithful who live in the same situations as those under the penal sanction of *minor excommunication* (in the terminology of the Eastern Code),[113] that is, they are deprived of reception of the Divine Eucharist.[114] What can be done in the Catholic Church to reintegrate them fully into the life of the Church and yet authentically continue to teach that marriage is indissoluble?

2. In the Orthodox Churches, divorces are granted on such a routine basis that the practice has now become countersign to the teaching that marriage is indissoluble?

In the area of successive marriages, perhaps is there a possible convergence of Catholic and Orthodox practice. Marriage and family life are rarely clear and never simple, so one cannot expect the proposal that follows to be perfect. If nothing else, it will remind us of the need for a pastoral and canonical response and give us food for thought. The challenge is articulated in *Relatio Synodi* of the 2014 Extraordinary Synod:

> The synod father[s] also considered the possibility of giving the divorced and remarried access to the Sacraments of Penance and the Eucharist. Some synod fathers insisted on maintaining the present regulations, because of the constitutive relationship between participation in the Eucharist and communion with the Church as well as the teaching on the indissoluble character of marriage. Others expressed a more individualized approach, permitting access in certain situations and with certain well-defined conditions, primarily in irreversible situations and those involving moral obligations towards

113 In the Eastern Code, such a sanction is referred to as *minor excommunication* ("Those punished with minor excommunication are deprived of the reception of the Eucharist" [*CCEO* c. 1431 §1]). This penalty has no counterpart in the Latin Code and in fact was absent from the 1917 codification. One commentator refers to it as a partial penalty in that one is not deprived of all the goods and is divisible, that is, the effects of minor excommunication are separable and must be determined in the sentence. With minor excommunication, one could also be prevented from participating in the Divine Liturgy or entering a church during liturgical celebrations.
The Latin Code declares that an excommunicated person is forbidden "to celebrate the sacraments or sacramental or to receive the sacraments" (*CIC* c. 1331 §1, 2°).

114 For 93 years, American Catholics who attempted remarriage after divorce were automatically excommunicated in accordance with a decision of the U.S. bishops at the Third Plenary Council of Baltimore (1884). On 4 May 1977 the National Conference of Catholic Bishops requested that the penalty be repealed. On 22 October 1977, the request was granted by Pope Paul VI. See James I. O'Connor, ed., *Canon Law Digest* (Chicago: Canon Law Digest, 1978) 8:1213-1214.

> children who would have to endure unjust suffering. Access to the sacraments might take place if preceded by a penitential practice, determined by the diocesan bishop. The subject needs to be thoroughly examined, bearing in mind the distinction between an objective sinful situation and extenuating circumstances, given that 'imputability and responsibility for an action can be diminished or even nullified by ignorance, inadvertence, duress, fear, habit, inordinate attachments, and other psychological or social factors' (*Catechism of the Catholic Church*, 1735).[115]

Penance

The Latin Church generally confines the imposition of penance to the sacrament of reconciliation. However, the extra-sacramental imposition of penances, e.g., acts of piety and charity as a means to heal, reform and make reparation has a long-standing tradition in the Eastern Churches. The Eastern Code, in its treatment of penal sanctions, introduces the possibility of the imposition of penance in penal sanctions and emphasizes the healing power of penance.[116] Why not avail ourselves of a traditional, effective remedy also to the situation of remarried Catholics?[117]

Penance for those in successive marriages has a long-standing tradition in the Church fathers.

Saint Basil, in canon 4, states that persons who are in second or third marriages are to be given gradated penances: Such persons were restricted only to listening to the Divine Liturgy for a period of several years without receiving the Eucharist and, after manifesting signs of repentance admitting them to the Eucharist.

> As regards trigamy and polygamy we have decreed the same Canon as in the case of digamy (i.e., second marriage), analogously. For it is a year in the case of digamy, but two years for the others. As for those who are guilty of trigamy (i.e., a third marriage), they are excommunicated for the space of three years and often four years. For *such a marriage is*

115 *Relatio Synodi* n. 52: http://press.vatican.va/content/salastampa/en/bollettino/pubblico/2014/10/18/0770/03044.html (accessed November 6, 2014).

116 "Unless another penalty is determined by law, according to the ancient traditions of the Eastern Churches, penalties can be imposed that require some serious work of religion or piety or charity to be performed, such as certain prayers, a pious pilgrimage, a special fast, alms, spiritual retreats": *CCEO* c. 1426 §1.

117 Penance before remarriage is required in the Orthodox Church in America. Coptic priests indicate that penance is also required in their Church.

no longer to be called a marriage, but polygamy, or rather mitigated fornication. But it behooves us not to exclude them entirely from the Church, but instead to entitle them to listening in some two years or three, and thereafter to permit them to be co-standers, though obliged to abstain from communion with that which is good (i.e., the Eucharist), and then after exhibiting some fruit of repentance, let them be restored to the status of persons entitled to communion.[118]

A careful reading of canon 4 of St. Basil reveals that nothing is said about whether the parties in second or third marriages are obliged to depart from such a union before being admitted to the communion. However, canon 9 of St. Basil reveals that a man whose wife has abandoned him is not to be considered an adulterer and is apparently permitted to remain with the woman in the second union:

> *So that a woman who deserts her husband becomes an adulteress in case she comes to another man. The man, on the other hand, whom she has left is pardonable, and a woman who cohabits with him is not to be condemned.* If, however, a man deserts his wife and comes to another woman, he too becomes an adulterer because he is making her be an adulteress; and the woman cohabiting with him is an adulteress, because she has taken another woman's husband for herself.[119]

The substance of these canons is incorporated into canon 87 of the "Quinisext" Council of Trullo:

> *If, therefore, a woman appears to have departed from her husband without a good reason, the man deserves to be pardoned, while the woman deserves a penance. The pardon shall be given to him so that he may have communion with the Church.* Any husband, however, who abandons his lawful wife, and takes another, according to the Lord's decision, is subject to the judgment attached to adultery. *It has been canonically decreed by our Fathers that such men shall serve a year as weepers, two years as listeners, three years as kneelers, and during the seventh year shall stand together with the faithful,*

118 The English translation is taken from St. Basil, c. 4. *The Rudder of the Orthodox Catholic Church: The Compilation of the Holy Canons by Saint Nicodemus and Agapius* (New York: Luna Printing Co., 1983) [abbreviated *Rudder*] 792 [emphasis added].
119 St. Basil c. 9: *Rudder*, 797 [emphasis added].

and thus be deemed worthy to partake of the prosphora if indeed they verily repent with tears.[120]

These texts demonstrate that penance for those in successive marriages is a venerable tradition for the most part ignored by the Catholic and the Orthodox Churches, but one that needs to be explored further. Perhaps both the Orthodox and the Catholic Churches could accept the challenge to formulate a pastoral approach that does not abdicate responsibility to consider the facts of the former marriage, the spiritual state of the faithful who are seeking to remarry, and the possibility that persons who remarry are not automatically excluded from full communion with the Church.

Dispensation

The first aspect of this proposal, penance, is a *pastoral* response to the problem of a marital breakdown and a successive marital union. In the Catholic Church, the traditional *canonical response* to the situtation has been a tribunal adjudication of the validity of the marriage or, less frequently, a dissolution of a non-consummated or non-sacramental marriage.[121] The "good faith" solution proposed for the past forty years and condemned, while compassionate, lacks the juridical clarity required in a matter dealing with the public good. It might also place too much of a burden on the conscience of the faithful. Is there another way?

When Catholic canonists hear the word *oikonomia*, the "knee-jerk" reaction is that law has been abandoned and a "feel good" approach has been adopted. A more nuanced response – but still nonetheless incorrect – is that *economy* is an Orthodox institution that has no place in Catholic teaching or practice. However, Catholics do have a developed, codified notion of economy: the *dispensation*.

Ivan Zuzek, the canonist most responsible for the revision of the Eastern Code, considered it important to demonstrate the institution of *economy* is indeed found in the common law of the Eastern Churches. Father Zuzek might have been motivated to make this argument because the Eastern Code, according to the general principles that were to be operative in the articulation of it, indicated

120 Quinisext Council, c. 87: *Rudder*, 391 [emphasis added]. Canons from the Quinisext Council are cited in the Eastern Code.

121 "It must be discerned with certainty by means of the external forum established by the church whether there is objectively such a nullity of marriage. The discipline of the church, while it confirms the exclusive competence of ecclesiastical tribunals with respect to the examination of the validity of the marriage of Catholics, also offers new ways to demonstrate the nullity of a previous marriage in order to exclude as far as possible every divergence between the truth verifiable in the judicial process and the objective truth known by a correct conscience." Müller, "Communion."

that the future code was to be truly *Eastern*. How could it be Eastern if the institution of *economy* was not present?

Zuzek points out the the canonical insitution of *dispensation* is the Catholic expression of *economy*. The notion of dispensation, that is, a juridic remedy regarding demands of the law for a specific individual, is an institution found in both the Latin Code and the Eastern Code.[122]

A dispensation is an administrative act, not a legislative act, that relaxes "the obligation contained in a law but does not affect the juridicial stability of the law itself, which retains its force and is not thereby abrogated."[123] Thus, the prohibition against marrying a non-baptized person can be relaxed in the case of an individual Catholic while the law itself remains in place. The value expressed in the canon, that Catholics are to marry baptized persons, still has its place.

For example, the impediment of disparity of worship (*CCEO* c. 803 §1/*CIC* c. 1086 §1) invalidates the marriage of a Catholic with a non-baptized persons; put simply, Catholics are forbidden to marry the non-baptized. This is a provision of law that was promulgated in 1983 and 1990 for all the Catholic Churches.

Yet, dispensations from this obligation are granted in certain circumstances (the Catholic party is obliged to promise to preserve his/her own faith and to do what is possible to have the children baptized and educated in the Catholic Church) and marriages between Catholics and the non-baptized are celebrated. The dispensation from the impediment permits them to enter into a non-sacramental marriage and receive communion. But the law retains its juridical stability. This is the beauty of the nature of a dispensation.

Perhaps a canonical remedy for the situation of divorced and remarried Catholics would be a dispensation from the obligation to abstain from the Eucharist. Please note that this is not a proposal to dispense from the impediment of ligamen.[124] Rather, it would be a dispensation from restraints imposed in Eastern Code canon 712 ("Those who are publicly unworthy are forbidden to receive the Divine Eucharist") and Latin Code canon 915 ("Those who have been excommunicated or interdicted after the imposition or declaration of the penalty and others obstinately persevering in manifest grave sin are not to be admitted to holy communion").

Some Catholic canonists would argue that the penance has no meaning as long as the persons remain in irregular marital unions, i.e., "persevering in manifest grave sin" and, consequently, cannot be admitted to the Eucharist. This is

122 *CCEO* c. 1536 §1/*CIC* c. 85.
123 See Augustine Mendonça, "Singular Administrative Acts," in *The Canon Law: Letter and Spirit*, ed. Gerard Sheehy et al. (Collegeville, MN: Liturgical Press, 1995) 48-49.
124 *CCEO* c. 802/*CIC* c. 1085.

a broad moral judgement—or presumption—with canonical consequences that probably should not be made in appraising all situations.

We must acknowledge that neither penalties nor penances can always be expected to return to the status *ante quo*—penalties for abortion or murder cannot revivify the victim. However, the penalties and penances do serve their purpose in healing the offender and repairing damages done to the ecclesial community. In the case of faithful living an irregular marital union, we can examine the validity of the marriage (if the parties submit the case to our tribunal) and, if nothing is to be done and the individuals merit a dispensation, impose appropriate healing penance and grant a canonical dispensation.

As is the case with any dispensation, it must be based on a genuine reason such as the spiritual welfare of the individual. The dispensation does not affect the juridical stability of the law itself which prohibits the reception of the Eucharist by those who are generally considered unworthy because of their irregular unions, but does address the spiritual needs of individuals.

It seems important that the judgment regarding admissibility to communion requires the intervention of the authority of the bishop, perhaps creation of eparchial/diocesan penitentiaries. To leave it to the parish priest would inevitably lead to inconsistent application and abuse.

This canonical dispensation to be admitted to the Eucharist says nothing about the validity or non-validity of the former marriage; the current marital union is canonically "tolerated" as a concession to human weakness. With regard to the invalidity of the previous marriage, a tribunal must still proceed with the adjudication of the validity of the former marriage. If the marriage is declared to be invalid, then the current union can receive the blessing of the Church. Of course, the need for a dispensation would no longer exist.

Keys of Peter

The two-faceted proposed solution comprising a penance and dispensation is awkward and unsatisfying to canonists who relish charity.[125] The solution may not be neat, clean, and clear, but family life never is. Perhaps someone in this room or a future reader will formulate another canonical remedy. But we must do something: the current practices of the Orthodox and Catholic Churches are ineffective in their teaching and harmful in their consequences. In the words of the *Relatio Synodi* of the III Extraordinary General Assembly of the Synod of Bishops:

125 For the author, it was interesting that negative criticism from Catholics focused on the aspect of the dispensation, while the Orthodox resisted the imposition of penance.

> All these situations require a constructive response, seeking to transform them into opportunities which can lead to an actual marriage and a family in conformity with the Gospel."[126]
>
> The necessity for courageous pastoral choices was particularly evident at the Synod. Strongly reconfirming their faithfulness to the Gospel of the Family and acknowledging that separation and divorce are always wounds which causes deep suffering to the married couple and to their children, the synod fathers felt the urgent need to embark on a new pastoral course based on the present reality of weaknesses within the family, knowing oftentimes that couples are more 'enduring' situations of suffering than freely choosing them. These situations vary because of personal, cultural and socio-economic factors. Therefore, solutions need to be considered in a variety of ways, as suggested by Pope St. John Paul II (cf. *Familiaris Consortio*, 84).[127]

In closing, in giving Peter the keys of the kingdom,[128] Jesus gave to him and his successors the power to resolve any challenges. The powers of Hades cannot prevail against them! The pope and the bishops have the power to address this situation;[128] we canonists need to give them the tools. Let us begin a conversation.

126 *Relatio Synodi*, n. 43.
127 *Relatio Synodi*, n. 45.
128 Mt 16:18.

SEMINAR

PROOFS BY WITNESSES IN MARRIAGE NULLITY TRIALS

Rev. Peter O. Akpoghiran, JCD

Witness testimony comprises one of the most important instruments of proof in marriage nullity trials in the 1983 Code of Canon Law. Already with the submission of a petition for a declaration of nullity, the petitioner is required to indicate not only the facts upon which the assertion is made, but also the proofs that will be adduced to support the petitioner's claim. This includes naming possible witnesses who will support the allegations made (c. 1504, 2°). Since the burden of proof rests on the one who makes an assertion to the court (c. 1526 §1), witness testimony forms a substantive body of evidence that either strengthens or weakens the petitioner's claim or the respondent's exception to it. In addition, probative value cannot be attributed to the judicial confessions and declarations of the parties alone unless they are thoroughly corroborated by the other circumstances of the case and by other elements of proofs. (c. 1536 §2).

Since proof by witnesses frequently plays a central role in a canonical trial, the procedural law of the 1983 code provides extensive norms governing its admissibility and evaluation. The instruction *Dignitas connubii*, issued on January 25, 2005, by the Pontifical Council for Legislative Texts (*DC*) elaborates on the manner in which the norms of the code are to be applied in marriage nullity trials. These norms address, among other things, those who may function as a witness, the manner of questioning witnesses, and the evaluation of their testimony.

When witness testimony has been obtained and incorporated into the acts, the judge must evaluate the evidence based on the norms offered by the code and the Instruction. This is a critical phase of the trial since the evidence received forms a basis for the court to fulfill its duty of investigating the truth and rendering judgment based precisely on the results of that investigation. To this end, the evaluation of witness testimony requires that the court consider the character and uprightness of witnesses, the sources of their information (personal experience, opinion, rumor, or hearsay), the extent to which their testimonies corroborate other proofs, and the internal consistency of the depositions themselves.

Dignitas connubii reiterates many of the provisions already found in Book VII of the Code of Canon Law regarding the admissibility of witnesses and the evaluation of witness testimony. However, it also contains several norms that clarify and elaborate on the norms of the code. For example, it states that in evaluating testimonies, the judge is to consider when the witnesses came to know what they are asserting, e.g., whether or not it was during a non-suspect time (*DC* article 201, 3°). It is important, then, to consider the role and evaluation of witness testimony in light of the Instruction and its ultimate purpose: the more efficient administration of justice in ecclesiastical marriage nullity trials.

This article is a study of, and a commentary on, the norms governing proof by witnesses in marriage nullity trials in the Code of Canon Law and the Instruction *Dignitas connubii*. It seeks to answer the following questions: Who can and who cannot be a witness? What are the principles concerning the introduction and admission of witnesses? How and by whom are depositions to be taken? And how is the testimony to be evaluated? The answers to these questions are provided below.

I. Proofs in General

The word *proof* comes from *probare,* which means to make a thing credible, to show, or demonstrate; it also means to convince one of a thing.[1] In civil law, a proof is the logically sufficient reason for assenting to the truth of a proposition advanced; it includes everything that may be adduced at a trial, within the legal rules, for the purpose of producing a conviction in the mind of the judge or jury.[2] The code itself does not define proof; but in the canonical tradition, a judicial proof is "a demonstration of a dubious or contested fact through legitimate arguments made to a judge."[3] Another more specific classical definition states that proof is a judicial act by which a judge comes to a certain clarity about a doubtful and controverted matter through documents, witnesses, or suitable arguments.[4] To *prove* something means to establish the truth or validity of an assertion by the presentation of arguments or evidence.[5]

Proofs are distinguished by reason of their formality: judicial proof and extrajudicial proof. Judicial proofs are those formally brought to the judge in his or her capacity as judge in the course of the trial, while extrajudicial proofs are those that arise outside of the trial. Extrajudicial proofs may be brought into the judicial forum by being presented during the trial according to the norm of law. That is, the judge may decree the admission of such information as judicial

1 *A Latin Dictionary,* eds., Charton T. Lewis and Charles Short (Oxford: Clarendon Press, 1958) s.v. "Probo."

2 *Black's Law Dictionary,* 6th ed. (1990), s.v. "Proof."

3 Francisco X. Wernz, *Ius Decretalium,* vol. 5 (Prati: Giachetti, 1914) 450.

4 Francisco Schmalzgrueber, *Ius Ecclesiasticum Universum,* vol. 4 (Rome: Ex Typographia Rev. Cam. Apostolicae, 1843) 28-29.

5 *The American Heritage Dictionary*, 3rd ed. (Boston: Houghton Mifflin Company, 1996) s.v. "Prove."

proof, which can considerably broaden the amount of information available to the court.[6]

Proofs can also be distinguished as direct and indirect. Direct proofs are those through which the controverted fact is established immediately from what was personally deduced by those proposing them, while indirect proofs are those through which the controverted fact is established inductively from other relevant facts.[7] Direct proofs are those whose probative value comes from their very nature such as a judicial confession, a witness testimony, an expert report, or a public ecclesiastical or civil document.

Indirect proofs, on the other hand, are *admincula,* circumstances, indices, and presumptions.[8] Indirect proofs or presumptions are so-called because they do not directly establish the existence of a fact; however, they lead one to conclude the existence of a fact according to other facts and circumstances related to the matter. The judge uses direct forms of proofs to establish facts about the parties, their pattern of behavior, and their marriage and then proceeds to educe from these facts conclusions about the intentions of the parties and the juridic significance of these intentions. The second stage of the judge's reasoning is an exercise in indirect proofs.[9]

Proofs are also distinguished by reason of their effects according to whether or not they are sufficient to enable the judge to arrive at a moral certainty. Thus, there is full proof (*probatio plena*) and semi-full proof (*probatio semiplena*). Full proof such as an authentic document is that which is sufficient for the judge to form a conviction and allows the judge to decide the case. On the other hand, incomplete or semi-full proof is that which is insufficient to evince a conviction in the mind of the judge unless it is supplemented by other proofs and by other circumstances of the case. Some examples of full proof are the deposition of two witnesses above reproach concerning the same point; public documents or others of the same weight, a presumption of law, and a confession of the respondent.

6 James H. Provost, "Remarks Concerning Proofs and Presumptions," *The Jurist* 39 (1979) 457.

7 John Beal, "The Substance of Things Hoped For: Proving Simulation of Matrimonial Consent," *The Jurist* 55 (1995) 749. [Henceforth, "Proving Simulation"].

8 Beal, "Proving Simulation," 766. An *adminiculum* is something such as a declaration of a party, an extrajudicial confession, a document, or a witness's deposition that supports and lends to another proof probative weight that it does not have in itself. Circumstances are facts that do not bear directly on the principal issue of a trial but are sufficiently germane to the principal issue to form the basis of certain inferences or deductions about it. Indices are facts relevant to but distinct from the controverted fact central to the trial. It reveals or points to the existence of a distinct and as yet unknown fact in virtue of a nexus between the two facts. And a presumption "is a probable conjecture about an uncertain matter" (c. 1584). For more on these distinctions see Beal, "Proving Simulation," 766-773.

9 Beal, "Proving Simulation," 765.

Examples of semi-full proofs are the deposition of one witness and private documents.

II. General Principles of Proofs

There are certain principles that govern proofs in general. These are found in canons 1526-1529 of the 1983 code and articles 156-157 and 160-161 of *Dignitas connubii*. In the code, they are placed immediately under the title: "Proofs" – thereby suggesting that the norms are meant to regulate the presentation, admission, and evaluation of proofs and to assist the judge in verifying the truth of the facts alleged in the trial. Since witness testimony is a means of proof, therefore, it is necessary to examine these general norms on proofs.

1. ***The burden of proof:*** The burden of proof rests upon the person who makes the allegation.[10] This norm is derived from the Roman law principle that the burden of proof rests on the one who asserts, not on the one who denies. In the ecclesiastical marriage nullity process, the petitioner must prove that the marriage is invalid since the presumption of law is that the marriage is valid. (c. 1060). The petitioner therefore, and not the judge, has the burden of proving the invalidity of the marriage. Accordingly, if the petitioner is unable to prove the alleged invalidity of the marriage, the judge renders a negative decision, and upholds the validity of the marriage.

   The norm also applies to the respondent by reason of exception. An exception is any defense made by the respondent through the judicial use of facts and arguments to impede, extinguish, or overthrow the action of the petitioner. The respondent can reply to the claim of the petition by pleading an exception. As such, the respondent assumes the burden of proof by establishing the counterclaims made in response to the petition.

   The norm also applies indirectly to the judge. For although it is up to the one who asserts a fact to produce the necessary proof, the code accords to the judge the role of evaluating the proofs (c. 1608). The code also instructs the judge to collect proofs on his or her own initiative not only in defense of the public good, but also every time the search for the truth and justice demands it. (cf. c. 1452 §1) Furthermore, the judge has the right and duty to supply for the negligence of the parties in furnishing proofs or in lodging exceptions whenever the judge considers it necessary to avoid a gravely unjust judgment.[11]

2. ***Matters not needing proof.*** The following do not need proof: 1° matters presumed by the law itself; 2° facts alleged by one of the contending parties and admitted by the other unless the law or the judge

10 C. 1526 §1. See also *DC*, article 156 §1.

11 C. 1452 §2.

nevertheless requires proof.[12] Presumptions of law require no proof. A presumption is a probable conjecture about an uncertain matter. This presumption may either be a presumption of law, which is based in the law itself, or a human presumption, which is a personal conjecture of the judge (c. 1584). Some examples of things presumed by the law are: the validity of marriage (c. 1060), the consummation of a marriage after the cohabitation of the parties (c. 1061 §2), and the external manifestation of consent conforming to the internal matrimonial consent (c. 1101 §1). However, these presumptions yield in the face of contrary evidence, and in fact the challenging of any of these presumptions is at the heart of marriage nullity process. Moreover, the agreement of the parties on some fact does not, however, discharge them from the burden of proof in all cases. The law or the judge can oppose it, if, for example, the judge has reasons to believe that there is collusion between the parties.

3. ***The admissibility of proofs.*** "Proofs of any kind which seem useful for adjudicating the case and are licit can be brought forward."[13] According to *Dignitas connubii*: "Proofs of any kind which seem useful for understanding the cause and are licit can be brought forward. Proofs which are illicit, whether in themselves or in the manner in which they are acquired, are neither to be brought forward nor admitted (cf. c. 1527 §1)."[14] The production of the proofs in a trial is not and cannot be left to the will of the parties but must follow the norms established by the law. Consequently, proofs of any kind are permitted but they must be licit and pertinent to the case and they must be admitted by the judge. The proofs have to be lawful *(licitae)* because of the moral principle that the end does not justify the means. In addition, the judge respects the dignity of persons pursuant to natural law and its interpretation by ecclesiastical teachings. For example, no one is obliged to exhibit documents that cannot be communicated without danger of harm or of violating a secret.[15] Thus, the judge can refuse to admit a proof that was obtained through some illicit means.

   If controversies arise regarding the admissibility of any evidence, the judge must decide the matter expeditiously. "If a party insists that a proof rejected by a judge be accepted, the judge is to decide the matter as promptly as possible (*expeditissime*)."[16] Against this decision of the judge there is no possibility of appeal to a superior court (c. 1629, 5°), but the question can be proposed again if and when there is a second instance process.

---

12 C. 1526 §2. See also *DC,* article 156 §2.

13 C. 1527 §1.

14 *DC,* article 157 §1.

15 C. 1546 §1.

16 C. 1527 §2.

4. ***The refusal to testify.*** "If a party or a witness refuses to appear before the judge to testify, it is permissible to hear them through a lay person designated by the judge or to require of them a declaration either before a notary public or in any other legitimate manner."[17] This is a new canon although a similar norm is found in article 5 of the 1973 *Procedural Norms for Drawing UpA Process of Dissolution of the Bond of Marriage in Favor of the Faith.*[18] The designation of a layperson to receive the testimony was initially reserved to the competence of the bishop: "If a party or witness refuses to appear before a catholic priest to testify, that person may be heard by a layperson designated by the bishop; if that is not even possible, it is required of them to make a declaration before a notary or in any another lawful manner."[19] The canon was later amended to its present form, in response to the proposal of a consultor, to give to the judge the competence to designate the person to collect the testimony.[20] The purpose of canon 1528 is to respect "the freedom of conscience of one who refuses to appear before a catholic priest."[21]

5. ***The prohibition against evidence gathering before the Joinder of the Issue.*** "Except for a grave cause, the judge is not to proceed to collect the proofs before the joinder of the issue."[22] According to *Dignitas connubii*: "Without prejudice to art. 120, the tribunal is not proceed to collecting the proofs before the formulation of the doubt has been set in accordance with art. 135, except for a grave reason, since the formulation of the doubt is to delimit those things which are to be investigated. (cf. c. 1529)."[23] The instruction states that the judge can only collect proofs before the joinder of the issue to determine the tribunal's competence and the petitioner's procedural capacity. According to article 120: "The *praeses* can and must, if the case requires, institute a preliminary

---

17 C. 1528. See also *DC,* article 161 §1.

18 Sacred Congregation for the Doctrine of the Faith, Instruction *Ut notum est pro solutione matrimonii in favorem fidei,* December 6, 1973: *Enchiridion Vaticanum,* 4 (Bologna: Editoriale Dehoniano, 1978) 1788-1799. Article 5 §1 stated that if a given witness was a non-Catholic and refused to present him/herself and make a deposition before a Catholic priest, a document containing the deposition made concerning this matter before a notary public or other trustworthy person may be accepted. This fact must be expressly noted in the acts. See also *CLD* 8, ed. James O'Connor (Mundelein, IL: St. Mary of the Lake Seminary, 1978) 1180. The same norm is found in article 15 §1 of the 2001 *Normae de conficiendo processu pro solutione vinculi matrimonialis in favorem fidei* issued by the Congregation for the Doctine of the Faith on April 30, 2001. For the English translation and a detailed commentary on the 2001 Norms see Alan A. McCormark, "A Commentary on the Norms for Favor of the Faith Cases," *The Jurist* 65 (2005) 268-337.

19 *Coetus de processibus,* October 27, 1978: *Communicationes* 11 (1979) 98.

20 *Communicationes* 11 (1979) 99. Canon 1528 reads that "if a party or a witness refuses to appear before the judge to testify, it is permissible to hear them through a lay person designated by the judge or to require of them a declaration either before a notary public or in any other legitimate manner."

21 *Coetus de processibus,* November 3, 1976: *Communicationes* 8 (1976) 188.

22 C. 1529.

23 *DC,* article 160.

investigation regarding the question of the tribunal's competence and of the petitioner's legitimate standing in the trial. In regard to the merits of the cause the judge can only institute an investigation in order to admit or reject the *libellus*, if the *libellus* should seem to lack any basis whatsoever; he can do this only in order to see whether it could happen that some basis could appear from the process."[24]

Thus, before the joinder of the issue, the judge cannot proceed to collect proofs unless for a grave cause. Thus, the practice of gathering witness testimony even before the petition for a declaration of nullity of marriage has been formally submitted to the tribunal should be discouraged. In other words, with regards to the gathering of proofs in order to determine the merits of the case before the joinder of issue, "it is not the judge's responsibility to verify whether the allegations of the petitioner are true or not." [25] The judge can only gather proofs before the joinder of issues due to some grave cause such as in the case of the danger of the death of a witness or in the case of someone leaving on a faraway journey. The 1917 code (c. 1730) stated that before the joinder of the issue, the judge was not to proceed to receive testimony except in the case of contumacy or unless the deposition of the witness would be undertaken with difficulty or a witness might die or depart the place or for some other just cause.[26] The substitution of the word "grave" for "just" in the 1983 code was initially debated but was retained nevertheless to counter abuses in some places where the instruction of the case usually took place before the joinder of the issue, and was even done by the procurator or advocate.[27]

III. Definitions, and types of witnesses and their testimonies

1. ***Definitions and types of witnesses***. A witness is a person distinct from the judge and the parties who is summoned to trial to make known his or her observations concerning the disputed facts. At times the observations of the witness are obtained from the senses; at other times, they are simply deduced by logical reasoning. In this, the witness is different from an expert, because the expert always produces his or her knowledge or conclusions by the use of some art or science.[28] The assertions of the witness are called testimonies or testimonial proofs. A testimonial proof is a procedural act consisting in a declaration of

24 *DC,* article 120 §§1-2.

25 Zenon Grocholewski, "Canons 1505 and 1529: The Gathering of Proofs Before the Joinder of the Issues," in *Roman Replies and CLSA Advisory Opinions 1984-1993*, ed. Patrick J. Cogan (Washington, DC: CLSA, 1995) 460. For more on the preliminary investigation before the instruction of the case, see Robert Sanson, "A Preliminary Investigation for Marriage Annulment?" *Studia canonica* 11 (1977) 37-66.

26 *CIC*/1917 c. 1730

27 1982 Schema: *Communicationes* 16 (1984) 64.

28 Franciscus Roberti, *De Processibus,* vol. 2 (Rome: Pontificium Institutum Utriusque Iuris, 1926) 41.

knowledge or information regarding a past fact in the case before the judge by a person extraneous to the case.[29] A witness can also be said to be a person distinct from the judge and the parties, legitimately summoned to an ecclesiastical trial to testify to the truth regarding some fact that the witness has seen or heard to be included in the canonical process.

Witnesses differ according to their status before the court. These are substantive witnesses, qualified witnesses, expert witnesses, summoned witnesses, and spontaneous witnesses. Substantive witnesses are those who testify to what they have observed while qualified witnesses are those who testify to acts observed or done in fulfillment of their office such as bishops, pastors, deacons, and notaries. For example, a pastor is a qualified witness in those matters that is strictly connected to his pastoral office such as ministering baptism or witnessing marriage. Furthermore, those persons are also called witnesses whose presence at the solemnization of a marriage is required for its validity (cf. c. 1108 §1). While the sacred minister in a marriage celebration may become a qualified witness in a subsequent marriage nullity trial, the two witnesses required in conjunction with the sacred minister to constitute canonical form do not become qualified witnesses. They offer their testimony as substantive witnesses.

Expert witnesses are those who are called upon to establish some fact or to ascertain the true nature of some matter based on their art or science (c. 1574). They are persons trained in an art or science, or who are otherwise experienced in a matter pertaining to the object of the controversy. Furthermore, some are summoned witnesses, that is, those who have been called to testify and others are spontaneous witnesses, that is, those who come to the tribunal on their own accord or send information to the tribunal on their own such as the current civil law spouse of one of the principals. Witnesses can be heard sworn or unsworn (c. 1562); they may be certain or vacillating (c. 1572, 3°); some are unsuitable (c. 1550 §1) and others are disqualified if, for reasons stated in the law, they are excluded from testifying (c. 1550 §2). Finally, some are suspect if, for a just reason such as bitter enmity toward one of the parties, they are excluded from testifying by the judge (c. 1555).[30]

2. ***Types of witness testimonies.*** There are also various kinds of witnesses according to the nature of their testimonies. Witnesses are corroboative when they testify concordantly to the same fact, that is, they agree in their testimony. They are singular when their testimonies do not agree with each other. Singular witnesses in turn are of different kinds. First,

---

29 Ibid.

30 Lawrence Wrenn, "Trials in General," in *The Code of Canon Law: A Text and Commentary*, eds. James Coriden, Thomas Green, and Donald Heintschel (London: Geoffrey Chapman, 1996) 981. [Henceforth, "Trials"].

they are adversative when their testimonies regarding the same fact are contrary or in opposition to each other. For example, one states that Titus was killed in his house, the other in the metro train. Second, singular witnesses are diversative when they testify to different facts having no connection with each other. Third, singular witnesses are cumulative when their testimonies, though differing in circumstances, can be harmonized. For example, one witness states that she saw Joan's father threatening the daughter when she refused to marry John, another that Joan's father had mentioned that he threatened the daughter over the matter of the marriage. Although these testimonies differ in specifics, they nonetheless can be harmonized in proving the same fact. Of the three kinds of singular testimonies, it is only in regard to cumulative testimony can the judge attain moral certainty about the fact.

Testimonies also vary according to their source. Some witnesses testify from personal experiences (*de scientia*), hearsay (*de auditu*), or rumor (*de fama*). Some merely give an opinion of their own (*de credulitate*) and others are character witnesses (*de credibilitate*). Witnesses *de scientia* are in turn distinguished as eyewitnesses or ear witnesses depending on whether they saw or heard first hand that which they testify about. Witnesses who report a version of an event they heard from others are called hearsay witnesses. Direct hearsay witnesses hear of the event from those who saw or experienced it. And indirect hearsay witnesses hear of the event from those who themselves merely heard of it.

Furthermore, some witnesses testify based on rumor; they are not witnesses in the strict probatory sense of the word. And then there are character witnesses who limit themselves to clarifying the credibility of a party in the trial. They indirectly admit the judicial declarations of a party.

In conclusion, proof by witnesses is often indispensable for the historical reconstruction of the relevant facts which is necessary for the pronouncement of a sentence by the judge. Therefore, it is incumbent on the judge to examine witnesses and evaluate their testimonies according to the norm of law.

IV. The admissibility and rejection of witnesses

"Proof by means of witnesses is always allowed under the direction of the judge in cases of any kind."[31] The source for canon 1547 is canon 1754 of the 1917 code. The same principle is enunciated in both canons. Canon law has always held testimonial proof in great esteem. Even in the documentary process, testimonial proof is allowed, especially if documents cannot be obtained, are lost, or destroyed. Moreover, in the daily practice of our tribunals, with its emphasis on the matrimonial nullity process, testimonial proof necessarily con-

31 C. 1547. See also *DC,* article 193.

stitutes a substantial part of the proof. Thus, the first canon in the chapter of the 1983 code on proof by witnesses states that this mode of proof is admitted in all cases under the direction of the judge (c. 1547).

Some have argued against the use of witnesses in documentary process.[32] Nonetheless, canonical tradition supports the use of proof by witnesses to prove the nullity of a marriage in the documentary process. For example, the Commission for the Authentic Interpretation of the 1917 code declared that any type of proof could be used to prove that no dispensation was granted from an impediment provided that the proof of this was likewise certain.[33] Although changes have been made in the norms concerning the documentary process in the 1983 code, its fundamental judicial nature remains the same. Furthermore, the fact that the canonical tradition accepts testimonial proof in the documentary process is proven in a rotal decision *coram* Fidecicchi of January 13, 1948. According to the 1917 code, a person who is bound by a previous marriage bond, even though not consummated, cannot validly contract another marriage with due regard for privilege of the faith cases (1917 *CIC* c. 1069). Thus, the *turnus* stated that for any marriage to be declared null under the impediment of prior bond, it must be absolutely apparent that there is such an impediment from a certain and authentic document subject to no contradiction or exception (1917 *CIC* c. 1990), from another legitimate means which begets equal certitude of the contracted marriage, or from the depositions of credible witnesses.[34] Therefore, in light of the canonical tradition testimonial proof is admissible in the documentary or summary process if it will help the judge beget moral certainty in the case. Not only does canonical tradition support the use of witnesses in the documentary process, but practical court experience in summary cases also shows that witnesses are an important means of establishing the fact of non-baptism in cases of disparity of worship.

As canon 1547 states, proof by witnesses is always admitted under the direction of the judge according to the modalities established by law. By mandating that proof by witnesses be admitted only under the direction of the judge, canon 1547 preserves the judge's role in directing the course of the trial.[35] Moreover, the expression, "under the moderation of the judge" indicates that the judge is to admit, reject, and interrogate witnesses, introduce witnesses *ex officio* in cases involving the public interest (cc. 1478 §4 and 1550 §1), curb an excess number of witnesses (c. 1553), or decide whether a witness should be excluded (c. 1555). It is also up to the judge to assess whether the testimony is sincere or whether it has been altered due to bad faith, the self-interest of the party, or other factors.

32 Robert Bourgon, "Proofs," *The Canon Law: Letter and Spirit* (Collegeville, MN: The Liturgical Press, 1995) 880.

33 Pontifical Commission for the Authentic Interpretation of the Code of Canon Law, *responsa,* July 16, 1931, *AAS* 23 (1931) 353-356.

34 *C.* Fidecicchi, January 13, 1948, *RRDec* 40 (1948) 18.

35 Cox, "Proofs," 1678.

V. The obligation of witnesses to respond and tell the truth

"When the judge questions witnesses legitimately, they must tell the truth."[36] When legitimately questioned, the witness has a grave, moral and juridic obligation to respond and speak the truth. The interrogation is legitimate when it is done by a competent judge or his or her delegate or an auditor. (c. 1528). This norm has two sides to it: the obligation to testify which concerns every person legitimately questioned (with some exception) and the obligation to tell the truth. The obligation to tell the truth is violated not only by telling a falsehood, but also by concealing the truth.[37]

An earlier draft of canon 1548 (i.e., *schema canonum de iure precessuali* c. 190 §3) stated that witnesses who knowingly affirm falsehood or hide the truth when legitimately questioned by the judge can be punished according the norm of law.[38] This penal clause disappeared in the revised code, and as such the obligation indicated in canon 1548 §1 acquires a greater moral weight.[39]

The function of witness affects the public good, those called upon to give testimony are to accept and fulfill that function rightly. Nonetheless, the necessity of testifying is not absolute since it can be supplied by other means; therefore, the law does not insist on it if its observance would impede a greater good or could not be fulfilled without excessive inconvenience.

VI. The exception from the obligation to testify

Without prejudice to canon 1550 §2, 2°, which exempts priests and others from testifying in respect of all knowledge gained from sacramental confession, the following are exempted from the obligation to respond: 1° clerics regarding what has been made known to them by reason of sacred ministry; civil officials, physicians, midwives, advocates, notaries, and others bound by professional secrecy even by reason of having given advice, regarding those matters subject to this secrecy; 2° those who fear that from their own testimony ill repute, dangerous hardships, or other grave evils will befall them, their spouses, or persons related to them by consanguinity or affinity.[40]

An earlier draft of this canon (i.e., *schema canonum de iure processuali* c. 190) read that pastors and other priests, in what pertained to things that were

36 C. 1548 §1. See also *DC,* article 194 §1. This canon has as its sources 1917 *CIC* c. 1755 §1 and *Provida mater* article 121 §1.

37 Canon 63 distinguishes between "subreption," which is concealment of the truth, and "obreption," which is a statement of falsehood.

38 *Coetus de processibus,* November 21, 1978, *Communicationes* 11 (1979) 108-109.

39 José Maria Serrano Ruiz, "De testibus et attestationibus," *Commento al Codice di Diritto Canonico,* ed. Pio Vito Pinto (Vaticana: Libreria Editrice Vaticana, 2001) 900.

40 C. 1548 §2. See also *DC,* article 196, §2, 2°.

revealed to them by reason of sacred ministry outside of sacramental confession, were exempted from the obligation of responding when legitimately questioned by the judge.[41] There were suggestions that the norm should begin with: "Ministers of the Church..." One consultor preferred this because of the places where lay persons perform matrimonial investigations. But other consultors noted that the lay persons referred to are provided for by the words "others who are bound to secrecy of office." A suggestion was also made that "all priests" replace "pastors and other priests." But the consultors preferred rather that it should read "clerics, in what pertains to..."[42]

The use of the word "clerics" in canon 1548 §2 means that the exemption is applicable to bishops, priests, and deacons concerning any information confided to them by reason of the sacred ministry. Also, the phrase "and others bound by professional secrecy even by reason of having given advice" includes, besides civil officials, physicians, midwives, advocates, and notaries, "all others who exercise similar offices or who not exercising any office, gave advice asked of them. For those things that were revealed to someone while seeking advice fall under the secrecy of office.

The "professional secrecy" mentioned in canon 1548 §2, 1° means the secret that has been entrusted to an office holder or to someone by virtue of some title by an explicit or implicit prior agreement with the person divulging theinformation. The secret of office obliges not merely by reason of a respect for the private good, but also by reason of the common good. For it is necessary that people should be free to confer with experts without fear of their secrets being divulged. Another reason for the exemption is that people are not always able to provide for their own needs but need the help and counsel of those with special knowledge. And unless this secret was observed, people would be deterred from seeking counsel, to the great detriment of the spiritual or material order.[43]

However, professional secrecy no longer obliges as long as the person keeping the secret is freed by the party from its obligation. Therefore, upon release from the obligation, the person is obliged to respond to the judge. A witness, then, who has been released from the obligation of professional confidentiality is obligated to inform the judge of what he or she knows that was covered by professional secrecy since he or she is now subject to the general rule that witnesses must tell the truth to a judge who lawfully questions them (c. 1548 §1).

But not infrequently those bound by professional secrecy have refused to give testimony even when the parties themselves have freed them from the obligation of keeping the secret. A witness who is bound by professional confidentiality

41 *Coetus de processibus,* November 21, 1978, *Communicationes* 11 (1979) 108.

42 *Communicationes* 11 (1979) 108-109.

43 Roberti, 43.

cannot assert a right of exemption if the person to whom the confidentiality pertains releases him or her from the obligation relating to it.[44]

Also exempted from the obligation to respond when legitimately questioned by the judge are those who fear that from their testimony ill repute, dangerous hardships (or harassments), or other grave evils will befall them, their spouses, or persons closely related to them by consanguinity or affinity (c. 1548 §2). This is a demonstrative listing of damages to which a witness might be exposed and which exempt the witness from testifying. The code does not determine the decree of consanguinity or affinity for the use of the term "closely related." This leaves the determination up to the prudent discretion of the judge.[45] The 1917 code (c. 1755 §2, 2°) indicated the relationship was to any degree of the direct line and the first degree of the collateral line. During the code revision process, the *coetus* on procedures was asked simply to restate the grade of consanguinity and affinity as it was in the 1917 code. All the consultors except one, however, agreed that the determination of the grade should be left to the discretion of the judge.[46]

In interpreting canon 1548 §2, 2° (i.e., about the possible harm that might come to a potential witness) it is important to refer to canon 1598 §1. According to canon 1598 §1: "After the proofs have been collected, the judge must permit the parties and their advocates, under penalty of nullity, to inspect at the tribunal chancery the acts not yet known to them; furthermore, a copy of the acts can also be given to advocates who request one. In cases pertaining to the public good to avoid a most grave danger the judge can decree that a specific act must be shown to no one; the judge is to take care, however, that the right of defense always remains intact."[47]

The purpose of canon 1598 §1 is to ensure a fair trial. Indeed, it is impossible to conceptualize a fair trial without the right to be heard and to respond to the allegations lodged. "One cannot conceive of a just judgment without the contention, that is, without the concrete possibility granted to each party in the case to be heard and to be able to know and contradict the requests, proofs, and deductions adopted by the opposing party or *ex officio*."[48]

44 Klaus Lüdicke and Ronny E. Jenkins, *Dignitas Connubii: Norms and Commentary* (Washington DC: Canon Law Society of America, 2006) 330.

45 García Faílde, 1249.

46 *Coetus de processibus,* November 21, 1978. *Communicationes* 11 (1979) 109.

47 C. 1598 §1.

48 John Paul II, Allocution of January 26, 1989: *AAS* 81 (1989) 923. Translations from William H. Woestman, *Papal Allocutions to the Roman Rota, 1939-2002.* Ottawa: Saint Paul University, 2002. All subsequent translations of papal allocutions will be taken from this source.

Consequently, the parties have the right to examine the acts of the case. The right of defense includes the right to be heard, to put forth one's argument and to support the argument with evidence, to know the arguments of the opposing party, and to dispute and contradict these arguments.[49] It is violated when a court precludes or denies either party the faculty of knowing the proofs brought forward by the other party, of defending themselves, and contradicting the proofs. "If however, the tribunal, whether in good or bad faith, precludes or denies either party the possibility of knowing the proofs or of defending themselves and contradicting the proofs, without doubt the right of defense is to be said to have been violated and consequently the sentence is vitiated by irremediable nullity."[50]

However, if the judge thinks that to avoid very serious dangers some act is not to be shown to the parties, the advocates of the parties, having first taken an oath or made a promise to observe secrecy, may study the same act.[51] Moreover, before the examination of the acts, the judge can also bind the parties to take an oath or promise that they will use the knowledge gained through the inspection of the acts only for their legitimate defense in the canonical forum.[52] A party who refuses to take an oath or make such a promise is considered to have renounced the right of examining the acts. "But if a party refuses to take an oath or, as the case may be, make a promise, he will be considered to have renounced the faculty of examining the acts, unless particular law establishes otherwise."[53] Obviously a *de facto* defense is not required for the validity of the process provided its concrete possibility is always present. Therefore the parties can renounce the exercise of the right of defense in a contentious trial.[54]

The dangers to be avoided must be serious and concrete and not vague, generic, or abstract. In a decree *coram* Colagiovanni of March 30, 1993,[55] the *turnus* held that the right of access to the acts is not absolute but must be tempered with another principle, namely, the necessity of avoiding serious harm to the "public good" mentioned in the second part of canon 1598 §1. For this reason, serious consideration must be given to these dangers of serious harm (not only for the Church as the canon expressly states, that is to say, the public good, but also for the party and so the private good). These dangers must be evaluated not abstractly, but in individual circumstances, and in their personal, social, and juridical (especially civil law) situations.[56] Furthermore, the *turnus* stated that the types of harm implied in canon 1598 can be of various kinds, not excluding

49 François Morlot, "Le droit de dèfense, en particulier dans la publication des actes," *Studia canonica* 30 (1996) 136.

50 *C.* Bruno, July 15, 1993, *Monitor Ecclesiasticus* 119 (1994) 331.

51 *DC,* article 234. See also c. 1455 §3.

52 *DC,* article 232 §1.

53 *DC*, article 232 §2.

54 Pope John Paul II, *AAS* 81 (1989) 923.

55 *C.* Colagiovanni, March 30, 1993, *Monitor Ecclesiasticus* 119 (1994) 535-544. Translation from Augustine Mendonça, *Studia canonica* 33 (1999) 320-326.

56 *C.* Colagiovanni, March 30, 1993, *Monitor Ecclesiasticus* 119 (1994) 537.

actions in civil courts for economic damages, if the alleged facts presented in an ecclesiastical trial can injure a person's good reputation in those countries where the so-called "separation of State and Church or any religious denomination" is strictly enforced.[57]

According to the rotal auditors, there may not be a serious problem if only a particular judicial act or some particular judicial acts are not communicated to the parties. But there may be serious difficulty when in particular cases harm is feared not just from the publication of a single document (as foreseen by the canon), but also from any part that essentially integrates the entire probatory context itself, or, more seriously, is the very foundation of the proof. This can happen especially when a marriage nullity case is judged on grounds of psychic incapacity (c. 1095). The risk may be all the more serious when a respondent who is opposed to the nullity, fearing harm from the revelation of such personal facts, threatens that he or she is ready to have recourse to the civil authority to protect his or her private good. Perhaps this could pave the way for the intervention of civil authority to interpret canonical norms.[58] "Therefore, whereas most certainly c. 1598 §1 must be strictly observed, one must be very prudent in deducing the nullity of the process or of the sentence from the application of the second part of this canon in order to prevent very serious harm to the Church."[59]

In any case, closely related to the harm that might possibly come to witnesses who testify is the case of witnesses who want to do so only on condition that their names be withheld from at least one of the parties, or both of them. Indeed, "Tribunals encounter from time to time a witness who will testify only if his or her name identity as the one making the statement is not revealed to the parties."[60] The 1983 Code of Canon Law does not admit of such confidentiality, either in canon 1554 or in canons 1678-1680, which deal with the special procedures for marriage cases. A matrimonial case touches the fate and status of the parties in a matter of the greatest personal importance; and so they are entitled in natural justice to be fully acquainted with the evidence according to which the judges will decide their ecclesial status. Hence, canon 1598 accords the parties the right to have access to the acts.

However, the acceptance and use in trial of such "secret evidence" is completely repugnant to the modern mind and to the contemporary sense of justice. Evidently such a "right" is in no way countenanced by canon 1598.[61] The right to confidentiality, therefore, precludes other persons from access to the acts, for they have no right to know them. However, it cannot bar one or both of the parties from access to the acts, for they have a strict and inviolable right to this

57 Ibid., 538.
58 Ibid., 540.
59 Ibid.
60 Lüdicke and Jenkins, 331.
61 *C.* Burke, June 11, 1992, *Studia canonica* 26 (1992) 493.

direct knowledge. "Not to respect this right would be to tolerate a sort of secret chamber process whereby evidence could be used against a person of which he or she is unaware and has therefore no opportunity of rebutting...If priorities are respected, a court cannot sacrifice the justice and integrity of the current judicial hearing to possible issues – however delicate – that may arise at some future time. To invert priorities here – i.e., to allow the witness' relative right to confidentiality to take precedence over the party's absolute right to publication – is to run the gravest danger of provoking the nullity of a sentence."[62]

Some reasonable steps can be taken to avoid possible future dangers that might result from the publication of the acts to the parties. For example, witnesses should be reminded that the tribunal is more interested in knowledge and facts than in mere opinion; what mainly matters is what the witness knows to be true. From the outset witnesses should be told of the natural and fundamental right of both parties to be informed of all the evidence adduced. If there is some particular statement or document that a witness strongly thinks ought not to be communicated to one or both parties, he or she should be requested to indicate it specifically and give the reasons why it should be treated with reserve. The tribunal can then prudently decide whether such a particular item of evidence is to be treated as reserved under canon 1598. It is to weigh both the importance of the evidence itself as well as the reasonableness of the witness's fear of very grave danger resulting from its publication to the parties.

In the unlikely event that a particular witness was called to give evidence and refused to accept the aforementioned provisions, "this arguably provides good reason for excluding him or her from that trial (cf. 1555). It is clear that the fairness of a trial is less prejudiced by the absence of one such witness than by the inadequate protection of the rights of the parties themselves."[63]

VII. Those who can and cannot be witnesses

"All persons can be witnesses unless the law expressly excludes them in whole or in part."[64] This norm states both a principle and an exception. The principle is that everyone is considered competent to testify and the exception is that some persons are expressly disqualified by natural or positive law, in whole or in part from testifying. Those persons expressly excluded by law from testifying are minors under the age of fourteen, the mentally challenged, those who fulfill a function incompatible with that of witnesses, and priests and others who have in any way obtained knowledge of pertinent facts on the occasion of sacramental confession.

62 C. Burke, June 11, 1992, *Studia canonica* 26 (1992) 493.

63 C. Burke, June 11, 1992, *Studia canonica* 26 (1992) 493-494.

64 C. 1549. See also *DC,* article 195. The sources for this canon are c. 1756 1917 *CIC* and *Provida mater,* article 118. There are no comments regarding this canon in *Communicationes*. *Coetus de processibus,* November 21, 1978, *Communicationes* 11 (1979) 109.

1. ***Those disqualified from being witnesses.*** "Minors below the fourteenth year of age and those of limited mental capacity are not allowed to give testimony; they can, however, be heard by a decree of the judge which declares such a hearing expedient."[65] A person may have the natural capacity to observe events and relate them to others but still be canonically disqualified from being a witness in an ecclesiastical court.

   Canon law also disqualifies from testifying in an ecclesiastical trial those with limited mental capacity. These are those who suffer from some sickness on account of which they neither perceive facts rightly nor communicate intelligently with others. Witnesses must be of sane mind either at the time that the facts were learned or at the time of testimony. Hence, those of impaired mind are excluded because of the state of their faculties which prevents them from seeing and comprehending sufficiently to provide testimony to justify a judicial sentence.[66]

   Article 196 §1 of *Dignitas connubii* and canon 1550 §1 state that the judge may admit minors who are under the age of fourteen and those of limited mental capacity to testify if the judge thinks it advisable to do so. However, no guidelines are offered regarding the probative weight of such testimony unlike the 1917 code which stated that "their testimony shall be of value only as an indication of and in support of the proof."[67] It is advisable then that the judge should be guided by the availability of other proofs and the amount of valuable information likely to be secured from such persons before admitting their testimonies.

   Furthermore, canon 1550 §1 states that when the judge considers it opportune to hear these categories of persons, the judge must issue a decree. "A decree is to be issued in writing, with the reasons at least summarily expressed if it is a decision."[68] Thus, it is not enough simply to admit these categories of persons to testify; the decision of the judge to admit minors under fourteen years or those of limited mental capacity must be issued by decree indicating, at least in summary form the reasons for the decision.

1. ***Those incapable of being witnesses.*** While minors below the age of fourteen and those persons with limited mental capacity are disqualified from testifying, there are others who are incapable of being witnesses. The following are considered incapable: 1° the parties in the case or those who stand for the parties at the trial, the judge and the judge's assistants, the advocate, and others who assist or have assisted the parties in the same case; 2° priests regarding all matters which they have come to know from sacramental confession even if the penitent seeks

65 C. 1550 §1. The sources for this canon are cc. 1757 §1; 1758 1917 *CIC* and *Provida mater,* artcles 119 §1; 120.

66 R. Naz, "Témoins Judiciaires," in *Dictionnaire de Droit Canonique,* vol. 7 (Paris: Librairie Letouzey et Ané, 1965) 1174-1175.

67 1917 *CIC* c. 1758.

68 C. 51.

their disclosure; moreover, matters heard by anyone and in any way on the occasion of confession cannot be accepted even as an indication of the truth.[69]

While the judge may decree, with reasons, that minors below the age of fourteen and those of diminished mental capacity may testify in a trial, in the case of those incapable, the judge is not able to make exceptions to allow these persons in order for them to testify. During the code revision process, it was suggested that instead of the term *incapaces,* the term *inhabiles* should be used to identify those who are incapable of testifying since it expresses more appropriately the juridic prohibition intended. The consultors, however, maintained that *incapaces* was more appropriate because it denotes the juridic incapacity rather than physical or moral suitability.[70] Those incapable of functioning as witnesses are the parties, guardians, judges and their assistants, advocates, and confessors.

The parties in the case and those who stand in the trial in their name (i.e., the procurator, guardian, curator, or legal representative) are disqualified from testifying because one cannot be a witness and a party in his or her own case at the same time. Matrimonial trials would be a travesty of justice if the same persons were both the parties and witnesses.

The 1917 code expressly stated that spouses, relatives, and in-laws were incapable of being witnesses for or against each other except in marriage cases (1917 *CIC* c. 1757 §3). During the code revision process, it was initially stated that in cases which concern the public good or the status of persons, the spouses of the parties and those related to them by blood or marriage are also admitted as witnesses; in other cases, however, they can be admitted according to the decree of the judge.[71] But two consultors recommended that this canon should be deleted because the spouses and their blood relatives are not considered as incapable of giving testimony and therefore there was no reason to retain the canon. A vote was taken and the canon was removed.[72] In other words, relatives can testify as witnesses in cases concerning the persons to whom they are related. Indeed, since matrimonial cases deal with the status of the parties and the public good is involved, the former code allowed relatives to testify as witnesses in the cases of their relatives (1917 *CIC* c. 1974).

---

69 C. 1550 §2. See also *DC,* article 196 §2, 2°. The sources for this canon are 1917 *CIC* c. 1757 §3 and *Provida mater,* article 119 §3.

70 *Coetus de processibus, Communicationes* 11 (1979) 110.

71 *Coetus de processibus,* November 21, 1978, *Communicationes* 11 (1979) 110.

72 *Communicationes* 11 (1979) 110.

Those who take the place of the parties such as guardians cannot also be witnesses in the cases of their wards. Minors and those who lack the use of reason can stand trial only through their parents, guardians or curators.[73] Minors and those lacking the use of reason do not generally enjoy procedural capacity (*ius standi in iudicio*); as such the procedural capacity is offset by parents, guardians, and curators. Since the parties are debarred from testifying as witnesses, guardians likewise are not permitted to testify as witnesses. They give their deposition as parties in the case and not as witnesses and hence enjoy the prerogatives of the parties and are bound by any restrictions on them.

The judge and his or her assistants are also disqualified from giving testimony. This is not only to guarantee their impartiality and freedom but also the integrity of the judicial system. The judge not only directs the *iter* of the trial itself but more significantly also determines the definitive response to the question before the court.[74] A judge as a witness poses a grave harm to the credible administration of justice. "As the adjudicator of the matter before the court, the judge must always remain free of bias or prejudice, not only in fact, but also in appearance. So too, by extension, must other officers of the court whose participation in the process bears on the course and outcome of a case."[75]

Advocates and procurators who assist or had assisted the parties in the same case are also disqualified from giving testimony. The procurator differs from the advocate in that the former acts as a type of guardian in a trial specifically taking the place of a party who is impeded in some way while the latter is one who by his advice provides legal and technical help to a party in the case.[76] In most cases, however, the two functions are entrusted to one person. The procurator-advocate is unqualified to appear as a witness a case in which he or she exercises or had exercised the office. The functions of the parties and guardians, the judge and his or her assistants, the procurator-advocates and others who assist or had assisted the parties in the case should not be assumed by persons who may be likely witnesses in the same case. According to *Dignitas connubii*: "care should be taken lest these functions be assumed by persons who through their testimony could make a contribution toward ascer-

73 C. 1478 and *DC,* article 196 §2, 2°.

74 Ronny E Jenkins, "Safeguarding the Administration of Justice: Judicial Abstention and Recusal in Canonical Perspective." *Periodica* 93 (2004) 389; 396.

75 Jenkins, 389-397. For more on the duties of the judge, see Antoni Stankiewicz, "I doveri del giudice," *Studi Giuridici* 29 (1994) 299-321.

76 *C.* Boccafola, July 25, 1989, *Rotae Romanae Tribunal Decreta* 7 (1989) 146.

taining the truth."[77] In other words, those who are foreseen to function as witnesses should not have any other role in the trial.[78]

Priests and those who have in any way obtained knowledge on the occasion of sacramental confession are also disqualified from testifying regarding the facts obtained in this manner. The disqualification established by positive law affects not only sins revealed in the confession, but also extends to all information known from the confession received. The disqualification cannot be lifted even with the permission of the penitent on account of a public scandal that may have duly arisen from the actions of the penitent before he or she went to confession. And whatever is revealed from this knowledge even with the permission of the penitent cannot be taken as an indication of the truth. Indeed, the sacramental confession is absolutely outside the external forum.[79]

The sources for canon 1550 §2, 2° are canon 1757 §3 of the 1917 code and article 119 §3, 2° of *Provida mater,* both of which stated in part that priests were disqualified from testifying in what pertained to the things they knew from sacramental confession, even if they were released from the bond of the seal. An earlier draft of canon 1550 §2, 2° (i.e., *schema canonum de iure processuali* c. 192 §2, 2°) initially retained the 1917 code text. A consultor, however, commented that in the common opinion of theologians, a priest cannot be released from the bond of the seal of sacramental confession. Therefore, he proposed that the canon should read: "even if the penitent has requested their disclosure" in place of "even if they are released from the bond of the seal." The suggestion was accepted by all the other consultors.[80]

The sacramental seal is the strict and inviolable obligation of keeping secret whatever has been related to the confessor to obtain absolution. The revelation of the secret would render the sacrament odious and onerous.[81] The secrecy of the confessional transcends even the will of the penitent to protect the good of the Church and the sacrament on behalf of all the faithful. Thus, even if the penitent should offer to release the confessor, the law does not permit the confessor to act on the release.[82] The obligation of the seal flows from natural law, that is, justice,

77 *DC,* article 196 §2, 1°.

78 Lüdicke and Jenkins, 334.

79 Roberti, 47-48.

80 *Coetus de processibus,* November 21, 1978, *Communicationes* 11 (1979) 110.

81 Thomas Green, "Penalties for Individual Delicts," in *New Commentary on the Code of Canon Law*, ed. John P. Beal et al. (New York/Mahwah, NJ: Paulist Press, 2000) 1592. [Henceforth, "Penalties,"].

82 J. James Cuneo, "Canons 983 and 984: Confidentiality of the Seal of Confession in connection with Post-abortion Counseling" in *CLSA Advisory Opinions 1984-1993,* ed. Patrick J. Cogan (Washington, DC: Canon Law Society of America, 1995) 298.

lest the penitent's good name be damaged or he or she suffer some other harm. It also flows from divine positive law, that is, from the precept of confessing one's sins and also from ecclesiastical positive law, determining divine law and punishing its violations.[83] Its obligation does not expire with the passing of time, but continues on even after the death of the penitent. It demands silence from the confessor in respect to everyone, including the penitent himself or herself outside confession.[84]

The prohibition against revealing matters learned from sacramental confession is absolute. "The sacramental seal is inviolable; therefore it is absolutely forbidden (*nefas*) for a confessor to betray in any way a penitent in words or in any manner and for any reason."[85] The source for canon 983 §1 is canon 889 §1 of the 1917 code, which stated that the sacramental seal was inviolable. Therefore, a confessor must diligently (*caveat diligenter*) take care that neither by words nor by signs nor in any manner whatever does he betray the sins of another.[86]

De Paolis states that the use of the term *nefas* in canon 983 §1, which replaced *caveat diligenter* in canon 889 §1 of the 1917 code, denotes the special relation of the confessional seal to God. The seal in the new code is used only to express an obligation that the confessor has as confessor, and he is not to betray the penitent by revealing his or her sins. The confessor hears sins in the forum of God; God alone remits sins although by the ministry of the Church. What is heard in the forum of God must always be kept in that forum. There can never be any reason, however grave, that permits the revelation in a human forum of sins which the penitent confessed to God in the sacramental forum. It follows, then, that the seal is inviolable. It does not follow from human ecclesiastical law, but from divine law.[87]

The use of the term *nefas* in canon 983 §1 is to stress the gravity of the violation of the norm such that there are no exceptions to the norm: The confession of sins is protected by an inviolable sacramental seal; and this is true even if he or she has not been absolved. The seal of confession is understood to be the obligation to observe secrecy regarding what has been revealed in sacramental confession. The lips of the priest are sealed in an inviolable manner. The seal is necessary to protect the

83 William H. Woestman, *Sacraments: Initiation, Penance, Anointing of the Sick* (Ottawa: Saint Paul University, 2004) 273.

84 John Roos, "The Seal of Confession," *Canon Law Studies*, no. 413 (Washington, DC: The Catholic University of America, 1960) 64.

85 C. 983 §1.

86 1917 *CIC* c. 889 §1.

87 Velasio De Paolis, "De delictis contra sanctitatem sacramenti paenitentiae," *Periodica* 79 (1990) 190-191.

good of the sacrament and the good of the penitent. The Church teaches that the faithful are bound to confess their sins through individual confession (c. 988 §1). It would, therefore, be burdensome for the faithful to confess their sins as taught by the Church if confessors were not bound by the strictest obligation to preserve the seal of confession. There is a violation of the seal when the identity of the penitent and his or her sins are exposed to a third party. Even if there is no danger of disclosure of the penitent to others, any use of sacramental knowledge to the detriment of the penitent is prohibited.

On the other hand, the sacramental seal does not exist if an individual tells a priest something outside confession and says "this is under the seal" or "under confessional secrecy." Such a case is not in fact a confession. The seal does not also exist if the individual intends only spiritual direction and not confession in view of absolution.[88]

Canon 1550 §2 also states that those things heard by anyone in any manner whatsoever on the occasion of a confession cannot be used even as an indication of the truth. This means that the disqualification includes all persons, priests and lay persons, who intentionally, that is, through malice, curiosity or in the capacity of interpreter, or accidentally in any manner whatsoever, came either mediately or immediately, directly or indirectly, to the knowledge of something revealed in confession, not only sins but all information, made orally or by writing or by signs to the priest. Similarly, "The interpreter, if there is one, and all others who in any way have knowledge of sins from confession are also obliged to observe secrecy."[89] Thus, besides the interpreter, the list of those disqualified from testifying in a formal process also includes the theologian whom the confessor would have consulted concerning the penitent with the permission of the latter. It also includes whoever read the confession written down by others and misplaced somewhere. Whatever these persons might have heard on the occasion of confession cannot be the subject of a deposition in a trial even as an indication of the truth.

In conclusion, while minors under fourteen and those of limited mental capacity may be permitted to testify in court with the special permission of the judge, on the contrary, disqualified witnesses are never to be called to testify: if they are summoned, they are not to respond; if they respond, their testimonies are not to be heard.

---

88 William H. Woestman, *Sacraments: Initiation, Penance, Anointing of the Sick* (Ottawa: Saint Paul University, 2004) 273.

89 C. 983 §2.

VIII. The introduction, number, exclusion, and citation of witnesses

1. ***The introduction and renunciation of witnesses.*** "The party who has introduced a witness can renounce the examination of that witness; the opposing party, however, can request that the witness be examined nevertheless."[90] The introduction of witnesses is a petition made to the judge by either or both parties so that the named witness is heard to prove an action or exception. The sources for canon 1551 are canon 1759 of the 1917 code and article 132 of *Provida mater,* which explicitly listed the parties, the promoter of justice, and the defender of the bond as having the faculty to present witnesses. However, an earlier draft of canon 1551 (i.e., *schema canonum de iure processuali* c. 194) stated that the party who has introduced the witness can renounce the examination of the witness; the opposing party can, notwithstanding this renunciation, request that the witness be examined.[91] A consultative organ proposed that the faculty to introduce witnesses should be attributed also to the judge and the promoter of justice. The consultors responded, however, that the judge already has such a faculty and that even the promoter of justice also clearly has the faculty when he is involved in the case.[92]

2. In another meeting of the consultors, one of them suggested that canon 1759 of the 1917 code should be retained so that those who can introduce witnesses should be listed. The response was that it would be superfluous to retain the text in the former code as it is clear that there is no limitation on who can introduce witnesses in the code.[93] Consequently, the parties are not the only ones who can introduce witnesses; the defender of the bond, in virtue of canon 1432 and the promoter of justice if one is involved can also do so (cc. 1430-1434). Moreover, the judge, in virtue of canon 1452 §2, can also introduce witnesses.[94] But if witnesses are introduced by the judge *ex officio*, the decree in which the examination of these witnesses is ordered must indicate the individual witnesses and the points of the examination.[95]

   When proof through witnesses is requested, their names and domicile are to be communicated to the tribunal.[96] In addition, the party naming the witnesses is to provide the points on which each witness should be examined. The party must do so within the time limit set by the

90 C. 1551. See also *DC,* article 197.

91 *Coetus de processibus,* November 21, 1978, *Communicationes* 11 (1979) 111.

92 *Communicationes* 11 (1979) 111.

93 1980 Schema, *Communicationes* 16 (1984) 65. Canon 1479 §1 is now canon 1527 §1, which states that proofs of any kind which seem useful for adjudicating the case and are licit can be brought forward.

94 Canon 1452 §2 prescribes that the judge can supply for the negligence of the parties in furnishing proofs or in lodging exceptions whenever the judge considers it necessary in order to avoid a gravely unjust judgment.

95 Lega-Bartoccetti, 681.

96 C. 1552 §1. See also, *DC,* article 198.

judge; otherwise, the request to question the witness is considered abandoned.[97] On the other hand, the party who has introduced a witness can renounce the examination of that witness. The party does so by notifying the court of his or her intention to retract the witness. Notwithstanding the renunciation, the other party or the defender of the bond can demand that that witness should be examined. According to *Dignitas connubii,* article 197: "A party who has proposed a witness can renounce the examination of the witness; but the other party or the defender of the bond can ask that the witness be examined anyway (cf. 1551)."[98] To be valid, the renunciation must be put in writing and properly signed. It must be communicated to the other party and in light of *Dignitas connubii* (art. 197) to the defender of the bond; they must accept or at least not oppose the request, and the judge must admit it.[99]

The 1983 code suppressed the provision in the 1917 code which stated that if witnesses spontaneously presented themselves with the intention of giving testimony, it was up to the judge to admit or reject their testimony as he deemed it expedient (1917 *CIC* c. 1760 §1). Although the current law is silent on the issue of spontaneous witnesses, nevertheless, cases might still arise whereby such witnesses may send on their own accord written statements to the judge. The provision of the former code on judicial discretion still seems relevant in such cases.

3. ***The number of witnesses.*** "It is for the judge to curb an excessive number of witnesses."[100]Ordinarily, the names of the principal witnesses are provided in the *libellus* (c. 1504, 2°). Nonetheless, as the trial progresses, additional witnesses may be introduced by the parties, the judge, the defender of the bond, or the promoter of justice, if one is involved in the trial. At the same time, the judge has the right to restrict the number of witnesses lest they become too numerous and thereby cause delays in the judicial process.[101] No pre-determined number of witnesses can be established in any given case. However, the judge can also restrict the number of witnesses when the witnesses introduced do not pertain directly to the proof or when the case is considered instructed with fewer witnesses.
Thus, if a party insists that a witness otherwise qualified to testify but rejected by a judge should be accepted, the judge is to decide the matter as promptly as possible (c. 1527 §2). The judge has the right and obligation to limit excessive number of witnesses according to the quality and gravity of the case and according to his or her prudent discretion. The

97 C. 1552 §2.
98 *DC,* article 197.
99 C. 1524 §3.
100 C. 1553. The sources for this canon are c. 1762 1917 *CIC* and *Provida mater,* article 123 §2.
101 *DC,* article 157 §3.

decision of the judge cannot be appealed except to the appellate tribunal at the prosecution of the appeal.

4. ***Communicating the names of the witnesses to parties.*** "Before the witnesses are examined, their names are to be communicated to the parties; if in the prudent judgment of the judge, however, that cannot be done without grave difficulty, it is to be done at least before the publication of the testimonies."[102] The sources of this canon are canon 1763 of the 1917 code and article 126 of *Provida mater.* In the 1917 code, it was the duty of the parties to make known the names of the witnesses to each other (1917 *CIC* c. 1763). *Provida mater,* however, placed the responsibility on the court instead (article 126 §1). Nonetheless, in an earlier draft of the present canon 1554 (i.e., *schema canonum de iure processuali* c. 197), the parties were obliged to do so.[103] However, some consultors were not pleased that the parties had to make the names of the witnesses known to each other and proposed instead that such communication be done *ex officio* by the court. Another consultor responded that the issue should not be decided by the code, which should say only that the names of the witnesses must be communicated to the parties. The canon was then modified and assumed its present form.[104]

However, although the new code does not specify who is to make known the names of possible witnesses to the parties, in practice, most tribunals do so. The notification is done through the public postal services or through other very secure means established by particular law, and the fact of notification and its method must be evident in the acts (cf. c. 1509 §§1-2). The purpose for the communication of witnesses' names to the parties is to enable them to make exceptions that particular witnesses be excluded if they so desire. A party can request that a witness be excluded provided that a just cause for the exclusion is shown before the witness is questioned (c. 1555).

Connected to the above is the practice of some tribunals in not disclosing the identity of the witness to the parties. There is unquestionably a direct connection between the witnesss and the testimony of the witness. These two elements, namely, the identity of the witness and the testimony of the witness, constitute proof. These two elements must be provided so the parties have the occasion to exercise the right of defense assured by natural and positive ecclesiastical law. When exercising self-defense, the interested party should not have to speculate which witness may perhaps have provided a particular testimony. The specific author of a specific testimony should be provided to the party so that, if neces-

102 C. 1554. See also *DC,* article 199.

103 *Coetus de processibus,* November 21, 1978, *Communicationes* 11 (1979) 112.

104 *Communicationes* 11 (1979) 112.

sary, appropriate defense can be exercised in the trial. The practice of publishing the acts to the parties without disclosing the identity of the witness to the party promotes "a suspicious culture of secrecy. It does not promote a culture of transparency which is the basis for a judgement based in that moral certitude which results from a process which seeks to discover the spendor of truth, the *veritatis splendor*."[105] On the other hand: "Proofs are not to be admitted under secrecy, unless for a grave reason and as long as their communication with the advocates of the parties has been guaranteed, without prejudice to articles 230 and 234 (cf. c. 1598 §1)."[106]

5. ***The exclusion of witnesses.*** The parties can request, for a just cause, the exclusion of a witness introduced by the other party or by themselves. (c. 1555) The judge can also exclude a legally disqualified witness *ex officio*. (c. 1550). The burden in proving the defects of the witness, however, falls on the party who has requested the exclusion or on the judge if he or she is the one who has excluded a witness *ex officio*.

   The request to exclude a witness is usually done before his or her examination. Canon 1555 states that a party may request that a witness be excluded provided a just cause for the exclusion is established before the witness is examined. During the code revision process, what is now canon 1555 initially had two paragraphs. Paragraph one stated that except for legally disqualified witnesses, at the request of a party, the judge could exclude other witnesses if a just cause for the exclusion was demonstrated. And paragraph two stated that the discussion to exclude the witness, if perhaps it was to take place, was to occur before the conclusion of the case, unless particular law determined otherwise.[107]

   Two consultors proposed that the exclusion of the witness should be made before the examination of the witness only, and the other consultors agreed. Therefore, they agreed that paragraph one should be modified to read that a party may request that a witness be excluded provided a just cause for exclusion is established before the witness is examined. The relator proposed that the second paragraph should be deleted since the issue was evident. The proposition was accepted by the other consultors, with the exception of one.[108] Thus, according to canon 1555, the exclusion of witnesses is to be done for a just cause before their examination.

---

105 John A. Renken, "Personally Identifying Witness Statements," in *Roman Replies and CLSA Advisory Opinions 2014*, eds. Sharon A. Euart, John A. Alesandro, and Thomas J. Green (CLSA, Washington, D.C.) 87-88.

106 *DC*, article 157 §2.

107 *Coetus de processibus*, November 21, 1978, *Communicationes* 11 (1979) 112.

108 *Communicationes* 11 (1979) 112.

6. ***The citation of witnesses.*** "The citation of a witness occurs through a decree of the judge legitimately communicated to the witness."[109] The citation of witnesses is to be done through the public postal services or by some other very secure method according to particular law; and the fact of the notification and its method must be evident in the acts (c. 1509).

IX. The examination of witnesses

"Witnesses must be examined at the tribunal unless the judge deems otherwise." [110] The best practice for the objective collection of proofs from parties and witnesses is precisely the judicial deposition. This means the deposition of the person using questions based on the specific ground or grounds of nullity determined in the formulation of the doubt. The questions are prepared by the judge, with input from the parties and the defender of the bond, but previously unseen by the deponent, and then answered by the party or witness in the presence of a notary. This questioning can also be done by an auditor, at the direction of the judge, and in a place that is more convenient for the person being deposed.[111]

The practice of most tribunals is to interview witnesses by means of questionnaire sent to witnesses through the postal system. The witnesses are then asked to prepare their written responses and return them to the tribunal after they have sworn to the truth of the information contained in the documents. Several reasons have arisen for this practice. Some ecclesiastical tribunals do not have the power to subpoena witnesses to appear before it. Also, many tribunals do not have sufficient resources for the transcription of the oral deposition of witnesses. Furthermore, the transcription of interviews can take an unusually long time such that it causes an undue delay of the process. In addition, many witnesses due to health or financial reasons are unable to come physically to the tribunal or some other designated place for an oral interview. Moreover, some dioceses encompass a vast geographical territory such that it would cause a great inconvienence either to wait for a witness to find the time and means to travel to the tribunal or to expect the parties to bear the travel expenses to be incurred by the witness who is to travel to the tribunal or some other place designated by the Church.

Another method often used by some tribunals in the interrogation of witnesses is the telephone interview. During the code revision process, a consultor proposed that a norm should be added stating that for a grave cause a judicial deposition could be taken by telephone provided that the judge or notary guaranteed the authenticity of the deposition. However, this proposition did not please the other consultors. It was argued that such a norm could give rise to abuses and

---

109 C. 1556.

110 C. 1558 §1; *DC,* article 126 §1.

111 Raymond Burke, "The Nullity of Marriage Process as the Search for Truth," *Monitor Ecclesiasticus,* 129 (2014) 146.

in addition, there could be doubts about the identity or freedom of the witness, etc. Besides, it was also argued, the practice of receiving deposition by telephone is not reprobated in what was to become canon 1558.[112]

Grocholewski has argued that interrogation by letter or by telephone may not be used as an ordinary means of questioning the witnesses. For the intention of the legislator in canon 1558 is that the interrogation be carried out in the presence of the person doing the questioning. In an interrogation by letter, one cannot be sure about the observance of canon 1560 §1, according to which the individual witnesses are to be questioned separately. It can happen that the witnesses, in writing their depositions or testimonies, consult one another. "In the same way, one cannot be sure about the fulfillment of this requirement in an interrogation by phone, insofar as one witness might have already heard the testimony given by another witness present in the same room or speaking on another telephone extension."[113]

Grocholewski further argued that the prescript of canon 1561 regarding the presence of a notary and of the defender of the bond, the promoter of justice, and the advocates of the parties during the examination of the witnesses cannot be fulfilled through an interrogation by letter or telephone. "In such an interrogation there is also less certainty about the oath prescribed by canon 1562, §2 (together with c. 1534) and it is less possible to verify the identity of the party or the witness in keeping with canon 1563 (together with c. 1534)."[114]

Furthermore, according to Grocholewski, in an interrogation by letter it is impossible to observe the prescription of canon 1565 §1 that prohibits the communication of the questions to the witnesses ahead of time. Besides, in an interrogation by telephone the observance of the prescription of canon 1566 is doubtful, which requires that the witnesses are to give testimony orally and that they are not to read from written memoranda unless there is a question of calculations and accounts. Moreover, canons 1567-1569, which determine the duties of the notary, also presuppose a direct interrogation. Therefore, there can be no doubt that the interrogation of the witnesses by letter or telephone does not correspond to the kind of interrogation prescribed by canons 1556-1570 and 1678.[115]

---

112 *Coetus de processibus,* November 22, 1978: *Communicationes* 11 (1979) 114. Canon 1558 §§1-3 states that witnesses must be examined at the tribunal unless the judge deems otherwise. Cardinals, patriarchs, bishops, and those who possess a similar favor by civil law are to be heard in the place they select. The judge is to decide where to hear those for whom it is impossible or difficult to come to the tribunal because of distance, sickness, or some impediment, without prejudice to be prescripts of cc. 1418 and 1469, §2.

113 Zenon Grocholewski, "Interrogation by Letter or Telephone," in *CLSA Advisory Opinions 1984-1993*, ed. Patrick J. Cogan (Washington, DC: Canon Law Society of America, 1995) 461.

114 Ibid., 461-462.

115 Ibid., 462.

Noting that rotal jurisprudence does not support depositions by letter or by telephone, Grocholewski also noted that canonical legislation does not provide for interrogation by letter or by telephone even in the case of a party or witness who is far away or for another reason cannot come to the tribunal in which the case is being heard. "Thus, even in reference to these circumstances, canon 1558 §3 still speaks of an interrogation in a concrete place to be determined by the judge, that is, it still speaks of a direct interrogation."[116]

Moreover, continued Grocholewski, an interrogation by letter or telephone is not provided for by the legislator even when a witness refuses to appear before the judge to testify. In considering this kind of case, the code provides that it is permitted to hear the person through another person assigned by the judge or to seek the person's declaration before a notary, or in any other legitimate manner (c. 1528). The expression, "or in any other legitimate manner" must be interpreted in light of the two means clearly demonstrated in canon 1528, namely, that a person may be heard lawfully by a person appointed by the judge and that a witness can make a declaration before a notary public and in light of the canons on judicial examination of parties and witnesses (cc. 1530-1534; 1556-1570; 1678).

Grocholewski further stated that depositions and testimonies made in this fashion have an uncertain probative force because they amount to a complete surrender of the rights of the judge or auditor to direct and control the examination of witnesses according to the norm of law. Furthermore, depositions carried out in such manner easily lend themselves to fraud, falsification, corruption, or undue interference of the parties and their advocates in the examination of the witnesses. There is no guarantee of the identity of the person who answers the telephone or of the person who really composed the written responses. "One cannot exclude a fraudulent substitution of persons or the possibility that the written responses were dictated by another person. Yet the judge, in order to pronounce a sentence in favor of the petitioner, must have moral certainty (cf., c. 1608), namely that which 'is characterized ... by the exclusion of every well-founded or reasonable doubt.'"[117] However, according to Grocholewski, "interrogation by letter or telephone could be justified only by the most exceptional circumstances."[118]

It seems the practice of tribunals gathering evidence by written statements is not illegitimate *per se* as it can be done in exceptional cases. For example, according to Beal, the code foresees situations where witnesses will not or cannot come to the tribunal to be interviewed by the judge. For example, canon 1418 asserts the right of any tribunal to call upon the services of another tribunal to instruct a case or to communicate acts. Moreover, to limit the interpretation of the phrase "or in any other legitimate manner" in canon 1528 to only the two op-

116 Ibid., 463.
117 Ibid., 464.
118 Ibid.

tions mentioned in the canon, namely for the judge to designate a lay person to interrogate the person or to require the person swear an affidavit before a notary public is unduly restrictive.[119] In other words, the hearing of a party or witness before a designated lay person or the making of a declaration before a notary are not the only options available when a person refuses to appear before the judge.

According to Beal, there seems to be no compelling reason not to interpret canon 1528 to include situations where a party or a witness would, in the judgment of a tribunal, refuse or be reluctant to appear personally because of the expense or other hardship or where obstacles to the person's appearance before the tribunal would unduly delay the disposition of the case. "Thus, canon 1528 accepts the legitimacy of receiving testimony from parties and witnesses by their written and notarized statements at least when they refuse to appear before the judge."[120]

However, according to Beal, when written responses are completed at home and returned to the tribunal by mail, the tribunal is unable to verify that the responses were actually prepared by the persons who have signed them. Furthermore, the possibility of collusion between a party and a witness or cooperation among witnesses exists when depositions are prepared in private. Moreover, in written depositions or affidavits, there is no personal interaction between the judge and the affiant or deponent. As such, the judge is deprived of the opportunity to observe the demeanor of the person and to note indications of vacillation or uncertainty during his or her testimony. This can make it extraordinarily difficult for the judge to determine the probative value to be attributed to an affidavit or written deposition.[121]

Moreover, when a tribunal instructs cases solely by written depositions from witnesses, it may unwittingly prejudice the process against those with limited ability to express themselves in writing. When tribunals deal with those whose writing skills are weak, direct interviews may be the only way to assure that the parties receive a fair hearing of their case. Face-to-face examination of witnesses by the judge serves an important purpose of facilitating accurate decision-making on the part of the judge. Thus, those who do not have any opportunity in the course of the process to make their case directly and personally to the judge, the ultimate decision-maker, are apt to feel that their participation in the process was considerably less than meaningful.[122]

---

119 John Beal, "Making Connections: Procedural Law and Substantive Law," in *The Jurist* 54 (1994) 161-162. Canon 1528 states that if a party or a witness refuses to appear before the judge to testify, it is permissible to hear them through a lay person designated by the judge or to require of them a declaration either before a notary public or in any other legitimate manner.

120 Ibid., 162.

121 Ibid., 160.

122 Ibid., 160-161.

In conclusion, Beal stated that in determining whether and to what extent tribunals need to use written depositions or affidavits rather than oral testimony, tribunals need to search for a balance between efficient and economic instruction of cases and the demands of the truth. He suggested that tribunals may accept written affidavits or depositions at the beginning of the process and follow up later with personal interviews with those whose statements seem incomplete, confusing, or in need of further clarifications. "In searching for this delicate balance, tribunals have to find a way to get the evidence they need at a price they can afford."[123]

Tribunals that use a written questionnaire are to find a way of verifying that the responses were actually prepared by the persons who have signed them and there is no collusion between a party and a witness or cooperation among witnesses. Moreover, written questionnaires should not be structured in such a way that the witness answers "yes" or "no" questions only. This can make it extraordinarily difficult for the judge to determine the probative value to be attributed to such a written deposition. The questions should be asked in such a way as to give the witness ample opportunity for free self-expression.

In conclusion, the norm is for tribunals to conduct the examination of witnesses face-to-face. A face-to-face interview enables the identity and freedom of witnesses to be certainly established, to observe the body language of the party or witness, which tells as much about what is not being said as well as about what is being said, and to more easily weigh the probative value of what is being said. Moreover, the oral interview is better suited to those witnesses who prefer to express themselves orally. Even if a witness has good writing skills, a written deposition deprives the judge of the opportunity of immediately asking further questions to clarify and expand on certain points that witnesses may raise during the interview. The code stipulates that questions should be adapted to the intelligence of witnesses (c. 1564). Where written interrogatories are streamlined, witnesses answer questions as they understand them, or may even collude with the party or others to answer them.

However, a tribunal may resort to gathering testimony by telephone or by written deposition or affidavit in certain circumstances. For example, when witnesses cannot come to the tribunal without grave difficulties or inconveniences or when the oral deposition of witnesses and the subsequent transcription thereof will unduly delay the process. A court may also gather evidence by telephone or by written deposition as a follow-up to clarify or elaborate on what witnesses had said earlier. A written examination may also be necessary if the witness is unable to communicate orally and an interpreter familiar with sign language cannot be obtained.

123 Ibid., 163.

X. The evaluation of witness testimony

"In evaluating testimony, the judge, after having requested testimonial letters if necessary, is to consider the following: 1° what the condition or reputation of the person is; 2° whether the testimony derives from personal knowledge, especially from what has been seen or heard personally, or whether from opinion, rumor, or hearsay; 3° whether the witness is reliable and firmly consistent or inconsistent, uncertain, or vacillating; 4° whether the witness has co-witnesses to the testimony or is supported or not by other elements of proof."[124]

In addition to the aforementioned four general criteria, *Dignitas connubii* following in the footsteps of *Provida mater* adds a fifth criterion, namely, the time a witness acquired the knowledge. For example, according to *Dignitas connubii* article 201: "In evaluating the testimonies, the judge, having sought, if necessary, testimonial letters, is to consider:

> 1° what is the condition of the person and whether he is honest;
>
> 2° whether he is testifying from his own knowledge, especially from what he has seen and heard, or rather from his opinion, from a rumor, or from what he has heard from others;
>
> 3° when he came to know what he is asserting, especially whether it was *tempore non suspecto,* that is, when the parties had not yet considered introducing the cause;
>
> 4° whether the witness is consistent and firmly coherent with himself, or rather changeable, uncertain or wavering;
>
> 5° whether there are other witnesses to what is testified, or whether or not it is confirmed by other elements of proof (cf. can. 1572)."[125]

After the examination of witnesses and other legal provisions have been observed such as the publication of the acts and the conclusion of the case, the judge must weigh the probative value of the testimony obtained. The judge must assiduously look into the credibility of each witness and also inquire whether the witnesses have testified from their personal knowledge or from rumor or hearsay, or merely gave an opinion. Even when a witness gives an opinion, the judge is to examine whether it is supported by sufficient facts. The judge must also examine whether the testimony is internally consistent, whether it is in agreement with other testimony, and whether it is tainted by falsehood or subornation.

The Code of Canon Law and *Dignitas connubii* establishes five criteria for the evaluation of witness testimony. They are the moral criterion, namely, the condi-

124 C. 1572.
125 *DC,* article 201.

tion and integrity of the witness; the mental criterion, that is, the source of the witness's knowledge, and the temporal criterion, that is, the time in relation to the marriage that the knowledge was acquired. Others are the material criterion, namely, the internal consistency of the testimony, and the numerical criterion, that is, the singularity of the witness's testimony or its corroboration by other witnesses' testimony. These criteria have been established to assist the judge to form a conviction in his or her mind regarding the probative value to assign to each witness testimony.

1. ***The moral criterion for the evaluation of witness testimony: The condition and honesty of the witness.*** The first criterion given for evaluating testimonial proof is the condition of the witness. The term "condition" refers to the witness's age, life experiences, religious, educational, and cultural background, and relationship to the parties. It can also include whether the witness is a cleric, a religious, a lay person. These elements bear on the probative value of the testimony of the witness because they assist the court in determining the witness's freedom, intelligence, and knowledge regarding the controverted matter.

   The honesty of a witness is also relevant in evaluating witness testimony. Honesty refers properly to the witness's moral qualities, e.g., whether he or she is a perjurer or a credible person. The fundamental quality of a good witness is credibility. Greater weight is attributed to the testimony of a credible witness than to that of a person who has little or no credibility before the court. Thus, with a lucid and an independent mind, the judge should be able to access, according to his or her conscience, whether the witness is worthy of trust and whether the witness has spoken the truth.

2. ***The mental criterion for the evaluation of witness testimony: The source of the information.*** The mental criterion for evaluating witness testimony pertains to how the witness came about the information that has been made to the tribunal. Is it first-hand information, an opinion, a rumor, or hearsay? First-hand witnesses are those who testify about a thing which they perceived with their own senses, that is, they saw or heard the thing with their own eyes or ears. The witness statements are given full probatory value when they are supported by detailed facts that the witness has seen or heard personally. Therefore, it is necessary that the deponent should faithfully narrate the facts that he or she knows and anything that the witness preserved in his or her memory.

   The opinions of witnesses are not testimony properly speaking. Witnesses who state their opinion regarding an event do not as such beget full proof of the fact. Rather, their opinion can be regarded as an indication of, and an aid to proof. And this indication or aid is strong or weak depending on whether the witness gives reasons for his or her opinion.

It is often difficult to obtain first-hand witnesses in some marriage nullity cases. Opinions in themselves do not provide full proof unless they are supported by other circumstances or arguments. Thus, when witnesses offer opinions based on their observations of a marriage and give reasons or facts to support their opinions, such testimony can be given probative value.

The judge also needs to evaluate whether the information proffered to the tribunal is based on rumor. A rumor is the common opinion of people or of a majority of the people of a community about a person or a fact. A rumor can proceed from certain and reliable persons who tell others that they were present when an event occurred or it can originate from an unknown source or author. Testimony founded on rumor does not provide full proof. It enjoys a presumption which must be corroborated by other adminicular proofs, or weighed in light of other elements of proofs for it to cause moral certainty in the mind of the judge. For a rumor to have probative value, it must have the following qualities: First, it must be uniform, strong, constant, and enduring, that is, it must not be vague, unimportant, or contradictory. Second, it must have originated from honest and credible persons. And third, there must also be a probable cause for the rumor that made people to believe it. Thus, if the rumor did not originate from reliable sources, but merely from gossip, or there was no probable cause for it, the rumor must be regarded as false, and thus without value.

Information offered to the tribunal may also be based on hearsay, and the judge needs to evaluate whether this is so. Hearsay witnesses are those who testify to what they have heard from others, and not from personal experience.There are two kinds of hearsay witnesses: direct and indirect. Direct hearsay witnesses are those who heard of the event from those who experienced it and indirect hearsay witnesses are those who heard of the event only from those who in turn merely heard of it. The differences among opinion witnesses, hearsay witnesses, and rumor witnesses are that an opinion witness gives his or her personal opinion, a hearsay witness relates what he or she has learned from another person's report, and a rumor witness reports an opinion that a town, community, city, or people have concerning a certain person or fact.

Witnesses also sometimes receive their information from one common source. Thus, in evaluating testimony, especially those based on hearsay or rumor, the judge should be particularly careful of weighing statements that have one common source. The judge should not be led astray by the repetition of the same statements from many witnesses. The cumulative effect of mere numbers can often be very misleading. Hearsay testimony, however, can be credible insofar as it is strengthened by other circumstances, conjectures, or presumptions, or other proofs, provided the source of their knowledge merits credence and they learned of such matters at a non-suspect time.[126] Did the witness give details of time, place, names, motives, etc? The judge must weigh other proofs such as the parties' dispositions, other witnesses' testimony, and the circumstances before, during, and after the marriage to be convinced. However, if other sources of proof can prove the alleged fact, heresay testimony may not be used.

3. ***The temporal criterion for the evaluation of witness testimony: The time the information was obtained.*** The judge must also take note of the time when the witness acquired his or her knowledge. "When a witness introduces into the trial a statement he or she claims a party made, the judge must verify whether the statement was made to the witness during a non-suspect time."[127] A non suspect time is when there was no thought of raising the question of the nullity of a marriage, and there were no other reasons for concealing the truth or telling a falsehood.[128] A suspect time runs from when a party begins to raise the question of the invalidity of the marriage or for an unspecified reason has an interest in concealing or distorting the truth. If a witness learned of a fact from a party or another person in *tempore non suspecto,* then the credibility of the witness is beyond doubt.

   Probative value is not assigned to information that was obtained *tempore suspecto.* The reason for this is that when a party is intent on impugning the validity of his or her marriage, the person is naturally less objective in his or her statements. The person makes statements designed to achieve the desired objective, namely, the nullity of the marriage. For example, if a witness testified that the party had firmly stated several times before the marriage began that divorce or adultery was an option, their testimony would be considered credible. However, if the witnesses testified that the party told them that he or she considered divorce as an option or was unfaithful before and during the marriage only after the party began preparing to file a petition for a declaration of nullity of the marriage, then the value of such testimonies will be regarded as suspect. Thus, the time the witness obtained his or her knowledge has an influence on the truthfulness, veracity, and reliability of the information.

4. ***The material criterion for the evaluation of witness testimony: The consisteny or inconsistency in the testimony.*** Another criterion for determining the probative value of a witness's testimony is its internal consistency or inconsistency; uncertainty, or vacillation. If

126 C. Pinto, June 17, 1974, *RRDec* 66 (1974) 447.

127 Lüdicke and Jenkins, 341.

128 Sacred Congregation of the Sacraments, May 7, 1923, *Decree and Rules of Procedure for Cases on Non-consummation of Marriage, AAS* 15 (1923) 406.

the testimony of a witness is internally consistent, it is to be accorded greater weight than if it is inconsistent or internally contradictory. A testimony may sometimes contain incidental discrepancies. When there are contradictions in the testimony of a witness, the judge must establish that the contradictions bear on the substance of the case, and not merely on accidental discrepancies. If the witness is consistent in the fundamental facts, his or her statement should be accorded full probative value.

A witness may also vacillate or be doubtful. A vacillating witness is one who is fearful or wavering in his or her testimony while a doubtful witness is one who is not sure of what he or she has said. A doubtful witness does not merit any credibility because he or she is not sure of the truth. A witness who simply vacillates merits some credibility but not full proof.

5. ***The numerical criterion for the evaluation of witness testimony: Corroborative and singular testimony.*** The testimony of each witness must be assessed in light of the other testimonies before the court, whether it conforms to or corroborates other witnesses' testimony, or is unsupported. Canon 1790 of the 1917 code (*schema canonum de iure processuali* c. 220), which stated that if witnesses disagreed among themselves the judge was to consider whether their testimonies were mutually contradictory, merely different, or supplementary was suppressed because it was considered superfluous.[129]

Corroborative witnesses are two or more witnesses above reproach who testify from personal knowledge and unanimously to the same fact. Corroborative witnesses provide full proof. The scripture says that a judicial fact can be established on the testimony of two or three.[130] Full proof is not obtained by accumulating many witnesses, but from witnesses who know the facts first hand and give testimony that is in agreement with each other, without major discrepancies.

Corroborative witnesses also provide full proof even when they disagree about an incidental matter. For example, minor discrepancies among witnesses on the duration of the dating period, date of the marriage, time of separation, etc., are oftentimes unimportant details which do not discredit the value of their testimony. In fact, such discrepancies are rather a sign that there was no collusion among the witnesses. Moreover, such discrepancies can be explained in that some witnesses recall some facts more easily than others after a lapse of time. Nonetheless, it is for the judge to seek to resolve the apparently discrepant testimonies,

129 *Communicationes* 11 (1979) 120.

130 Deut. 19:15b; Mt. 18:6.

or to decide, from the condition, character, and certainty of the witnesses, which testimonies must be believed.

Moreover, in evaluating the testimonies, the judge must examine whether there is subornation or collusion involving a party and the witnesses. Subornation occurs when a party in a case tells a witness to testify in the party's favor against the truth, in exchange for gifts or some promises. Collusion is something similar, but it does not involve bribery. Collusion occurs when a witness favors one party over another in opposition to the truth. Collusion is usually evident in terms of very striking similarities in the words used in the testimony. Thus, if several witnesses use the same words, phrases, etc, the judge may have reason to suspect collusion with or the coaching of the witnesses. The testimony of witnesses who have colluded with one another or with the party has no probative value.

On the other hand, singular witnesses are two or more witnesses who give testimony about different facts in such a way that each gives his or her individual testimony and none agrees. Singular witnesses are adversative, diversative, or cumulative. Singular witnesses are adversative when the testimony of one is entirely contrary to that of another so that the testimony of both cannot be true at the same time. For example, one testifies that John was baptized and another that John was never baptized. In singular adversative testimonies, only one witness is correct; the other is incorrect. Neither one constitutes proof until the truth becomes evident by means of other elements of proofs. When two depositions are contradictory so that it is impossible to know where the truth lies, their probative value is null. The judge must critically examine the adversative testimonies and decide in favor of the witness who makes sense and whose statements are confirmed by other proofs in the case.

On the other hand, singular witnesses are diversative when they testify about different facts on the case which are neither contradictory nor connected with each other. The facts stated in singular diversative testimonies are not related to each other, and each is accorded the probative weight given to singular testimonies.

On the other hand, singular witnesses are cumulative when they testify about events, which though different in minor details nevertheless agree on the same fact. For example, one witness states that the respondent said before the marriage was contracted that he had no intention of being faithful; another states that the respondent continued to maintain an extra-marital relationship during the marriage. In cumulative singular testimony, the testimony may differ on some inconsequential details regarding the same fact or or they may be different facts but they contain some common elements or some pattern that not only mutually support and complement each other but also cumulatively establish the fact.

In conclusion, the testimonial acts in marriage cases often contain a combination of corroborative and singular adversative, diversative, and cumulative testimony. Some parts of a testimony may contain events related by other witnesses in substantially the same way or somewhat differently. Some testimony may refer to events apparently unknown by other witnesses or related differently; and sometimes their observations about the same event are quite contradictory.

Thus, the rule of thumb for evaluating such testimony is as follows: corrobortive testimonies that are beyond reproach are probative, singular cumulative testimonies are also probative, singular diversative testimonies are unhelpful, and singular adversative testimony are accorded little or no probative weight until the other circumstances of the case establish the fact-in-question.

In evaluating witness testimony, the judge must also weigh "other elements of proof" to determine whether or not they support the testimony (c. 1572, 4°). The use of the phrase "other elements of proof" indicates that the judge carefully to consider the circumstances antecedent, concomitant, and subsequent to the marriage,

XI. The testimony of only one witness and character witnesses

"The testimony of one witness cannot produce full proof unless it concerns a qualified witness making a deposition concerning matters done *ex officio,* or unless the circumstances of things and persons suggest otherwise."[131] As a general rule, the deposition of a single witness does not constitute full proof. This is so because at least two witnesses who are credible and whose testimonies substantially agree with each other on the facts of the case are required to beget full proof. But the testimony of a sole witness can constitute full proof in certain cases. For example, if the judge can establish that no other witnesses are available and the testimony of the sole witness is supported by other elements of proof such as documents and by good arguments, such a testimony can lead to the moral conviction which the judge needs to pronounce a sentence.

Indeed, there are instances when only one witness testimony can be admitted. For example, some persons for various reasons migrate far from the place in which they contracted marriage and have lost contact with the family members or friends who might serve as witnesses. Also, some witnesses may not be Catholics and refuse to cooperate with an ecclesiastical court; or some witnesses may

131 C. 1573. See also *DC,* article 202.

be bitterly alienated from a party in the case as a result of feuds or other severe misunderstandings. Furthermore, some marriages occurred such a long time ago that those who could have known about the marriage are either dead or in such ill-health that no testimony can be obtained from them It is not possible to list all the circumstances in which only one witness is available; nonetheless, in cases in which more than one witness cannot be found by any means or only with difficulty, the deposition of a single witness is sufficient proof. The judge, however, must consider and state in the sentence the reasons why other witnesses have not been presented. The evaluation of only a single witness must be done in light of other proofs and indices, especially when the testimony of a single witness is exceptionally insightful, internally consistent, based on personal knowledge, and supported by the circumstances of the case. The the practice of admitting only one witness remains the exception.

There are instances when only one witness has been introduced and admitted. For example, some persons for various reasons migrate far from the place in which they contracted marriage and have lost contact with the family members or friends who might serve as witnesses. Also, some witnesses who have been introduced may change their minds or may be hostile to the judicial ecclesiastical proceedings and refuse to cooperate with the Tribunal. Furthermore, some potential witnesses may be bitterly alienated from the other party as a result of feuds or other severe misunderstandings and as such decline to provide testimony. At other times, the events needing corroboration are so remote in time that the whereabouts of witnesses are unknown, or the witness is suffering from some ailment that make them unable to perceive facts rightly or communicate intelligently with others, or the witness may in fact be deceased. At other times, several witnesses may have been cited but only one responded or only one could provide corroborative proof. It is not possible to list all the circumstances in which only one witness is available. In any case, the judge must consider the reasons why such is the case.

Under the regime of the Pio-Benedictine code, there was only one condition when the testimony of a single witness could constitute full proof, namely, that that person was a qualified witness who testified to things done in an official capacity (1917 *CIC* c. 1791). The 1983 code, however, provides for two exceptions to that rule, namely, that the person be a qualified witness testifying to things done in an official capacity and that the circumstances of things and persons indicate otherwise (c. 1573). Thus, the phrase "unless circumstances of things and persons suggest otherwise" reflects a change from the 1917 code. This important modification, which also reflects doctrine and jurisprudence, can be considered a characteristic of the spirit of the new code which gives the judge more discretion in the evaluation of proofs. Several factors help to explain this development.

One, following the promulgation of the 1917 code, there were debates regarding whether the rule that the testimony of a single witness did not constitute full proof, except that of a qualified witness, was absolute in all cases. For example, Lega and Bartoccetti argued that although canon 1791 stated that the testimony of only one witness did not provide full proof and that this was generally true. Nonetheless, they argued that the law did not, in some cases, preclude the testimony of a single witness from providing the proof that begets moral certitude in the mind of the judge, if it were supported by circumstances of things and persons.[132]

Another factor that contributed to the expansion of the exception in canon 1791 §1 is that Pius XII in his 1942 allocution to the Roman Rota had noted that moral certitude can be derived from an aggregate of indications and proofs which, when taken together and embraced in light of the entire case, could provide the necessary elements for arriving at a safe and sound definitive judgment. According to the Pontiff, sometimes moral certainty is derived only from an aggregate of indications and proofs which, taken singly, do not provide the foundation for true certitude, but which, when taken together, no longer leaves room for any reasonable doubt on the part of a person of sound judgment. The simultaneous presence of all these separate indications and proofs can have sufficient basis only in the existence of a common origin or foundation from which they spring, that is, in objective truth and reality.[133]

In such a case, therefore, certainty arises from the wise application of a principle which is absolutely secure and universally valid, namely the principle of a sufficient reason. Consequently, if in giving the reasons for his or her decision, the judge states that the proofs which have been adduced, considered separately, cannot be judged sufficient, "but that, taken together and embraced in a survey of the whole situation, they provide the necessary elements for arriving at a safe definitive judgment, it must be acknowledged that such reasoning is in general sound and legitimate."[134]

Furthermore, several Rotal decisions had held that moral certainty could be obtained from the testimony of a sole witness when it was considered alongside other pertinent elements.[135] In particular, one notes *coram* Felici of July 17, 1952 (*RRDec* 44 [1952] 450), wherein it was stated that although there was only one first-hand witness, nevertheless:

---

132 Michaële Lega and Victorio Bartoccetti *Commentarius in Iudicia Ecclesiastica,* vol. 2 (Rome: Libreria Cattolica, 1950) 724.

133 Pius XII, Allocution of October 1st, 1942, *AAS* 34 (1942) 340.

134 Pius XII, Allocution of October 1st, 1942, *AAS* 34 (1942) 340.

135 For example, *Coram* Mattioli, November 7, 1951, *RRDec* 43 (1951) 688; *Coram* Wynen, January 31, 1952, *RRDec* 44 (1952) 45; July 18, 1956, *RRDec* 48 (1956) 684; *Coram* Felici, July 17, 1952, *RRDec* 44 (1952) 445; April 2, 1957, *RRDec* 49 (1957) 785; *Coram* Lefebvre, January 28, 1961, *RRDec* 53 (1961) 27; *Coram.* Bejan, April 27, 1966, *RRDec* 58 (1966) 246; *Coram* Rodgers, November 14, 1967, *RRDec* 59 (1967) 785.

i) This witness was of the highest credibility.

ii) The plaintiff had a very good character and was regarded as exemplary because of her desire for Christian perfection, her constant care for her family, and the excellent education of her children.

iii) The respondent did not dare openly to refute the allegation of coercion made by the plaintiff even though it was much to his advantage to have done so.

iv) Many circumstances following the marriage supported the plaintiff's case. As such there was moral certainty that the coercion alleged by the plaintiff, grave and unjust and which nullified the marriage, was in truth actually present.

Furthermore, Felici, who later became the President of the Commission for the Revision of the Code, also noted in his February 21, 1977, address to the Apostolic Chancery that with regard to testimonial proof, "we know that *unus testis, nullus testis,* at least if the deponent is not a qualified witness and testifies *ex officio.* The presumption of canon 1791 §1 [*CIC*/17], can and has been overcome in practice through the occurrence of other proofs, which in themselves are perhaps insufficient, but which have reinforced and given probative value to the deposition of *unus testis* beyond reproach."[136]

Thus, with these developments in doctrine and jurisprudence, the 1983 code indicates that the testimony of a non-qualified single witness can be admitted provided other circumstances of things and persons support the testimony.

What are these "circumstances of things and persons"? They are indications and proofs which, though insufficient in themselves to support a judgment, can together reinforce and give probative value to the deposition of one witness beyond doubt.[137] Thus, the aggregate of other proofs such as the judicial confession of the parties, documents, expert report, presumptions, and indices, when combined with the testimony of a sole witness can provide sufficient basis for the judge to come to moral certitude.

"Unless full proofs are present from other sources, in evaluating the deposition of the parties in accord with canon 1536, the judge is to use witnesses regarding the credibility of the parties, if possible, as well as other indications and aids."[138] Character witnesses testify to the trustworthiness of a party in a case. They help the court in excluding any possible fraud by the parties by establishing the moral and religious character of the parties. Character witnesses are required

---

136 Pericle Felici, "Judicial Formalities and Evaluation of Evidence in the Canonical Process," *The Jurist* 38 [1978] 156.
137 Ibid., 156-157.
138 C. 1679.

in formal contentious cases when, for example, only one witness testimony could be secured by the tribunal and there seems to be moral certainty in the mind of the judge regarding the invalidity of the marriage.

XII. Moral certitude in the evaluation of witness testimony.

The purpose of gathering proofs, especially witness testimony, is to enable the judge reach moral certainty in the determination of the case. Moral certitude is the sound definitive judgment in a certain matter that excludes all reasonable doubt to the contrary. It is the determination of the mind to a given judgment as opposed to another. The removal of all positive valid arguments in favor of the contradictory judgment is an essential factor of moral certainty. When this occurs, the mind is compelled to give full assent to the judgment made, which is the only reasonable one left.[139] "Such objectively founded moral certainty does not exist if there are motives in favor of the reality of the contrary judgment, which a sound, serious, and competent judgment pronounces to be at least in some way worthy of attention, and which consequently make it necessary to admit the contrary as not only absolutely possible, but also in a certain sense probable."[140]

Therefore, moral certainty excludes all reasonable doubt; the arguments adduced to the contrary retain no probability. There is probability or quasi-certitude, which does not exclude all reasonable doubt and admits of a fundamental fear of error. On the other hand, there is an absolute certitude in which all possible doubt about the truth of the matter and the insufficiency of proof to the contrary is totally excluded. Moral certitude lies between the two extremes of quasi-certainty or probability and absolute certainty. It is characterized on the positive side by the exclusion of well-founded or reasonable doubt, and in this respect it is essentially distinguished from the quasi-certainty which has been mentioned. "On the negative side, it does admit the absolute possibility of the contrary; and in this it differs from absolute certainty. Moral certainty is necessary and sufficient for the rendering of a judgment."[141]

Furthermore, moral certitude depends on the conclusiveness of the arguments upon which it is based. The judge can claim to have no doubts to the contrary only if he or she has truly evaluated the conclusive character of the arguments that have led him to reach moral certitude. The formation of moral certitude is an act by which the judge takes cognizance of certain, largely objective factors. It is not a means by which the judge reaches a decision regarding his or her own intentions in the matter. "Moral certitude is not grounded in what the judge might want to result from the process, but in what he or she is compelled to conclude re-

139 Arthur Caron, "The Concept of Moral Certitude in Canonical Decisions," *The Jurist* 19 (1959) 14-15.

140 Pius XII, Allocution of October 1, 1942, *AAS* 34 (1942) 340.

141 Pius XII, Allocution of October 1, 1942, *AAS* 34 (1942) 339-340.

garding the case based on a careful and thorough consideration of the law and the facts."[142] Thus, moral certitude is neither a matter of absolute certainty, in which every possible doubt about the truth of the facts to be judged is totally excluded nor is it a purely subjective certainty based on personal opinion or sentiment.[143]

Moreover, moral certitude is different from "a preponderance of the proofs" or a "preponderance of the evidence." A "preponderance of evidence," which is the standard of proof in civil law cases, is evidence which is of greater weight or more convincing than the evidence which is offered in opposition to it, that is, evidence which as a whole shows that the fact sought to be proven is more probable than not. "It is that degree of proof which is more probable than not."[144] In canonical marriage nullity cases, what is required is not a preponderance of evidence, since the legal presumption is in favor of the validity of the marriage (c. 1060) but moral certainty that the nullity of the marriage in question has been proven. A judge who is unable to reach moral certainty of nullity does not state that the validity of the marriage has been proven but that its nullity has not been proven. "In order to have the moral certainty necessary by law, a preponderance of the proofs and indications is not sufficient, but it is required that any prudent positive doubt of making an error, in law or in fact, is excluded, even if the mere possibility of the contrary remains. The judge must derive this certainty from those things which have been carried out and proven in the process (*ex actis et probatis*) (can. 1608, §2)."[145]

The judge derives this moral certitude *ex actis et probatis* (c. 1608 §2). It is derived *ex actis* because *quod non est in actis, non est in mundo*. The judge also draws this certainty *ex probatis* because the proofs *in casu* cannot give credence to what the witnesses have said without critically evaluating the alleged facts and comparing each proof with the others. The *acta et probatis* are those things which are done or carried out during the course of the process and proven by the evidence advanced in the process. The *acta* refer also to the assertions and denials, the petitions, and the objections advanced within the trial. The *probata* are not merely the pieces of evidence advanced but that which is proven by that evidenced. "Naturally, the judge's certitude must take into account everything

142 Lüdicke and Jenkins, 396.

143 Antoni Stankiewicz, "Moral Certainty and the Search for the Objective Truth," *L'Osservatore Romano,* English edition (March 9, 2005) 7.

144 *Black's Law Dictionary,* s.v. "Preponderance of evidence." In canonical marriage nullity cases, what is required is not a preponderance of evidence, since marriage enjoys the favor of the law (c. 1060) but moral certainty that the nullity of the marriage in question has been proven. A judge who is unable to reach moral certainty of nullity does not state that the validity of the marriage has been proven but that its nullity has not been proven.

145 *DC,* article 247 §2.

that has been carried out and proven in the process; the judge is not at liberty to ignore certain elements that do not agree with his conclusion."[146]

Furthermore, the judge also arrives at a moral certainty "after a diligent study of the cause" (*DC* article 247 §5). The judge in evaluating the testimonies of witnesses must also derive moral certainty from his or her conscience – *ex sua conscientia* – (*c* 1608 §3). This expression must not be distorted to mean that the judge evaluates the proofs according to his or her personal knowledge or opinion. Rather, it must be objective and demonstrable. Conscience here does not refer to the moral conscience, which prescribes and prohibits certain actions, but to the cognitive faculty applied to the examination of judicial *acta et probata*. Therefore, when evaluating the evidence, the judge is not precisely employing his or her capacity to develop a moral conviction but is using his or her intellectual capacity to evaluate the judicial proofs.[147]

Not infrequently, the judge cannot attain moral certainty regarding the alleged invalidity of a marriage. In such a case, the judge is obliged to pronounce that the nullity of the marriage has not been proven and accordingly, in effect, declare in favor of the validity of the marriage since marriage enjoys the favor of law (c. 1060).

The judge who has attained moral certainty or who could not attain moral certainty in a case is bound to provide reasons and arguments for this decision. After evaluating the testimony of witnesses and the other proofs, when the judge has arrived at a decision, he or she is obliged to set forth the motives and reasons in law and in fact in a judicial sentence (c. 1611, 3°). A sentence which does not contain the motives or reasons for the decision is remediably null (c. 1622, 2°).

A summation all that was said by witnesses is insufficient. The judge must evaluate the objectivity and strength of the testimonies relative to the allegations of the invalidity of the marriage. The judge articulates the reasons and arguments regarding the probative value assigned to the facts and proofs that led to his or her decision. If a sole judge conducted the marriage nullity trial, then he alone writes the sentence. However, in a collegial court, as a rule, it is the task of the *ponens* (c. 1429; *DC* article 47 §1) to draft the sentence based on the arguments that the judges presented in their written opinions and discussion. The objections of a dissenting judge, if there is one, can also be accounted for in the sentence to demonstrate the breadth of the court's consideration of the matter. However, the sentence should give no indication regarding the vote itself, whether or not it was unanimous or, if it was not unanimous, how the judges voted.[148]

146 William L. Daniel, "The Notion of Moral Certitude in Canonical Tradition and in the Dynamism of the Judicial Process," in *Studies in Church Law* 6 (2010) 244.
147 Ibid., 245.
148 Lüdicke and Jenkins, 404.

It is the duty of the judge who drafts the decision to give it a convincing legal and factual basis in light of the conclusions drawn by the judges. And the sentence, along with the motivation underlying it, must be approved by the individual judges. This does not mean that all the judges are responsible for the way the sentence is written and its motivation. On the contrary, its approval by the individual judges means that the sentence, along with its motivating reasons, is a collegial decision. "Of course, the disposition of the sentence, and, indeed, the motivation for the sentence itself, is also an expression of the collegial court, even if the motivation was not reached by a collegial act."[149]

Furthermore, the sentence must be neither excessively brief nor excessively lengthy. The presentation of the facts ought to be done prudently and cautiously to avoid any offense to the parties, the witnesses, the judges and the other ministers of the tribunals.[150] In summation, the judge must not merely be convinced of his or decision in the sentence; he or she must also carefully and systematically outline the arguments underlying the decision and the way in which it was arrived at.

XIII. General Conclusion.

Proofs by witnesses in marriage nullity trials constitute the principal means of proving marriage nullity cases. The vindication of rights is one of the objects of a trial in a church court (c. 1400, §1, 1°). In marriage nullity cases the Church is not simply dealing with the determination of a person's state in the Church, namely whether the person is still bond by a previous marriage or is free to enter into a new marriage. The Church is also concerned with with safeguarding and promoting the sanctity of matrimony which is a source of divine grace and a means of sanctification for the spouses and for the Church. The norms regarding witness testimony are meant to discover the truth, administer justice, safeguard the rights of the parties, and promote the sanctity of marriage which has been raised by Christ to the dignity of a sacrament. These norms are meant to help the judge better carry out his or her function.

Proof by witnesses has been always held in high esteem in the judicial process. It remains one of the important proofs by which the judge reaches moral certainty in a marriage nullity case. Indeed, it is a necessary means for the judge to have a deeper understanding of the background and dating experiences of the parties, the wedding, the marriage itself, and the reasons for its breakdown. Therefore, the judge must not only be morally certain that the depositions of the parties are verified or established by means of the proofs, especially by witness testimony, but also convincingly state the reasons on which the decision is based. When the validity of the bond of marriage is challenged before a competent tri-

149 Ibid., 405.
150 Cf. *DC,* article 254 §1.

bunal, the Church cautiously examines the petition to ensure that the decision to be reached is a just one based on the law and the facts. Witness testimony is an indispensable means of proof for the administration of justice and the establishment of the truth in marriage nullity processes.

Seminar

Laypeople as "Protagonists in the Church": Pathways for the Future

Anne Asselin, JCD

Introduction

In March of this year, Pope Francis told the participants at a conference on the mission of the laity, held at the Pontifical Lateran University in Rome, that the lay faithful, in virtue of their baptism, "are protagonists in the work of evangelization and human promotion."[1] If we are members of the People of God, he said, we are "inseparably a disciple and a missionary." This is the premise from which we must all begin, a common foundation for all of us who belong to the Mother Church. But what does this mean exactly, for the laity?

Merriam-Webster defines "protagonist" as: 1) the principal character in a literary work (as a drama or story) or the leading actor, character, or participant in a literary work or real event; 2) the leader, a proponent or a supporter of a cause, an advocate; the champion of a cause.

Francis had used the expression several times before this, not surprisingly since one of the important trademarks in the South American pastoral field is the protagonistic role of the laity in the Church. It gives life to basic ecclesial communities, reaffirms the centrality of the Word of God, the usefulness of home missions, Sunday celebrations presided by laypeople, and a commitment to the poor. The Provincial Superior of the Augustinian Recollects of Brazil, Province of Saint Rita of Cascia, explains how the laity has been invited and encouraged in their mission: "Those who visit our parishes will be surprised by the presence of the laity, their availability and joy to serve the Church, and the love with which they treat us, fruit of the care and dedication that we give them in our parishes."[2]

---

1 Francis, message to the participants of a conference held at the Pontifical Lateran University, "The Mission of Lay Christians in the City," 7-8 March 2014, http://w2.vatican.va/content/ francesco/en/messages/pont-messages/2014/documents/papa-francesco_20140307_messaggio-convegno-laici.html (accessed July 9, 2014).

2 N. Pérez-Aradros, "The Laity Are the Protagonists of the Church in Our Parishes," interview of 12 February 2012, in *Order of Augustinian Recollects News*, February 2012, http://www.agustinosrecoletos.com/news/view/4-noticias-actualidad/3299-nicolas-perez-aradros-los-laicos-son-los-protagonistas-de-la-iglesia-en-nuestras-parroquias?lang=en_US (accessed July 16, 2014).

At their May 2006 meeting, the Latin American Episcopal Conference, CELAM (Consejo Episcopal Latinoamericano), endorsed three key concepts of the Church in Latin America: the option for the poor, small Christian communities (CEBs or *Communidades Eclesiales de Base*), and the opposition to economic development that worsens the fate of the poor.[3] And the laity is a central force in all these initiatives.

With this in mind, it is understandable that Francis calls so frequently on the laity to join priests, deacons and religious in the new evangelization project, to be "protagonists": 1) when he addressed the members of Pontifical Council for Health Pastoral Care on Saturday, in November 2013, and referred to the elderly who had always been "protagonists" or "leaders in the Church";[4] 2) at the beginning of Lent, this year, he reminded members of the Italian Federation of Spiritual Exercises that the "protagonist of spiritual life is always the Holy Spirit";[5] 3) in his 2014 message to the International Labour Organization, he encouraged participants to look for new avenues to foster solidarity among people, new avenues focused on the development of the human person as the *protagonista* or central actor;[6] 5) he used the Italian word *protagonista* again, when he said that we should not distinguish among those who help and those who are helped. This way, it becomes an encounter, not a source of tension and, therefore, who is the *protagonista*, the leader?[7] And finally, 6) in *Evangelii gaudium*, article 122, when he says that "each people is the creator of their own culture and the protagonist of their own history...," and, further on in the same article, that the Holy Spirit is the principal agent (*protagonista*) of the missionary activity of the People of God.[8]

3 R.S. Pelton, "A Church in Flux," in *Notre Dame Magazine*, Winter 2007-2008, http://magazine.nd.edu/news/1345-a-church-in-flux/ (accessed July 15, 2014).

4 Francis, address to the participants of the 28th international conference sponsored by the Pontifical Council for Health Care Workers, 23 November 2013, http://w2.vatican.va/content/ francesco/en/speeches/2013/november/documents/papa-francesco_20131123_conferenza-operatori-sanitari.html (accessed July 9, 2014).

5 Idem, address to the participants in the Assembly of the Italian Federation of Spiritual Exercises (IFSE), 3 March 2014, http://w2.vatican.va/content/francesco/en/speeches/2014/march/ documents/papa-francesco_20140303_federaz-esercizi-spirituali.html (accessed July 9, 2014).

6 Idem, message on the occasion of the 103rd session of the conference of the International Labour Organization, 28 May - 12 June 2014, http://w2.vatican.va/content/francesco/en/messages/ pont-messages/2014/documents/papa-francesco_20140522_messaggio-ilo.htm (accessed July 9, 2014).

7 Idem, address to the Sant'Egidio community, 15 June 2014, http://w2.vatican.va/content/francesco/en/speeches/2014/june/documents/papa-francesco_20140615_comunita-sant-egidio.html (accessed July 9, 2014).

8 Idem, apostolic exhortation on the proclamation of the Gospel in today's world *Evangelii gaudium*, 24 November 2013, art. 122, in *AAS*, 105 (2013), p. 1071, English version in Vatican Press, art. 122, p. 99.

So, lay people are to be protagonists, leaders, but in what way and of what? In his book *The Future Church*, John Allen says that "party lines, and ways of doing business that have dominated Catholicism in the forty-plus years since the close of the Second Vatican Council in 1965 … are being turned on their head by a series of new forces reshaping the global Church … Catholics in the twenty-first century won't just need hustle … above all, they'll need imagination. They'll need the capacity to reconsider how they think about Church and what they do with their faith because otherwise Catholicism won't rise to the occasion of these new challenges – it'll be steamrolled by them."[9]

There is therefore a pressing call for the laity to organize its protagonistic role in the social, political and economic realms of society. We need to discover and invent the means of permeating these realities, and it must become a normal element of the life of the Church. It is fine to say that lay believers are on the front line of the Church, but how can they concretely do this? Evidently, firstly by the example of their own Christian life; but for this, they need to have a firmer knowledge of this right and duty, individually or grouped in associations or movements, in places where the Church "cannot become salt of the earth unless by means of [the laity]."[10] In his latest book, Cardinal Rino Fisichella, President of the Pontifical Council for Promoting the New Evangelization, foresees that any action undertaken by the laity in the mission of new evangelization "will be all the more effective the more they are able to bring with them the community to which they belong, which encourages them in their mission, sustains them in their difficulties and remains as their place of reference …"[11]

So, as we consider our response to Francis' call to the laity to take on a front role in the evangelization mission and the need for us – canonists as well – to rise to these new challenges facing the Church, I propose that we briefly look back at the treatment of the laity's mission in a few select Church documents. Then, we will turn to the situation of lay ministry in the Church today and end by seeking pathways for the future.

I – The Mission of the Laity in Selected Church Documents

1.1 – The Second Vatican Council

There is definitely no need to return at length to conciliar documents that we all know very well. But in order to lay the foundation for our reflection today, let us very briefly recall a few key teachings in relation to the laity in the Church.

---

9 J.L. Allen, *The Future Church: How Ten Trends Are Revolutionizing the Catholic Church*, Kindle edition, (New York/London/Toronto/Sydney/Auckland, Doubleday Religious Publishing Group, 2009) [= Allen, *The Future Church*] 1.

10 *Lumen gentium*, 33.

11 R. Fisichella, *The New Evangelization: Responding to the Challenge of Indifference*, (Balwyn: Freedom Publishing Pty. Ltd., 2012), 115.

Lumen gentium 32 teaches us that among the people of God, there is a "wonderful diversity": "For just as in one body we have many members, yet all the members have not the same function, so we, the many, are one body in Christ, but severally members one of another." There is a "common dignity, as members from their regeneration in Christ, having the same filial grace and the same vocation to perfection; possessing in common one salvation, one hope and one undivided charity." Between the people of God, there is also equality: "There is, therefore, in Christ and in the Church no inequality on the basis of race or nationality, social condition or sex, because 'there is neither Jew nor Greek: there is neither bond nor free: there is neither male nor female. For you are all one in Christ Jesus'." We know these passages by heart, but what has it meant in the everyday life of the Church?

In *Lumen gentium* 10, we also see that the common priesthood of the faithful and the ministerial priesthood are different but interrelated: "Though they differ from one another in essence and not only in degree, the common priesthood of the faithful and the ministerial or hierarchical priesthood are nonetheless interrelated: each of them in its own special way is a participation in the one priesthood of Christ." The English translation differs from the Latin text which says: "The common priesthood of the faithful and the ministerial priesthood, although they differ in essence ..."[12] It seems similar but we can see that in the Latin text, the Council fathers wanted first to emphasize the relationship between the two before going on to the difference.[13]

Lay faithful and ordained faithful are also interrelated, but what does this mean exactly? Here again, the Latin text says "*ad invicem tamen ordinantur,*" and each is "ordered" to the other. To me, this term is stronger than "interrelated." It means that they are meant for each other,[14] they are connected to each other, related to one another, having a mutual or reciprocal relation, a close and shared relationship. I am certain that each one of us, priest or layperson, can think of someone who has particularly inspired us, someone with whom we have enjoyed a meaningful ministerial relationship. As a layperson, I can think of special priests who have called on me. I am sure the same is true of priests who have been encouraged in their ministry by a layperson. It is this interrelation that has brought us from a Church-hierarchy to a Church-ministry, from a clergy-laity relationship to a community-ministries relation.

Presbyterorum ordinis 9 also mentions this relationship:

---

12 *Sacerdotium autem commune fidelium et sacerdotium ministeriale seu hierarchicum, licet essentia et non gradu tantum differant, ad invicem tamen ordinantur; unum enim et alterum suo peculiari modo de uno Christi sacerdotio participant.*

13 See H.R. McCord, "Priests and Laity in the One Priesthood of Christ," in *Origins*, 40 (2010) 120.

14 Ibid.

> Priests must sincerely acknowledge and promote the dignity of the laity and the part proper to them in the mission of the Church ... Likewise, they should confidently entrust to the laity duties in the service of the Church, allowing them freedom and room for action; in fact, they should invite them on suitable occasions to undertake works on their own initiative.

It is the response to this call that makes the difference between a vibrant community and one that is dying, a place where members are called forth, encouraged in their response to this call, and supported in their discernment and their apostolate or their ministry.

1.2 – *Christifideles laici*

It is in John Paul II's post-synodal exhortation *Christifideles laici* that we read that the laity has an "essential and irreplaceable role" in the work of the new evangelization, but it does warn:

> that the post-conciliar path of the lay faithful has not been without its difficulties and dangers. In particular, two temptations can be cited which they have not always known how to avoid: the temptation of being so strongly interested in Church services and tasks that some fail to become actively engaged in their responsibilities in the professional, social, cultural and political world; and the temptation of legitimizing the unwarranted separation of faith from life, that is, a separation of the Gospel's acceptance from the actual living of the Gospel in various situations in the world.[15]

One may read in this a judgment that laypeople who are actively involved in the "business of the Church" risk the danger of losing touch with the "real world." Although this may be true in some cases, I believe the exhortation calls on all of us to seek a better unity between faith and everyday life. And in this, laity has a key role.

1.3 – The 1997 interdicasterial instruction *Ecclesiae de mysterio*

15 John Paul II, post-synodal apostolic exhortation *Christifideles laici*, no. 2, 30 December 1988, in *AAS*, 81 (1989), pp. 393-521, English translation in *Origins*, 18 (1988-1989), pp. 561-595.

This instruction[16] on the collaboration of the laity to the ministry of the ordained is well known to canonists and theologians as well. Its definite legislative flavour, while remaining an instruction, gave rise to a multitude of canonical commentaries. The effect was "more psychological" than juridical for it suggested that it represented the thought of the entire Roman Curia on the subject. It was definitely meant to correct what was perceived as an abusive situation – laypeople taking on a ministerial role that was not theirs.

However, what was most regretful with this text is that it remained silent on the new ecclesial identity of laypeople associated in a stable manner to pastoral ministry. There is an underlying message that lay ministry is more a dangerous concession than a true ministry.[17] Its aim was most certainly not to discourage laypeople from participating actively in the Church's mission. Rather it was meant to correct abuses, but disgruntled laypeople, priests and even bishops did think at the time that it might have been better to direct these remarks to the few dioceses where abuses had been found. In hindsight, now that clearer heads have prevailed, one might look at it in a more positive light: that it made us stop and take stock, forced us in one way to come up with a clearer definition of ordained ministry and lay ministry.

1.4 – *Co-Workers* in the Vineyard of the Lord

Whereas the 1997 Instruction was reluctant to allow the use of the term "minister" for laypeople, the USCCB document, *Co-Workers in the Vineyard of the Lord*,[18] embraces the ecclesial reality that is lay ministry: "The further call of some persons to lay ecclesial ministry adds a special grace by which the Holy Spirit 'makes them fit and ready to undertake various tasks and offices for the renewal and building up of the Church'."[19] The document provides four characteristics for lay ecclesial ministry:

a. Authorization of the hierarchy to serve publicly in the local church;

b. Leadership in a particular area of ministry;

c. Close mutual collaboration with the pastoral ministry of bishops, priests, and deacons;

---

16 Congregation for the Clergy et al., Instruction on Some Questions Regarding Collaboration of Nonordained Faithful in Priests' Sacred Ministry *Ecclesiae de mysterio*, 15 August 1997, in *AAS*, 89 (1997), pp. 852-877, English translation in *Origins*, 27 (1997-1998) 397, 399-409.

17 See B. Sesboüé, *Rome et les laïcs: une nouvelle pièce au débat: l'Instruction romaine du 15 août 1997* (Paris : Desclée de Brouwer, 1998) 68.

18 United States Conference of Catholic Bishops, *Co-Workers in the Vineyard of the Lord: A Resource for Guiding the Development of Lay Ecclesial Ministry* (Washington: USCCB, 2005) [= *Co-Workers*].

19 *Co-Workers* 25, citing *Lumen gentium*, 12.

d. Preparation and formation appropriate to the level of responsibilities that are assigned to them.

Going even further, *Co-Workers* recognizes that "when called to ministry," laypeople "take on a new relationship to the mission of the Church and to the other ministers who work to accomplish it."[20] But it cautions that their "call, however, should not foster an elitism that places lay ecclesial ministers above or outside the laity. Like Jesus, they are called to serve and not to be served."[21]

Co-Workers is a remarkable document that goes a long way in furthering the theological reflection on lay ministry and stresses the essential need for formation for lay ministers, along with proper certification and authorization.

1.5 – *Evangelii gaudium*

In his apostolic exhortation *Evangelii gaudium*, Pope Francis has certainly made it clear that he wants a more active role for the laity in the Church because "laypeople are, put simply, the vast majority of the people of God."[22] By this very fact, they must take on more of a responsibility in the Church's mission. The Pope has cautioned that it cannot be left all to the bishops, priests and deacons and he decries the fact that there are not enough laypeople taking on this work. Why is this? Sometimes, laypeople feel they are not up to the task because the formation they are offered is inadequate. Sometimes, it is because of "an excessive clericalism that keeps them away from decision-making."[23]

However, the Pope is definite about the role he sees for laypeople: one that will have more to do with "a greater penetration of Christian values in the social, political and economic sectors." He notices that lay ministries remain too often "tied to tasks within the Church, without a real commitment to applying the Gospel to the transformation of society."[24]

As you know, *Evangelii gaudium* followed the Synod on New Evangelization. The role of the laity in evangelization is certainly not news to anyone. In the Pope's words there lies an invitation to "broaden" the role of laity, to not keep them tied to tasks within the Church but to send them "out" in society. He wishes to see more laypeople in leadership roles, including women and youth, and he has proven he means what he says in two recent decisions affecting his own entourage: the creation of the Council for the Economy, with eight cardinals and

---

20 *Co-Workers* 25.
21 Ibid.
22 Francis, *Evangelii gaudium*, no. 102.
23 Ibid.
24 Ibid.

seven laypersons,[25] and the creation of the Pontifical Commission for the Protection of Minors in which he appointed four women and four men (a cardinal and two Jesuits, and five laypersons).[26] These members will be free to decide what issues they are going to deal with, how they are going to work and who else will join the commission, and it will make its recommendations directly to the Holy Father without having to communicate through other Vatican departments. This, to me, is an example of having confidence in lay leadership.

II – Lay Ministry – Today's Situation

I have chosen to speak of "lay ministry" in this second part of my paper because this is and has been for quite some time the main focus of canon law's treatment of the laity's involvement in the mission. "Lay" because it is a service done by laypeople, rooted in the sacraments of initiation, not in the sacrament of ordination. "Ecclesial" because it is done within and for the Church community. "Minister" because it is a participation in the threefold ministry of Christ. The lay minister is called to service in the Church but not necessarily to a lifelong commitment.[27]

As we look at this form of ministry, two points must be kept in mind: (1) lay ministry, we all know, differs from lay apostolate in that it is exercised in response to a calling – a personal calling and a hierarchical calling; and (2) it has mostly referred to "ministry around the altar" or pertaining mainly to sacramental ministry.

2.1 – Are lay ecclesial ministers (LEMs) declining in numbers?

The latest Center for Applied Research in the Apostolate (CARA) statistics reveal that there are now, in 2014, approximately 38,000 priests in the US; there were 46,000 in 2000. There are also 38,000 LEMs in 2014 whereas there were 30,000 in 2000. What is interesting is that, according again to CARA, there were 553 parish life coordinators nationwide in 2005, and now there are only 388 as some of them have retired, others were encouraged to leave or otherwise left parish leadership. But as there were about 2,800 parishes without a resident pastor in 2000, there are now 3,500 and the numbers are expected to grow.[28]

25 Francis, motu proprio establishing a new coordinating agency for the economic and administrative affairs of the Holy See and the Vatican City State *Fidelis et dispensator prudens*, 24 February 2014, http://w2.vatican.va/content/francesco/en/motu_proprio/documents/papa-francesco-motu-proprio_20140224_fidelis-dispensator-et-prudens.html (accessed July 14, 2014).

26 See F. Lombardi, statement on Pope Francis' institution of the Commission on the Protection of Minors, 22 March 2014, http://www.news.va/en/news/pope-francis-establishes-commission-on-protection (accessed July 14, 2014).

27 See *Co-Workers* 11-12.

28 See CARA, "United States Data over Time," http://cara.georgetown.edu/CARAServices/ requestedchurchstats.html (accessed July 16, 2014).

These facts seem to contradict each other. The number of parishes without a pastor is rising, but parish life coordinators are fewer in number. Yet, there is the same number of LEMs as there are priests. What does this mean? If parishes increasingly are without a pastor, what does this mean for our traditional ecclesiology, the priest-pastor leading the parish? Is this the reason bishops seem reluctant to hand over parishes to LEMs? Or are laypeople staying away from parish coordination or being kept away? Is their ministry now extending beyond the church walls?

2.2 – The Eucharistic parish and the pastor

The celebration of the Eucharist is the expression of the mystery of the Church and its structure. If, increasingly, Sunday Eucharist is unavailable to parishioners or replaced by a Liturgy of the Word, what does this mean for our official ecclesiology? Canon 213 affirms the right that Christian faithful have to receive the Word of God and the sacraments from their pastors, and canon 1247 lays out the obligation to attend Mass on Sundays. Increasingly, the lay ecclesial minister has been asked to take on the ministry of the Word, where allowed, and a part of sacramental ministry when it cannot be assured by ordained ministers. There remains only what is "left over" for the priest, what laypeople cannot do under any circumstances.[29]

2.3 – The LEM – a back-up ministry?

In view of what we have just said, what exactly is lay ecclesial ministry? Is it simply a ministry that we call upon because of a lack of ordained ministers? I believe this is, as Archbishop-designate Cupich of Chicago[30] said in 2011, when he was Bishop of Spokane, "an insufficient way of looking at the phenomenon."[31] Unfortunately, too often, lay ministry has been closely associated with what I may call "ministry around the altar," and it has sometimes found itself in competition with ordained ministry. May we say that lay ministry has perhaps focused almost entirely on those people already *in* the Church and neglected to look outward to those *outside* the Church? Lines have become blurred, in some places, between the role of the ordained minister and the role of the lay minister.[32] This

29 See B. Sesboüé, "Lay Ecclesial Ministers: A Theological Look into the Future," Theological Trends, in *The Way*, 42/3 (2003) [= Sesboüé, "Lay Ecclesial Ministers"] 58-60.

30 At the time of this conference, the installation of Archbishop Cupich had yet to happen.

31 B. Cupich, interview "Advancing Excellence in Lay Ecclesial Ministry," at the National Symposium on Lay Ecclesial Ministry, August 2-5 2011, Collegeville, Minnesota, http://lem symposium.wordpress.com/2011/08/24/bishop-blase-cupich-advancing-excellence/ (accessed February 20, 2014).

32 See C.E. Olson, "The Role of the Laity: An Examination of Vatican II and *Christifideles Laici*," in *Ignatius Insight*, 1 October 2006, http://www.ignatiusinsight.com/features2006/print 2006/colson_rolelaity_oct06.html (accessed February 20, 2014).

situation also runs the risk of giving the impression that the *in* faithful are all around the altar. Anyone in the pew is *out* and his or her service to the mission is not essential. Has the situation of the lay ecclesial minister been misinterpreted or does it merit further thought? Is it meant to fill a gap in a static model of church ministry or should we venture into a more dynamic and inventive way of serving?

III – Lay Mission – Pathways for the Future

After the Second Vatican Council, the Church was meant to undergo an *aggiornamento* if it was to respond to the needs of the modern world. In the twenty-first century, we are now facing situations that we could not have even imagined a few decades ago: the largest Catholic population is no longer in Europe and North America but in Africa, Asia, and Latin America; the pressures of secularization and globalization; interreligious relationships that now include Islam; an aging population; laypeople being called to compensate for the lack of clergy; scientific advances that strain the Church's moral teaching.[33]

Lay ecclesial ministry must continue. Its usefulness no longer needs to be affirmed. But how is it called to continue? Should it develop in ways that will respond to the needs of the modern world? A common frame of reference is required that will ensure that this form of ministry not only meets these new situations but also remains faithful to the Church's tradition. *Co-Workers* provides a frame of reference for Church leaders wanting to be more effective in ordering and integrating lay ecclesial ministry within the structures of the parish and of the diocese, but should it take on a new form? If so, it needs to be understood, organized and adequately prepared for its mission.

3.1 – A theology of lay ministry that is understood

One thing, I believe, must be recognized: a layperson who responds to the call from the hierarchy to serve the Church publicly and with the proper authorization from the bishop serves as a lay minister. This is something more than the universal call to holiness. It is still rooted in baptism, but it is something more. Without wanting to create yet another "Church elite," we need to realize that it distinguishes the layperson. Becoming part of a "superior" group is not the meaning of ministry as a service, but we must recognize that, as Bernard Sesboüé, the Jesuit theologian, says, we therefore have a "third existential pole"

33 See Allen, *The Future Church*, 2-3.

in the Church.[34] These are people who are coming forward, wanting to help the Church. They are already married or otherwise engaged with life's tasks, but they are responding to a call, a call that takes time to discern. For them, it is a process, a spiritual journey. If they respond positively to this call, then they enter into a special relationship with their pastor, with their bishop. This, according to Sesboüé, creates a third pole within the Church, a group of faithful who come forward, because of a charism, and it needs to be recognized, laying aside the oft-repeated fear of clericalizing the laity or creating yet another elite group in the Church.[35] These conclusions lose sight of ministry as a service.

Lay ministers enter into a new relationship with the bishop. As he should know his seminarians and his priests, so should he know the laypeople training for ministry. As well, although they are not seeking ordination, they should be recognized officially by the Church. There is certainly the well-known procedure of commissioning, either by a letter or by a liturgy, but what about the recognition of a new identity? It is too soon in the history of lay ecclesial ministry to speak of commissioning these people sacramentally, but they are still in a "sacramental relationship" with the pastors, with the bishop. It is this sacramental relationship, not sacramental ordination, but a relationship with the bishop that requires recognition and organization. Laypeople, in general, do not strive to shed themselves of their lay identity.[36] However, they do wish to be supported and recognized in the Church as having entered into a new relationship with the bishop and the faithful. They need to know they are recognized as such as they need to recognize themselves as having a different pastoral responsibility – lay apostolate and lay ministry are not to be in conflict with each other but complementary to each other.[37] The lay apostolate that all the faithful are called to is of critical importance: "The vocation to bring the spirit of Christ into the arenas of secular life from within, i.e. into the family, work and profession, trade and commerce, politics and government, mass media, science and culture and national

34 See B. Sesboüé, *N'ayez pas peur! Regards sur l'Église et les ministères aujourd'hui*, Pascal Thomas – Pratiques chrétiennes, no.12 (Paris: Desclée de Brouwer, 1996) 141-143. This new theology of lay ministry was also adopted in the USCCB report, Subcommittee on Lay Ministry, "Lay Ecclesial Ministry: State of the Questions, Toward a Theology of Lay Ecclesial Ministry," conclusion 8, in *Origins*, 29 (2000) 502; in *Co-Workers* 12. See also A. Borras, "Remodelage des paroisses: libres propos d'un canoniste à partir de trois cas de remodelage paroissial," in *Esprit et Vie*, no. 62, 112 (2002) 18; N. Provencher, "Un regard théologique sur nos pratiques ministérielles," in *Studia canonica*, 29 (1995) 368.

35 See Sesboüé, "Lay Ecclesial Ministers," 66.

36 On the need to explore the experience of the lay minister being "in the middle" which presents a dilemma for the traditional understanding of vocations, see also E.P Hahnenberg, "Theology of Lay Ecclesial Ministry: Future Trajectories," in Z. Fox ed., *Lay Ecclesial Ministry: Pathways Toward the Future* (Lanham, MD: Rowman & Littlefield Publishers, Inc., 2010) 74.

37 See Sesboüé, "Lay Ecclesial Ministers," 62-65.

and international relations."[38] However, the recognition of the importance of one does not diminish the need for the other. Is lay ministry meant to support this apostolate "in the world"?

3.2 – The organization of the lay mission

3.2.1 – In the public sphere

We know that the Church must not only be indentified with clerics. In the past, whenever a public stance had to be taken to represent the Catholic Church, it was always to a bishop or a priest that one would go. Quite frequently, it is still the case today. There is nothing wrong with this, but does this mean that laypeople are not qualified to represent the Church publicly? "It is not a good argument to say that the clergy are better prepared theologically than the laity. Laypeople can also be theologically well prepared."[39]

It is now well received that laypeople can teach and assume leadership positions in seminaries, as well as in Catholic and ecclesiastical faculties and universities. If they are theologically fit to teach in the public sphere, they certainly can do so in the field of communications. In his apostolic letter founding the Pontifical Council for New Evangelization, *Ubicumque et semper*, Pope Benedict XVI entrusted to this council the task of studying and fostering "the use of modern forms of communications, as instruments for the new evangelization."[40] The world of communications definitely has a functional aspect, but, moreover, it is a universe of thought with enormous potential. Canon 822, §1, reminds us that pastors "are to make ample use of the means of social communication" and much has been done in this regard in the past few years. But this is definitely an initiative in which laypeople could take the leadership.

As one example of this form of evangelization, the USCCB has already acknowledged the usefulness of the world of communications in evangelizing as it organized its Catholic Communication Campaign in parishes around the United States in May 2014. The collection funds several Catholic projects, including the *For Your Marriage* campaign and coverage of important events. Half the donations collected stay in the diocese to support local communications needs.

3.2.2 – In lay apostolate

38 F. Arinze (Cardinal), interview on the role of the laity, 9 October 2013, in *The Catholic World Report*, http://www.catholicworldreport.com/Item/2629/cardinal_arinze_on_the_role_of_the_ laity.aspx (accessed July 21, 2014).

39 F. Arinze, *The Layperson's Distinctive Role*, Kindle edition (San Francisco: Ignatius Press, 2013) 655.

40 Benedict XVI, apostolic letter *motu proprio* establishing the Pontifical Council for the New Evangelization *Ubicumque et semper*, 21 September 2010, art. 3, in *AAS*, 102 (2010), p. 792, English translation in *Origins*, 40 (2010) 396.

Lay apostolate is an enormous task, varied and broad. It is the task of all Catholic faitful and no one can do it alone. Experience has proven that a concerted effort in parishes and dioceses is useful. Councils directed specifically to apostolate could be established: "In dioceses, insofar as possible, there should be councils which assist the apostolic work of the Church either in the field of evangelization and sanctification or in the charitable, social, or other spheres."[41] In places where it is possible, councils specifically set up by the laity for lay apostolate could be helpful in spearheading action on the social, cultural and political levels. They could be on the parish, diocesan, regional or national level, with statutes approved by the bishop or the bishops' conference.[42]

On the topic of councils, Pope Francis has invited us take a fresh look at our structures: "There are ecclesial structures which can hamper efforts at evangelization, yet even good structures are only helpful when there is a life constantly driving, sustaining and assessing them."[43] He wants us to examine our structures to see whether they are in place and function in such a way as to further the cause of new evangelization or whether they are a detriment to the cause. Do our diocesan and parochial councils and committees facilitate new evangelization or are they in place merely to maintain the *status quo*? Are they innovative and forward-looking? Do laypeople feel they have an active place in these structures, a voice? Again, in the exhortation, Francis sets the tone:

> We can count on many laypersons, although still not nearly enough, who have a deeply-rooted sense of community and great fidelity to the tasks of charity, catechesis and the celebration of the faith. At the same time, a clear awareness of this responsibility of the laity, grounded in their baptism and confirmation, does not appear in the same way in all places. In some cases, it is because laypersons have not been given the formation needed to take on important responsibilities. In others, it is because in their particular Churches room has not been made for them to speak and to act, due to an excessive clericalism which keeps them away from decision-making.[44]

Catholic professional associations are already well known, whether they are associations of medical professionals, teachers or legal practitioners. Members of these associations should have a regular contact with diocesan councils, namely the diocesan pastoral councils and apostolate councils, or be assured of a representation on these councils. Perhaps a closer liaison with Catholic sponsorship corporations might be worthwhile as these are called to take on greater roles in the future.

41 *Apostolicam actuositatem*, 26.

42 See Arinze, *The Layperson's Distinctive Role*, 893-913.

43 *Evangelii gaudium*, art. 26.

44 Ibid., art. 102.

3.2.3 – In ecclesial movements and new communities

A lot has been said about ecclesial movements and new communities, some of it good and forward-looking, and some of it, let us be honest, downright scary. These mostly lay movements and communities have risen in the Church largely in the last fifty or so years. They seek to harmonize the lives of the faithful, their families, their work, and their surroundings with the Lord, to seek a personal encounter with Christ. In his exhortation *Evangelii gaudium*, Pope Francis invites us to embrace these institutions as an extension of the parish:

> We must admit, though, that the call to review and renew our parishes has not yet sufficed to bring them nearer to people, to make them environments of living communion and participation, and to make them completely mission-oriented.
>
> Other Church institutions, basic communities and small communities, movements, and forms of association are a source of enrichment for the Church, raised up by the Spirit for evangelizing different areas and sectors. Frequently they bring a new evangelizing fervour and a new capacity for dialogue with the world whereby the Church is renewed. But it will prove beneficial for them not to lose contact with the rich reality of the local parish and to participate readily in the overall pastoral activity of the particular Church. This kind of integration will prevent them from concentrating only on part of the Gospel or the Church, or becoming nomads without roots.[45]

In 2006, the Pontifical Council for the Laity published a *Directory of International Associations of the Faithful* approved by the Council at the universal Church level, which may be regarded as ecclesial movements or new communities. There are also those which function at the national or diocesan levels.[46]

As signs of the Holy Spirit's intervention, these movements and communities should be encouraged. But it is also true that, given their great diversity, they have sometimes been a challenge for bishops preoccupied with coordinating their apostolate with the existing structures of the Church. To this end, the Canadian Conference of Catholic Bishops has published *Criteria for the Discernment of Ecclesial Movements and Associations*, a useful guide for a bishop in evaluating the ecclesiality of a movement or a community: accountability, implantation

45 *Evangelii gaudium*, art. 28-29.

46 See Arinze, *The Layperson's Distinctive Role*, 1140.

within a parish, authentic doctrine, complementarity with other movements or associations, social involvement, and holiness.[47]

When ecclesial movements and new communities function well, they "can help the local Church avoid the mentality of being a maintenance Church by bringing with them the freshness of missionary enthusiasm rather than an attitude of business as usual."[48] In support of these new initiatives, the Pontifical Council for the Laity has organized a world congress, 20-22 November 2014, for ecclesial movements and new communities that will gather delegates of large international associations of the faithful recognized by or in dialogue with the Holy See. This initiative has received the support of some 80 associations from all the continents of the world. *Evangelii gaudium* is considered the *vademecum* for this gathering.

3.3 – Formation

Co-Workers has insisted on the necessity for the proper formation of lay ecclesial ministers and lists four areas:

a. Human qualities critical to form wholesome relationships and necessary to be apt instruments of God's love and compassion.
b. A spirituality and practice of prayer that root them in God's Trinitarian life grounding and animating all they do in ministry.
c. Adequate knowledge in theological and pastoral studies, along with the intellectual skill to use it among the people and cultures of our country.
d. The practical pastoral abilities called for in their particular ministry.[49]

A solid formation of the laity is essential for it engages the discernment that is critical if laypeople are to know what their gifts are and understand how these gifts should serve the Church. Although formation has mainly been the privilege of lay ecclesial ministers called to parish ministry, if their protagonistic role is to take root, it should be broadened to include laypeople called to this particular mission. Formation should provide them with a background in theology, in missiology, in ecclesiology, and in canon law. To this end, new evangelization should be included "as an integral dimension of the mission of every theological

47 See Canadian Conference of Catholic Bishops, Criteria for the Discernment of Ecclesial Movements and Associations, 5 September 2006, at http://www.cccb.ca/site/eng/commissions-committees-and-aboriginal-council/national-commissions/doctrine/documents/2059-new-ecclesial-movements-a-associations (accessed July 30, 2014).

48 See Arinze, *The Layperson's Distinctive Role*, 1218.

49 *Co-Workers*, p. 33.

faculty and a department of new evangelization studies should be established in Catholic universities."[50]

3.4 – Laypeople and ordained ministers as collaborators

For an effective collaborative effort of the ordained and the laity, pastors are called to "show the way" in facilitating the development of new ministries and new forms of apostolate. Formation on collaborative ministry will be necessary for them, both at the seminary level and as continuing education. Laypeople called to ministry will benefit from proper formation on the theology of ministries – both ordained and non-ordained – and on methods for fruitful collaboration.

On this topic, Cardinal Arinze shared his views on the main impediments facing laypeople who would want to exercise their mission:

> ignorance on the part of some clerics or of some laypeople on what the Church teaches as distinctive of the lay apostolate; ignorance of correct and dynamic theology on the Church and on the differing roles of laity, clerics, and religious; fear on the part of clerics or of the laity if laypeople are encouraged to 'take on their own distinctive role'; the lay apostolate seen as a power struggle between clerics and laypeople. This could make the clergy afraid and the laity unnecessarily aggressive; the lay apostolate seen as parallel authority in the Church or as a threat to the clerics; fear of the unknown shown in the spirit that says: "There is no need to change. The clergy have given good leadership in the past and we had better not experiment with the new ideas"; fear shown in the following mentality: "The laity do not know theology. This idea of 'the layperson's distinctive role' is going to bring confusion into the Church." The response is: "If the laity do not have enough theological formation, give it to them." The importance of theological and other formation is stressed in the final chapter in my book. Let priest chaplains to the laity be tip-top! We do not promote Church apostolate by ignorance.[51]

---

50 See XIII Synod of Bishops, Final Propositions, no. 30, at http://www.vatican.va/news_services/press/sinodo/documents/bollettino_25_xiii-ordinaria-2012/02_inglese/b33_02.htm (accessed January 9, 2014).

51 F. Arinze, interview with *Catholic World Report* on the role of the laity, 9 October 2013, at http://www.catholicworldreport.com/Item/2629/cardinal_arinze_on_the_role_of_the_laity.aspx (accessed July 8, 2014).

Conclusion

Where do we go from here? Do we maintain the *status quo* or do we dare to go where no one has gone before? Clearly, great strides have been made with regards to the involvement of the laity in the Church. But I believe it is crucial that we proceed with a clear understanding of the proper theology of their mission and ministry. Although several laypeople will choose to exercise their apostolate in a more private way, several should and must be called to a more public engagement. Lay ministry should not be limited to internal Church matters but given a formal frame that will propel its influence and action outwards. Their mission is not essentially filling in for priests. There is a need for this, at times, but I do not believe that laypeople are merely called to suppletory functions. In the same vein, we can no longer equate and limit leadership in the Church to the ordained faithful. A spirit of shared mission, among equals, each called to their own form of leadership is the only way forward. Pope Francis has warned that power struggles in the Church should not exist and that true power is measured by the service one renders for the Church and the faithful.

We have mentioned movements as an important structure in which laypeople can exercise their particular mission and provide leadership in the Church. Adequately organized, they can lead in the changing face of the Church.

Formation is key to this, adequate and solid. If we seek to have good seminaries, so should we seek to have good centres, institutes and faculties offering a comprehensive formation for the laity. Just as important is ensuring adequate support for laypeople who will accept this important call. They must be assured of the same protection for their job as are priests and religious.

There should no longer be disagreements about the need for laypeople in decision-making roles in the Church. Perhaps this aspect will be helped along by the Roman Curia. Cardinal Rodriguez Maradiaga, Chair of the Council of Cardinals appointed by Pope Francis to look at the reform of the Curia, and Cardinal Gracias, also a member of this Council, have both spoken of the possibility of having a Congregation for the Laity, which would absorb the responsibilities of the present councils dealing with laity and family: "Bishops have their own dicastery, religious people and the clergy have theirs, but the laity is the majority of the Church and they only have a council."[52] Time will tell if this is to become a reality.

Lay protagonists, either as leaders or agents of new evangelization, are meant to be seen as a revolutionizing trend, not linked to the shortage of priests but assets that the Church cannot do without. They can be sent out to help, to listen, to

52 O. Rodriguez Maradiaga, interview with T. Reese for the *National Catholic Reporter*, 11 July 2014, at http://ncronline.org/blogs/faith-and-justice/cardinals-rodriguez-gracias-open-about-curia-reform (accessed July 11, 2014).

preach, to heal, to lead. Time will tell whether we will be holding on to a familiar model of Church or whether we will boldly look at new ways in which the laity can be called to serve. They are, after all, there in great numbers. In Cardinal John Henry Newman's words when asked what he thought of the laity, "Well, we'd look pretty silly without them."

Seminar

Diocesan Indebtedness: Will We Be Selling the Cathedral?

Diane L. Barr, JD, JCD, PhD

I. Introduction

Our Changing Church Landscape

As we meet here in St. Louis this week, the work of only the third Extraordinary Synod of Bishops continues to meet in Rome. We live in exciting times for canon lawyers – at least I'm excited by the questions that are being asked and the work that is being done to reshape the world we live in on so many fronts.

We have all heard the renewed call for evangelization and seeing the work we have always done through a clearer lens of the mission of the Church. In my own diocese, we have very actively worked to focus and clarify that vision in a very practical way. Our parishes have embraced the approach of Sherry Waddell in her book *Forming Intentional Disciples* or the programmatic format of our local ministry entitled "Discovering Christ." Or perhaps you have picked up the book entitled *Rebuilt Parish*, authored by a team from one of our local parishes in Baltimore. We are in a time of extraordinary energy and excitement and those of us with administrative responsibilities in the Church need to reflect and embrace that energy in our own ministry. It seems a daunting task since a new attitude is required for renewed action and understanding.

What is An Administrator to Do Now?

What can we do to deal with these issues in a way that will support evangelization and manage in a way that is consistent with the call of the Holy Father who said:

> As the faithful and prudent administrator has a vocation to care attentively for those goods that have been entrusted to him, so the Church is conscious of her call to safeguard and carefully administer her goods in light of her mission of evangelization, with special care for the needy. In particular, the responsibility of the economic and financial sectors of the Holy See is intimately linked to its own particular mission,

> not only in its service to the Holy Father in the exercise of his universal ministry but also with respect to how they correspond to the common good in light of integral human development. Pope Francis, Moto proprio - *Fidelis Dispensator et Prudens*, February 24, 2014.

We are being challenged as administrators to bring that focus on mission to everything we do. Whether it is direct ministry to an individual or the collective actions of our administrative offices we need to be sure we are focused on that mission. We have to be certain that everyone we work with "gets the mission" so that vision can be constitutive in every decision we make. No more automatic pilot or road of least resistance.

II. How Did We Get Here?

One word of caution about this presentation – you will have noticed that I am NOT a CPA or the former manager of a bank. I have worked in dioceses of varying sizes so am familiar with some approaches to diocesan financial administration. I present here what I have learned personally, and from others.

The Many Ways Dioceses (and their Parishes) Get Into Debt

I would be remiss if I did not state the obvious here. Dioceses get into debt by spending more than they take in. Going into debt can be properly intentional, such as taking on a new mortgage for new facilities, or it can be the result of poor oversight of investments or parishes, or simply poor budgeting at the diocesan level. We live in a time when there are many challenges in every diocese. I am sure some of the following list will be familiar to you:

- **Appointment of a new bishop or pastor** – Financial support is about relationships and when those relationships change, so might the financial support. The financial knowledge and acumen of a new leader will also directly affect the bottom line in many ways.

- **Demographic Issues - Growing or Shrinking populations** – The need to provide for ministry to more people than before on a limited income; (South and West) or the need to support shrinking populations that still have large infrastructures and institutions (Northeast).

- **Increasing costs to educate future clergy** – This may involve educating men at the college and seminary level, as well as providing appropriate training for priests who serve our dioceses from other countries. Education costs of all sorts are continuing to increase every year.

- **Aging Clergy** – This means we may have to budget to increase the available contributions for the priest pension fund. More men are retiring, yet after the great Recession, income may be more limited. This is a canonical requirement and one that must be met, but what is its priority?

- **Aging Facilities** – Every diocese has a list of deferred maintenance requests for its Cathedral, schools or other buildings. If parishes cannot afford such costs, where will the funding come from?

- **Building New Facilities** – Every diocese has some areas that are growing so fast they need to build – whether it is a new church hall or a new church itself. Building costs have only gotten higher with time as competition in a global marketplace has accelerated the price of materials. Those costs do not even include the land. Dioceses are going to shorter term solutions – can we rent space in an appropriate place instead of building a church when we do not know if we will need one in that spot in ten years due to changing demographics? How do we oversee the building process for individual facilities in a way that minimizes expenses (read keeps building change orders to a minimum) and assures the construction of quality facilities? Seminary training does not usually include a license in architecture or building construction for our priests – do we need specialists for this process? Do we have processes in place to deal with the unexpected failure or compromise of our facilities?

- **Unclear Priorities for Diocesan Budget** – An attempt to do and be everything for everyone all the time means that there is no real prioritization of vision and resources – we often leave things in place once they are established and do not question their existence since it would not be "nice" and what would that say about that ministry or effort that was once valuable – was it wrong? What about the people who work there – are they to be fired? They are family, are they not?

- **Poor Parish Budgeting Practices** – Parishes submit inadequate or fantasy budgets for review by the diocese and fall short on an on-going basis – this results in lack of timely and proper payment of Cathedraticum and other shared expenses – any shortfall is born by the diocese in every case and has an impact on other compliant parishes who are effected with higher costs for shared insurance or other costs.

- **Delayed or Unsuccessful Parish Reorganization Processes** – Dioceses may delay reorganization or parish cooperative efforts for many reasons, with expensive financial results – parishes that are not financially viable can be left to "survive" through neglect – their inability to pay staff or support programs can result in serious diocesan deficits if they are unable to pay for shared services.

- **Delayed or Unsuccessful Diocesan Schools Reorganization** – Similar to the issues involving parishes, but schools may require heavy infusions of capital to allow them to keep their doors open through an entire school year; this can mean complete diocesan support of all expenses including salary, building support and payment of any other budget items that cannot be covered due to a tuition shortfall.

- **Growing Expenses for Technology and Outreach** – The next generations are connected through technology and investment in this aspect of ministry is crucial to our future. We will need to invest heavily in the infrastructure and support necessary to engage in this area. Are we prepared to do this? What will this mean to various cultural populations in my diocese?

- **Lack of Technology to Oversee Parish Financial Practices** – Local bookkeepers are using inadequate software systems for parish records and dioceses do not have arrangements for transfers of funds from parishes to diocesan accounts for payment of Cathedraticum or other income;

- **Poor Investments** – The days of a diocese having a single investment manager are hopefully long over, but it may still cause great harm to a diocese and its parishes if not properly monitored and managed.

- **Unknown future for sexual misconduct cases** – We need to continue to support and expand our work in child and youth protection areas – local laws may change, cases may emerge or other issues may arise here that affect the financial future of a diocese.

- These are just some of the ways dioceses and parishes get into debt although the list is not exhaustive. Let us move on to the other side – seeking to deal with debt.

III. What Can We Do About It Now?

College of Consultors and Diocesan Finance Council - We must use the expertise available in our own dioceses including the members of the College of Consultors and the Diocesan Finance Council. The appointees to the second group should not be "yes" people and the retired, but those who can challenge the

CFO and the diocesan administrators to look beyond the usual structures and solutions. I believe the laity in our dioceses are eager to take on these responsibilities and can lead us in a positive direction. They have to be part of any solution or our attempts to change the situation will be unsuccessful.

Our Basic Challenges Include:

- **Harder to borrow** – It is harder to qualify for loans or refinancing;
- **Need to Have More Collateral** – While interest rates are low, we may have to put up more collateral for longer periods of time;
- **Debt Service Issues** – Borrowing money means that we will have to service debt before doing other things with those funds;
- **Uniqueness of Our Structures** – Most banks do not understand our structures and limitations and are nervous about possible liability from child sexual abuse cases;
- **The Great Recession Lives On** – Parish income can be unreliable given the economic conditions in the US and other places thus Cathedraticum can be unreliable as a source of income;
- **Roman Approval** – May need to go to Rome to receive approval of the transaction.

Avoiding Indebtedness and Getting Out of the Debt We Already Have

- **Spend Less** – This may seem obvious, but can be a true trial for any diocesan bishop or pastor. We have also moved into an era of a very public call by the Holy Father to live with and serve the poor. Simplicity and a renewed sense of mission can make this option a reality. What we save we also apply to our debt.
- **Institute Mission Based Budgeting** – There are many ways to build a budget, but mission based budgeting should be designed to make sure all who serve at the diocesan or parish levels look first at how their work serves the mission of Gospel. Many say that any work of the Church meets this criteria, but we live in a time when it is important to be sure that all not only understand that message in a private individual way, but that everything they do must meet this criteria. This is also an opportunity for those of us in diocesan administration to work with the CFO and her or his team to make such a budget a reality.

- **End Automatic Hiring** – Our biggest expense, whether at the diocesan or at the parish level, is supporting people. When an employee leaves, regardless of the reason, the position should not be filled automatically, but the question of when and if it should be filled has to be addressed. When income is limited, a delay in hiring for a particular position can give the administrator greater financial flexibility. If you have to cut a position, it is always easier to cut one that is vacant than one that is occupied.

- **Institute Advance Technology Options for Diocesan and Parish Management** – Many dioceses have begun requiring that their parishes adopt QuickBooks On-line for their accounts. This allows dioceses to better monitor the income of particular locations and assist those parishes that may need help in handling financial concerns. It can also serve as an early warning system for drops in income or other problems.

  Dioceses have also required that parishes adopt some type of Electronic Funds Transfer (EFT) to stabilize their contribution base. Envelop systems are a thing of the past in many places. Some dioceses have required their parishes to allow a "sweep" of parish accounts on a particular schedule to provide for payment of Cathedraticum in a timely fashion. Electronic transfer of other funds allows for an efficient and transparent method of financial management.

- **Institute True Oversight of Parish Finances through Active Audit Processes** – We all know which of our pastors are financially sophisticated and which are not. Establishing an active audit process with a follow-up protocol to assist local parishes with the issues uncovered will result in better financial management and hopefully will avoid questionable financial practices that harm the parish and the reputation of others. Just because you conduct an audit does not mean that the recommendations that result from that review are actually implemented at the parish. It is important to establish a mechanism to ensure accountability on this front.

- **Increase Development Efforts** – Development efforts have become even more sophisticated over the last decade. These efforts involve not only the Catholics in the pews, but can expand the reach of Church efforts by partnering with other likeminded agencies or foundations. In my own diocese, we have just finished a capital campaign that was originally supposed to raise $100 million, but has been so successful over the last five years that we will soon reach the $150 million mark. Transparency in these efforts will be essential in the future since donors have many more options than ever before. If we want to keep them donating to the Church, we have to include our people in our decisions and continue to seek their assistance and leadership in these efforts.

- **Establish an Education Trust for Clergy and/or Laity** – Many development professionals will tell you that our people are eager to support these efforts because they realize the needs for our future.

- **Selling Assets We Already Own** – There are times when it is essential to sell assets to pay down debt. We may also have to do this should the covenants on any bank loans or bonds demand it due to a short fall in our finances. Do we really need to land-bank property in a given area or keep open an unused convent or church?

- **Make Owned Property Produce Income** – Should we manage it in a way that supports the mission of the Church, but also provides revenue in some way? Rental of property can produce unrelated business income, but that may be an acceptable alternative to leaving the property unused. Better yet, can the property be used on temporary basis with one of our likeminded partners? What about housing a head start program in an underutilized school or allowing the farming of a piece of agricultural land so that a portion or all of the produce raised goes to a local food bank?

- **Reorganizing Schools and Parishes** – When parishes and schools sell their unused properties as a result of a consolidation or reorganization, the funds from those sales are first used to pay any outstanding debt which includes any outstanding balances to diocesan coffers for pension and other outstanding unpaid expenses. The remainder of these funds can be used to improve and enhance remaining schools and learning opportunities.

- **Establishing Restricted Funds for Emergency Use** – These can be for emergency capital improvements or for other types of issues including educating the laity, supporting youth and child protection efforts, etc.

IV. What If We Owe More Than We Can Pay?

Bankruptcy

At last count I think we have had fifteen dioceses file for bankruptcy over the last twenty years. Some continue in that process even today and many are linked to situations involving the sexual abuse of minors. This is a last resort in any diocese given the limitations on the management of Church funds.

V. Reflecting the Law of the Church in Our Civil Structures

I want to focus on an area where a renewed sense of mission can have a major impact on our work and that is the actual structuring of our apostolates and ministries.

Have you considered whether your diocesan structures reflect the mission of the diocese? This can often be a difficult question. When I was at the meeting of national financial administrators a few weeks ago, one question came from the floor: How do you get a bishop to make the decision about what is important beyond the support and promotion of vocations? If everything is important, nothing ends up being important. Prioritizing the mission of our dioceses is the first step in truly beginning this broader conversation about how to support that mission. Have you really looked at your diocesan structures in the last five years? I think these questions are essential:

- Are the canonical and legal entities in my diocese structured to maximize the mission of the Gospel?
- Are we structuring the apostolates and institutions we have to allow us to be nimble and creative rather than settled and static?
- Do the structures we have actually reflect the canonical requirements of our own law?
- Are parishes recognized as separate juridic persons, not only in theory but in the way they are managed and supported?
- Do other entities need to have that same canonical autonomy to fully undertake the mission to which they have been assigned?

The basic ways dioceses are structured have generally not changed across the US. There are three basic approaches:

- **Bishop is a corporation sole under state law** and holds in trust the property of the parishes of the diocese as well as a variety of other supportive entities such as a cemetery fund, a pooled investment fund, and an interparish deposit and loan fund.
- **Bishop is a corporation sole under state law and parishes are individually incorporated under state law** – The usual structure is to have the bishop as president, a vicar general as vice-president, the pastor as secretary-treasurer with two lay parishioners appointed by the bishop as the other members of the board. Property is titled in the name of the parish, but has a condition of approval of the bishop attached to the deed. Other

entities within the diocese are separately incorporated such as Catholic Charities, the priest retirement fund, the lay pension fund, the cemetery trust, as well as the interparish deposit and loan fund.

I prefer this particular method of organization since, in my opinion, it tends to reflect the canonical structures of the parish as a juridic person. It is convenient for diocesan officials since organizing and supporting a structure where parishes are individually incorporated is a challenging task, but it can be done. It is advantageous in creating another type of consultative body at the parish level that can provide a positive contribution to the overall management of the parish at every level; financial, legal and administrative. It also recognizes the role of the laity in a very significant way.

- **Diocesan Trusts** – The diocese has established a number of trusts that hold and manage the assets of the diocese. These may be pooled parish property, retirement support assets, education assets, etc. Some dioceses have individual parish trusts with the Bishop as sole trustee (Harrisburg).

  This type of structure can be advantageous as far as efficiency and proper protection under civil law, but again the statutory requirements that exist for the establishment and support of these entities must be observed in order to obtain the protections available under civil law. It can be more cumbersome to change if circumstances warrant it, depending on the laws of the local jurisdiction.

Changing from One Structure to Another

Proper legal advice should be sought before any changes are made so that the decision-makers are aware of the potential consequences of their decision. When a diocese goes from a corporation sole model to another there is often the question of reflecting that change in the ownership of property. This may necessitate a change in title which can trigger the potential payment of taxes as a result of the transfer.

Educating Our Priests and Our People

Regardless of the structures we have in place, it is imperative that we educate our priests and people about their purpose and make sure they are involved in the administration of these entities.

Incorporating Other Entities

Many of the apostolates and works of the Church start with the actions of just a few people and over time grow and develop into something much bigger. One of the mission questions for me is how these apostolates are to be structured in relationship to the diocese itself. Again, proper legal advice should be taken, but if the mission and apostolate is to be overseen and controlled by the laity, the appropriate independent structure should be established with a determinative board. The role of the diocese in the mission of the group should be clarified and put into writing. A number of ministries have been given this independent character – these include Catholic Charities or other local entities.

Diocesan Schools

A number of dioceses around the country are experimenting with a variety of Catholic school support models. They often involve the establishment of a new corporate entity with a determinative board. Again, the school's sponsor, administrative and financial relationship with the parish or diocese should be properly established from the beginning.

Cemetery board

As an administrator I must decide whether this entity should take ownership of all the parish and diocesan cemeteries in the diocese or if it should simply contract to manage these entities with the actual ownership remaining with the parishes and diocesan entities themselves.

Interparish Loan Funds

This is another entity that has often been established only by some limited guidelines from the diocesan bishop. The funds are pooled for investment and distribution is often controlled solely by the diocesan bishop. Given that this is an entity where parish funds are being received and loaned, a more formalized structure is likely necessary that will truly reflect the independence of the use of the funds. Establishing this as an independent entity with a board of well-trained pastors and laity can provide better stability and safeguards for the funds used in this manner as envisioned by Church law.

Priest Retirement Funds

Many dioceses have already incorporated these funds and established an appropriate board of pastors to oversee the investment of these monies. This independence allows the presbyterate to take ownership of its own future and to understand the workings of their own future support. At present most priest funds are determined benefit funds that are dependent on the vagaries of the stock market. A review of who may benefit from such a fund may also be in order since the question of "being in good standing" as a priest for pension eligibility has broader justice implications.

Catholic Charities and Similar Entities

Many dioceses have already separately incorporated these entities to provide them with the autonomy they need to work in the broader community and to received appropriately designated state funds.

VI. Conclusions

As administrators, we face many challenges as we oversee the work of the Church. Financial management is key to what we do. We must be sure that our efforts support the mission of the Church in its efforts to spread the Gospel everywhere. Responsible stewardship of our resources is one of the foundations of those efforts.

Seminar

The Office for Promoter of Justice: Once Thought Nearly Irrelevant Again Becomes Relevant

Rev. Thomas T. Brundage, JCL

When it came time to choose a topic for my dissertation for the licentiate degree in canon law at the Catholic University of America in the early 1990's, I consulted with my father, Dr. James A. Brundage, as to what topic I should choose. Having directed hundreds of dissertations over a fifty year period as a professor of Medieval History, his advice (which I accepted), was to make the topic extremely narrow and of little interest to anyone.

Since the 1990's, however, the subject of the office of promoter of justice has become less narrow and of greater interest not only to canonists but to all who oversee the administration of justice in our local dioceses.

In this presentation, I will look at this topic from five angles. I will first present a brief history of the office of promoter of justice; second, study the intent of the lawmakers in providing such an office; third, provide an overview of the 1983 Code of Canon Law and the office of the promoter; fourth (and perhaps most daunting), trace the evolution of this office over the past two decades; and finally, to offer a few observations on the importance of this office.

A Brief History of the Office or Promoter of Justice [1]

There is no consensus among commentators of the origin of this office. Nevertheless, the first express mention of the promoter of justice as a diocesan official comes from the Archdiocese of Paris in 1274 where one could find a Promoter *Fiscalis Episcopi Parisensis*.[2]

1 Much of these early sections of the presentation were mined from my 1992 dissertation *The Promoter of Justice under the 1983 Code*, November, 1991, The Catholic University of America.

2 The duty of the promoter here is not clear. See Celestin Tanon, *Histoire des Justices des Eqlises et Communautes Ecclesliastiques* de Paris (Paris: L. Larose, 1883) 341. See also Adbemar Esmein, *History of Continental Criminal Procedure* (Boston: Little, Brown and Company, 1925-1931) 158.

In commentaries on the 1983 code, there is mention that historically, the offices of defender of the bond and the promoter of justice may be connected.[3] The office of defender was instituted after that of the promoter and some commentaries argue that a defender is simply a different form of a promoter of justice.

The promoter also served as a prosecutor during the Inquisition. [4]

By the nineteenth century, through custom, usage, various decrees and instructions, the office of promoter of justice existed with certain rights and obligations. Among the promoter's tasks at this time were the accusations of marriages to be invalid by reason of an impediment, participation in criminal and disciplinary trials of clerics, and involvement in contentious cases involving the public good.

In 1880 it was decreed that each diocese must have a *procurator fiscalis* whose duty was to ensure that the judicial process occurs according to the law.[5]

Prior to the codification of the church law in 1917, the office of promoter of justice entailed a variety of functions. He often owed his existence to local customs and legislation and at that time he was at the mercy of the whims of the local ordinary. This lack of uniformity was remedied by the promulgation of the 1917 Code of Canon Law.

This code clearly described the appointment, tenure, and qualifications of the promoter (cc. 1588, 1589, 1613), the causes in which the promoter must intervene (c. 1586), the role of the promoter in criminal proceedings (c. 1934), matrimonial proceedings (cc. 1970, 1971), contentious proceedings (cc. 1734, 1850), and the prosecution of cases that pertain to the common good (cc. 1586, 1934, 1955, 1971). Procedural acts expedited without proper notification of the promoter would be null (c. 1587). In canonization cases, the promoter of justice would be called the promoter of faith (cc. 2010 §2; 2011 §1)

---

3 Lawrence Wrenn, commentary on canons 1430-1436, in *The Code of Canon Law: A Text and Commentary*, ed. James A. Coriden et. al, (New York/Mahwah, NJ: Paulist Press 2000) 1628-1630.

4 Carmelo de Diego-Lora, commentary on c. 1430 in *Exegetical Commentary on the Code of Canon Law*, Volume IV/1, ed. Ernest Caparros (Montréal: Wilson & Lafleur, 2004) 762.

5 S.C. Ep. et Reg., *Instr.* June 11, 1888. *Collectanea S.C. de Prop. Fide*, v. II, n. 1534; *AAS* 13 (1880) 324-336*; Codex Iuris Canonici Fontes* (Rome: Typis Polyglottis Vaticanis, 1923-1932), n. 2005. Also see John Glynn, "The Promotor of Justice," *Canon law studies*, 101 (Washington, DC: The Catholic University of America Press, 1936) 3-14, where he indicates that the title *fiscalis* was used for the promotor at this stage in history because at times the promoter was involved in monetary connected issues for the diocese, such as the collection of all the property, financial, and personal rights pertaining to the public good.

In cases of a professed religious dismissed from a clerical order, the promoter would assume the function of the defender of the religious profession (cc. 655 §2; 1589 §2).

In the period between the promulgation of the codes, there was considerable debate among canonists regarding the public impediments to marriage and the promoter's duty to impugn certain marriages.[6]

In order to clarify further the procedural law on marriage (and hence the duties of the promoter of justice), the Sacred Congregation of the Sacraments in 1936 promulgated the instruction *Provida Mater Ecclesia.* This instruction provided a clear and practical instance of the role of the promoter in marriage cases.

Neither of the two important post-conciliar documents addressing tribunal practice during the period between the two codes, *The American Procedural Norms* and *Causas Matrimoniales*, provided any substantive changes in the law regarding the function of the promoter of justice.[7]

A review of the schema leading to the promulgation of the 1983 Code of Canon Law indicates that there was not an extended discussion of the office of promoter of justice during the revision process.

The intent of the lawmaker in providing for the office of promoter of justice

In summary, this brief history of the office of the promoter of justice indicates that for at least a thousand years, the Christian faithful have found it necessary to employ an officer in their court system who would speak for the public, watch out for the public good, and be mandated with both the right and duty to intervene when gross injustice was being committed in the name of the law.

In a general sense, the history of this office indicates that the legislator has been concerned that true justice be reached in any given case. The promoter has been a safeguard against improper procedural activity as well as a vigilant guardian of the integrity of the ecclesiastical judicial process. As a significant office representing the Christian faithful, the office of promoter of justice has been developed to truly promote justice.

6 Before the code, any Catholic could impugn a marriage that was null by reason of an impediment of a public nature. See Decisio VIII, *coram* Many, June 27, 1916, *S. Romanae Rotae Decisiones Seu Sententiae* (henceforth *SRRDS*) 19 (1916) 202-212; *Acta Apostolicae Sedis* (henceforth *AAS*) IX (1917) 242; *Fontes*, 1076.

7 S.C. Pub. Eccl., *Provisional Norms for Marriage Annulment Cases in the United States*, April 28, 1970, in *Canon Law Digest* 7, 951-966. Also see Blessed Pope Paul VI, Motu proprio *Causas Matrimoniales*, March 28, 1971, *AAS* 63 (1971) 441.

Many of us who practice canon law have probably experienced situations where the letter of the law was applied to a certain matter but at the end of the day, justice was not provided for those needing relief. The office of promoter of justice almost acts as an administrator of equity, to stand above our legal processes to ensure the fair administration of justice.

An overview of the 1983 Code of Canon Law and the office of the promoter of Justice

Canons 1430-1437 outline the main requirements made of a promoter of justice. Every diocese is required to have one who is to be appointed either permanently or on an ad hoc basis (c. 1436 §2). As an official of the Church, the requirements for holding offices (cc. 146-183) are applicable and it should be noted that the promoter must be in communion with the Church (c. 149).

The Code of Canon Law has some specific requirements for those to be appointed promoter of justice. In order to be a candidate for this office, according to canon 1435, one may be a cleric or lay person, must possess an unimpaired reputation, hold a doctorate or licentiate in canon law, and be proven in prudence and zeal for justice.

The code's main purpose in having a promoter of justice is to provide for the "public good" (c. 1430). First, the promoter is to be appointed for all contentious cases in which the public good could be at stake and for all penal cases. Secondly, the promoter is bound by office to provide for the "public good."

What precisely constitutes the "public good"? First, it should be noted that the good mentioned here must be the "public" good. This good is not primarily the private good of an individual. The public good of a community may in some instances involve the private good of an individual or of the community. For instance, a lawsuit between two pastors, while a private matter between the two, becomes a public matter because of the public offices held by them and the resulting scandal that would follow an action. Nevertheless, when the case ceases to be public in nature, the promoter should withdraw from the case.

Secondly, the good mentioned above would be those related to situations that directly address the welfare of the Christian community. The "good" would be those actions and decisions that benefit the faith community as a whole and its relationship with God. It is the duty of the promoter to protect the faithful of the diocese from whatever could become a source of scandal.[8]

Issues that should be addressed in assessing whether the "public good" is at stake in a given case would include the public status of the person(s) involved,

8 Joseph Noval, "De Processibus," in *Commentarium in Codicem Iuris Canonici*, v. IV, (Rome: Augustae Taurinorum, 1920) 569.

notoriety of the event(s), the damage experienced by third persons who are defenseless, and the scandal caused to the faithful.

In view of the different interpretations of what constitutes the "public good," when can it be ascertained that the "public good" is in fact at stake?

First, the "public good" is involved when the bishop decides it is (c. 1431 §1).

Secondly, the "public good" is at stake when the law says that it is. For instance, canon 1696 declares that any marital separation case involves the "public good." Also, the promoter is obliged to intervene in all penal cases (c. 1430). Finally, the public good is at stake in cases that are obviously public, for example, when it is a highly publicized matter involving well-known people.

The promoter is bound to intervene in contentious cases and it is the task of the diocesan bishop to determine if the public good is at stake (c. 1431 §1).

Strictly speaking, the promoter is not a member of the tribunal. The office is exercised in and before the tribunal as a public party.[9]

More germane to our contemporary canonical scene are issues related to penal matters. Canon 1430 states that the promoter of justice is to be involved in all penal cases. Here the promoter acts as the prosecutor of the crime, somewhat analogous to a district attorney in the American legal system. The promoter acts as the petitioner before the tribunal (c. 1721 §2). Because the accusation of a crime pertains to the "public good" (the good of the Christian community is always at stake when an accusation of criminal behavior is made against one of its members), the promoter is bound by office to intervene in all penal cases. Also in such cases the promoter may appeal whenever the reparation of scandal or the restitution of justice has not been sufficiently provided for (c. 1727 §2).

In the development of a penal procedure, the promoter of justice plays a crucial role. Once the ordinary has decreed that a judicial penal process is to begin, he gives the acts of the investigation to the promoter of justice. The promoter of justice then is to present a *libellus* of accusation to the judge (c. 1721 §1). The promoter constituted as such is to act as the petitioner before the tribunal (c. 1721 §2)

In order to protect the community against the disruptive behavior of the accused, at any stage of the penal process, the ordinary can temporarily remove the accused from the sacred ministry or from any ecclesiastical office or function, impose or prohibit residence in a given place or territory, or prohibit public participation in the Eucharist (c. 1722).

9 See de Diego-Lora, commentary on c. 1430, 761-777.

Besides a citation of the accused, it is required that the ordinary must also consult the promoter of justice on this matter. Measures such as the above are prompted by a concern for the integrity of the process, the protection of the freedom of witnesses and the expediting of the course of justice.

The promoter of justice also has the right, in any stage of the trial, to renounce the instance at the order of or with the consent of the ordinary (c. 1724 §1). The pivotal role of the ordinary in the penal process is seen here because the promoter is powerless to act without the consent of the former.

In general, the laws regarding appeals (cc. 1628-1640) apply to penal cases. Canon 1727 §2, however, provides the promoter with a wide discretionary ability to appeal a decision that seems unjust.

The evolution of the office of promoter of justice over the last two decades

In this section, I will briefly outline the role of the promoter in marriage cases and then spend more time on the role of the promoter in penal matters.

Canon 1691 indicates that the "public good" is involved in all marriage nullity cases. However, in light of canon 1431, it is the task of the diocesan bishop to decide if a particular marriage case indeed threatens the public good, or if the nature of the matter itself clearly indicates the necessity of the intervention of the promoter of justice.

It is common knowledge that most tribunals today in the United States deal primarily with marriage nullity cases. The Code of Canon Law presents several options for the promoter of justice in marriage cases.

The promoter of justice is capable of challenging a marriage if the nullity has become public, if the marriage cannot be convalidated or this is not expedient (c. 1674 §2). Clearly, the above-cited reasons for a promoter to act as petitioner would be a rare occurrence under the 1983 code.

In the course of intervening in a marriage case, the promoter has the right to be present at the examination of the parties, the witnesses, and the experts (c. 1678 §1, 1°). Likewise, the promoter may inspect the judicial acts even though not published and has the right to review the documents produced by the parties (c. 1678 §1, 2°).

In marital separation cases, canon 1696 states that cases involving the separation of spouses (cc. 1692-1696) pertain to the "public good." Therefore, the promoter of justice is obliged to intervene in all cases. The cases of separation are normally processed according to the oral contentious process. However, the promoter (or one of the parties) also has the right, in marriage separation cases, to seek an ordinary contentious process (c. 1693 §1). This would enable a slower and more deliberate process to occur should the promoter believe that separation case is being expedited with undue haste.

An issue that has become a problem for some American tribunals is so-called "serial marriages." With more and more Americans embarking not only on their second marriage, but on their third and fourth marriages, tribunals are more often seeing these multiple and successive marriages. Typically these cases involve a non-Catholic who has successively contracted a series of two or more marriages with other non-Catholics and now seeks to marry a Catholic.

In a June 18, 1987 letter from the Supreme Tribunal of the Apostolic Signatura to the Apostolic Pro-Nuncio of the United States, tribunals are enjoined to attack serially the validity of the marriages in question. In those tribunals that use another method of proceeding in declaring the nullity of several marriages, the defender of the bond, or any other person involved in the matter, is now bound to denounce the abuse to the competent promoter of justice. By reason of the "public good" the promoter will be held to attack the decisions respecting the successive marriages, and also a new marriage if it is entered. Thus, here is an example of a situation where the promoter is now bound, by Signatura jurisprudence, to attack the validity of marriage.

Attacking the validity of marriages in such a fashion as instructed by the Signatura could conceivably present a pastoral problem for tribunals, especially if new marriages have been contracted. The process of adjudicating several marriage cases may be very lengthy. Court personnel will need to be guided by pastoral sensitivity and a sense of canonical equity in addressing such issues.

Another issue is whether the promoter of justice may attack the validity of marriages where the official witness failed to make a proper investigation of past marriages, and unknown to at least one of the parties, witnessed the marriage of a couple although one of them had a previous valid union. It is plausible that in order to protect the public good, the promoter, unknown to the ignorant party if such knowledge would cause grave difficulty, may function as the petitioner in this situation. The pastoral considerations noted above seem equally relevant in this context.

In *Dignitas connubii*, promulgated in 1995, the office of promoter of justice is mentioned twenty one times.

Some notable insights into the role of the promoter include article 53, §3, which states "the same person, but not in the same cause, can carry out the office of defender of the Bond and promoter of justice (cf. c. 1436, §1).

Other issues relating to marriage law include his or her appointment, incompatible offices, and removal (art. 53), the failure to cite (art. 60), qualifications (art. 54), the right to act in the case as the equivalent to the petitioner, and incidental cases (art. 223)

Article 57 indicates a special concern for the promoter to safeguard procedural law in marriage cases. Provisions for substitutes are provided in articles 55 and 69.

Article 279 adds that "a party who considers himself aggrieved by a sentence, the defender of the bond and likewise the promoter of justice, if he had taken part in the trial, has a right to appeal from the sentence ... "

The role of the promoter in cases of the sexual abuse of minors.

A lot of water has passed under our canonical bridges since the early 1990's, most obviously with the immense damage done to the Church's reputation in light of the clerical sex abuse scandals. Once whispered to be an American problem, then a problem of the English-speaking world, it is from at least the 1940's to the late 1980's a world-wide epidemic.

Fortunately, for most American dioceses, new accusations of sexual abuse occurring in the near past have become rare. [10]

Nevertheless, our canonical world has been on the front lines of facing these horrendous crimes along with our safe environment directors and associated personnel. The following are some of the highlights on how the office of promoter has evolved.

Already in the early 1990's as the abuse crisis spread throughout the United States, in canonical circles there was much written and talked about what was perceived as the lack of existing law to formally prosecute a priest who had abused a child. Issues such the age of the victim, prescription, etc., made the penal procedure, especially as it related to canon 1395 §2, problematic at best.

At the 1994 CLSA Convention in Atlanta, Msgr. John Alesandro outlined the struggles that bishops and canonists face in cases of dismissal from the clerical

10 See United States Conference of Catholic Bishops, "2013 Annual Report on the Implementation of the Charter for the Protection of Children and Young People," at http://www.usccb.org/issues-and-action/child-and-youth-protection/reports-and-research.cfm (accessed December 16, 2014).

state.[11] Various attempts, up to that point, to make the procedure more usable together with requests for derogations, were rejected largely on the basis of the due process rights of the accused.

In that same year, Pope John Paul II ratified a set of particular laws for the United States (and later extended to Ireland) to make trials more functional [12] which led in part to the 1995 document of the USCCB, *Canonical Delicts Involving Sexual Misconduct and Dismissal from the Clerical State.*

Two other pertinent documents of the Holy See make mention of the promoter but do not make substantive changes in the promoters duties.

Sacramentorum Sanctitatis Tutela, the Apostolic Letter given Motu proprio, promulgated in 2001 (and revised in 2010), states: "In tribunals established by Ordinaries or Hierarchs, for the cases of the more grave delicts reserved to the Congregation for the Doctrine of the Faith, the functions of judge, promoter of justice, notary and legal representative could be validly performed only by priests."

The Norms current in force are articulated in *Delicta Graviora,* the text which was approved by the Pope Benedict XVI on May 21, 2010.

The promoter of justice is mentioned six times in the thirty-one articles and it should be noted that *Delicta Graviora* applies to several delicts besides the sexual abuse of minors. [13]

Article 9, paragraph 2 states that "this Supreme Tribunal also judges other delicts of which a defendant is accused by the Promoter of Justice, by reason of connection of person and complicity."

The prerequisites needed to be appointed as the promoter of justice are outlined as such in Article 11 which reads, "To present and sustain an accusation a Promoter of Justice is to be appointed, who is to be a priest, possessing a doctorate in canon law, outstanding in good morals, prudence, and expertise in the law. He is to carry out his office in all grades of judgment."

11 See John Alesandro, "Dismissal From the Clerical State in Cases of Sexual Misconduct: Recent Derogations" *CLSA Proceedings*, 56 (Washington, DC: Canon Law Society of America, 1994) 28-62. For an excellent overview on how the church removes men from the clerical state for sexual abuse, see John Alesandro, "Removal from the Clerical State for the Sexual Abuse of Minors," *Studia canonica* (47), 2013, 295-339.

12 Secretariat of State, *Rescript* (April 25, 1994), in *Roman Replies and Advisory Opinions, 1994*, ed. Kevin Vann and James Donlon (Washington, DC: Canon Law Society of America, 1994) 20-21.

13 Other delicts include delicts against the faith, e.g., heresy, apostasy and schism, throwing away the Sacred Host, delicts against the sanctity of the sacrament of penance, etc.

These prerequisites are restated in article 14, although article 15 references canon 1421 whereby "the Congregation for the Doctrine of the Faith may dispense from the requirements of the priesthood and of a doctorate in Canon Law."

Article 19 provides for the safety of the community referencing canon 1722 and the provision that to "prevent scandals, protect the freedom of witnesses, and guard the course of justice, the ordinary, after having heard the promoter of justice, and cited the accused, at any stage of the process, can exclude from the sacred ministry," along with provisions forbidding residence and public participation in the Holy Eucharist.

Article 19 goes on to make provision that the promoter may request the presiding judge to exercise the same authority as the ordinary in limiting the public ministry of the accused. This, indeed, is an expansion of the governmental authority not only of the presiding judge but also the promoter of justice in that his request is the linchpin to preventing the accused any exercise of public ministry.

Articles 23 and 26, §2, addresses the role of the promoter in the appellate stage of a process.

Article 23 allows the promoter to bring forward a specifically different accusation whereby allowing the Supreme Tribunal to admit and judge it as if in first instance.

In regards to appealing a sentence, Article 26, §2 reads: "The right of the Promoter of Justice of the Congregation to challenge a sentence runs from the day on which the sentence of first instance is made known to this same Promoter." This provision addresses the real life delays that sometimes hamper our legal systems by interjecting a technicality that could potentially extinguishing the ability of a court to render judgment on the accused.

The *Special Faculties* granted to the Congregation for Clergy in 2009 should also be considered. These faculties pertain to the documents and processes relating to the loss of the clerical state and with dispensation from obligations arising from sacred ordination, including the obligation of celibacy for the clergy who have abandoned their ministry.

The *Special Faculties* require the appointment and intervention of a promoter of justice. A *votum* of the promoter of justice is required, whereby there is a brief description of the situation at hand, and a testament that the norms of law have been observed and that the rights of the priest has been protected. This *votum* is part of the *acta* of the case and the ordinary is compelled to take into consideration the observations of the promoter.

Should the promoter have observations that either the procedural laws have not been followed or the rights of the cleric are not protected, surely the ordinary would want to halt the process and return it to the place where there has been a canonical irregularity.

Starting in 1995, the Archdiocese of Milwaukee, among others, worked with the CLSA on the issue of administrative tribunals. Through a long evolution, eventually what was called an "Archdiocesan Court of Equity" was established and still exists today. [14]

Employing the rarely used oral contentious process, section 4 of the "Norms for the Archdiocesan Court of Equity" provides that in every case, a promoter is appointed by the diocesan bishop and that the promoter possess an "unimpaired reputation, be knowledgeable about the rights and obligations of the Christian faithful, and be proven in prudence and the zeal for justice."[15]

These norms leave maximum flexibility for the ordinary in appointing a promoter for the Court of Equity. The promoter does not need to be a cleric or even have a canon law degree.

Article 6, section 4d, states: "If the promoter of justice is not cited in a case, the acts are valid if, the promoter of justice is in fact present or, prior to the sentence, is afforded opportunity to inspect the acts of the case and to intervene."

Article 7, section 7 also allows for the promoter to question the parties to a case as well as their witnesses as part of the oral contentious process.

Having reviewed some of the major documents that have evolved over the last two decades, what exactly is the role of a promoter in a judicial penal process?

The role of the promoter is outlined in canon 1721: "If the ordinary has decreed that a judicial penal process must be initiated, he is to hand over the acts of the investigation to the promoter of justice who is to present a libellus of accusation to the judge according to the norm of cann. 1502 and 1504." Canons 1502 and 1504 relate primarily to what is necessary for a valid libellus.

Paragraph 2 states: "The promoter of justice appointed to the higher tribunal acts as the petitioner before that tribunal."

---

14 See my presentation to the 2001 Annual Convention in Albuquerque, NM entitled "Canonical Issues in Due Process," found in *CLSA Proceedings* 63 (Washington, DC: Canon Law Society of America, 2001) 37-48

15 See the "Norms for Archdiocesan Court of Equity" in the Archdiocese of Milwaukee available at http://www.archmil.org/Resources/ArchdiocesanCourtofEquity.htm (accessed December 16, 2014).

In general, the promoter's duty to the court is four-fold: to support the allegation if credible; to organize the evidence; to argue the case for an appropriate penalty; and to appeal the case if necessary.

Having received the acts of the preliminary investigation from the ordinary, the promoter reviews the acts to verify that they contain credible factual evidence that a crime has been committed.

In preparing the libellus, the promoter should outline the purpose of the trial and present the evidence that a crime has occurred. The promoter is to present the evidence so that the court can make a final decision with moral certitude.

In courts of second instance, the role of the promoter is basically the same as in the first instance.

To conclude, the title of this presentation may lend itself to a suggestion that the substantive law regarding the promoter of justice has shifted dramatically in recent decades. In reality it has not, as there have been only minor adjustments to the office.

One can view this situation as either a bottle half full or half empty. The lack of specificity regarding the interventions of a promoter of justice allows for flexibility on behalf of the court in seeking justice. Nevertheless, that flexibility could be easily abused by an overly zealous or prejudiced promoter.

Promoters of justice that I have consulted have indicated that the lack of specificity of exactly what the promoter does leaves them at times moving forward into uncharted canonical practices. Again, this can be seen both positively and negatively. Positively in the sense that for law to grow and evolve, someone has to be pushing into uncharted waters. Negatively, at what point does a lack of procedures lead to unethical or sloppy canonical practices?

What is new, and has shifted more attention to the office of the promoter of justice in the canonical world, is that, especially in cases of allegations of the sexual abuse of minors, the office of promoter of justice is crucial, indeed, indispensable.

Since the crisis over the clerical abuse scandals are most certainly the largest canonical time bomb of our lifetimes, the key position of the promoter of justice is not as I began, a topic both "narrow" or of little interest to anyone. To understand this is to understand the immensely helpful role of Monsignor, and now Bishop, Charles Scicluna as the promoter of justice for the Congregation for the Doctrine of the Faith.

As the promoter of Justice for the C.D.F, then Msgr. Scicluna put a human and credible face on the sincere efforts of the church to punish those who have abused children as well to make reparations for the sins of the past

Since trials concerning these crimes were seldom held prior to the 1990's, those who studied canon law prior to the 1990's often have a steep learning curve, as in my own experience, the office of promoter of justice was rarely addressed when I was a student of canon law. Few foresaw the wave after wave of abuse cases looming in the near future.

As noted in the beginning of this text, canon law provides for an office with enough flexibility to effectively carry out the successful prosecution of those clerics guilty of the sexual abuse of minors. It is the role of the promoter to seek true justice in each case and to a certain extent, to be the conscience for the other canonical officers in these matters.

Seminar

Building from the Ground Up: Creating the Personal Ordinariate of the Chair of Saint Peter

Margaret Chalmers, JD, JCD, PhD

Yesterday morning, Bishop Vann gave his perspective on how the Personal Ordinariates, and the Personal Ordinariate of the Chair of St. Peter in particular, came into being. My presentation is going to be complementary with his, but from my own perspectives. The first is as a canonist tasked with helping to create the actual canonical structure of the Ordinariate, and the second is as someone who is married to a former Anglican priest who is now a priest of the Ordinariate. There is the old adage about how one shouldn't watch either laws or sausages being made. This presentation is going to be a blatant violation of that adage.

As a pastoral response to groups of Anglicans who for many years had been requesting some sort of corporate reunion with the Catholic Church, on November 4, 2009, Pope Benedict XVI promulgated the Apostolic Constitution, *Anglicanorum Coetibus*. The Constitution established a new canonical structure to permit groups of Anglicans to be received corporately into the Catholic Church while retaining elements of their distinctive spiritual and liturgical patrimony. It was an incredibly generous gesture by Pope Benedict, and an unusual one as well. Instead of entrusting this new endeavor to the Pontifical Council for Christian Unity, it was the Congregation for the Doctrine of the Faith who was entrusted with overseeing the creation and implementation of this new entity in the Church. This unusual path to Christian unity was a harbinger that this was going to be a different kind of entity.

I personally knew we would be charting new territory when, in the first few months of the Ordinariate, we canon law types were having a serious discussion about whether our Ordinary could exercise legislative power because canon 391, the one giving the Ordinary executive, legislative, and judicial power, was left out of the list of the Ordinary's powers. We knew he could exercise executive power and, since they told us we could have a tribunal, we presumed that he had judicial power. But we were not sure if he could legislate, which would have been problematic since we were about to promulgate an entire ministry manual's worth of particular law. But after having gotten the unofficial answer of "of course he can legislate, we only left that canon out so you wouldn't feel pressured to have a tribunal," and then when we pushed for a more definitive answer, what came back was: " It may be presumed, therefore, that he has the same powers and prerogatives as a territorial/diocesan Ordinary. The canons cited in the Complementary Norms are meant to be indicative, not prescriptive." And then they added this: " … there is perhaps a bit of disconnect between an American vs. Italian style to canonical interpretation … when I read our consulter the passage in your email (referring to the fact that there is nothing canonically which gives the Ordinary the power to legislate particular law), there was a slightly confused pause followed by this response: 'But the point is that there is nothing which prohibits it'." As the mother of two little boys, I knew very well we were in trouble because there is a lot of mischief you can get into under the rubric of "but mom, you didn't tell us we couldn't!"

Another official indication that we were in new territory was that there was much discussion swirling around about whether the Ordinariate could have vicars, since the power exercised by our Ordinary was clearly described as being vicarious. The Ordinariate in England originally did not have vicars for this reason. For us in North America, not having a Vicar General or Episcopal Vicars would be a serious problem, given that our territory is so big that we had to anticipate that our Ordinary would frequently be out of contact on planes where we might not be able to reach him for hours. Cardinal Wuerl was kind enough to solve that problem for us by simply giving us a Vicar General. We weren't about to go arguing with Cardinal Wuerl over this, and very soon after we were once again informed by CDF that yes, we of course could and should have vicars, regardless of what our founding text said or didn't say.

So I have decided that the Ordinariate is very much like a duck-billed platypus, which is, as we know, a mammal that lays eggs. You can tell the platypus repeatedly that she is a mammal and shouldn't be able to lay eggs, but in the end, we have a mammal who lays eggs. In a similar fashion, there have been a number of questions raised about the nature and powers of the Ordinariate, pointing out that there are elements of it that are both unexpected and canonically odd. I can only agree with that statement, but as God made the platypus, CDF created us, and we are good in their sight.

Initial Considerations

It is not often that a canonist gets the opportunity to help build something new in the Church. In the case of the Ordinariate, that is exactly what we have had the chance to do. It has been, and continues to be, a challenge – one where I don't have the answers to the questions that I and others have raised and continue to raise. The answers are evolving as the Ordinariate evolves.

It should also be noted that the concrete planning for the structures of the Ordinariate began just six weeks before it was officially created. So from the beginning, the creation and evolution of the North American Ordinariate has been happening on the fly – much like building a moving go-cart where all you have are attached wheels, an awkward place to sit, and you are looking for a place to attach a steering wheel. From day one of its creation we had Anglican communities like the ones Bishop Vann mentioned in Fort Worth and their individual members who had already been received into the Latin Church that needed to change jurisdiction; we had Anglican communities clamoring to be received; we had hundreds of applications for ordination; applicants that needed processing, forming, and winnowing, and only a handful of people tasked with making this happen. And on top of that, we had to set up some sort of functional administration to handle it all.

I want to refer you to an article written by Fr. Kristen Paver, the Chancellor for the Personal Ordinariate of Our Lady of Walsingham. At the last CLSGBI meeting he gave a comprehensive overview of the canonical questions and issues that arose out of *Anglicanorum Coetibus* and the working answers the Ordinariates have developed to those questions. His presentation is what I call the academic presentation of the questions raised by our founding documents. So instead of rehashing his work, this presentation is going to focus on the practical, day-to-day, and often surprising canonical challenges that we faced, how they were dealt with, and the further questions that these challenges have produced. *Anglicanorum Coetibus* was a blueprint for building the Ordinariates, but that's really all it was. CDF has left the actual building out of these structures up to the Ordinariates themselves, and it has been quite an adventure.

I do not generally quote the onetime Secretary of Defense, Donald Rumsfeld. However, in this case Secretary Rumsfeld made a statement that is apropos to the creation of this new jurisdiction. He stated that in pursuing any endeavor, knowledge can be classified according to three distinct 'types.' There are the 'known knowns,' the 'known unknowns,' and the 'unknown unknowns.'

The 'known knowns' refer to those distinctive elements of the situation that we know about or those things that have been defined for us. The 'known unknowns' refer to those elements of the situation where we know what we don't know and can work to come up with answers. And then there are the most frustrating, the most confusing, the most time-consuming elements, and, potentially for this audience, the most entertaining, the 'unknown unknowns.' These are not just those things that we anticipate we don't know, but the entirely new and unexpected issues that one could never have anticipated that need solutions.

With the creation of the Ordinariate, there were very few 'known knowns' starting out. Much of the creation of the Ordinariate has been in the realm of 'known unknowns' – things we knew we were going to have to figure out as we go along. And then there are the 'unknown unknowns.' These have tended to crop up frequently and when we least expect them. Even more frustrating is that they often appear when you think that the answer is something that you actually know.

For example, what are these Personal Ordinariates for Anglicans? We are told that they are new structures in the Catholic Church created by Pope Emeritus Benedict that are meant to be a home for former Anglicans who want to be Catholic but who want to retain parts of their unique ecclesiastical identity. The three Ordinariates are currently in England and Wales, Australia and the Torres Straits, and North America which encompasses both the United States and Canada.

As stated, the Ordinariates are meant to be a home for former Anglicans and, at first glance, this may seem reasonably straightforward: a 'known known.' In reality what we found is that this question isn't even close to being straightforward, starting with the most basic question of "Who counts as being Anglican?" Obviously there are those national Anglican churches that are in communion with the Archbishop of Canterbury. Those clearly count as Anglican – including the Episcopalians in the United States and the Anglican Church in Canada. However, the Anglican churches have been fragmenting over the course of the last fifty years over various issues, the most well-known being women's ordination, and issues regarding sexual morality and marriage.

Unlike both the English and Australian Ordinariates, this is particularly complicated here in the United States where we have a veritable alphabet soup of groups who claim to be Anglican: the Episcopalians, the Anglican Catholic Church (ACC), Anglican Church in North America (ACNA), the Anglican Church in America (ACA), the Charismatic Episcopal Church, and some individual Episcopalian dioceses that have broken off and are going it alone. There is even an Anglican Orthodox Church – a branch of western Orthodoxy that uses the Anglican 1928 Book of Common Prayer. Then there is the African-American Methodist Episcopal Church, the African Methodist Episcopal Church, and all other flavors of Methodists, who are a long-ago break-off of the Episcopalians. So determining who was eligible for membership in the Ordinariate was not a straightforward question, and one that required clarification from the Congregation of the Doctrine of the Faith.

As an interesting and unusual canonical side note, when questions about our creation and founding documents have arisen, they continue to be answered directly by CDF, and not by other dicasteries that would usually answer such questions. We must assume that these answers are authoritative clarifications for us, despite the unusual source.

The basic answer we have been given to the question "Who is Anglican?" is that if you claim to be Anglican and your church is a direct branch of Anglicanism, you are Anglican for the purposes of membership. In addition, a baptised Catholic who has not completed the Sacraments of Initiation, and subsequently returns to the Church through the Ordinariate, may also be a member and receive the Sacrament of Confirmation or the Sacrament of the Eucharist or both (Complementary Norms, art. 5§2).

This brings me to membership and its surrounding issues. Though personal parishes can register members if they qualify for membership in that particular parish, there are few examples of how one implements a registered membership on a broader diocesan level. Religious orders clearly have members and their own jurisdiction, but that is not a diocesan model and it does not include lay people. Opus Dei incardinates priests, but their lay members are members of their local diocese, not of Opus Dei. And members of churches are generally members by birth or marriage, not by registration. So creating a *sui iuris* model for a diocesan-wide membership registry was an innovation in the Church.

There were many questions raised when *Anglicanorum Coetibus* was issued about whether a person who is a member of the Ordinariate is also a member of their territorial diocese. This was not clear from *AC*, and canonists disagreed on the answer. Article 10 of the Decrees of Erection states that "if a member notifies the Ordinary in writing that no longer wants to be a member of the Ordinariate, the person automatically becomes a member of the Diocese in which he is domiciled." If the person who belonged to the Ordinariate "automatically becomes a member of the diocese," then it logically follows that he did not belong to the diocese as a member of the Ordinariate. Therefore, one can argue that the document did not create a "dual" jurisdiction. However, there were certainly well-reasoned arguments put forth to support the notion of dual jurisdiction.

The problem with this argument is that at some point one has to make a practical choice whose arguments to adopt because you actually have to start making day-to-day decisions based on that choice. What it came down to was that allowing people to have dual jurisdictions is an administrative nightmare: Who is responsible for registering and maintaining sacramental records? Since a decision had to be made, it was made in favor of exercising exclusive jurisdiction.

However, that notion of registration = jurisdiction = Ordinariate membership is a very different model. It also raised the question, "Who keeps the records of membership? The Ordinariate parish or the Ordinariate chancery?" *Anglicanorum Coetibus* is not clear on this point. Ultimately, we created an Ordinariate database to track our members, but trying to keep it current with people joining, people leaving or dying, and registering the baptisms and reception of new members, is quite a challenge.

So how does one become a member? To be a member of the Ordinariate, one has to be eligible and one has to indicate in writing that one desires membership. Given that c. 111 gives minors who have completed their fourteenth year the right to freely choose baptism in the Latin or other ritual Church, by extension if follows that if the person is fourteen or over, that person must indicate in writing their own desire to enter the Ordinariate or to remain in the Latin Church. From our standpoint this is necessary but very difficult for administrative purposes because parents typically register their entire family, including their adolescents. Furthermore, once we developed standard applications we had to make sure that both spouses signed the form, because often one spouse filled out the form for the entire family. On day one of the Ordinariate's creation we already had stacks of letters indicating a desire for membership. But oftentimes the letter was signed by one member of the family, or at best the two parents. We have had to go back and actively track down the names and ages of all of the children, and then get signatures from all of the family members fourteen and older. This project by itself took up an incredible amount of time.

The question also arose regarding what to do about a person who is not proximate to an established Ordinariate community yet who wants to join the Ordinariate. Interestingly, there is nothing in *AC* or the complementary norms that allows us to refuse membership to someone who is eligible to join. So as soon as we receive their letter and they are put in our system, they change jurisdictions and become a member of the Ordinariate. However, practically speaking, because their nearest Ordinariate community may be six hundred miles away, they are treated like an Eastern Catholic without a ritual parish close by and are cared for by their local Latin diocese. In this same way, our members, or soon-to-be-members, are using the tribunal of the local Latin diocese until the Ordinariate has its own tribunal.

Finally, we have run into an interesting problem, an 'unknown unknown,' that was absolutely unanticipated regarding Ordinariate membership and that is unique to North America. Since the turn of the century, there has been a close relationship between the Episcopal Church and the Orthodox Church, though that relationship has recently cooled. When Orthodox families immigrated to the United States at the turn of the last century, many were told that if they could not find an Orthodox church to attend, to attend the Episcopal Church because 1) the Orthodox did not want their members becoming Catholic, and 2) the Anglicans and the Orthodox have a similar polity. So we now have a number of second and third generation Anglicans whose surnames would clearly indicate their Eastern descent.

In addition, we have a number of Anglicans married to Orthodox. Over the past thirty years or so, we've had a number of Anglicans grow dissatisfied with their Anglican churches, and decide to join an Orthodox Church, sometimes a Western branch of Orthodoxy. Because of the inherent cultural differences, after a few years, many of them choose to return to some form of Anglicanism after having been baptized and/or chrismated Orthodox. With all of the splits within Orthodoxy, we have had to determine who was considered to be Orthodox, on top of who was considered to be Anglican! This required specific rulings from

CDF regarding these circumstances, which again is an unusual canonical source for such decisions. However, CDF has determined that if the person was ever Anglican they are eligible for the Ordinariate; however, if they have been chrismated Orthodox then they are treated like Orthodox regarding being able to have access to our sacraments prior to their formal reception.

Besides having different membership issues, there are different challenges within the three Ordinariates arising from the differences in the local or national Anglican liturgical practices. You heard Bishop Vann mention liturgy as being part of the Anglican Patrimony. While most Ordinariate members would likely agree with that statement, there would likely not be common agreement on what that liturgy should look or sound like.

One might think that this would be a 'known known' because Anglicans use the *Book of Common Prayer* (known as the *BCP*). Well, yes, sort of. There are many *BCP*'s – some written specifically with local variations for a particular country, others were updated versions of the original. So there are the 1549 and 1552 versions, 1604, the 1662, the 1928, and for the United States the 1979 version, which allowed for two liturgies: Rite one with traditional language (think of "plighting one's troth") and Rite two with modern language.

Though the Anglican Church in England uses the 1662 *Book of Common Prayer* (my understanding is that the English Parliament has to approve any changes to their *BCP*, and they haven't been able to agree on a change), most of the English Anglo-Catholic priests (Anglican priests with Catholic sympathies and sensibilities) were actually using the Catholic *Novus Ordo* liturgy for their expression of catholicity. However, since this was largely unregulated, there was room for ample creativity. The English Anglicans also used an English translation of the Extraordinary Form, called The English Missal. Ironically, this means that the Anglicans in the United States and Canada have a stronger emotional tie to the language of the *Book of Common Prayer* than the English Ordinariate does.

Here in the United States, it is even more varied. Most Episcopalian churches use some form of the 1979 *BCP* that contains both a modern and traditional liturgy, though there is nothing preventing them from using the older forms, or getting creative with the rites within the *BCP*. Many of the break-away Anglican groups used the 1928 prayerbook, and some communities even used the ancient Sarum rite. Some Episcopal churches liked to experiment with using the *BCP* from other countries. And in Canada, the groups interested in the Ordinariate were using the 1962 Canadian *BCP*, with no one using its more contemporary version.

So the North American Ordinariate faces a challenge that the other Ordinariates do not have. We are not only trying to move our clergy and people from being Anglicans to being Catholics, and not only are we bringing Anglicans who are from different branches of Anglicanism into communion with each other, but we are bringing into communion Anglicans with different liturgical sensibilities into a single jurisdiction with a common liturgy. And as we know from our own experience, it is difficult to get the "maniple crowd" and the "praise music crowd" to mix. There has been a traditional Mass and other liturgical rites approved specifically for Ordinariate use, but they use language out of the older prayer book that some in the Ordinariates are uncomfortable with. Given these challenges, it may be some time before the liturgical tensions get worked out.

Another challenge for us and for the Australian Ordinariate is that we are geographically spread out over thousands of miles, and in our case, two countries. This is further complicated for us because it is quicker to get from our parishes in Baltimore to London than it is to get from our parish in Vancouver to our parish in Miami. This poses a challenge to building a community when your nearest Ordinariate parish may be a few states or provinces away. It makes collegiality, unity, and uniformity difficult in groups that are already arriving from different ecclesiastical practices and sensibilities.

One last challenge I'd like to mention: we have a presbyterate made up exclusively of former Anglican clergy. The Anglican Church on the exterior looks very much like the Catholic Church. For example, they have bishops, priests, and deacons, they incardinate and excardinate their clergy, they have sacraments, they have similar vestments, they have something that looks like a pastoral council, etc. However, though we often use the same words for many things, the underlying concepts and the theology of those words can be vastly different.

This became clear to me personally after I married an Episcopalian and we spent the first five years of our marriage defining terms and asking the question, "So what do you mean by that?" We found that not asking that question resulted in some rather profound misunderstandings. One of the challenges at the outset has been trying to educate our new clergy that just because you know the word, does not mean that you know what that word means in a Catholic context.

This profound difference in the way we do things really came home when we had a very well-meaning community who was worried about the financial well-being of their priest. So their newly minted parish council had their parish lawyer draft a very generous employment and retirement contract to offer their priest to make sure that he was given generous terms and a substantial retirement package. It was a very lovely and caring gesture and, as we all know, an absolute violation of canon law. The more you think it through, the worse it gets. And then we had to explain to these very well-meaning people why a parish council can't offer either an employment contract or a retirement package to their priest.

What is an Ordinariate?

So now that we've discussed the challenges of membership, liturgy, distance and terminology, we get to the question, What exactly is the Ordinariate? What is it that is being built? This is certainly a 'known unknown.' I have found that I must use analogies, and think in analogies, because there is no comparable entity within the Church. So in an attempt to define the canonical identity of the Ordinariate: it is like taking one part *sui iuris* church, one part diocese, one part religious order, one part military Ordinariate, put in a jar and shake. The Ordinariate has bits of all of these entities – but is not exactly like any of them.

Jurisdictionally and functionally, we are like both a diocese and a *sui iuris* Church. As my English counterpart of the Personal Ordinariate of our Lady of Walsingham puts it:

> In the English translation the Apostolic Constitution states that these Ordinariates are 'juridically comparable to a diocese' and refers in a footnote to the same expression used in the Apostolic Constitution, *Spirituali militum curae*, which introduced the structure of the Military Ordinariate after the promulgation of the 1983 code. This would seem, therefore, to propose some sort of equivalence between these two types of personal jurisdictions.
>
> However, the Latin texts of both documents show that the original verbs used are not the same. In the case of Personal Ordinariates, these are juridically '*aequantur*' to a diocese, whereas Military Ordinariates are juridically '*assimilantur*' to a diocese.[1] The first verb would seem to be stronger than the second: 'to be equal to' sometimes would appear to be a greater identity than 'to be similar/like' something. Thus, the Latin text of the Constitution would seem to suggest that there is an equality between a diocese and a Personal Ordinariate.[2]

Like a diocesan bishop, our Ordinary belongs to both the United States Conference of Catholic Bishops (USCCB) and the Canadian Conference of Catholic Bishops (CCCB). We are like a diocese in that we have exclusive jurisdiction over our people. Our curia is set up like a diocese or eparchy. Our territory covers all of the territory of the United States and Canada. Our priests are incardinated into the Ordinariate. If they also have faculties from, and function within, the

1 A look at Ochoa. X. *Index Verborum ac Locutionum Codicis Iuris Canonici*, Città del Vaticano, 1984, shows that this verb is not used anywhere in the 1983 code, so it is not possible to look in comparable places for clarity of meaning. See K. Paver, *The Ordinariates, the Church, and Canon Law*, unpublished, 2014, p. 2.

2 Ibid.

local diocese they are like an Eastern priest whose parish's territory overlaps the geographical boundaries of the local diocese. They may be helping out in the local Latin diocese, but they reside within their own territory. Ordinariate priests are not like religious priests who can be asked to leave a diocese, in that an Ordinariate priest is always in his own territory if he resides anywhere in the United States or Canada. Like a church *sui iuris*, while we have jurisdiction over our people, there are times when we must entrust our people into the care of the local diocese if they are not near one of our parishes.

The Ordinariate also has some elements in common with religious orders. Since we have a married Ordinary who currently is not a bishop, our Ordinary functions somewhat like a mitered abbot. If the Ordinary is a former Anglican bishop, he can be given permission to wear "the insignia of the Episcopal office" like a mitered abbot is permitted to do. Like religious priests, Ordinariate priests can be assigned to a local Latin diocese and care for a local parish. Our priests are also able to work outside of a parish in what might be considered a secular job – much like many religious priests do when they work in universities, hospitals, or other apostolates.

We are also like the Military Ordinariate both in that we are a structure equal to a diocese, and one must belong to a particular class of people, a class not based on ethnicity, to be a member. Since we do not yet have a tribunal we must send nullity cases to the local diocesan tribunal, much like the Military Ordinariate often has local tribunals handle cases that they would also have jurisdiction to adjudicate. Also, our priests can be made members of their local diocesan presbyteral council, and are encouraged to become a part of the life of the Latin diocese in which his parish is located so that he can have some form of local priestly community and collegiality.

After determining what a Personal Ordinariate is (or is like), we then had to determine how to build it. The instruction that it was "comparable to a diocese" helped greatly because we knew that if a diocese could do something, we were expected to do it too. However, we were starting from scratch, and we were and continue to be in governmental terms, an "unfunded mandate." At the beginning we had no resources, no money, an Ordinary, a borrowed Vicar General, and a volunteer chancellor. We were soon joined by a very experienced volunteer civil lawyer, Mark Chopko. After our first round of ordinations, we were able to add a vicar for clergy and, after a second round of ordinations, we added a vicar for finance. After the Canadians joined us as a deanery, we then added the Canadian Dean. Our Ordinary was in Houston, our vicar general was in Washington D.C., the Chancellor was in Greenville, SC, and our Vicar for Clergy was in Fort Worth, TX. This made curial meetings a bit of a challenge!

So what must be first? That question quickly became a two-parter: 1) How do you set up a functional juridical structure, and 2) How do you bring in and form communities, and form and ordain former Anglican clergy into it?

We are still slowly trying to set up a functional juridical structure. One challenge we faced is that when the Ordinariate came into creation on January 1, 2012, we already had a stack of letters requesting membership in accord with *Anglicanorum Coetibus*, and we had a stack of clergy- petitions-for-ordination files in process. Unlike when a diocese splits and one is dividing resources, we started off with the need to create a diocese from scratch, with one tiny office located in a seminary, a chancery in three states and four cities, and only one person who had experience with Catholic governance. Questions immediately arose, like, how does one start issuing decrees when one does not yet have a canonical notary appointed to notarize them? Where does one create the myriad decrees, permissions, rescripts, dimissorial letters, and other canonical documents that one needs to make a chancery function?

The fact that resources were so scarce necessitated a form of ecclesiastical triage, in that while we may have had a roomful of very serious issues that needed immediate attention, with our limited resources, we could only deal with the most serious ones. It was very frustrating in that we could see these issues out there, but we truly did not, and still do not, have the time, resources, or manpower to deal with them. For example, we did not have the compiled information, time, money, or manpower to send letters acknowledging a person's membership in the Ordinariate until our second year. Thank goodness for not being bound to the impossible – a mantra I frequently repeat.

One of the first big projects we were able to complete was a ministry manual that created policies and particular law for everything we could think of. And I want to thank you, colleagues, and particularly those of you who post your policy manuals online, and to you who responded generously to my pleas for help. It is likely that parts of our policy manual would look familiar to you.

Creating a policy manual to act as particular law was critical, given that many of our priests and their communities have come from ecclesial jurisdictions that have been in turmoil with no consistency or regulation. Additionally, we have far-flung communities and no way to monitor them. It was our goal to create clear guidelines, to make clear rules, to have defined expectations, to follow them, and to apply them consistently. This was one way we could bind all of our people and all of our communities to the same rules and reduce the chance that we would be seen as playing favorites among our communities. Given that we are building something new, we thought that having defined norms was like the steel structure that supports a building – we could build all the beautiful elements around it, but it provided the general shape and structure, and gave strength and stability to the edifice it supports. Without that support, the whole building can easily collapse. So the Ordinariate has attempted to create a safe and reasonably predictable ecclesiastical home for our clergy and their neophyte communities. Furthermore, since most of our clergy was accustomed to having significant liturgical and administrative freedom in their Anglican jurisdictions, it was also a means to try to keep the clerical creativity somewhat in check.

We are also wrestling with how we should set up our parishes, given the profound scale of difference between Catholic and Anglican churches. Most of our communities are exceedingly small by Catholic standards. In the United States, an average Episcopal parish has between sixty-six and ninety-four people – not families – individuals. Many groups coming into the Ordinariate have under fifty people in them, and some are considerably smaller. Some come in bringing property with them, but many did not. Some groups have no children in them, or are so small that their viability is questionable. We have chosen at this point to create quasi-parishes with administrators for the larger groups who have property, and to have either public associations, or some other small non-juridic grouping with administrators for the small ones. This is to make sure that our groups are stable and viable before we create something permanent that would take a lot of effort to eliminate should they fail. We are just now assessing our larger groups with an eye to establishing them as parishes. We made our priests administrators rather than pastors, because many of the men being ordained were not known to our Ordinary. While we had paper files on them, files do not always convey the full picture of the priest. We decided that we'd move slowly so that personnel problems could be identified and dealt with before we made any more permanent assignments.

At the same time we were putting together the basic structures for a chancery and parishes, we were also in the middle of bringing in, forming, and ordaining former Anglican clergy, most of whom were married. This brought up all kinds of questions: How do you create a collegial presbyterate out of men who were not all in communion to start with? Who live in an area from Vancouver to Miami, from San Diego to New Brunswick? Coming from years of difficult relationships with their former bishops and dioceses? How do you take these men (and their communities) and make them Catholic?

Formation for our priests has been a huge challenge, and we have had to rely on local dioceses to help us with the formation of our new communities. Our communities are spread out all over North America, and they have little money and few resources. Clergy formation has had to occur by electronic means. It is certainly not the ideal method of formation, and it is dreadful for building community and collegiality among our clergy, yet there was no other viable way to do it. As with so many things in the Ordinariate, what is practical and possible has had to suffice because there simply was no other way.

We are also confronted with a challenge that is both ancient and new to the Latin Church: How do we deal with the reality of married clergy? Having a married clergy presents all sort of interesting issues – some predictable and obvious, some not. These differences were underscored when Cardinal Müller from CDF came to visit Houston last year, and we had to have two drivers at the ready for him. This was because the primary driver was a young priest whose wife was expecting the imminent delivery of their third child and he needed to be able to get to a hospital quickly if she went into labor. That same priest and his family made quite a stir during the Ordinariate visit to Rome. You should have seen the faces in the crowd watching the priest in his cassock walking around with the baby-carrier on his back and his toddler daughter inside! There were more pictures taken of him and Caroline than of the group of Cardinals walking by.

But a married clergy raises a number of issues, some obvious, some not so obvious.

The first issues that people think of are financial: how to support a family on a priest's stipend. Depending on the diocese, we have found that it is actually less of an issue than it might seem to be, given that many dioceses provide considerable indirect compensation to their priests. People also think about what might happen if the priest's marriage is in trouble. But these are the obvious issues.

But there are less obvious issues that are no less important. One issue that ought to come to mind for canonists has to do with the implementation of the Charter and norms. Under almost all current diocesan policies, priests who are fathers or grandfathers would be barred from driving carpool, going on family campouts, changing diapers, babysitting their kids – particularly if the kids have friends over – or picking up their fifteen year old daughter and her friends who are stranded at the mall or movie theater. We had to very carefully craft a policy that holds "Father" to a certain standard when he is acting in a ministerial capacity, but allows "Dad" to be husband and father when he is clearly acting as a parent. It is a very delicate balance that requires us to caution our priests to use a high level of prudence in whatever role they happen to be playing. To maintain the restrictions placed on celibate priests is simply untenable in a family setting, and likely would cause significant problems within a priest's marriage.

Another question: how do you craft transfer policies for married clergy? Many of our priests have outside jobs in addition to taking care of a small community. Their wives also have jobs. Many of our priests own their own homes. Under what circumstances can a married priest be assigned to another parish? If the parish is halfway across the country, who pays for the moving expenses, particularly since the Ordinariate is itself practicing evangelical poverty? Yet, because the overwhelming majority of our priests were ordained for a particular community, we have few "spare" priests able to pick up the slack if we have a parish vacancy. We have not yet worked out how these issues will be resolved.

Another issue has to do with priests' wives. In both the Eastern Catholic Churches and the Orthodox Churches, the *Matushka*, or *Presbytera*, or *Khouria*, has a recognized theology, title, and role that obviously the Latin Church has not had for over a millennium. And while the Anglican church had particular roles that clergy wives were expected to play, that has been changing over the last thirty years or so. Believe me when I tell you, most Catholics have no idea what to do with the concept of a priest's wife! How does that troublesome Bible verse about "the two becoming one" (Mk. 10:8) play out in this context? The Orthodox have some very interesting thoughts on this. But this raises some interesting issues. Since our clergy-candidates are all converts, must their wives also be Catholic? Like diaconal candidates, must the wife consent for the husband to be ordained? Our answer to that, by the way, is yes. How much control can the Ordinariate exercise over the priest's wife's employment? Can she be politically active or run for political office? Is there such a thing as "fitting employment" for a priest's wife? What if she takes a job that may not be in keeping with a Catholic understanding of "fitting employment?" We don't know. In August of this year, the Diocese of Charleston had what may be the first-in-a-millennium funeral celebrated by a Latin bishop for the wife of the first Latin married priest in the United States. What sort of liturgical dignity, if any, is given for the wife of a priest? Practically speaking, which way does the body face? These are questions that are still being worked out.

And then there are the "PK's," a moniker given to "priest's kids." Kids also raise some issues. Should the kids be expected to go to Catholic school if there is one nearby? Should Catholic schools or parishes subsidize or comp tuition if the priest can't afford the school? What does it say to the Catholic community if the priest and his wife choose to send their children to public school or they choose to home school?

And speaking of scarce resources, the Ordinariate is in the unfortunate circumstance where we do not have the resources to take care of a priest if something happens to him. We required any clerical applicant to demonstrate that he is financially secure, although that has not been fool-proof. Our priests are specifically authorized by *AC* to hold secular jobs to help them support themselves and their families. But if something happens, and a priest is somehow unable to work, we have a real problem. Since the door is open for priests to have other employment, this also opens the door to what is "fitting" employment for a Catholic priest. Can we require him to support himself doing some sort of secular work if we do not have a place to put him and do not have the resources to support him? Must secular work take place in fields such as academics that are within the greater Catholic ambit, or could a priest do something like sell insurance or be a banker?

The financial viability of the Ordinariate is an ongoing concern. Our communities are tiny, and though we have a tax on our communities, the paucity of the return mirrors the tininess of the community. It is the embodiment of the maxim: "You can't squeeze blood out of a turnip." As a result, we have had to rely on the generosity of the greater Catholic Church to help us, though we hope that as our communities grow this will increasingly be less of an issue. But it makes the competent administration of the Ordinariate a serious issue if resources do not exist to cover all of the needed personnel and functions.

Finally, I want to talk about "weirdness." Part of our job as canonists is to keep the "weirdness" at bay. That has been a significant challenge, and is certainly well within the category of 'unknown unknowns.'

I don't know how much canonists pay attention to what is happening in the Episcopal Church and the wider Anglican communion, but there is considerable weirdness going on there. They have dioceses seceding; they have new Anglican jurisdictions being formed, folding, and reforming. There are Anglicans refusing the oversight of their bishops. Liturgically, all manner of unregulated liturgies are being done: they do "U2charists." They have new and interesting religious, ecumenical, interfaith "religious communities," and hermitages being formed, with very little regulation or oversight. There is plenty of nasty litigation over property and assets. It is a bit of a free-for-all. This is the ecclesiastical milieu from which our communities emerged. Many of the folks approaching us are not used to having a specific way of doing things, much less used to "the Catholic way of doing things." So they don't understand why we balk when they want to bring with them such things as "religious ecumenical communities" of habited married women.

We constantly have to explain to our people that part of being Catholic means that we actually have rules for the way that we do things, and that these rules generally are in place for a good reason. We are doing our level best to keep their ecclesiastical insanity on their side of the Tiber. While we value the Anglican Patrimony, that part of the patrimony we don't want, and we are actively trying to avoid having it imported into out context.

The other aspect of weirdness is having to keep the unhealthy folks from within the Catholic Church from taking advantage of our youth and inexperience. For example, we were surprised to learn that one of our parishes had been in conversation with a Catholic group that had some difficulty finding an ecclesiastical home. To circumvent their difficulties with the local diocese, they wanted to lease some of our parish property to put a boy's boarding school on it without bothering to consult or even inform the broader Ordinariate leadership. Just what a brand-new Catholic jurisdiction who had just gotten their insurance needs: a Catholic boy's boarding school! We very quickly had to shut that deal down and explain that, in fact, they could not circumvent our leadership and take advantage of our parish's inexperience.

The Ordinariate is doing its best to move forward and forge its own independent identity. To do this we must always go back to the Holy Father's direction regarding what our mission and what our charism is to be. Our first question to ask must always and necessarily be, "Is this decision, or activity, or outreach, in keeping with our patrimony and tradition?" The second question we must ask is, "Is what is being done or requested distinctly a part of our patrimony tradition or not?" The decision that something is not of our patrimony is in no way a commentary on whether it is worthy, or useful, or spiritually beneficial. It simply means that it is not something that promotes the distinct mission and charism of the Ordinariate.

Since our creation, we have worked hard in fleshing out Pope Benedict's vision – a concrete step towards reconciliation and Christian unity within the Catholic church. It has been both terrifying and challenging. We are continuing to enflesh that vision in such a way that the Ordinariates add their own distinctive patrimony to the life of the Church. And while we still have a way to go, we are profoundly grateful for this opportunity that Pope Benedict has given us.

To all of my colleagues who have been dealing with us over the last three years, I want to thank you for your patience, understanding and assistance. Please understand that we in the Ordinariate are all still learning and figuring this out. We have only been at this for three short years: We are mere babes in church-time. So please be patient with us; we are maturing as fast as we can. And most of all, please keep us in your prayers. Thank you.

SEMINAR

EXECUTIVE OFFICES OF GOVERNANCE IN THE PARTICULAR CHURCH

Rev. James J. Conn, S.J.[1]*, JD, JCD*

Introduction

The topic of this presentation arose from a conversation at a CLSA Board of Governors meeting about the variety of organizational structures currently in place in diocesan curias in the English-speaking world, and especially in the territory of the United States Conference of Catholic Bishops. Participants in the conversation observed how various management models have been adopted which address the many areas of service and supervision that either the law of the Church or the demands of effective pastoral ministry require of particular churches of different sizes, history and complexity. Some of these areas are common to most not-for-profit organizations: mission and identity, personnel, finance, planning, buildings and grounds, fund raising, communications, information technology, public relations – to name but a few. Other areas are more specific to the Church's spiritual goals and objectives: evangelization, worship, catechesis, education, priestly formation, and works of charity. All of these areas and many more are related either directly or indirectly to the Church's threefold mission of teaching, governing, and sanctifying and to the executive, legislative, and judicial power of the diocesan bishop, some of which he shares with his vicars and delegates.

My own initial thoughts of conducting a survey of the various organizational and governance structures employed by U.S. dioceses were quickly dismissed as I perceived how burdensome a task this would be. My focus changed to a consideration of the roles of the vicar general and episcopal vicar(s), the moderator of the curia, and the chancellor. Two of them are new to the 1983 code: the moderator of the curia and the episcopal vicar; they are also optional. While it would be interesting to know whether and how these offices have been implemented, such a study might have been too complex and its success too doubtful. Instead I decided to examine these roles from the perspective of official documents, especially the code and *Apostolorum successores (AS),* the Congregation for Bishops'

1 Ordinary Professor of Canon Law (on leave), Pontifical Gregorian University; Professor of the Practice of Canon Law, Boston College.

2004 Directory for the Pastoral Ministry of Bishops.[2] This presentation will review and comment on those texts. At its conclusion, it will consider briefly the complementary functions, as specified in the code, of the diocesan bishop and the local ordinary.

The Diocesan Curia

The context of the treatment of the vicars, the moderator, and the chancellor in both the code (cc. 469-494) and *AS* (nos. 176-181) is that of the diocesan curia. The code divides its chapter on the curia, after six introductory canons, into three articles: Vicars General and Episcopal Vicars; the Chancellor, Other Notaries, and the Archives; and the Finance Council and the Finance Officer. On the other hand, *AS* contains one general section on the curia and one section each on Coordination of Different Offices; the Vicar General and Episcopal Vicars; the Chancellor of the Curia and Other Notaries; the Diocesan Tribunal; and Diocesan Pastoral Structures. The code defines the curia in canon 469 as follows:

> The diocesan curia consists of those institutions and persons which assist the bishop in the governance of the whole diocese, especially in guiding pastoral action, in caring for the administration of the diocese, and in exercising judicial power.

AS repeats this definition in no. 176, adding the words of Pope St. John Paul II in the only specific reference made to the diocesan curia in his 2003 Postsynodal Apostolic Exhortation *Pastores gregis*,[3] no. 45, where he recalls the Synod Fathers' discussion of the curia: "Due attention was given to the Diocesan Curia as the structure employed by the Bishop to express his pastoral charity in its different aspects."

The Directory goes on to explain that the bishop enjoys a good measure of discretion in structuring his curia:

> Without changing the essential structure of the diocesan curia indicated by canon 469-494 of the Code of Canon Law, the Bishop may supplement it with other offices. These may have ordinary or delegated powers, above all of a pastoral nature, depending on the needs of the diocese, its size, and local custom.

It is not easy to determine what is meant here by the phrase, "especially of a pastoral nature." Which supplementary offices would not be "of a pastoral

2 22 February 2004. Libreria Editrice Vaticana, 2004. It should be noted that this text is a revision of *Ecclesiae imago*, 22 February 1973, Typis Polyglottis Vaticanis, 1973. Its value to this presentation is minimal inasmuch as it antedated the code by a decade.

3 16 October 2003, *AAS* 96 (2004) 825-924.

nature"? Would they be those that we might consider more strictly "administrative," such as those dealing with facilities or information technology? These are not likely to be considered ecclesiastical offices; much less other support support functions in the curia (maintenance, food service, et cetera). If the "especially pastoral" offices in question are endowed with ordinary power, they ought to be ecclesiastical offices in the sense of canon 145 §1: "any function constituted in a stable manner by divine or ecclesiastical ordinance to be exercised for a spiritual purpose"; and canon 131 §1, which provides that the "ordinary power of governance is that which is joined to a certain office by the law itself."

These supplementary offices mentioned in *AS* are not those established in universal law, but, if they are to be stable, they should be established by the legislative power of the bishop along with those ordinary powers, rights, and obligations attached to them. The bishop should be conscious that such designation of a function as an ecclesiastical office obliges him to observe the general norms on ecclesiastical offices – including their conferral and loss – to be found in canons 145-196. It is within the bishop's discretion to determine which offices not established and required by universal law he wishes to establish as ecclesiastical offices. Even with respect to those offices established by the code, some may be employed or not, as the bishop sees fit, or given the scope that the bishop chooses (as with episcopal vicars), or even with the powers determined by law either restricted or expanded.[4] In any case, it is important – sometimes even for the validity of acts – to avoid confusion, to ensure good governance, and to provide for fair evaluation and eventual discipline, that the scope of obligations and rights of all office holders be clearly determined in advance by appropriate documents.

As for appointment to curial offices, the code succinctly provides in canon 470 that "the "appointment of those who exercise offices in the diocesan curia pertains to the diocesan bishop." This does not mean, of course, that the bishop must sign off on every "new hire" in his pastoral center or whatever the diocesan curia is called. We could say that the code is referring only to ecclesiastical offices in the strict sense, or that the bishop is delegating his authority to someone else. The notion of which powers are suitable for delegation will be considered later

The Directory calls upon the bishop to appoint as "heads of curial office ... those who distinguish themselves by competence in their respective fields of expertise, by pastoral zeal and by the integrity of their Christian life."[5] It goes on to recommend that these appointments be made after opportune consultation with clergy and laity alike. When appointees are priests, the Directory offers this admonition:

4 See canons 479 §§ 1 and 2 and 134 §3.

5 Particular law could provide further detail on the requirements for offices proper to the diocese, and even to offices established by universal law which itself is silent about the requirements for appointees, for example, the chancellor.

> When appointing priests to these positions, the Bishop should see to it that they exercise *some other ministry involving the care of souls*, so as to keep alive their apostolic zeal and to avoid developing a damaging bureaucratic mentality through lack of direct contact with the faithful.

Finally, the Directory offers a prudent word of advice to a newly appointed diocesan bishop. Conscious that the structures of a curial office transcend changes in personnel (including, we may presume, the bishop himself), the new bishop should familiarize himself with the administrative praxis of the diocese and as far as possible make it his own. At the same time, he is not to hesitate to introduce (adeptly, we would hope) improvements and to correct what does not fully conform to canonical discipline.

Coordination in the Curia

The next topic among the general principles that concern the functioning of a diocesan curia is that of coordination. Canon 473 §1 reads as follows:

> A diocesan bishop must take care that all the affairs which belong to the administration of the whole diocese are duly coordinated and are ordered to attain more suitably the good of the portion of the people of God entrusted to him.

It is worth recalling here the definition of the curia we read in canon 470: namely, to assist the bishop 1) in the governance of the whole diocese, especially in guiding pastoral action; 2) in caring for the administration of the diocese; and 3) and in exercising judicial power. Obviously, the third of these areas of assistance is entrusted to the judicial vicar and other officers of the tribunal. While these are part of the curia, their functions are delineated in detail in Book VII of the code, as canon 472 recalls. But while it makes due reference to Book VII, canon 472 goes on the say, however, that "the prescripts of the following canons," 473ff., "are to be observed regarding those things which pertain to the administration of the diocese." In other words, while the tribunal enjoys autonomy concerning its judicial function, its administrative dimensions – such as finance, support staff, physical plant resources, etc., remain subject to the coordinating responsibility of the bishop. The term "administration" seems to have different meanings in canon 469 and 473 §1. In the former, the meaning appears more restrictive and not directly related to the bishop's core pastoral office. But in canon 473 §1, "administration" seems to have a broader, more inclusive sense requiring the bishop's pastoral solicitude which can be exercised in a variety of ways, but, in the context of the curia, especially by coordination.

How does the bishop go about this coordinating activity? We find part of the answer in canon 473 §2, which reads as follows:

> It is for the diocesan bishop himself to coordinate the pastoral action of the vicars general or episcopal vicars. When it is expedient, a moderator of the curia can be appointed who must be a priest, and who, under the authority of the bishop, is to coordinate those things which pertain to the treatment of administrative affairs and to take care that the other members of the curia properly fulfill the office entrusted to them.

We should note first of all that the bishop himself is to coordinate the pastoral action of the vicars general or episcopal vicars. It is probably safe to assume that the bishop himself is to exercise this function even if there is one vicar general and one or more episcopal vicars. The conciliar decree *Christus Dominus* 17, which is cited in the code as a source of canon 473 §2, calls for harmonious action among the various diocesan undertakings, "whether their object be catechetical, missionary, charitable, social, family, educational, or any other pastoral end." These areas of concern are related more closely to the bishop's pastoral role and therefore require his more urgent supervision either directly, or, as canon 473 §2 implies, through his vicars whose pastoral action the bishop himself coordinates. The code cites as a source for canon 473 §2 *Christus Dominus* 26, which deals with coadjutor and auxiliary bishops, and 27, which treats the officers and councils of a diocesan curia. No. 177 of *AS* simply affirms that the duty of coordination of diocesan pastoral activity "naturally" belongs to the bishop; it goes on to say that "it is on him that the Vicars general and episcopal Vicars directly depend." It is they alone who, along with the diocesan bishop himself, are constituted by canon 473 §4 as members of an episcopal council which the bishop can establish if he judges it expedient (yet another optional provision) in order "to foster pastoral action more suitably." The term "vicar" carries with it the notion of standing in the place of the one with proper power and therefore of sharing it in a more than simply ancillary manner.[6] This privileged role of the vicar general and episcopal vicar in carrying out the pastoral care of the diocese is further grounded in the vicars' sharing in the bishop's sanctifying office. Canon 968, for example, gives the local ordinary (and therefore vicars general and episcopal vicars by reason of c. 134 §2) the *ex officio* faculty to hear confessions. Such involvement in the care of souls is a reason for the requirement of canon 478 §1 that the vicars be priests.[7] The distinguishing function of the vicars general and episcopal vicars, then, concerns governance and pastoral action rather than administration in a more narrow subsidiary sense.

---

6 Other vicars mentioned in the code are vicars apostolic, vicars forane, parochial vicars, and religious vicars.

7 Canon 1108 similarly gives local ordinaries the ex officio faculty to assist at marriage, though deacons and, extraordinarily, lay persons can be delegated to do the same.

Moderator of the Curia

While the diocesan bishop is personally responsible for coordinating the pastoral action of the vicars, canon 473 §2 goes on to provide for the possible appointment of an officer new to the 1983 code, namely, the moderator of the curia. The canon reads as follows:

> Where it is expedient, a moderator of the curia can be appointed who must be a priest and who, under the authority of the bishop, is to coordinate those things which pertain to the treatment of administrative affairs and to take care that the other members of the curia properly fulfill the office entrusted to them.

A variety of circumstances will determine whether or not such an appointment is expedient. Among the more obvious are the size and complexity of the diocese and its curial structure. Another factor could be the management style of the diocesan bishop himself. He may be a skillful and experienced administrator who prefers a "hands-on" involvement in organizational matters and in the supervision of subordinates at every level and in matters that go beyond the "pastoral action" which the code, as we have seen, entrusts to him personally. The question can be raised, of course, whether such a bishop has duly discerned how best to devote his time and energy, especially when certain functions are principally entrusted to him by the nature of his office and by the law, and should not be sacrificed in favor of administrative activity that the law also entrusts to his vicars. Principal among the bishop's duties are the ministry of the Word of God and of the Church's sacramental life.[8]

The term "moderator" is used in a variety of places in the code: associations, consecrated life, parishes, and schools. It is a generic term that can be given greater specificity in particular or proper law; it does not necessarily involve the exercise of jurisdiction or governance. In the context of the diocesan curia, where, as we have seen, ample flexibility is given to the diocesan bishop to determine how he wishes to govern his diocese, the role of the moderator of the curia can be tailored to the bishop's preference. But in its use of the term "administrative affairs" in contrast to "pastoral action," canon 473 §2 appears to understand administration in a more restrictive sense, referring to the everyday ancillary functions of a complex organization. The moderator's coordination of those activities and his supervision of the personnel who carry them out can free the bishop to attend to matters of greater moment.

The only qualification for the office of moderator of the curia specified in canon 473 §2 is that he be a priest. Canon 473 §3, however, expresses a further preference:

8 See *Christus Dominus* 12-15.

> Unless in the judgment of the bishop local circumstances suggest otherwise, the vicar general, or if there are several, one of the vicars general is to be appointed moderator of the curia.

Why must the moderator of the curia be a priest, and why the preference that a vicar general be appointed moderator if there is to be one at all? The moderator's task, after all, seems largely an administrative one (in the more restrictive, ancillary sense of administration), and could probably be carried out efficiently by a professionally qualified layperson. But it is perhaps because of the relationship among the various functions of a diocesan curia that there should be a single "chief operating officer" who is a priest. As we will see, the vicar general often acts as the bishop's *vicem gerens* or alter ego. Even though the bishop himself is charged with coordinating the pastoral action of the vicars, there are likely to be occasions when the duties of the moderator will have an impact on the functions of the vicars (general, episcopal, and judicial). To the degree that the moderator may be required to exercise authority over them, it may be considered more fitting and less awkward that he be not only a brother priest but a fellow vicar as well.

In concluding its treatment of curial coordination, no. 177 of *AS* offers an important word of advice:

> In directing and coordinating all the work of the diocesan agencies, the Bishop will keep in mind, as a general principle, that diocesan structures should always be at the service of the good of souls and that administrative demands should not take precedence over the care of persons. Therefore, he should see that the operation is smooth and efficient, avoiding all unnecessary complexity or bureaucracy and always directed toward its proper supernatural end.

Vicar General

Canon 475 §1 provides that "[i]n each diocese the diocesan bishop must appoint a vicar general"; the requirement is new to the 1983 code. In the 1917 code (c. 366 §1) the office was to be established "as often as the correct governance of the diocese requires it." The office of vicar general, even in the memory of older American Catholic churchmen, was often viewed as an honorific and not reflective of the busy "chief operating officer" that our current documents suggest. Holders of the office in certain dioceses were senior priests with wide experience in "the chancery" to whom a bishop could turn for discreet advice and support. This may still remain the case even today in certain places in the English-speaking world. But the requirement that the office be filled suggests that today the breadth and complexity of the diocesan bishop's task demand that his burden be shared. His power is ordinary, that is, attached to the office, and the scope of his concern, as stated in canon 475 §1 is identical with what canon 469 attributes to the whole diocesan curia, namely, to assist the bishop "in the governance of the whole diocese." The comprehensive role of the vicar general best explains the provision of canon 475 §2: "As a general rule, one vicar general is to be appointed unless the size of the diocese, the number of inhabitants, or other pastoral reasons suggest otherwise."[9]

It is worthy of note that the code makes special provision for the curial offices of auxiliary bishops. A coadjutor bishop or an auxiliary with special faculties (c. 403, §§2 and 3) are to be appointed vicar general by the diocesan bishop, and they are to be entrusted before others with tasks that need a special mandate (c. 406 §1). With regard to the curial offices to be assigned to any other auxiliary bishop, canon 406 §2 makes the following provision:

> Unless the apostolic letter has provided otherwise and without prejudice to the provision of §1, a diocesan bishop is to appoint his auxiliary or auxiliaries as vicars general or at least as episcopal vicars, dependent only on his authority or that of the coadjutor bishop or auxiliary bishop mentioned in can. 403 §2.

It is not uncommon that in a large diocese where there are several auxiliary bishops, all of them are appointed as vicars general in order not to create odious comparisons among them or to have a presbyter-vicar general "outrank" an auxiliary bishop-episcopal vicar. While it is probably the case that in such situations it is clear to those on the inside who is really in charge, such arrangements are not so obvious to persons on the outside.

AS 178 leaves no doubt about the unique importance of the vicar general, calling him "the preeminent official of the diocesan curia,"[10] but multiple preeminence can be confusing. *AS* 178 recognizes the difficulty created by a plurality of vicars general when it says:

> Since they all have the same power over the whole diocese, clear coordination of their activity is necessary, observing what the Code lays down regarding favors granted by different Ordinaries, and, in general, regarding the exercise of their respective competence.

---

9 The prior code made that same provision in canon 366 §3, adding to size a diversity of rites as another reason for appointing more than one vicar general. There were no further "pastoral reasons" foreseen.

10 Vatican II made the same assertion in *Christus Dominus* 27.

What the code lays down can be found in canon 65. Consideration of its provision will follow comments on the episcopal vicar. Likewise, comment on the appointment and qualifications of the vicar general will be made there.

Episcopal Vicars

Vatican II, even though it did not specifically require the appointment of a vicar general as did the 1983 code, introduced the figure of the episcopal vicar as an option for appointment by the diocesan bishop when "the good government of the diocese requires it."[11] This is the source of canon 476 which reads:

> Whenever the correct government of the diocese requires it, the diocesan bishop can also[12] appoint one or more episcopal vicars, namely, those who in a specific part of the diocese or in a certain type of affairs or over the faithful of a specific rite or over certain groups of persons possess the same ordinary power which a vicar general has by universal law, according to the norms of the following canons.

The code amplifies the possible circumscription of the episcopal vicar's authority by adding "over certain groups of persons" to "the faithful of a specific rite" envisioned by *CD* 27.[13]

The postconciliar reorganization of diocesan curias witnessed the appearance of a wide variety of officers identified as vicars.[14] Whether or not the appointing bishops envisioned them as episcopal vicars as authorized by the Council is unclear. It was not until the promulgation of the code, however, that the requirement that the episcopal vicars be priests was clearly affirmed in canon 478 §1.[15] While there is nothing in the law that expressly prohibits the use of the term "vicar" without the adjective "general" or "episcopal," it is probably more fitting, even if the officer is a priest and the bishop does not intend that he have the faculties of a local ordinary, that another term be chosen, such as "direc-

11 Ibid.

12 In addition to the required appointment of a vicar general.

13 It is noteworthy that canon 366 §3 of the 1917 code identified the presence of the faithful of varied rites as a reason for the appointment of more than one vicar general. Would it have been envisioned that his competence be limited to the faithful of a specific rite? The resolution of this question could have been a motive for the introduction of the new figure of the episcopal vicar.

14 Some women religious working in diocesan curias with responsibility for relations between the bishop and institutes of consecrated life, are even today referred to as "vicars for religious."

15 Even *Ecclesiae Sanctae* 14, which is cited as a source of that canon, is silent on this question. So is *Ecclesiae imago*, which might have mentioned it at no. 202. It is likely that priesthood was simply a presumed requirement.

tor," "coordinator," or even "delegate."[16] Clarity is best preserved when a priest whom the diocesan bishop intends to appoint as an episcopal vicar according to the prescripts of law be in fact called and known as an episcopal vicar.

How is the authority of the episcopal vicar circumscribed? The code specifies territory, affairs (business or subject matter), and groups of persons. Elsewhere the law tends to favor territoriality as a criterion for determining a superior's authority and a subject's subordination by reason of domicile, etc. This is true of particular churches (c. 372) and parishes (c. 518) "as a general rule." Both admit of exceptions on the basis of pastoral expedience. The specification of an episcopal vicar's authority, however, is not expressly subject to such a general rule, except, perhaps, by analogy. Territoriality, of course, is the easiest criterion to apply because it is the most clearly objective. It can be defined by geographical markers such as rivers, streams, and streets, or by civilly determined subdivisions such as counties. Canon 136 in Book I on the General Norms of the code address how the ordinary power of governance is exercised when either the superior or subjects are outside the territory or when travelers are actually in the territory. This question becomes more complex when there is a non-territorial criterion for determining the superior's competence.

Examples of "affairs" as a criterion could include Catholic schools, adult faith formation, youth ministry, and catechesis. But note the similarity and overlap of those categories. Others could be liturgy, ecumenical relations and interreligious dialogue, and the very general "canonical affairs." Which issues does the last of these *not* include? There is significant overlap among these categories as well. Groups of persons can have cumulative jurisdiction by a variety of episcopal vicars: for example, clergy, religious, the deaf, Hispanic Catholics, university students (c. 813) and those devoted to the extraordinary form of the liturgy. And how are language or ethnic groups to be determined (an equally vexing issue in the case of non-territorial parishes)?

Canon 479 provides for the scope and limits of vicars' authority. The power of the vicar general is determined first in §1:

> By virtue of office, the vicar general has the executive power over the whole diocese which belongs to the diocesan bishop by law, namely, the power to place all administrative acts except those, however, which the bishop has reserved to himself or which require a special mandate by the bishop by law.

---

16 Use of the term "delegate," of courses, suggests an exercise of delegated jurisdiction, which raises the thorny question of the extent of canon 129 §2's "cooperation" of the laity in the executive power of governance. This is beyond the scope of this presentation.

The limits of the episcopal vicar's power are similar and specified in canon 479 §2 as follows:

> By the law itself an episcopal vicar has the same power mentioned in §1 but only over the specific part of the territory or the type of affairs or the faithful of a specific rite or group for which he was appointed, except those cases which the bishop has reserved to himself or to a vicar general or which require a special mandate of the bishop by law.

Both the vicar general and the episcopal vicar are limited in the scope of their power by those acts which the law itself reserves to the bishop and therefore require a special mandate to place. How do we know which acts these are? The question is answered in canon 134 §3:

> Within the context of executive power, those things which in the canons are attributed by name to the diocesan bishop are understood to belong only to a diocesan bishop and the others made equivalent to him in can. 381 §2, excluding the vicar general and episcopal vicar except by special mandate.

By contrast, when the canons – or any other ecclesiastical law – attributes an act of executive power to the local ordinary, the vicar general and episcopal vicar are included, as canon 134 §2 provides. Acts authorized by special mandate are subject to the norms governing delegated power. And just as the diocesan bishop can expand the vicars' power by means of the special mandate, so can he limit their ordinary power as local ordinaries by reserving certain of them to himself, or certain of the episcopal vicar's powers which the vicar general might continue to enjoy. These could include powers that affect the validity of an act.

More complex is the limitation of the scope to the episcopal vicar's powers by reason of his appointment as vicar for certain business or certain persons. Which episcopal vicar is competent to give dispensations from the form of marriage or from impediments to marriage? Which one has competence over the appointment of religion teachers or the censure of a cleric. And when does an "episcopal vicar for the new evangelization" act as a local ordinary? All of these matters need to be addressed in clear and complete decrees establishing an episcopal vicar's office or appointing a priest as episcopal vicar. Such clarity is crucial for the appointee himself, for his fellow vicars, and for the clergy and faithful who have recourse to them. As *AS* 178 asserts:

> When appointing an episcopal Vicar, the Bishop will take care to define clearly the extent of his faculties. In this way he will avoid overlapping areas of competence or, what would

be worse, uncertainty on the part of the Vicar himself or the faithful.

Even when appointments are clearly delineated and promulgated, there will still be overlapping jurisdiction among all of those who hold the executive power of governance: the diocesan bishop, the vicar(s) general, and the episcopal vicar(s). There are advantages to having a variety of subjects of executive power; these could include differences in location, availability, and administrative style. The universal law has provisions that help to avoid conflicts. The first, to be found among the code's general norms on rescripts, is canon 65 §2, which provides as follows:

> A favor denied by a vicar general or by an episcopal vicar cannot be granted validly by another vicar of the same bishop even if the reasons for the denial have been obtained from the vicar who denied it.

This norm reflects the unity of authority that exists within the governing activity of two or more vicars of a diocesan bishop. Once a negative decision is made, a petitioner cannot play vicars against each other. The diocesan bishop, on the other hand, as the hierarchical principle guarantees, can be, in effect, a means of recourse as canon 65 §3 explains:

> A favor denied by a vicar general or by an episcopal vicar and afterwards obtained from the diocesan bishop without any mention made of this denial is invalid. A favor denied by a diocesan bishop, even if mention is made of the denial, cannot be obtained validly from his vicar general or episcopal vicar without the consent of the bishop.

Implicitly, of course, the law allows the diocesan bishop to overturn the negative response of the vicar if mention is made of the vicar's denial. At the same time, the law acknowledges that more than one authority may become involved in the handling of the same matter. Canon 139 addresses this question in the following two paragraphs:

> §1. Unless the law determines otherwise, the fact that a person approaches some competent authority, even a higher one, does not suspend the executive power, whether ordinary or delegated, of another competent authority.
>
> §2. Nevertheless, a lower authority is not to become involved in cases submitted to a higher authority except for a grave and urgent cause; in this case, the lower authority is immediately to notify the higher about the matter.

Prudence and good government suggest that the bishop will ordinarily respect the judgments his vicars make. They are bound, after all, to be of one mind with him as canon 480 provides:

> A vicar general and an episcopal vicar must report to the diocesan bishop concerning the more important affairs which are to be handled and have been handled, and they are never to act contrary to the intention and mind of the diocesan bishop.

These open lines of communication, used perhaps at meetings of an episcopal council, are another means of avoiding conflict and the duplication of effort. As for a commonality of mind and heart between the bishop and his vicars, experience will determine how present it is in fact. A vicar might misunderstand a bishop's desires and intentions or even willfully act contrary to them in violation of canon 480's provision. In such a case, the act of the vicar would be valid by virtue of canon 10 since canon 480 does not include an invalidating clause. The exception would be in the case of the errant vicar acting in virtue of a special mandate. In that instance canon 133 §2 holds that the delegate who acts "in some manner other than that determined in the mandate is not considered to exceed the limits of the mandate unless the manner was prescribed for validity by the one delegating."

Patterns of action – whether unwitting or willful – by a vicar contrary to the mind of the bishop suggest that removal from office is opportune. Canon 477 §1 provides: "The diocesan bishop freely appoints a vicar general and episcopal vicar and can freely remove them ... An episcopal vicar who is not an auxiliary bishop is to be appointed only for a time to be determined in the act of appointment." What does "freely appoints" and "freely removes" mean? In this context "freely" means at least that the bishop is not required to have anyone's advice or consent. Does "freely" suggest that the general norm of canon 193 need not be observed with regard to the cause for removal? That norm varies according to the duration of the appointment in question: it can be for an indefinite time, for a definite period, or "at the prudent discretion of the competent authority." Although the 1983 code does not say so in precisely the same terms, canon 366 §2 the 1917 code provides: "The Vicar General is designated freely by the Bishop, who can remove him at his discretion (*ad nutum*)." The 1983 code uses the term "*ad nutum*" only once, in canon 682 §2, in the context of the removal of a religious from ecclesiastical office; the action can be taken either by the entrusting authority or the religious superior, each merely informing the other with no requirement that the reasons for the removal be given. This provision is meant to preserve the autonomy of both authorities and does not suggest that the cause be anything less than the just one required by canon 193 §3 for the removal of an officer appointed at the prudent discretion of a competent authority. For the removal of a vicar general, such a just cause can be the bishop's prudent desire to appoint a new vicar general.

An episcopal vicar, on the other hand, is to be appointed for a definite period of time, and canon 193 §2 requires a grave cause for the removal of such an officeholder before the time has elapsed. It is unclear why the law prescribes a definite period for the appointment of an episcopal vicar. Why should his office and not that of the vicar general be so determined? It is perhaps because of the newness of the figure itself. If, for example, a bishop should create an episcopal vicariate for some new subject matter or group, sufficient time may be needed to assess the usefulness of such an office. At the same time, *Ecclesiae Sanctae* 14, which treats the office of episcopal vicar and is cited in the code as a source of canon 477, recognizes both questions at issue here, namely, the definite term and the free removal. Blessed Pope Paul VI's 1966 Motu proprio reads as follows:

> Episcopal vicars who are not auxiliary bishops shall be nominated for a limited period to be determined in the act of nomination; they may however be removed from office at the wish (*ad nutum*) of the bishop.

The specificity of the norm of canon 477 along with the acknowledgement of *ES* of the apparent contradiction (between a fixed period and an appointment *ad nutum*) trumps the general norm of canon 193 §2 which calls for a grave reason to remove someone from an office established for a limited time before its expiration. The standard for the removal of an episcopal vicar is therefore the same as that set for a vicar general.

Qualifications for both offices are the same and are listed in canon 478 §1: priesthood; age (at least 30 although *AS* 178 prefers 40 or older); academic achievement (a license or doctorate in canon law or theology or expertise in these disciplines); and attributes including sound doctrine, integrity, prudence, and experience in handling business. Excluded by §2, apparently to avoid conflicts of interest, are the canon penitentiary and men related to the bishop by blood up to the fourth degree. Canon 1420 §1 also provides that the judicial vicar be "distinct from the vicar general unless the small size of the diocese or the small number of cases suggests otherwise." While this distinction between officeholders may appear to avoid too heavy a workload for a single person, it is more likely that here too the norm has been established to avoid conflicts or their appearance. A judicial vicar may otherwise find himself adjudicating a case that involves his own administrative act. For this reason, it seems prudent to extend this distinction to the episcopal vicar as well.

Chancellor

The more senior clergy and faithful in the United States will recall a time when the diocesan chancellor was considered the bishop's "right hand man" and perhaps the most central and powerful figure in diocesan governance after the bishop himself. The diocesan curia was commonly referred to, and is often still known as "the chancery." Divisions of canonical responsibility and expertise have traditionally been "tribunal" and "chancery," where the former involved the adjudication of cases according to the norms of Book IV of the 1917 code and Book VII of the current one, while "chancery" dealt by contrast with all other matters of administration and governance. If the exercise of the power of governance was involved, delegation was required. This alternate preeminence of the chancellor (and his vice-chancellor and assistants) was largely a matter of custom; how it developed is beyond the scope of this presentation, but it is clear that under the 1917 code (canon 372), the *de iure* role of the chancellor was nearly identical with what the 1983 code provides, except for the former requirement that the chancellor be a priest. The current role of the chancellor is delineated in canon 482 §1 as follows:

> In every curia a chancellor is to be appointed whose principal function, unless particular law establishes otherwise, is to take care that the acts of the curia are gathered, arranged, and safeguarded in the archive of the curia.

The same canon in §3 further provides that the chancellor, and the vice chancellor if there is one, are by reason of those roles notaries and secretaries of the curia.

The code sets no specific qualifications for the chancellor's appointment. *AS* 176, as discussed above, says that the bishop should take "care not to entrust offices or tasks to those lacking the necessary skills."[17] What are the requisite skills for a diocesan chancellor? It is likely that his job description will exceed the minimal elements of the code's description of the chancellor as the curia's chief notary and archivist. *AS* 179, as befits a Directory,[18] amplifies the job description and provides some qualifications. It divides the office into three curial functions: archivist, notary, and secretary. The first is probably self-evident. The notary's role, *AS* explains,

> . . . has a particular canonical importance since the notary's signature bears witness to juridical acts, whether judicial or administrative, that is, it "certifies" the juridical identity of the document, thereby confirming the act itself and attesting that it has been properly recorded in writing.

AS goes on to describe how the chancellor as notary can be of further assistance to the bishop:

---

17 See footnote 5 *supra*.

18 Canon 31 §1 provides that general executory decrees, among which directories are numbered, "more precisely determine the methods to be observed in applying the law ... "

> The Bishop should enlist the help of the chancellor and the notaries in the preparation of juridical documents, such as different kinds of juridical acts, decrees, or indults, so that the wording of the documents will be precise and clear.

While this suggestion may emphasize the technical dimension of the chancellor's juridical activity, it could readily be expanded, either in particular law or in curial custom and praxis, to make of the chancellor the canonical expert in the curia, especially when the bishop and his vicars are neither trained nor experienced in canonical science. The chancellor can assist the bishop by recalling for him his rights and duties and those of other officials and of clergy and laity alike, especially when these may not be widely known or are abused. Similarly, the chancellor, if qualified by his or her training, can be available to others in the diocese for canonical counsel, especially when they are not in conflict with the interests of the diocese.

This role of the chancellor as the chief canonical expert in the diocese has developed in a number of places, and is especially consistent with the role of a lay chancellor, who may be in a better position than a cleric to be candid and objective in providing canonical advice.[19] This expanded description of the chancellor's office could well be further delineated in particular law, as canon 482 §1 allows. More ample canonical responsibility for the chancellor is preferable, in my opinion, to the establishment of an "office of canonical affairs" if that office were to be "out of the loop" with regard to day-to-day diocesan business. By contrast, one might expect to find the chancellor at the center of curial affairs. Likewise, the practice of relegating to the tribunal all matters that are perceived as being of canonical moment creates similar problems, along with the danger, discussed above, of mixing the exercise of executive and judicial power.[20]

The third function of the chancellor as described in *AS* 179 is that of secretary of the curia. It reads as follows:

> This office involves overseeing the good ordering of curial administrative tasks, in close collaboration with the Vicar general and, if there is one, with the Moderator of the curia.

AS promptly goes on to remand to particular law specification of the relationship between the chancellor and other officers of the curia. What is meant here by "administrative tasks" recalls a familiar ambiguity. Is "administrative" synonymous with "executive" or does it have a more ancillary meaning? If we choose the latter meaning, we could more easily assign to a lay chancellor a wide range of supervisory responsibility for which he or she had outstanding qualifica-

19 Members of institutes of consecrated life may be similarly situated.

20 Tribunal officers would have to be properly delegated in order validly to place acts of the executive power of governance.

tions, while reserving to a vicar-moderator matters that were more suited to his priestly identity. It will be important to discern carefully how to balance tailoring a job description to the strengths (and weaknesses) of a particular person with finding the best person to appoint to a pre-determined office having objective qualifications for carrying it out.

AS 179 supplies for the silence of the code when it enumerates some qualification of a diocesan chancellor:

> The member of the faithful who is entrusted with the office of chancellor must be of good reputation and above all suspicion, with canonical ability and experience in the management of administrative affairs.

Special training in archive management, civil law, and business administration could be very useful, as well as competence in Latin and in languages used in the diocese. Just as particular law can further specify the chancellor's functions and relations with other officers of the curia, so can it determine qualifications for appointment.

Canon 485 provides for the free removal of the chancellor by the diocesan bishop but not by the diocesan administrator without the consent of the college of consultors. "Free removal" as we saw with regard to vicars, implies service *ad nutum*, and while vicars lose office at the vacancy of the see, the chancellor does not.

The Diocesan Bishop and the Local Ordinary

We have already discussed how in a particular church the diocesan bishop (and his equivalent in law) and the vicar(s) general and episcopal vicar(s) are all local ordinaries. When the law attributes an act to the local ordinary all are included unless the diocesan bishop has reserved it to himself or to the vicar general. If, on the other hand, the law attributes an act to the diocesan bishop, the vicars are excluded and can act validly only by the bishop's special mandate.[21] It is interesting that canon 134 §3 has no cited source in the 1983 code. Canon 199 §1 of the 1917 code provides a general norm that has no exactly parallel canon in the current law. It says: "Whoever has the ordinary power of jurisdiction can delegate it to another in whole or in part, unless it is expressly provided otherwise by law." Canon 137 §1 of the 1983 code makes a similar assertion in the passive voice: "Ordinary executive power can be delegated both for a single act and for all cases unless the law expressly provides otherwise." While legislative power cannot be validly delegated (c. 135 §2), there is no similarly broad prohibition of

21 See canons 134 §§ 2 and 3.

the delegation of executive power.[22] Indeed, the reference to the special mandate in canon 134 §3 implies that any act of executive power reserved by the law to the diocesan bishop can be conferred as long as its delegation is not expressly prohibited.

Just as a diocesan bishop enjoys broad discretion in organizing his diocesan curia and in establishing or not establishing espiscopal vicars and a moderator of the curia, so does he exercise discretion in conferring on his vicars (or others) a special mandate to place acts that the law attributes only to him. Likewise, he can choose to restrict the faculties conferred by the law itself upon the local ordinaries subordinate to him. While it is beyond the scope of this presentation to comment on the large number of such competencies, it seemed useful to list at least some of them with a view to making some general concluding observations.

Powers/Functions/Faculties Reserved to the Diocesan Bishop

Canon	
87	to dispense from disciplinary laws
98, 2	to appoint a guardian
145 § 2; 157	to make appointments to ecclesiastical offices
234-236	to establish seminaries
239	to approve seminary spiritual directors
241	to admit students to the major seminary
243	to approve the seminary rule
253	to appoint seminary teachers
259	to oversee the governance and administration of the seminary
263	to provide for seminary finances
267-269	to incardinate and excardinate clerics
271	to permit clerics to serve outside the diocese
277 §3	to set norms to safeguard celibate chastity
297	to consent to a personal prelature to function in the diocese
312	to erect a public association
320	to suppress a public association
470	to appoint officers of the diocesan curia
515	to erect parishes
517 §2	to appoints non-priests to participate in the pastoral care of a parish
524	to appoint pastors
536	to decide if there are to be parish pastoral councils
547	to appoint parochial vicars

22 Without prejudice to the provisions of canons 883 and 884, the power of orders belonging to the bishop cannot be delegated.

557	to appoint rectors
579	to erect diocesan institutes of consecrated life (IVC)
595	to approve and dispense from constitutions of diocesan IVCs
603-604	to constitute hermits and consecrated virgins in the diocese
609 §1	to consent to the erection of a religious house
612	to consent to changes in the scope of a religious house
628	to conduct visitations of religious
678	to supervise religious regarding the care of souls, public exercise of divine worship other works of the apostolate
679	to prohibit a religious for a most grave cause from residing in the diocese
772 §1	to issue norms for preaching
775	to issue norms for catechetics
801	to give consent for the establishment of schools by religious institutes
802	to establish schools
804	to regulate and watch over Catholic religious instruction.
806 §1	to visit all Catholic schools and issue prescripts for them
810 §2	to exercise vigilance over Catholic universities
813	to provide for the pastoral care of university students
814	to send clergy to study at ecclesiastical faculties
821	to establish theological institutes
838	to regulate the liturgy according to the norm of law
844 §4	to determine "another grave necessity" for Catholic ministers to admit Protestants to receive the holy Eucharist, penance, and the anointing of the sick
860 §2	to permit baptisms in hospitals outside of necessity
863	to reserve to himself the baptism of persons 14 or older
874 §1, 2°	to set another age than 16 for godparents
883-884	to enable presbyters to be the minister of confirmation
935	to set norms carrying the Eucharist
943	to issue prescripts for exposition and reposition of
the	Eucharist
944 §2	to regulate processions with the Eucharist
961 §2	to judge whether the conditions for general absolution are met
967 §1	to deny a bishop the faculty to hear confessions licitly

1002	to issue prescripts for communal celebrations of the anointing of the sick
1017	to permit another bishop to ordain in his diocese
1028	to instruct ordinands about obligations of their new order
1112 §1	to delegate lay persons to assist at marriage
1165 §2	to grant radical sanations
1206	to dedicate sacred places and to entrust the dedication to a presbyter
1207	to bless a church and delegate a presbyter to do so
1215	to consent to the building of a church.
1222	to reduce a church to profane but not sordid use
1244 §2	to establish feasts and penances but only for individual instances
1248 §2	to issue prescripts for Sunday celebrations without a priest
1261 §2	to admonish the faithful to contribute to the support of the Church
1263	to establish a tax
1308 §3	to reduce Mass obligations
1419	to judge in first instance
1421	to appoint judges
1431 §1	to call for intervention of the promoter of justice
1483	to approve advocates
1692	to issue a decree of separation of spouses
1699	to accept a *libellus* for the instruction of a non-consummation case
1740	to remove a pastor

Some Competencies of Local Ordinaries

Canon	
88	to dispense from diocesan laws
305 §2	to exercise vigilance over diocesan associations
311	to foster cooperation among associations in a diocese
324 §2	to confirm the spiritual director of a private association
325 §2	to exercise authority over pious legacies left to private associations
390	to permit a visiting bishop to exercise pontifical functions
527 §2	to place a pastor in possession of a parish and to dispense from the method
527 §3	to set a time limit for taking possession
533 §1	to permit a pastor to reside outside of a parish house.
550 §1	to permit a parochial vicar live outside the parish.

559	to see to it that non-parochial liturgical functions do not harm parishes
560	to provide for liturgical functions in non-parochial churches
562	to oversee non-parochial churches
563	to remove a rector for a just cause
565	to appoint and install chaplains
637	to receive accounts from autonomous monasteries
638 §4	to consent to extraordinary administration by autonomous monasteries
686 §1	to consent to have an exclaustrated religious cleric live in the diocese
780	to take care that catechists are prepared
804 §2	to be vigilant over teachers of religion
805	to appoint and remove religion teachers
806 §2	to be vigilant over the quality of Catholic schools
826-827	to grant the *imprimatur*
830	to entrust books to censors
833	to receive some professions of faith
839 §2	to be vigilant over popular piety
858 §2	to order that some non-parochial churches have a baptismal font
860 §1	to permit baptism in private houses for a grave reason
861 §2	to designate an extraordinary minister of baptism
905 §2	to give priests the faculty to binate and trinate
930 §1	to permit an aged or infirm priest to celebrate Mass in public when seated
933	to permit Mass in a non-Catholic church
934 §1, 2°	to permit the reservation of the Eucharist in places other than parochial and religious churches
943	to designate a lay minister of exposition
957	to supervise Mass obligations in churches of seculars
967 §2	to give the portable faculty to hear confessions to incardinated and domiciled priests
968 §1	to hear confessions *ex officio*
969 §1	to give the faculty to priests to hear confessions
974	to revoke the faculty to hear confessions
1071	to permit otherwise prohibited marriages
1077 §1	to prohibit marriage
1078-1080	to dispense from matrimonial impediments
1102 §3	to permit a marriage on condition past or present
1108	to assist at marriage and to delegate clerics to do so
1115	to permit marriage outside the proper parish of either party

1118 §1	to permit sacramental marriage in a non-parochial church or oratory
1118 §2	to permit sacramental marriage in a decent non-sacred place
1125	to permit mixed marriage
1127 §2	to dispense from the canonical form of marriage
1130	to permit a secret marriage
1144 §2	to permit Pauline-privilege interrogations before baptism or to dispense from them
1153 §1	to permit separation of spouses in case of danger
1168	to permit the lay faithful to administer sacramentals
1172	to permit exorcism
1183	to permit funerals of unbaptized infants or baptized non-Catholics.
1184 §2	to be consulted in doubt about denying Christian burial
1196	to dispense from private vows
1211	to suspend worship in a violated sacred place
1225	to prohibit rites from celebration in oratiries
1226	to permit private chapels
1228	to permit rites in private chapels
1230	to approve shrines
1232	to approve statutes of diocesan shrines
1241 §2	to designate cemeteries for blessing
1265 §1	to permit private begging for pious purposes
1266	to order collections in all churches and oratories
open	to the faithful.
1320	to coerce religious with penalties in matters of his competence (see can. 678)
1355-1356	to remit penalties
1684	to decree a *vetitum*

Conclusion

Patterns can be noticed among the functions that are reserved to the diocesan bishop. Their subject matter can be identified as persons and institution of great importance in the life of the local church. These include clerics, religious, seminaries, parishes, schools, universities, churches, pastors, preaching, catechesis, and sacraments. They involve possibly indefinite-term appointments and the erection of ecclesiastical entities that will have long-range consequences for the diocese and for his successors in office. Some call for the issuance of norms and prescripts that, even if they are not legislative acts but general executory decrees, have the qualities of generality and permanence which are associated with law.

By contrast, the competencies of the local ordinary lack this kind of generality and permanence. They tend rather to include matters that can arise frequently and whose disposition may not require significant discretion such as, for example, the granting of routine dispensations from impediments to marriage, permission for mixed marriages, and the dispensation from the form of marriage. Less long-term appointments, such as those of teachers of religion and chaplains, are not likely to have a significant impact on the life of the diocese. If experience shows that certain of these matters call for the decision of higher authority because of their sensitivity, peculiarly local importance, or a pattern of erroneous judgments by subordinates, the bishop is be free to reserve them to his own judgment.

Documents such as *Christus Dominus*, *Pastores gregis*, and *Apostolorum successores* reveal the wide-ranging responsibilities that extend far beyond the specific issues of the two lists provided above. For a bishop to be the kind of evangelizer, preacher, and teacher of faith and morals called for in the twenty-first century; the voice of the Church in dealing with public officials; the principal agent of ecumenism and interreligious dialogue in the diocese; and an informed participant in the worldwide work of the episcopal college, he must be prepared to allow his vicars to attend to much of the day-to-day business of the diocese. At the same time, he should be able to see the close connection between the functions reserved to him by law and these and other roles that demand his attention. He should be discerning and cautious before delegating the major duties imposed by law and risking the sacrifice of excellent opportunities for exercising his proper role of priest, prophet, and pastor.

While the law of the Church leaves ample room for episcopal discretion in both diocesan organization and in the restriction and extension of his vicars' authority, non-obligatory provisions of law should not be seen as among the many equally appropriate ways of proceeding, but as norms for behavior which only experience, prayerful discernment, and cautious judgment should trump.

SEMINAR

THE "NEWNESS" OF THE NEW EVANGELIZATION AND CANON LAW

James-Daniel Flynn, JCL

Among the legacies of Pope St. John Paul II is the popularity of the term "new evangelization." John Paul used the term with regularity, and in some ecclesial circles, its use has subsequently become ubiquitous. In its ubiquity, the term is in danger of becoming virtually meaningless – by synonymous usage with nearly every component of the Church's mission, the powerful idea of the new evangelization can easily be swallowed up into the broader missionary nature of the Church.

For that reason, it is a valuable use of our time to consider what is unique about the new evangelization – what particularizes it within the ordinary missionary identity of the Church herself. The question can be asked this way: What is so "new" about the new evangelization?

This paper will discuss the mission, methodology, and the subject of the "new evangelization," and consider the relationship of the new evangelization to the Code of Canon Law, especially with regard to some general principles of canon law and ecclesiology that can be extrapolated from the code. Finally, it will offer some suggestions for the means by which canonists, ecclesial administrators, and diocesan bishops in particular, can serve the mission of the new evangelization.

Of course, proper exegesis of a term requires a consideration of its history, and the history of the term "new evangelization" is critical to understanding it. This paper will discuss the term's history organically, by considering the mission and methodology of the new evangelization, followed by a more systematic treatment.

Mission of the New Evangelization

In a real sense, the mission of the new evangelization is "sanctity," or more concretely, a pastoral plan in application of the universal call to holiness articulated in the fifth chapter of *Lumen gentium*, the pastoral constitution on the Church. The Council says that "it is evident to everyone, that all the faithful of

Christ of whatever rank or status, are called to the fullness of the Christian life and to the perfection of charity."[1]

The constitution continues:

> The classes and duties of life are many, but holiness is one – that sanctity which is cultivated by all who are moved by the Spirit of God, and who obey the voice of the Father and worship God the Father in spirit and in truth ... All the faithful of Christ are invited to strive for the holiness and perfection of their own proper state. Indeed they have an obligation to so strive.[2]

The profound invitation of the Second Vatican Council – the invitation to holiness – is, without question, inextricably tied up in the mission of the new evangelization.

The universal call to holiness was a fundamental component of the ministry of John Paul II. In *Christifidelis Laici*, he stated that "holiness must be called a fundamental presupposition and an irreplaceable condition for everyone in fulfilling the mission of salvation within the Church."[3] The universal call to holiness was at the heart of the pastoral plan for the Church he undertook, which included the new evangelization.

In the Apostolic Letter *Novo Millenio Innuente,* John Paul said that "I have no hesitation in saying that all pastoral initiatives must be set in relation to holiness."[4] A pastoral plan for holiness, said John Paul, "implies the conviction that, since baptism is a true entry into the holiness of God through incorporation into Christ and the indwelling of his Spirit, it would be a contradiction to settle for a life of mediocrity, marked by a minimalist ethic and a shallow religiosity."[5]

In further reflection on the new evangelization, the Holy Father remarked that "the time has come to re-propose wholeheartedly to everyone *this high stan-*

1 Vatican II, dogmatic constitution *Lumen gentium*, 40, in *Vatican Council II: The Conciliar and Post Conciliar Documents*, ed. Austin Flannery (Northport, NY: Costello Publishing Co., 1992) 397.

2 Ibid., no. 41, 398.

3 John Paul II, apostolic exhortation *Christifidelis Laici,* December 30, 1988, no. 17. See http://www.vatican.va/holy_father/john_paul_ii/apost_exhortations/documents/hf_jp-ii_exh_30121988_christifideles-laici_en.html (accessed December 17, 2014). Hereafter *CL*.

4 John Paul II, apostolic letter, *Novo Millenio Innuente*, January 6, 2001 no. 30. See http://www.vatican.va/holy_father/john_paul_ii/apost_letters/documents/hf_jp-ii_apl_20010106_novo-millennio-ineunte_en.html (accessed December 17, 2014). Hereafter *NMI*.

5 *NMI*, no. 31.

dard of ordinary Christian living: the whole life of the Christian community and of Christian families must lead in this direction. It is also clear however that the paths to holiness are personal and call for a genuine '*training in holiness*,' adapted to people's needs."[6]

The new evangelization can be understood as a part of the "pastoral plan for holiness of life" which John Paul called for. Pope Francis rearticulated this call as the formation of "missionary disciples." In a period of aggressive secularization, the disintegration of the family, and the abandonment of human rights, such a pastoral plan is desperately needed in the life of the Church.

But it would be a mistake to call the need for such a plan, or even the actualization of such a plan, "new." In reality, the term "universal call to holiness," articulates in a novel, and winsome way, the mission at the heart of the Church since its foundation in Jesus Christ.

One need only look to the work of the great apologist Frank Sheed, or that of St. Francis de Sales, or the Benedictine cultivators of Christendom, or the desert fathers for that matter, to know that developing a theology and a pastoral program of "training in holiness" accessible to Christians in all states of life is the very fabric of the Church's identity.

In fact the exhortation of Christ to "be perfect, just as your heavenly Father is perfect,"[7] was addressed to a multitude – to the crowds assembled for the Sermon on the Mount. The universal invitation to holiness is the invitation of Christ himself.

We cannot, therefore, suggest that what is "new" about the new evangelization is its emphasis on the universal call to holiness of all believers.

Admittedly, it might be fair to argue that in the period immediately prior to the Council, secularization, and an inflexible institutionalism coupled with clericalism in some corners of the Church had, for some, muddled this mission. But it would be disingenuous to suggest that the universal call to holiness and a pastoral plan for its implementation is a novelty of either the Council or the post-conciliar era. John Paul expressed it thusly:

> It is not therefore a matter of inventing a 'new programme.' The programme already exists: it is the plan found in the Gospel and in the living Tradition, it is the same as ever. Ultimately, it has its centre in Christ himself, who is to be known, loved and imitated, so that in him we may live the life of the Trinity, and

6 *NMI*, no. 31. Emphasis in the original.
7 Matthew 5:38. New American Bible.

with him transform history until its fulfilment in the heavenly Jerusalem. [8]

Methodology

If promoting the universal call to holiness is not the "newness" of the new evangelization, it seems fair to ask if the "newness" of the new evangelization arises from its methodology. Certainly, John Paul emphasized the imperative of new modes of pastoral activity as a fundamental component of the new evangelization.

In his address to the CELAM meeting in Port-au-Prince, Haiti, in 1983, John Paul further addressed the need and methods of a new evangelization: "The commemoration of the half millennium of evangelization," he told the Latin American bishops "will gain its full energy if it is a commitment, not to re-evangelize but to a new evangelization, *new in its ardor, methods and expression.*"[9]

In 1993, in Denver, John Paul reemphasized this with the young people gathered for World Youth Day, encouraging the crowd to creative and dynamic apostolic activity. "The Church needs your energies, your enthusiasm, your youthful ideals," he told them, "now more than ever, in a world that is often without light and without the courage of noble ideals, people need the fresh, vital spirituality of the Gospel."[10]

The entire pontificate of John Paul was a call to a creative, dynamic apostolate – to new approaches to communicating the Gospel. Benedict XVI and Pope Francis have both echoed this call. *Evangelii nuntiandi,* the great work of Pope Paul VI, to be beatified in just a few days, was entirely a call to new enthusiasm and new urgency in the task of evangelization.[11]

The response to the encouragement of the Church is astounding. We are living, as John Paul said, in a new springtime of evangelization. We are witness to a beautiful blossoming of new energy for evangelization – to new modes of spiritual expression, new energy for proclamation, and new engagement with technology for the proclamation of the Gospel.

---

8 *NMI*, no. 29.

9 John Paul II. Opening Address to the Nineteenth General Assembly of CELAM, March 9, 1983, Port-au-Prince, Haiti, L'Osservatore Romano, English Edition 16/780 (April 18, 1983), no. 9. Italics have been added for emphasis.

10 John Paul II. Homily at the 8th World Youth Day, August 15, 1993, Denver, Colorado. See http://www.vatican.va/holy_father/john_paul_ii/homilies/1993/documents/hf_jp-ii_hom_19930815_gmg-denver_en.html (accessed December 17, 2014).

11 Paul VI, apostolic exhortation *Evangelii Nuntiandi*, December 8, 1975. See http://www.vatican.va/holy_father/paul_vi/apost_exhortations/documents/hf_p-vi_exh_19751208_evangelii-nuntiandi_en.html (accessed December 17, 2014).

But renewal is not the same as novelty and methodology is not the "newness" of the new evangelization. Certainly, the Church is innovating for the sake of the Kingdom and the innovation in evangelization is shared among clerics, religious, and laity. But innovation in the proclamation of the Kingdom is a hallmark of Christian evangelization.

The beauty of the Gospel, as St. Augustine said, is "ever ancient and ever new." And, in his magnificent *Essay On the Development of Christian Doctrine*, Blessed John Henry Newman observed that the promotion of the Gospel "changes ... in order to remain the same. In a higher world it is otherwise, but here below to live is to change, and to be perfect is to have changed often."[12]

If the methodology of the new evangelization is enthusiasm, commitment, and creativity, this methodology is in precise continuity with the Church's evangelical efforts since her foundation.

New answers – and new modes of evangelization – are but changing responses to the circumstances of time and place. The Church has innovated in response to the challenge of evangelization in new cultures even from the moment that Paul preached at the Aeropagus.[13]

The methodologies of the civilizing monks of St. Benedict, the missionary Jesuits of St. Ignatius of Loyola, the television evangelism of Venerable Fulton Sheen, and the methodology of the laity of the Neocatechumenal Way, or Communion and Liberation, or FOCUS, are all organic responses to the particular needs and realities of cultures, and an earnest effort to present Christ therein.

Of course, evangelical and catechetical methodology is proved in the test of time, with the guidance of the Holy Spirit, and through the judgment of competent ecclesiastical authorities. It would be a mistake to confuse novelty with success.

The only metric for evaluating new methods of evangelization is the degree to which they lead to a transformative encounter with Jesus Christ and his Church.

Christ, himself, and not any mode of communication, is what matters in the work of evangelization. John Paul articulates this clearly: "The kingdom of God is not a concept, a doctrine, or a program subject to free interpretation," he said,

---

12 John Henry Newman. "Essay on the Development of Christian Doctrine," 1.1.7. See http://www.newmanreader.org/works/development/chapter1.html (accessed December 17, 2014).

13 See Acts 17.

"but it is before all else *a person* with the face and name of Jesus of Nazareth, the image of the invisible God."[14]

In the "springtime of evangelization," some methodologies and approaches will be found effective, and others will be found wanting. Some will be found consistent with truth, and some will be found to be aberrational. Already, many modes of evangelization initiated in the post-conciliar era have been found wanting, and have begun to diminish. This is consistent with the history of evangelization in the life of the Church. What will remain, and what matters, are those methods that bring souls into a transformative encounter with Jesus Christ, in the context of the Church and her sacramental life.

As an aside, consider a particularly remarkable fact of the new evangelization, namely, the new enthusiasm with which very ancient articulations of the Gospel are being proclaimed. The fervent interest among young and devout Catholics in the Extraordinary Form of the Roman Rite; in classical Catholic works of art, literature, and poetry; and in traditional expressions of religious piety, bespeak the great treasure in the repository of Christian culture, and the value of continuity in the Church's evangelical efforts, even as new approaches are tried. Pope Francis has expressed the importance of evangelization along the "*via pulchritudinis*" – the way of beauty – particularly in the realm of the sacred liturgy.[15] A separate and very interesting paper could be written on the canonical consequences of this phenomenon.

History of "The New Evangelization"

To this point, it is clear that neither the mission nor the methodology of the new evangelization are precisely where "newness" can be found. Our mission is sanctity. Our methods are a response to the needs of culture.

On these fronts, consider the recent observations of Archbishop Charles Chaput. Speaking to a gathering of bishops in Mexico City last year, the archbishop remarked that "we need to grasp that the 'new' evangelization is finally very much like the 'old' evangelization. We need to understand the hopes and fears of today's world, and especially its young adults. And we need to master the new technologies and methods to reach people as they are today. But programs and

14 John Paul II. encyclical letter *Redemptoris Missio*. December 30, 1990, no. 18. See http://www.vatican.va/holy_father/john_paul_ii/encyclicals/documents/hf_jp-ii_enc_07121990_redemptoris-missio_en.html (accessed December 17, 2014).

15 Francis. Apostolic exhortation *Evangelii Gaudium*. November 24, 2013, no. 24. See http://www.vatican.va/evangelii-gaudium/en/ (accessed December 17, 2014).

techniques don't convert the human heart. Only the witness of other people can do that."[16]

The new evangelization is, in fact, very much like the old evangelization – evangelization that leads people to encounter Christ, to be zealous for the Gospel, and to seek the heroism of the ordinary Christian life. Nevertheless, John Paul suggested a "new evangelization" with a particular concept in mind. A consideration of the term's history and context gives insight into what makes the "new evangelization *new*."

In 1979, the newly elected John Paul II, the first Polish Pope and the former Archbishop of Krakow, made a historic visit to Soviet-controlled Poland. His visit has been called the "nine days that changed the world." In a nine-day pilgrimage, John Paul witnessed to the vibrancy and endurance of Catholic faith in a place where radically statist secularism had worked to eradicate the influence of the Church in national politics and culture. In short, John Paul's visit was the beginning of an effort to reanimate the Soviet bloc with the spirit of the Gospel.

Christianity had come to Poland in 966, with the baptism of Mieszko I, the father of the Polish state. For nearly a millennium, the Polish people had produced saints and missionaries, holy families and holy vocations, in the context of a Christian nation. But the establishment of Poland as a satellite state of the Soviet Union at the conclusion of the Second World War inaugurated an era of secular, materialist, and communist indoctrination on the part of party organizers and state officials.

It was in this context, speaking in the ruins of a once proudly-Christian Poland, that John Paul observed that "*a new evangelization* has begun, as if it were a new proclamation, even if in reality it is the same as ever."[17] The context is everything. When John Paul referred to the new evangelization, he was expressing a commitment to the re-Christianization of a nation with deep ecclesial roots. The idea he expressed in Poland was distinct from both catechesis and missionary activity *ad gentes*.

In Poland, John Paul called for a cultural *aggiornamento* for a people once formed by a Church that had become ever more irrelevant to their lives.

---

16 Charles J. Chaput, *The New Evangelization: Responsibilities and Challenges for the American Continent.* November 16, 2013, Mexico City. See http://catholicphilly.com/2013/11/think-tank/homilies-speeches/the-new-evangelization-responsibilities-and-challenges-for-the-american-continent/ (accessed December 17, 2014).

17 John Paul II, Homily at the Shrine of the Holy Cross, Mogila, Poland, 9 June 1979. See http://www.vatican.va/holy_father/john_paul_ii/homilies/1979/documents/hf_jp-ii_hom_19790609_polonia-mogila-nowa-huta_en.html (accessed December 17, 2014).

In *Redemptoris missio,* issued in 1990, John Paul called "the new evangelization of Christian peoples" to be the Church's "universal mission." *Redemptoris missio* clarified with precision those who were the subjects for this new evangelization:

> There is an intermediate situation, particularly in countries with ancient Christian roots, and occasionally in the younger Churches as well, where entire groups of the baptized have lost a living sense of the faith, or even no longer consider themselves members of the Church, and live a life far removed from Christ and his Gospel. In this case what is needed is a 'new evangelization' or a 're-evangelization.'[18]

The new evangelization is the mission of preaching Christ anew to Christians, to the baptized themselves, to those who have been catechized and rejected the faith, or even perhaps to those who have been baptized and yet have never heard the Gospel or responded to it.

In *Christifidelis Laici*, John Paul takes the concept even further – explaining that the mission of the new evangelization "is to ... *remake the Christian fabric of the ecclesial community itself*."[19]

Raymond Cardinal Burke offers further reflection on this point. "For the Church to remake her own fabric requires that she acknowledge a rupture in her life caused by the failure to see the organic nature of her life, received from Christ, faithfully down the centuries, the gift of the Holy Spirit for the evangelization of the world."[20]

The subjects of the new evangelization – Christians, and the ecclesial community, namely Christian institutions – are perhaps most clearly what makes the new evangelization new. The new evangelization is not catechesis for Christians living in devout families and devout cultures, nor is it the *ad gentes* proclamation of the Gospel to those entirely untouched by the Church of Christ. Instead, the subjects of the new evangelization are Christian people, institutions, and cultures in need of receiving a new and revitalizing encounter with Jesus Christ.

What is new, therefore, in the new evangelization is a formal recognition of the effects of secularization on Christian culture and Christian families. There

---

18 John Paul II, encyclical letter, *Redemptoris Missio*. December 7, 1990, no. 33. See http://www.vatican.va/holy_father/john_paul_ii/encyclicals/documents/hf_jp-ii_enc_07121990_redemptoris-missio_en.html (accessed December 17, 2014).

19 *CL*, no. 34. Italics in the original.

20 Raymond Burke. *Canon Law at the Service of Justice and Freedom in the Church as the People of God.* August 30, 2012, Nairobi. See http://www.zenit.org/en/articles/cardinal-burke-to-kenya-canon-law-convention (accessed 17 December, 2014).

are some Catholics and Catholic institutions that have, as it were, lost a sense of commitment to the apostolic mission of the Gospel, and perhaps even lost crucial aspects of the fullness of Christian life and identity. The new evangelization is a response to that loss – a commitment to present Christ anew to Christians and to the Church herself. Western Christians are living, as it were, in a post-Christian culture: the new evangelization is an invitation to commit more deeply to the Christian life.

In terms more comfortable to canonists, the new evangelization can be articulated as a call to full communion – to a communion of faith, governance and sacraments – that involves people and institutions which are Christian, yet lack the formation, devotion, and identity which comes from actively living in full communion with the Church.

There are two canonical principles important to understanding and engaging in the work of the new evangelization.

Catholic Identity

The first is the notion of Catholic identity expressed as in canon 96 of the Code of the Canon Law. "By baptism," the canon reads, "one is incorporated into the Church of Christ and is constituted a person in it with the duties and rights which are proper to Christians in keeping with their condition, insofar as they are in ecclesiastical communion and unless a legitimately issued sanction stands in the way."

Canon 96 is a consequence of the soteriology and ecclesiology by which baptism, though perhaps not a volitional act on the part of the baptized, confers an indelible character and definitively incorporates a person into a spiritual and temporal reality – the Church of Christ. This is a repudiation of the sort of theological formulation that places volition at the center of ecclesial identity – the modern notion that a person might enter or leave the Church entirely through their own choice. Canon 849 is even clearer on this point – the baptized, it says "are reborn as children of God, and, configured to Christ by an indelible character, are incorporated into the Church."

Canonists understand that the ontological consequences of baptism – the conferral of a sacramental character, and the capacity for full communion with the Church herself – are not abrogated entirely by human volitional acts.

Obviously, full communion with the Church is lost through the application of the penalty of excommunication. It is, in real ways, wounded through the loss of faith, a disregard for the precepts of the Church, a disregard for the legitimate governance of the Church, or for a general repudiation of the faith which might not rise to the level of heresy, apostasy, or schism. However, no matter how badly the bonds of ecclesial communion might be harmed or even severed by acts of volition, the capacity for communion, conferred in baptism, can neither be surrendered nor withdrawn by any human act.

Benedict XVI's motu proprio *Omnium in mentem,* issued in 2009, seems to affirm this point. It removed from canons 1086, 1117, and 1124 the canonical consequences of defecting from the Church by a formal act. By eliminating this, the Holy Father affirmed the durability of the juridic and ontological consequences of baptism.[21]

The durability of Catholic identity seems, to canonists, to be obvious. But we face, at least in the west, a popular crisis of understanding regarding the Catholic identity of believers.

Those who have worked in tribunal ministry can probably recount how frequently even seasoned pastors are confused with the question of ecclesial identity. Tribunal ministers can recall instances in which they have been called upon to explain that, despite never having worshipped in a Catholic Church, or having long ago abandoned the practice of the faith, or even having been ordained in some other Christian community, a person baptized in the Catholic Church is still held to the requirements of canonical form because they are still, and ever shall be, Catholic.

More popularly, the Church is often confronted – *ad intra* and *ad extra* – with the idea that those who have repudiated the doctrinal teachings of the Church, or ceased to practice the faith, are, by their repudiation, capable of surrendering the juridic and ontological consequences of baptism. The popular opinion regarding politicians, which says that one "can't be Catholic and be pro-choice," seems to evoke this idea. What is very obviously meant by the phrase is that a Catholic may not, with integrity, promote the legal protection of abortion without repudiating Catholic doctrine. A Catholic politician who publicly denies the teachings of the Church – who may, in fact, work against the very fundamentals of human dignity – causes grave scandal, and may well imperil her or his eternal salvation. A person in such a circumstance may well sever the bonds of full communion which, by virtue of canon 209, he or she is obliged to maintain. It seems that this ought to be the subject of appropriate penalties or consequences prescribed by the Church, in order to both call to conversion and to mitigate scandal.

However, the fact remains that a person who undermines or rejects the teachings of the Catholic Church, even very publicly, remains a Catholic. A person incorporated into the Church of Christ can, of course, be damned to eternal punishment by the consequence of sin and thus be impeded from enjoying the full

21 Benedict XVI. Motu proprio *Omnium in mentem.* October 26, 2009. See http://www.vatican.va/holy_father/benedict_xvi/apost_letters/documents/hf_ben-xvi_apl_20091026_codex-iuris-canonici_en.html (accessed December 17, 2014).

fruits of Christian initiation. Yet the moral consequences of sin, even the eternal consequences, should not be confused with the juridical, soteriological and ecclesiological consequences of baptism.

This may seem to be a semantic issue. But the consequences of baptism are at the heart of the new evangelization. John Paul's call to a new evangelization is a call to zealous evangelization of those who are baptized into the life of the Church. To respond requires recognition that the subjects of the new evangelization are fellow Christians, brothers and sisters in Christ, who possess the theological character of baptism, together with the aptitude for the theological virtues of faith, hope, and charity. Here is found an invaluable tool in the work of the new evangelization: sharing the Good News that baptism gives the gift of human dignity, of the dignity of being re-created in the image of Christ, of becoming co-heirs with Christ to the fullness of the Kingdom, and inheritors of the great riches of the Christian tradition. Baptism gives us the capacity to love as God loves.

In a materialistic and undignified culture, in what Pope Francis calls the "throw-away" culture, the dignity of baptism stands as a point of profound attraction.

Consider the case of the pro-choice politician, the one who might be told that his political position renders him a non-Catholic. Such a declaration, while perhaps in an attempt to remedy scandal, could suggest a certain surrender of ecclesiological and soteriological realities. Perhaps a more suitable approach, for the common good and for the politician's spiritual welfare, is extrapolated from the principles of canon law. Bound by canon law, such a person might receive a declaration that he or she may not be Catholic and an active proponent of "abortion rights," with an appropriate application of the consequences of obstinacy, as outlined in canon 915. At the same time, she or he might be presented with the good news that, because he or she is baptized, he or she may be set free from intellectual or moral error and not be ensnared in supporting what the Church cannot, and never will, condone.

Another example is the profusion of those who identify themselves as ex-Catholics. It is commonly suggested that such a group would constitute one of the largest religious groups in the United States. But approaching ex-Catholics with a proclamation of the capacities and dignities imparted to them in baptism, and by membership in the Church, bestows upon them an awareness they may never have had – that they have been transformed, and that by baptism, they already have the capacity to love as God loves. Such awareness is a powerful instrument of deeper conversion.

Finally, we observe a problematic tendency in the project of the new evangelization: to place primacy to upon a person's *kerygmatic* experience – the infusion of a subjective experience of faith – in the narrative of Christian identity.

"I was Catholic," such a person might say, "but not *really* Catholic." This kind of language correlates the Catholic experience to a pattern more familiar among American evangelical Christians. The *kerygmatic* experience is doubtlessly important. But apostolates dedicated to the new evangelization should be careful to recognize the primacy of baptism in the assessment of Christian identity, precisely because of its centrality to the mission of the new evangelization – which is an awakening of the awareness of Christian identity, its meaning, and its potential.

Of equal importance, ecclesial recognition of the Catholic identity of the baptized underscores the fundamental obligations of those entrusted with the *curae animarum.*

The new evangelization is an extension of the right of the baptized, articulated in canon 213: "to receive assistance from the sacred pastors out of the spiritual goods of the Church, especially the word of God and the sacraments." A proper understanding of Catholic identity, and of the mandate to engage in the work of the new evangelization, will remind a pastor, and for that matter, a diocesan bishop, of his obligation to engage those Catholics who will never darken the door of the Church, and who nevertheless, while entrusted to their care, have both right and the need of the word of God and the sacraments.

According to the Center for Applied Research in the Apostolate, in May of 2014, 24% of American Catholics could be estimated to attend Mass weekly.[22] In 2011, well over half of self-identified millennial Catholics reported being neither registered in a parish nor regularly attending Mass.[23] To definitively count among the faithful not only those who participate in sacramental life, but also those Catholics who are inactive in the faith – who are, as Pope Francis would say on the existential peripheries – demonstrates the magnitude of the new evangelization's mission, and assists pastors in focusing new effort.

Institutional Identity

The new evangelization is not only evangelization to the baptized. It is also, as John Paul said, an effort to "remake the very fabric of ecclesial identity."[24] In the motu proprio *Ubicumque et semper,* Pope Benedict XVI elaborated, saying that "what all the Churches living in traditionally Christian territories need is a

22 Statistical data from the Center for Applied Research in the Apostolate, Frequently Requested Church Statistics. See http://cara.georgetown.edu/CARAServices/requestedchurchstats.html (accessed December 17, 2014).

23 Statistical data from the Center for Applied Research in the Apostolate, Nineteen Sixty-four Research Blog at http://nineteensixty-four.blogspot.com/search?updated-min=2011-01-01T00:00:00-05:00&updated-max=2012-01-01T00:00:00-05:00&max-results=33 (accessed December 17, 2014).

24 *CL,* no. 34.

renewed missionary impulse, an expression of a new, generous openness to the gift of grace."[25]

The renewal of missionary impulse is essential for all elements of the Church's hierarchical constitution. Diocesan and parochial curias too often depend on a business model of organization, instead of a model organized around the mission of salvation. The bishop who wishes to engage in the new evangelization must first consider the structures of his own curia – to examine the extent to which he has allowed it to be overrun with the priority of the "bottom line." Is the bishop's curia a Eucharistic community, or is it a business office? This is the first question he must ask.

This recognition also suggests that Catholic ecclesial institutions including universities, hospitals, schools, etc., are all essential collaborators in the work of the new evangelization. It also implies that they are themselves subjects of the new evangelization. Consider again the implications of this for the diocesan bishop. The scope of evangelical ministry for a diocesan bishop includes not only those in the parishes of his territory, but also those apostolates which exercise ministry in it. Catholic institutions, whether those formed as juridic persons by decree of the competent ecclesiastical authority, or those which are apostolates of juridic persons (as is often the case for healthcare and educational institutions), are the subjects of the bishop's mandate to the new evangelization. He is called to engage those institutions in a pastoral plan, with new methods, ardor, and enthusiasm, all of which is committed to their growth in holiness, of purpose and of mission.

In many places, it is likely that large Catholic apostolates, such as universities or hospitals, have considerably more resources than does the diocesan bishop, with more personnel, larger visibility, and a broader network of support. In such cases, the diocesan bishop may understandably hesitate to exercise the power of governance, by, for example, holding a university accountable to the norms of *Ex corde ecclesiae*,[26] or a hospital accountable to the *Ethical and Religious Directives*.[27] Very often, the complexity of such institutions poses difficulty for a bishop who is not trained in business, healthcare, or university administration.

25 Benedict XVI, apostolic letter issued motu proprio, *Ubicumque et semper*. September 21, 2010, Introduction. See http://www.vatican.va/holy_father/benedict_xvi/apost_letters/documents/hf_ben-xvi_apl_20100921_ubicumque-et-semper_en.html (accessed December 17, 2014).

26 John Paul II. apostolic constitution *Ex corde ecclesiae*. August 15, 1990. See: http://www.vatican.va/holy_father/john_paul_ii/apost_constitutions/documents/hf_jp-ii_apc_15081990_ex-corde-ecclesiae_en.html (accessed December 17, 2014).

27 United States Conference of Catholic Bishops. *Ethical and Religious Directives for Health Care Institutions*, 5th Edition. November 17, 2009. See: http://www.usccb.org/issues-and-action/human-life-and-dignity/health-care/upload/Ethical-Religious-Directives-Catholic-Health-Care-Services-fifth-edition-2009.pdf (accessed December 17, 2014).

Understandably, these circumstances may cause a bishop to limit the exercise of the power of governance with regard to these apostolates.

As a consequence of these factors, a diocesan bishop may well be uncertain, and understandably so, of the degree to which a large Catholic apostolate in his diocese is actually compliant with the norms which govern it, and uncertain of how to approach the question. But the call of the new evangelization is precisely the call to engage Catholic institutions in order to, when necessary, reanimate them with the spirit of the Gospel, ensure their fidelity to the governance of the Church, and enlist their aid in the broader apostolic activity of the particular Church.

If the new evangelization is a call to "remake the fabric of the ecclesial community,"[28] then the diocesan bishop ought to see in it a mandate to exercise the governance and oversight authority he possesses with regard to Catholic apostolic activity. Governance should not imply draconian or unduly paternalistic approaches to engagement with the Catholic apostolates in his territory. The new evangelization is precisely that – evangelical. If the bishop wishes to reanimate a struggling Catholic university, for example, with the spirit of the Gospel, and of missionary discipleship, he will develop a relationship with its administrators and students, frequently offer the sacraments there, and provide the resources for evangelization and pastoral care of its community. But a bishop committed to the new evangelization will also recognize his responsibility in governance. For the sake of institutions and for the sake of the People of God, an evangelical bishop will require institutional fidelity to the normative expectations of the Church, and respond with appropriate measures when such fidelity is lacking.

In short, the new evangelization of Catholic institutions sees the application of the law, even the penal or restrictive application of the law, as service to the sanctity – the Christianization – of the institution itself, which enables greater collaboration or relationship with the pastoral efforts of the Church. Expecting, and assisting in, the application and accountability to the law are themselves evangelical and pastoral overtures of the diocesan bishop.

Lessons for the future

There is value to a brief conclusion of the phenomena that led to the need for a new evangelization, and what response canonists can offer in light of those circumstances.

Of course, the broadest phenomena that necessitated the new evangelization is external to Church, or at least broader than the Church itself, namely, the kind of cultural secularization of the twentieth and twenty-first century, characteristic, perhaps, of western history since the time of the Enlightenment and the

28 *CL*, no. 34.

Protestant Reformation. This secularization is perhaps most clearly embodied in the sexual revolution and its consequences. This philosophical and cultural climate has, arguably, precipitated the disintegration of the family, the ubiquity of contraception and pornography, and the destruction of the unborn child in the womb. The same philosophical climate, though manifest in a variety of particular circumstances, has contributed to the mass de-Christianization of the west, particularly in Europe and Oceania, but increasingly in the United States and North America.

But within the Church, certain phenomena can also be recognized as contributory to instances of institutional and personal decline of authentic Christian formation. Among them can be included the regular occurrence of ecclesial antinomianism. Canonists know that a disregard for the law can lead to chaos and confusion in the life of the Church, and that chaos and confusion can lead to disengagement.

Canonists, particularly those in diocesan administration, would do well to note that many of the apostolates and initiatives developing in response to the call of the new evangelization are, in some ways, a-nomian. They often develop without any juridic relationships to the hierarchical constitution of the Church, and often in forms and expressions which defy the categories and possibilities of the law. This is not likely the consequence of intentional antinomianism. Instead, it is a consequence of ignorance about the role canon law plays in the life of the Church, its importance, its wisdom and purpose.

Law is, of course, formational. As John Paul wrote in *Sacrae Disciplinae Leges*, law "facilitates ... an orderly development in the life both of the ecclesial society and of the individual persons who belong to it."[29] Law reflects the theology and anthropology of Christian revelation. It also reflects the wisdom of the Church, with regard to the praxis most conducive to salvation. Finally, it reflects considered experience in the protection of rights, appropriate disposition and administration of temporal goods, and the exercise of apostolate.

Diocesan bishops and canonists who wish to support the initiatives and apostolic projects of the new evangelization would do well to expose their proponents to canon law, to explain its value and role in the history and life of the Church, and to ensure that canon law supports and shapes the initiatives of the new evangelization. Indeed, the new evangelization calls for a significant effort to educate all of the faithful about the role canon law plays in the life of the Church.

Consider, for example, the profusion of lay-run apostolic initiatives dedicated to evangelization, undertaken with great fidelity to the doctrinal teaching of the Church, but unincorporated according to the norms for juridic persons or asso-

29 John Paul II, apostolic constitution *Sacrae disciplinae leges*, January 25, 1983, *AAS* 75/2 (1983).

ciations established in Books I and II of the Code of Canon Law. A bishop would do well to encourage such groups to present themselves for approval as ecclesial associations or persons, and to support that formation with the expertise of his curia. This would ensure that benefactors receive the protection which comes with properly developed statutes, that they themselves are able to exercise proper oversight required of them as bishops by the law, and that the apostolates themselves have the standing to make acts of hierarchical recourse when appropriate.

Or consider the new forms of consecrated life which have developed in response to the call for the new evangelization. To ensure the protection of rights for consecrated persons, and proper internal ordering, a bishop would do well to help such communities to establish themselves in accord with the norms of Book II, Part III of the code. Persons who are "consecrated," so to speak, in extra-canonical communities might find themselves with very little protection of rights when they wish to undertake some act of recourse.

It may well be that some new forms of consecrated life seem inconsistent with any of the institutional models available to institutes of religious consecration. For that reason, it may be true that the law must develop in order to accommodate the movement of the Holy Spirit. But it may also be true that a mode of apostolic living is incongruous with the menu of options presented by the code because it is imprudent, impractical, or inconsistent with Christian anthropology. In that case, and in probably many others, the law does justice by tempering the impulses of apostolic creativity with the wisdom of experience borne in the history of Holy Mother Church.

In short, by subjecting themselves to the dictates of the law, new apostolic movements and initiatives have the opportunity to be formed along a path of wisdom, that could well ensure the long-term viability of their creative endeavors. Bishops and other ecclesial administrators would do well to make the law, and its formative capacity, available to the initiatives and apostolates of the new evangelization.

In *Evangelii gaudium*, Pope Francis spoke of ecclesial responsibility to "'*the baptized whose lives do not reflect the demands of Baptism,'* who lack a meaningful relationship to the Church and no longer experience the consolation born of faith. The Church, in her maternal concern, tries to help them experience a conversion which will restore the joy of faith to their hearts and inspire a commitment to the Gospel."[30] Canon law is an aid to that conversion. In the application of our ministry may canonist help to restore joy in Jesus Christ, and inspire in the Church a deeper commitment to the Gospel.

30 Francis, apostolic exhortation, *Evangelii Gaudium*, November 24, 2014, no. 15. See http://w2.vatican.va/content/francesco/en/apost_exhortations/documents/papa-francesco_esortazione-ap_20131124_evangelii-gaudium.html (accessed December 17, 2014). Pope Francis is actually quoting Pope Benedict XVI in a homily he preached at the closing of the Synod of Bishops, 28 October, 2012. He said: "A third aspect concerns *the baptized whose lives do not reflect the demands of Baptism.* During the Synod, it was emphasized that such people are found in all continents, especially in the most secularized countries. The Church is particularly concerned that they should encounter Jesus Christ anew, rediscover the joy of faith and return to religious practice in the community of the faithful." See http://www.vatican.va/holy_father/benedict_xvi/homilies/2012/documents/hf_ben-xvi_hom_20121028_conclusione-sinodo_en.html (accessed December 17, 2014).

Seminar

Practical Guidelines for Aging Institutes

Sr. Amy Hereford, CSJ, JD, JCD

Background

This paper is based on my doctoral research on the role of law in the life-cycle of a religious institutes. The project began with an historical case study, the history of the Sisters of St. Joseph of Carondelet, of which I am a member. The historical overview focused on three key moments in the history of the institute, its initial foundation, its establishment in North America and the renewal of the congregation in response to the Second Vatican Council. While this case study was used throughout the project as the primary example of the life-cycle of a religious institute, general statistical information on religious institutes in the United States was also incorporated to enhance a broader understanding and applicability. While it discusses religious institutes of women in the United States, it may have broader application to societies of apostolic life, mens' institutes and societies and those outside the United States.

The project turned next to the notion of the life-cycle of an organization, applying studies of this concept to the historical case study presented in the first section. Drawn from the field of biology, the concept of life-cycle was applied to organizations in the mid-20th century in the fields of economics and management studies. Exploring an organization's social system from a longitudinal perspective is particularly helpful in analyzing the role of law in religious institutes, because most of the relevant change in law of an organization occurs at key moments of institutional change in the life-cycle.

Because a religious institute is greater than the sum of its sociological parts, the project moved to a theological analysis of the nature of a religious institute, focusing on the development of the nature of the institute through its life-cycle; an institute is not a static institution, but a dynamic entity in an unfolding life.

The final section turned to the central question of the project, critiquing the role that law plays in the course of the life-cycle of a religious institute. It reviewed particular points of canon law and civil law that come in to play in the various stages in the life-cycle of the institute. Then, turning to the issue of the influence and contribution of law and jurisprudence in the life-cycle of a religious institute, it analyzed the appropriate use of law in a Christian community as it seeks to follow its particular way of living the Gospel: it examined the methodology of law as a useful tool in helping to engage issues and challenges, and in formulating responses. The legislative process can bring disparate voices together to articulate a common vision and establish the structures and processes that will further that vision. Laws made by the community serve to memorialize that process, and provide guidance for the ongoing life of the community and a point of reference as the members move out in pursuit of their common vocation. External laws can serve as a measure or κανών to help the institute evaluate its way of life and to guide relations *ad extra*. Finally, it sought to provide guidance for those who find themselves in the states of foundation or ending in the United States in the early 21st century. This final section on practical guidelines for aging institutes will be the focus of this presentation.

The Second Vatican Council foresaw that there would be institutes that would not "possess hope for further development," mandating that such institutes "should be forbidden to receive novices in the future." It further provided that "if it is possible, these should be combined with other more flourishing communities and monasteries whose scope and spirit is similar."[1] *Perfectae caritatis* did not anticipate the current situation, in which the overwhelming majority of institutes, in a particular territory such as the United States, do not "posses hope of further development," and thus there are not enough "flourishing communities and monasteries" to receive all those that are declining.

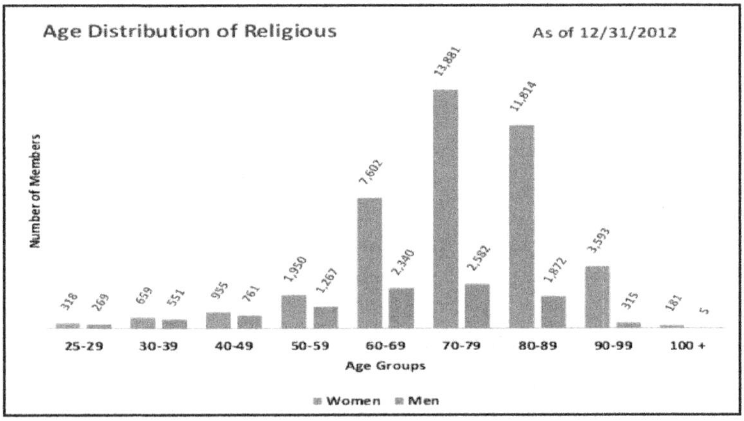

Ecclesiae Sanctae repeated the preference expressed in *Perfectae caritatis* that declining institutes be joined with "more vigorous institutes," and added the caution that "individual religious ... should be consulted before and all should

1 Vatican II, decree *Perfectae caritatis,* in *Vatican Council II: The Conciliar and Post-Conciliar Documents*, ed. Austin Flannery (Northport, NY: Costello Publishing, 1992) 611-623.

be done with charity."[2] For declining institutes, combining with a larger, more stable institute has the advantage of 1) ensuring adequate care is given to the members and 2) providing for the institute's apostolic works. Such a combination of institutes should also preserve the spiritual patrimony of the declining institute,[3] which is incorporated into the new institute. However preservation of the spiritual patrimony has not always been a reality.[4]

Due to the large number of institutes that are facing irreversible decline in the early twenty-first century in the United States,[5] it is highly unlikely that many of the declining institutes will be able to find flourishing institutes with whom to merge. Even if institutes decide to merge, the median age will remain high, even if there are more members in the resulting institute. If the current trends continue, many will likely face the end of their institutes in the coming decades. This paper explores the issues and concerns facing these institutes and practical guidelines for assisting them.

Practical Guidelines for Religious Institutes in Decline

By 2020, in the United States, the last of the large cohorts of members of religious institutes will have moved from active ministry into retirement or semi-retirement. According to projections of the National Religious Retirement Office, 90 percent of the members in women's communities will be over the age of seventy.[6] While the demographics will vary slightly from one institute to another, an institute of fifty members would have five members under the age of seventy, most of them in their sixties. It has been opined that between 75 percent and 90 percent of current religious institutes will cease to exist in the next twenty years.[7] If this is correct, between 300 and 350 institutes are currently in their last decades, and need to address the juridical issues necessary for this period in

---

2 Paul VI, motu proprio *Ecclesiae Sanctae II*, in *Vatican Council II: The Conciliar and Post-Conciliar Documents*, ed. Austin Flannery (Northport, NY: Costello Publishing, 1992) 624-633.

3 *CIC* c. 578.

4 Catherine C. Darcy, *The Institute of the Sisters of Mercy of the Americas: The Canonical Development of the Proposed Governance Model* (Lanham, MD: University Press of America, 1993) 115.

5 David J. Nygren and Miriam D. Ukeritis, *The Future of Religious Orders in the United States: Transformation and Commitment* (Westport CT: Praeger, 1993); *NRRO Annual Report* (Washington, DC: National Religious Retirement Office, 2013); Marjory Gallagher, "The Future of Small Religious Institutes: Merging and Other Issues," *Canon Law Society of America Proceedings* 57 (1995) 201–15.

6 See *2013 NRRO Annual Report* for complete lists of all statistics cited.

7 Diarmuid O'Murchu, *Consecrated Religious Life: The Changing Paradigms* (Maryknoll, NY: Orbis, 2005) 115; Ted Dunn, "Refounding Religious Life: A Choice for Transformational Change," *Human Development* (2009) 5-13; Miriam D. Ukeritis, "The Rise and Fall of Catholic Religious Orders: A Social Movement Perspective," *Journal for the Scientific Study of Religion* 34, no. 4 (December 1, 1995): 545–46.

their life-cycle. Over the past decades, institutes have merged, or affiliated with one another.[8] However, given the large number of institutes facing decline, and the relatively small number of institutes that show signs that they will continue to flourish, it is unlikely that there will be sufficient numbers of institutes large enough and stable enough to welcome and support the declining institutes. These institutes will likely face extinction or completion[9] in the next twenty years, particularly when merger and aggregation are not options.

The Motu proprio *Ecclesiae Sanctae* gave three criteria that give evidence of an institute in decline: "the small number of religious in proportion to the age of the institute or the monastery, the lack of candidates over a period of several years, the advanced age of the majority of its members."[10] Institutes that show these indicators of decline and are in the final generation of their life-cycle face a number of challenges, however three critical issues become increasingly acute, arising, as they do, at a time when the institute's and members' energies and resources are declining. These issues are:

1. Providing ongoing leadership for the institute.

2. Providing care for aging members, in addition to health-care, this includes pastoral care and support of the all the members, those facing the challenges of aging and those moving out of full-time ministry, as well as those still in active ministry.

3. Providing leadership in the sponsored ministries.[11]

While some general statements can be made about the demographics and challenges of institutes, it is also true that each institute is unique in its history, its resources and its situation. Some institutes are related to others of similar charism, some are not. Some communities are provinces of a larger institute, with other provinces in the United States or abroad, while others are free-standing. Some institutes are diocesan, others are pontifical. Some are concentrated in one local area, others are spread over several cities, or even across much of the United States and beyond. Institutes vary by number of members, and the skill and experience of their members. Many continue to sponsor schools, hospitals and other ministries, some have significant property holdings, others have none of these.

---

8 Canons 582, 580. See Dan Ward, "Covenant Relationship," *RCRI 8* (Fall, 2012) 4-8.

9 Theo Sponselee, Ad Leys and Cees van Dam, "Explorations on the 'Completion' of Religious Institutes," *RCRI 8* (Fall, 2012) 9-22.

10 *ES II*, 41.

11 Amy Hereford, "Small and Aging Institutes, Issues and Options," *Religious Law and Consultation Newsletter* 113 (2011) 5.

In 1986, the National Conference of Catholic Bishops and the leadership conferences of men and women religious formed the National Religious Retirement Office (NRRO) to address "the significant lack of retirement savings among religious communities in the United States."[12] The office has been collecting data on the retirement needs of religious in the United States and the retirement assets available in the various institutes to support their aging members. Though not every religious institute participates in their survey, this survey provides the best data available, both on the demographics of religious institutes and on their ability to care for their aging members.

In an effort to quantify the retirement needs of the various institutes, NRRO has been collecting and collating data on the unfunded retirement liability of religious institutes since its inception. Each year participating institutes complete a survey that elicits information about the institutes' demographics and financial resources. From this information, NRRO is able to project those institutes that have sufficient funding to care for all their members (100 percent funded), and those that do not have enough resources to care for their members (less than 100% funded). Through the ongoing work of NRRO, the overall ability of institutes to care for their aging members has improved significantly. While the level of funding has improved, only about one third of the institutes are over 80 percent funded according to the office's 2013 annual report.[13] Institutes facing their final decades are doing so with a scarcity of resources to care for their aging members; that scarcity is likely to become increasingly acute in the coming years.

Aging membership and dwindling resources can overwhelm leaders and members gathered in chapter, as they seek to make arrangements for their coming years. Often institute leadership and chapters turn their attention to the new challenges of mission and justice, to the day-to-day administration, or to some hoped-for "transformation" into a bright new future. When they address future challenges, chapters resolutions may include a preference for "retaining our identity," and a charge to leadership to explore the institute's options.[14] The daily work of institute leadership is occupied with caring for aging members, healthcare, funerals and administration. There is little time or energy left to address the bigger question of managing institutional decline. Studies of the life-cycle of an organization show that this is typical of an organization in decline.[15]

12 See NNRO, *Backgrounder: Retirement Fund for Religious* (Washington, DC: USCCB, 2014).

13 *2013 NRRO Annual Report*, 6.

14 See Dunn, "Refounding Religious Life: A Choice for Transformational Change," 5-13; Fintan Sheeran, "Transformation of Religious Life: Practical Learnings," *InFormation* 20, no. 1 (Spring 2011) 2–4; Sandra M. Schneiders, *Prophets in Their Own Country: Women Religious Bearing Witness to the Gospel in a Troubled Church* (Maryknoll, NY: Orbis Books, 2011).

15 Ichak Adizes, *Managing Corporate Lifecycles*, rev. ed. (New York: Prentice Hall Press, 1999) 167.

An institute can turn to its spiritual heritage and its charism, to help it face the challenges of the later stages of the institute's life-cycle. The courage and resilience of the founding generation can be an inspiration to the aging generation in meeting the challenges it faces. Trust in God, who inspired the institute's first generation, and each generation over the institute's long history, may help the institute and its leadership to have the courage for their task. "Do not let your hearts be troubled. You have faith in God; have faith also in me. In my Father's house, there are many dwelling places. If there were not, would I have told you that I am going to prepare a place for you?"[16] Jesus is preparing a place for the institute and its members, they can take courage and set out, and along the way, they need not fear because Jesus also proclaims "I am the way"[17] that leads to where you are going. Taking courage from the sustaining presence of God, institutes must make practical preparation for their coming years of decline.

Institutes may be critically near the end of their ability to provide their own leadership. Yet they may be only vaguely aware that, at some point in the future, they will no longer be able to continue as they have in the past. Members gradually adjust to the inevitable decline, to the diminishment of energies and capacities, but they fail to engage the larger issues of the end of the institute's life-journey. The leadership spends time and attention on the daily challenges of administration, and on attending to aging and dying members, but rarely engage the mortality of the institute itself. Individuals and communities must engage the sense of loss, guilt, anger, and grieving[18] that can arise as the institute comes to face and accept its reality.

As an institute moves into its final generation, there are certain decisions it must make. One decision is the overall structure that it wishes to pursue. Sometimes this is determined for it, because only one option is possible. Briefly, the options are these. First, the institute can remain as it is and avoid any planning. In this case, likely the institute will flounder at some point, and those outside the institute will come in to make decisions which may or may not be in the best interests of the remaining members or the legacy of the institute. This is a poor choice, but it is the default position. Second, the institute could seek to merge with a larger institute,[19] but at this point in many institutes' life-cycles this choice seems to demand too much commitment of time and resources, and in the end it does not result in a viable institute.[20] A modification of this would be to seek an aggregation to another institute,[21] or non-canonical relationship with another

16 Jn. 14.

17 Jn. 14.

18 Luisa Saffiotti and Raymond Dlugos, "Engaging Resistance in the Service of Communal Discernment." Authors' notes from their presentation at *Transformation of Religious Life in North America*, St. Louis, MO, April 19, 2012.

19 *CIC* c. 582.

20 Sponselee, et al., 20.

21 *CIC* c. 580.

institute. This path is often being termed a "covenant relationship" between two institutes.[22] If there is a larger more stable institute available, this is a possibility. However, in the United States at this time, a large number of institutes are seeking sponsoring institutes, and only a handful of institutes are in a position to provide this form of sponsorship. This second option has been explored in detail elsewhere, and will not be discussed further here. In any case, it is unlikely to be a viable option for many more institutes.[23] Finally, an institute could choose to engage its final decades by looking outside the institute for partners to ensure the care of its members, the dignified transition or ending of all its responsibilities and the settling of its legacy. Institutes often experience difficulty in coming to discuss and eventually embrace this option. However, once they do, they often report experiencing a certain freedom from the demands of keeping up appearances. Their choices are difficult, even painful, but they experience the peace from knowing that they are making more realistic choices for their institute.

Once an institute acknowledges that it is coming to the end of its life-cycle, it can begin to move into a period of adjusting to this reality, and begin putting plans in place for the coming years. These plans will center around four principal tasks which will overlap, but which occur more or less sequentially. The first task is transitioning sponsorship. If the institute continues to have ministries for which it provides leadership, financial support or canonical sponsorship, it must transition these relationships. The second task is providing for elder-care; the institute cares for its aging members, and they must begin to explore ways of providing this care as the last members begin to need care themselves. The leader of one such institute described the challenge of this task as follows: "The last three sisters can't push their own wheelchairs."[24] The third task is turning over the administration of the institute's assets and operations to non-members. As long as the institute is able to provide effective oversight of elder-care and administration, the institute can retain its own canonical leadership. The final task is to nominate an individual, or group of individuals, who can provide canonical leadership for the institute and its members, and provide effective oversight of elder-care and administration. These tasks will be examined in sequence.

Transitioning Sponsorship

A fundamental part of the life and work of religious institutes is carrying on the mission of Jesus.[25] Many religious institutes carried out their apostolic works in institutions that provided health-care, education, social and pastoral services

---

22 Amy Hereford, "Canon 580: Aggregation and Covenants," *Roman Replies and CLSA Advisory Opinions* (Washington, DC: CLSA, 2012), 83–86. See Ward, "Covenant Relationship," 4-8.

23 Hereford, "Canon 580: Aggregation and Covenants." See Ward, "Covenant Relationship," 4-8; Hereford, "Small and Aging Institutes," 5.

24 Sister Mary Louise Kelly, interview with author, March 7, 2012.

25 *LG*, 43.

to millions of people. Sponsorship is the term that has come to be used for the relationship between a religious institute and its institutional ministries. Over the past fifty years, many of these institutional ministries were separately incorporated, due to several factors, including the increasing complexity of the ministries and their regulation, and rising concern with liability and litigation arising from the ministries. When the ministries were initially founded, members of the founding institute carried out all the roles, including direct service, administration and oversight. In time, and with the decrease in membership, fewer members were available for direct service, though often members remained in important administrative positions and the institute retained control of the ministry's board of directors. Over the past ten years, members have all but disappeared from direct service and administrative positions, and it is only with difficulty that institutes are able to responsibly exercise control over the boards of directors or member boards. From a canonical point of view, ministries started by the institute remain an integral part of the religious institute as a single juridic person, even if they are separately incorporated under civil law.[26] For this reason, the institute retains the canonical responsibility to ensure that the ministry is carried out according to its own mission, that it remains in communion with the Church, and that the assets are administered as ecclesiastical goods.[27]

As an institute comes to the point of acknowledging its decline, it must consider making other arrangements for these sponsored ministries.[28] They may seek to transfer sponsorship to another juridic person, either another religious institute or a diocese. However, there are few religious institutes capable of accepting sponsorship of these ministries. In addition, some dioceses have expressed reluctance to accept responsibility for the ministries, often due to the financial or administrative burden, or to the potential for civil liability. In the case of a school, there are three options for being a Catholic school as set out in canon 803 §1. A Catholic school is understood as one which 1) "a competent ecclesiastical authority … directs" or 2) "a public ecclesiastical juridic person directs," or 3) "ecclesiastical authority recognizes as such through a written document."[29] Thus if a school is unable to find a successor sponsor, in the form of a religious institute or a diocese, or other juridic person, they may seek to be recognized in a written document, without seeking a sponsor. Alternatively, a ministry may seek independent status as a juridic person.[30] In order to operate *in nomine ecclesiae,* a public juridic person would be required. In the case of a ministry which oper-

26 Robert T. Kennedy, "McGrath, Maida, Michiels: Introduction to a Study of the Canonical and Civil-Law Status of Church-Related Institutions in the United States," *Jurist* 50 (1990) 351–401.

27 Amy Hereford, "Transitioning Sponsorship," *Religious Law and Consultation Newsletter* 136 (2013): 1–4.

28 Sponselee, et al., 11.

29 *CIC* 803 §1.

30 Sharon Holland, "Vatican Expert Unpacks Canonical PJP Process," *Health Progress* 90, no. 5 (September 2011) 50–62.

ates in several dioceses, the ministry might seek to become a pontifical public juridic person, as is the case with some hospital systems in the United States.[31] In most cases, the ministry would seek to become a diocesan public juridic person.[32] Some institutes are questioning the need for ongoing juridical sponsorship, particularly for ministries that provide social service.

Providing Elder-care

Providing elder-care for the remaining members of the institute, who have given their lives in service, is an important obligation for the declining institute.[33] Most institutes in the United States do not have sufficient resources to care for their elderly members. According to a 2012 report, the religious institutes in the United States, considered as a whole, will need an estimated $13.3 billion to care for all the elderly religious, and they have $8.6 billion in reserve, leaving a $4.7 billion shortfall.[34] While this is a staggering sum, the shortfall had been double that amount just ten years before. Institutes may employ several practices to enhance their financial position, including financial planning and fund-raising. Increasingly, institutes are turning to laypersons to assist in these tasks. Most, but not all, religious institutes participate in Social Security programs, which can help fill the deficit in the institute's retirement resources.[35] There are two areas of concern in elder-care, retirement assets and the retirement facility.

Some institutes have chosen to place their retirement assets in a charitable trust. This was initially done, primarily, to protect retirement assets from civil liability, and secondarily, to ensure that the institute and its leaders continued to reserve these assets for retirement needs, rather than diverting them to operations.[36] The charitable trust is a separate legal entity, and as a rule, the leadership of the religious institute serve as trustees. With this arrangement, no alienation is involved because the assets and their control remain in the religious institute. Under trust law, the religious institute, as "settlor," dedicates a portion of its resources, in trust, for the care of its elderly members. As a fiduciary entity, the

31 Melanie Evans, "Ascending in Healthcare," *Modern Healthcare* (May 14, 2007), 1–4; Nancy Mulvihil, "Public Juridic Person Ensures Catholic Presence," *Health Progress* 77, no. 1 (Feb. 1996) 25–37; Robert J. Murray, "Religious Communities and Their Mission," *Journal of Religion and Health* 41, no. 2 (June 2002) 131–51.

32 *CIC* cc. 312-320.

33 Sponselee, et al., 14.

34 NRRO, *NRRO Annual Report* (Washington, DC: National Religious Retirement Office, 2012).

35 CARA and NRRO, *Planning for Retirement and Mission: Best Practices* (Washington DC: Nation, 2006).

36 Peter Campbell, "Temporalities for Religious - Six Practical Cases: II. Financial and Civil Law Considerations," *Canon Law Society of America Proceedings* 46 (Washington, DC: CLSA, 1984) 82–97; Joan E. Brophy and Daniel W. Luther, "Protecting Retirement Assets," *Legal Bulletin* 68 (1997) 3–12; Amy Hereford and Laura Reicks, "Charitable Trusts Twenty Five Years Later," *Legal Bulletin* 73 (2002) 17–37.

charitable trust must dedicate its assets perpetually to carrying out the charitable purposes of the trust, which are generally stated to be "providing care for the aged and/or infirm members of the institute." The trustees are responsible for administering the assets of the trust, for disbursing assets for the care of the beneficiaries, and for fund development, through investment and/or fund-raising.

Up to the present, religious institutes have made it a practice to have institute leadership serving as trustees, in accord with the advice of civil and canon lawyers.[37] However, for a declining institute, it is increasingly difficult for the leadership to continue to carry out this role. The purpose clause of the trust ensures that the assets can only be used for "providing care for the aged and/or infirm members of the institute." Non-member trustees may be appointed to carry out that role. The assets are dedicated in trust, and cannot be used for purposes other than care of the members. For this reason, if this is done with care, the appointment of non-member trustees may not be an alienation, because they remain dedicated to institute purposes through the trust document.

Initially, non-member trustees can serve with certain powers of the trust reserved to the leadership of the institute, as has been done with sponsored ministries in the past. These non-member trustees may be retired professionals, who may be willing to serve in a voluntary capacity, due to a long-standing relationship with the institute. In this case, it will be important to foresee the need for successor trustees. Alternatively, they may be paid, commercial trustees. In this case, the institute must have sufficient resources to pay the fees; however, it will obviate the need for a successor. In either case, the institute will retain oversight of the trust, receiving periodic reports and approving investment plans, spending rules and disbursement of funds. If an institute has not established its retirement resources in a separate trust, it may nevertheless seek a similar arrangement for transferring administration of retirement assets to non-members.

A second area of concern for elder-care is the retirement facility. Some institutes have their own retirement facility that may have begun as an internal infirmary for the sisters. If the retirement facility is now separately incorporated, then it may be treated like a sponsored ministry, discussed above, and the institute makes plans for the transitioning of the sponsorship. In this case, they will seek a sponsor who is able to continue to govern and manage the facility, at least as long as it is needed by the members. The institute will contract with the new sponsor for the care of its members in the facility. Generally, this issue is included in the negotiations for the transfer of sponsorship of the facility.[38] Licensing of the

37 Hereford and Reicks, 17–37.

38 Jenny Beatrice, "Sisters of St. Joseph of Carondelet and Benedictine Health System Enter Co-Sponsorship of Nazareth Living Center," *St. Louis Today*, July 10, 2009.

facility must be planned with care, in order to ensure that the members are able to make use of government assistance programs, and still remain at the facility.[39]

If the elder-care facility remains an internal infirmary for the community, and is not separately incorporated or licensed, the institute will have to determine how to sustain their elder-care. They may choose to close their facility and sell it, using the funds to care for the members in another facility. They may separately incorporate their facility, and treat it as a sponsored ministry, as above. Or they may choose some intermediate course, which transfers the responsibility for care of the members and management of the facility to non-members in exchange for the transfer of the future value of the facility, in an arrangement like a "reverse mortgage." Some institutes share their facilities with members of other religious institutes, or collaborate with several other institutes in the area to find an effective way to provide elder-care for their members.[40]

As these arrangements are made, it is important to have clear communication and role definition for those caring for the elderly religious, those providing pastoral care for the members, and the institute's leadership. "Each administrator needs to have clear roles and responsibilities to prevent conflict or duplication of services. Although the administrators are ultimately accountable to the president or provincial and/or the general or provincial council, institute leadership should not be involved in the day to day management of the facility."[41]

Transitioning Administration

Having ensured the appropriate transition of sponsorship, and the elder-care of members, the institute leadership has the ongoing tasks of the administration of the temporal affairs of the institute itself, of the canonical leadership and pastoral care of the institute and its members.

In the United States, religious institutes generally establish civil corporations for handling their temporal affairs.[42] Somewhat analogous to a juridic person in canon law, a corporation is:

> a legal entity entirely separate and distinct from the individuals who compose it, with the capacity of continuous existence or succession, and having the capacity of such legal entity, of taking, holding and conveying property, suing and being sued,

---

39 See the fine work done in CARA and NRRO, "Planning for Retirement and Mission: Best Practices."

40 Ibid.

41 Ibid., 10.

42 Amy Hereford, "Requirements for Corporation Documents of Religious Orders," *Legal Bulletin* 78 (2004) 11.

> and exercising such other powers as may be conferred on it by law, just as a natural person may.[43]

An institute's corporation may be organized as a membership corporation, as is generally done for monastic communities, or as a non-member corporation. If organized as a member corporation, all the members of the institute are members of the corporation; this is not the case in a non-member corporation. In either case, the elected leadership of the institute serves as the board of directors of the corporation, either *ex-officio* or by appointment.[44]

A declining institute may choose to appoint non-members to the board of directors of its institute corporation. These directors would be charged with carrying on the temporal affairs of the institute while the institute's leadership would retain oversight, through certain reserve powers, such as appointment of directors, approval of budget, receiving the audit, amendment of the articles and bylaws, and dissolution of the corporation, as has been done for sponsored ministry corporations.[45] The institute's leadership, sitting as the board of directors, would have to revise its corporate articles and bylaws to provide for this change. This practice would be similar to the practice in the Netherlands of establishing a juridic person for administration, separate from the religious institute's *de jure* juridic person, and entrusting the leadership of that juridic person for administration to non-members.[46]

The task of the new non-member directors of the institute's corporation would be to oversee the ongoing temporal activities of the institute and manage its temporal affairs. Knowing that the institute is in irreversible decline, they would complete the work of transferring or closing any activities of the institute that are not related to the care of the members or to sustainable activities of the institute. They would manage the institute's property, sell any under-utilized property, and consolidate and down-size the institute's infrastructure.

During this time, the canonical leadership of the institute would continue to carry out the canonical and pastoral leadership of the institute and its members. They would attend to other critical tasks such as settling the institute's archives and its cemetery.[47] They would also hold the reserve powers for the institute's corporation, its retirement trust, and continue to oversee elder-care. Eventually, when there are no longer activities of the corporation, it may be closed or "wound up," or it may be made a subsidiary of the trust. This is appropriate

43 Bryan Garner, ed., *Black's Law Dictionary* (St. Paul, MN: West, 2009), s.v. "corporation."

44 Hereford 17.

45 Peter Campbell, "Evolving Sponsorship and Corporate Structures," *Health Progress* 76, no. 4 (1995) 39.

46 Sponselee, et al., 18.

47 Ibid., 11.

especially if the elder-care is in another corporation and there is a trust holding the retirement assets.

One model for carrying out the three tasks described so far, namely sponsored ministries, elder-care and administration of the institute's activities and assets, is Canadian Religious Stewardship. Erected by a decree of the Congregation for Institutes of Consecrated Life and Societies of Apostolic Life on December 8, 2010,[48] following extensive consultation with Congregation and with institutes interested in participation, the pontifical public juridic person has five purposes:

1. To assist religious institutes by managing and safeguarding their ecclesiastical temporal goods and assuring their proper administration in accordance with canon and civil law

2. To provide personal care programs and services for the membership of these institutes

3. To accept ownership of ecclesiastical temporal goods in those instances where the institute wishes to divest itself of property, in accordance with the requirements of canon law

4. When opportune, to accept governance responsibilities for any or all health-care, educational, religious and social service ministries presently supported by the institute

5. With the consent of the relevant diocesan bishop, and, if appropriate, to accept sponsorship of an institute's ministry.[49]

The juridic person's statutes require that the president "shall be a perpetually professed member of an institute of consecrated life or society of apostolic life. The other members are to be in full communion with the Catholic Church, but they may be religious or lay persons."[50] The juridic person established Canadian Catholic Congregational Management, a Canadian civil corporation to provide needed services. The Canadian Religious Stewardship is intended only for the temporal affairs of the institutes and societies; there is no plan to succeed to the canonical leadership of the institutes, or to become a religious institute itself.[51] This represents a positive, coordinated step forward in addressing the needs of declining institutes.

---

48 Francis G. Morrisey, "New PJP Model 'A Leap Of Faith,'" *Health Progress* 92, no. 2 (April 2011) 68.

49 Ibid., 69.

50 Ibid.

51 Ibid.

Canonical Administrator

In the steps described up until this point, the declining institute has retained its canonical leadership, while entrusting operations and administrative matters into the hands of non-members. Religious leadership remains in office as long as possible, for specifically canonical functions, for the pastoral care of the members, and to exercise the reserve powers for the civil corporation and the charitable trust. When there are no longer members who have sufficient energy and competence to exercise these roles, then they must seek an alternative way to ensure that these important needs are met, for example, by entrusting them to a canonical administrator, also called a canonical trustee or a canonical steward.[52]

Canon 623 states that "to be validly appointed or elected to the office of superior, members must have been perpetually or definitively professed for an appropriate period of time, to be determined by their own law or, for major Superiors, by the constitutions."[53] Constitutions provide similar qualifications for councilors. Thus, a person who is not a perpetually professed member cannot serve as superior or supreme moderator, or as councilors. However, in a declining institute, the time will come when there is no member able to serve in this role. In addition, while there may be someone able to serve as superior, there may not be sufficient members to serve as councilors. At that point, the institute must seek an alternative. There is little precedent for the situation of a religious institute that does not have its own canonical leadership. There have been individual examples of the use of a delegate or administrator, appointed to a religious institute from outside the institute, for a limited period of time, when the institute was facing particular challenges.[54]

The use of a canonical administrator, or administrative team is one alternative that has been suggested as an option for declining institutes, who are without members able to serve in canonical leadership.[55] The appointment of such an administrator would involved a derogation of universal law and of the institute's own constitutions.[56] For pontifical institutes, the appointment of a canonical administrator would be within the competence of the Apostolic See, specifically the Congregation for Institutes of Consecrated Life and Societies of Apostolic Life.[57]

---

52 Sponselee, et.al, 20.

53 *CIC* c. 623.

54 Benedict XVI, *Nomina del delegato Pontificio per la congregazione dei Legionari Di Cristo*, Press Office of the Holy See, July 9, 2008. The text can be seen at http://www.regnumchristi.org/italiano/articulos/articulo.phtml?id=30425&se=362&ca=966&te=821 (accessed December 15, 2014); Ward, "Covenant Relationship," 6.

55 See Ward, "Covenant Relationship," 8; Sponselee, et al. 17 ff.

56 *CIC* c. 623.

57 In the case of an institute of one of the Eastern Churches *sui iuris*, the Congregation for Eastern Churches would be competent.

"An institute of diocesan right remains under the special care of the diocesan bishop."[58] Because of this special care, the diocesan bishop of the principal house 1) "approves the constitutions and confirms any changes lawfully introduced into them," 2) "deals with major affairs which exceed the power of the internal authority of the institute,"[59] and 3) "grants a dispensation from the constitutions in particular cases."[60] The appointment of a canonical administrator to carry out functions entrusted to the supreme moderator in the constitutions would probably not be introduced as a change in the constitutions. However, it would certainly be a "major affair" exceeding the power of the internal authority of the institute, and would require a dispensation from the constitutions. It also requires a derogation from universal law. The diocesan bishop is competent to dispense from universal law, whenever he judges that it contributes to the spiritual good of the faithful in his territory.[61] Thus a diocesan bishop is competent to appoint an administrator to carry out the functions of canonical leadership in the diocesan institute.

For further guidance in this situation, we can look to a parallel place in the code, namely canon 318 §1, which provides for replacing the moderator of public associations of the faithful, in extraordinary circumstances. It states: "in special circumstances and where grave reasons require it, the ecclesiastical authority mentioned in can. 312§1 can designate a trustee (*commissarium)* who is to direct the association for a time in its name."[62] The canon does not apply to religious institutes, but its principle may be applied *mutatis mutandi,* in the "special circumstance" and "grave reason" of a religious institute that is not able to provide its own supreme moderator. This canon states that the canonical trustee would serve "for a time," that is, not indefinitely as would be the need in a declining religious institute.

While the appointment of a canonical administrative team is within the competence of ecclesiastical authority, a declining institute may nominate someone, indicating the person or persons, to whom they wish to entrust the responsibility for their care, in their declining years. Such a nomination would assist the ecclesiastical authority in appointing an administrator, who could protect the autonomy of the institute, while the ecclesiastical authority retains certain oversight responsibilities.[63]

In examining how this role is to be carried out, it is important to remember that the governance of religious institutes is never done alone, each superior is required to have a council,[64] whose advice or consent must be sought for more

58 *CIC* c. 594.
59 *CIC* c. 595 §1.
60 *CIC* c. 595 §2.
61 *CIC* c. 87 §1.
62 *CIC* c. 318 §1.
63 *CIC* cc. 591–595. See also: Sponselee, et al., 19.
64 *CIC* c. 627.

important decisions, particularly when they touch the rights of members, or the disposition of temporal goods.[65] Likewise, every juridic person is required to have a finance council, or at least two counselors,[66] and the governance of dioceses and parishes require certain councilors or advisors.[67] These canonical precedents indicate that someone serving as administrator for a declining religious institute should also not serve alone. It may be advantageous to select three persons to serve in this role, in accord with this canonical principle. In this way there will be some checks and balances among them, it will ensure that there is always one of the three available, and will enable the group to have multiple competencies. Relevant competencies include: ensuring the pastoral needs of the members are met in their waning years, overseeing elder-care and assisting in decision-making regarding health-care, and attending to legal and financial issues. It is important that persons selected for the canonical administrative team bring one or more of these or other relevant skills and experience.

The institute, even in its declining years, retains its right to autonomy (*justa autonomia*) as specified in canon 586.[68] The canonical administrative team must be aware of and respect this autonomy. It is important that administrators be personally disinterested, i.e., that they not have a personal financial or other interest in the life of the institute, which may be in conflict with the interest of the institute or its members. For this reason, while the assistance of the local bishop may be useful, even called for in the case of diocesan institutes,[69] the bishop or diocesan officials are not be the most appropriate persons to serve as administrators.[70]

In the case of a declining institute, the canonical administrator may be required to serve in this capacity for a number of years, even decades, through the life of the last remaining member of the institute. Therefore, it will be important to give some attention to succession of administrators. If there is an office or an organization that can supply the administrator, this may be preferable to selecting one person or three individuals, with no designation of a successor in the case of the inability of one or more of them to continue their service.

It will also be important to provide some forum of accountability for the administrator. It is important that the religious have the assurance that someone is overseeing the administrator, into whose hands they have entrusted their lives, and ending years of the life of their institute. Conferences of major superiors are established to "deal with affairs which are common to all, and work to es-

---

65 See *CIC* cc. 638 §3; 647 §§1, 2; 656 §3; 684 §1; 688 §2; 690 §1; and 694 §2.

66 *CIC* c. 1280; See also Francis G. Morrisey, "Alienation and Administration," *Health Progress* 79, no. 5 (October 1998) 28, for the principle that the general council serves as finance council for a religious institute.

67 *CIC* cc. 423; 495ff; 511; 536 and 537.

68 *CIC* c. 586.

69 *CIC* cc. 594 and 595.

70 Sponselee, et al., 19.

tablish suitable coordination," while "respecting the autonomy, nature and spirit of each."[71] As such, conferences of major superiors may be in the best position to provide the service of oversight of canonical administrators of religious institutes within their territories.[72] These conferences may be able to work together to provide ways of assisting institutes in this important phase of their lives, and to provide the forum of accountability for those charged with the responsibility of canonical administration for the religious institute.

Chapter of Affairs for Completion

The declining institute needs to address four principal tasks: 1) transitioning sponsorship, 2) providing for elder-care, 3) transferring administration to non-members and 4) preparing for the appointment of non-members as canonical administrators of the institute. Some of these tasks are well under way, as an institute comes to recognize that it is in irreversible decline, others remain still to be addressed. An institute that recognizes that it is coming to its end, should hold a chapter of affairs for completion, in which it specifically addresses each of these four tasks, and any other tasks related to the settling of the affairs of the institute, such as celebrating and memorializing its life and entrusting its legacy to others.[73] This chapter should not be the final chapter of the institute, since it should be celebrated when there are sufficient members who can participate fully, and have sufficient energy to address the challenges that it presents. Subsequent chapters may serve to further refine the plan, or may simply be a "true sign of [the institute's] unity in charity," and an opportunity to "foster appropriate renewal in accord with [the institute's] patrimony,"[74] in keeping with the situation of the institute and its remaining members. Some institutes will celebrate this chapter of affairs for completion in its regular cycle of chapters, usually every four to six years as provided in the constitutions.[75] Other institutes will call a special chapter as the chapter of affairs for completion; this enables the institute's leadership and the chapter to focus on this task, and adequately prepare for the chapter and celebrate it, without the important, but more routine matters that can be taken up in the regular chapter of affairs. The special chapter also ensures a continuity of leadership throughout the chapter preparation, celebration and initial implementation.

The chapter of affairs for completion should address the four tasks outlined above, namely sponsorship, elder-care, civil administration and canonical administration. While the institute may still have a number of members, and years and even decades still to live, the chapter will draw up a testament that provides the direction for its future. Sponsorship may already be transferred, but if not, it

71 *CIC* c. 708.
72 Sponselee, et al., 20.
73 Ibid., 10; See also Ward 6.
74 *CIC* c. 631.
75 *CIC* c. 632.

should provide direction for this matter. Choices regarding elder-care should be specified, along with a plan for transferring the administrative responsibilities to non-members. And finally, the institute may indicate its preference regarding civil and canonical administration. The testament would express the chapter's choice regarding the disposition of remaining assets and properties, and the care of the cemetery and archives. Such a testament can serve to assist both civil and canonical administrators as they carry out their fiduciary roles on behalf of the institute and its members. It can also assist ecclesiastical authorities in their role of better ensuring the welfare of institutes of religious life and their members.[76]

Covenant Agreements

In the United States, there is increased interest among religious institutes in developing covenant relationships in order to assist in the final decades of the institute's life-cycle. These covenants may come in many forms. In its simplest form, a single smaller institute enters into relationship with a single larger institute that can provide the range of services that the smaller institute will need over the course of its declining years, including elder-care, management and administration, and finally canonical leadership. In other cases, a smaller institute may enter into various covenants and agreements with different institutes and/or commercial entities in order to provide the services needed.

In an example of the simples form, the two institutes would enter into an agreement covering the following areas:

1. Ensuring that sponsored ministries receive adequate oversight and/or are transferred to other sponsors;

2. Assisting with the management of assets, investments, and retirement funds of the smaller institute;

3. Assisting in the health-care of members, including permitting members of the smaller institute to live in the health-care facility of the larger institute, and/or overseeing the health-care of members in other facilities. Ensuring that the members participate in government benefit programs and obtain other funding;

4. Oversight of the operations and administration of the smaller institute. This may include an agreement to act as the business and finance office of the smaller institute, or simply overseeing those functions as they are currently in place in the smaller institute. This includes oversight of finance, personnel, and property;

---

76 *CIC* c. 591.

5. Managing the real property of the smaller institute and assisting in the sale of properties that are no longer needed. This may also include allowing use of the larger institute's space for housing and offices;

6. Ensuring that the smaller institute meets its civil and canonical obligations, including assistance in civil and canonical leadership.[77]

Initially, the covenant relationship involves support of the elder-care of the members, and the management and administration of the institute's affairs. Eventually, the smaller institute will no longer be able to oversee these functions, and will no longer have sufficient members to serve in canonical leadership of the institute. At this time, the smaller institute will petition the competent authority to have its own governance suppressed, relieving it of the responsibility to have a supreme moderator and council. At this time, the institute, with the support of the larger institute will nominate a member of the larger institute, or the larger institute's superior and council, to provide canonical administrators for the duration of the life of the institute.

In the United States, there are hundreds of communities of women religious whose average age is approaching 80 years.[78] For this reason, it is likely that there will not be enough larger stable institutes available to covenant with all the institutes that will be needing this type of support. Thus institutes may find it necessary to build a network of relationships with various religious institutes, regional or national networks of institutes, and commercial service providers that will be able to support and assist them in the coming decades. It is common in the United States, for religious institutes to use a memorandum of understanding to document their agreements because it is seen as less formal. In those cases where an institute is seeking to obtain services of a commercial entity, a formal contract is used, and the institute will take care to ensure that its own leadership, or some other fiduciary is overseeing the services of the commercial entity.

Further Considerations

There are several important issues that require attention in any attempt to develop a plan for a declining institute. It is critical for an institute to begin planning for its completion early enough that it has the members, resources and energy to develop and implement a plan. Since the institute is already aging, it is necessary to schedule the planning and the chapter in keeping with the energy and needs of members.

Appropriate attention must be given to the pastoral needs of members as they experience understandable grieving and the sense of loss. It is important to encourage members to face the institute's decline realistically, and with a firm trust

77 Hereford, "Canon 580," 83-84.

78 See *2013 NRRO Annual Report*, 3-5.

in God's loving providence. Plans made for the completion of the institute must also ensure that each of the members have "everything that is necessary to fulfill the purpose of their vocation."[79] While the planning process focuses on the common good for the institute as a whole, it may happen that some members are unable to embrace the direction chosen by the chapter of affairs for completion. "While no member can stonewall and refuse to let the group move forward, the member can choose to walk another path. This will usually be either dispensation from vows, or transfer to another institute or another form of consecrated life."[80] Particular attention must be given to members who are significantly younger than the majority of members. If there are members still active, care must be taken to enable them to continue to live a vibrant religious life, even if the decision for completion is made for the benefit of the majority who are retired and aging. These members too have the right to receive from the institute "everything necessary for the fulfillment of their vocation." Pastoral sensitivity and creativity will be needed to "imagine the future of religious life in the next fifty years."[81]

As planning is made for a declining institute, it is primarily the average age, not the size of the institute that is critical to consider. An institute may still have several hundred members, but if its median age is near eighty or even above, and it has few if any members under the age of sixty, it is time to engage in some realistic planning regarding its future. Such an institute lacks the capacity to attract and retain new members. It may continue to have members for several decades, however, with each passing year, their energy and resources for planning continue to decline. It is important for these institutes to begin now to ensure that their legacy of service, spirit and ministry are secured for their members and for the future. Through the process, the institute, its leadership and members can rely on the words of Jesus: "I am with you always ... I have prepared a place for you."[82] The same God, who was present at the founding of the institute and throughout its history, will be present, sustaining the institute and its members, as it faces the challenge of today and tomorrow.

---

79 *CIC* c. 670.

80 Amy Hereford, "Alternatives for Aging Institutes: Issues and Options," *RCRI Bulletin* 6 (2011) 15.

81 Hereford, Amy. *Religious Life at the Crossroads*, xiv. This book explores the movements in religious life today and the currents that are emerging among the smaller cohorts of younger religious in mainstream communities of religious women. Tracing the history of religious life, including the impact of Vatican II, it examines some of the theological sources for the reinvention of religious life today, and re-imagines the meaning of vows, community, and mission. *Giving Voice* and *Sisters2.0* are national organizations that of younger women religious that help them develop future oriented initiatives.

82 Mt. 28:20, Jn. 14:3.

SEMINAR

ECUMENICAL ACTIVITY IN THE TRIBUNAL: DIGNITAS CONNUBII, ARTICLES 2-4

Rev. Michael Joyce, CM, JCD

1. Introduction

Articles 2, 3, and 4 of *Dignitas connubii* are striking in their novelty. They appear to be a significant innovation in matrimonial procedures for the Latin Church. The Instruction acknowledges and incorporates the substantial marriage law of the Orthodox Churches and of ecclesial communities not in full communion with the Catholic Church. Such acknowledgement, much less incorporation, had not previously been a part of the law of the Latin Church.

A great number of marriage causes that come before Latin tribunals in the United States include at least one party who was a baptized non-Catholic. These people have been treated as subject to, and only subject to, the law of the Latin Catholic Church. *Dignitas connubii* now calls upon the ministers of Latin tribunals to acknowledge other laws to which a baptized non-Catholic may be subject because of their membership in some other church or ecclesial community.

This commentary will examine articles 2, 3, and 4 of *Dignitas connubii* to find what is required of tribunal officials in causes that involve at least one principal party who is a member of a non-Catholic Eastern Church or of an ecclesial community not in full communion with the Catholic Church. It will then explore ways in which judicial ministers can fulfill those requirements. It will expose various avenues that can be further explored. The examination only purports to begin an understanding of the new directions toward which these three articles of *Dignitas connubii* lead.

This analysis will follow a standard exegesis of the articles according to the canons of the Code of Canon Law in its introductory canons. Since the articles entail working with other Churches or ecclesial communities or even different religious traditions, the beliefs, worship, and discipline of those groups also come into consideration.

There is a proper distinction to be kept in mind between ecumenism and interfaith relations. Ecumenism is activity that occurs between Christian churches and ecclesial communities and interfaith relations are between members of the

Christian faith and members of other faith traditions. Both ecumenical and interfaith relations are present in the articles from *Dignitas connubii* under consideration.

The first task at hand to understand the articles is to examine their text and context (c. 17). While the Instruction is not law *per se,* it clarifies the prescripts of law (canon 34 §1). Therefore, the principles of the interpretation of ecclesiastical law are applicable to the Instruction itself.

Prior to examining the text of the three articles, it may be helpful first to recall the general context of the Instruction as well. The primary text for the Instruction is the revised Code of Canon Law. The Introduction to *Dignitas connubii* explicitly states that the revised code occasioned the need for a new instruction for the revised procedures for ecclesiastical declarations of nullity.[1] The previous instruction for matrimonial procedures, *Provida Mater,* had not been applicable for a number of years due to the motu proprio *Causas matrimoniales* given by Pope Paul VI on March 28, 1971 and various procedural norms subsequently developed by various episcopal conferences and approved by the Holy See for use until the 1983 effectiveness of the revised code.

The context of the revised code places *Dignitas connubii* in a broader milieu; namely, Vatican Council II.[2] As Pope St. John Paul II explained in his apostolic constitution promulgating the revised Code of Canon Law, this code complements the teaching of the Second Vatican Council, incorporates the new from the treasury of tradition, and emphasizes the Church's self-understanding as set forth in *Lumen gentium* and *Gaudium et spes.*

This broader context includes the decree on ecumenism *Unitatis redintegratio* and the declaration on religious freedom *Dignitas humanae.* Both of these documents relate to the Church's renewed self-understanding and its relationship to other Churches and ecclesial communities as well as to other religious traditions. This relationship is markedly different than the ecclesiology of the 1917 Code of Canon Law and the instruction *Provida Mater.*

Another context for the interpretation of *Dignitas connubii* is the Code of Canon Law of the Eastern Churches. Although the Instruction is only for members of the Latin Church,[3] the articles under consideration refer to members of non-Catholic Eastern Churches, of ecclesial communities, and even to those who

---

1 Pontifical Council for Legislative Texts, *Instruction to be observed by diocesan and interdiocesan tribunals in handling causes of the nullity of marriage, Dignitas connubii* (Vatican City, 2005: Libreria Editrice Vatican) p. 13.

2 John Paul II, apostolic constitution *Sacrae disciplinae legis,* January 25, 193, *Code of Canon Law: Latin English Edition, New English Translation* (Canon Law Society of America, Washington, D.C.: 2012), xxx-xxxi.

3 *DC,* art. 1 §1.

are not baptized. The Code of Canon Law of the Eastern Churches considers these persons and directs tribunals that operate according to it how to treat such persons.

2. Article 2, §1: Applicable Substantive Law on Marriage

Although article 1, §2 implies that the Instruction concerns only procedural law, article 2, §1 notes that the marriages of Catholics, even if only one of the parties is Catholic, are governed by divine law as well as canon law. The entire article addresses what substantive law is applicable to the determination of the validity of a marriage. The Church holds that divine law governs all people and therefore all marriages. This particular section also applies civil law to marriages involving Catholics for those matters that are purely civil, e.g. civil registration of marriage. The section is an exact reiteration of canon 1059 to which it refers. The canon also contains the phrase, "without prejudice to the competence of civil authority concerning the merely civil effects of the same marriage."[4] There is one exception to the directions of this section even though it does not explicitly mention the exception and it is the law for the canonical form of marriage. That subject is addressed later by article 4 §1, 2°.

Article 2, §2, 1° is taken verbatim from canon 780, §2, 1° of the Code of Canons of the Eastern Churches. Article 2, §2, 2° is slight different from §2, 2° of the canon. This difference is stylistic rather than substantial. Both the canon and the article refer to the matrimonial law used by ecclesial communities that do not have their proper law. All of article 2 of *Dignitas connubii* is contained in canon 780 of the Code of Canons of the Eastern Churches.

Article 1, §1 applies the Instruction only to the tribunals of the Latin Church. This application follows from canon 1 of the Code of Canon Law which restricts the force of the canons it contains to the Latin Church. Instructions clarify prescriptions of the law and elaborate on methods observed in fulfilling them (canon 34, §1). Ordinances of instructions do not derogate from the law and if the ordinances cannot be reconciled with the prescription of law, they lack all force (canon 34, §2). Since article 2 of *Dignitas connubii* comes from the Code of Canons of the Eastern Churches and not from the Code of Canon Law, is it possible that article 2 lacks all force?

The resolution of this question is found in the *fontes* of canon 780 of the Code of Canons of the Eastern Churches. It has already been noted that article 2, §1 is a restatement of canon 1059 of the Code of Canon Law. This part of the ordinance is applicable because it is a restatement of a prescript of law for the Latin Church. Article 2, §2 is an addition to what is contained in canon 1059 and is found in canon 780 of the Code of Canons of the Eastern Churches. However,

4 "*salva competentia civilis potestatis circa mere civiles eiusdem matrimonii effectus.*" (canon 1059)

the *fontes* for canon 780, §2, 1° refer to the decree *Unitatis redintegratio* and the declaration *Dignitatis humanae* from the Second Vatican Council. The decree and the declaration were promulgated for the entire Catholic Church, Eastern and Western and are effective in the whole Church.

It is appropriate to use the proper law of the churches and ecclesial communities for the members of those churches and communities because the members received their religious formation in part from that proper law. Their matrimonial consent and intention are presumed to be informed by that law because of their religious formation. This practice takes place in the Catholic Church. It is fitting in ecumenical activity that the Catholic Church acknowledges a similar effectiveness in other churches and ecclesial communities.

While the conciliar decree and the declaration are effective for the Latin Church, as well for the Eastern Churches, their juridical "force" appears to be lacking for the Latin Church in that it has not been formulated in legal language as it has in the Eastern Churches in their canon 780.[5] Canon 19 of the Code of Canon Law is applicable here. The Latin legislation for acknowledging the applicability of proper marriage law for members of non-Catholic churches and ecclesial communities is lacking in the procedural law for matrimonial causes in the Latin code. Canon 19 provides for the use of laws issued in similar matters and the general principles of law applied with canonical equity. Thus, judges in Latin tribunals can, and possibly must, apply canon 780 of the Code of Canons of the Eastern Church in hearing the causes of marriages involving members of churches and ecclesial communities that are not in full communion with the Catholic Church.

How does the decree *Unitas redintegratio* apply the ecclesiastical law of separated churches and ecclesial communities to Catholic matrimonial causes of invalidity? The reference to number 16 is in chapter III of the decree which concerns churches and ecclesial communities separated from the Roman Apostolic See.[6] It is contained in number I of the chapter, entitled "the special position of the eastern churches."[7] The chapter distinguishes between the Eastern non-Catholic churches and the ecclesial communities separated from the Apostolic See not only because of the differences of causes of separation but also because of differences of "serious matters concerning belief and the structure of

5 George D. Gallaro, "The Mysteries of Vocation" in *Comparative Sacramental Discipline in the CCEO and CIC* edited by Francis J. Marini (Washington, D.C.: Canon Law Society of America, 2003), p.p. 184-185.

6 "Cap. III. De ecclesiis et de communitatibus ecclesialibus a sed apostolica Romana seiunctis." See Norman Tanner, ed., *Decrees of the Ecumenical Councils* (Washington, D.C.: Georgetown University Press, 1990), vol. II: 915.

7 "*I. De ecclesiarum orientalium peculiari consideration.*" See Ibid., II: 916

the church."[8] As the decree goes on to consider the eastern Orthodox churches, it extols its treasury and notes that the western church has drawn from it extensively ". . . in liturgical practice, spiritual tradition, and canon law."[9]

After presenting the liturgical treasury of the Eastern Churches, the council fathers continued in number 16 to present the disciplinary resources that these churches have. They observed that the churches followed their own disciplines from the earliest of times which were approved by the fathers of the church and by synods, including ecumenical councils. The diversity of customs and observances adds to the Church's beauty and helps it carry out its mission. The council then solemnly declared that "the churches of the east, while mindful of the necessary unity of the whole church, have the right to govern themselves according to the disciplines proper to themselves ... "[10] The decree makes no declaration about the status of ecclesiastical discipline in other separated churches and ecclesial communities in the west.

The *fontes* for canon 780, §2 of the Code of Canons of the Eastern Churches also refer to a paragraph from the declaration on religious freedom *Dignitatis humanae.* This paragraph of number 4 begins "*His igitur.*" It states the freedom of all religious communities in conducting their affairs in their own way. The Council, then, acknowledged the right of churches and ecclesial communities not in full communion with the Catholic Church to have their own discipline and church order.

Article 2 §1 acknowledges that marriages involving a Catholic are governed by canon law as well as divine law. The Catholic Church holds that all marriages, whether the spouses are Catholic or not, are governed by divine law since all human beings are created by God and are subject to the order for all of created reality that God established at the beginning of creation. Catholics are also governed by canon law as part of their membership in the Catholic Church.[11] Matrimonial law in the Catholic Church is contained not only in the Code of Canon Law but also in other legislation that might be promulgated. A member of an eastern Catholic Church is governed by the Code of Canons of the Eastern Churches. If the marriage is between an Eastern Catholic and a Latin Catholic, both canonical disciplines apply.

3. Article 2, §2: Further Applications

---

8 " ... *gravitate quaestionum ad fidem et structuram ecclesiasticam pertinentiam.*" Ibid., II 915.

9 " ... *in rebus liturgicis, intraditione spirituali et in ordine iuridico* ... " Ibid., II: 916.

10 " ... *ecclesias orientis, memores necessariae unitatis totius ecclesiae, facultatem habere se secundum proprias disciplinas regendi, . . .(De oecumensismo* 16)."

11 Canon 205: "Those baptized are fully in the communion of the Catholic Church on this earth who are joined with Christ in its visible structure by the bonds of the profession of faith, the sacraments, and ecclesiastical governance."

Section 2 of the article determines what law governs the marriage between a Catholic party and a baptized Christian who is not a member of the Catholic Church. These marriages are called mixed marriages. The section contains two parts. The first part states that the proper law of the church or ecclesial community to which the non-Catholic party belongs, provided that the community has its own proper matrimonial law, also governs the marriage along with divine law and canon law. Mixed marriages then are possibly governed by two ecclesiastical legal systems, Latin Catholic canon law and the law of the church or ecclesial community to which the non-Catholic spouse belongs, in addition to divine law and frequently to civil law.

This section has special significance in that it acknowledges that churches and ecclesial communities have the right and power to govern themselves and their members. In the 1917 Code of Canon Law, all baptized Christians were treated as members of the Catholic Church.[12] As mentioned above, the Code of Canons of the Eastern Churches, promulgated in 1990, acknowledged the effectiveness of ecclesiastical law used by churches and ecclesial communities not in communion with the Catholic Church. The Latin Church in *Dignitas connubii* also recognizes their right to govern themselves in accord with paragraph 4 of *Dignitias humanae.*

The term "church" ordinarily refers to those Christian communities that possess the sacrament of order validly maintained through apostolic succession. On the other hand, "ecclesial community" usually refers to Christian communities that do not have a valid sacrament of order due to a lack of apostolic succession. There is a question about whether these ecclesial communities have the power to govern themselves since they lack the sacrament of order. One school of thought holds that the power of order is required for the power of governance. Another school holds that the powers are separate and that one is not required for the exercise of the other. This presentation does not address this question. However, the disupute must be acknowledged although both the Code of Canons of the Eastern Churches and *Dignitas connubii* admit the governance power of ecclesial communities that lack the power of order.

4. Article 2, §2, 1°: Churches and Ecclesial Communities that have proper law for marriage

A challenge is to determine if a church or an ecclesial community has its proper law for marriage. The Eastern Orthodox Churches generally use a compilation of canons from the first six ecumenical councils and regional synods for their canonical legislation. This work is entitled *Pedalion*, or *The Rudder.*[13] Pope St. John Paul II makes two references to a relationship between the Code of Canons

12 Stanislaus Woywod, *A Practical Commentary on the Code of Canon Law,* rev. by Callistus Smith (New York: Joseph F. Wagner, Inc., 1957), p. 47.

13 http://www.orthodoxchurchbritishisles.com/

of Eastern Churches and the Orthodox canons in the apostolic constitution *Sacri Canones*,[14] October 18, 1990. *The Rudder* is not a codification of canons. Eastern Orthodox Churches have not codified their legislation. Their canonical tradition is similar to that of the Latin Church prior to the promulgation of the 1917 Code of Canon Law. While *The Rudder* is a collection of Eastern Orthodox legislation, it simply collects and comments on it much like the *Corpus Iuris Canonici.* It does not codify the canons.

Another challenge is to enter into the mindset of the legal system used by the church or ecclesial community. While the canonical system of the Latin Church is primarily based in the civil law (commonly referred to as Roman Law), the legal system of another church or ecclesial community not in full communion with the Catholic Church may be based on a different system of law. Furthermore, these churches and ecclesial communities may not have the same perception of the role of law or church order in the structuring of the church or community that the Catholic Church has.

This admission of the power of governance in churches and ecclesial communities not in full communion with the Catholic Church is a very concrete experience of the *novus habitus mentis* Pope Paul VI called for in the revision of the Code of Canon Law. This new mindset calls us to recognize these churches and ecclesial communities as actual members of the Church of Christ having their unique heritages.

A particular example of the challenge to understand the legal tradition of other churches and communities is the institute of *economia* or **economy** in the Orthodox Churches.[15] This institute recognizes that the spirit of the law and its principles supersede the mere application of the letter of the law. It is only applied in nonessential matters. **Economy** is always a general exception to the rule and it lifts the legal consequences that follow from the violation of a law. It is granted by a competent authority. It is not applied randomly or arbitrarily. Defined regulations govern its application. The right to exercise **economy** is the sole prerogative of the legislator; i.e. a council or a holy synod of bishops. It can be delegated to individual bishops by the synod but they must conform to limits prescribed by canons and to the express authorization of the superior legislative authority. **Economy** does not establish precedent.

Some of the grounds of nullity are more extensive in *The Rudder* than in the 1983 Code of Canon Law. The impediment of consanguinity extends there to the

---

14 John Paul II, apostolic constitution *Sacri canones,* in *Code of Canons of the Eastern Churches: Latin-English Edition, New English Translation,* (Washington, D.C.: Canon Law Society of America, 2001), pp. xxi-xxii.

15 http://www.goarch.org/ourfaith/ourfaith7071; The Concept of "Economy."

seventh degree.[16] These marriages are prohibited. Similarly, the diriment impediment of affinity is more extensive.[17] These two impediments are the only ones mentioned in *The Rudder.* Spiritual affinity, that is, affinity by reason of baptism can be an invalidating impediment. The wives of priests are also subject to the impediment of spiritual affinity.

Some ecclesial communities also have proper law concerning marriage. The Anglican Communion has canon law as part of its tradition. Each of the member churches legislates for itself. The Episcopal Church in the United States holds a general convention every four years at which it issues its canons. Such a convention was held in 2012.[18] There were two canons on marriage; canon 18 regarding the solemnization of Holy Matrimony, and canon 19 concerning regulations respecting Holy Matrimony. The regulations are about the preservation of marriage, the dissolution of marriage, and remarriage. None of the canons speak directly to the possible invalidity of a marriage.

5. Article 2, §2, 2°: Churches and Ecclesial Communities that do not have proper law for marriage

Article 2, §2, 2° addresses churches and ecclesial communities that do not have their own proper marriage law. While some ecclesial communities do have a proper law for marriage, rarely do those laws address what may affect the validity of marriage. Some of these ecclesial communities directly refer to the civil marriage law.[19] Even if these communities or churches do not have their proper marriage law, the members are still subject to the civil law applicable to marriage. The grounds for invalidity vary from state to state. In the State of Missouri the impediment of consanguinity in the direct line and to the second degree render marriages invalid.[20] Mental incapacity is also a ground for invalidity, as is bigamy. Most states have an impediment of age. Usually, the parties must be eighteen (18) to marry validly without parental consent. Thus, if a member of an ecclesial community that does not have its proper matrimonial law who was not yet eighteen years old attempted marriage, he or she would be subject to the impediment by reason of being bound to the civil law for marriage.

Some states allow marriages to be declared invalid for a cause that arose later in the marriage but was not necessarily present at the beginning. The State of New York allows a marriage to be annulled after a person has been incurably

16 Ibid., Chapter 1: Concerning Consanguinity, or Blood Relationship, that is to say, of one Lineage or Kindred, pp. 1761-1762.

17 Ibid., Chapter 4: Concerning marriages between two kindred by affinity in which the one kindred furnishes two parties lineally, pp. 1764-1765.

18 http://extranet.generalconvention.org/staff/files/download/6994

19 See for example Ibid., canon 18, Section 1.

20 http://www.moga.mo.gov/statutes/C400-499/4510000020.HTM. For the ground of bigamy, see http://www.moga.mo.gov/statutes/C400-499/4510000030.HTM.

mentally ill for five years.[21] According to ecclesiastical tradition, the validity of a marriage takes effect at the moment consent is exchanged and this event is a matter of divine law. If an impeding factor develops later in the union, the bond is still effective because the perpetuity of the marriage was established earlier when consent was exchanged. Thus, the New York law is contrary to divine law and lacks effect before an ecclesiastical tribunal.

While the article 2 of *Dignitas connubii* accepts, or "canonizes," civil law for churches and ecclesial communities that are not in full communion with the Catholic Church, the Catholic Church does not always acknowledge the findings of civil courts in matrimonial matters. If a member of the church or ecclesial community not in full communion with the Catholic Church sought an annulment or declaration of invalidity in the civil courts, the person must still seek a similar finding from a tribunal of the Latin Catholic Church.

On the other hand, does the Catholic Church acknowledge the findings of a church that has its own ecclesiastical procedures for finding a marriage invalid? If the Catholic Church accepts the proper matrimonial law of a church or an ecclesiastical community that is not in full communion, it seems to follow that if the church has procedures in place for the investigation of a marriage and those procedures find the marriage invalid, the Catholic Church should accept the finding and not reduplicate the efforts. However, such does not appear to be the practice in the Catholic Church as article 4 of *Dignitas connubii* seems to indicate. The usual practice among Orthodox churches is to allow second, and even third, marriages without solemnization and without declaring the previous marriage invalid. However, a previously married Orthodox member is required to have the marriage declared invalid by the Catholic Church if she or he wishes to marry a Catholic.

6. Article 3: Competence of Latin Catholic Tribunals

Article 3, §1: For the Baptized

The first section of article 3 claims the right of the Church to hear a matrimonial cause from a baptized person. The text is the same as that of canon 1671. At its face, this claim can appear to be an affront to churches and ecclesial communities separated from the Apostolic See. However, the 1917 Code of Canon Law claimed the right as both **proper** *(proprio)* and **exclusive** *(exclusivo).*[22] *I*n canon 1617 the Church establishes its right to respond to a matrimonial cause from any validly baptized person. The assertion is based upon the Church's obligation to care for matters that are spiritual in nature. The marriage is the subject of the question before the ecclesiastical court. The spouses are principal parties in the resolution of the question but they are not in question themselves. Marriage

21 http://public.leginfo.state.ny.us

22 Canon 1960 from the 1917 *Code of Canon Law.*

between two baptized persons is a sacrament. The Church has the charge to care for the sacraments. Thus it is responsible for determining if a marriage between Christians truly existed if it is called into question.

The claim does not deny a baptized member of a church or ecclesial community not in full communion with the Catholic Church to seek resolution from an ecclesiastical judge in her or his church or ecclesial community. Thus the Catholic Church no longer claims the **exclusive** right to investigative matrimonial causes as was claimed in the Pio-Benedictine code. A member of a church or ecclesial community not in full communion with the Catholic Church is also free as a baptized person to approach a competent ecclesiastical court of the Catholic Church. However, the Catholic Church does not have the exclusive right to consider the cause as was previously the case under the 1917 code.

Article 3, §2: For the Unbaptized

The second section of the article addresses the situation in which an ecclesiastical judge of the Catholic Church can consider a cause of nullity of marriage of non-Catholics, baptized or not. The judge can address such a cause when it is necessary to establish the freedom to marry of one of the parties before the Catholic Church even if one or both of the parties is unbaptized and not subject to any ecclesiastical law.

Such an action requires that the person submit a libellus.[23] According to article 92 §1, 2°, the promoter of justice can present the libellus when a marriage is revealed as invalid and cannot be convalidated or the convalidation would not be expedient. The non-Catholic party may be opposed to seek a declaration of invalidity of his or her first marriage because of religious convictions. The right of the promoter of justice to question the nullity is asserted in canon 1674, 2°. Two conditions are necessary for the promoter to exercise this right. The first is that the marriage is obviously invalid, and the second is that it is either impossible or inexpedient to convalidate the marriage.

This right of the promoter of justice to impugn the validity of a marriage might provide some opportunity to resolve difficult pastoral situations in which a Catholic desires to have his or her marriage recognized as valid in the Catholic Church but the non-Catholic partner is unwilling to cooperate in ecclesiastical proceedings. If there is a possibility that the invalidity of the non-Catholic's first marriage is publicly known and there is no possibility of reconciliation with the first partner, the promoter of justice can present a libellus before the appropriate tribunal instead of the non-Catholic party.

23 Article 114.

Article 3, §3: For Civil Effects

The third section of article 3 refers questions of the merely civil effects of marriage to the civil forum. This article reiterates canon 1672 verbatim. The Church acknowledges that civil governments have jurisdiction over the merely civil effects of marriage. Particular law, through the use of concordats, may retain the right of ecclesiastical courts to resolve matters that might otherwise be addressed by the civil courts. This section is also pertinent to those ecclesial communities that use the applicable civil law for their matrimonial law.

7. Article 4: Law for Non-Catholic Marriages

Article 4, §1, 1°: Time of the Celebration of the Marriage

Article 4 directs the ecclesiastical judge to the law to be used when judging nullity causes of non-Catholics. The first section of the article is about baptized non-Catholics and the second section considers unbaptized person. Each section contains two numbers.

Paragraph one of the first section first states that the law to be used is the law that was in force at the time the marriage was celebrated. It also refers the judge back to article 2, §2. This reference is to the proper law of the church or ecclesial community to which the non-Catholic party belongs, if the community has its own marriage law or to the law used by the ecclesial community if it lacks its own marriage law. Thus, if an ecclesiastical judge is considering the cause of two baptized non-Catholics, the judge must use the substantive law proper to the church or ecclesial community of the principals, if the community has substantive law concerning marriage. As noted above, most ecclesial communities use the civil law for their substantive law.

Churches and ecclesial communities, as well as civil jurisdictions, change their laws from time to time. The Latin Catholic Church significantly changed its matrimonial law in 1983. As mentioned above, the Episcopal Church in America revises its canon law every four years. The judge must carefully attend to what law was in effect at the time that consent was exchanged between the spouses.

Article 4, §1, 2°: Form of the Celebration of the Marriage

The second number of the section addresses the form to be used in the celebration of marriage. This number acknowledges that the Latin Church recognizes the form prescribed or accepted by the church or ecclesial community to which the non-Catholic party belonged. There is an additional requirement in the number for members of a non-Catholic Eastern Church. These marriages must be celebrated with a sacred rite. This latter obligation uses the language of canon

828 §2 of the Code of Canons of the Eastern Churches when it uses the term "sacred rite."

Canon 828 requires the presence of a local hierarch, a local pastor, or a priest who has been give the faculty of blessing the marriage for Eastern Catholics, along with at least two witnesses. The second section of the canon requires the intervention of the priest who assists and blesses the marriage to make the celebration a "sacred rite."[24] Neither Eastern nor Latin deacons are capable of blessing the marriage. *Dignitas connubii* requires the blessing for members of non-Catholic Eastern Churches.

Article 4, §2, 1°: Canonical Procedural Law

Section 2 of article 4 concerns decisions about the nullity of marriage contracted by two unbaptized persons. Number one of the article states that the cause is heard according to canonical procedural law. Canon 11 of the Code of Canon Law indicates that merely ecclesiastical law binds only members of the Catholic Church. Thus at first glance, it may appear that unbaptized persons are not bound to the canonical procedures of the Church. However, section 2 is directed to the ecclesiastical judge who has been approached by an unbaptized person to consider the cause according to article 3, §2. The unbaptized person then is affected by ecclesiastical law in the determination and protection of their rights in the procedures because the tribunal which she or he has approached must follow the canonical procedures.

Article 4, §2, 2°: Law Binding Persons at the Time

Article 2 of the Instruction applied the proper law of churches and ecclesial communities along with divine law to the marriages of Catholics and baptized non-Catholics. Section 2, number 2 similarly applies divine law and the law to which the non-baptized parties were subject at the time they entered the marriage in question. All non-baptized persons, as well as baptized person, are subject to the civil law. Some unbaptized persons may also be subject to their proper religious law depending upon their membership to a specific religious, such as Jews, Muslims, or Hindus, among others.[25]

---

24 Victor J. Popishil, *Eastern Catholic Marriage Law according to the Code of Canons of the Eastern Churches,* Brooklyn, N.Y.: Saint Maron Publications, 1991, p. 226. Popishil indicates that the Coptic Church of Egypt allows deacons to give the blessing. The Ethiopian Church requires the reception of the Eucharist for validity.

25 See Popishil, pp. 210-212 on the use of Islamic and other religious laws in Islamic countries.

8. Conclusions

While Article 2 of *Dignitas connubii* is not law since it is an instruction, it nonetheless directs the ecclesiastical judge to use the directives of *Unitas redintegratio, Dignitias humanae,* and the legislation of the Code of Canons of the Eastern Churches in adjudicating matrimonial causes involving members of churches and ecclesial communities that are not in full communion with the Catholic Church. *Dignitas connubii* follows the lead of the Code of Canons of the Eastern Churches and takes an ecumenical step forth by accepting law from churches and ecclesial communities not in communion with the Apostolic See.

Article 2 "canonizes" the ecclesiastical discipline of other churches and ecclesial communities when applicable. The acceptance of the canonical traditions and church orders from these groups is an implementation of *Unitas redintegratio* and *Dignitias humanae.* This article may be challenge to the ecclesiastical judge to become cognizant of those traditions and orders. While the judge may not be conversant with those aspects of churches and ecclesial communities not in full communion with the Catholic Church, he or she can approach members of those groups who are knowledgeable in their own traditions and learn from them what law might be applicable in causes before them.

A judge may need to appoint an expert in causes that involve mixed marriages who is knowledgeable in the canon law or church practice of the non-Catholic party. He or she may not be acquainted with the discipline of the church or ecclesial community of the non-Catholic party. Since that person was bound to the law, the judge can appoint an expert in that law to aid in the instruction of the cause about the applicable law.

The fact that *Dignitas connubii* refers indirectly in article 3, §2 to the possibility of the promoter of justice raising a question of nullity of a marriage in accordance with articles 92 and 93 of the Instruction opens the possibility of presenting causes to an ecclesiastical judge that may not have seemed possible. There are regions of the United States in which some evangelical communities have such anti-Catholic sensibilities that a member of such a community would be adamantly opposed to approaching a tribunal. In such an instance, might not the promoter of justice present the cause for the sake of the interested Catholic party? There is the challenging work of determining that the nullity of the previous marriage has already been revealed. However, the pastoral responsibility of caring for the Catholic party presents a proper motivation for assuming the task.

Another indirect and discreet challenge that these three articles from *Dignitas connubii* present to the ecclesiastical judge is to enter into a dialogical relationship with other churches and ecclesiastical communities that are not in full communion with the Catholic Church. Such a stance used in the various dialogs listens carefully to the beliefs and traditions of the other party without abandoning one's own position or attempting to refute the position of the other. It involves a true learning. When the Second Vatican Council acknowledged the rich treasure that particularly the Eastern Churches have in their doctrine, worship, and discipline, it admitted that those churches also possess truth. The ecclesiastical judge is in a position to learn that truth in the course of the investigation of the possible nullity of mixed marriages and applying the law of those churches, and possibly ecclesial communities, to the question before the court.

It would also be remiss not to acknowledge the existence of the newly-established Special Commission for the study of the reform of the matrimonial processes in canon law. One of the members of the commission is Bishop Dimitri Salachas, Apostolic Exarch of the Greek Byzantine Catholic Church. Although it appears that any such reform will be for the Latin Church, the fact that a learned and distinguished member of an Eastern Church is at the table suggests that the commission will be performing its task from a wider perspective than simply a Western mindset. Certainly, the Commission will be mindful of the new direction that articles 2, 3, and 4 of *Dignitas connubii* has set, and will incorporate it in some fashion into its work.

SEMINAR

MARRIAGES OF ORIENTAL CATHOLICS AT LATIN PARISHES: CANONICAL CONSIDERATIONS

Very Rev. Francis J. Marini, JD, JCOD

INTRODUCTION

The recent increases in the immigration of Eastern European, Middle Eastern and Far Eastern Christians to the United States is resulting in the more or less permanent presence of increasing numbers of Catholics who are ascribed in the Oriental Catholic Churches *sui iuris* rather then the Latin Church *sui iuris* to which the overwhelming majority of Catholics in the United States has traditionally belonged. This phenomenon has created an urgency to readdress the interritual issues and concerns with which the Catholic Church in the United States has been dealing for more than one hundred years. The purpose of this intervention is to discuss the canonical issues which relate directly to the pastoral care of Oriental Catholics who are seeking to enter into marriage at the local Latin parishes where they reside.

At the outset, it is important to acknowledge that there is a certain distinction among the sacraments which has important pastoral and canonical implications. That is because some sacraments are validly and licitly administered to Catholics regardless of the ascription of the faithful; there are some sacraments which should be administered according to the ritual proper to the Church *sui iuris* to which the Catholic is ascribed by law; but if not they are validly administered nonetheless; and then there are some sacraments which are not validly administered if attention is not paid to interritual issues by the competent authorities. As we all know well from our canonical training and practice, marriage is one of the sacraments that falls into this last category.

This presentation will attempt to address the more common canonical issues typically encountered in the pastoral care of Oriental Catholics who present themselves for marriage in a Latin parish in the place where they are living, and will address the marriage of an Oriental Catholic with another Oriental Catholic, with a Latin Catholic, with a baptized non-Catholic and with an un-baptized non-Catholic. We will try to discuss the topics in a way which simplifies rather than complicates their pastoral care. The focus will be on pastoral issues which arise at the parochial, chancery and tribunal levels because canonists are called upon to provide guidance in all of these areas. The emphasis of this presentation will be practical as opposed to theoretical. While the focus of this discussion is the situation of Oriental Catholics requesting pastoral care in Latin parishes, which is the situation most frequently encountered in the West, the relevant canonical principles would apply equally to any situation in which the faithful of one church *sui iuris* require pastoral care in a parish of a different church *sui iuris*, especially if the churches *sui iuris* are of different rites.

THE SACRAMENTS AND ORIENTAL CATHOLICS IN GENERAL

Preliminary Considerations

Before we discuss the topic of marriage specifically, certain fundamental canonical concepts and provisions which are especially important in any discussion of interritual matters should be reviewed and a certain precision in their use employed. These canonical concepts and terms are: "rite," "church *sui iuris,*" and "ascription."

The concept of "rite" in the *ius vigens* is not the one which had been employed in canonical literature prior to the coming into force of the *Codex Canunum Ecclesiarum Orientalium* (the *CCEO* or Eastern code) on 1 October 1991. In the Eastern code, the Supreme Legislator has drawn a distinction between the term "rite," which was formerly used to identify both the broad geographical and cultural tradition (e.g., Byzantine) and the organized church structures which participated in that tradition (e.g., Romanian Greek-Catholic, Melkite Greek-Catholic, etc.), and the new term "church *sui iuris.*" Thus, whereas prior to the *CCEO*, canonists used to talk about both the Antiochene Rite and also the Maronite Rite, the *CCEO* clearly distinguishes between the two concepts as follows:

> *CCEO* Canon 28, §1. A rite is the liturgical, theological, spiritual and disciplinary patrimony, culture and circumstances of history of a distinct people, by which its own manner of living the faith is manifested in each Church *sui iuris*.
>
> §2. The rites treated in this code, unless otherwise stated, are those which arise from the Alexandrian, Antiochene, Armenian, Chaldean and Constantinopolitan [Byzantine] traditions.
>
> *CCEO* Canon 27. A group of Christian faithful united by a hierarchy according to the norm of law which the supreme authority of the Church expressly or tacitly recognizes as *sui iuris* is called in this Code a Church *sui iuris*.

Thus, the concept of "rite" is much broader than "church *sui iuris*," such that a rite can, and usually does, include a number of churches *sui iuris*, which are distinct from each other hierarchically and in other ways, yet all belong to a common rite. This is most clearly seen in the Constantinopolitan or Byzantine Rite in which there are thirteen churches *sui iuris* which are all Byzantine or Constantinopolitan or more commonly "Greek-Catholic." So, now we ought to refer only to one of the six liturgical, theological, spiritual and disciplinary patrimonies of the Catholic Church as a rite: namely, the five Oriental or Eastern rites listed in *CCEO* c. 28, §2 and the one Occidental or Western rite.

Similarly, we no longer refer to the Maronite Rite or the Ukrainian Rite, but to the Maronite Church *sui iuris* or the Ukrainian Church *sui iuris* to refer to one of the twenty-one Oriental hierarchically organized groups of Christian faithful recognized by the Supreme Authority of the Church;[1] namely: the Coptic Church *sui iuris* and the Ethiopian Church *sui iuris* of the Alexandrian Rite; the Malankara Church *sui iuris*, the Maronite Church *sui iuris* and the Syriac Church *sui iuris* of the Antiochene or West Syrian Rite; the Armenian Church *sui iuris* of the Armenian Rite; the Chaldean Church *sui iuris* and the Malabar Church *sui iuris* of the Chaldean or East Syrian Rite; and the Albanian Church *sui iuris*, the Bielorussian Church *sui iuris*, the Bulgarian Church *sui iuris*, the Croatian or Krizevci Church *sui iuris*, the (Hellenic) Greek Church *sui iuris*, the Greek-Melkite Church *sui iuris*, the Italo-Albanian or Italo-Greek Church *sui iuris*, the Romanian Church *sui iuris*, the Russian Church *sui iuris*, the Ruthenian Church *sui iuris*, the Slovak Church *sui iuris*, the Ukrainian Church *sui iuris*, and the Hungarian Church *sui iuris* of the Byzantine or Constantinopolitan or Greek Catholic Rite; as well as to the one such group which belongs to the Occidental Rite; namely the Latin Church *sui iuris*.[2] By logical extension, we now speak of a Maronite Catholic or a Latin Catholic to refer to an individual member of the Maronite Church *sui iuris* or the Latin Church *sui iuris*. The term "Roman Catholic" should not be employed indiscriminately or as a synonym for "Latin Catholic" because all faithful belonging to the universal Roman Catholic Church are by definition Roman Catholics. That is, all Latin Catholics are Roman Catholics, but not all Roman Catholics are Latin Catholics.

The concept of ascription or enrollment refers to becoming or being a member of one of the Churches *sui iuris*. Both the *Codex Iuris Canonici* of 1983 (the 83*CIC*)[3] and the *CCEO*[4] read *in pari materia* make it quite clear that an indi-

1 *Annuario Pontificio* 2012 at p. 1140.

2 As an aside observation, under the new definitions, it is questionable whether the two venerable Western liturgical traditions in Milan, Italy and Toledo, Spain are properly called either the Ambrosian Rite and the Mozarabic Rite or the Ambrosian Church *sui iuris* and the Mozarabic Church *sui iuris* because neither tradition seems to completely meet either definition.

3 83*CIC* cc. 111 & 112.

4 *CCEO* cc. 29, 30, 37 & 38.

vidual Catholic cannot be a member of the Catholic Church in general or even in one of the rites in general, rather each Catholic must be ascribed or enrolled in one of the churches *sui iuris*. Ascription occurs in only three circumstances: 1) when a person is baptized in the Catholic Church; or 2) when a baptized non-Catholic enters into full communion with the Catholic Church; or 3) when a Catholic validly transfers from one church *sui iuris* to another. There are only two methods of ascription: the ordinary or *ipso iure* method in which the ascription is effected by operation of law, and the extraordinary or optional method in which the person to be ascribed or those who act on his or her behalf have some choice in regard to ascription. These methods will be more fully discussed below under the topics of entering into full communion with the Catholic Church and transfers of ascription. But the most important point is that ascription can never happen by any other method, and the law is very clear that attending and receiving the sacraments at a parish of a church *sui iuris* other than the one to which a person is canonically ascribed, even if formally committed to the pastoral care of a hierarch or pastor of that other church *sui iuris*, cannot effect a transfer of ascription, no matter for how long or for how many generations this may have continued.[5] In fact, the law requires that all ascriptions and transfers of ascription be properly recorded in the baptismal register of the parish where a baptism was celebrated, including a Latin parish.[6] The topic of ascription will appear often in our discussion because so may other things depend on recognition of the proper ascription. Suffice it to say at this point that attention to ascription will greatly simply the identification and resolution of issues relating to Oriental Catholics in the parish, chancery and tribunal.

THE SACRAMENT OF MARRIAGE IN PARTICULAR

The Form of Marriage

We all know that the sacrament of marriage is one in which jurisdiction does affect the validity of the sacrament. This is because the observance of the Catholic or canonical form of marriage is required for validity. The relevant canons are:

> 83*CIC* Canon 1108, §1. Only those marriages are valid which are contracted in the presence of the local ordinary or the pastor or a priest or deacon delegated by either of them, who assist, and in the presence of two witnesses, according to the rules expressed in the following canons, with due regard for

5 83*CIC* c. 112,§ 2, and *CCEO* c. 38.

6 *CCEO* c. 37.

the exceptions mentioned in cann. 144,[7] 1112, §1,[8] 1116,[9] and 1127, §§ 1[10] and 2.[11]

§2. The one assisting at a marriage is understood to be only that person who, present at the ceremony, asks for the contractants' manifestation of consent and receives it in the name of the Church.

CCEO Canon 828, §1. Only those marriages are valid which are celebrated with a sacred rite, in the presence of the local hierarch, local pastor, or a priest who has been given the faculty of blessing the marriage by either of them, and at least two witnesses, according, however to the prescriptions of the following canons, with due regard for the exceptions mentioned in cann. 832[12] and 834, §2.[13]

§2. That rite which is considered a sacred rite is the intervention a priest assisting and blessing.

The Latin code and the Oriental code are not identical in regard to the form of marriage, and in fact there are substantial differences between them. For this reason, careful attention must be paid to the question of jurisdiction in any marriage in which an Oriental Catholic is a party.

However, the matter of jurisdiction is not problematic in all weddings involving Oriental Catholics. For instance, if the proposed marriage is between a Latin Catholic and an Oriental Catholic, the proper pastor for either of them has jurisdiction to validly marry the couple.[14] The problem of jurisdiction is crucial only in weddings in which neither the bride nor the groom is a member of the church *sui iuris* of the officiating priest. Examples of this are two Oriental Catholics who wish to marry before the local Latin pastor or an Oriental Catholic who wishes to enter into a mixed religion or disparity of worship marriage before the local Latin pastor. In such cases, in addition to any other considerations which

7 *Ecclesia supplet* in cases of factual or legal common error and in positive and probable doubt of law or fact.
8 The delegation of lay persons to witness marriages.
9 The extraordinary form of marriage.
10 The marriage of a Catholic to an Orthodox who is free to marry under Catholic law before an Orthodox priest is illicit but valid.
11 The dispensation of the canonical form of marriage.
12 The extraordinary form of marriage.
13 The marriage of a Catholic to an Orthodox who is free to marry under Catholic law before an Orthodox priest is illicit but valid.
14 83*CIC* c. 1109 and *CCEO* c. 829, §1.

may apply,[15] it is necessary to know if the local Latin pastor is the proper pastor for the Oriental Catholic. This is important because if he is not, then it is necessary to obtain delegation to officiate at the wedding from the competent authority in order to achieve the canonical form of marriage.

In the case of those Eastern Catholics who have a hierarchy in the United States, there will usually be a proper pastor of their own church *sui iuris* and there will always be an eparchial bishop or exarch who can bless the marriage or delegate any Catholic priest, including a Latin priest, to do so within his eparchy or exarchate.[16] Eastern Catholic hierarchies have been established in the United States for the following ten (10) Eastern Catholic Churches *sui iuris*: the Maronite Church, the Malankara Church, the Syriac Church, the Greek-Melkite Church, the Romanian Church, the Ruthenian Church, the Ukrainian Church, the Chaldean Church, the Malabar Church, and the Armenian Church.[17] Additionally the faithful of the Croatian or Krizevci Church *sui iuris*, the Hungarian Church *sui iuris* and the Slovak Church *sui iuris* have been entrusted to the Bishops of the Ruthenian eparchies in whose territory they reside,[18] and thus for the purposes of our topic, the local Ruthenian pastor is the proper pastor and the local Ruthenian bishop is the proper bishop for those Oriental faithful.

There are eight (8) Eastern Catholic Churches *sui iuris* which do not have hierarchies in the United States: the Coptic Church, the Ethiopian Church, the Albanian Church, the Bielorussian Church, the Bulgarian Church, the (Hellenic) Greek Church, the Italo-Albanian or Italo-Greek Church, and the Russian Church. For Oriental Catholics ascribed in these churches *sui iuris*, there are two issues which must be addressed: the identification of their proper pastor and the identification of their proper hierarch/bishop. A careless approach to these issues will usually result in a marriage which does not take place according to the canonical form and one which is therefore invalid. While this sometimes creates an easy solution for a tribunal when such a marriage fails, more often it creates a problem for the spouses, chancery officials, and parish priests when the invalidity is later discovered during the marriage and a radical sanation or renewal of consent is required to correct the situation.

---

15 Such as the need for the mixed religion permission or the disparity of worship dispensation from the proper bishop or the current *praxis Curiae Romanae* that the Holy See's permission is necessary for marriages according to a ritual which is not the proper ritual for either party to the marriage, which goes to liceity at most but is *praeter legem* and not found in either code.

16 *CCEO* c. 830, § 1.

17 See the current edition of the *Annuario Pontificio* and the current edition of the *Official Catholic Directory*.

18 See Papal *bullae* of May 1924 erecting the Ruthenian Eparchy in the United States and appointing the Most Reverend Basil Takach as the first Eparch for Carpatho-Rusyn (Ruthenian) Greek Catholics and also for Hungarian, Slovak, and Croatian Greek Catholics.

Sometimes, there is a misplaced reliance on *CCEO* canon 916 as to the jurisdiction of the local Latin pastor and ordinary; and the pertinent sections of the canon provide as follows:

> *CCEO* Canon 916, §4. If there is no pastor for the Christian faithful of a certain Church *sui iuris*, the eparchial bishop of these people can appoint the pastor of another Church *sui iuris* to look after them as their proper pastor, but with the consent of the eparchial bishop of the pastor who is to be appointed.
>
> §5. In places where no exarchy has been constituted for the Christian faithful of a certain Church *sui iuris*, the hierarch of another Church *sui iuris*, even the Latin Church, of the place is to be considered the proper hierarch of these faithful, with due regard for the prescription of can. 101;[19] if, however, there are several hierarchs, that one is to be considered their proper hierarch who has been appointed as such by the Apostolic See or, if it is a question of Christian faithful who belong to a patriarchal Church, by the patriarch with the assent of the Apostolic See.

Now, it seems that there is an assumption that in the absence of a pastor or hierarchy for the faithful of a particular Oriental Church *sui iuris*, the local Latin pastor and the local Latin Ordinary are the "default pastor" and "default hierarch" for them. However, as one can plainly see, that is not what the canon provides. As to the proper pastor, *CCEO* canon 916, §4 does not itself provide one, rather it allows for one to be appointed from another church *sui iuris* (including the Latin Church) but this is only possible if there is an eparchial bishop or exarch for the faithful without a proper pastor, and then only with the permission of the eparchial or diocesan bishop of the pastor to be appointed. In the United States, this possibility is only available among the Latin Church *sui iuris* and the Eastern Catholic Churches *sui iuris* for whom there are eparchies or exarchates established here.

Independently of this provision, the establishment of these Oriental eparchies and exarchates in the United States has largely eliminated the uncertainty as to the proper pastor for Oriental Catholics since either parishes or missions have been established with territorial jurisdiction or else the Oriental eparchial bishops have designated pastors of other churches *sui iuris* with the consent of their bishops to function as the proper pastor for their faithful in a particular geographical area. However, prior to the establishment of these Oriental jurisdictions, there was uncertainty in the United States regarding the proper pastor for Oriental Catholics until this was eventually remedied by a *ius speciale* enacted by the Apostolic See making the local Latin pastor the proper pastor for Oriental Catho-

19 Concerning the rights and obligations of the Oriental patriarchs.

lics living in places where there was no pastor of their own Church *sui iuris*.[20] Since this *ius speciale* remains in force,[21] in the absence of other provisions, the local Latin pastor remains the default proper pastor for Oriental Catholics in their territory who do not have a pastor of their own Church *sui iuris*. Occasionally this has proved dispositive in the adjudication of marriage annulments in which Catholic form has been questioned. However, because another priest may have been designated as the proper pastor by the eparchial bishop or exarch, it cannot simply be assumed that the local Latin pastor is always the proper pastor for every Oriental Catholic without his or her own. This does not mean that pastoral care should not be provided for Oriental Catholics if the local Latin pastor is in the best position to do so, but it does mean that for purposes of acts which depend for their validity on the power of governance or jurisdiction, such as the canonical form of marriage, the question of whether the local Latin pastor is the proper pastor for particular Oriental Catholics in the area without a pastor of their own church *sui iuris* should be carefully investigated before a canonical act requiring jurisdiction for validity is attempted. Clearly, the *ius speciale* does mean that the local Latin pastor is the proper pastor for those Eastern Catholics who have neither a pastor of their own church *sui iuris* in the area nor a hierarchy of their own church *sui iuris* in the United States.

Similarly, it cannot be assumed that *CCEO* canon 916, §5 applies in such a way as to automatically make the local Latin ordinary the hierarch for Oriental Catholics without their own hierarchy. This is because the Apostolic See has in fact made a few special provisions in this regard,[22] and also because the canon means that if the Latin ordinary is the sole Catholic hierarch, which is certainly not the case in the United States, since many of the Oriental Catholic Churches *sui iuris* have their own hierarchies here, and hence their proper hierarchs to grant matrimonial permissions, dispensations and delegations. However, for those Oriental Catholic Churches *sui iuris* which do not yet have their own hierarchy in the United States and for whom no special provision has been made by the Apostolic See, the identification of a proper hierarch would be a problem

20 See *ius speciale* for Ruthenians in the United States provided in the letter from the Sacred Congregation for the Oriental Church, dated 30 May 1955, Prot. N. 803/48, as extended to "all Orientals (in the United States) who find themselves in the same situation" by an announcement in ian-feb 1982 edition of *Servizio Informazione Congregazione Orientale*, at p. 16 and confirmed in a letter from the Most Reverend Pio Laghi, Apostolic Delegate, to the Most Reverend John R. Roach, President of the National Conference of Catholic Bishops, dated 24 June 1982. See *Roman Replies and CLSA Advisory Opinions 1984*, at pp. 5-9.

21 This provision is not revoked under by *CCEO* c. 6, 1° as a particular law contradictory to the canons of the *CCEO*, because it is not contradictory to *CCEO* c. 915, §4, but supplementary to it by merely providing another method of determining a proper pastor for Oriental Catholics without their own.

22 Namely, that the faithful of the Croatian or Kriźevei Church, the Hungarian Church, and the Slovak Church have been entrusted to the pastoral care of the Ruthenian Eparchial Bishops.

were it not for another *ius speciale* from the Apostolic See which does provide that the local Latin ordinary is the proper hierarch for Oriental Catholics living within the territory of his diocese who do not have a hierarchy of their own.[23] This *ius speciale* is unaffected by the promulgation of the *CCEO* and remains in force.[24] It is also very clear in the current legislation specifically as to matrimonial dispensations, that the local Latin bishop can dispense Oriental Catholics actually present in his diocese who do not have their own hierarchy.[25] However, failure to give adequate attention to the ascription of Oriental Catholics can still affect the validity of marriage, and American tribunals have declared marriages null on the grounds of an undispensed diriment impediment in cases where an Oriental Catholic was married by a Latin priest who was in fact the proper pastor but where a diriment impediment was invalidly dispensed by the local Latin ordinary because there was a hierarchy established for the Oriental Catholic party, thus depriving the local Latin bishop of jurisdiction over the Oriental Catholic.

A practical example of how inattention to ascription can affect the validity of marriage is an actual tribunal case in which a Catholic man was married to a baptized non-Catholic by a Latin priest and the local Latin ordinary had granted the Mixed Religion permission. The man was known to the Latin pastor because he was a life-long parishioner, having been baptized at the parish, as was his father. However, the paternal grandfather was a Maronite Catholic born in Lebanon and married to another Maronite Catholic immigrant to the United States at the local Latin parish long before there was a Maronite Eparchy in the United States. The only clue to this was the very obvious Middle Eastern surname. The family actually believed that they were Latin Catholics, although they knew and were very proud that their ancestors were Lebanese Maronites from a particular village in Lebanon. Of course, canonically, the man was a Maronite Catholic. There was a canonically erected Maronite parish not too far away, and the Maronite eparchy had been established, but delegation was never sought. The marriage was an-

23 The special provisions on this point made by the Apostolic See prior to the *CCEO*; namely, that the Latin ordinaries have the power to grant dispensations for Eastern Catholics who have no ordinary (hierarch) of their own in the United States, remain in force. These provisions are contained in a Private Reply from the Sacred Congregation for the Oriental Church, dated 24 July 1948, found at *Canon Law Digest* 3: 50 - 51 (based on the usual Quinquennial Faculties *in vigore* at the time), as necessarily modified by the subsequent M.p. *De Episcoporum muneribus* (giving new norms for the dispensing power of bishops), 15 June 1966, LVIII *AAS* 467ff, *Canon Law Digest* 6: 394. See also the letter from the Sacred Congregation for the Oriental Churches, dated 24 May 1982, Prot. N. 106/82, concerning the exclusive jurisdiction of Eastern hierarchs over their faithful, i.e., that it is not cumulative with the Latin ordinaries, found at *Roman Replies and CLSA Advisory Opinions 1984*, pp. 5-9, at p. 6, which confirms by implication that the Latin ordinaries retain jurisdiction if there is no Eastern hierarch.

24 Since this provision is not revoked under by *CCEO* c. 6, 1° as a particular law contradictory to the canons of the *CCEO*, and in fact is precisely the kind of action by the Apostolic See contemplated by *CCEO* c. 916, §5.

25 See 83*CIC* c. 1078, §1 as clarified by *CCEO* c. 795, §1.

nulled on the grounds of defective form of marriage, the tribunal ruling that the principle of *ecclesia supplet* did not supply the power of governance since this was a case of ignorance, not error.

Substantive Matrimonial Law in General

The reason we must be concerned about the substantive matrimonial law is simple; substantive law binds the parties subject to it. Let us consider the provisions of both codes relative to this issue; namely, 1983 *CIC* canons 1 and 1059, and *CCEO* canons 1 and 780, §1:

> 83*CIC* canon 1. The canons of this Code affect only the Latin Church.
>
> 83*CIC* canon 1059. Even if only one party is Catholic, the marriage of Catholics is regulated not only by divine law but also by canon law, with due regard for the competence of civil authority concerning the merely civil effects of such a marriage.
>
> *CCEO* canon 1. The canons of this Code affect all and solely the Eastern Catholic Churches, unless, with regard to relations with the Latin Church, it is expressly stated otherwise.
>
> *CCEO* canon 780, §1. Even if only one party is Catholic, the marriage of Catholics is regulated not only by divine law but also by canon law, with due regard for the competence of civil authority concerning the merely civil effects of such a marriage

In practical application, these canons require that a Latin Catholic be subject to the substantive matrimonial law found in the 1983*CIC*, and an Oriental Catholic be subject to the substantive matrimonial law found in the *CCEO*. But since the *CCEO* also permits the legislation of particular law by an Oriental Catholic Church *sui iuris* in certain matrimonial matters,[26] this also means that an Oriental Catholic be subject to any substantive matrimonial law of his or her own Church *sui iuris*. Therefore, in marriages involving Oriental Catholics, the inescapable implication is that both the substantive matrimonial law binding the bride and that binding the groom must be satisfied. This is because both parties must be free to marry, and each party's freedom to marry is determined by the substantive matrimonial law which binds him or her. This is true whether we are considering an interritual marriage between a Latin Catholic and an Oriental Catholic, or a marriage between two Oriental Catholics of the same or different Churches *sui*

26 E.g., the age of marriage can be increased by particular law under *CCEO* Canon 800, § 2; marriage by proxy is invalid unless permitted by particular law under *CCEO* Canon 837, §2.

iuris, or a mixed religion or disparity of worship marriage involving an Oriental Catholic. In actual practice, the substantive matrimonial law of the 83*CIC* and of the *CCEO* are essentially the same, but there are some notable exceptions. The differences occur in connection with certain diriment impediments, matrimonial consent, the form of marriage, and marriage by proxy.

Diriment Impediments

The diriment impediments are those of public propriety and spiritual relationship. Both codes contain the impediment of public propriety,[27] and both codes agree that the diriment impediment of public propriety arises from an invalid marriage and from notorious and/or public concubinage, but the *CCEO* includes a third basis for incurring this impediment; namely, from a marriage which is attempted without complying with the canonical form of marriage, so-called "lack of form" cases. In doing this, the *CCEO* distinguishes between marriages which are invalid due to some provision of substantive matrimonial law, such as a diriment impediment, and marriages in which the parties are canonically free to marry, but simply do not observe the required (canonical) form of marriage. Even though there is some opinion that a marriage attempted without canonical form could give rise to the impediment of public propriety after cohabitation,[28] the question is far from clear.[29] While it is very clear under the 83*CIC* that this impediment does not arise merely because of the civil marriage, even if consummated, absent the establishment of cohabitation, I would suggest that a properly strict interpretation of 83*CIC* canon 1093 would hold that the impediment is not necessarily incurred as a result of a marriage which is invalid due to lack of form even with cohabitation.[30] At the very least, there is a *dubium iuris* under the 83*CIC*. *CCEO* canon 810, § 1 avoids this problem by specifically including "lack of form" marriages among the situations which establish this impediment.

27 83*CIC* c. 1093 and *CCEO* c. 810.

28 See William J. Doheny, C.S.C., J.U.D., *Canonical Procedure in Matrimonial Cases, Second Edition*, Volume I (Milwaukee: The Bruce Publishing Company, 1948), at p. 711. Note that Doheny bases this opinion on the reasoning that the cohabitation raises the impediment under the "public and notorious concubinage" aspect of the prior Latin legislation, 1917*CIC* canon 1078, and not because of the attempted marriage without canonical form.

29 This is because marriages which are invalid due to lack of form have not been traditionally considered as putative marriages, and therefore they do not, *ipso facto*, give rise to the impediment. See Pontifical Commission for the Authentic Interpretation of the Code of Canon Law, Opinion of 12 March 1929, XXI *AAS* 179, also found in *Canon Law Digest* 1: 516-517; James A. Coriden, Thomas J. Green and Donald E. Heintschel, eds., *The Code of Canon Law, a Text and Commentary* (New York and Mahwah: Paulist Press, 1985), at p. 773; Doheny, at p. 711.

30 The reason I say this is because cohabitation alone does not seem to amount, in and of itself, to "public and notorious concubinage," at least not without additional facts which make it "notorious," such as actual knowledge among the people that the parties were not married in Church and resultant scandal in the parish, etc.

As a result, when doing a pre-nuptial investigation involving an Oriental Catholic who was in a prior lack of form marriage, inquiry must always be made as to whether either party to the proposed marriage is a blood relative in the first degree of the direct line of the former spouse of the other party in the lack of form marriage, and if so, a dispensation must be sought from the competent authority.

The two codes also differ on the matter of spiritual relationship. This impediment of spiritual relationship exists in the Oriental code, but not in the present Latin code.[31] The *CCEO* provides:

> *CCEO* Canon 811, §1. From baptism there arises a spiritual relationship between a sponsor and the baptized person and the parents of the same that invalidates marriage.
>
> §2. If a baptism is repeated under condition, a spiritual relationship does not arise, unless the same sponsor was employed for the second ceremony.

Thus, if a Latin Catholic man were to marry a Latin Catholic woman in a Latin Church after 1983 according to the Latin ritual, and the groom is the godfather of the bride, there is no impediment. But if an Oriental Catholic man were to marry a Latin woman before a Latin pastor and the Oriental Catholic man were the godfather of the Latin woman's son, the marriage would be invalid unless the diriment impediment of spiritual relationship were properly dispensed by the Oriental Catholic bishop, if there is one, or if there is not, by the local Latin bishop even though this is not an impediment under the Latin code.[32]

---

31 This impediment existed under the former Latin legislation. The diriment impediment extended only to the minister and the baptized person and the sponsor(s) and the baptized person under 1917*CIC* canons 1079 and 768; but the parents of the baptized person were also included under the pre-1917*CIC* legislation. See Pietro Cardinal Gasparri, *Tractatus Canonicus de Matrimonio, editio nova ad mentem Codicis I. C.* (Romae: Typis Polyglottis Vaticanis, 1932), Volumen I, nn. 749 - 763, at p. 454ff; and the authorities cited in reference to 1917*CIC* canons 768 and 1079 in *Codex Iuris Canonici, Pii X Pontificis Maximi iussu digestus Benedicti Papae XV auctoritate promulgatus, praefatione, fontium annotatione et indice analytico-alphabetico ab Emo. Petro Card. Gasparri auctus* (New York: P. J. Kenedy & Sons, 1918); at pp. 221 - 222, fn. 4 and 308, fn. 2.

32 Because the local Latin ordinary has the power to dispense Oriental Catholics from most impediments of ecclesiastical law if they are residing in his diocese, that is, if there is no hierarchy erected for their own church *sui iuris*. See 83*CIC* c. 1078, §1 as clarified by *CCEO* c. 795, §1. Even though the Latin Church is not explicitly mentioned, the canons relate to the power to dispense and so should be interpreted broadly.

Matrimonial Consent

The only issue relating to matrimonial consent is that of conditional consent. The two codes differ on the substantive law of matrimonial consent given under condition.

> 83*CIC* Canon 1102, §1. Marriage based on a condition concerning the future cannot be contracted validly.
>
> §2. Marriage based on a condition concerning the past or the present is valid or invalid, insofar as the subject matter of the condition exists or not.
>
> *CCEO* Canon 826 - Marriage based on a condition cannot be validly celebrated.

The Latin code invalidates consent if the condition refers to the future, because otherwise the validity of the matrimonial consent is dependent on some future event, and the consent is not absolute at the time it is given; but it permits conditional consent as long as the fulfillment of the condition can be verified at the time of the consent, i.e., the condition refers to the past or the present, because the consent is absolute at the time it is given if the condition has been met.

The Oriental code follows the long-standing Oriental tradition and simply invalidates all conditional matrimonial consents because the attachment of any condition at all indicates some kind of limitation of the consent, and calls into question whether it is absolute or not.

The practical effect of this difference can result in matrimonial consent which could be valid for a Latin spouse but invalid for an Oriental spouse. Therefore, in all marriages involving Oriental Catholics, the pastoral preparation should be especially sensitive to the possibility of any kind of condition. If any kind of condition is revealed on the part of either the man or the woman, the matter should be referred to the chancery for decision and directions. This particular issue can be very complicated, and there is an argument which can be made that *CCEO* canon 826 is phrased quite broadly, and could be read so as to invalidate any marriage entered into under condition in which one of the parties is an Eastern Catholic and a condition is placed by either party, even by a Latin Catholic party. This is really an interesting argument because, if one of the spouses were a non-Catholic, that is exactly how a tribunal, Latin or Eastern, would apply the law. That is, in a mixed religion or disparity of worship marriage, it would apply the substantive law on condition which bound the Catholic party, whether it is 1983*CIC* canon 1102 or *CCEO* canon 826, to the non-Catholic party, and would adjudicate the case based on how the law applied to the facts. While the argument is intriguing, the better reasoned analysis is that the substantive matrimonial law which binds the Catholic man controls the validity of his consent and the substantive matrimonial law which binds the Catholic woman controls the validity of her consent which should be applied here. The only time in which the one party's substantive law can be applied to the other party is in a mixed religion or disparity of worship marriage case precisely because there is no substantive matrimonial law for the non-Catholic party.[33]

The Sacred Rite of Marriage

Returning now to the Catholic or canonical form of marriage, we have already observed that the provisions of the Latin code and the Oriental code as to form are not identical and that the differences between the two codes can have important consequences which go to the validity of the sacrament of marriage. Assuming then, that we have addressed and resolved the issue of jurisdiction in a particular wedding, we must still address the substantive matrimonial law as it relates to marriages involving Oriental Catholics. We know from the legislative history of the *CCEO* that a deliberate effort was made to have consistency between the Latin code and Oriental code insofar as this was consonant with maintaining the authentic Oriental traditions of the *sacri canones* or *fonti* of the Oriental code. That effort was not always successful, and so we find in the Oriental code a provision for the extraordinary form of marriage[34] similar to that found in the Latin code even though this is quite foreign to the Oriental tradition.[35] That having been said, there are some important differences, and Catholic or canonical form of marriage is one of them. The two codes are in total agreement as to the form of marriage requiring the marriage to take place before the proper ordinary/hierarch or proper pastor or a priest properly delegated and two witnesses.

But the codes differ in that the Latin code permits a deacon to assist at a marriage, and defines assistance as asking for the consents and receiving them in the name of the Church, whereas in the Oriental code the form of marriage also requires a "sacred rite" which it defines as the intervention of a priest (*interventu sacerdotis*) assisting and blessing. The use of the word *sacerdos* is deliberate and excludes – and is intended to exclude – a deacon because in the Oriental tradition, deacons cannot give a blessing. In other words, under the Oriental code, the hierarch or priest is the minister of marriage. It is important to recognize this distinction if even one party to a wedding is an Oriental Catholic. Why? Because this is a substantive provision binding on the Oriental Catholic and it goes to validity for the Oriental Catholic. So, if two Oriental Catholics; or a Latin Catholic and an Oriental Catholic; or an Oriental Catholic and a baptized non-Catholic or

33 Of course, if a baptized non-Catholic in a mixed religion marriage belongs to a Church or ecclesial community which has its own proper matrimonial law, that law must be applied to the baptized non-Catholic. See *CCEO* canon 780, §2.

34 See *CCEO* c. 832.

35 The sole *fons* for this canon is canon 89 of the *M.p,* of Pius XII, *Crebrae allatae sunt*, 22 Feb. 1949.

an un-baptized person are married according to the Latin ritual with all appropriate permissions and dispensations and, if necessary, delegation, the marriage would still be invalid if it were witnessed by a deacon because the Catholic form of marriage for the Oriental Catholic would not have been observed precisely because there would not have been a "sacred rite" as defined by the Oriental code. Although a few Oriental canonists have opined that it is possible for a Latin deacon to validly assist at marriages involving Oriental Catholics,[36] the majority of Oriental canonists, including myself, think otherwise; and in any event, it seems only prudent to avoid the issue entirely. Thus, the actual praxis of most Oriental eparchies and exarchates in the United States when granting delegation for a marriage to take place according to the Latin ritual is to state explicitly in the rescript that delegation is granted to a named Latin priest with the faculty to subdelegate to a priest and not to a deacon.

Marriage by Proxy

There is also a significant difference between the two codes when it comes to marriage by proxy. 83*CIC* canon 1105 permits a marriage to be entered into validly by proxy, but, because of the opportunity for fraud and abuse, it creates a process intended to assure that the parties are entering the marriage freely and knowingly, and it allows for a change of mind; and the observance of all of these safeguards goes to validity. *CCEO* canon 837, §2 simply forbids marriage by proxy, but it does allow a Church *sui iuris* to enact particular law permitting it as long as safeguards for its celebration are also provided. Although marriages by proxy are rare, if they are encountered, it would probably be in cases involving immigrants, and this difference between the Latin and Oriental codes can have practical consequences when an Oriental Catholic is involved in a proxy marriage. The issue here is whether *CCEO* canon 837, §2 is applicable when the marriage is celebrated according to the Latin ritual. Clearly, if the party who consented to marriage by proxy is the Eastern Catholic, the provisions of the Eastern code apply and the marriage would be invalid because the Eastern Catholic could not marry by proxy even though the Latin Catholic could. The more problematic issue is whether an interritual marriage is valid where one party's law allows a marriage by proxy and the other party's law does not, and the party whose law permits it appears by proxy. The text of *CCEO* canon 837, §2 is very broad; it does not say that an Eastern Catholic may not give a proxy, it says that marriage by proxy "cannot be validly celebrated" (*valide celebrari non potest*) unless the sole exception that particular law allows it is applicable. In practical application, the canon means that an Eastern Catholic whose Church *sui iuris* does not permit marriage by proxy cannot validly marry by proxy whether he or she is the party appearing by proxy or it is the other party who is appearing by

36 Most notably, the late distinguished Ukrainian canonist Archimandrite Victor J. Pospishil. See his *Eastern Catholic Marriage Law* (Brooklyn, NY: Saint Maron Publications, 1991), at p. 372. Pospishil believed that this would be permissible under the maxim *locus regit actum* because he considers witnessing a marriage to be a procedural act.

proxy. The only time a marriage by proxy can validly be entered into is when the law binding both parties permits it, and then, only if the conditions for a proxy marriage in both laws are observed.

FREQUENTLY ENCOUNTERED RELATED PASTORAL ISSUES

Entering into Full Communion

A pastoral situation involving ascription is often encountered when a baptized non-Catholic is received into full communion with the Catholic Church. The law on this subject is not found in the 83*CIC*, however this *lacuna* in the Latin code has been filled by the Supreme Legislator with *CCEO* canons 35 and 896 to 901 inclusive, which clearly apply by their very nature and substance to all cases of ascription.

The basic provision is that Baptized non-Catholics received into full communion with the Catholic Church are ascribed *ipso iure* to the church *sui iuris* of the same rite whence they came.[37] Historically in the West, this has not been a difficult issue because most baptized non-Catholics have been members of the various Protestant denominations, and thus come from a Western culture and from an ecclesial community which can be historically traced back to the Latin Church *sui iuris*. So when Protestants are received into full communion, they have been assumed to become Latin Catholics, and indeed this is the correct ascription under the *ius vigens*. However, we must be clear that the ascription is by operation of law based on the church or ecclesial community of origin and not based upon the parish at which an individual is received. This principle is best demonstrated by examples. If a baptized non-Catholic who is a member of the Church of England were to be received into the Catholic Church after appropriate catechesis he or she is ascribed *ipso iure* to the Latin Church *sui iuris* regardless of whether the reception took place in a Latin parish or an Oriental Catholic parish. Similarly, if a Romanian Orthodox person were to be received into full communion with the Catholic Church, he or she is ascribed to the Romanian Greek-Catholic Church *sui iuris*, whether the reception took place at a Latin parish, a Romanian Greek-Catholic parish, or an Armenian Catholic parish. So, it is important to correctly identify the correlative Catholic Church *sui iuris* to a given non-Catholic Church, and to make a notation of the proper ascription in the record of reception.[38]

---

37 *CCEO* c. 35.

38 This is not always an easy task, especially in the case of some of the less well-known Oriental Orthodox Churches. A convenient English resource on this is "A Guide for Determining Ascription to the Proper Church *Sui Iuris* for Baptized Non-Catholics Coming into Full Communion with the Catholic Church" found as an Appendix in *Comparative Sacramental Discipline in the CCEO and CIC – A Handbook for the Pastoral Care of Members of Other Catholic Churches Sui Iuris* (Washington, DC: Canon Law Society of America, 2003).

One situation sometimes encountered is the case of the child of an Orthodox parent and a Catholic parent (it does not matter which parent is the Orthodox and which is the Catholic), and the parents have had the child baptized, chrismated and communicated in the Orthodox Church, but later want the child to become Catholic. Usually, but not always, this occurs when there has been a civil divorce and the Catholic mother is the custodial parent. There will be several pastoral issues involved, not the least of which is whether the Orthodox father objects to the child becoming Catholic, but prescinding from those issues, it is sometimes assumed that a child in this situation will be ascribed to the church *sui iuris* of the Catholic parent upon being received into the Catholic Church. There is no canonical basis for this assumption, and the ordinary rule of *CCEO* c. 35 applies in that the child is *ipso iure* ascribed in the Catholic Church *sui iuris* which corresponds to the Orthodox Church into which the child was baptized. If the Catholic parent and the child wish to enroll the child to the same Catholic Church *sui iuris* as the Catholic parent in such a situation, it will be necessary to use the processes for transfer of ascription.

Transfer of Ascription

It may seem at first blush extraneous to discuss the subject of transfer of ascription in the present discussion, but it is appropriate to do so because, when the subject does arise, it is frequently in connection with the sacrament of marriage.

First of all, it is very important to know that the principles of ecclesiology regarding the Oriental Catholic Churches enunciated at Vatican II have resulted in a prohibition by the Supreme Legislator of any attempts, direct or indirect, to induce a member of the faithful to transfer his or her ascription. This prohibition is explicit and provides as follows:

> *CCEO* canon 31. No one can presume in any way to induce the Christian faithful to transfer to another Church *sui iuris*.

The penalty is as follows:

> *CCEO* canon 1465. One who, belonging to any Church *sui iuris*, including the Latin Church, and exercising an office, a ministry or another function in the Church, has presumed to induce any member of the Christian faithful whatever to transfer to another Church *sui iuris*, contrary to can. 31 is to be punished with an appropriate penalty.

Therefore, in bringing up or discussing this subject, it is important that in explaining to a member of the faithful his or her options in regard to transfer of ascription, nothing is said or implied which would violate the letter or even the spirit of this prohibition. In this regard, we should be aware that sometimes the financial benefits of reduced tuition for persons belonging to a Latin parish can become an unintended enticement to Eastern Catholic faithful whose children are attending a Latin parochial school.

There are only two methods of transfer of ascription: transfer by election; and transfer with the consent of the Apostolic See. Transfer by election applies exclusively to the situation of interritual marriages where both spouses are Catholic, but ascribed to two different churches *sui iuris*, and refers to the privilege conferred by the law upon one of the spouses to transfer to the church *sui iuris* of the other spouse. The motive for this provision seems to be promoting unity in family worship. However, the provisions of the two codes are not in complete agreement, as can readily be seen by comparing them.

> 83*CIC* canon 112, §1. After the reception of baptism, the following are enrolled in another Ritual Church *sui iuris*:
>
> 1° a person who has obtained permission from the Apostolic See;
>
> 2° a spouse who declares at the time of marriage or during marriage that he or she is transferring to the Ritual Church *sui iuris* of the other spouse; but when the marriage has ended, that person can freely return to the Latin Church;
>
> 3° before the completion of the fourteenth year of age, the children of those mentioned in nn. 1 and 2 as well as, in a mixed marriage, the children of the Catholic party who has legitimately transferred to another ritual Church; on completion of their fourteenth year, however, they can return to the Latin Church.
>
> *CCEO* canon 33. A wife is at liberty to transfer to the Church of the husband at the celebration of or during the marriage; when the marriage has ended, she can freely return to the original Church *sui iuris*.

The difference in the language of the Latin code and Oriental code was deliberate, and means that a Latin Catholic, whether the husband or the wife, married to an Oriental Catholic can transfer by simple election to the Oriental Catholic Church *sui iuris* of his or her spouse; but only an Oriental Catholic wife has the right to transfer by election to the church *sui iuris* of her husband (either another Oriental Catholic Church or the Latin Church); an Oriental Catholic husband does not have this right. The reasons for the difference appear to be the Oriental tradition of maintaining church ascription through the identity of the father and the desire to protect the numerically smaller Oriental Catholic Churches *sui iuris* from a mass exodus of members who have immigrated. The manner of making the election is not specified in the canons, and therefore it could be accomplished by a simple declaration. However, in order to establish the election with certitude, the common praxis is for the electing spouse to do so in writing in the presence of the parish priest of the parish of the church *sui iuris* to which the spouse wishes to transfer and two witnesses, and that the election be recorded and the church of baptism notified as in the case of formal transfers of ascription.[39]

The other method of transfer of ascription is with the consent of the Apostolic See, and it is clear that the requirement of consent is not a mere formality. On the contrary, this requirement is a true *lex irritans* because the consent goes to validity.[40] There are two kinds of consent: formal consent and presumed consent. The formal process is the traditional transfer process pursuant to *CCEO* canon 32, §1 and 83*CIC* canon 112, §1, 1° whereby a written petition from the person seeking to transfer and articulating the reasons for the request is submitted through the Apostolic Nunciature to the competent dicastery of the Roman Curia, which is always the Congregation for the Oriental Churches because this process will always involve at least one Oriental Church *sui iuris*, along with proof of present ascription (usually a baptismal certificate), the written *votum* of the sponsoring pastor, and the written *votum* of the local diocesan or eparchial bishop of the church *sui iuris* to which transfer is sought (the Bishop *ad quem*). If the petition is granted, a rescript will be issued by the Congregation which must then be executed[41] and recorded[42] in order to become effective.

The process of the presumed consent of the Apostolic See is new with the *CCEO* and the canon reads as follows:

> *CCEO* c. 32, §2. In the case of Christian faithful of an eparchy of a certain Church *sui iuris* who petition to transfer to another Church *sui iuris* which has its own eparchy in the same territory, this consent of the Apostolic See is presumed, provided that the eparchial bishops of both eparchies consent to the transfer in writing.

Now although the process is fairly clear, there was initially a *dubium* whether transfers from or to the Latin Church *sui iuris* could be accomplished by this presumed consent since there is no similar canon in the 83*CIC* and the *CCEO* provision does not specifically mention the Latin Church. However, this *dubium* was resolved in 1993 by an Authentic Interpretation of 83*CIC* Canon 112, §1,

---

39 See the following discussion of transfers of ascription with the consent of the Apostolic See.

40 Although 83*CIC* c. 112, §1 is not so clear about this, the intent of the Supreme Legislator is very clear in the supplementary provision *CCEO* c. 32, §1 (*valide*).

41 *CCEO* c. 36.

42 *CCEO* c. 37.

1° which allows the same presumption even when the Latin Church *sui iuris* is involved.[43] For this process to be available, there must be a diocese or eparchy canonically erected in the same territory so that there are two bishops who have jurisdiction over the same geographical area involved in the process. For the purposes of this process, an exarchate is treated as an eparchy since the law does not expressly provide otherwise.[44] Therefore, this process for the presumed consent of the Apostolic See can be employed for a transfer of a Latin Catholic to any of these Eastern Catholic Churches *sui iuris* or for the transfer of a member of any of these Eastern Catholic Churches *sui iuris* to the Latin Church. In actual practice, the process normally involves a written petition from the person seeking to transfer articulating the reasons for the request submitted to the bishop *ad quem*, along with proof of present ascription (usually a baptismal certificate) and the written *votum* of the sponsoring pastor. The bishop *ad quem*, if he is favorable to the petition, then writes to the bishop *ab quo* requesting his written *votum* on the request. If the bishop *ab quo* grants his *nihil obstat*, then the bishop *ad quem* issues a rescript granting the transfer, which must then be sent to the parish priest for execution and recording in accordance with law.[45] The process for the presumed consent of the Apostolic See cannot be employed for a transfer of a Latin Catholic to any of the Eastern Catholic Churches *sui iuris* who do not have a hierarchy in the United States or for the transfer of a member of any of these Eastern Catholic Churches *sui iuris* to the Latin Church.

It is important to note that under both transfers by election and transfers with the formal or presumed consent of the Apostolic See, children under fourteen years of age who are ascribed to the church *sui iuris* of the transferring parent, transfer *ipso iure* along with their parent(s).[46] For this reason, it is important to include the names, dates of birth and baptism certificates of any children under fourteen years of age along with the petition and also to notify their parishes of baptism of their transfers. Although the children transfer *ipso iure*, failure to name them in the petition or election and to include them in the execution and recording of the rescript and to notify their parish of baptism of their transfer will cause confusion and sometimes even provoke an invalid marriage, so it is a prudent practice to do so in all cases in which children under fourteen years of age are transferring ascription with a parent.

CONCLUSION

Oriental Catholics in general owe a great debt to the Latin Church *sui iuris* in the United States for welcoming immigrants who belong to these ancient Oriental traditions and for fostering pastoral care in their own rite where possible, as well as for providing pastoral care where it is not yet possible to have a priest of

43 See Authentic Interpretation found at *AAS* LXXXV [1993] p. 81.

44 *CCEO* c. 313.

45 *CCEO* cc. 36 and 37.

46 83*CIC* c. 112, §1, 3° and *CCEO* c. 34.

their own church *sui iuris* to minister to them. Similarly, the Oriental Catholic clergy could not function effectively in the United States without the fraternal encouragement and support of the Latin bishops and clergy. The legacy of the ecclesiological insights of the Fathers of Vatican II has certainly contributed to the modern openness and acceptance among the Catholic Churches *sui iuris*. Indeed, it is because of this awareness among the Catholic clergy of the vitality and richness of all the Catholic Churches *sui iuris* that so much progress has been made so quickly.

That having been acknowledged, there are two matters which could promote even greater progress. Firstly, greater awareness of and respect for the proper ascription of Oriental Catholics on the parochial level should be promoted because this will make life much easier both for the faithful and for the clergy. Secondly, since it appears that the presence of large numbers of Oriental Catholics in the United States will be more or less permanent, the Latin dioceses should encourage the establishment of parishes of their own church *sui iuris* for the Oriental faithful where this is practical sooner rather than later. Delays in doing so can cause serious damage to the ability of a particular Oriental Catholic Church *sui iuris* to survive, especially the smaller churches. The creation of parishes and hierarchies for the various Oriental Churches *sui iuris* in the United States has had nothing but positive results, and has increased the public image of the Catholic Church while at the same time relieving the Latin parishes, chanceries and tribunals from some burdensome and often difficult processes. Finally, the presence of the various Oriental Churches *sui iuris* alongside the Latin Church bears the best witness that our Church is truly and literally "Catholic."

Seminar

The Unfinished Business of the Eastern Code

Most Rev. David Motiuk, JCOD

INTRODUCTION

I am delighted to have been invited to speak at the Canon Law Society of America. It not only provides me with an opportunity to share a few thoughts on a topic that is dear to my heart, but also an opportunity to be with friends who share a passion for the ministry of canon law within the Church. For this I am grateful.

We are marking two significant events in the life of the universal Catholic Church. First, the 50th anniversary of the Second Vatican Council, *Orientalium ecclesiarum*, the Decree on the Eastern Churches. Second, we are on the eve of the 25th anniversary of the Eastern Code, *Codex canonum Ecclesiarum orientalium*, which Pope St. John Paul II promulgated with the apostolic constitution *Sacri canones* on October 18, 1990.

Some time ago, a Church official asked me at one particular chance meeting what problems I had with my married clergy. This was his first question after introductions. He was obviously well acquainted with my writings on the matter of the restoration of the right of the Eastern Catholic Churches in North America to ordain both celibate and married clergy, a right that had been suspended in the late 19th century. I responded by explaining that it was my position that the Second Vatican Council and the Eastern code had supported the Eastern Churches in their restoration and renewal and that certain matters, including the topic at hand, which had been abrogated having been integrally reordered. Perhaps my explanation was not completely satisfactory as he went on to say that the Eastern Catholic Churches in North America are on Latin territory and would have to act accordingly.

That exchange got me thinking.

Given the reality of hundreds of thousands of Eastern Christians outside their original patriarchal territories – the "old country," and given ever greater mobility of peoples today, who are oftentimes fleeing poverty and persecution, perhaps the fruits of the conciliar Decree on the Eastern Churches and the Eastern code have not yet been fully realized or have even gone far enough in providing an adequate response to the pastoral needs of the Eastern Catholic faithful in North America and like places. Perhaps some unfinished business remains here.

To provide some reflections on the topic, we begin at the beginning with an overview of the immigration en masse of Eastern Christians to North America starting in the late 1800's, then a look at the representation today of Eastern Catholics Churches in Canada and the United States. Then let us review the more salient points of the 1964 conciliar Decree on the Eastern Churches, *Orientalium ecclesiarum*, the backdrop as it were of the Eastern code.

With this foundation in mind, we are then ready to treat certain canonical-pastoral issues affecting the Eastern Catholic Churches which are not adequately addressed by the Eastern code. Much of the study focuses, in particular, on the question of the hotly debated and much desired extension of patriarchal jurisdiction throughout the world and several related issues. Other issues worthy of our attention included the on-going debate of the ordination of married priests, the particular law of the Churches *sui iuris*, and episcopal conferences and assemblies of hierarchies.

We conclude our reflections by pondering the question whether Eastern Christians in the New World are a curse or a blessing? In other words, what is the mission of the Eastern Catholic Churches in regards to the new evangelization?

EARLY IMMIGRATION OF EASTERN CATHOLICS TO NORTH AMERICA

As a Canadian Ukrainian Catholic, my experience of early immigration to North America of Eastern Christians is seen primarily through the lens of my ancestry. Regardless of nationality, our immigration stories are similar.

By the latter half of the nineteenth century, four million Ukrainians found themselves among the patchwork of nationalities constituting the Austro-Hungarian Empire. Most were peasants, at the bottom of the social ladder. Everyday life meant overpopulation, shortage of land, unemployment, political and social oppression, and starvation. Emigration was their only hope of survival.

Across the Atlantic Ocean, Sir John A. MacDonald had embarked upon Canada's "manifest destiny" of building a transcontinental nation, uniting Canada from the Atlantic Ocean to the Pacific.

MacDonald. Ukrainians and other Europeans. A match made in heaven.

When the Eastern immigrants came, and they did by the tens of thousands, they found themselves without spiritual care. Back at home, faith was of the utmost importance. One group of shepherdless Ukrainian Catholics from Mundare,

Alberta, wrote to Most Rev. Domenico Sbaretti, Apostolic Delegate to Canada, on August 30, 1909 in these words:

> We, the undersigned representatives of seven Greek Catholic Churches of Alberta, send this petition to Your Highness praying for the following:
>
> We, the members of the Greek Catholic Church expressing the wishes of the people of our nationality and religion, pray that you appoint a Greek Catholic bishop in Canada of Ruthenian nationality, or give power over us to the Ruthenian bishop of Philadelphia Pa., or appoint a substitute for the Greek Catholic bishop in the United States for Canada.
>
> This we ask for the following reasons:
>
> The present rule of the Roman Catholic bishops is foreign to us. They do not understand the spirit of our ritual, our ritual being different from the Roman Catholic, and also this brings much harm to our people as many of them being dissatisfied join the Greek Orthodox Church, which is not united with Rome.
>
> And also our people refuse to have their Church property given to the Roman Catholic bishops, which they would be glad to give to a Ruthenian Greek Catholic bishop.
>
> We pray you to do this favour for us and to direct us as to what should be done further in this case.
>
> We remain yours most obedient,
>
> The delegates of seven churches in Alberta,
> Mike Korchyski, Secretary.

The first of 54 signatures attached to the letter is one Ivan (John) Motiuk, who immigrated to Canada in 1899 with his brother Stefan, my great-grandfather.

Their request and many others were rewarded with the appointment of a bishop for Ukrainian Catholics in Canada in 1912 in the person of Bishop Nykyta Budka, who for his martyrdom, was beatified by Pope St. John Paul II in 2001.

The Ukrainian Catholic Church in the United States tell a similar story; however, their bishop, Bishop Soter Ortynsky, was appointed earlier in 1907, the first Eastern Catholic bishop in the western hemisphere.

Eastern Catholic Churches in Canada and the United States

The 22 Eastern Catholic Churches represented worldwide arose from the following five major traditions:

1. Alexandrian Churches
   - Coptic, Ethiopian

2. Antiochene or West Syrian Churches
   - Maronite, Syriac, Syro-Malankara

3. Armenian Church
   - Armenian

4. Chaldean or East Syrian Churches
   - Chaldean, Syro-Malabar

5. Constantinopolitan or Byzantine Churches
   - Albanian, Belarusian, Bulgarian, Croatian, Greek, Hungarian, Italo-Albanian, Macedonian, Melkite, Romanian, Russian, Ruthenian, Slovak, Ukrainian

Eastern Catholics make up a small percentage, relatively speaking, of the overall number of Catholics in the world – 17.5 million (2013 *Annuario pontificio)*, compared to the number of Roman Catholics – over 1.2 billion.

Of all Eastern Catholics, Syriac Christians make up some 47 percent and Byzantine Christians 46 percent. The three largest Eastern Churches are the Byzantine Ukrainian Catholic Church – 4.3 million (25 percent); the Syriac Syro-Malabar Catholic Church – 3.9 million (22 percent); and the Maronite Catholic Church of Lebanon – 3.29 million (19 percent).

In North America, many of the Eastern Catholic Churches are represented, with some 844,000 faithful in total, served by 27 bishops:

Armenian Catholics – 36,000 faithful

Chaldean Catholics – 188,200

Maronite Catholics – 171,000

Melkite Catholics – 59,000

Romanian Catholics – 6,240

Ruthenian or Byzantine Catholics – 84,227

Slovak Catholics – 5,000

Syriac Catholics – 22,000

Syro-Malabar Catholics – 100,700

Syro-Malankar Catholics – 10,100

Ukrainian Catholics – 161,614

These numbers are a good approximation and represent statistics provided by the Churches *sui iuris* themselves to various agencies, such as the *Annuario pontificio*, the Canadian Conference of Catholic Bishops' *Yearbook*, and the American *Official Catholic Directory* (P.J. Kenedy & Sons). Yet, in truth, the numbers can vary substantially depending to whom and for whom they are reported, influenced at times on whether the reporting criteria corresponds to taxation systems as opposed to grant applications.

The following information paints a more detailed picture as to the size and location of the Eastern Catholic Churches in North America. Note that at times the jurisdiction of a given bishop and his eparchy (equivalent to a diocese) may span both Canada and the United States.

Antiochene or Western Syrian Tradition

Maronite Church
Canada
- Eparchy of Saint-Maron de Montréal of the Maronites (85,900 faithful, Montréal, QC, www.cathedralstmaron.org)

United States
- Eparchy of St. Maron of Brooklyn (33,200, Brooklyn, NY, www.stmaron.org)
- Eparchy of Our Lady of Lebanon (51,900, St. Louis, MO, www.eparchy.org)

Syriac Church
Canada and United States (dual jurisdiction)
- Eparchy of Our Lady of Deliverance in the United States and Canada (22,000, Bayonne, NJ, www.ourladyofdeliverance.org)

Syro-Malankara Church
United States
- Apostolic Exarchate for the Syro-Malankara Catholics in the United States (10,100, Elmont, NY, http://syromalankarausa.org)

Armenian Tradition

Armenian Church
Canada and the United States (dual jurisdiction)
- Eparchy of Our Lady of Nareg in the United States and Canada (36,000, Glendale, CA, www.armeniancatholic.org)

Chaldean or East Syrian Tradition

Chaldean Church

Canada

- Eparchy of Mar Addai (18,500, Toronto, ON, www.chaldeanchurch.com)

United States

- Eparchy of St. Thomas the Apostle (104,800, Southfield, MI, www.chaldean.org)
- Eparchy of St. Peter the Apostle (65,000, El Cajon, CA, www.kaldu.org)

Syro-Malabar Church

Canada and United States

- Eparchy of St. Thomas of Chicago; and Apostolic Visitator for the Syro-Malabarese in Canada (100,700, Elmhurst, IL, www.stthomasdiocese.org)

Constantinopolitan or Byzantine Tradition

Melkite Church

Canada

- Eparchy of Saint-Sauveur de Montréal (35,000, Montréal, QC, www.melkite.org)

United States

- Eparchy of Newton (24,000, Roslindale, MA, www.melkite.org)

Romanian Church

Canada and United States (dual jurisdiction)

- Eparchy of Saint George in Canton (6,240, Canton, OH, www.romaniancatholic.org)

Ruthenian Church

United States

- Archeparchy of Pittsburgh (58,200, Pittsburgh, PA, www.archeparchy.org)
- Eparchy of Passaic (14,729, West Paterson, NJ, www.eparchyofpassaic.com)
- Eparchy of Parma (8,887, Parma, OH, www.parma.org)
- Holy Protection of Mary Eparchy of Phoenix (2,411, Phoenix, AZ, www.eparchyofphoenix.org)

Slovak Church

Canada

- Eparchy of Saints Cyril and Methodius in Toronto (5,000, Unionville, ON, www.slovakeparchy.ca)

Ukrainian Church

Canada

- Archeparchy of Winnipeg (30,400, Winnipeg, MB, www.archeparchy.ca)
- Eparchy of Edmonton (28,750, Edmonton, AB, www.edmontoneparchy.com)
- Eparchy of Toronto (37,900, Toronto, ON, www.ucet.ca)
- Eparchy of Saskatoon (6,817, Saskatoon, SK, www.skeparchy.org)

- Eparchy of New Westminster (7,500, New Westminster, BC, www.nweparchy.ca)

United States

- Archeparchy of Philadelphia (15,779, Philadelphia, PA, www.ukrarcheparchy.us)
- Eparchy of Stamford (13,783, Stamford, CT, www.stamforddio.org)
- Eparchy of Chicago (10,000, Chicago, IL, www.esnucc.org)
- Saint Josaphat Eparchy of Parma (10,685, Parma, OH, www.stjosaphateparchy.org)

DECREE ON THE EASTERN CATHOLIC CHURCHES

In preparation for the Second Vatican Council, the Ante-preparatory Commission in 1959 sent out a request to the bishops throughout the world for suggested topics that might be considered for discussion. Among the proposals were matters directly related to the Eastern Catholic Churches.

Early on in the drafting process of what was originally titled the "Decree on the Eastern Churches," the question arose as to the need at all for a separate decree. Some argued that the sections on what today we call "Churches *sui iuris*" and on the patriarchal structure within the universal Catholic Church could be incorporated into the Dogmatic Constitution on the Church and in the Decree on the Pastoral Office of Bishops in the Church, given that these matters concern not only the Eastern Churches but the universal Church.

However, out of concern that specific problems experienced by the Eastern Churches might not be dealt with, in the end the decision was made to proceed with a separate decree. Patriarch Maximos IV, of the Melkite Church, defended this position for the following reasons:

1. The universal Church needs to resist the Latinization of the Eastern Churches by preserving the patriarchal and synodal prerogatives, restoring authentic Eastern canonical discipline, and promoting inter-ritual and inter-confessional collaboration with the Eastern Orthodox Churches.

2. Existing Eastern legislation, at times contrary to the Eastern tradition, for example, the prohibition of Latinization in general and the recognition of the valid administration of the mystery of chrismation (sacrament of confirmation) by Eastern priests, would not have been properly addressed if not dealt with in a separate decree.

3. A separate decree on the Eastern Churches would facilitate the establishment of a commission on inter-ecclesial matters.

4. The problems raised above would not have been adequately addressed if dispersed among the other conciliar documents.

The decree, with the addition of "Catholic" in the title to exclude any possibility of doubt as to the subject matter, was approved on November 20, 1964. 2,110 Fathers voted in favour, 39 against. The decree was promulgated by Pope Paul VI the following day, November 21.

Introduction (art. 1)

Article 1 introduces the Decree by expressing solicitude for the Eastern Churches:

> The catholic church highly esteems the institutions, liturgical rites, ecclesiastical traditions and way of christian life of the eastern churches. For in them, as renowned for their venerable antiquity, shines forth a tradition which exists through the fathers from the apostles and which constitutes part of the divinely revealed and undivided heritage of the whole church... (English translation, N.P. Tanner, ed., *Decrees of the Ecumenical Councils*, vol. 2, London and Washington, Sheed & Ward and Georgetown University Press, 1990).

In order that the Eastern Churches "flourish and fulfill with fresh apostolic vigour the task entrusted to them," the Fathers of the Second Vatican Council enumerated four categories of principles which govern the Eastern Churches: 1) those affecting the universal Church; 2) those given in the decree itself; 3) those originating from the synod of bishops of the Eastern Churches; and; 4) those issued by the Apostolic See of Rome for the Eastern Churches.

Individual Churches or Rites (arts. 2-4)

Articles 2-4 address that which pertains to the universal Church, not only to the Eastern Churches.

Article 2 introduces the notion of individual churches or rites. Today, the Eastern code differentiates between these two concepts in terms of a "Church *sui iuris*," which is an expression of the living Church, that is, the people of God of a given Eastern Catholic or Latin Church, and "rite," which is the manner in which that Church expresses its faith:

> Can. 27 - A community of the Christian faithful, which is joined together by a hierarchy according to the norm of law and which is expressly or tacitly recognized as *sui iuris* by

> the supreme authority of the Church, is called in this Code a Church *sui iuris*.
>
> Can. 28 - §1. A rite is a liturgical, theological, spiritual and disciplinary heritage, differentiated by the culture and the circumstances of the history of peoples, which is expressed by each Church *sui iuris* in its own manner of living the faith.

The individual Churches, both Eastern and Latin, share in a fundamental equality regarding dignity, rights and obligations: "Thus the same churches enjoy equal dignity, so that none of them ranks higher than the others by reason of rite" (art. 3). The right to preach the gospel is specifically mentioned among the rights and obligations of all the faithful: They enjoy the same rights and bound by the same laws, even as regards preaching the gospel throughout the world (see Mark 16:15), under the direction of the Roman Pontiff" (ibid). Until the Second Vatican Council, this right was curtailed regarding the Eastern Churches. Indeed, in some circles, the thought prevails that the Eastern Churches have the right to preach the Gospel, that is, to evangelize, only among their own ethnic peoples.

Article 4 addresses four matters:

1. The preservation and enlargement of all Churches *sui iuris*, through the erection of parishes and the constitution of a proper hierarchy. This matter has been and continues to be a point of controversy in that, although it has been commonplace for Latin hierarchies to be established in traditionally Eastern territories, the erection of Eastern Catholic hierarchies amidst Latins has not always been readily accepted.

2. Better inter-church relations are to be fostered: "Ordinaries of the various individual churches who exercise jurisdiction in the same territory should take care to further unity of action, after taking counsel among themselves in periodic meetings."

3. Programs of priestly formation are to include instruction aimed at a better understanding of the Churches *sui iuris*, especially regarding inter-ritual matters. The laity themselves, East and West, are to receive instruction regarding the rites and their laws. Lay, religious and clergy formation programs include some instruction in this regard; more can be done especially where there are significant numbers of Eastern Christians in a given region or country.

4. All Catholics, East and West, are to observe their own rite according to their ability throughout the world. They are not to transfer their membership from one Church *sui iuris* to another with due regard for recourse to the Apostolic See. Baptised non-Catholics entering into communion with the Catholic Church should keep their own rite. These

norms, in many instances, are rarely adhered to in many parts of the world.

Safeguarding the Spiritual Heritage of the Eastern Churches (arts. 5-6)

Article 5 affirms that the ecclesiology and the spiritual heritage of the Eastern Churches belong to the common heritage of the universal Church: "Thus this synod not only bestows due esteem and rightful praise on this ecclesiastical and spiritual heritage but firmly regards it as the heritage of the whole church of Christ."

In addition, the Council now accords all Churches, East and West, the right and obligation to rule themselves: "Hence it solemnly declares that the churches of both east and west enjoy the right, and are bound by duty, to govern themselves in accordance with their own particular rules, seeing that they are recommended by venerable antiquity, are more suited to the customs of their faithful and seem more suitable for assuring the good of souls."

Article 6 declares the rightfulness of Eastern discipline, any foreign influence to this discipline being contrary to the spirit of the Council: "All eastern Christians should know and be certain that they may and should always preserve their own lawful liturgical rites and way of life, and that changes should be made only by reason of their proper and organic development. All these things are to be observed with the greatest fidelity by the eastern Christians themselves."

Those whose ecclesiastical offices or ministries have frequent contact with Eastern Christians are to be educated in the "knowledge and practice of the rites, law, teaching, history and nature of eastern Christians, in keeping with the importance of the office they hold."

Eastern Patriarchs (arts. 7-11)

Articles 7-11 put forward foundational principles regarding the most controversial issues regarding the patriarchal institute.

Article 7 recognizes the ancient origin of the institute especially that of the pentarchy, that is, the ancient patriarchal Churches of Rome, Constantinople, Alexandria, Antioch and Jerusalem. The term "Eastern patriarch" is defined as "a bishop who possess jurisdiction over all the bishops (including metropolitans), clergy and faithful of his own territory or rite in accordance with the norm of law and without prejudice to the primacy of the Roman pontiff."

Addressing the question of Eastern bishops constituted outside their patriarchal territory, the decree adds: "Whenever an ordinary of a rite is appointed outside the boundaries of his patriarchal territory, he remains attached to the hierarchy of the patriarchate of the same rite in accordance with the norm of law." On March 25, 1970, the Congregation for the Eastern Churches issued norms regarding aggregate bishops, their election, nomination and participation in their synod of bishops (*AAS*, 62 [1970], p. 179; *CLD*, vol. 7, p. 9). For many, these norms fell short in that patriarchs did not receive the much desired jurisdiction over the hierarchs outside their patriarchates; such jurisdiction was reserved to the Apostolic See. The lack of extension of patriarchal jurisdiction outside the original territory continues to be one of the greatest *lacunae* following the Second Vatican Council and the Eastern code.

Today, most of the Eastern Catholic patriarchs were constituted in relatively recent times in comparison to the ancient sees of the pentarchy. Article 8, states that regardless of the time of their origin, "they are all equal by reason of their patriarchal dignity, allowance being made for a certain precedence of honour among them, sanctioned by law."

Article 9 addresses the re-establishment of the rights and privileges of patriarchs and the determination of their ordinary power. Patriarchs in their capacity as "father and chief" of their Church are to have their rights and privileges "restored in accordance with the ancient traditions of each church and the decrees of ecumenical synods." These include the election of patriarchs, appointment of bishops, regulation of liturgy and canon law, and autonomous rule of the clergy and laity.

The same article defines that patriarchs with their synods constitute the highest tribunal for all matters concerning the patriarchate, and have the right to erect new eparchies and appoint bishops within the confines of their patriarchal territory, without prejudice to the right of the Roman Pontiff to intervene in individual cases.

Article 10 clarifies that whatever refers to patriarchs equally applies to major archbishops, in accordance with the norm of law.

According to article 11, the erection of new patriarchates are reserved to an ecumenical council or the Roman Pontiff.

Regulation of the Sacraments (arts. 12-18)

Article 12 introduces the norms regarding the administration of the sacraments, or mysteries as they are often known in the Eastern Churches. The Council confirms and commends the ancient Eastern canonical discipline of the sacraments and their celebration and administration. Where this discipline has been lost, through latinization, for example, it is to be restored.

The articles in this section address in brief more urgent matters concerning the sacraments of chrismation (confirmation), Divine Eucharist, penance, sacred orders and marriage, while deferring to the anticipated Eastern code the further delineation on the general norms regulating the sacraments.

Articles 13-14 completely restores the ancient discipline of the Eastern Churches regarding the administration of chrismation by priests which is ordinarily reserved to bishops in the Latin Church, save for the initiation of adults: "Thus priests can confer this sacrament, using chrism blessed by a patriarch or a bishop."

The norm addresses any doubt on the part of the Latin Church, which in some instances considered the act invalid by priests of the Eastern Churches. "All eastern priests can validly confer this sacrament, either together with baptism or separately, on the faithful of any rite, including the Latin rite, provided they observe the precepts for liceity of common and special law." The norm continues, "Priests of the Latin rite, in accordance with the faculties which they enjoy for the administration of this sacrament, can also confer it on the faithful of the eastern churches, without prejudice to the rite, provided they have observed the prescriptions for liceity of common or special law."

Regarding the celebration of the Divine Eucharist, article 15 raises two matters: 1) the Divine Liturgy, and 2) the reception of the Divine Eucharist. The particular law of each Church *sui iuris* is to be observed regarding the Sunday obligation: "So that the faithful may be able more easily to comply with this rule, it is decreed that the time for fulfilling this obligation runs from vespers the day before until the end of the Sunday or feast-day." "It is strongly recommended to the faithful to receive the holy eucharist on these days, indeed more frequently still and even daily."

The faculty to administer the sacrament of penance by priests of any rite, once duly granted by their own hierarch and without restriction, is understood as having been extended for the whole territory of that hierarch, and applies to the faithful of any rite in that territory (art. 16). Any territorial restriction on that jurisdiction must be expressly indicated by the hierarch.

The permanent diaconate is to be restored in those Eastern Churches *sui iuris* in which it has fallen into disuse (art. 17). The institution of minor orders and the subdiaconate, as well as their rights and obligations, is governed solely by the particular law of the Eastern Churches.

Where mixed marriages of Eastern Catholics and baptized Eastern non-Catholics are concerned, canonical form is required for liceity only (art. 18). However, for validity, the presence of a sacred minister is sufficient, provided the other requirements of law are observed.

Divine Worship (arts. 19-23)

This section provides norms on various liturgical matters: sacred seasons, the Divine Office, and the use of the vernacular in the Divine Liturgy.

Article 19 treats feast-days common to all Eastern Catholic Churches, and those proper to each Church *sui iuris*. The competent authority to establish, transfer or abolish feasts-days in the former is an ecumenical council or the Apostolic See, and in the latter the synod of bishops in addition to the Apostolic See.

Regarding working towards a common date for Easter, the patriarchs and other ecclesiastical authorities in a given region or country are to strive towards an agreement in order to promote Christian unity (art. 20).

Eastern Catholics living outside the country or territory of their own rite can follow local custom with regard to feast-days and days of penance (art. 21). Families of mixed rite may observe this law according to one and the same rite in order to protect the unity of the family.

Eastern clergy and religious, with the active participation of the lay faithful where possible, are to publicly celebrate the divine praises in accordance with the rules and traditions of their own rite (art. 22).

It belongs to the patriarch with his synod of bishops to approve translations of liturgical texts, after a report has been made to the Apostolic See (art. 23).

Contact with Our Brothers and Sisters of Separated Churches (arts. 24-29)

While much of the draft material on the means of approaching the separated Christians was transferred to the Decree on Ecumenism, some norms remained within the decree where unity among Eastern Christians, Catholic and Orthodox, are concerned.

Article 24 introduces the section and addresses the unique mission of Eastern Catholics in promoting ecumenism: "To the eastern churches maintaining communion with the apostolic Roman see belongs the special responsibility of furthering the unity of all Christians, especially eastern Christians, according to the principles of this synod's decree on ecumenism." The decree lists several concrete examples as to how this might be accomplished: prayer, example by one's life, religious fidelity towards the ancient eastern traditions, greater mutual understanding, common works, and a sensitive appreciation of realities and feelings.

The reception of lay faithful from separated Eastern Churches into the Catholic Church is to be accomplished through the reception of a simple profession of the Catholic faith. For the reception of clerics and the exercise of their orders, which are explicitly recognized as valid by the decree, the norms established by the competent authority are to be followed (art. 25).

The remaining articles in this section regulate *communicatio in sacris*, that is, the sacramental and liturgical fellowship with separated Christians. The decree adopts a new and more lenient approach to common participation in worship with Eastern non-Catholics, recognizing these Churches' true priesthood and valid sacraments (art. 26).

More specifically, provided that the danger of error, scandal and indifferentism are avoided, separated Eastern Christians can receive the sacraments of penance, Divine Eucharist, and anointing of the sick in the Catholic Church if they make the request of their own accord and are properly disposed (art. 27).

Likewise, Catholics can receive these same sacraments from non-Catholic ministers in whose Church the considered sacraments are valid by the Catholic Church when: 1) necessity requires it; 2) genuine spiritual advantage suggests it; and 3) access to a Catholic minister is physically or morally impossible (art. 27).

Concerning common participation in worship of Catholics and Eastern non-Catholics, sharing is permitted regarding sacred functions, things and places, provided these same principles are kept in mind (art. 28).

Finally, article 29 states that *communicatio in sacris* is entrusted to the supervision and control of the local ordinaries, who are to issue further practical norms guiding relations among Christians, first having consulted among themselves and, if need be, the ordinaries of the separated Eastern Churches.

Conclusion (art. 30)

The decree concludes with an expression of the Council's joy in the "fruitful and active co-operation of eastern and western catholic churches" (art. 30) and declares that the present provisions are in force for Eastern Catholics until such time as all Eastern Christians "come together into the fullness of union." Until then all Christians are to pray unceasingly for Christian unity.

EXTENSION OF PATRIARCHAL JURISDICTION THROUGHOUT THE WORLD

The question of the extension of the authority of a patriarch outside the original territory of his patriarchal church was one of the most debated topics concerning the Eastern Churches at the Second Vatican Council. The debate carried over into the drafting process of the Eastern code. It remains an unresolved issue even today, with unfortunate pastoral consequences. In order to understand the issue better, some context is helpful here.

Historical overview

From the earliest of times, the Church at Rome exerted claims of papal authority over the other four patriarchs (Constantinople, Alexandria, Antioch and Jerusalem), which together comprised the pentarchy within the Roman Empire. The disputes primarily centred along doctrinal, theological, linguistic, political and geographical lines. A growing mistrust between East-West relations eventually led to schism.

In particular, conflicting claims of jurisdiction arose between the Eastern and Western Churches. In time the situation arose whereby regions and countries throughout the world were claimed as either Latin or Eastern territory, albeit under the authority of the Apostolic See of Rome. Certain principles developed regarding territorial authority, beginning already with the First Ecumenical Council of Nicaea in 325.

The axiom "one bishop, one church" arose with Nicaea I. The Council Fathers decreed that there were not to be two bishops in the same city, basing themselves on the teachings of Saint Ignatius of Antioch (+107): "Where the bishop is, therein are the multitudes, just as where Jesus Christ is, therein is the catholic Church." In other words, the Council directed that when the responsibilities became too great for any one bishop, the territory was to be divided.

The principle of one bishop, one church remained intact until the Fourth Lateran Ecumenical Council (1215). This council followed closely on the heels of the failed Fourth Crusade (1202-1204), which was diverted to Constantinople by profit-seeking Venetians against the pope's will. When the city fell to the crusaders in 1204, East-West relations were dealt another if not fatal blow. Pope Innocent III, in a mistaken belief that it would promote unity among the Eastern and Western Churches, erected a Latin patriarchate in Constantinople, deposing its Eastern counterpart.

The Fourth Lateran Council, attended by 404 bishops of which only two were from the East, addressed the need, for the first time in history, to provide for the pastoral care of the faithful of another Church *sui iuris*, namely, Byzantine Christians, living within the same territory. Constitution 9 prescribed that the Latin bishops appoint priests for the Eastern faithful, who could then serve them in their own rite and language.

The same constitution went further: "We altogether forbid one and the same city or diocese to have more than one bishop, as if it were a body with several heads like a monster. But if ... necessity demands it, the bishop of the place may appoint, after careful deliberation, a catholic bishop who is appropriate for the nations in question and who will be his vicar in the aforesaid matters and will be obedient and subject to him in all things."

This innovation became the basis for the principle of jurisdiction of Latin bishops over Eastern Catholics who lacked their own hierarchy. This principle continues to be the norm throughout the world, including North America, and has its application in particular where new communities of Eastern Catholics have immigrated, but as of yet have no pastors or bishops of their own.

As new lands were discovered or conquered throughout the world, the Church accompanied the explorers, establishing supportive church and parish structures for the new communities. As a result, Latin jurisdiction throughout the world continued to grow.

Today, the Roman Catholic Church exercises exclusive jurisdiction over all regions and countries throughout the world, save for that which is overseen by the Congregation for the Eastern Churches: Egypt and the Sinai Peninsula, Eritrea and northern Ethiopia, southern Albania, Bulgaria, Cyrpus, Greece, Iran, Iraq, Lebanon, Palestine, Syria, Jordan, and Turkey.

Current situation

The Second Vatican Council recognized an equality among rites. Yet a remnant remains of the 18th century doctrine on the pre-eminence of the Latin rite over all others (*praestantia ritus latini*). This doctrine was first expressed by Pope Benedict XIV in his Constitution *Etsi pastoralis* (1742), which regarded the Latin rite as the "Holy Roman Church, mother and teacher of all Churches."

The principle of exclusive jurisdiction of the Latin Church finds an application in the Eastern code concerning the pastoral care of Eastern Catholics residing outside their patriarchal territories, and who have neither a pastor nor a bishop of their own.

> Can. 916, §5. In places where not even an exarchy has been erected for the Christian faithful of a certain Church *sui iuris*, the local hierarch of another Church *sui iuris*, even the Latin Church, is to be considered as the proper hierarch of these faithful, with due regard for can. 101.
>
> If, however, there are several local hierarchs, that one whom the Apostolic See has designated is to be considered as their proper hierarch or, if it concerns the Christian faithful of a

> certain patriarchal Church, the one whom the patriarch has designated with the assent of the Apostolic See.

In North America, where several Eastern and Roman Catholic bishops share jurisdiction in a given area, the presumption still remains that the Latin Church exercises exclusive authority over such Eastern Christians. This need not be the case. Each arrangement needs to be carefully reviewed with the intervention of the Apostolic See. At times it may be more pastorally prudent for Eastern Catholics who lack their own hierarch or pastor to receive their pastoral care from another Eastern Catholic Church *sui iuris*, given their similar liturgical, spiritual and theological expressions.

A better solution to the immediate problem would be the extension of patriarchal jurisdiction throughout the world. It seems more appropriate for a patriarch to oversee the pastoral care of his own faithful wherever they find themselves, especially in significant numbers, rather than being the subjects of a Church *sui iuris* other than their own.

A case in point. Following the collapse of the Soviet Union in the late 1980's-early 1990's, hundreds of thousands of Ukrainians left Ukraine in search of a better way of life for themselves and their families. For example, it is estimated that in Italy today there are some 700,000 Ukrainians, 80 percent from western Ukraine; 200,000 in Spain, 70 percent from western Ukraine; 75,000 in Portugal, 80 percent from western Ukraine; and 10,000 in Ireland, coming from all over Ukraine (source Caritas Ukraine). Given that Ukrainian Catholics are strongest numerically in western Ukraine, it stands to reason that any destination country which has a high percentage of people from western Ukraine must also have a high percentage of Ukrainian Catholics.

The Ukrainian Catholic Church in Italy and Spain, in particular, is already highly organized. In Italy, there are over 140 pastoral centres served by 30 priests and an additional 22 priest-students. In Spain, there are 40 pastoral centres served by 18 parishes (Source Pastoral-Missionary Institute of the Ukrainian Catholic Church). Despite the fact that a Ukrainian Catholic bishop has served for many years as Apostolic Administrator in these countries, the Ukrainian Catholic faithful and priests are directly subject to the local Latin ordinary, which poses certain pastoral and administrative challenges. The Ukrainian Catholic major archbishop's influence in the matter is greatly diminished in that these faithful fall outside the territory of his patriarchal church. Matters are further complicated in that many of the Ukrainian Catholic priests serving in these countries are married, which is often frowned upon by the local Latin bishops, not unlike the situation Ukrainian Catholics found themselves in North America in the late 1800's.

Another case in point. The horrific situation of on-going conflict and lack of peace in the Middle East has devastated the Christian population in these lands.

Middle East Christians are in decline. Christians in Lebanon in 1970 represented 55 percent of the population; today they number 39 percent or 1,600,000. Christians in Syria in 2011 represented 10 percent of the population; in 2013, 9 percent or 2,000,000. In Iraq, in 1980, 10 percent; in 2013, 1 percent at under 300,000. In Israel, in 1948, 20 percent; in 2013, 2 percent or 147,000. In Palestine, in 2000, 2 percent; in 2013, 1 percent or 40,000. In Egypt, in 1980, 12 percent; in 2013, 10 percent or 8,000,000. The only Middle East country that has seen an increase in its Christian population is Jordan, which has been become a centre for refugees: in 2000, 6 percent of the population were Christian; in 2013 it is estimated at 10 percent or 620,000 (Source Catholic Near East Welfare Association Canada). One might ask, to where are they fleeing? Many have or will find themselves in North America, where they may find an already existing parish of their own Church *sui iuris*. Others will be less fortunate.

The extension of patriarchal jurisdiction outside the patriarchal territory would provide greater pastoral care for these Christians in need wherever in the world they find themselves.

Second Vatican Council and the Eastern Code

Let us turn our attention more specifically to how the Second Vatican Council and the Eastern code treat the matter of the extension of patriarchal authority outside the original territory.

It is worthwhile to recall the mandate given by Pope Paul VI to the Pontifical Commission for the Revision of the Eastern Code of Canon Law on March 18, 1970:

> Both [Code] Commissions were instituted for the precise purpose to prepare a Code, and to proceed in an orderly fashion arranging the laws, and not to make or enact on their own authority laws themselves. The norms shall be upheld, while the principles themselves shall be derived from the sources of the laws, and neither former nor the latter can be altered. In other words, the men assigned to the Commission are arrangers of these laws, and not authors or creators (*Nuntia*, 1 [1975], 7).

The papal mandate was clear: prepare a code true to the conciliar teachings and the patrimony of the Eastern Churches.

The Pontifical Commission, following the first session of its second plenary meeting on November 5, 1988, presented the following question on patriarchal jurisdiction to Pope John Paul II:

> The undersigned propose that the question of the extension of patriarchal jurisdiction over all the faithful of the autonomous church also outside the territory of the patriarchate, be discussed first of all and that there be a solution before proceeding to the other questions (*Nuntia*, 29 [1989], 27).

The pope's response was communicated to the Commission on November 10, 1988:

> Relative to the "Motion" of the 5th of this month, signed by the "Plenary Codification Commission," assembled these days, it is my task to communicate to you that the Holy Father authorizes the Assembly to discuss the question posed, but holding firm to what has been decided by the ecumenical councils which have foreseen patriarchal jurisdiction only in the territory in the patriarchate and in particular what the Second Vatican Council established, which did not accede to the request to extend such jurisdiction outside the boundaries of the patriarchate ... It is necessary that the present assembly present to the Holy Father a draft of a code that entirely conforms to the Eastern traditions and to the conciliar decisions (*Nuntia*, 29 [1989], 27).

One might pose the question, does any one Church *sui iuris* have an exclusive canonical right to a specific territory? More fundamentally, does any one Church *sui iuris* have the right to preach the gospel, especially in North America?

The current pastoral situation in North America and beyond calls for a rethinking of the principle of territoriality and the right and obligation of the patriarch and others to provide pastoral care for their faithful everywhere in the world.

There is hope. The Eastern code does foresee the possibility that the territorial boundaries of the patriarchal church can be modified. Canon 146, in particular, treats the resolution of any questions which arise concerning existing territorial boundaries, whereby the Roman Pontiff has the authority to resolve the doubt. Furthermore, the Roman Pontiff also has the authority to extend these boundaries.

> Can. 146, §2. If any doubt concerning the territorial boundaries of the patriarchal church arises or if it is a question of the modification of boundaries, it is for the synod of bishops of the patriarchal church to investigate the matter. After hearing the superior administrative authority of each Church *sui iuris* concerned, and after discussing the matter in the synod, it is up to the same synod to present a properly documented petition for the resolution of the doubt or for the modification

of the boundaries to the Roman Pontiff. It is for the Roman Pontiff alone to resolve the doubt authentically or to decree a modification of the boundaries.

"Modification" of the patriarchal territory need not be limited only to small incremental changes, for example, where it can be demonstrated that the patriarch historically exercised jurisdiction beyond the current confines of his Church *sui iuris*, which was lost in times of national realignment in times of war or conflict.

"Modification" may also present new possibilities. It can be argued that the authority foreseen in the Eastern code, whereby the Roman Pontiff alone, that is, without the convocation of an ecumenical council, could modify the territorial boundaries of a Church *sui iuris* to regions or countries currently outside that Church's boundaries, even extending them worldwide.

The Eastern Catholic Churches, alone or even all together, might consider pursuing this avenue by way of resolving what has become an impasse. If successful in their petition, the pastoral situation of their faithful would be greatly improved.

Bishops Constituted outside the Patriarchal Territory

The Eastern Catholic bishops who are constituted outside the territorial boundaries of the patriarchal church have all the same rights and obligations as the other bishops of their Church *sui iuris* (c. 150, §1). However, and understandably so, their deliberative vote can be restricted given that they might influence the outcome of a specific matter treated at a synod of bishops and yet not be bound by that decision in their own respective eparchies (c. 102, §2).

Regardless of whether the vote of bishops outside the patriarchal territory is restricted or not, the Eastern code categorizes laws enacted by the synod of bishops according to disciplinary laws or liturgical laws (c. 150, §2).

Disciplinary laws

If the laws are disciplinary, they have the force of law only within the territorial boundaries of the patriarchal church.

Bishops constituted outside the territorial boundaries of the patriarchal church can attribute the force of law to disciplinary laws and other decisions of the synod of bishops by making them eparchial law, if they so choose. Also, the Apostolic See can intervene in a given matter and make these same laws and decisions particular law for that Church *sui iuris* everywhere in the world.

While the Eastern Catholic bishops argue for the extension of patriarchal jurisdiction throughout the world, it must be said that at the same time some are fearful as to what this means concretely when it comes to the relative autonomy they currently enjoy in the governance of their individual eparchies.

Liturgical laws

If the laws legislated by the synod of bishops are liturgical laws, they have the force of law everywhere in the world.

The Eastern code, like that of the Latin code, does not for the most part determine liturgical matters, rather leaving them to the prescripts of the liturgical books themselves (*CCEO* c. 3).

However, Title XVI of the Eastern code on "Divine Worship and Especially the Sacraments" does provide general norms on baptism, chrismation with holy Myron, the Divine Eucharist, penance, the anointing of the sick, sacred ordination, and marriage, as well as sacramentals, sacred times and places, veneration of the saints, and vows and oaths.

These general liturgical norms were further defined for all Eastern Catholic Churches in 1996 by the Congregation for the Eastern Churches by way of An Instruction for Applying the Liturgical Prescriptions of the Code of Canons of the Eastern Churches. Known as the Liturgical Instruction, it can be likened to the Constitution on the Sacred Liturgy, *Sacrosanctum concilium*, in which the Second Vatican Council set forth certain principles which would guide the renewal and growth of the liturgy in Latin Church.

The Eastern Liturgical Instruction at the outset speaks of the inalienable value of the particular heritage of the Eastern Churches and the richness of the Eastern liturgical patrimony, quoting from the conciliar Decree on Ecumenism:

> All should recognize that to know, venerate, preserve and cherish the right liturgical and spiritual heritage of the eastern churches is of supreme importance for the faithful preservation of the fullness of Christian tradition, and for bringing about reconciliation between eastern and western Christians (no. 15).

The need for the Eastern Liturgical Instruction is summarized in article 5 as follows:

> The liturgical laws valid for all the Eastern Churches are important because they provide the general orientation. However, being distributed among various texts, they risk remaining ignored, poorly coordinated and poorly interpreted.

> It seemed opportune, therefore, to gather them in a systematic whole, completing them with further clarification: thus, the intent of the instruction, presented to the Eastern Churches which are in full communion with the Apostolic See, is to help them fully realize their own identity.

More specifically, the Liturgical Instruction sets out four objectives:

1. Eastern liturgical patrimony. "To lead to a more profound understanding of the immense richness of the authentic Eastern traditions, which are to be scrupulously maintained and communicated to all the faithful";

2. Identification and recovery. "To arrange the liturgical norms valid for all the Catholic Eastern Churches in an organic summary and to introduce recovery, where necessary, of the Eastern liturgical authenticity, according to the Tradition which each Eastern Church has inherited from the Apostles through the Fathers";

3. Liturgical formation. "To exhort a permanent liturgical formation to be organized on a solid basis, for both the clergy – beginning with seminarians and formation institutes – and the people of God through schools of mystagogical catechesis;" and

4. Liturgical Directories. "To list the principles in common for the elaboration of Liturgical Directories for the individual Churches *sui iuris*" (no. 5).

The truth of the matter is that in many places in the world, including North America, the Eastern Churches have been heavily Latinized. The Eastern Liturgical Instruction is an attempt to restore that which was lost:

> The frequent comparison with the Roman liturgy is intended to highlight the Eastern uniqueness, which risks being compromised or even eliminated in the contact with the Latin Church, her institutions, her doctrinal elaboration, her liturgical practices, and her internal organization which is often more developed also because of more favourable historical vicissitudes (ibid.).

Much work remains to be done on the part of the Eastern Churches in the application of the Eastern Liturgical Instruction. Two agents can be identified in the slow progress towards authentic Eastern liturgical renewal:

First, on the part of the Apostolic See. While it is true that the Eastern Liturgical Instruction limited itself to the formulation of principles and norms valid for all the Eastern Churches – a welcomed tool at that – the Apostolic See had foreseen the formulation of more detailed norms for those Eastern Churches belonging to the same liturgical family, for example, those belonging to the Constantinopolitan or Byzantine Tradition.

Towards this end, the Eastern Liturgical Instruction prescribed: "Every single Church *sui iuris* belonging to such families will provide, according to methods that will be specified, for the elaboration of a corpus of norms which adapt the present document and the one that will be elaborated for her entire liturgical family to her own specific situation" (no. 6). Nearly twenty years later, no action has been taken in this direction.

Second, on the part of the individual Eastern Churches. The Eastern Churches themselves, in general, have been slow to develop their own individual liturgical directories as called for by the Eastern Liturgical Instruction, despite the offer by the Apostolic See to "provide experts to collaborate with the individual Churches *sui iuris* for the elaboration of such particular norms, if the Churches believe they have the need and request it. At the end of the process, the Liturgical Directory for each individual Church *sui iuris* will be presented to the Holy See."

To date, it does not seem that any of the Eastern Churches have done so. At times, personnel and resources are lacking. At other times, a certain coziness with entrenched Latin practices, for example, delaying First Holy Communion to the age of reason, has produced some reluctance on the part of some to move forward, again, so that the Eastern Churches may "fully realize their identity" and fully accepting their responsibility in the mission of evangelization.

Ius speciale

The matter of the extension of patriarchal jurisdiction outside the original territory of a given Church *sui iuris* having been set aside by the pope, the Eastern code foresees that the Eastern Catholic Churches could however avail themselves of an *ius speciale*, which would enable them to provide greater pastoral care for their faithful throughout the world.

The context is as such: In that same letter of Pope John Paul II of November 10, 1988 to the Pontifical Commission for the Revision of the Eastern Code of Canon Law, he writes:

> In any case, for those churches which find themselves in special situations with regard to their faithful residing outside the territory of the same, the Holy Father will be happy to consider, in light of the promulgated Code, the proposals elaborated by the synods with clear reference to the norms of the Code which if he should consider it opportune to specify

> with a *special law* (*ius speciale*) and *for a time* (*ad tempus*) (*Nuntia*, 29 [1989], 27).

By way of example, the Ukrainian Catholic Church took up the offer to petition the pope for a *ius speciale* soon after the promulgation of the Eastern code in 1990. Indeed, it was one of the very first issues that that Church addressed when communism collapsed in the former Soviet Union and Cardinal Myroslav Lubachivsky returned to Lviv, Ukraine, in 1991.

Cardinal Lubachivsky, in 1992, at the very first synod of bishops he convoked, raised the matter of providing pastoral care for the hundreds of thousands of his faithful in the so-called "diaspora," who had carried the faith while the Mother Church in Ukraine suffered persecution.

The synod of bishops drafted a proposed *ius speciale* which sought to grant wider rights and responsibilities to the head of the Ukrainian Catholic Church in relation to this faithful outside Ukraine. The draft, which modifies canons 148-149 of the Eastern code, proposed certain adaptations (italics added to draw out differences in the two texts):

Eastern Code	*Proposal – Ukrainian Catholic Church*
Can. 148, §1. It is the right and the obligation of the patriarch *to seek appropriate information* concerning the Christian faithful who reside outside the territorial boundaries of the Church over which he presides, *even through a visitor* sent by himself with the *assent of the Apostolic See.*	**Can. 148,** §1. It is the right and the obligation of the patriarch *to care for* the faithful which reside outside the territorial boundaries of his patriarchal Church, and, *having informed the Apostolic See, to visit them, either by himself, or through a visitator* sent by himself.
§2. The *visitor*, before he begins his function, is to go to the eparchial bishop of those faithful and present his letter of appointment.	§2. *The patriarch is to inform in due time the bishop of those faithful of his visit*; the *visitator*, before he begins his function, is to go to the eparchial bishop of those faithful and present his letter of appointment.
§3. When the visitation is completed, the *visitor is to send a report to the patriarch*, who, after discussing the matter in the synod of bishops of the patriarchal Church, can propose suitable measures to the Apostolic See, in view of providing everywhere in the world for the protection and enhancement of the spiritual good of the Christian faithful of the Church over which he presides, *even through the erection of parishes and exarchies or eparchies of their own.*	§3. When the visitation is completed, the *patriarch*, having discussed the matter in the synod of bishops of the patriarchal Church, can propose suitable measures to the Apostolic See, with a view to providing everywhere in the world for the protection and enhancement of the spiritual good of the Christian faithful of his Church, *even the appointment of bishops, according to the norms of the canons on the election of bishops, and through the erection of their own eparchies and exarchies with the permission of the Apostolic See.*
Can. 149 - *To fill the office of eparchial bishop*, coadjutor bishop or auxiliary bishop outside the territorial boundaries of the patriarchal Church, *the synod of bishops* of the patriarchal Church *elects*, according to the norms of the canons on the election of bishops, *at least three candidates* and *proposes them through the patriarch to the Roman Pontiff for appointment.* Secrecy is to be observed, even toward the candidates, by all who in any way know the results of the election.	**Can. 149** – *To fill the office of the eparchial bishop*, coadjutor bishop or auxiliary bishop outside the territorial boundaries of the patriarchal Church, *the synod of bishops* of the patriarchal Church *elects*, according to the norms of the canons on the election of bishops, *at least three candidates. It is then the right of the head of the Church to select one of the candidates, and the consent of the Apostolic See, to appoint him.*

The proposal raises several issues:

It is the primary responsibility of the patriarch to see to it that pastoral care is provided for the faithful of his Church *sui iuris* throughout the world, not only in the original territory of his Church. There is a significant difference in the patriarch having the right to seek appropriate information regarding his faithful as opposed to having the right recognized in law to provide active and ongoing pastoral care without the intervention of the Apostolic See in each and every instance. Cardinal Lubachivsky and the synod of bishops sought the latter.

Whether the patriarch decides to visit his faithful outside his territory in person or through a delegate, the proposed *ius speciale* sees such pastoral visitations as part of the normal life of a Church *sui iuris*. Rather than the patriarch requiring the "assent" of the Apostolic See to conduct such visitations, the proposal suggested that notification to the same authority would suffice.

In the event that the patriarch conducts the pastoral visit himself, the proposal requires him to notify the local bishop in advance, who in turn can inform the faithful, religious, monastic and clergy of the upcoming visit and make the necessary liturgical and other preparations suitable for receiving the father and head of his Church *sui iuris*.

Upon completion of the visitation, the patriarch, in discussion with the synod of bishops, is to make concrete proposals to the Apostolic See in order to provide for the spiritual care of his faithful worldwide. The Eastern code foresees possible outcomes including the establishment of parishes, exarchies and eparchies, which would require the consent of the Apostolic See in order to proceed. The proposed *ius speciale* goes further: It explicitly includes the appointment of bishops where required, according to the norms of the canons on the election of bishops. The difference perhaps is subtle; however, the synod of bishops considered it their right and obligation to initiate the process to nominate bishops where eparchies were considered necessary, albeit with the permission of the Apostolic See.

Perhaps the boldest and most far-reaching initiative of part of the synod of bishops of the Ukrainian Catholic Church was the request to derogate from the Eastern code regarding the appointment of bishops outside Ukraine. Within Ukraine, the synod of bishops has the right to elect bishops directly within Ukraine, provided the candidates have received the assent of the Roman Pontiff in advance (c. 110, §3; see also canons on the election of bishops, cc. 180-189). Outside Ukraine, the synod of bishops elects at least three candidates for a given episcopal office and presents the list to the Roman Pontiff for his appointment, who also has the right to appoint someone not included in the list (c. 149). The proposed *ius speciale* gives the right of appointment to the patriarch, with the consent of the Apostolic See.

The proposed *ius speciale* was presented to the Roman Pontiff shortly after the 1992 synod of bishops. It was rejected without reason. The same proposal was resubmitted in 1994 without success. A new proposal is under review by the synod of bishops of the Ukrainian Catholic Church for submission to the Apostolic See.

To date it seems that no *ius speciale* has been granted to any of the Eastern Catholic Churches which adequately address the need to provide better pastoral care for the growing number of Eastern Catholic faithful outside their original territories.

ORDINATION OF MARRIED CANDIDATES TO THE PRIESTHOOD

Having set aside the issue of the extension of patriarchal jurisdiction outside the patriarchal territory, let us turn our attention to several other issues left incomplete regarding the Eastern Code, starting with married clergy.

Over time, the Eastern and Western Churches developed a different discipline on clerical celibacy and the ordination of married candidates to the priesthood. These differences were highlighted when Eastern Christians began immigrating in large numbers to North America in the late 1800's. In the "old country" by far the majority of priests were married, with celibate clergy found primarily in monasteries and among religious communities. The arrival of married clergy to provide pastoral care for their faithful in the "new world" met with opposition on the part of the established Roman Catholic Church, who for already hundreds of years knew only a celibate clergy, citing married clergy as scandalous and a potential cause of great harm to religion and the ecclesiastical discipline of the Church.

The Apostolic See intervened by issuing various decrees starting in 1890 which quickly led to the suspension of the right of the Eastern Catholic bishops in North America and beyond to ordain married men to the priesthood or even to accept them from Europe. The most famous of these decrees is *Qua sollerti*, issued by the Congregation for the Propagation of the Faith on December 23, 1929, regarding Eastern clerics from Europe who desired to go to North, Central and South America, and Australia to minister to the faithful of their own Church *sui iuris*. Article 6, in particular, reads: "Secular priests who have a wife shall not be admitted to exercise the sacred ministry in these countries, but only celibate priests or widowers" (*AAS*, 22 [1930], pp. 99-105; *CLD*, vol. 1, pp. 17-24).

Qua sollerti is often cited in error in studies regarding the prohibition against the acceptance and ordination of Ukrainian Catholic married priests in Canada and the United States. Article 18 of the decree states: "Ruthenians, however, who go the United States of America or to Canada to exercise spiritual ministry under the jurisdiction of Ordinaries of their own rite, are to observe the special decrees which have been enacted by this Sacred Eastern Congregation." The Congregation was referring to the decrees *Fidelibus ruthenis* (August 18, 1913) for Canada and *Ea semper* (June 14, 1907) for the United States. Both decrees already contained the same prohibitions; however, it is important to note the distinction, to which we will return shortly.

Amidst an early attempt to produce an Eastern code, *Cleri sanctitati* (1957) – one of four motu proprios promulgated by Pope Pius XII – continued to hold celibacy in high regard while recognizing the legitimacy of married clergy in the Eastern Churches. The two pertinent canons are:

> Canon 68. The celibacy of the clergy, which corresponds and fits better with their state and the celebration of the divine mysteries, as it is witnessed by the unanimous tradition of both the Eastern as well as the Latin Church, shall be held in esteem by all.
>
> Canon 71. In regard to married men who wish to be admitted to the subdiaconate or major orders, either absolutely or with a dispensation either from the patriarch of the local Hierarch, but not from a syncellus, or even to those who are to be excluded from their reception, these Apostolic Letters do not change anything in the present discipline of each Eastern rite.

In other words, the prohibition against ordaining and accepting married candidates to the priesthood in certain countries, including North America, remained unchanged.

Cleri sanctitati did, however, make one notable innovation, with far-reaching and long-lasting consequences: What was once individual prohibitive decrees affecting certain regions, countries and Churches *sui iuris* now became common law for all the Eastern Churches throughout the world.

At first glance, the 1990 Eastern code seemed to have settled the matter once and for all, restoring the rights of the Eastern Churches to ordain married men to the priesthood not only in their original patriarchal territories, but everywhere:

> Can. 373. Clerical celibacy chosen for the sake of the kingdom of heaven and highly suited to the priesthood is to be greatly esteemed everywhere, according to the tradition of the entire Church; likewise, the state of married clerics, sanctioned in the practice of primitive Church and in the Eastern Churches through the ages, is to be held in honor.

However, some were quick to point out that this norm needs to be read in light of the requirements for candidates for sacred ordination, in particular:

> Can. 758, §3. The particular law of each Church *sui iuris* or special norms established by the Apostolic See are to be followed in admitting married men to sacred orders.

In other words, some circles continue to argue that the prohibitions from the late 1800's and early 1900's have not been abrogated by the 1990 Eastern code and are still in effect.

The Ukrainian Catholic Church in North America, for its part, has tested the waters over the years.

Bishop, now Blessed-martyr, Nykyta Budka, the first Ukrainian Catholic bishop appointed in Canada, soon after his appointment, ordained several married men to the priesthood for the United States following the death of their own hierarch Bishop Soter Ortynsky in 1916.

Bishop Basil Ladyka successfully petitioned the Eastern Congregation in 1947 to accept some 35 married priests in Canada who found themselves as displaced persons following World War II; at the same time, permission was likewise extended by the Congregation into the United States.

Again in 1958, the Ukrainian Catholic hierarchy in Canada and the United States successfully petitioned the Eastern Congregation to accept and ordain married seminarians from the Archeparchy of Lviv, whose studies had been interrupted when the War broke out.

Starting in the early 1970's, individual Ukrainian Catholic bishops in Canada began ordaining married priests in individual cases, first having unsuccessfully petitioned the Apostolic See for permission. The Apostolic See understandably reacted in each of these instances.

More recently, the Ukrainian Catholic hierarchy in North America adopted the practice of ordaining both celibate and married clergy in virtue of canon 373, arguing that the prohibitive clauses of 1913 *Fidelibus ruthenis* decree for Canada, and the 1907 *Ea semper* decree for the United States – and their successive decrees, issued for a ten year period – have all expired. It does not seem that any particular law referenced in canon 758, §3 exists.

Other Churches *sui iuris* have similar stories.

Most recently, the cause has been taken up by the North American Orthodox-Catholic Theological Consultation. In their 2014 Statement, "On the Occasion of the 85th Anniversary of the Promulgation of the Decree *Cum data fuerit*," they write:

> The Theological Commission 'encourages the lifting of the restrictions regarding the ordination of married men to the priesthood in the Eastern Catholic Churches of North America. This action would affirm the ancient and legitimate Eastern Christian tradition, and would assure the Orthodox that, in the event of the restoration of full communion between the two Churches, the traditions of the Orthodox Church would not be questioned. We are convinced that this action would enhance the spiritual lives of Eastern Catholics and would encourage the restoration of unity between Catholic and Orthodox Christians.'

In February 2014, Pope Francis granted permission for the ordination of a married Maronite man to the priesthood in Saint Louis, Missouri, the first in the history of the Maronite Catholic Church in the United States.

Following on the footsteps of this ordination, in a May 27, 2014 news conference, Pope Francis responded to a question about the possibility of revising the rule of celibacy for Roman Catholic priests, cited the example of Eastern Catholics. He said, "The Catholic Church has married priests – Greek Catholics, Coptic Catholics, those of oriental rites. Celibacy is not a question of dogma, but rather a rule of life that I greatly appreciate, as I believe it is a gift for the Church. But, since it is not a dogma of faith, the door is always open."

In any event, the canonical issue of ordaining Eastern Catholic married priests in some parts of the world remains unresolved. Though it must be said that not all Eastern Catholic bishops, even in North America, are supportive of a married priesthood; however, there seems to be a growing but not yet a united front in this regard.

PARTICULAR LAW OF THE CHURCHES *SUI IURIS*

Notion and current status

The 1983 Latin code and the 1990 Eastern code are both products of the Second Vatican Council. They give life to the conciliar teaching and, together with the 1988 apostolic constitution *Pastor bonus* on the reform of the Roman Curia, form one body of canon law for the universal Church, complementing each other while at the same time allowing for legitimate diversity.

Pope John Paul II in promulgating the Eastern code said:

> The *Code of Canons of the Eastern Churches* should be considered as a new complement in the teaching proposed by the Second Vatican Council. By the publication of this Code, the canonical ordering of the whole Church is thus at length completed, following as it does the *Code of Canon Law* of the Latin Church, promulgated in 1983, and the "Apostolic Constitution on the Roman Curia" of 1988, which is added to both codes as the primary instrument of the Roman Pontiff for 'the communion that binds together, as it were, the whole Church" (Apostolic Constitution *Sacri canones*).

Yet the work of updating the canonical discipline of the universal Church is still incomplete. The Latin code, which comprises the common law for the entire Latin Church worldwide, foresaw the need for complementary norms to be undertaken by the various episcopal conferences. Similarly, the Eastern code concerns primarily that which is common to all the Eastern Catholic Churches, yet at the same time it also foresees the need for particular law. In such manner, both codes emphasize the principle of subsidiarity whereby decisions are entrusted to the lowest level of governance capable of fulfilling them properly.

The Eastern code defines common law and particular law in the following terms:

> Can. 1493. §1. Under the name "common law" in this Code come, besides the laws and legitimate customs of the entire Church, also the laws and legitimate customs common to all the Eastern Churches.
>
> §2. However, under the name "particular law" come all laws, legitimate customs, statutes and other norms of law, which are neither common to the entire Church nor to all the Eastern Churches.

Particular law can be enacted by the Roman Pontiff and by the Apostolic See – pontifical law – for one or several of the Churches *sui iuris*. Particular law can also be enacted by the synod of bishops in a patriarchal or major archiepiscopal church; the council of hierarchs in a metropolitan church; and the hierarch for all other churches.

Each of the 21 Eastern Churches *sui iuris* needs to codify their own particular law in order to express more fully the unique and legitimate diversity of the universal Catholic Church.

Matters to be treated by the particular law include: the election, rights, and obligations of patriarchs, major archbishops, metropolitans and bishops; the function and authority of the synod of bishops and council of hierarchs; various eparchial bodies, including the college of consultors, presbyteral council, and finance council; pastors and parishes; clerics, religious, monastics and lay faithful; evangelization and the teaching office of the Church; sacraments and Divine worship; Christian unity; temporal goods; trials, procedures and penal sanctions.

To date, only eight of the 21 Eastern Catholic Churches *sui iuris* have completed their particular law: Byzantine (Ruthenian) Metropolitan Church – Pittsburgh (1999), Italo-Albanian (two eparchies and a territorial abbacy, 2010), Maronite Patriarchal Church (promulgated 1996; under revision), Melkite Patriarchal Church (published 2004 and 2012, under revision), Syro-Malabar Major Archiepiscopal Church (promulgated piecemeal starting in 1995; published in one collection in 2013), Syriac Patriarchal Church (1991), Syro-Malankara Major Archiepiscopal Church (2012), and the Ukrainian Major Archiepiscopal Church (published 2012, under revision).

The remaining 14 Eastern Churches *sui iuris* have yet to complete their particular law. Towards this end, personnel, time and expertise are a contributing factor for many of the Eastern Churches given that their faithful may number only a few thousand worldwide or whose structure may not even include a bishop as their hierarch.

It is interesting to note that in the work completed to date, some Churches in promulgating their particular law have restricted themselves to respond simply to the 150 or so canons in the Eastern code, while others have gone beyond the immediate need by providing norms on a wide variety of topics and areas. The published texts range from 47 articles (some 10 pages) to 220 articles plus appendices (175 pages). The scope and nature of each project are very different. It may well be the intention of the Churches that have initially promulgated their particular law by limiting their responses to the areas directly raised by the Eastern code, that is, the 150 canons, only to return to the task at hand and augment their particular law at a later date.

Promulgation and competency

A canonical question arises as to who is the competent authority authorized to promulgate the particular law of a Church *sui iuris*. The Apostolic See or each Eastern Catholic Church itself?

By way of recourse to 1983 Latin code, particular laws – more specifically, general decrees and general executory decrees – enacted by episcopal conferences for their country or region must be first reviewed by the Apostolic See and granted *recognitio* prior to being promulgated by that conference. The Latin code states:

> Can. 455. §1. The Bishop's Conference can make general decrees only in cases where the universal law has so prescribed, or by special mandate of the Apostolic See, either on its own initiative or at the request of the Conference itself.
>
> §2. For the decrees mentioned in §1 validly to be enacted at a plenary meeting, they must receive at least two thirds of the votes of those who belong to the Conference with a deliberative vote. These decrees do not oblige until they have been reviewed [*recognito*] by the Apostolic See and lawfully promulgated.

The Eastern code designates the synod of bishops in patriarchal and major archiepiscopal churches as the competent authority for enacting particular law for their Churches *sui iuris*. There is no requirement for written approval from the Apostolic See prior to promulgation:

> Can. 110. §1. The synod of bishops of the patriarchal Church is exclusively competent to make laws for the entire patriarchal Church that obtain force according to the norm of can. 150, §§2 and 3.

Canon 150 limits the force of law of these laws to within the territorial boundaries of the Church, unless they are liturgical laws in which case they have the force of law everywhere in the world (§2). However, eparchial bishops constituted outside the territorial boundaries can attribute the force of law to disciplinary laws and other decisions of their Church, that is, by making it eparchial law (§3).

In the case of metropolitan churches, the council of hierarchs is the competent authority to enact particular laws and norms for their churches (c. 167, §1). However, like the Latin episcopal conferences, such laws and norms cannot be validly promulgated until *recognitio* from the Apostolic See has been received. Furthermore, metropolitans on behalf of their metropolitan church are required in addition to inform the Apostolic See of other acts of the council of hierarchs (§2). No such notification is required for patriarchs and major archbishops.

A church *sui iuris* which is neither patriarchal, major archiepiscopal nor metropolitan depends immediately upon the Apostolic See, and as such, the hierarch who presides over it requires the consent of the Apostolic See in enacting particular laws (c. 176).

Having said this, in practice, some confusion remains as to who is the competent authority to enact and promulgate particular law for the Eastern Churches, in particular, for the patriarchal and major archiepiscopal churches.

The Maronite Church, a patriarchal church, was the first to promulgate their particular law in its entirety; however, prior to its promulgation, the draft was sent to the Congregation for the Eastern Churches for review. Similarly, the Syro-Malankara Church, a major archiepiscopal church, asked for and received *recognitio* to promulgate their particular law by the Apostolic See. On the other hand, the Syro-Malabar Church and the Ukrainian Church, both major archiepiscopal churches, did not present their particular law to the Apostolic See prior to approval.

Further clarification in this regard is required, while recognizing the principle of subsidiarity and the right and obligation of the Eastern Churches to govern themselves "in accordance with the ancient traditions of each church and the decrees of the ecumenical synods" (Decree on the Eastern Churches, no. 9).

Work remaining

Some of the Eastern Churches have done well in promulgating their particular law. Others are well into the process. Still others are only beginning. Overall, much work remains in the preparation and promulgation of the particular law of each Church *sui iuris*.

Twenty-five years ago, Pope John Paul II, in promulgating the Eastern code, urged the Eastern Churches to take upon themselves the challenge and the responsibility of renewing their particular law for their benefit of their faithful:

> [F]ull attention should be given to all those things that this Code entrusts to the particular law of the individual Churches *sui iuris*, which are not considered necessary to the common good of all the Eastern Churches. Our intention regarding these things is that those who enjoy legislative power in each of the Churches should take counsel as soon as possible for particular norms, keeping in mind the traditions of their own rite and the precepts of the Second Vatican Council (Apostolic Constitution, *Sacri canones*).

Only once all the Eastern Churches complete their particular law will Pope St. John Paul II's desire, following the tone and direction set by the Second Vatican Council and the Eastern Code, will the canonical ordering of the whole Church be completed, thereby enriching the communion of the Catholic Church in its expression of unity and legitimate diversity.

EPISCOPAL CONFERENCES AND ASSEMBLIES OF HIERARCHIES

Both the Latin and Eastern codes call for common pastoral coordination among bishops of the different Churches *sui iuris*, especially where jurisdictions coincide in a given region or country. The bishops do so through episcopal conferences in the Latin Church and assemblies of hierarchs of several Churches *sui iuris* in the Eastern Churches. The purpose and membership of the episcopal groupings, which are notably quite similar, are spelled out in the following canons:

> *CIC* can. 447. A conference of bishops, a permanent institution, is a group of bishops of some nation or certain territory who jointly exercise certain pastoral functions for the Christian faithful of their territory in order to promote the greater good which the Church offers to humanity, especially through forms and programs of the apostolate fittingly adapted to the circumstances of time and place, according to the norm of law.
>
> Can. 450 §1. To a conference of bishops belong by the law itself all diocesan bishops in the territory, those equivalent to them in law, coadjutor bishops, auxiliary bishops, and other titular bishops who perform in the same territory a special function entrusted to them by the Apostolic See or conference of bishops. Ordinaries of another rite can also be invited though in such a way that they have only a consultative vote unless the statutes of the conference of bishops decree otherwise.
>
> *CCEO* can. 322 §1. Where it seems advisable in the judgement of the Apostolic See, periodic assemblies are to be held of patriarchs, metropolitans of metropolitan Churches *sui iuris*, eparchial bishops, and, if the statutes so state, other local hierarchs of various Churches *sui iuris*, even of the Latin Church, exercising their authority in the same nation or region.
>
> The purpose of these meetings is that, by sharing the insights of wisdom born of experience and by the exchange of views, the pooling of their resources is achieved for the common good of the Churches, so that unity of action is fostered, common works are facilitated, the good of religion is more readily promoted and ecclesiastical discipline is preserved more effectively.

The manner in which decisions are assigned the force of law in both the episcopal conferences and assemblies of hierarchs are rather comparable. Decisions can only have juridical binding force if: 1) the matter does not exceed the competence of the conference or assembly; 2) has been passed by at least two-thirds of the members having a deliberative vote; and 3) are approved by the Apostolic See (*CIC* c. 455; *CCEO* c. 322, §§2-3). Furthermore, explicit to the assembly of hierarchs (c. 322, §2), and implicit to the episcopal conference, decisions cannot be prejudicial to the rite of any Church *sui iuris*.

However, unique to assemblies of hierarchs, is the exhortation of the Eastern code to include the participation, where possible, of hierarchs of Churches that are not yet in full communion with the Catholic Church (c. 322, §4). Yet, this possibility need not be excluded from the reality of episcopal conferences in that the statutes could determine the nature and extent of such ecumenical cooperation.

In regions and countries where Eastern and Latin Catholic bishops work side by side, it is not unusual that they become members in each others' episcopal groupings, which is the reality in the Canadian Conference of Catholic Bishops (CCCB) and the United States Conference of Catholic Bishops (USCCB). The common pastoral action that has resulted through such cooperation has been insurmountable, especially where the bishops speak with one voice on various issues, for example, the sanctity of life, the poor and marginalized, and the environment.

In recent years, the USCCB, which is also divided into regions where local assemblies of bishops from a given region, state or several states, created "Region 15," comprised of all the Eastern Catholic bishops in the United States. Although these Eastern bishops have met in common regularly for many years through their "Eastern Catholic Associates," Region 15 provides a mechanism within the USCCB for the Eastern bishops to discuss and present matters from the point of view of the Christian East, thereby making a valuable contribution to the life of the Catholic Church in the United States.

Similarly, the CCCB is divided into four regional episcopal assemblies: Western, Quebec, Ontario and Atlantic. The Catholic Church in Canada would benefit from a similar grouping of Eastern Catholic bishops either through an assembly of hierarchs or a region of their own.

At the same time, caution must be exercised not to overextend the competency of the respective episcopal conference of assembly of hierarchies. By way of illustration, the 2002 USCCB Charter for the Protection of Children and Young People, in responding to allegations of sexual abuse of minors by Catholic clergy, brought about binding legislation upon the Eastern Catholic Churches in the United States. This is not to say that the Eastern Catholic Churches need not be vigilant in respect to providing safer environments for youth and vulnerable adults; however, the competent authority to provide legislation in these matters are the synod of bishops and council of hierarchs, and not Latin episcopal conferences.

A similar situation recently arose in Canada also regarding protocols to deal with sexual abuse and the protection of minors and vulnerable adults. The Canadian Conference of Catholic Bishops was responding to the 2011 Congregation for the Doctrine of the Faith's Circular Letter To Assist Episcopal Conferences in Developing Guidelines for Dealing with Cases of Sexual Abuses of Minors Perpetuated by Clerics. The CCCB's initial intention was to include the Eastern Catholic Churches in Canada under its legislation and protocols. While the norms of Pope John Paul II's motu proprio *Sacramentorum sanctitatis tutela*, which provide the background for the Circular Letter, apply both to Latin and Eastern clerics, again, the competent authority to develop suitable procedures for assisting the victims of sexual abuse are the synod of bishops and councils of hierarchs, and not Latin episcopal conferences.

EASTERN CHRISTIANS IN THE NEW WORLD: CURSE OR BLESSING?

When we think of Eastern Christians in the West, can use different images to describe the same reality: immigration, Boat People, displaced persons, ethnic cleansing, exodus, expatriates, holocaust, human migration, Long Walk of the Navajo, Nakba, population transfer, refugees, rural exodus, slave trade, stateless nation, Trail of Tears, Ummah, etc.

In the realm of the Church, the most frequently applied term in relation to Eastern Christians outside their original homeland is the "diaspora." Diaspora, from the Greek διασπορά, refers to a scattering, a dispersion: the movement, migration, or scattering of people away from an established or ancestral homeland; people dispersed by whatever cause to more than one location; people settled far from their ancestral homelands.

The word refers historically to mass-dispersions of people with common roots, particularly movements of an involuntary nature, such as: the expulsion of Jews from the Middle East; the African Trans-Atlantic slave trade; the southern Chinese during the "coolie" slave trade; and Tibetans who fled their homeland with the Dalai Lama in 1959 to escape the invasion and occupation by China.

Biblically, the first mention of a diaspora, created as a result of exile, is found in the Septuagint: "Therefore thus said the Lord ... I will give you up to dispersion [diaspora] among all the kingdoms of the earth" (Jeremiah 34:17). Diaspora was later used to refer to the population of Jews exiled from Israel in 587 BC by the Babylonians, and from Judea in 70 AD by the Roman Empire.

In this sense, diaspora invokes a collective memory of one's homeland, a rootedness. It often involves a strong hope and desire eventually to return home. In exile, one's very identity is shaped by the "old country," and a commitment to maintain and restore that which was lost.

Yet, perhaps diaspora can take on another definition, one offered by the Christian East. For the Ancient Greeks, diaspora referred to the citizens of a dominant city-state who emigrated to a conquered land with the purpose of colonization. The term derives from the verb διασπείρω (*diaspeirō*), "I scatter," "I spread about," and that form διά (*dia*), "between, through, across" + the verb σπείρω (*speirō*), "I sow, I scatter."

In this sense, one with more positive overtures, can be applied to Eastern Christians in a Western World. Immigration has resulted in new opportunities for spreading the Good News of the Gospel message. One Catholic Church, 22 Catholic Churches – Unity in Diversity. One faith, diverse liturgies, theologies, spiritualities, disciplines, cultures and histories. One Church, two lungs.

Pope St. John Paul II, in his Apostolic Letter *Orientale lumen*, Light From the East, invites us to listen to the Churches of the East, who are

> living interpreters of the treasure of tradition they preserve, inasmuch as in contemplating it, before my eyes appear elements of great significance for a fuller and more thorough understanding of the Christian experience. These elements are capable of giving a more complete Christian response to the expectations of the men and women of today. Indeed, in comparison to any other culture, the Christian East has a unique and privileged role as the original setting where the Church was born (no. 5).

The reality of Eastern Christians in the western world is here to stay. Some of these faithful will return to their homeland, when the reasons for which they fled turn cease to exist. However, many will stay. Yet, for some 150 years now, Eastern Christians have been immigrating to North America. For them, this is not a diaspora of a longing to return, but a diaspora of rootedness, a sowing of new seeds in a new land. This is home.

What might this mean for the spreading of the Gospel?

MISSION OF THE EASTERN CATHOLIC CHURCHES

What then is the mission of the Eastern Catholic Churches in light of the New Evangelization called for by Pope Emeritus Benedict XVI and acted upon by Pope Francis?

The question can be approached from two points of view. On one hand, what do the Eastern Catholic Churches themselves say about their role in evangelization? On the other hand, what does the Apostolic See have to say in this regard?

An international symposium was held in Gaming, Austria from March 4-6, 2009 on the mission of the Greek Catholic Churches in Central and Eastern Europe. The symposium was hosted by the International Theological Institute in cooperation with the Institut für Theologie und Geschichte des Christlichen Ostens, Katholisch-Theologische Fakultät der Universität Wien, and the Ukrainian Catholic University – Lviv, Ukraine. Some 150 participants attended the gathering, including 17 bishops, leading scholars, students, clergy and lay persons from over 20 countries. The Acts of the symposium were published under the auspices of the International Theological Institute by Svichado (Lviv, 2013).

The symposium centred its attention on the contributions that the Eastern Catholic Churches of Central and Eastern Europe are called to make to the broader Christian community and to the world at large. The findings are equally applicable to North America.

The symposium's communiqué summarizes its findings in terms of vocation and ecumenical dialogue:

> The urgent and life-giving vocation of Greek Catholics is to integrate and synthesize the patristic, liturgical, canonical, cultural, and mystical tradition of the Christian East with a living witness to the catholicity and universality of the Gospel of Jesus Christ.
>
> In this regard, Eastern Catholics have much to offer their Latin brothers and sisters. Roman Catholic participants of the conference, especially its convener, Christoph Cardinal Schönborn, reiterated the hope of Western Christians that Greek Catholics, as well as Orthodox, can help people in the West better experience liturgical beauty and holiness, offsetting a "flattened" sense of the sacred in an increasingly secularized post-Enlightenment world.
>
> In recent decades in ecumenical dialogue, Eastern Catholics have often been deemed a 'problem.' The conference affirmed that an objectifying and patronizing critique of Greek Catholics as an ecumenical obstacle has reached a dead end. The miraculous revival and evident vigor of Central and Eastern European Greek Catholics must be explained only by God's will and bounty. This revival also suggests that discussions of unity without the Greek Catholics, stigmatized

> as the 'Uniates,' will not generate new answers to the question of East-West religious reconciliation.

Among the most promising proposals put forth from the symposium was the decision on the part of the participants to petition then Pope Benedict XVI to consider the topic of the Eastern Catholic Churches at an upcoming papal synod. While we do not know whether Pope Francis will act on the request, we do have a glimpse into the mind of Pope Emeritus Benedict XVI on the mission of the Eastern Catholic Churches through His Beatitude Lubomyr Husar, Major Archbishop Emeritus of the Ukrainian Catholic Church.

Cardinal Husar, was unable to attend the symposium in person, however, he wrote a rather interesting and revealing greeting to the participants, summarizing two written encounters he had prior to his retirement with Pope Benedict on the very mission of the Eastern Catholic Churches.

In 2005, Cardinal Husar sent Pope Benedict XVI a greeting on behalf of the bishops of the Ukrainian Catholic Church who were meeting for their annual synod. In the letter, His Beatitude posed two questions to the Roman Pontiff: First, what is the role of the Ukrainian Catholic Church within the Universal Church, and second, what is the Ukrainian Catholic Church's particular role in fostering Christian unity?

In his response, Cardinal Angelo Sodano, Secretary of State, writes – in full concord with the Roman Pontiff, concludes Cardinal Husar – that the answer to the first question is to treasure the Eastern Tradition for the benefit of the entire Church; and second, to be an example for the non-Catholic brethren on what the full communion with the Catholic Church means.

Cardinal Husar, in the same greeting to the symposium participants, writes that Pope Benedict XVI himself reiterated this very mission of the Eastern Catholic Churches in a March 2006 letter to His Beatitude on the occasion of the commemoration of the 60th Anniversary of the Soviet regime's attempt to liquidate the Ukrainian Catholic Church. Cardinal Husar writes:

> To my mind, the two answers are very clear. Much difficulty has arisen in the course of the decades – even centuries – by the not respecting of these, one could say, self-evident truths, from various sides. It has been a constant endeavour of true ecumenists to help us be ourselves 'fully Oriental and fully Catholic' and to make the communion with the Apostolic See fully understandable and fully respectful of legitimate aspirations. This endeavour has not yet been completed. There still remains a strong residue of the fatal *praestantia ritus*

> *latini*, which can be described as a one-sided understanding of catholicity.
>
> What I have said above is really nothing new. It has been stated already many times before this. This, however, need not discourage us, because in the process of being fully Catholic and being of real service to the cause of the Church's unity, we are learning what catholicity and what Church unity really mean. Yes, this process of learning has not been without much suffering, but neither has it been without hope. Experience has shown that trying other roads or solutions leads nowhere. What the Holy Father has repeated in his above mentioned letters remains the only right road.

The symposium communiqué summarizes these papal sentiments in this way:

> Pope Benedict XVI stressed that Greek Catholic Churches are called to be faithful to the Eastern tradition and to witness to it in the Catholic communion. They will thus be an example to Orthodox Christians of the meaning of living in communion with the Catholic Church. This communion has led to a multifaceted mutual enrichment of Eastern and Western traditions ... Today, with the encouragement of the highest authorities in the Catholic Church, the recovery of authentic Eastern Christian identity is being actively fostered.

CONCLUSION

The 50th Anniversary of the Second Vatican Council's Decree on the Eastern Catholic Churches, *Orientalium ecclesiarum*, and the approaching 25th Anniversary of the Eastern code have provided us with opportunity to reflect on two of the most important documents affecting the life of the Eastern Catholic Churches in recent history.

Much has been done by way of implementing the conciliar teachings and the revised canonical discipline regarding the Eastern Churches. Understandably, much more remains to be done. Twenty-five years and fifty years are relatively small in the life of the Church. It will take considerably more time to fully realize the fruits of the Second Vatican Council and to bring about the much hoped for renewal.

The mission of the Eastern Catholic Churches in relation to their contribution towards the new evangelization remains unclear. Are they called to evangelize solely along their ethnic lines, as some would have it? Or are the Eastern Churches also called to share the joy of the Gospel with all peoples in all places, beyond their lands of origin and nationality? The latter seems more hopeful, especially in the context of North America, which in reality has become to a great extent missionary territory once again.

In this light, resolving the issue of the extension of the jurisdiction of the patriarch beyond the original territory, that is, the "old country," seems even more crucial today. Much of the "unfinished business" of the Eastern code is related in one way or another to this question. Yet it seems we have reached an impasse in this regard. It was hoped that the matter would have been treated in the Eastern code, picking up where the Second Vatican Council left off regarding the restored rights and privileges of the patriarchal institute. Instead, when the Code Commission sought clarification on the question of patriarchal jurisdiction, a reminder of their papal mandate made it clear that the members are "arrangers of these laws, and not authors or creators." Neither the Second Vatican Council nor the Eastern code were able to bring about any resolution on the matter.

The plight of Eastern Christians in the Middle East and ever increasing tensions in eastern Ukraine and elsewhere require that the impasse be revisited by the Roman Pontiff, together with the heads of the Eastern Catholic Churches. Just as it would be seem impossible to conceive of the Roman Catholic Church without the pope, it is equally inconceivable to think of the Eastern Catholic Churches without their patriarch, the head and father of their Churches *sui iuris*; his ministry is more than symbolic – it is crucial in providing pastoral care to his faithful throughout the world.

The Second Vatican Council desired that the Eastern Catholic Churches, in the context of the universal Church, once again "flourish and fulfill with fresh apostolic vigour the task entrusted to them" (*OE*, no. 1), namely, to carry on the mission entrusted by God to the Church, to evangelize.

The Eastern Catholic Churches need themselves to be more active in the mission of evangelization, being convinced that their role is to share the Good News and to move beyond the ghetto of being "ethnic churches." It seems from the 2009 International Symposium on the Mission of the Greek Catholic Churches in Central and Eastern Europe that they are prepared to do so. The conclusion of the symposium communiqué states:

> The participants reached a consensus that Greek Catholics should not rest on the spiritual laurels of their martyrs. Rather, it is time for all Greek Catholics to roll up their sleeves and apply themselves with the faith of their fathers to the challenges of Christian unity and of being a witness in the twenty-first century.

"Fully Eastern. Fully Catholic." A papal dream or a work in progress? Unfinished business.

Appendix

An Overview of

Eastern Catholic Churches Worldwide

(Source: Catholic Near East Welfare Association – 2013)

Alexandrian

1. Coptic Catholic Church (patriarchate): Cairo, [163,849], Egypt (1741)

2. Ethiopian Catholic Church (metropolia): Addis Ababa, [208,093], Ethiopia, Eritrea (1846)

Antiochene or West Syrian

1. Maronite Church (patriarchate): Bkerke, [3,105,278], Lebanon, Cyprus, Jordan, Israel, Palestinian Authority, Egypt, Syria, Argentina, Brazil, **United States**, Australia, **Canada**, Mexico

2. Syriac Catholic Church (patriarchate): Beirut,[131,692], Lebanon, Iraq, Jordan, Kuwait, Palestinian Authority, Egypt, Sudan, Syria, Turkey, **United States and Canada**, Venezuela

3. Syro-Malankara Catholic Church (major archepiscopate): Trivandrum, [412,640], India, **United States**

Armenian

1. Armenian Catholic Church (patriarchate): Beirut, [375,182], Lebanon, Iran, Iraq, Egypt, Syria, Turkey, Jordan, Palestinian Authority, Ukraine, France, Greece, Latin America, Argentina, Romania, **United States**, **Canada**, Eastern Europe

Chaldean or East Syrian

1. Chaldean Catholic Church (patriarchate): Baghdad, [418,194], Iraq, Iran, Lebanon, Egypt, Syria, Turkey, **United States**

2. Syro-Malabar Catholic Church (major archepiscopate): Ernakulam, [3,902,089], India, Middle East, Europe, **Canada**, **United States**

Constantinopolitan or Byzantine

1. Albanian Catholic Church (apostolic administration): [3,510], Albania

2. Belarusian Catholic Church (no established hierarchy at present): [10,000], Belarus

3. Bulgarian Greek Catholic Church (apostolic exarchate): Sofia, [10,107], Bulgaria

4. Byzantine Church of Croatia, Serbia and Montenegro (an eparchy and an apostolic exarchate): Križevci, Ruski Krstur [21,480] + [22,653], Croatia, Serbia, and Montenegro

5. Greek Byzantine Catholic Church (two apostolic exarchates): Athens, [2,325], Greece, Turkey

6. Hungarian Greek Catholic Church (an eparchy and an apostolic exarchate): Nyiregyháza, [290,000], Hungary

7. Italo-Albanian Catholic Church (two eparchies and a territorial abbacy): [63,240], Italy

8. Macedonian Catholic Church (an apostolic exarchate): Skopje, [11,491], Republic of Macedonia

9. Melkite Greek Catholic Church (patriarchate): Damascus, [1,346,635], Syria, Lebanon, Jordan, Israel, Brazil, **Canada**, **United States**, Mexico, Iraq, Egypt and Sudan, Kuwait, Australia, Venezuela, Argentina

10. Romanian Church United with Rome (major archiepiscopate): Blaj, [776,529] Romania, **United States**

11. Russian Catholic Church (two apostolic exarchates, at present with no published hierarchs): Russia, China; currently about 20 parishes and communities scattered around the world, including five in Russia itself, answering to bishops of other jurisdictions

12. Ruthenian Catholic Church (a *sui juris* metropolia, an eparchy, and an apostolic exarchate): Uzhhorod, Pittsburgh, [594,465], **United States**, Ukraine, Czech Republic

13. Slovak Catholic Church (metropolia and an eparchy): Prešov, [243,335], Slovakia, **Canada**

14. Ukrainian Catholic Church (major archiepiscopate): Kiev, [4,223,425], Ukraine, Poland, **Canada**, **United States**, Great Britain, Australia, Germany and Scandinavia, France, Brazil, Argentina

SEMINAR

DEVELOPMENT OF THE CHAIR OF THE SAINT PETER ORDINARIATE: A BISHOP'S PERSPECTIVE

Most Rev. Kevin Vann, JCD

Dear friends here at the CLSA,

It is wonderful to be back with you here again after all of these years when I was in regular attendance at CLSA meetings, and when I was a member of the Board of Governors in the early 1990's. The last time I was in a seminar setting like this was around 1987 or 1988 when I gave a seminar on Canon 1098 of the Code of Canon Law. Perhaps the only thing that has changed since those days is that my once red hair is now a thing of the past!

The title of this seminar is "Development of the Chair of St. Peter Ordinariate: A Bishop's Perspective." I write these words with great gratitude to those clergy and lay members who made this great leap, sometimes at no small cost, with whom I was privileged to journey these past years. I also want to particularly thank Cardinal Donald Wuerl, who chaired the committee that I was part of to establish the Ordinariate in the United States; to Cardinal William Levada, who asked me to be of assistance; and to Msgr. Jeffrey Steenson, now Ordinary of the Personal Ordinariate of the Chair of St. Peter. I also wish to make special mention of Msgr. James Hart, who served the Diocese of Fort Worth with great dedication as Chancellor, and is stationed at St. Elizabeth Ann Seton Church in Keller, Texas. My reflections are certainly a Bishop's perspective – or rather a pastor's perspective, and perhaps unique because of the history that I 'inherited' in Texas and because a great part of my life took on the call of walking with, and accompanying, so many people on this challenging and courageous journey of faith. It was more than just one parish or a few people … it was, in the end, three communities of Christ's faithful (in Fort Worth alone), and at least ten priests (I include here not only the Ordinariate clergy, but the Pastoral Provision priests who were already in service when I arrived in Fort Worth in 2005.

One of the great images I have in all of this is one occasion in the sacristy of St. Patrick's Cathedral in Fort Worth. I was getting ready to celebrate Mass along with Msgr. Steenson. Also present at the same time was Msgr. James Hart, who served the Diocese of Fort Worth as the Chancellor at a very critical time and was a great help to me personally. As Msgr. Hart and Msgr. Steenson were conversing in the sacristy, I could not help but think that how seemingly short years before they were both together at another time at St. Andrew's Episcopal Church, just two blocks over from St. Patrick's! Msgr. Steenson was the Rector of St. Andrew's and Msgr. Hart was the curate! A short distance away to be sure, but in some ways a distance of centuries had been crossed and healed!

The outline of this presentation is going to be a brief history of how I got involved in all of this, followed by what I term catechetical, canonical, pastoral and "clergy" reflections. This follows, in some way, the headings found in *Anglicanorum Coetibus* and the *Complementary Norms* (Articles 5 and 6 of the norms, for example.) My sources are not many: Certainly, *Anglicanorum Coetibus*, some personal testimonies from some of the priests who made this great step, and my own recollections. Putting this together has not been difficult – the challenge is finding the time to do it – but for me this has been a "labor of love" and a time to give thanks to the Lord for what I believe to be one of the tangible fruits of the Second Vatican Council impulse toward ecumenism.

HISTORY

When I was appointed the Bishop of Fort Worth, among the many phone calls and letters that I received, was a phone call from Msgr. William Stetson, a good friend and a member of the CLSA. He had been the Regional Vicar of Opus Dei in the Midwest and he and I were active in the national and regional CLSA at about the same time. He said that he planned on coming to my ordination, not only because we were friends, but also because of the presence of a number of Pastoral Provision priests in the Diocese of Fort Worth, and an entire community that had been received into the Church, St. Mary the Virgin in Arlington, Texas, during the time of my late predecessor Bishop Joseph Delaney. At that point, I had some vague recollection of the Pastoral Provision, as I had known then Bishop Bernard Law, then Bishop of the Diocese of Springfield-Cape Girardeau, Missouri, when I was in the seminary, and knew that he was associated after that time with the Pastoral Provision. I knew that I had met Father Parker at some point, one of the first priests to be received under the Pastoral Provision. But, that was it!

However, shortly after my ordination as Bishop of Fort Worth, I was invited by Father Alan Hawkins, the then pastor of St. Mary the Virgin, to be the principal celebrant for the parish feast day of the Assumption. He was a gracious guide as I celebrated Mass for the first time from the Book of Divine Worship. I met a number of people who had made the journey "across the Tiber" years before. From that time on, I began to meet more and more people who could best be described as "Anglo-Catholic" and who certainly had yearnings and prayers for full communion. I was asked to speak early on as well at a meeting of the priests of the Episcopal Diocese of Fort Worth, under the leadership of Bishop Jack Iker, and he and I became friends and usually tried to have lunch on a monthly basis. I sensed some of those same questions and desires at the early meeting with their priests. You see, the Catholic Diocese of Fort Worth was in many ways "co-terminus" in history and geography with the Episcopal Diocese of Fort Worth. As one of their priests noted in a presentation in San Antonio years ago:

> As most of you know, the Episcopal Diocese of Fort Worth has been a rather interesting diocese over the years as it has fought its way through the deterioration of the Episcopal Church. From its beginning in 1983, it has been blessed with a majority of Anglo-Catholic clergy who have continued to support a very courageous Bishop who was witnessing for the Faith in an atmosphere that was rapidly becoming impossible. Let me note that the diocese had watched some of its best clergy leaving for the Catholic Church under the pastoral provision … Many more followed including our host here at St. Mary's. We are grateful for their witness.

I also found that the interest in full communion among certain sections of the Diocese of Fort Worth was not only here, but also in Houston, at Our Lady of Walsingham, and at Our Lady of the Atonement in San Antonio. Thus, this movement for full communion has been described as having its "epicenter" in Texas, and indeed across the South and the Southwest.

My involvement with these pastoral provision priests and communities, who contributed a great deal to the life of the Catholic Diocese of Fort Worth, eventually resulted in me being appointed "Vice-Delegate" of the Pastoral Provision, under Archbishop Myers as ecclesiastical delegate, with special responsibility for Texas. This involvement leads directly to the next dramatic step in the journey, namely June 16, 2008 at 3:00 PM at the Catholic Center for the Diocese of Fort Worth!

Even prior to this day, there was one more meeting which served as a prelude. Father Hart and I were invited to a meeting of the Society of the Holy Cross, an association among Episcopalian clergy that were dedicated to living a Catholic life and with a commitment toward full communion with the Holy See. One in this group, now pastor of St. Mary the Virgin in Arlington, Texas, during the course of the prayer and discussion stood up and said that "we are hoping that someone will reach out their hand to us." At around this same time, some of that group had accompanied Bishop Iker on a pilgrimage to England, and then to Rome. They met with now Cardinal Bernard Law, that year serving as the Ecclesiastical Delegate for the Pastoral Provision. In the words of one of those who made this journey:

> With the gracious help of our good friend, Fr. Alan Hawkins, who made arrangements for us to have a meeting with his Eminence, Bernard Cardinal Law, we received from the

> Cardinal some Godly advice. At that meeting, Cardinal Law indicated that the Catholic Church was aware of the current difficulties faced by Anglo-Catholics, and particularly the Anglo-Catholic Diocese of Fort Worth. He said to us in essence that we needed to 'make an offer,' that is, to make a proposal on how the Catholic Church might respond to the crises in our branch of Christendom. This advice was well received and we were most grateful for his support. It was another indication to us of what God was calling us to do. It was after this pilgrimage that four priests in that group began meeting with the knowledge and support of our Bishop. As is stated in the presentation, 'we came to realize that, like the Prodigal Son in the Gospel, it is up to us to make the initiative to return to the rock from whence we were hewn.' In essence, that trip crystallized for us the need to work for the goal of the unity with the See of Peter now. Since that time we have worked, prayed, met, and prepared for the meeting that took place with Bishop Vann two years later.

The proposal that was made on that June day by Father Charles Hough, III (then Canon to the Ordinary), Fr. William Crary, Fr. Christopher Stainbrook, and Fr. Louis Tobola consisted in summary of the following points:

1. We now believe that the See of Peter is essential, not optional;

2. We believe a "Magisterium" is needed desperately;

3. We believe the Catholic Faith is True;

4. We believe that the Anglican Communions shares the fatal flaws of the Episcopal Church;

5. We believe our polity is in error;

6. We believe we are not the only ones: this finding contains a history of the Episcopal Diocese of Fort Worth;

7. We believe Pope Benedict XVI understands our plight;

8. We believe there is a charism which the Anglican ethos has to offer the Universal Church.

At that meeting, we spoke of the long context of the impulse toward full communion, going back to the Oxford Movement and the work of the Second Vatican Council, to make clear that this proposal did not arise only out of present-day challenges. I had the distinct impression that I was, as it were, standing on "holy ground" and that history was unfolding in front of me at that very moment. This meeting concluded with the following proposal:

We request that the Catholic Diocese of Fort Worth provide guidance and assistance as we look for a new way that would lead our diocese into full communion with the Holy See.

We believe that this guidance is necessary for the following reasons:

> 1. We cannot adequately prepare for such a proposal without input from those to whom the proposal is to be made;
>
> 2. Such guidance would help us work through the complicated aspects of this proposal;
>
> 3. With this guidance, the Holy Spirit could affect more quickly the healing of the broken Body of Christ.

Should you consent, we are glad to offer ourselves for this important work and stand ready to work with those you might designate.

After some thought and reflection, I submitted this proposal to the then Ecclesiastical Delegate for the Pastoral Provision, Archbishop John Myers, who submitted it to the Congregation for the Doctrine of the Faith. After this meeting, I had a similar meeting with about eight younger priests of the Episcopal Diocese of Fort Worth who submitted a similar proposal, which I in turn also submitted to the Congregation for the Doctrine of the Faith.

An unfortunate note in all of this was that this proposal was leaked to the press by a retired priest in the Episcopal Diocese of Fort Worth, which then made the *Dallas Morning News* and the *Fort Worth Star Telegram*. This obviously caused a great deal of discord which, unfortunately, affected a number of individuals and communities. However, the priests that I met with, and some of the second group, persisted in their desire for full communion with groups in their parishes and among themselves.

It turns out that several similar proposals had been made to the Holy See and on November 4, 2009, the Memorial of St. Charles Borromeo, *Anglicanorum Coetibus* was promulgated. This, to many, was seen as an "answer to prayer" and indeed I would say, a confirmation of hope, prayer and diligent work toward full communion, and it was only about a year and one half after that momentous meeting with the first group of Episcopal priests in the Chancery in Fort Worth!

Following the promulgation of *Anglicanorum Coetibus*, I was asked by Cardinal George, having heard from Cardinal Levada, to be on the three Bishop Commission to establish the Ordinariate in the United States. Cardinal Wuerl served as the Chair, and I served along with Bishop Robert McManus of Worcester, Massachusetts. Cardinal Levada made a presentation to the United States Conference of Catholic Bishop, and in the course of our meetings, Cardinal Wuerl, Bishop McManus and I made several presentations to the Bishops' Conference. The end "juridical and canonical" result was the establishment of the Personal Ordinariate of the Chair of St. Peter with Msgr. Jeffrey Steenson, here present with us today, as the Ordinary. The Mass of Institution was held for the Personal Ordinariate of the Chair of St. Peter, and Msgr. Steenson was installed as Ordinary on Sunday, February 12, 2012 at the Co-Cathedral of the Sacred Heart in Houston. It was a day of great joy for all.

Given this history, which for me is a necessary way to convey to you how, in God's providence, I became involved in this project, I would like to turn now to three areas which would certainly be part of a "Bishop's perspective" and which certainly reflect my experience. They would be catechetical, canonical and what I would call "pastoral care" for priests.

CATECHETICAL

With such obvious needs as catechesis as foundational to all of this, where does one begin? Paragraph 5 of No. 1 of *Anglicanorum Coetibus* states that "*The Catechism of the Catholic Church* is the authoritative expression of the Catholic Faith professed by members of the Ordinariate." Our commission decided, with the help of Fr. James Massa, then of the USCCB staff, that the catechism for the United States would be the *United States Catholic Catechism for Adults*.

I turned to my director of Faith Formation for the Diocese, Mr. Lucas Pollice, for help in this critical area, and he in turn, composed an approach for the unique circumstances of this venture. The attached program[1] was developed to cover July through the following June, and was developed by Lucas and myself and our Faith Formation department with the unique background of these folks in mind. The outline we used was eventually adopted as a template for other dioceses who were working with other communities. We approached a couple, Rosary and Bert Guidry, who were RCIA catechists at St. Michael's parish in Bedford, Texas, for assistance. They have described this process as a real gift to themselves.

At that time, there was one community under the leadership of Fr. Timothy Perkins (formerly of St. Mark's Episcopal in Arlington) who was in the process

1 The program was distributed in hard copy at the 76th Annual Canon Law Society Convention in St. Louis, Missouri, in October 2014. To obtain a copy, please contact the Canon Law Society of America.

of discernment. Fr. Perkins had been meeting with them for about one year. Later another community came into being under the leadership of Fr. Charles Hough, III. Shortly after this, there was another nearly entire community from St. Timothy's Episcopal Church in Fort Worth, who discerned their desire to come into full communion under the leadership of their pastor, Fr. Christopher Stainbrook. Bear in mind that Fathers Hough, Stainbrook and Perkins were part of the initial group of priests that came to see me. Father Perkins was the priest that had a made a plea two years earlier for someone to "reach out to them."

Lucas and the Guidry's began to meet with this community weekly at one of the local Catholic campus ministry centers. They attended Sunday Mass at St. Maria Goretti Church in Arlington, Texas, and received much pastoral care and support from the parish and the pastor, Father James Gigliotti, TOR. The two communities with which we were working were communities by the names of St. Peter the Rock in the Arlington/Metro area, and St. John Vianney further South near what is called Cleburne, Texas. I remember that the Diocese of Fort Worth had a lot of miles to cover, so to accommodate the geography of the diocese, we worked with these two communities. Eventually, they became one community. It was a very joyful day when, in September of 2009 we received this group into the Church, along with Fr. Perkins and his wife Jody, and Father Hough and his wife Marilyn.

I will note this a little further along in the process, but for those who needed canonical help on previous marriages and could not be received at the time of the rest of the community, we celebrated the Rite of Welcome for them so they could still be a tangible part of this grand celebration. I would say above all that this was not a hurried process, but a journey of discernment and study of several years in all. Remember that the announcement of the Apostolic Constitution was November 4, 2009. The discernment and study with these folks had already begun even before that. Following the publication of the Apostolic Constitution, the work of the commission for the United States began and it took the better part of a year. The group from St. Peter the Rock, with the members of the St. John Vianney community, were received into the Church in September 2011, in anticipation of the official decree establishing the Ordinariate of the Chair of St. Peter on January 1, 2012, the Solemnity of the Mother of God.

At about the same time, another catechesis process was begun for the community of the parish of St. Timothy of the Episcopal Diocese of Fort Worth. The process was different as the needs were somewhat different. This was one parish of probably about 100 families that already had a parish identity, unlike the above two communities which were made up of faithful from several different parishes. The announcement of their intention to leave the Episcopal Church meant that they had to leave their Church home of many years, which was certainly accompanied by loss and grief. However, thanks to the generosity of Father David Bristow, who is a former priest of the Episcopal Diocese of Fort Worth and in service at the venerable St. Mary of the Assumption in downtown Fort Worth, they found their place and home to worship. They were received into the Church on May 27, 2012, and had the name of St. Timothy's Ordinariate Community at St. Mary of the Assumption Church.

CANONICAL

Chief among the canonical concerns that first presented themselves were, as might be expected, former bonds of marriage for parishioners who would be received. I would like to acknowledge the Tribunal staff of the Diocesan Tribunal of the Diocese of Fort Worth for their care and pastoral concern and the extra efforts that were made for these folks. Meg Hogan and Anna Marie Chamblee went above and beyond to help in this way. I might add that the first element of catechesis for all of these communities was in fact all of the questions surrounding previous marriages. As I recall, I took some of those sessions with the communities, and worked with the parish priests who were going to be received so that they, who were accompanying their folks, could help with this. Our Tribunal had attended to these cases with extra care, and where possible attended to the protocol numbers so that they could be moved ahead, given the historical import of all of this. A particular pastoral concern was helping Catholics who thought that they had left this behind, but now found this facing them once again. With careful pastoral care all were helped.

One point that we made with all of this, that ties into the catechetical concerns, was that the process for reception into full communion, even though spread over ten months, was not an academic year, but rather a process of learning and discernment for which there could be no time line. As I mentioned earlier as well, for those who could not be received in September with the others, they were afforded the Rite of Welcome during the reception celebration. I also might add – even with the "eye-brows" that might be raised, that we were able to use the "Frater/Soror" solution for some couples … at their suggestion. As I mentioned earlier, of necessity these canonical proceedings for prior marriages were very much connected with the catechetical content and how the Church understands the sacrament of marriage, with its qualities of permanence, fidelity and openness to children.

Once the Ordinariate was established in Houston in 2012, the communities of St. Timothy and Our Lady of Walsingham in Houston were officially established as Ordinariate parishes. The community of St. Peter the Rock became part of St. Mary the Virgin in Arlington, and Father Timothy Perkins was appointed pastor. The process of its transfer was slowed because of my transfer to Orange and is now in process again. The process necessarily involved the alienation of property, and the suppression of one canonical entity and erection of another. Because of the size and nature of St. Mary the Virgin, this is a transaction that will have to go to the Holy See.

PASTORAL CARE FOR PRIESTS

I would subdivide this section into two parts: formation and ongoing support, and care for families as well. Formation of priests is essential because this is explicitly in Article 6 of the complementary norms.

During the course of the deliberations of the Commission, the question of formation of future clergy took a major place, in addition to the catechetical dimension. After much deliberation and consultation, it was decided that the formation for candidates for the Ordinariate would take place at St. Mary's Seminary in Houston, since the Archdiocese of Houston already had an Anglican use community, Our Lady of Walsingham. Msgr. Steenson was already a professor of Patristics at St. Mary's Seminary. As the time was drawing nearer for an announcement of the establishment of an Ordinariate here in the United States, a curriculum for formation was drawn up by the faculty of St. Mary's Seminary in Houston. Initially it was to involve distance learning, as well as a gathering of candidates monthly at the seminary for the four pillars of formation. Granted that at first the matter seemed to be rushed, nonetheless with the impending establishment of the Ordinariate it was deemed important to begin to develop a formation process that would be ready to receive candidates.

There was at least enough interest in the State of Texas that a number of candidates would be interviewed to begin the process. Their dossiers were prepared and sent to the Congregation for the Doctrine of the Faith, in a manner similar to that of the Pastoral Provision. With the establishment of the Ordinariate on January 1, 2012 the initial governing Council was Cardinal Wuerl, Bishop McManus and myself. The interviews were conducted and dossiers completed in light of Number 6, paragraph 1 of the *Complementary Norms*:

> In consideration of Anglican ecclesial tradition and practice, the Ordinary may present to the Holy Father a request for the admission of married men to the presbyterate in the Ordinariate, after a process of discernment based on objective criteria and the needs of the Ordinariate. These objective criteria are determined by the Ordinary in consultation with the local Episcopal Conference and must be approved by the Holy See.

Paragraph 2 is also relevant when it says that:

> Those who have been previously ordained in the Catholic Church and subsequently have become Anglicans may not exercise sacred ministry in the Ordinariate. Anglican clergy who are in irregular marriage situations may not be accepted for Holy Orders in the Ordinariate.

In these three years, the formation process has matured greatly, and as I now give you the current statistics for the Ordinariate, I will note that next February, approximately three years after the establishment of the Personal Ordinariate of the Chair of St. Peter, a Pastoral Center will be dedicated in Houston, near the Church of Our Lady of Walsingham, which has been designated by the Holy See as the "Principal Church." In addition, a house of formation for Ordinariate Clergy is nearly ready as well. A lot to be grateful for in these years!

The second part of this section entitled "Pastoral Care for Clergy" comes from my own personal experience with the men themselves. A lot of this is rooted in the years that I spent as Vicar for Priests for Bishop Lucas in Springfield, Illinois, and during which they and I seemed to live instinctively, just as were the years in Fort Worth and now in Orange.

My friends, the Guidry's, said that their role in the catechetical formation of the communities was a blessing that they never would have expected and that they received much more than they gave. I would say in a parallel fashion that this was my experience with the priests with whom I journeyed who came into the Ordinariate. Frankly, their experience was in a sense a "conviction" for me, as I often wondered if I would have the courage to do what they did. They gave up everything – some of which still is a memory for them – friends and relationships of the past and the loss of their relationship with their beloved Bishop, who in fact was a friend of mine.

I believed that it was a mission and an imperative call that I support them as much as I could, together with the priests of the Diocese of Fort Worth. They were invited and welcomed to Diocesan celebrations and Masses, clergy gatherings and retreats. We assisted them with finding spiritual directors as well. Since some had young families, and even those who did not, I assisted them in finding some employment during the transition times. For insurance purposes, I included them in the seminarian budget so that they would have insurance. My predecessor, Bishop Delaney, did the same for the pioneer pastoral provision candidates. We would have monthly daytime prayer and luncheon meetings, and they were always free to call me on my cell phone just as were any of the priests of Fort Worth. I – we – did what we could to journey with them in a time of transition from leaving one home before reaching the other.

Just as a point of context, I would also say that during this same time, the number of seminarians studying for the Diocese of Fort Worth grew from eleven to nearly thirty. There truly was no wonderment or confusion among the Catholic people of the Diocese of Fort Worth. This was due, in part, I believe to the men whom I would call the "pioneers" of the Pastoral Provision who, to this day, are still serving in the Diocese of Fort Worth and to whom I salute and give much credit: Fr. Alan Hawkins, Fr. David Bristow, and Msgr. James Hart who ably served as Chancellor of the Diocese for several years. Their courageous example in uncharted territory led the way for the men of the Ordinariate to follow. At the end of June of 2012, just two months before I found out that I was being transferred, I had the privilege to ordain six men to the priesthood for the Personal Ordinariate of the Chair of St. Peter. It was truly one of the highlights and greatest blessings of my life.

I would close these reflections with the words of Fr. Timothy Perkins, whom I consider a good friend, on the journey of the Ordinariate. His sentiments are mine truly.

> Finally, because of the difficulties that have been a formative part of our spiritual pilgrimage, the tone of some of this address might seem a bit negative. I can say without exaggerating that I and many faithful people whom I have known for years are happier in the service of the Lord than we can remember being. God continually provides for our needs through the ministry of the Holy Catholic Church; and we confidently trust in him to lead us into a bright future of love and service to the glory of his Name, the benefit of his Church, and the proclamation of the good news of salvation to the world Christ came to save.

When I was suddenly thrust into the office of the Diocesan Bishop in Fort Worth on July 13, 2005, I had no idea of what had come upon me. I had no idea what the Lord had in store, and indeed any of us can say that. However, what I can say now is that the sacred history of the Anglo-Catholic movement in the South of the United States, certainly hearkening back all the way to the Oxford Movement and Blessed John Henry Newman, certainly brought me to sacred ground where I fearfully tread at times. Yet, right in front of me, in the lives of the priests and their communities with whom I journeyed, I saw in some small way one of the breaches of the Reformation being healed in a way that I never could have expected. The constant exhortation of then Cardinal Joseph Ratzinger and now Pope Saint John Paul II "to be generous" to the groups of Anglicans who were seeking full communion became for me a defining moment in my life and ministry that continues to this day! God bless you all, and thank you so much: It is great to be here with all of you again!

Seminar

Ministry to Hispanics
Rev. Manuel Viera, OFM, JCL

Ever since Michael Joyce emailed me requesting that I make a presentation at this Convention on the topic of "Sacramental Issues in Ministry to Hispanics" in the context of the convention theme, "The Unity of the Church: Challenges and Prospects," I have questioned myself, "Why did I say yes?" However, I have to thank Father Joyce as it has given me the opportunity to reflect on *some* of the issues regarding ministry to the Hispanics. The topic is too broad, and I am unable to address or even hint at all of the issues regarding the sacraments. I apologize if some specific issue is not addressed.

I – Who are we?

Migration is not a new reality on these shores. The very founding of the nation is based on the migration of people from all over seeking a better life. Each nation and generation brings their own challenges, concerns and blessings. Migrants challenge our views by expanding our horizon to see the world from a different perspective, blessing us with a unique and different outlook at life and the grace of God present in our midst.

Migration of Spanish speaking persons to the territory that is today considered the United States dates back to the conquest itself. Way before the landing of the Mayflower in 1620 at Plymouth Rock, the "Kingdom of New Mexico" was claimed for the Spanish crown in 1540 and the city of Saint Augustine, Florida was founded in 1565. Henceforth, the Spanish speaking presence from Mexico and other Spanish speaking nations has been a constant reality in the United States. Some of the present territory of the United States at one time was part of the territory of Mexico. Many Texans and New Mexicans have been quoted to say that their families did not cross the international border, that the international border crossed them.[1]

1 This is the subject of the work of Josue David Cisneros. *The Border Crossed Us: Rhetorics of Borders, Citizenship, and Latina/o Identity (*Tuscaloosa: The University of Alabama Press, 2014). *Project MUSE.* According to their website (http://muse.jhu.edu/), *Project MUSE* is a leading provider of digital humanities and social services content. Since 1995, its electronic journal collections have supported a wide array of research needs at academic, public, special and school libraries worldwide. *MUSE* books and journals, from leading university presses and scholarly societies, currently include 333,270 articles and 657,520 chapters by 241 publishers.

In understanding the complexity of the issues regarding Hispanics there are several concepts that need to be before us for the sake of clarity. The terms "Hispanic" and "Latino/a" are generic terms that identify peoples of several countries and cultures whose official language is Spanish. While using the term Hispanic/Latino facilitates some of the studies and discussions in different circles,[2] at the same time the term is inadequate to describe all the complexities of grouping together such a large population in a single phrase. There are twenty to twenty-two countries where Spanish is the official language, depending on how the counting is done. The official language of Belize is English, but Spanish is also widely used, and Equatorial Guinea in Africa, has two official languages, Spanish and French.

While the number of nations is easy to count, that is not the case for the number of different cultures that inhabit these lands. Some of the cultures retain their own languages – I have encountered people from Oaxaca, Mexico and Guatemala that either do not speak Spanish, or their Spanish is very poor at best. They speak and know their native indigenous languages. However they are considered to be Hispanics/Latinos because of their place of origin.

The 2010 national census indicates that Hispanics are approximately 16.3 percent of the total US population; while to some it may seem not significant enough, the 2010 figures represents a 43 percent population increase among Hispanic compared to 4.9 percent increase among non-Hispanics. In some areas of the country the population increase is more alarming. In areas where the Hispanic population still is a great minority (3 to 7 percent of the total population) the increase has been between 70 and 120 percent. In those same areas, the non-Hispanic population has shown an increase of 3 to 5 percent.

According to the statistics posted on the web of the United States Conference of Catholic Bishops, the Hispanic population in the United States as of July 1, 2011 was 52.0 million. Hispanics constituted 16.7 percent of the nation's total population. The Hispanic population in the United States is second in size worldwide, only Mexico (112 million) had a larger Hispanic population than did the United States, as of 2010.[3] The top nine nations represented in the United States are: Mexicans (64.9 percent); Puerto Ricans (9.2 percent); Cubans (3.7 percent); Salvadorans (3.6 percent); Dominicans (3.0 percent); Guatemalans (2.2 percent); Colombians (1.9 percent); Hondurans (1.4 percent); Ecuadorians (1.3 percent), and Peruvians (1.2 percent)[4].

---

2 E.g. Hispanic Vote, Hispanic Ministry, Hispanic Migration, etc...

3 http://www.usccb.org/issues-and-action/cultural-diversity/hispanic-latino/demographics/hispanic-latino-demographics.cfm (accessed June 15, 2014),

4 http://www.usccb.org/issues-and-action/cultural-diversity/hispanic-latino/demographics/hispanic-latino-population-by-origin.cfm (accessed June 15, 2014).

Some estimate that Hispanics constitute approximately forty percent of the Catholic population in the United States.[5] A recent publication of the Pew Research Center[6] demonstrates a shift taking place among Latinos where nearly one-in-four consider themselves former Catholics. As canonists we are well aware that there is no such canonical institute known as "former Catholics" after Benedict XVI's October 26, 2009 Motu propio *Omnium in Mente.* At the same time as pastors of souls who are called to have "the odor of the sheep,"[7] we are fully aware of those who, for different reasons, do not consider themselves members of the fold. While reasons for departure have little to do with migration to the United States, it is a fact that evangelical churches have been gaining members in Latin America, and we cannot ignore the factors that migration and the present culture in the United States have in departure from the faith.

What can we learn from the recent publication by the Pew Research Center? First, that the majority of Hispanics in the United States continue to consider themselves Roman Catholics, but as already mentioned, this affiliation is declining. The majority of those who have departed consider themselves either unaffiliated or Evangelical Protestants.[8] The decline has been operative for a few decades with approximately a 12 percent decline since 2010. In the same period the Evangelical Protestants have had an increase of 4 percent, and the unaffiliated an increase of 8 percent. The study breaks down the change by gender, age, education, foreign born, and those born in the United States. Insofar as age is concerned, there is a 15 percent decline among those aged 18-29, and a 14 percent decline among those aged 30-49. While the decline of Catholic affiliation is more pronounced among younger generations of Hispanics, 44 percent of Catholics under the age of 50 are Hispanic. Those who have completed high school share the same 14 percent as those who have gone to college. There is a 15 percent decline among the foreign born, and an 8 percent decline among those born in the United States.

While the decline should be reason for concern, we also need to be aware that the Hispanic community makes up an increasing large share of the US Catholic population. The Pew Research surveys states that 33 percent of the US Catholic population is Hispanic. We must be conscious that not all Hispanic Catholics agree with all that the Church teaches: 72 percent disagree with the Church's position on birth control; 64 percent disagree with the Church's view

5 Hoffman Ospino. *Hispanic Ministry in the Twenty-First Century: Present and Future* (Miami, FL: Convivum Press, 2010), Kindle edition.

6 PewResearch Center, May 7, 2014, "The Shifting Religious Identity of Latinos in the United States," http://www.perforum.org/files/2015/05/Latinos-Religion-07-22-full-report.pdf (accessed June 15, 2014).

7 "This I ask you: be shepherds, with the "odor of the sheep", make it real, as shepherds among your flock, fishers of men." Pope Francis, Homily at the Chrism Mass, March 28, 2013.

8 See Pew, "Shifting Religious Identity of Latinos," 5.

on divorce and remarriage; 57 percent seldom or never go to confession. However a great majority, 70 percent, have a devotion to Mary and/or the Saints. An increasing number of Hispanic Catholics consider themselves to have some association with the Catholic Charismatic Renewal.[9]

The Hispanic community is perceived as one which values the role of the family, especially of an extended family with the *abuelos, tios* and *primos*. At the same time, the value of marriage and its importance is questionable, with nearly 42 percent of Hispanic children in the United States born out of wedlock, and half of the births to Hispanic women are to single mothers.[10] A significant number of couples are either living together in concubinage, or married outside of the required canonical form.

In spite of the cultural differences there is the common threat to faith and language that unites the Hispanic experience. Father Virgilio Elizondo captures the essence of this unity in his book *Galilean Journey: The Mexican-American Promise*: "Our Mexican-American people is everywhere; and, as different as we are from one another, we are a distinct people, we have a common soul. *Somos un pueblo*!"[11]

II – Where does Ministry to Hispanics take place?

Ministry to the Hispanic community takes place in several modalities depending on the way that it has been constituted in each diocese.

The predominant place for ministry is the parish or quasi-parish, whether it be territorial or personal. Most ministry takes place in territorial parishes. In some dioceses and cities, the presence of Hispanics is great and several parishes minister to the community. In other dioceses ministry takes place in designated parishes although not officially erected as personal parishes. In the Diocese of Camden several parishes were combined into one: the decree established the new parish as both territorial and personal – personal for the Spanish speaking community of the city; territorial for everyone else.[12]

The parish is the best setting for ministry to take place, as "the parish offers an obvious example of the apostolate on the community level inasmuch as it brings together the many human differences within its boundaries and merges

9 See Ospino.

10 Ibid.

11 Virgilio Elizondo, *Galilean-Journey: The Mexican American Promise*. (Maryknoll, NY: Orbis Books, 1983), Kindle edition.

12 Establishment of Divine Mercy Parish in Vineland, NJ. http://divinemercyparishvld.com/?page_id=1339 (accessed October 27, 2014).

them into the universality of the Church."[13] This merging into the universality of the Church presents a great gift and challenge when multiple cultural realities are found within the local parish. The influx of new membership is not always welcomed as it challenges the status-quo of the community. The presence of new cultures demands a certain openness and willingness to change. My experience has shown that this is not an easy task, not only between Hispanics and other cultural entities, but among Hispanics themselves. I have ministered in several parishes in New Mexico where there has been a constant tension between the Hispanics whose families have been in the area for generations, and the Hispanics that constitute the group of "new arrivals" from Mexico. It was not always a welcoming experience. I have experienced the same in Cincinnati with the lack of welcoming of Hispanics by the non-Hispanic community. This lack of welcoming has been from the faithful as well as the clergy.

There are other models of ministry also present in other dioceses. One of those models that I am familiar with is where ministry is organized around "centers" where migrants can gather to worship and be Church. While some of the "centers of ministry" are located within a parish, or use the parish facilities, they are not necessarily considered to be part of the parish community but as a quasi-standalone community. This type of ministerial organization seems to be in line with the Apostolic Constitution of Pius XII, *Exul Familia.*[14] Chapter 4 (numbers 32-40) of that Constitution directed local ordinaries to provide for migrants within their dioceses whether they had a domicile, quasi-domicile, or no domicile at all. Efforts were to be made to entrust priests of their language or nationality with the care of migrants and to supply them with the same authority as that of a pastor.

In the Archdiocese of Cincinnati, where I worked for many years in Hispanic ministry, the model used was centers of ministry or mission not directly connected to a parish. One of the places of ministry is a church that once served as a parish church. That parish community was suppressed and the church building was given to the care of the Hispanic community as a center of ministry but not as a parish. The sacramental records are kept at the territorial parish: there is no further involvement from the territorial parish in the ministry. The priest in charge is referred as a "pastor," although canonically he is not one: he is better identified as a rector with the authority of a pastor for that community. In another location, the place where I was ministering used the buildings of the local territorial parish, but it was considered a separate ministry that simply used the space of the parish. Rent was paid by the Hispanic ministry to the parish for the use of the church, office and parish hall. Slowly the pastor and I began to work toward

---

13 Paul VI, Decree on the Apostolate of the Laity, *Apostolicam Actuositatem*, November 18, 1965, no. 10, www.vatican.va/.../vat-ii_decree_1965118_apostolicam-actuositatem_en.html (accessed June 15, 2014).

14 Pius XII, Apostolic Constitution, *Exul Familia*, August 1, 1952, http://www.papalencyclicals.net/Pius12/p12exsul.html (accessed June 15, 2014).

an integration of both communities as one parish community. I have been gone for over three years and the process is not yet completed.

I am also aware of another place, not to be named to protect the guilty parties, where the local pastor did not allow Hispanics to use his new parish building for fear that it would be trashed. He would allow the Hispanic community to celebrate the Eucharist in the parish hall as long as there were no other "parish" activities that would preclude the Hispanics from using the place. I believe that situation has already been dealt with, but I mentioned it because these situations are encountered in our dioceses when dealing with Hispanics or other minorities. These situations do not speak well of the universality of the Church.

There might be other models of ministry to the Hispanic community that I am not aware of. The important issue is that ministry takes place in a way that the gifts are honored, challenges are dealt with, and ultimately, the rights of people to the spiritual goods of the Church are provided for (cf. canons 213, 214).

III – Language of Ministry and the Liturgical Books

Spanish is the main language of ministry to Hispanics in the United States. Yet we need to be aware that among those who are second or third generation Hispanics born in the United States, the use of Spanish as a main language has dropped. In January 1985 Spanish was established as an official liturgical language in the United States.[15] Prior to this the use of liturgical books in Spanish was ruled by a decree of the National Conference of Catholic Bishops of April 2, 1964 and confirmed by the Apostolic see: other vernacular languages were permitted in the celebration with a congregation as long as the approved translations of the particular language were used. The end result was a lack of uniformity as liturgical books from Spain, Mexico, Argentina, etc., were being used. To this day we see different books being used from one parish to another at the discre-

---

15 On September 11, 1984, the Administrative Committee approved Spanish as a liturgical language for the United States. The approval of Spanish as a Liturgical language in the United States would enable the National Conference of Bishops to exercise authority over the texts use in the Spanish language in the dioceses of the United States. The Congregation for Divine Worship confirmed the decision (Prot. CD 382/84) and was communicated to the Bishop James W. Malone, president of the conference, in a letter dated January 19, 1985. It is worth noting some of the points made in the letter of confirmation:

> 1. This Congregation approves that a single version of Spanish-language liturgical books, approved by the National Conference of Catholic Bishops and confirmed by the Apostolic See be available for uniform use in the dioceses of the United States of America.
>
> 2. In order not to multiply further the different versions of the same texts, it would be preferable if the Spanish text for use in the United States of America, especially as regards the celebration of the Mass and the Sacraments, be a version already approved by an Episcopal Conference and confirmed by the Apostolic See.

tion of the presider even for those liturgical rites that have approved books for use in the Dioceses of the United States.

The arduous work of preparing a set of Spanish-language liturgical books for the United States has been a long haul, and the process continues.[16] As liturgical books are promulgated, the use of liturgical books from other Spanish-speaking Episcopal Conferences is supposed to cease, although that is not what is taking place. The approved books are not being used mainly due to a lack of awareness of their availability, and partially due to some poor language or editorial decisions in the translations themselves. It is worth noting that the Congregation for Divine Worship and the Discipline of the Sacraments did not grant approval for a Spanish translation for the *Book of Blessings* for the United States.[17]

In an effort to deal with a multicultural presence, abridged bilingual liturgical books have also been published. My experience with these abridged liturgical books is mixed: I have found them to be helpful during bilingual celebrations, yet have found them lacking when the chapter or portion of the rite that I need is the one that has been left out of the abridged publication. Not too long ago I was asked to preside at a funeral at a parish for a Hispanic child. The parish informed me that they had the Spanish books and that there was no need for me to bring my own. When I got there the bilingual funeral rite was the one that the parish had. Unfortunately, the chapters on funerals for children were omitted from the official abridged bilingual edition.

It is proper to include a note regarding bilingual celebrations. The ideal situation is that the liturgical celebrations are celebrated in one main language. However, there is often a need to have multiple language celebrations in order to emphasize the unity of the community in its diversity – e.g. the Easter Triduum and

16 Liturgical Books published by the United States Conference of Catholic Bishops: *Cuidado Pastoral de los Enfermos: Ritos de la Unción y del Viático* (1984); *Rito de la Iniciación Cristiana de Adultos* (Confirmed of period of five years 11-6-1990 PN 770/99), *Ritual de las Exequias Cristianas* (1999, PN 1551/93/L), *Order of Blessing for the Fifteenth Birthday* (2007 PN 1709/05/L), *Ritual del Matrimonio* (recognition 9/25/2008, PN 1707/05/L, effective date of use September 2010); *Rito de Bendición de una Creature en el Vientre* (Recognitio 12/8/2011 PN 1422/08/L), *Leccionario* (Recognitio 6/12/2013, PN 69/10/L not yet in print but to be published by the USCCB with a must use date of Pentecost 2015 (5/24/2015). However, there are indications that the publication would not be done on time due to typographical errors on the manuscript). The *Misal Romano for the United States* is still in Rome for a recognitio.

17 Congregation for Divine Worship and the Discipline of the Sacraments, March 9, 2012, Protocol Number 539/11/L.

some special diocesan or parochial celebrations. The United States Conference of Catholic Guidelines has issued guidelines in preparing these celebrations.[18]

IV - Issues Regarding Individual Sacraments

Insofar as the sacraments are concerned, I do not believe that there are canonical issues that are specific and uniquely "Hispanic." The issues and concerns cross the multifaceted reality of the Church. As canonists we look at the concerns and issues from the perspective of the norm of law. And the norm of law is the same universally for all, regardless of culture or language. At the same time, the cultural issues play a role in the way a given sacrament may be celebrated or at least the celebrations surrounding a given sacrament. Culture and traditional practices from the place of origin do dress up the celebrations giving it a full flavor of the enculturation of the liturgy.

Baptism

Most of the issues regarding the celebration of baptism center on the *padrinos* – godparents. The norm of law is clearly established in canons 872 through 874. This is an area where sensitivity is needed as there is a misunderstanding by some of the role of the *padrinos*. It is not unusual to hear from parents that the choice of *padrino* is prompted by a desire to identify who would take care of the child if they were deported, or if some other tragedy came upon them. A careful conversation regarding the protection of the child's best interest through the means of legal documentation, such as a power of attorney, rather than a godparent who shares the faith with the parents and the child, is often needed. One must take into consideration that in this culture to accept an invitation to be a *padrino/madrina* is to accept an invitation to be a part of the family: a relationship of *compadre/comadre* (coparents) is established. The *compadrazgo* establishes a lifelong relationship not only with the child, but with the parents as well. The *compadres* become members of the nuclear family. The establishing of this bond must be kept in mind as parents indicate that they have not baptized their child because they do not know whom to ask to be godparents. Also one must understand that it is a way of honoring friends. I have seen situations in which

18 From http://www.usccb.org/prayer-and-worship/the-mass/frequently-asked-questions/guidelines-for-a-multilingual-celebration-of-mass.cfm: In 1987, the Instituto Nacional Hispano de Liturgia and the Federation of Diocesan Liturgical Commissions collaborated to produce guidelines for multilingual Masses. The USCCB Committee on Divine Worship's Subcommittee on Divine Worship in Spanish revised them in January 2013. The purpose of these guidelines is to assist parishes and other communities faced with multicultural and multilingual celebrations of the Eucharist. These guidelines arise out of the experience of many parish liturgists, priests, and diocesan worship offices in their planning and celebration of such liturgies, and from a respect for the liturgical principles which comprise the rites of the Roman Missal. With the permission of the Federation of Diocesan Liturgical Commissions, these guidelines are revised and reprinted as a resource of the USCCB Secretariat of Divine Worship (accessed June 15, 2014).

the *padrino/madrina* impose themselves on the parents by declaring themselves. Sensitivity is needed, and at times permissions, when one who does not fulfill all the requirements of the canons has been chosen. However, care and due diligence needs to be exercised because any information concerning an exemption will be shared with the members of the community. Soon others would expect that same exemption and would question the minister, "Why did you allow it for them and not for us?"

Another concern is the post-baptismal request to change godparents when the relationship between the parties goes sour, or when the godparents no longer practice the Catholic faith. While the historical reality of who the godparents were when the sacrament was celebrated cannot be changed, there might be pastoral reasons to allow for a substitute in order to take on the responsibility of those who are no longer able to do so. Such a solution should not be used when the concern is with a relationship that has been broken due to some tensions or issues, or in those situations when the parties involved should be called to reconciliation. Some mediation can be offered to help them resolved their issues to the best of their abilities. However, when the original *padrinos* can no longer fulfill their obligation due to an abandonment of the faith, a substitute can be used. The substitute should be one who is able and willing to fulfill the office that was entrusted to another. The possibility of "substitute godparents" is addressed in a reply of November 13, 1984 from the Congregation of the Sacraments.[19]

A request is sometimes made to use more than one set of *padrinos*. Such a request can be based on two possible issues. First, the inability of the parents to say "no" to someone who wishes to be the *padrino/madrina*, or the inability to exercise their right to make a choice. Second, the culture honors as *padrinos* those who are contributing to the party after the celebration. Proper instruction should be done, and aid given to the parents, so the most suitable *padrinos* can be chosen according to the norms of the canons. At times the request for two *padrinos* or two *madrinas* is made, that is to say, two godparents of the same sex – a request that is not envisioned in the present canons. In the reply mentioned above, the Congregation saw no spiritual benefit to the child to warrant a dispensation from

19 In a reply from the Congregation for the Sacraments, 13 November 1984, Prot. Num 1032/84 reported in *Canon Law Digest* Volume 11, page 193, the following appears:

> 3. The nomination of a new sponsor by the bishop to take the place of the original sponsor who presented the candidate for baptism (c. 872) in the event of incapacity or death, is not foreseen in the new code, indeed it is specifically excluded for just reasons.
>
> There is nothing, however, to prevent the diocesan bishop for just reasons, from nominating even officially a *substitute* (emphasis on the original) of the sponsor who could be inscribed on the same baptismal register.

the norm of law of not allowing more than two godparents, and of one being a male and the other a female.[20]

An increasing problem is the baptism of Hispanic Catholics in other churches or ecclesial communities. Often the fact is discovered when the parents present the child for other sacraments of initiation. Non-Catholic communities often lack a strict interpretation regarding *padrinos* and allow parents to baptize their children without any specific requirements, and with the promise that it is "all the same." While such parents could incur the penalties mention in canon 1366,[21] all efforts should be made to reconcile them with the Church and to avoid the issues that could lead to a further alienation from the Church. The child should be welcome to the Church through the Rite of Christian Initiation for Children.

I believe that it would also be important to make some comments regarding the keeping of baptismal records. This can be addressed from two different perspectives. First, the recording of a baptism that takes place here in the United States, and second, obtaining a certificate from other countries.

When the sacrament is being celebrated in the United States, I strongly encourage a copy of the birth certificate be asked as a normal operating practice. First of all, the practice aids in verifying the information that is given with the proper spelling of names; it also ensures that the correct country of origin is placed in the baptismal book. I have seen a couple of situations where the child was being presented as being born in the United States when that was not true. The presentation of a birth certificate also gives the opportunity to check for possible errors in the birth certificate that might need to be corrected. I have spent a lot of time and energy at the probate courts of Butler County, Ohio, helping parents correct mistakes found in their children's birth certificates. Many times the errors are a result of language barriers at the hospital and the disparity of practice for the registration of a birth between the United States and Mexico. In Mexico, the official registration takes place at the court: the parents are to present their child within a year of birth, so the information given at the hospital might not be fully correct.[22] In some cases we encounter women who enter the hospital under an assumed name due to their immigration status. Other times the errors are due to the lack of knowledge regarding naming practices in the United States and the Latin American Countries. In Hispanic countries there is a convention of naming a child with two last names: the first, corresponding to the father, and the second,

20 Ibid. 2. In the case presented one can see neither a just cause nor a spiritual benefit for the baptismal candidate why the bishop should in virtue of canon 85, dispense from the norms which regulate the number and sex of the sponsors (c. 873).

21 Can. 1366: "Parents or those who take the place of parents who hand over their children to be baptized or educated in a non-Catholic religion are to be punished with a censure or other just penalty."

22 I have seen several birth certificates indicating that the child was registered 10 to 15 years after birth.

corresponding to the mother. Only the first of the two last names is carried to the next generation. Many women, when asked for their maiden name, confused it with the maternal last name. Corrections of the certificates are important for the sake of legal documentation and the possibility of dual nationalities. I must say that I have encountered more significant and serious errors where a male child was registered as a female, and a female child, as a male. In both cases the parents did not notice the error until the child was of school age.

Insofar as records from Mexico and other countries are concerned, significant efforts should be made to try to locate them. Ask for all the information necessary, including the closest main city to the place of birth. Verify the information given regarding the inability to obtain the record. For many the inability is simply the absence of a family member to visit the parish and personally obtain the certificate. The issue of correctness is also a serious problem. Recently, I dealt with a case where the baptismal certificate could not be located. The person had gone through life without a father and did not know who the biological father was. The certificate of birth had the individual as a child of a single mother with an unknown father. However, in the record of baptism, the name of a man as the father had been inserted. Luckily an aunt found a copy of the baptismal certificate that revealed the problem. Please verify with diocesan offices if indeed the parish in question was burnt or destroyed in some other natural disaster. Yes, there are cases where indeed a record cannot be found, and affidavits may be needed in accord with the norms of canon 876.[23]

Confirmation

There are two issues that I want to address regarding the sacrament of confirmation. First, the age of celebration. When you receive a certificate of confirmation, or see the annotation in the baptismal register, you may notice that it was celebrated while the child was an infant.[24] The long-standing custom of confirming below the age of seven was practiced in Spain and many of the Latin American countries. As far as I have been able to research, after the promulgation of the 1983 code most Episcopal Conferences of Latin America, including Spain, had determined an age for confirmation that was higher than seven years

23 Can. 876: "To prove the conferral of baptism, if prejudicial to no one, the declaration of one witness beyond all exception is sufficient or the oath of the one baptized if the person received baptism as an adult."

24 Cf. Age of Confirmation, Canon 788, Response form the Code Commission, *CLD* I: 348-349. The response was in the affirmative that the old practice in Spain and South America could continue.

old, although an argument can be developed in favor of the centennial and immemorial practice.[25]

Second, the issue of receiving a new name at confirmation. While there is a common practice in the United States to take on a new name at confirmation, the practice is not found in most Latin American countries. At least, that was not the practice in Cuba when I was confirmed, nor is it a common practice in Mexico. I am open to be being wrong on this topic. What I have found is a strange reaction when the idea of a confirmation name is proposed. While the act of not taking a new name speaks highly of the continuation of the sacraments of initiation, sometimes the name given at birth has no connection with the faith, and for an individual to take on the name of a patron saint or theological virtue would be helpful in their journey of faith.

First Eucharist

The celebration of the *Primera Comunión* is a big event in the life of a child. Adults who for some reason did not receive their first Eucharist often feel that it is too late for them to do so.

One of the issues frequently encountered is the request for *padrinos de la Primera Comunión* – that is, sponsors for First Communion. This practice is not universal. While I use the English word "sponsor," the proper word in Spanish is *padrino*. Please do not use *esponsores.*[26] The sponsor is one who accompanies the child to receive the Eucharist. It would make perfect sense if the sponsors were also the godparents of baptism, but this often is not the case. I have encountered the presentation of sponsors of first Eucharist who are not Catholics, or Catholics who are in an irregular union and cannot receive the Eucharist. Several parishes that I have consulted do allow *padrinos* of first Eucharist, and have no regulations regarding who can be in this role. I am not aware of any diocese that has regulations regarding the *padrinos* of first Eucharist. My practice has been not to allow them; partly because not all families request them, and partially because oftentimes the person chosen is not able to receive the sacraments. I have been successful in explaining to the parents that it is not a practice in the United States and that the law does not provide for such a role. At the same time

25 The Confirmation Policy for the Archdiocese of Santa Fe includes the following footnote: "The Archbishop of Santa Fe reserves the right to confirm infants (those under the age of 7) in accord with the centenary and immemorial custom established in New Mexico (c. 26). Requests are to be made directly to the Archbishop." See http://www.archdiocesesatafe.org/Offices/SacramentalPolicies/Confirmation.pdf (accessed June 15, 2014).

26 In the approved RCIA Rites in Spanish for the United States and in the Rite for Quinceañeras the word "esponsores" is used. The word is not found in the official dictionary of the *Real Academia Española.* However there is an entry with the English spelling "sponsor" to indicate someone who sponsors an event. See htttp://www.rae.es/ (accessed June 15, 2014).

I informed them that there is nothing preventing them from having honorary *padrinos* who would help with the festivities, but who would not sit or walk with the child during the celebration at the church. If a parish community decides to allow *padrinos* of first Eucharist there should be some regulations regarding the ability of the person to participate fully in the Eucharistic celebration.

In many of the Hispanic celebrations of first Eucharist, the child carries a candle. I have had mixed experiences with the practice. I do recall using one at my own first Communion. If all those who are receiving first Eucharist are Hispanics, and the parents have such a practice, it might be good to keep the practice and somehow connect it to the light of Christ received at baptism. However, in a mixed group, it would be important to seek some sense of uniformity for all.

Marriage

In the celebration of marriage there are a lot of cultural issues that come to take place. I will address only a few that I have encountered. There might be many others from your experience with Hispanics from different areas.

One common element is the use of *arras*. The Spanish ritual includes an exchange of coins. Usually there are thirteen coins that are exchanged back and forth. The official *Ritual del Matrimonio* approved for the United States has a blessing and exchange of the *arras* that is to be done after the blessing and exchange of the rings. After the blessing of the coins, the groom takes the coins and gives them to the bride, who in turn gives them back to the groom. During the exchange they say to each other: "Receive these coins as a sign of God's blessing and the goods that we will share."[27]

Similarly the use of a veil or a *lazo* is found in the approved liturgical books. In Spain, Cuba, and other countries, it takes the form of a veil that is placed over the head of the bride and the shoulder of the groom. In Mexico it takes the form of a rope, or a double rosary, that is placed upon the shoulders of both the bride and groom. This practice symbolizes the bond that now unites the parties. The veil/*lazo* is usually placed just before the Lord's Prayer at the Nuptial Mass. The rite for the United States calls for a blessing of the veil/*lazo* by the priest, and after the blessing, those who have been designated for this purpose[28] place the veil or *lazo* on the parties, then the Lord's Prayer is recited. The recitation of the Lord's Prayer is followed by the nuptial blessing. The rite does not indicate when the veil or *lazo* is removed; the common practice is just after the nuptial blessing but before the exchange of the sign of peace.[29]

27 Cf. *Ritual del Matrimonio*, Conferencia de Obispos de los Estados Unidos, 2010. Liturgical Press. Numbers 67b, 101b, 133.

28 In Mexico they are referred as *Padrinos del Lazo*

29 *Ritual del Matrimonio*, Conferencia de Obispos Católicos de los Estados Unidos 2010, Numbers 71b, 103b, 137

I just want to add a note regarding the attendants at a wedding. Sometimes it seems that the number of attendants, bridesmaids and groomsmen, is very large. A common practice, at least among Mexicans, is to invite as attendants all of those who are responsible for some aspect of the celebrations. They are referred as *padrinos* of a given object, or of the gift that they are providing. Be careful in reducing the numbers – especially at the last minute. I have encountered a couple of situations where the parties did not want to have a rehearsal, and on the day of the wedding, the entire family – both sides – were the *padrinos* wanting to be in the procession. Being upfront with the couple regarding the parish policy does help.

I believe that a note should be made regarding the marriages of undocumented immigrants. At times there is a difficulty in some counties in obtaining a marriage license due to the request for a social security number. The Catholic Legal Immigration Network has issued a statement regarding the inability of states to deny marriage licenses to undocumented immigrants.[30] When the difficulty to obtain a license is presented in a given county, there can be recourse to another county within the state. I am speaking of true difficulty, not of fear that the county clerk would report a case to immigration authorities. Some have proposed making use of institutes of law such as secret marriages found in c. 1130, the extraordinary form found in c. 1116, or seeking the permission of the local Ordinary as found in c. 1071 §1, 2° for a marriage that cannot be recognized or celebrated in accord with the norms of civil law. I will caution about making a rash decision to use one of these institutes without a proper search that the license has indeed been denied. I have taken the time to accompany the parties to the county clerk's office and established a working relationship with the staff to deal with the more difficult situations. With regard to the use of the institute of secret marriages, the secret will be very difficult to keep. I know of a particular situation where the parties agreed to keep and maintain the secret. After the celebration the minister and the two witnesses were invited to the couple's home for a meal. When the minister arrived he found the rest of the family waiting at home to celebrate the marriage that had just taken place secretly at the Church. The risks of allowing marriages that cannot be celebrated in accord with the norms of civil law have to be weighed in light of possible civil penalties incurred by the minister and/or the diocese. The canonical option is there if indeed the marriage cannot be recognized or celebrated in accord with the norms of civil law: this institute is not for cases where the couple, for whatever reason, does not want their marriage recognized by the civil authorities. The question should always be whether indeed there is a prohibition that impedes the celebration in the civil forum. In most cases that I have encountered, it is a matter of avoidance or fear, but not of inability.

30 "Undocumented Immigrants and the Right to Marry", https://cliniclegal.org/sites/default/files/Unauthorized%20Immigrants%20and%20the%20Right%20to%20Marry%20update%2010-26-10%20update%2012-13-11%20(2).pdf (accessed September 15, 2014).

V - Other Non-Sacramental Celebrations

There are other celebrations in connection with the Church that are expressions of the faith and culture of the Hispanic Community. Of great importance are the celebrations surrounding life and death – from birthday celebrations to anniversaries, and remembrance of the dead. Among the celebrations of life and birthdays, two have a special significance in some communities: the presentation of a child at the age of three and the *Quinceañeras*.

The presentation of a child at age three has increased in some areas. In some places it is reserved to girls honoring the Presentation of the Blessed Mother at the Temple at the age of three. However, the present practice as I have encountered it is for both boys and girls. There are no specific rituals; I simply use the blessing of a baptized child. When the request is made for a non-baptized child, I have encouraged the parents to baptize the child and let the celebration of the sacrament of baptism be the presentation. For some families the practice is quite elaborate with special dresses for the girls and formal wear for the boys.

The celebration of *Quinceañeras* also differs between nation and region. The United States has received approval from the Holy See for a rite of blessing for the fifteenth birthday. I am not aware of any other country that has an official rite or blessing with a *recognitio* from the Holy See. Parishes should have clear rules of what they will or will not allow in such celebrations. Care should be taken that it does not resemble a wedding. The number of attendants varies, as well as their role in the celebration. It was the practice in the community that I served not to allow the attendants to be in the procession, but to have the girl accompanied by her parents and *padrinos* of baptism.

With regard to celebrations of those who have "gone before us marked with the sign of faith," the celebration of the funeral is primary. Each cultural group has their own way to deal with the death of a loved one, and the pastoral solicitude of the Church should be present to the family during this difficult time. Working closely with the family is of great importance. It is my experience ministering among Mexican immigrants that they will want to return the body to Mexico for burial. Being aware of some of the difficulties that the family may encounter with such a decision is very useful. Make sure that they are aware of the closest consulate office and that they can access their services. The consulate can help in choosing a funeral home that is familiar with procedures. However, be careful with requests for monetary assistance as it can lead to abuse. It has been my practice to work with the funeral home to make sure that the information given is correct and that the person requesting it is indeed the responsible party. Often there are nine days of prayers that follow either the death or the funeral. There are several guides for the celebrations of the *novenarios,* including one that is published by Liguori Publications.

In dealing with death, one cannot ignore the cultural celebrations of the *Dias de los Muertos*, the day of the dead. These celebrations often include a Mass at a local cemetery or creating an altar of remembrance for the departed.

Hispanic religious experience is marked by the use of sacramentals and popular piety. Again each nation or region has its own ways of celebrating.

First, a note regarding the use of sacramentals and blessings of objects. It is my practice to ask what the object would be used for. Abuses do creep into the use of blessed objects, and superstitious beliefs abound. The problem is that most requests happen after Mass when there is no time to enter into a meaningful conversation with those involved.

Devotions to Mary are an important aspect of the Hispanic presence. Each nation or region has invocation or devotion to the Blessed Mother which is dear to them. The most common of all is the celebration of Our Lady of Guadalupe. The celebrations of Mary cannot be underestimated in ministering to the Hispanic population.

Devotions to the saints are also important. Once again this is localized and many requests may come from different cities to celebrate their patronal feast. Pastoral sensitivity should be used in accepting and denying a celebration. Be aware that once a practice is established, it is difficult to stop without alienating people.

As canonists and pastoral ministers, we should look at these celebrations as moments of evangelization. The guiding norm should be the "Directory on Popular Piety and the Liturgy: Principles and Guidelines" issued by the Congregation for Divine Worship in December of 2001.

Conclusion

These reflections are offered not as the last word on the issues of Hispanic ministry, but as a means to keep a conversation and discussion going regarding the many issues that are encountered when ministering to such a diverse culture and people.

I am not the expert on these matters, just one minister who has had to struggle to find ways to minister to the people that have been entrusted to my care by the Lord through the Church. I am simply one who has been asked by the Convention Planning Committee to address some of the issues involved, but primarily I am willing to be taught by others. Keep always in mind that there is not one answer that fits all, just as there is not one way to minister. As canonists we are guided by canon 1752, keeping before one's eyes that salvation of souls is the supreme law of the Church.

Seminar

From Generation to Generation: Challenge and Opportunity[1]

Sr. Patricia Wittberg, SC, PhD

I would like to begin this morning with a little mental/emotional exercise. How many of you graduated from high school in or around 1985? Just raise your hands. How many of you graduated from high school in or around 1975? In or around 1965? 1955? When those of you who graduated in the middle 1980's were seniors in high school, what was your impression of 1956? Of the clothing/hair styles of the mid-1950's? Of its music/slang? Of that era's overall "out-of-dateness"? How long ago was 1956 to you, emotionally? When those of you who graduated in the middle 1970's were seniors in high school, what was your impression of 1936 – right in the middle of the Great Depression? How long ago did that feel to you? For those of you who graduated in the middle 1960's, think about 1916 – how long ago did that feel to you when you were high school seniors? And for those of you who graduated in the middle 1950's, think of 1896. The point that I would like to make is that *the year you graduated from high school is that long ago to the class of 2014.*

Each generation is a *culture* – a specific way of looking at the world, a set of unquestioned assumptions, values, ways of talking, material artifacts such as dress, communications devices, etc. We can think of generational cultures as similar to ethnic cultures such as the cultures of African Americans, Latinos, or Appalachian whites. The Church has been called, ever since the second chapter of the Acts of the Apostles, to preach the Gospel to every people and nation in their own language: in words, symbols, and actions that will resonate with their particular culture. I would argue that, just as there are workshops to help Church people do this for various *ethnic groups* – to learn their language, to appreciate their values, to welcome them into our parishes, so must we make similar efforts to learn about generational cultures.

1 This presentation is based on Patricia Wittberg, *Catholic Cultures: How Parishes Can Respond to the Changing Faces of Catholicism Today*, forthcoming from Liturgical Press.

Where do generational cultures come from? According to sociologist Karl Mannheim,[2] two key formative factors shape a generation's worldview:

1. Our parents' environment before our birth: The kind of childhood experiences, and what was happening when our parents entered adulthood, affected the way they were to raise us when we were children.

2. Our childhood environment. We get this from our parents, whether or not our parents intend to impart a particular message to us. Children are like little sponges: just by observing the adults around them, they pick up an optimistic or a pessimistic view of the future, priorities about what things are important or unimportant (money, material things/toys, family togetherness, religion ...), and basic assumptions about how the world works. We do not question this worldview while we are children – it becomes the basic background from which we think and act.

3. Societal conditions at the beginning of our adulthood. At around age 18, we become cognitively able, for the first time, to form our own opinion on the childhood worldview we had absorbed unreflectively. We accept what seems right/true/consistent with the reality we see, and we reject what seems wrong/ inconsistent.

After we have formed our first adult opinions, Mannheim said, *these become the lenses through which we see the world ever afterward.* We engage in what Chris Mooney[3] describes as "motivated reasoning" – our previous opinions/emotions influence how we approach new facts. We disproportionately pay attention to information which supports our point of view and resist that which disconfirms it. Also, most people have a "social desirability bias" – we find disagreeing with all of our friends too unpleasant, so we tend to adopt the same opinions they do. As part of our bonding with them, we tell and re-tell each other stories/jokes/ metaphors, which reinforce the reasons why *our way* is the correct and logical way to think/act.

As an example of how this works out in real life (for white, middle class Americans, at least – there are also generational cultures for the African American community, for working class whites, for Iranians, Chinese, etc.), we might consider someone who was born in the 1920's and grew up in the Great Depression. Such a person would absorb in childhood attitudes that money is tight, that leftovers should never be wasted, that family and community are precious

2 Karl Mannheim, "The Problem of Generations," pp. 276-320 in Karl Mannheim, *Essays in the Sociology of Knowledge* (New York: Oxford University Press, 1952).

3 Chris Mooney, "The Science of Why We Don't Believe Science." *Mother Jones*, April 18, 2011. Downloaded from http://motherjones.com/print/106166.

resources to help out in hard times. With regard to the Catholic Church, many grew up in solely Catholic cultures – it may have been rare for them even to see a non-Catholic. When they came of age during World War II, they learned to sacrifice even more for a noble cause. These formative experiences would shape that generation's life ever afterward: They would save money and avoid going into debt, re-use plastic bags, give their kids the toys they themselves never had, respect government and authority, support keeping America militarily strong, and so forth. Leaving the Church is likely to be unthinkable to them: Catholicism has been bred into their blood and bones, so to speak.

But what growing up experiences will their 1950's era children have? They will be fortunate enough to experience material security – but have to hide under their desks during nuclear bomb drills. Their parents will expect them to respect civil and religious authority – while they consult Dr. Spock's child care book on how to foster their children's independence and initiative. And *The Baltimore Catechism* answers and the Latin Mass responses they had to memorize as children did not seem to favor independence and initiative very much! When these children turned eighteen in the 1960's, they had questions which targeted the inconsistencies in their upbringing – inconsistencies between what their parents said and what how they acted; inconsistencies between what they learned at home and at school and how changes in the larger society were rendering these lessons outdated. All upbringings have such inconsistencies. The 1960's young adults thus began to ask questions like:

- Could working all day in the same office job for forty years really fulfill one's need for a deeper meaning and purpose to life?

- Why save money if you have never experienced need as a child, or if inflation erodes the value of both debt and savings?

- How could America claim to be such a good country when it denied civil rights to African Americans or waged war in Viet Nam?

- Why build up military strength when it could lead to a nuclear holocaust?

And so we find the 1960's – antiwar protests, hippies, gurus, LSD, and so forth.

When generational shifts happen, the previous generation is often aghast. The young seem to be cavalierly discarding the very values and practices which their elders had worked so hard to defend. Even more confusingly, they often "mix and match" beliefs which their elders had assigned to opposite ideological camps, accepting some and refusing others. The elder generation has usually become so accustomed to viewing the world through one set of assumptions and values that they find it impossible to understand why the younger generation does not see things the same way.

Each generation thus has a distinct mindset or way of evaluating and approaching the world and the Church, which is layered on top of class, ethnic and other subcultural perspectives. While some authors divide things differently or use different terminology, most writers label the generational cohorts among white middle-class Americans as follows:

- The "Greatest Generation" (born 1915-1929)
- The "Silent Generation" (born 1930-1945)
- The "Baby Boomers" (born 1946-1961), often divided in half into "older" and "younger" cohorts born either before or after 1955.
- Generation X (born 1962-1981)
- The "Millennials" (born 1982-1995)
- A "Post-Millennial" Generation (born after 1995)

Catholic researchers have demarcated these generations slightly differently: combining most of the Greatest and Silent generations into one "Pre-Vatican II Generation" (born before 1943), and the rest of the Silent Generation and the Baby Boomers into a "Vatican II Generation" (born between 1943 and 1960) – a reflection of the profound effect of the second Vatican Council on American Catholics. The table[4] I have handed out describes some of the different experiences of Church which have formed each generation. Remember, however, that there are no hard and fast division points between the generations: at the edges, they blend into each other.

Passing the Faith from Generation to Generation

Pre-Vatican II Catholics

How will each of these generations experience Catholicism? For the Pre-Vatican II Generation and the older Vatican II Generation, Catholicism was in the very air they breathed. Today, the Pre-Vatican II Generation make up the majority of "strong Catholics": between one-half and two-thirds have reported attending Mass weekly or more often in every survey we have taken for the past 25 years, and 41% say they are "highly committed" to the Church. They are the

4 The referenced table was distributed at the 76th Annual Convention of the Canon Law Society of America in St. Louis, Missouri, in October 2014. To obtain a copy, please contact the Canon Law Society of America.

most likely to watch religious TV (42% do so), and to read religious books and periodicals. Compared to American Protestants their age, the Pre-Vatican II generation of Catholics are more strongly attached to their religion.

The Vatican II Generation: Born 1943-1960.

The Vatican II Generation includes most of the Baby Boomers, plus the youngest of the Silent Generation. The defining characteristic of this generational cohort is that its members experienced the changes of Vatican II prior to, or while entering, young adulthood. Like the Baby Boomers who comprise most of this age cohort, the Vatican II Generation could be divided into older and younger halves. The older Vatican II Catholics passed their childhood in the same kind of all-encompassing Catholic culture experienced by the Pre-Vatican II Generation, and they have early memories of the Latin Mass, *The Baltimore Catechism*, parochial schools with only sisters as teachers, and Catholic devotions such as May Crowning, Forty Hours, etc. Those who were born after 1955 are less likely to remember these experiences. The older members of the Vatican II Generation, therefore, experienced the changes that followed the Council as teenagers, and found them to be exciting and liberating when compared to the more traditional Catholicism of their childhood. They enthusiastically embraced guitar Masses and more "relevant" religion classes, and many also began to participate in social justice activities such as the United Farm Workers boycotts or the rallies for peace during the Viet Nam War. Even today, it is the older half of the Vatican II Generation which is disproportionately represented in organizations such as Pax Christi, Voice of the Faithful, or Call to Action. Because they had experienced being surrounded by a Catholic culture in their childhood – however stultifying they may later have defined it as being – they are more likely to remain Catholic and exercise their "voice" for change than they are to "exit" the Church.[5]

Several of the cultural changes which would become more evident in subsequent generations began with the Vatican II Generation. There was an abrupt drop-off in Mass attendance between the Pre-Vatican II and the Vatican II Generations, but only a gradual decline thereafter.[6] Both the Vatican II and later generations of Catholics are barely half as likely as the Pre-Vatican II Catholics to agree that the Catholic Church is the "One True Church," and twice as likely to

5 A. O. Hirschman, *Exit, Voice, and Loyalty: Responses to Decline in Firms, Organizations, and States* (Cambridge, MA: Harvard University Press, 1970).

6 Melissa A. Cidade, "Young Adult Catholics and the Church" Presentation at the Romero Center in Camden, NJ, May 29, 2011. Center for Applied Research in the Apostolate. See also Mark Gray, "C and E Catholics Decoded," CARA 1964 blog, September 6, 2011. http://www.nineteensixty-four.blogspot.com/search?updated-min=2011-01-01T00:00:00-05:00&updated-max=2012-01-01T00:00:00-05:00&max-results=33 (accessed September 27, 2011). Between 58% and 64% of Vatican II, Post-Vatican II, and Millennial Catholics attend Mass only a few times a year; only 36% of Pre-Vatican II Catholics attend that rarely.

believe that women should be ordained.[7] The Vatican II Generation of American Catholics is the first generation to make the distinction between being "spiritual" and being "religious," and the first to evince a sharp decline of trust in the institutional Church.[8] Catholic women of this generation were more likely than any other age cohort, and more likely than men their age, to state that their experiences with the Church had alienated them from it. The younger members of this generation begin to resemble subsequent generations in being more likely to "exit" Catholicism if they are dissatisfied, and less likely to remain and exercise their "voice" for change.[9]

The Post-Vatican II Generation: Born 1961-1981.

This generation is roughly coterminous with Generation X in secular literature. Catholics in this generational cohort received their entire religious formation in the post-Vatican II era. Unlike the previous generations, they had no experience of an all-encompassing Catholic environment to form their religious identity. By the time they were in grade school, the Baltimore Catechism, with its rote memorization, had been discarded in favor of more experiential religious education. Fewer members of this generation attended parochial schools, and few, if any, sisters taught them there. Distinctively Catholic devotions such as May Crowning, Forty Hours, and Benediction had been de-emphasized. "[T]he old system of Catholic faith transmission – which relied on concentrated Catholic residential neighborhoods, ethnic solidarity, strong Catholic schools, religious education designed to reinforce family and parish life, and 'thickly' Catholic cultures, practices, and rituals – had drastically eroded ... yet no alternative approach to effective intergenerational Catholic faith transmission had been devised" to replace it.[10]

The Post-Vatican II Generation's experience of the Church, therefore, was often of an institution in constant and disorienting flux, unable to articulate anything worth believing in. While nineteenth-century Catholics had struggled with the question of what it meant for them to be *American*, the Post-Vatican II Generation had to figure out what it meant for them to be *Catholic*.[11] Like

7 James D. Davidson, Andrea S. Williams, Richard A. Lamanna, Jan Stenftenagel, Kathleen Maas Weigert, William J. Whalen, and Patricia Wittberg, *The Search for Common Ground: What Unites and Divides Catholic Americans* (Huntington, IN: Our Sunday Visitor Press, 1997), 126, 130.

8 Vern L. Bengtson, *Families and Faith: How Religion is Passed Down across Generations* (New York: Oxford University Press, 2013), 31, and John P. Hoffman, "Declining Religious Authority? Confidence in the Leaders of Religious Organizations, 1973-2010," *Review of Religious Research* (2013) vol. 55 no. 1, 1-25.

9 Bengston, 36.

10 Christian Smith, Kyle Longest, Jonathan Hill, and Kari Christoffersen, *Young Catholic America: Emerging Adults In, Out of, and Gone from the Church*. (New York: Oxford University Press, 2014), 26.

11 Ibid., 23

the younger members of the Vatican II Generation, they are deeply suspicious of all institutions, including religious ones, believing them to be predominantly concerned with obsolete rules, with little to say about the world's most pressing problems.[12] Most Post-Vatican II Catholics remain relatively uninformed about religious history or Church teachings and consider religion irrelevant, preferring an eclectic, do-it-yourself spirituality. They are only half as likely as the Vatican II Generation, and less than one-third as likely as the Pre-Vatican II Generation, to say it is important to obey Church teaching they do not understand or agree with.[13] Contrary to the pattern of previous generations, most of the Post-Vatican II Generation have not returned to regular religious practice after they married and began their families.[14]

The Millennials: Born since 1982.

Millennials are two or more generations removed from pre-Vatican II Catholicism. Most have parents from the younger members of the Vatican II Generation or from the older members of the Post-Vatican II Generation, both of whom had had little or no experience with the traditional Catholic practices and catechesis that had formed previous age cohorts. They are the most diverse generation we have ever had. As you can see from Figure #1 on the back of the handout, fewer than half are non-Hispanic whites. So when we speak of Catholic Millennials, we are speaking of at least two different ethnic groups. To speak about non-Hispanic Millennial Catholic whites first of all, studies have found that they are:

- Unschooled in Catholicism – and they rarely practice it. Fewer than one-third of Catholic young adults think of themselves as practicing Catholics, or say that the sacraments are essential to their faith. Two-thirds say that missing Mass on Sunday is OK. As a reflection of this belief, more than one-third rarely or never attend Mass; another one-third do so only a few times a year.[15] And, for the first time, Millennial Catholic women are more likely never to attend Mass than the men are. Between 25-30 percent of Millennials claim no religion at all, and over 50 percent say they are "not religious" and would be embarrassed if anyone thought they were.[16] They associate "religious people" with intolerance and narrow-mindedness. An intolerant mindset deeply conflicts with a second strong Millennial characteristic. They are:

12 Tom Beaudoin, *Virtual Faith: The Irreverent Spiritual Quest of Generation X.* (San Francisco: Jossey-Bass, 1998), 41.

13 Davidson, et al., 127.

14 Mark Silk 2012.

15 Melissa A. Cidade, "Young Adult Catholics and the Church." Power Point presentation delivered at the Romero Center, Camden NJ, May 29, 2011. Available through the Center for Applied Research in the Apostolate, Georgetown University, Washington DC.

16 Robert D. Putnam and David E. Campbell, *American Grace: How Religion Divides and Unites Us*, (New York: Simon and Schuster, 2010) 124. This compares to 5-7% of Silent Generation and 10-15% of Baby Boomers who claim no religion.

- Post-Modern: They are reluctant to say that something is universally true – It might be "True *for me,*" but not for everyone. This includes religious teachings. Fewer than one-fourth say they form their opinions of what is right and wrong by looking at Catholic teaching. Millennials are also:

- Materialistic: In an annual poll conducted of college freshmen every year since the early 1960s, 75% of Millennial freshmen in 2005 said that it was essential or very important for them to be rich, as compared to 62 percent of Gen X freshmen in 1980 or 42 percent of Baby Boomer freshmen in 1966.[17] *The percentage of materialistic freshmen is actually higher at Catholic colleges than it is at non-religious or at evangelical colleges.* Catholic Millennials are less than half as likely as Protestants their age to say that the Bible or religious leaders have "a great deal" of influence on how they think about money.[18] Finally, critics accuse Millennials of being:

- Narcissistic: Sheltered and pampered by their "helicopter parents," they need constant praise and attention.[19]

For the most part, however, Catholic Millennials are not – yet – *anti*-religious. While they are, indeed, less likely to be strongly attached to their faith than Protestant Millennials are – a reversal of what was the case with the Pre-Vatican II Generation – they are also less likely than those raised Protestant to become atheists.[20] At least half strongly agree that they are proud to be Catholic.

But while many Millennials do remain Catholic in name, they are, by and large, only marginally attached to their faith. They are the least likely of all Christian young adults to pray once a day or more, to say that they believe in God, or to claim that their faith is "very" or "somewhat" important in shaping

---

17 John H. Pryor et al., "The American Freshman: Forty Year Trends." Cooperative Institutional Research Program, Higher Education Research Institute, UCLA, 52-53. Accessed via http://gseis.ucla.edu/heri/PDFs/40TrendsManuscript.pdf.

18 Christian Smith, with Melinda Lundquist Denton, *Soul Searching: The Religious and Spiritual Lives of American Teenagers* (New York: Oxford University Press, 2005).

19 Jean M. Twenge and W. Keith Campbell, *The Narcissism Epidemic: Living in the Age of Entitlement* (New York: Free Press, 2009). See also Jean M. Twenge and Joshua D. Foster, "Birth Cohort Increases in Narcissistic Personality Traits among American College Students, 1982-2009." *Social Psychological and Personality Science* 1:1 (2010), 99-106.

20 Mark Gray, "Young Adult Catholics Haven't Lost God's Number." Center for Applied Research in the Apostolate blog, Nineteen Sixty-Four. http://www.nineteensixty-four.blogspot.com/. See also Pew Forum on Religion and Public Life, "Faith in Flux: Changes in Religious Affiliation in the U. S." (Pew Research Center, Washington DC, 2009), 21, and Christian Smith and Patricia Snell, *Souls in Transition: The Religious and Spiritual Lives of Emerging Adults* (New York: Oxford, 2009), 109.

their daily life.[21] They are less active in their parishes, least likely to attend religious education sessions, least likely to be part of a youth group, prayer group or choir, and least likely to have talked with their priest or to have adult friends in their congregation.[22] Fewer than a quarter accept the Church's teaching authority on moral issues such as divorce, contraception, abortion, homosexuality, and nonmarital sex.[23] Most importantly, Millennial Catholics are among the least likely to think that it is important to marry another Catholic, and the most likely to say that they will probably not be attending a Catholic church in ten years.[24]

"Anti-Generations"

This picture may seem to contradict what we see in our parishes, where the youngest attendees are ostentatiously taking Communion on the tongue and flocking to Eucharistic Adoration, and where the youngest priests and habited sisters profess a rigorous orthodoxy. No generation, especially one as large and diverse as the Millennials, is one homogeneous mass. While over 90 percent of Catholic Millennials are only marginally attached to the Church,[25] a small minority has reacted to the egalitarianism, post-modernism, and tolerance of their generation *by aggressively promoting the exact opposite*:

- Instead of tolerance, they proclaim there is only one way to be a "real" Catholic;

- Instead of egalitarianism, the seminarians among them say that the priesthood is a special and holier state;

- Instead of post-modernism, they proclaim that there is only one truth.

The problem, of course, is that it is primarily this minority that is showing up in our seminaries and religious orders. This has, potentially, two extremely negative effects:

- Since the majority of Catholics – of *all* generations – are *not* becoming more conservative, having unusually conservative clergy may alienate

21 Christian Smith and Melissa Lundquist Denton, *Soul Searching: The Religious and Spiritual Lives of American Teenagers* (New York: Oxford University Press, 2005), 37-40.
22 Smith and Denton, 46, 51, 53, 60, 64.
23 William V. D'Antonio, James Davidson, Dean R. Hoge, and Mary L. Gautier, *American Catholics Today: New Realities of Their Faith and Their Church* (Lanham, MD: Rowman and Littlefield, 2007), 98-101.
24 Smith and Denton, 66; Smith and Snell, 140.
25 Christian Smith with Patricia Snell, *Souls in Transition: The Religious and Spiritual Lives of Emerging Adults* (New York: Oxford University Press, 2009), 167, and Dean R. Hoge et al., *Young Adult Catholics: Religion in the Culture of Choice* (Notre Dame IN: Notre Dame University Press, 2001), 71.

them from the Church. This is especially true of Catholic Millennial and Gen X women.[26]

- If the only young people who enter the priesthood or religious life are from this ultra-orthodox six percent, other young men and women who have vocations may ignore God's call because they do not think they would fit in – or because, as true children of their generation, the one thing they are intolerant of is the intolerance of the ultra-orthodox.

Ethnicity and Generation in Catholicism

In addition to the ultra-traditionalist cognitive minority, another important segment of Millennial Catholics to consider are Hispanics. As the handout shows, a full 54 percent of Millennial Catholics are Hispanic; only 39 percent are non-Hispanic whites. Hispanic Millennials remain more likely to agree with the Church theological teachings Christ's resurrection, on Mary as the Mother of God, and on the sacraments. They are also more likely to support its moral teachings on abortion and helping the poor. They are much more likely (86 percent as compared to 68 percent for non-Hispanic Millennials) to say that being Catholic is an important part of their identity, that the sacraments are essential to their relationship with God (86 percent as compared to 67 percent), that Catholicism contains a greater share of the truth than other religions (83 percent as compared to 50 percent), and that it is important to them that the younger generations of their family grow up Catholic (83 percent as compared to 71 percent).[27] And they are much *less* likely than non-Hispanic Millennial Catholics to say that one can be a good Catholic and still disagree with Church teachings on abortion (48 percent of Hispanic Millennials as compared to 64 percent of non-Hispanic Millennials), the Real Presence of Christ in the Eucharist (33 percent as compared to 51 percent) or the Resurrection (25 percent as compared to 41 percent).[28] However, as successive generations of Hispanic Catholics assimilate to American culture, they are beginning more and more to resemble non-Hispanic Catholics in their beliefs.[29] Already, similarly small percentages of Hispanic and non-Hispanic Millennial Catholics (29 percent and 24 percent) agree with the bishops' opposition to same-sex marriage, and a similar plurality (42 percent and 41 percent) say that being able to disagree with Church teachings and still be loyal to the Church is very meaningful to them.[30] The youngest generation

26 Dean R. Hoge and Jacqueline Wenger. *Evolving Visions of the Priesthood* (Collegeville MN: Liturgical Press 2003), 118.

27 William V. D'Antonio, Michele Dillon, and Mary L. Gautier, *American Catholics in Transition* (Lanham, MD: Rowman and Littlefield, 2013), 143.

28 D'Antonio, Dillon, and Gautier, 144.

29 *The CARA Report*, "Foreign-Born Hispanics Are More Socially Conservative" (Washington, DC: Center for Applied Research in the Apostolate, Winter 2014), vol. 19, no.3, 8.

30 D"Antonio, Dillon, and Gautier, 145.

of Hispanic-Americans are less likely to attend Mass regularly, to report praying frequently, or to consider themselves "strong" Catholics or "religious persons."[31] And, as we know, many are leaving Catholicism for Evangelical churches.

Millennial Catholic Women

Another ominous finding is that alienation from the Church is stronger among Catholic young adult women than it among their male counterparts.[32] *This is highly unusual.* In the past, Catholic women, like women in all other Christian denominations, have been *more* orthodox in their beliefs and *more* observant in their devotions and Mass attendance than men were. At least since the 1990's, however, these proportions have been reversed. While both genders of Millennial and GenX American Catholics are far less devout than their elders, *the women are even more alienated than the men are.* They are now less likely than men their age to say that the Church is an important part in their lives, and slightly less likely to say they would never leave Catholicism. While, for older generations, women reported attending weekly Mass in greater percentages than the men did (52 percent as compared to 35 percent in 1987), now both genders are equally likely to report this level of attendance.[33] Millennial women are more likely than men their age to disregard official Church teaching on contraception, abortion, divorce and remarriage, and same-sex sexual activity, and they are also more likely to say that they can disagree with certain aspects of Church teaching and still remain good Catholics.[34]

At the present, this alienation occurs primarily among non-Hispanic Millennial women, who, one study reports, "Stand out for their apparent disengagement from and indifference toward Catholicism."[35] Older Hispanic Catholic women still remain more devout, orthodox, and observant than both Hispanic and non-Hispanic Catholic men. But, as second and third generation Hispanic women assimilate to American culture, they may come more to resemble non-Hispanic Catholic women. Like their non-Hispanic sisters, the youngest generation of Hispanic Catholic women does not show significant differences with Hispanic Catholic men in Mass attendance, frequency of prayer, or agreement with Church teachings on issues of premarital sex, abortion, or homosexuality.[36]

---

31 Patricia Wittberg, "Religious Practice at the Intersection of Generation and Gender: A Case Study of American Catholicism." Paper read at the annual meeting of the Religious Research Association, Boston, November 9, 2013.

32 Davidson, et al., 141-154. See also Patricia Wittberg, *Building Strong Church Communities. A Sociological View* (Mahwah NJ: Paulist Press, 2013), 125, 180.

33 D'Antonio, Dillon, and Gautier, 91-92. See also Schwadel, 122.

34 D'Antonio, Dillon, and Gautier, 95-96, 149.

35 Ibid., 148.

36 Wittberg, 125, 180.

As one study notes, "that there is a generational split among women on the issue of loyalty and dissent presages the larger, significant shift in women's commitment to the Church ... The emergent generation divide among Catholic women suggests that younger women – and millennial and non-Hispanic women in particular – are not likely to stay within the fold of a church whose sexual teachings and church practices are out of step with their lived experiences."[37] It is likely, these authors state, that the women's alienation will also lead to a decline in the commitment of their husbands and children.[38]

There already is evidence that this is happening. The number of marriages celebrated in the Church fell 60 percent between 1972 and 2011 – from 415,487 to 165,400.[39] "To put it another way, this is a shift from 6.4 Church-sanctioned marriages per 1,000 U.S. Catholics in 1972 to 2.5 per 1,000 in 2011."[40] This decline is only partially because Millennials are more likely to postpone marriage; it is also due to Catholic Millennials' tendency – especially the rising percentage of Millennials who marry non-Catholics – to eschew Catholic weddings in favor of rites performed in other denominations, or in more exotic locations such as parks, beaches, or even Disney World. With fewer parents having Catholic-sanctioned marriages, the number of Catholic baptisms has declined as well – both absolutely and in proportion to the number of total births. The percentage of U.S. babies baptized Catholic dropped from a high of 33.9 percent in 1965 to 25.0 percent in 2004, to 20.1 percent in 2011.[41] First Communions have also declined.[42]

Another result of the alienation of Millennial and Post-Vatican II Catholic women is their reluctance to engage in Church service. According to several recent studies done by the Center for Applied Research in the Apostolate and the National Religious Vocation Conference, there are now, for the first time, fewer women than men who are interested in entering religious orders in the United States.[43] There are also fewer women interested in lay parish ministry.[44] Women

37 D'Antonio, Dillon, and Gautier, 96.

38 Ibid., 94.

39 "A New Catholic Subculture?" *The CARA Report,* (Winter 2014) vol. 19, no. 3, p. 11. See also Mark M. Gray, "Exclusive Analysis: National Catholic Marriage Rate Plummets." *Our Sunday Visitor*, June 26, 2011, http://www.osv.com/ (accessed July 12, 2011).

40 D'Antonio, Dillon, and Gautier, 108.

41 "Declining Proportion of Baptisms a Cause for Concern." *The CARA Report* (Summer 2013), vol.19 no.1, 3.

42 Smith, Longest, et al.,71.

43 Mark M. Gray and Mary L. Gautier, "Consideration of Priesthood and Religious Life among Never-Married U.S. Catholics." (Washington, DC: Center for Applied Research in the Apostolate, 2012), 9, 78, 99. See also Mary E. Bendyna and Mary L. Gautier, "Recent Vocations to Religious Life: A Report for the National Religious Vocation Conference." (Washington, DC: Center for Applied Research in the Apostolate, 2009), 25-27.

44 Dean R. Hoge and Marti R. Jewell, *The Next Generation of Pastoral Leaders: What the Church Needs to Know* (Chicago: Loyola University Press, 2010), 13, 18.

are more likely than men to say that parish ministry would not adequately use their gifts and talents. This, too, has implications for the Catholic Church in the future: "Besides the 'vocation crisis' to the priesthood and religious life, there is another crisis of lay vocational workers. The generation of DREs and youth ministers who sprouted up after the Second Vatican Council are now retiring and it is not at all clear who will replace them."[45]

What can we do about this?

I would like to conclude this presentation by calling us all to engage in cross-generational conversations, aimed at increasing our understanding of generational cultures within the Church and eliminating the stereotypes we have of each other. We could do this, first of all, by sharing stories.

- Older generations need to hear the stories of the young, in order to understand what meaning and emotional resonance which various Catholic practices/beliefs/artifacts have for them. When the old do this, they need always to remember that *"It doesn't mean the same thing to them as it did to me!"* – whether "It" is the rosary, Eucharistic Adoration, the Pope, the Magisterium, abortion, being gay, or being Catholic.

    - Sometimes "It" will refer to an actually different experience. For example, my own Baby Boomer memory of grade school religion class involved a sister in full habit and memorizing *The Baltimore Catechism*. A Millennial or GenXer is more likely to remember lying on the floor drawing rainbows and making collages.

    - Sometimes "It" will refer to the same thing but with an entirely different emotional valence. For example, the religious habit might have unpleasant overtones of discomfort, denial of one's sexuality, women's subordination, or purported "superiority" to the laity for sisters of the Silent Generation. To Gen X, the habit is a radical icon, indicating that you belong to something bigger than yourself; to Millennials it is "the Team Colors." Why would you not want to wear the team colors? Are you ashamed of your team?

    - Often "It" will be packaged differently with other practices/beliefs/artifacts. For example, the youth in a parish might be attracted to Latin chant, Eucharistic Adoration – and Buddhist meditation. Or they might be against abortion and for gay marriage.

---

45 Michael White and Tom Corcoran, *Rebuilt: Awakening the Faithful, Reaching the Lost, Making Church Matter* (Notre Dame, IN: Ave Maria Press, 2013), 225.

- The younger generation (especially that ultra-orthodox 5-10%!) also need to talk to the old, so that they understand why their elders discarded the traditional elements which the young now find to be so deeply mystical, and why their elders now react so negatively to their proposed revival of this or that tradition.

Jim Bishop, in his recent book *The Big Sort*,[46] complained that we are fracturing more and more into polarized populations whose members read different newspapers, watch different news networks, listen to different radio stations, live in different neighborhoods, and socialize only with those who think like they do. Chris Mooney[47] says that this tribalization increasingly leads to motivated reasoning and a social desirability bias. As a result, more and more, we see those with different beliefs as "The Other" and not really American – or not really Catholic.

I believe that Catholic Millennials are at a crossroads, as far as their affiliation with the Church is concerned. Many are deeply alienated by the polarization between warring factions who are still fighting the battles of 50 or more years ago. As a result, they may either

- **Give up on Catholicism altogether.** In which case, only a small number of Americans will be Catholic in coming generations, and our Church will become an encapsulated and miniscule minority, increasingly marginalized in its influence in the larger American society. I don't believe any of us want this.

OR, Millennials could, through their diversity and tolerance,

- **Lead us to a new unity and reconciliation** that is a source of life for the Church in the future, and a model for America as a whole of a way to emerge from its current polarized stasis. But before Millennial Catholics can do this, however, they need to be interested enough in the Church to actually join it. This is by no means a sure thing.

If Catholic Millennials are to take this second alternative, however, they need the help of those of us who are older, who soon will be passing the leadership of the Church to them. What I hope we can do in the next few minutes is to brainstorm on the kinds of help we might give. At a minimum, I would suggest:

- Arranging regular times/places – in each parish and religious community – where the various generations can engage in the kind of storytelling they need to do in order to understand each other.

46 Bill Bishop, *The Big Sort: Why the Clustering of Like-Minded America is Tearing Us Apart* (Boston: Houghton Mifflin, 2008).
47 See fn. 3, p. 344.

- Give Millennial Catholics positions of leadership and responsibility in our parishes, dioceses, and religious institutes.
- Explore and expand new ways to draw the 90% of less-observant Catholic young adults back to closer affiliation with and participation in the Church – whether that be tweets, blogs, podcasts, etc. – or some of the "old fashioned" devotions that resonate with them.

And do not forget that the Post-Millennial Generation is coming along – they are already in our grade schools and high schools. Within a decade they, too, will be looking at the Church as adults for the first time. What will they think of what they see?

OFFICER'S REPORT

REPORT OF THE PRESIDENT

Very Rev. Phillip J. Brown, pss, JCD

Review of Activities

a. New BOG
b. Seventy-fifth Annual Convention
c. CCLS Annual Meeting
d. January BOG meeting
e. Lecture, Faculty of Canon Law, Saint Paul University
f. Western Regional CLSA Meeting
g. April BOG meeting
h. CLSGBI Annual Meeting
i. Executive Coordinator Search
    a. Interim Plan
    b. New Executive Coordinator
j. Penal Law Symposium
k. National Penal Law Tribunal Study
l. CLSANZ Annual Conference
m. CLSA Seventy-sixth Annual Convention

Proposals/Issues/Concerns & Recommendations

n. PAB Proposed Annual Seminar
o. Relations with canon law schools
p. Presidential term of office
q. Executive Coordinator title
r. CLSA, CCLS, CLSGBI and CLSANZ Limited Joint Membership Proposal
s. International Federation of Canon Law Societies

INTRODUCTION

This is my last report as President. I want to begin by thanking the members of the Society, the BOG, Sr. Sharon Euart, Colleen, and Mary for the confidence you have placed in my leadership and your cooperation and assistance throughout the year. I think that it has been a successful term of office. The extended search for a new Executive Coordinator turned out to be the principal focus and necessarily distracted me from some of the other priorities I had enunciated when I stood for office. It is perhaps inevitable that when one holds a leadership position the exigencies of the moment overtake agendas and other priorities. However, I believe we have made good progress on most of the Society's projects over the course of the past year, and I leave office satisfied that we have accomplished all that we could under the circumstances

Working with the BOG could not have been a more pleasant or satisfying experience. I continue to be deeply impressed by their thoughtfulness, skill, and depth of reflection as canon lawyers. Together with our entire membership, they illustrate professionalism and a love for the Society and for canon law itself.

A number of significant tasks have been accomplished during the year, the most important of which was hiring Fr. Roger Keeler as our new Executive Coordinator. I note our very successful convention in Sacramento last October, the well-received Penal Law Workshop in Lutz, Florida, the establishment of a National Penal Law Tribunal Study Commission, and the appointment of Sr. Sharon Euart as chair of the Publications Advisory Board (PAB). The regional conferences went very well, including the meeting I was privileged to attend in Salt Lake City. I was also fortunate to attend the Canadian Canon Law Society Annual Convention in Sudbury, Ontario, the Canon Law Society of Great Britain and Ireland Annual Conference in May in Harrogate, England, and the Canon Law Society of Australia and New Zealand Conference in Sydney just a few weeks ago. Of equal note is the lecture I gave at the Faculty of Canon Law at Saint Paul University, Ottawa, last February.

I do believe younger and newer canonists have been getting involved in the Society. I would have liked to have made more progress on the revision of the *Code of Professional Responsibility*. It is important for us to produce a modern, up-to-date *Code* for our members, upon which our Professional Conduct Committee may rely if and when they are called upon to assess a case involving alleged unethical or otherwise unprofessional conduct on the part of a member. This is a task that I plan to turn my attention toward during my year as Past-President. I hope that we will be able to have this project completed within the next one to two years.

After elaborating on developments during the year, I would like to mention a few projects in which the Society is involved, or in which our participation has been proposed. Moreover, there are concerns or issues that have been discussed that I would like to place before you. Finally, I would like to mention a few recommendations for the consideration of the BOG that may eventually be brought before the general membership.

REVIEW OF ACTIVITIES

a. New BOG

A new Vice President, Msgr. Michael Souckar, was elected at the Sacramento convention last October. He joins Fr. Charles Antonicelli and Fr. Jim Conn, S.J, as the newest members of the BOG. Cathy Gilligan, Gerry Jorgensen, Zabrina Decker, Fr. Patrick Cooney, O.S.B. and Msgr. John Foster continued their terms, and although Fr. Tom Cronkleton's term as a consultor ended in Sacramento, he succeeded Fr. Greg Bittner in the Office of Treasurer. We said goodbye to Fr. Greg, Rita Joyce, and Dr. Margaret Chalmers, each of whom offered the BOG three years of exemplary service. I am also pleased to report that Rita has accepted appointment as Chair of the Research and Development Committee, and so will continue her long and valued service to the Society in that role.

The members of the Board exemplify a generous commitment of time and talent – an important characteristic of members of our Society – and we owe them all an ongoing debt of gratitude. I must reiterate what a pleasure and privilege it has been – and continues to be – to serve with them on the BOG.

b. Seventy-fifth Annual Convention

By all accounts, the Seventy-fifth Annual Convention of the CLSA in Sacramento was a tremendous success. The evaluations, with rare exception, gave all of the major addresses, seminars, and workshops very high marks. Hospitality was particularly outstanding and provided opportunities for networking, catching up with one another, and making new friends. Msgr. Ken Boccafola was extremely gratified to receive the Role of Law Award. We were enriched and blessed by the presence of Msgr. Pio Vito Pinto, Dean of the Roman Rota, Bishop Charles Scicluna, former Promoter of Justice for the Congregation for the Doctrine of the Faith, and Archbishop John Meyers of Newark, NJ. An exceptional convention is not something that comes together quickly. Rather, it is the product of many years of planning, with skills and insights gained over many years of convention experience. In a real sense, last year's convention was the visible culmination of all that Sr. Sharon Euart brought to the office of Executive Coordinator: contributions that will continue long into the future. The procedures she established, and professionalism that she inculcated into the operations of the EC's office, build on similar contributions of her predecessors, and we cannot thank Sr. Sharon and her predecessors enough. They have set a very high standard for the Society to maintain as we go forward.

c. CCLS Annual Meeting

Two weeks after our own annual convention I represented the CLSA at the Canadian Canon Law Society Annual Convention in Sudbury, Ontario. I was struck by the warm reception I received, together with the depth and strength of our relationship with the Canadian Society. The presentations at the convention were excellent. It was good to renew friendships with so many Canadian colleagues and to make new friends within the Society. As you perhaps know, a number of canonists belong to both the CLSA and the CCLS, and I would certainly encourage members of our Society to consider membership in the CCLS (and vice versa). Both societies offer excellent annual conventions, coupled with valuable opportunities for continuing education that could well forge stronger ties for mutual professional development. Could there eventually be a class of membership in our respective Societies that would permit attendance at one another's meetings? This is an idea that has in fact begun to circulate.

d. January BOG meeting

To facilitate ease of travel, the BOG held its January meeting at a location near Baltimore/Washington International Airport. With the new members of the BOG present, the meeting followed the usual agenda for this time of the year: committee reports, a review of the prior convention, and continued planning for the October 2014 convention. Because we were not yet prepared to offer the Executive Coordinator position to any of the applicants, the three presidential officers proposed, and the BOG accepted, an interim plan to maintain the functions of the OEC. This interim plan will be described in greater detail later in the report.

e. Lecture, Faculty of Canon Law, Saint Paul University

In February I travelled to Ottawa, Canada, where I delivered a lecture entitled: *Due Process and the Right of Defense: Fulcrum of Justice, Heart of the Law*, at the Faculty of Canon Law at Saint Paul University. I could not have been received more warmly nor had a better time. Dean Anne Asselin was especially gracious, as were Fr. Frank Morrisey and Robert Larivière (President of the Canadian Canon Law Society). The lecture was well-received, and I have been asked to provide a text for publication in *Studia canonica*. I had an excellent exchange with the students of the Faculty, encouraging those who are not members of the Society to join us and encouraging one and all to attend our convention. This experience persuaded me all the more of the importance of our relationship with our Canadian colleagues and with the Faculty of Canon Law at Saint Paul University

f. Western Regional CLSA Meeting

We are indeed fortunate to have such dedicated, able, cooperative, and helpful canonists as members of the BOG. In March I attended the Western Regional Meeting in Salt Lake City, Utah. I had a wonderful time and, once again, I could not have been received more graciously. Fr. Langes Silva and the other organizers are to be commended for an outstanding meeting, with very interesting presentations on Mormonism, Mormon-Catholic marriage issues, and an excellent series of presentations by Msgr. Pat Lagges on penal law especially as it pertains to the sexual abuse scandals. I updated the attendees on the activities of the CLSA, which I believe does a great deal to promote attendance at our national conventions. As Bishop Wester was not able to be present at the meeting, I was asked to preside at the convention Mass. The theme of my homily was "Justice Delayed is Justice Denied." I am personally very grateful to Langes for the gracious reception he and the others gave me.

g. April BOG meeting

The April BOG meeting proceeded according to the usual pattern. Although quite preoccupied with filling the Executive Coordinator position, we continued to plan and revise the 2014 Annual Convention program. Consideration was given to the nominees for election and to candidates for the Role of Law Award. Although convention planning is a very involved affair, the process of advance planning has been established effectively. By April we are finalizing aspects of the upcoming convention, while giving thought to the following year's convention. It is one of the pleasures of serving on the BOG: the procedures are well-established and long-standing – there is seldom a sense of pressure about upcoming events. We can take a very deliberate approach to deciding things like the theme of a convention or meeting, who will be invited to speak or give presentations, format, etc.

h. CLSGBI Annual Meeting

In May I attended the Annual Conference of the Canon Law Society of Great Britain and Ireland in Harrogate, England. What a wonderful experience! The CLSGBI meeting is smaller in scale, and a little more "laid back" than our annual meeting, yet equally enjoyable and helpful as a forum for networking, renewing old friendships, and making new ones. Msgr. Gordon Read, the President of the CLSGBI, was a most gracious host, ensuring a warm welcome. The meeting afforded me the opportunity to renew my contacts with Sr. Maria Casey, President of the Canon Law of Australia and New Zealand, and Patsy Gonsorcik, Vice President of the Anglophone sector of the Canadian Canon Law Society, who was attending on behalf of President Robert Larivière. Together with representatives from the Francophone sector of the CCLS, we were able to meet to discuss matters of mutual concern, including the possibility of allowing members from our respective Societies to attend any of our conventions and receive certain publications at a discounted rate.

i. Executive Coordinator Search

a. Interim Plan

As mentioned above, in January the BOG instituted an interim plan to maintain the CLSA office in Washington as we completed the process of finding a new Executive Coordinator. The basic plan involved having Colleen Crawford, our Executive Assistant, maintain the operations of the office with the assistance of Mary DeBroeck. Colleen has become very familiar with OEC operations and has demonstrated the prudence and discretion necessary to know when to ask for assistance and not to go out on a limb when responding to requests. With the agreement of her new employer, Sr. Sharon made herself available to the OEC, including spending time in the office to help Colleen with questions. Sr. Sharon was generous in being available by telephone and email to offer advice, counsel, and assistance when needed to address particular issues. Colleen and Mary fully lived up to and, in fact, surpassed expectations, and we are grateful for Sr. Sharon's continued devotion to the Society! Things continued to run smoothly during the interim before we found a new EC.

b. New Executive Coordinator

The search for a new Executive Coordinator was more complicated and protracted than we expected. In the end, however, we took the necessary time, evaluated candidates carefully, and were patient as we waited for the right candidate to come to the fore. Eventually Fr. Roger Keeler emerged as the best fit for the Society, we offered him the position and he accepted.

Roger had been teaching at the Oblate School in San Antonio and also working as Judicial Vicar for the Appellate Court of the Dioceses of Texas. The position of EC of the CLSA was appealing to him because of his past experience as a canonist, administrator, and pastoral minister, and because of his creativity and ability to think outside the box.

It is not an exaggeration to say that this is a momentous time for the Society as we move from the era of Sr. Sharon Euart, RSM, who provided such strong and excellent leadership for the executive office of the Society, to the era of Fr. Roger Keeler, who will no doubt bring a new style and a different kind of creativity and leadership to the office. Thus, we say "welcome" to Fr. Keeler, and "thank you" to Sr. Sharon for her leadership as Executive Coordinator and for her continuing contribution to the Society as Chair of PAB.

j. The Penal Law Symposium

The Penal Law Workshop in Lutz, Florida, sponsored by the Society at the end of March and early April, was a great success. This has led to a proposal by PAB to sponsor another seminar next year, the focus of which would be marriage. PAB also recommends that presenters publish material based on the content and findings of the seminar. If individuals continue to participate in these workshops, PAB may consider an annual intensive workshop on a range of canonical topics.

k. National Penal Law Tribunal Study Commission

A resolution was passed at last year's convention calling for a study of the possibility of a National Tribunal for Penal Law. Archbishop Kurtz, President of the USCCB, endorsed the idea and has asked that the CLSA produce something for, and in collaboration with, the USCCB. The matter has been delegated to Archbishop Broglio, Chairman of the Canonical Affairs Committee of the USCCB. I met with Archbishop Broglio to discuss what we had in mind, and he encouraged the idea as well. His term as Chair of the Canonical Affairs Committee ends this fall and Archbishop Bernie Hebda of Newark will assume the new Chair. Archbishop Broglio has been in touch with Archbishop Hebda to brief him on the project, and we are eager to begin work with him this fall. I have asked Msgr. Fred Easton to act as Chair of a Study Commission, and approached Msgr. Jack Alessandro to be Associate Chair. Frs. Larry DiNardo and Mark O'Connell, with Msgr. Michael Padazinski, have agreed to serve on the Commission. They will report back to the President of the Society and the BOG as work progresses. It will ultimately be up to the President to determine how to share the results with the USCCB and facilitate any other forms of collaboration.

l. CLSANZ Annual Conference

As part of my duties as President, in September I attended the annual conference of the Canon Law Society of Australia and New Zealand in Sydney, Australia. Another great trip although a very long one! There was no overarching theme for the conference. Fr. Gerard Kelley gave a presentation on "Vatican II's Theology of *Communio,*" and Sr. Maria Casey, RSJ, President of the Society, spoke on "The Unopened Gifts of *Communio* from the Code." Mr. Robert Larivière, President of the Canadian Society, offered a workshop on "Grave Lack of Due Discretion of Judgment," Msgr. Brendan Daly addressed "Amalgamating Parishes," and Msgr. David Price spoke on "Advocacy in Matrimonial Cases." Dr. Rodger Austin addressed the convention on "The Bishop's Pastoral Governance: Council, Code and Beyond," and Fr. Frank Morrissey, OMI, on "Dealing Justly with Complaints against Church Personnel."

m. CLSA Seventy-sixth Annual Convention

As we gather together in St. Louis for our Annual Meeting, I want once again to thank the BOG for a wonderful and productive year during my tenure as President. We are indeed fortunate to have such dedicated, able, cooperative, and helpful canonists as members of the BOG. It was a joy to work with Fr. John Vaughan, first as President and then as Past-President, with Msgr. Michael Souckar, as Vice-President/President Elect, and with Sr. Sharon Euart, Colleen, and Mary in the OEC. All of them have made the job easier and much more productive than it otherwise would have been: their support, encouragement, and assistance are deeply appreciated. I, of course, pledge the same support and assistance to Michael as he takes over the reins at this meeting. I leave office with a very bright outlook for the future potential of the Society as it relies on wonderful traditions and works with the demonstrated leadership and hard work of those in official positions.

Before concluding my report I would like to highlight a few projects in progress and point to issues or concerns of which members should be aware. I will also make several recommendations to the Society and the Board for future consideration.

PROJECTS/ISSUES/CONCERNS & RECOMMENDATIONS

n. PAB Proposed Annual Seminar

The PAB has made a proposal for the establishment of an annual spring seminar that could produce publications for the Society. This is based on the success of the Penal Law seminar in Florida this past spring. I believe this is an excellent proposal that will succeed very well with Sr. Sharon Euart at the helm. I want to give the idea my strong endorsement, as it seems to reflect the attitude of the other current members of the BOG as well. Because the BOG has given this proposal its provisional approval, we can look forward to a seminar next spring on a marriage topic. I encourage the BOG to continue planning and seeking approval for an annual spring seminar.

o. Relations with canon law schools

Our relationship with the various canon law schools remains an important priority and we should continue to foster those relationships carefully. Our membership comes from the graduates of these institutions, and therefore it is crucial that we maintain very good relations with them. We also need to be attentive to the service we offer our membership who are alumni, and also to ways we might encourage others to pursue canon law studies.

p. Presidential term of office

During the CCLS meeting last October and again at the CLSGBI meeting in May, the Presidents of the other Societies were curious about how our presidential term of office system worked. I explained the three-year term structure with one year as Vice President, one year as President, and one as Past-President. Each of the other Presidents expressed the opinion that they would find it very difficult to hold office under that structure, because he or she has very little time to advance his or her priorities and follow up before the term ends. I had to agree with them based on my experience this past year. The Presidents of the other Societies recommended re-visiting this structure and suggested we consider a three-year term like their own or, at the very least, a two year term. I realize this would be a substantial change for the CLSA, as the presidential office has been structured this way for quite some time – if not from the beginning. Nevertheless, I do believe that the President would be more effective if she or he had at least a two-year term as President. I personally prefer the three-year model currently in place in the other Societies. How this would be structured in relation to the other presidential offices would have to be explored. I certainly understand the difficulty that might be involved in getting religious superiors to agree to a three-year term, although it could be argued that they currently have to agree to a three-year term as it is, given the existing structure of Vice President/President-Elect + President + Past President. Perhaps the Office of Vice President would not have to be automatically tied to that of the President.
Lengthening the term would help to express that governance of the Society rests entirely with the elected officers of the BOG, with the President in the presiding role.

I recognize a proposal to change the term of office might provoke considerable debate, yet a healthy debate about this issue would not be a bad thing: it would likely strengthen the Society, whatever the outcome. Thus, it is my hope that the BOG will discuss the question and make a prudent decision about whether or not it should be placed before the membership at large.

q. Executive Coordinator Title

There has been some discussion by the BOG about possibly changing the title of the Executive Coordinator to "Executive Director." "Executive Director" is a title with a well-understood meaning in civil law, which is not the case with respect to the title "Executive Coordinator." Thus, we might want to consider that "Executive Director" would lend greater clarity to the civil law aspects of Society governance and administration, which could be helpful. It was pointed out during the contracting process that changing the title to "Executive Director" would require a constitutional amendment, since "Executive Coordinator" is the title used in our Constitution. I would like to recommend that the BOG decide formally if we want to move to the title "Executive Director," and if so, follow the process for requesting a constitutional amendment to that effect at next year's convention (October 2015).

r. CLSA, CCLS, CLSGBI and CLSANZ Limited Joint Membership Proposal

As mentioned in my report, the Presidents of the CLSA, CCLS, CLSGBI and CLSANZ have had several conversations about the possibility of creating some form of limited joint membership that would allow members to attend one another's annual meetings at member rates, and to receive publications at member rates. I have brought these discussions to the attention of the BOG and recommend that they be pursued, wherever they may lead. Such a proposal could foster greater cooperation and collaboration between Societies (which is already quite good), and could encourage greater understanding among canonists from around the world. Convention programs could be coordinated in such a way that it gives rise to increased scholarly activity. All of this could lead to the overall growth and development of canon law worldwide with an obvious benefit for all of our members.

s. International Federation of Canon Law Societies

I would also encourage consideration for the establishment of some sort of international federation of canon law societies, starting in particular with English-speaking countries. The relationship between the CLSA, CCLS, CLSGBI and CLSANZ already seems to be evolving somewhat in this direction, and I could see great benefits in formalizing this development in ways that will ensure that each Society maintains its independence. The opportunities for cooperation and collaboration could be myriad, and I believe it would enhance and strengthen each of our respective Societies. There seems to be some enthusiasm for this idea among leaders of the four Societies, and therefore I would recommend at least engaging in a thorough discussion of the possibility. If there seems to be a consensus that this would be a good idea, I would definitely encourage moving forward with concrete proposals to create such a federation.

Officer's Report

Report of the Treasurer
Rev. Thomas E. Cronkleton, Jr., JCD

This is my first report to the Society as Treasurer. I want to thank Sister Sharon Euart, RSM, our former Executive Coordinator, and Colleen Crawford, our Executive Assistant, for the excellent work they have done. I am always amazed at how much they have been able to accomplish with so little. I am grateful for the assistance of the Resource and Asset Management Committee and for their valuable input. I am also enjoying working with Father Roger Keeler, our new Executive Coordinator.

We divide our financial operations into 4 Units: General Operations, Publications, Conventions, and Scholarships. Each unit strives to have a balanced budget, but a positive balance in Publications can be used to offset a negative balance in General Operations. Conventions seek to have a balanced budget. The Scholarship Unit and the funds represented are only used for the scholarships and the operational expenses of this Unit. I will highlight below a few items contained in the reports that follow.

I am pleased to be able to point out that we completed Fiscal Year 2013-2014 in the black. This was due to differing reasons depending upon the Unit, which will be discussed below.

General Operations Unit:

In the General Operations Unit, the main source of income is dues. Both our collection of dues from New Members and dues from Current Members exceeded our expectations. We collected $2,500.00 more in New Members dues and $11,800.00 in Current Member dues, for a total of $14,300.00 of additional revenue.

Because of the additional time needed to recruit a new Executive Coordinator, the Office of the Executive Coordinator was vacant. We, therefore, had savings in this area of $38,352.00. As a result of this vacancy, we had additional expenses with the Executive Assistant and Administrative Assistant positions, partly through their working additional hours.

One of the things we added for the Executive Assistant and Administrative Assistant positions was health benefits, and one of the things we added for the Executive Assistant was a 403(b) Thrift Savings Retirement Program. We realized savings in these areas, since we were not able to get them in place until the second half of the fiscal year.

The expense for the Board of Governors meetings were less than budgeted, because we were able to keep travel and meeting space expenses down. We also had savings from the Standing Committees.

We had some additional unbudgeted expenses for the process of transitioning to a new Executive Coordinator. These expenses included conference calls and meetings initiated by the search committee, as well as candidate interviews and travel.

One of the services we have added for the membership is the webinars. These have been very successful and popular. During this last Fiscal Year 2013-2014, webinars were offered at no-cost to members of the Society, and we will continue to fund them at no-cost to members for this current year too.

We also had a Penal Law Workshop, which was very well attended. It brought some additional income over expenses.

Due to the additional revenues and the various savings, we did not have to utilize the Prior Year Realized Net Assets to meet our expenses. This happened, however, mainly because of the vacancy in the Executive Coordinator position, the delay in providing benefits, and the Board of Governors and Standing Committees spending less than budgeted. This is not likely to happen for this fiscal year, 2014-2015.

Historically the Publications Unit has been a revenue-producing area for the Society. Over the last few years this has become less and less so, and this year no additional revenue was produced by the Publications Unit that could be used for the General Operations Unit. Fortunately, we did not need this revenue. The General Operations Unit needs to become more and more self-sufficient. The main source of income for the General Operations Unit is dues. For the last 3 years, the General Operations Unit was budgeted to use the Prior Year Realized Net Assets in order to balance the budget. While budgeted to do so, we did not have to use them. We may, in the future, need to consider a dues increase.

The Investments in the General Operations Unit have been experiencing positive growth the last few years. Below are the quarterly balances for the last three years:

General Operations Investment Fund (CUIT Balance Fund)

Date	Fund Balance
December 31, 2011	$545,113.60
March 31, 2011	$593,318.42
June 30, 2012	$585,252.27
September 30, 2012	$616,230.86
December 31, 2012	$624,659.45
March 31, 2013	$668,626.16
June 30, 2013	$680,025.21
September 30, 2013	$708,690.03
December 31, 2013	$757,643.34
March 31, 2014	$769,264.93
June 30, 2014	$797,237.52

The growth has been due both to a positive return in the Market over this period, and from expenses being less than income for the General Operations Unit.

The Balance Sheet for the General Operations Unit shows the gains in the Market, and a positive balance.

Publications Unit:

The Publications Unit had a slight negative year of -$82.83, because expenses exceeded income. This was due to the revenues from Sales of Publications being about 75% of what was anticipated. We did, therefore, realize some savings from other related fees. We do not, however, have many publications in the pipeline, so in the future we may not be able to anticipate much income from the Publications Unit for use in the General Operations Unit.

The Balance Sheet for the Publications Unit shows the inventory we have, and some reserves. The Balance Sheet is positive for the Publications Unit.

Conventions Unit:

The Conventions Unit had a positive return for last year's Convention and Pre-Convention Workshops in Sacramento, California. This was due to programs that attracted more than anticipated attendance. Additionally, we did not have the anticipated $5,500.00 expense for speaker travel, resulting in further savings.

The Balance Sheet for the Conventions Unit is positive, and we have some reserves in case our expenses should exceed our income.

Scholarship Unit:

We are operating the Scholarship Unit on the basis of the total return from the Scholarship Investment Fund. Up to 5% of the total market value of the Scholarship Investment Fund is used to fund the Scholarship Unit. The total market value is computed on the basis of a three (3) year rolling quarterly average, with the ending quarter on December 31 - immediately preceding the January Board of Governors' meeting. This sum is used for scholarship awards, administration and fundraising efforts. The financial report shows the income and expenses in the unit.

Since the inception of the Licentiate Scholarship Fund as of June 30, 2014, $400,396.71 has been donated to the Scholarship Fund. We have given out over the same period $229,177.58 in scholarships to 27 recipients.

The Investments in the Scholarship Unit have been experiencing positive growth the last few years. Below are the quarterly balances:

[Licentiate] Scholarship Investment Fund (CUIT Balanced Fund)

Date	**Fund Balance**
December 31, 2011	$434,505.86
March 31, 2011	$472,929.58
June 30, 2012	$466,500.09
September 30, 2012	$491,192.89
December 31, 2012	$497,911.19
March 31, 2013	$532,956.72
June 30, 2013	$542,042.79
September 30, 2013	$564,891.34
December 31, 2013	$603,911.62
March 31, 2014	$613,175.11
June 30, 2014	$635,471.89

The growth has been due both to a positive return in the Market over this period, and from donations to the Scholarship Fund.

The Balance Sheet for the Scholarship Unit shows the gains in the marke and a positive balance.

Doctoral Scholarship:

At the 2013 General Meeting of the Canon Law Society, the membership voted to establish a Doctoral Scholarship by moving $50,000.00 from the General Operations Investment Fund. At the January 2014 meeting of the Board of Governors, a resolution was made to transfer the $50,000.00 approved by the Membership from the General Operations Investment Fund to a new Doctoral Scholarship Investment Fund. The Doctoral Scholarship Fund will be managed separately from the Licentiate Scholarship Fund. Work is underway to accomplish this.

Christian Brothers Investment Services:

Our investments are with Christian Brothers Investment Services in two of their funds: the CUIT Balanced Fund and the CUIT Money Market Fund (formerly RCT Flex Cash Fund). The CUIT Balanced Fund is 60% equities and 40% bonds. The equities portion is large cap, and the bonds are intermediate term, with average effective duration of 5.02 years. Intermediate bond funds have exposure to declining value when the interest rates go up. CBIS, however, has been reducing the duration on the bonds so that there will be less exposure to rising interest rates. The CUIT Money Market, like most money market accounts, has less than half a percent return. This will continue until interest rates are raised by the Federal Reserve. Both investments vehicles are performing close to or above their bench marks.

Accountants' Review:

Linton, Shafer, Warfield & Garrett, PA, did a review of fiscal years ending June 30, 2014 and June 30, 2013. A review is an intermediate analysis which is less rigorous than an audit and more rigorous than a compilation. A review primarily applies analytical procedures to our financial data and makes inquiries of our management. This is the second year for a review, and next year will have an audit. We will also need to have an audit next year due to the change in Executive Coordinators. Mr. Joseph M. McCathran, CPA, who was the principal in the review of our financials, did some extra testing in the areas of higher risk, such as the Publications Unit and investments. His additional testing indentified no unusual activities that warranted further attention.

Most importantly, the Review done by Linton, Shafer, Warfield & Garret, PA stated:

> Based upon our review, we are not aware of any material modifications that should be made to the accompanying financial statements in order for them to be in conformity with accounting principles generally accepted in the United States of America.

We have received a positive report. The Independent Accounts' Review Report follows in this booklet.

Budget and Budget vs. Actual Reports:

The 2014-2014 Budget Report and the 2013-2014 Budget vs. Actual Reports follow.

LSWG
Linton Shafer Warfield & Garrett, P.A.
CERTIFIED PUBLIC ACCOUNTANTS

Jennifer P. Clingan, CPA
Edward T. Garrett, CPA
Meredith C. Harshman, CPA
Kevin R. Hessler, CPA
Lisa D. Landaverde, CPA
Donald C. Linton, CPA, CFP, PFS
Joseph M. McCathran, CPA
Brian E. Rippeon, CPA
Barbara Cline-Roman, CPA
Ronald W. Shafer, CPA
Douglas C. Warfield, CPA, CVA

Independent Accountant's Review Report

Board of Governors
Canon Law Society of America

We have reviewed the accompanying statements of financial position of Canon Law Society of America (a nonprofit organization) as of June 30, 2014 and 2013, and the related statements of activities and changes in net assets, and cash flows for the years then ended. A review includes primarily applying analytical procedures to management's financial data and making inquiries of the organization's management. A review is substantially less in scope than an audit, the objective of which is the expression of an opinion regarding the financial statements as a whole. Accordingly, we do not express such an opinion.

Management is responsible for the preparation and fair presentation of the financial statements in accordance with accounting principles generally accepted in the United States of America and for designing, implementing, and maintaining internal control relevant to the preparation and fair presentation of the financial statements.

Our responsibility is to conduct the reviews in accordance with Statements on Standards for Accounting and Review Services issued by the American Institute of Certified Public Accountants. Those standards require us to perform procedures to obtain limited assurance that there are no material modifications that should be made to the financial statements. We believe that the results of our procedures provide a reasonable basis for our report.

Based on our review, we are not aware of any material modifications that should be made to the accompanying financial statements in order for them to be in conformity with accounting principles generally accepted in the United States of America.

932 Hungerford Drive, Suite 29B • Rockville, Maryland 20850-1752 • 240-314-7075 • FAX 240-314-7079
ROCKVILLE • FREDERICK
www.lswgcpa.com

Our review was made primarily for the purpose of expressing a conclusion that there are no material modifications that should be made to the financial statements in order for them to be in conformity with accounting principles generally accepted in the United States of America. The Schedules of Program Services and Supporting Services for the years ended June 30, 2014 and 2013 included as supplementary information are presented for purposes of additional analysis and are not a required part of the basic financial statements. Such information has been subjected to the inquiry and analytical procedures applied in the review of the basic financial statements, and we did not become aware of any material modification that should be made to such information.

Linton Shafer Warfield & Garrett, P.A.
August 27, 2014

STATEMENT OF FINANCIAL POSITION
June 30, 2014 and 2013

	2014	2013
Assets		
Current Assets		
Cash	273,977	197,258
Cash - scholarship fund	17,133	25,534
Accounts receivable	2,996	3,866
Inventory	80,318	99,401
Prepaid expenses	19,347	18,814
Total Current Assets	393,771	344,873
Furniture and Equipment - at cost		
Furniture and equipment	17,765	17,765
Less: accumulated depreciation	(14,304)	(12,622)
Furniture and Equipment, Net	3,461	5,143
Other Assets		
Investments	797,237	680,025
Investment - scholarship fund	635,472	542,043
Total Other Assets	1,432,709	1,222,068
Total Assets	**1,829,941**	**1,572,084**
Liabilities and Net Assets		
Current Liabilities		
Accounts payable	30	30
Royalties payable	-	553
Deferred revenue	25,085	13,060
Total Current Liabilities	25,115	13,643
Total Liabilities	25,115	13,643
Net Assets		
Unrestricted		
Undesignated	1,058,632	902,375
Board designated - publications	87,733	87,816
Total Unrestricted	1,146,365	990,191
Temporarily restricted	658,461	568,251
Total Net Assets	1,804,826	1,558,441
Total Liabilities and Net Assets	**1,829,941**	**1,572,084**

See Accountant's Review Report and accompanying notes.

STATEMENT OF ACTIVITIES AND CHANGES IN NET ASSETS

For the Year Ended June 30, 2014

	UNRESTRICTED				
	Undesignated	Publications	Total	Temporarily Restricted	Total
Revenue					
Membership dues	$263,675	$ -	$263,675	$ -	$263,675
Convention, workshops	175,956	-	175,956	-	175,956
Sale of publications	-	67,204	67,204	-	67,204
Contributions	-	-	-	12,495	12,495
Interest and dividends	10,876	-	10,876	8,767	19,643
Royalties	-	8,246	8,246	-	8,246
Reprint permissions	-	-	-	-	-
Lay Ecclesial Ministry Grant	-	-	-	-	-
Other Income	-	-	-	-	-
Appreciation on fair value of investments	106,347	-	106,347	84,769	191,116
Net assets released from restrictions	19,362	-	19,362	(19,362)	-
Total Revenue	576,216	75,450	651,666	87,119	738,785
Expenses					
Program Services					
Publications	-	75,533	75,533	-	75,533
Convention, workshops	157,350	-	157,350	-	157,350
Membership services	8,839	-	8,839	-	8,839
Committees	22,202	-	22,202	-	22,202
Lay Ecclesial Work Group	72	-	72	-	72
Holy See/Australia	10,801	-	10,801	-	10,801
Scholarship fund	19,290	-	19,920	-	19,920
Total Program Services	218,554	75,533	294,087	-	294,087
Supporting Services	198,313	-	198,313	-	198,313
Total Expenses	416,867	75,533	492,400	-	492,400
Changes in Net Assets	159,349	(83)	159,266	87,119	246,385
Net Assets - Beginning	902,375	87,816	990,191	568,250	1,558,441
Equity transfer	(3,092)	-	(3,092)	3,092	-
Net Assets - Ending	1,058,632	87,733	1,146,365	658,461	1,804,826

Statement of Activities and Changes in Net Assets

For the Year Ended June 30, 2013

	UNRESTRICTED				
	Undesignated	Publications	Total	Temporarily Restricted	Total 2013
Revenue					
Membership dues	$243,100	$ -	$243,100	$ -	$243,100
Convention, workshops	172,508	-	172,508	-	172,508
Sale of publications	-	114,490	114,490	-	
Contributions	-	-	-	9,243	9,423
Interest and dividends	7,625	-	7,625	6,193	13,818
Royalties	-	7,645	7,645	-	7,645
Reprint permissions	-	-	-	-	
Lay Ecclesial Ministry Grant	-	-	-	-	
Other Income	3,578	-	3,578	-	3,578
Appreciation on fair value of investments	87,150	-	87,150	69,459	156,609
Net assets released from restrictions	33,599	-	33,599	(33,599)	-
Total Revenue	547,560	122,135	669,695	51,296	720,991
Expenses					
Program Services					
Publications	-	89,585	89,585	-	89,585
Convention, workshops	185,738	-	185,738	-	185,738
Membership services	11,576	-	11,576	-	11,576
Committees	1,093	-	1,093	-	1,093
Lay Ecclesial Work Group	5,033	-	5,033	-	5,033
Holy See/Australia	11,091	-	11,091	-	11,091
Scholarship fund	28,566	-	28,566	-	28,566
Total Program Services	243,098	89,585	332,682	-	332,682
Supporting Services	215,823	-	215,823	-	215,823
Total Expenses	458,921	89,585	548,506	-	548,506
Changes in Net Assets	88,639	32,550	121,190	51,296	172,485
Net Assets - Beginning	813,735	55,266	869,001	516,955	1,385,956
Equity transfer	-	-	-	-	-
Net Assets - Ending	$902,374	$87,816	$990,191	$568,251	$1,558,441

Statements of Cash Flows

For the Years Ended June 30, 2014 and June 30, 2013

	2014	2013
Increase (Decrease) in Cash		
Cash Flows From Operating Activities		
Changes in Net Assets	$246,385	$172,485
Adjustments to reconcile changes in net assets to net cash provided by (used in) operating activities:		
Depreciation	1,682	2,229
Unrealized (gain) on investments	(191,116)	(156,609)
Change in assets and liabilities:		
(Increase) Decrease in accounts receivable	870	(3,866)
(Increase) Decrease in prepaid expenses	(533)	(4,618)
(Increase) Decrease in inventory	19,083	1,303
Increase (Decrease) in royalties payable	(553)	143
Increase (Decrease) in deferred revenue	12,025	(14,240)
Net Cash Provided by Operating Activities	87,843	(3,173)
Cash Flows From Investing Activities		
Purchase of investments	(19,525)	(13,707)
Purchases of fixed assets	-	(1,219)
Net Cash Used in Investing Activities	(19,525)	(14,926)
Increase (Decrease) in Cash and Cash Equivalents	68,318	(18,099)
Cash Balance - Beginning of Year	222,792	240,891
Cash Balance - End of Year	291,110	$222,792
Supplemental Disclosures		
Income taxes paid	$ -	$ -
Interest paid	$ -	$ -

See Accountant's Review Report and accompanying notes.

NOTES TO FINANCIAL STATEMENTS
For the Year Ended June 30, 2014 and 2013

1. Nature of Activities

The Canon Law Society of America (CLSA) is a national, not-for-profit corporation, established in November 1939 in Washington DC to promote canonical and pastoral approaches to significant issues within the Roman Catholic Church. In addition to a publication service, CLSA conducts an annual convention and other symposia to promote a better understanding of church law and its pastoral applications. Major sources of gross income are from membership dues, sales of publications and books and annual convention.

2. Basis of Financial Statement Presentation

According to Financial Accounting Standards Board (FASB) Codification Standards, CLSA is required to report information regarding its financial position and activities according to three classes of net assets:

(1) **Unrestricted Net Assets** - represents resources that are currently available for support of CLSA's operations.

(2) **Temporarily Restricted Net Assets** - represents resources that may be utilized only in accordance with the restricted purposes established by CLSA's bylaws. When a restriction expires, temporarily restricted net assets are reclassified to unrestricted net assets and reported in the statement of activities and net assets as funds are released from temporary restrictions.

(3) **Permanently Restricted Net Assets** - represents resources for which the principal is to be maintained intact and the income, may only be spent in accordance with the intent of the donor. CLSA currently does not have any permanently restricted net assets.

The financial statements are prepared on the accrual basis of accounting, whereby, revenue is recognized when earned and expenses are recognized when incurred.

3. Summary of Significant Accounting Policies

Cash and cash equivalents – For purposes of the statement of cash flows, CLSA considers all cash accounts and all highly liquid debt instruments purchased with an initial maturity of three months or less to be cash equivalents.

Investments - Investments in marketable securities with readily determinable fair values are reported at their fair values in the statement of financial position. Investment income or loss (including gains and losses on investments, interest and dividends) is included in the statement of activities as an increase or decrease in unrestricted net assets unless the income or loss is restricted by donor or law.

Investments consist principally of two mutual funds. Fair value of investments in securities is based on the latest reported sales price at June 30, 2014 and 2013.

Accounts receivable - Accounts receivable are stated at the amount management expects to collect from outstanding balances. The provision for uncollectible accounts is based on management's evaluation of the collectability of accounts receivable. CLSA considers accounts receivable to be fully collectible; accordingly, no provision for doubtful accounts is required. Books and publication receivables are considered uncollectible if not collected within 90 days after the sale.

Inventory – The inventory of books and publications is valued at cost, on the first-in, first-out method.

Property and Equipment - Purchases of furniture and equipment are recorded at cost. CLSA's policy is to capitalize expenditures for equipment purchased in the amount of $1,000 or more. Depreciation is calculated over an estimated useful life of five to ten years using the straight-line method. Depreciation and amortization for the years ended June 30, 2014 and 2013 totaled $1,682 and $2,229.

Fair Value – Financial Accounting Standards Board (FASB) Codification Standards defines fair value, establishes a framework for measuring fair value, and expands disclosures about fair value measurements and establishes a hierarchy for valuation inputs.

Fair value is the price that would be received to sell an asset or paid to transfer a liability in an orderly transaction between market participants at the measurement date. A fair value measurement assumes that the transaction to sell the asset or transfer the liability occurs in the principal market for the asset or liability or, in the absence of a principal market, the most advantageous market. Valuation techniques that are consistent with the market, income or cost approach are used to measure fair value.

The fair value hierarchy prioritizes the inputs to valuation techniques used to measure fair value into three broad levels:

- Level 1 - inputs are based upon unadjusted quoted prices for identical instruments traded in active markets.

- Level 2 - inputs are based upon quoted prices for similar instruments in active markets, quoted prices for identical or similar instruments in markets that are not active, and model-based valuation techniques for which all significant assumptions are observable in the market or can be corroborated by observable market data for substantially the full term of the assets or liabilities.

• Level 3 - inputs are generally unobservable and typically reflect management's estimates of assumptions that market participants would use in pricing the asset or liability. The fair values are therefore determined using model-based techniques that include option pricing models, discounted cash flow models, and similar techniques.

Revenue Recognition - CLSA bills membership dues annually on a basis which conforms to CLSA's fiscal year-end. Dues, workshop and convention registrations received in advance of the next fiscal year are deferred and recognized as revenue in the subsequent year.

Contributions are recognized when the donor makes a promise to give to the Society that is, in substance, unconditional. Contributions received are recorded as unrestricted, temporarily restricted, or permanently restricted support depending on the absence or existence and nature of any donor restrictions. Contributions restricted by the donor are reported as increases in unrestricted net assets if the restrictions are met or expire in the fiscal year in which the contributions are recognized. When a restriction expires, temporarily restricted net assets are reclassified as unrestricted net assets. Revenue from convention and workshop registration fees are recognized when the events take place.

Tax Status - CLSA is exempt from federal income tax under Section 501(c)(3) of the Internal Revenue Code. CLSA has not been classified by the Internal Revenue Service as a private foundation. Income which is not related to the exempt purpose, less applicable deductions, is subject to Federal and state corporate income tax. CLSA is covered under a group religious exemption and is not required to file Form 990.

Expense Allocations - Directly identifiable expenses are charged to programs and supporting services. Overhead and expenses related to more than one function are not allocated but are included in supporting services.

Estimates - In preparing financial statements in conformity with generally accepted accounting principles, management is required to make estimates and assumptions that affect the reported amounts of assets and liabilities, the disclosure of contingent assets and liabilities at the date of the financial statements, and the reported amounts of revenues and expenses during the reporting period. Actual results could differ from those estimates.

Financial Instruments – CLSA's financial instruments consist of investments, accounts receivable, accounts payable and accrued expenses. It is management's opinion the CLSA is not exposed to significant interest rate or credit risk arising from these instruments. Unless otherwise noted, the fair values of these financial instruments are market values of these financial instruments, and approximate their carrying values.

4. Investments

Investments at June 30, 2014 and 2013, which are all considered level 1, consist of the following:

	Cost	**Market**
Total Investments 6/30/2014	$1,016,520	$1,432,709
Total Investments 6/30/2013	$996,994	$1,222,068

By fund type at June 30, 2014 and 2013:

	2014		**2013**	
	Cost	**Market**	**Cost**	**Market**
Unrestricted	$554,809	$797,237	$543,944	$680,025
Restricted	461,711	635,472	453,050	542,043
Total Investments	**$1,016,520**	**$1,432,709**	**$996,994**	**$1,222,068**

CLSA invests in a professionally managed portfolio that contains balanced funds. Such investments are exposed to various risks such as interest rates, market and credit. Due to the level of risk associated with such investments and the level of uncertainty related to changes in the value of such investments, it is at least reasonably possible that changes in risks in the near term would materially affect investment balances and the amounts reported in the financial statements.

Investment income, which is included in the Statement of Activities for the years ended June 30, 2014 and 2013 is comprised of the following:

	2014		**2013**	
	Temporarily Unrestricted	**Temporarily Restricted**	**Temporarily Unrestricted**	**Temporarily Restricted**
Net Unrealized gains	$106,347	$84,769	$87,150	$69,459
Interest and dividends	10,876	8,767	7,625	6,193
Net Investment Income	**$117,223**	**$93,536**	**$94,775**	**$75,652**

5. Concentration of Credit Risk

CLSA maintains its cash in bank deposit accounts, which at times, may exceed federally insured limits. CLSA has not experienced any losses in such accounts and believes it is not exposed to any significant financial risk on cash.

6. Commitments

Office Lease - CLSA leased office space in Washington DC for a 10 year period ending December 31, 2017. Monthly rent payments were increased during year 2013 from $1,564 to $1,743. Monthly rent payments for the sixth through the tenth year will be increased by the CPI each July 1st. Rent expense for the years ended June 30, 2014 and 2013 was $20,916 and $19,842, respectively. Minimum future rental obligations are: 2015 - $20,916; 2016 – 20,916; 2017 - $20,916.

Postage Lease - CLSA entered into a fifty-four month lease for a postage machine ending November 1, 2010 at which time it was converted to a month-to-month lease. The lease payment is $127 per quarter.

7. Board Designated Funds

The Board has designated that net income from the sales of publications and books be set aside for use only in the publication activities. As reported on the statement of activities, the net assets from publications decreased in fiscal year 2014 by $83 from $87,816 to $87,733. In fiscal year 2013 the publications net assets increased by $32,550.

8. Temporarily Restricted Net Assets

The activity in the temporarily restricted net assets for years 2014 and 2013 is as follows:

	Scholarship Fund	**Ministry Grant**	**Total**
Balance June 30, 2012	$514,941	$2,014	$516,955
Income	84,895	-	84,895
Expenses	(28,566)	(5,033)	(33,599)
Balance June 30, 2013	$571,270	$ (3,019)	$568,251
Income	106,481	-	106,481
Expenses	(19,290)	(72)	(19,362)
Transfer from Undesignated	-	3,092	3,092
Balance June 30,2014	$658,461	$ -	$658,461

9. Annual Meeting Site Reservation Agreements

CLSA has reserved hotel space for future annual meetings. The terms of these reservation agreements provide that a few will be assessed to CSLA if the reservation is canceled due to site change, within a specified period prior to the meeting dates.

10. Executive Coordinator's Contract

CLSA has contracted with Sisters of Mercy of the Americas South Central Community and Sister Sharon Euart to serve as their Executive Coordinator beginning August 1, 2008 and ending July 31, 2011. The agreement has been renewed extending the contract date to December 31, 2013.

11. Subsequent Events

Management has evaluated subsequent events through August 27, 2014, the date that the financial statements were available to be issued. There were no significant events to report.

Supplementary Information
Schedule of Program Services
For the Year Ended June 30, 2014

	2014	2013
Publications		
Cost of publications sold	$21,194	$25,092
Executive coordinator office	11,693	12,951
Royalty expense	1.977	2,863
Advertising	-	50
BrightKey	40,669	48,629
Total Publication Expenses	75,533	89,585
Convention and Pre-convention Workshop		
Coordination	108,992	131,500
Food service	2,418	1,371
Honoraria	9,200	8,300
Speakers' travel	-	3,721
Printing	4,688	5,591
Freight	678	648
Other	18,890	26,100
Postage	572	529
Convention chair	1,091	1,163
Liturgy	2,293	2,213
Supplies	5,974	3,611
Convention planning	1,946	219
Convention company	608	772
Total Convention and Pre-Convention Workshop	157,350	185,738
Membership Services		
Postage	3,373	6,289
Printing	4,025	5,239
Newsletter	39	48
Platform service webinar	1,402	-
Total Membership Services	8,839	11,576
Visit to Holy See and Australia Trip	10,801	11,091

	2014	2013
Committees		
Church governance	337	-
Resource & asset management	91	233
Nominations	2,143	33
Clergy	165	6
Laity	-	185
Other	19,466	461
Sacramental law	-	175
Total Committees	22,202	1,093
Lay Ecclesial Ministry Work Group	72	5,033
Scholarship Fund		
Scholarships paid	17,959	24,099
Scholarships expenses	1,331	4,467
Total Scholarship Fund	19,290	28,566
Total Program Services	$294,087	$332,682

See Accountants' Review Report and accompanying notes.

Supplementary Information

Schedule of Supporting Services
For the Year Ended June 30, 2014

	2014	2013
Board of Governors		
Rental housing	$12,508	$12,923
Travel	4,843	4,716
Food service	5,732	5,713
Other expenses	450	1,004
President	4,634	2,983
Vice President	552	265
Executive Coordinator Office	146,996	166,148
Depreciation expense	1,682	2,229
Rent expense	20,916	19,842
Total Supporting Services	$198,313	$215,823

Annual Budget
Fiscal Year 2014-2015

GENERAL OPERATIONS		
Income	$	286,815
Expenses	$	304,015
Excess/(Deficit)	**$**	**(17,200)**
PUBLICATIONS		
Income	$	95,000
Expenses	$	77,800
Excess/(Deficit)	**$**	**17,200**
CONVENTIONS		
Income	$	165,390
Expenses	$	165,390
Excess/(Deficit)	**$**	-
Subtotal Gen. Ops., Pub. & Conv. *	**$**	-
SCHOLARSHIP FUND		
Income	$	35,600
Expenses	$	23,775
Excess/(Deficit)	**$**	**11,825**
Grand Total *	**$**	**11,825**

Note: Since Scholarship income by definition belongs to the Scholarship Fund, it cannot be used to balance the overall budget. Hence, the first three CLSA "companies" as a whole need to achieve a balance independently, and the number labeled as "Grand Total" is not a simple "operational" profit. An "Excess" in the Scholarship Fund represents an increase in the fund, which is needed for the fund to grow.

General Operations Unit Summary *(by fiscal year)*

	Budget 14-15	Actual 13-14	Budget 13-14	Actual 12-13	Budget 12-13
INCOME					
Investment Income					
Interest/RCT	$ -	$ 10	$ -	$ 2	$ -
Dividends/CUIT	$ 6,000	$ 10,865	$ 6,000	$ 7,623	$ 6,000
Sub-total	**$ 6,000**	**$ 10,875**	**$ 6,000**	**$ 7,625**	**$ 6,000**
Portion of Prior Year Realized Net Asset Increase (Note 1)	**$ 48,815**		**$ 26,429**		**$ 24,012**
Dues Income					
New Member Dues	$ 12,000	$ 13,500	$ 11,000	$ 10,300	$ 10,000
Previous Year Member Dues	$ -	$ -	$ -	$ 400	$ -
Current Year Member Dues	$ 220,000	$ 226,800	$ 215,000	$ 232,400	$ 211,000
Sub-total	**$ 232,000**	**$ 240,300**	**$ 226,000**	**$ 243,100**	**$ 221,000**
Intensive Workshop Registration (Penal Law)		**$ 23,375**			
TOTAL INCOME	**$ 286,815**	**$ 274,550**	**$ 258,429**	**$ 250,725**	**$ 251,012**
EXPENSES					
Staff Compensations and Benefits (Note 2)	**$ 178,907**	**$ 112,065**	**$ 152,098**	**$ 139,053**	**$ 138,499**
Service Charges					
Bank Service Charges/Wells Fargo	$ 600	$ 696	$ 400	$ 458	$ 100
Flex Fund/RCT	$ 50	$ -	$ 50	$ 45	$ 100
Credit Card Fees	$ 4,000	$ 3,557	$ 4,500	$ 3,065	$ 4,000
Sub-total	**$ 4,650**	**$ 4,253**	**$ 4,950**	**$ 3,568**	**$ 4,200**
OEC Expenses (by account number)					
Postage Meter Lease	$ 900	$ 852	$ 900	$ 1,098	$ 900
Postage Meter Supplies	$ 175	$ 106	$ 150	$ 157	$ 200
Insurance & Workers	$ 1,100	$ 1,057	$ 2,200	$ 678	$ 2,200
Hospitality	$ 600	$ 484	$ 500	$ 449	$ 600
Postage/UPS/FedEx	$ 500	$ 628	$ 600	$ 472	$ 800
Office Supplies	$ 2,500	$ 2,122	$ 2,500	$ 2,323	$ 2,500
Telephone/ISP/DSL	$ 3,000	$ 2,943	$ 3,000	$ 3,284	$ 3,000
Travel	$ 1,000	$ 317	$ 500	$ 1,059	$ 2,500
Continuing Education (EC)	$ 1,000	$ -	$ -	$ -	$ 1,000
Taxes	$ 130	$ 80	$ 100	$ 130	$ 100

General Operations Unit Summary *(by fiscal year)*

	Budget 14-15	Actual 13-14	Budget 13-14	Actual 12-13	Budget 12-13
Furniture & Equipment	$ 1,000	$ 1,309	$ 1,000	$ 1,825	$ 1,500
Books and Periodicals	$ 300	$ 215	$ 400	$ 489	$ 500
Professional Collaboration w/ Nat'l Organizations	$ 500	$ -	$ 500	$ -	$ 500
Staffing Transition	$ -	$ -	$ -	$ 445	
Rent	$ 20,916	$ 20,916	$ 20,916	$ 19,842	$ 19,144
Copier Lease	$ -	$ -	$ -	$ 1,143	$ 3,500
Copier Maintenance	$ 800	$ 800	$ 800	$ 800	$ 800
Sub-total	**$ 34,421**	**$ 31,830**	**$ 34,066**	**$ 34,194**	**$ 39,744**
Professional Services					
Accountant/Auditor (Note 3)	$ 6,000	$ 5,700	$ 5,000	$ 3,600	$ 4,500
Web Design & Maintenance	$ 6,237	$ 6,237	$ 6,237	$ 5,390	$ 5,940
Legal Services	$ 500	$ -	$ 500	$ -	$ 500
Sub-total	**$ 12,737**	**$ 11,937**	**$ 11,737**	**$ 8,990**	**$ 10,940**
Member Services					
General Postage	$ 1,800	$ 897	$ 1,800	$ 1,392	$ 1,500
Newsletter Postage	$ 50	$ 39	$ 50	$ 48	$ 100
Proceedings Printing	$ 5,300	$ 4,025	$ 5,000	$ 5,239	$ 5,000
Proceedings Postage	$ 5,000	$ 2,476	$ 4,500	$ 4,897	$ 4,500
Sub-total	**$ 12,150**	**$ 7,437**	**$ 11,350**	**$ 11,576**	**$ 11,100**
Board of Governors, Meetings					
Food	$ 6,000	$ 5,732	$ 6,000	$ 5,713	$ 5,900
Lodging	$ 13,000	$ 12,508	$ 14,000	$ 12,923	$ 13,000
Meeting Space	$ 1,000	$ 450	$ 1,200	$ 999	$ 1,400
Postage/UPS	$ -	$ -	$ 50	$ -	$ 50
Supplies	$ 50	$ -	$ 50	$ 5	$ 50
Telephone	$ -	$ -	$ -	$ -	$ 100
Travel	$ 9,000	$ 4,843	$ 9,000	$ 4,715	$ 9,500
Rome or Australia Trip	$ 10,000	$ 10,801	$ 10,000	$ 11,091	$ 10,000
Sub-total	**$ 39,050**	**$ 34,335**	**$ 40,300**	**$ 35,446**	**$ 40,000**
Board of Governors, Officers					
President	$ 4,000	$ 4,634	$ 5,000	$ 2,983	$ 6,000
Vice President/Past President	$ 500	$ 552	$ 500	$ 265	$ 500
Treasurer/Secretary	$ 500	$ -	$ 500	$ -	$ 500
Sub-total	**$ 5,000**	**$ 5,186**	**$ 6,000**	**$ 3,248**	**$ 7,000**
Intensive Workshop Expense (Penal Law)		**$ 18,801**			
Committees					

General Operations Unit Summary *(by fiscal year)*

	Budget 14-15	Actual 13-14	Budget 13-14	Actual 12-13	Budget 12-13
Constitutional Committees (order of Const.)					
Nominations Committee	$ 1,800	$ 2,143	$ 1,800	$ 33	$ 1,800
Resolutions Committee	$ 100	$ -	$ 100	$ -	$ 100
Resource & Asset Management	$ 500	$ 91	$ 500	$ 233	$ 500
Professional Responsibilities Committee	$ -	$ -	$ -	$ -	$ -
Standing Committees (alphabetical)					
Church Governance Committee	$ 2,000	$ 337	$ 500	$ -	$ 500
Clergy Committee	$ 500	$ 165	$ 500	$ 6	$ 1,500
Institutes of Consecrated Life Committee	$ 150	$ -	$ 150	$ -	$ 150
Laity Committee	$ 2,500	$ -	$ 2,500	$ 185	$ 250
Research & Development	$ 1,500	$ 314	$ 1,500	$ 184	$ 1,500
Sacramental Law Committee	$ 1,000	$ -	$ 1,000	$ 175	$ 1,000
Committee Chair Orientation	$ 350	$ 629			
Approved Cmte. Work	$ 1,000	$ 36	$ 1,000	$ 452	$ 1,000
Sub-total	**$ 11,400**	**$ 3,715**	**$ 9,550**	**$ 1,268**	**$ 8,300**
Miscellaneous					
Platform Service Expense - Webinar (Note 4)	$ 3,200	$ 1,402	$ 1,000	$ -	$ 1,500
Depreciation		$ 1,682		$ 2,229	
Sub-total	**$ 3,200**	**$ 3,084**	**$ 1,000**	**$ 2,229**	**$ 1,500**
EC Staffing Transition	**$ 2,500**	**$ 7,516**			
Lay Ecc. Work Group Expense		**$ 72**	**$ -**	**$ 5,033**	**$ 5,000**
TOTAL EXPENSES	**$ 304,015**	**$ 240,231**	**$ 271,051**	**$ 244,605**	**$ 264,783**
EXCESS/DEFICIT	**$ (17,200)**	**$ 34,320**	**$ (12,622)**	**$ 6,120**	**$ (234,771)**

Publications Unit Summary *(by fiscal year)*

	Budget 14-15	Actual 13-14	Budget 13-14	Actual 12-13	Budget 12-13
INCOME					
Publication Sales	$ 75,000	$ 56,855	$ 75,000	$ 91,819	$ 80,000
Reprint Permissions	$ -	$ -	$ 500	$ -	$ 1,000
Royalty Income	$ 5,000	$ 8,246	$ 4,000	$ 7,645	$ 4,000
Shipping/Restocking - BrightKey	$ 15,000	$ 10,349	$ 20,000	$ 16,525	$ 20,000
Database Resolution					
TOTAL INCOME	**$ 95,000**	**$ 75,450**	**$ 99,500**	**$ 115,989**	**$ 105,000**
Cost of Goods Sold		$ 21,194		$ 25,092	
GROSS PROFIT	**$ 95,000**	**$ 54,256**		**$ 90,896**	
EXPENSES					
Compensation & Professional Services					
Staff Salary (Note 1)	$ 4,950	$ 4,514	$ 4,368	$ 3,850	$ 4,800
Accountant (Note 1)	$ 1,875	$ 1,900	$ 2,500	$ 1,600	$ 2,000
Publications Advisory Board	$ 2,500	$ 2,456	$ 2,200	$ 3,417	$ 2,200
Sub-total	**$ 9,325**	**$ 8,869**	**$ 9,068**	**$ 8,867**	**$ 9,000**
Royalties Paid					
Royalties/*CCEO*	$ 300	$ 166	$ 200	$ 284	$ 200
Royalties/*CIC*	$ 1,600	$ 1,534	$ 1,600	$ 2,086	$ 1,600
Royalties/*Dignitas Connubii*	$ 400	$ 203	$ 400	$ 391	$ 400
Royalties/*Selected Issues*	$ 100	$ 73	$ 50	$ 79	$ 50
Royalties/*Reception and Communion*	$ 25	$ -	$ 25	$ 24	$ 25
Sub-total	**$ 2,425**	**$ 1,977**	**$ 2,275**	**$ 2,864**	**$ 2,275**
Publication Expenses					
Advertising - Printing	$ 100	$ -	$ 500	$ 10	$ 500
Advertising - Electronic	$ 50	$ -	$ 100	$ 40	$ 100
Book Production	$ 15,000	$ -	$ 20,000	$ -	$ 20,000
Storage of Negatives	$ -	$ -	$ -	$ -	$ 100
Copyright Applications	$ 100	$ -	$ 150	$ -	$ 150
Outsourcing - BrightKey	$ 46,000	$ 39,175	$ 51,000	$ 47,640	$ 50,000
Sub-total	**$ 61,250**	**$ 39,175**	**$ 71,750**	**$ 47,690**	**$ 70,850**
Office of the Executive Coordinator					
Postage	$ 150	$ 74	$ 100	$ 234	$ 100
Supplies	$ 150	$ 91	$ 150	$ 109	$ 150
Sub-total	**$ 300**	**$ 165**	**$ 250**	**$ 343**	**$ 250**
Service Charges					
Bank Service Charges/Wells Fargo	$ 500	$ 555	$ 400	$ 476	$ 100
Credit Card Fees	$ 4,000	$ 2,104	$ 5,000	$ 3,264	$ 5,000
Sub-total	**$ 4,500**	**$ 2,659**	**$ 5,400**	**$ 3,740**	**$ 5,100**

Publications Unit Summary *(by fiscal year)*

	Budget 14-15	Actual 13-14	Budget 13-14	Actual 12-13	Budget 12-13
Miscellaneous					
Publications Contingencies	$ -	$ -	$ 500	$ -	$ 500
Sub-total	**$ -**	**$ -**	**$ 500**	**$ -**	**$ 500**
Database Resolution		$ 1,494	$ -	$ 989	$ 5,000
TOTAL EXPENSES	**$ 77,800**	**$ 54,338**	**$ 89,243**	**$ 64,493**	**$ 92,975**
EXCESS/DEFICIT	**$ 17,200**	**$ (83)**	**$ 10,257**	**$ 26,403**	**$ 12,025**
Self-Funded Projects (Note 2)					
Canon Law Digest Resolution					
Income	$ 2,517		$ 4,011		$ 5,000
Expenses		$ 1494		$ 989	
Total Excess/(Deficit)		$ 2,517		$ 4,011	

Note 1: This line item is apportioned between General Operations and Publications.

Note 2: These lines are for the Resolution approved by the membership at the 2010 convention. Since it includes designated funds and could stretch across many fiscal years, it is not included in the annual budget.

Conventions Unit Summary *(by fiscal year)*

	Budget 14-15	Actual 13-14	Budget 13-14	Actual 12-13	Budget 12-13
INCOME					
Convention Fees (Note 1)	$ 122,000	$ 132,850	$ 122,000	$ 121,500	$ 108,500
Pre-Convention W1 Fees (Note 2)	$ 10,450	$ 12,575	$ 9,625	$ 13,950	$ 6,250
Pre-Convention W2 Fees	$ 10,450	$ 10,775	$ 11,000	$ 12,900	$ 8,750
Exhibitors' Fees	$ 2,500	$ 2,725	$ 2,375	$ 3,165	$ 1,800
Sponsors' Donations	$ -	$ 1,200	$ -	$ 4,200	$ -
Additional Banquet Fees	$ 420	$ 480	$ 420	$ 650	$ 200
Guest Registrations	$ 500	$ 200	$ 500	$ 650	$ 200
Hotel Room Commission (Note 3)	$ 13,000	$ 15,151	$ 13,000	$ 15,493	$ 12,000
Surplus from Prev.Year (Note 4)	$ 6,070				
TOTAL INCOME	**$ 165,390**	**$ 175,956**	**$ 158,920**	**$ 172,508**	**$ 137,700**
EXPENSES					
Professional Services					
General Convention Chair	$ 1,300	$ 1,091	$ 1,500	$ 1,163	$ 1,800
Convention Liturgy Chair	$ 500	$ -	$ -	$ -	$ 600
Convention Planning Committee	$ 2,000	$ 1,946	$ 2,000	$ 219	$ 2,000
OEC	$ 2,200	$ 2,233	$ 1,500	$ 898	$ 1,500
Convention Company	$ 250	$ 608	$ 700	$ 772	$ 600
Sub-total	**$ 6,250**	**$ 5,878**	**$ 5,700**	**$ 3,052**	**$ 6,500**
Pre-Convention					
Honoraria	$ 3,000	$ 3,000	$ 3,000	$ 3,000	$ 3,000
Liturgy	$ 500	$ 500	$ 500	$ 500	$ 500
Printing	$ 100	$ -	$ 100	$ -	$ 150
Shipping	$ 50	$ 42	$ 50	$ 32	$ 50
Speaker's Travel & Lodging	$ 2,000	$ -	$ 2,500	$ 2,108	$ 2,500
Supplies	$ 150	$ 148	$ 150	$ 100	$ 150
Sub-total	**$ 5,800**	**$ 3,689**	**$ 6,300**	**$ 5,740**	**$ 6,350**
Convention					
Convention Company/Nix	$ 42,640	$ 42,249	$ 41,000	$ 40,677	$ 40,000
Convention Hotel (Note 5)	$ 69,500	$ 66,743	$ 63,000	$ 88,982	$ 45,700
Audio Visual	$ 13,000	$ 12,695	$ 12,000	$ 22,015	$ 8,500
Food (Note 6)	$ 2,000	$ 2,418	$ 2,300	$ 1,370	$ 2,000
Honoraria	$ 6,100	$ 6,200	$ 6,500	$ 5,300	$ 5,500
Liturgy	$ 2,000	$ 1,793	$ 2,000	$ 1,713	$ 2,000
Postage	$ 1,000	$ 572	$ 1,500	$ 529	$ 2,000
Printing	$ 4,000	$ 4,688	$ 4,000	$ 5,591	$ 4,000
Shipping	$ 700	$ 637	$ 700	$ 617	$ 650
Speaker's Travel	$ 2,500	$ -	$ 3,000	$ 1,613	$ 2,000
Supplies	$ 6,000	$ 5,826	$ 6,000	$ 3,511	$ 7,000
Telephone/Internet	$ -	$ -	$ 100	$ 7	$ 100
Other/Contingency	$ -	$ -		$ 1,841	
Sub-total	**$ 149,440**	**$ 143,820**	**$ 142,100**	**$ 173,766**	**$ 119,450**
Service Charges					
Bank Service Charges/Wells Fargo (Note 9)	$ 400	$ 451	$ 400	$ 333	$ 100

Conventions Unit Summary *(by fiscal year)*

	Budget 14-15	Actual 13-14	Budget 13-14	Actual 12-13	Budget 12-13
Credit Card Fees	$ 3,500	$ 3,512	$ 3,000	$ 2,845	$ 3,000
Sub-total	**$ 3,900**	**$ 3,962**	**$ 3,400**	**$ 3,178**	**$ 3,100**
TOTAL EXPENSES	**$ 165,390**	**$ 157,350**	**$ 157,500**	**$ 185,736**	**$ 135,400**
EXCESS/DEFICIT	**$ -**	**$ 18,607**	**$ 1,420**	**$ (13,228)**	**$ 2,300**

Note 1: FY 2014-2015 Budget assumes 305 attendees @ $400 ea.

Note 2: FY 2014-2015 Budget assumes 76 pre-convention attendees (38 per workshop) @ $275 ea.

Note 3: This line represents the hotel room commission we receive as a result of the work of NIX; this commission was previously included in the hotel bill.

Note 4: This line item reflects surplus in the convention unit from FY 2013-2014, used to balance the overall budget for 2014-2015.

Note 5: This item reflects general convention expenses with the contracted hotel, including one lunch for convention attendees.

Note 6: This line item reflects expenses for volunteer snacks, food/liquor for the presidential suite, and the banquet wine.

Scholarship Unit Summary *(by fiscal year)*

	Budget 14-15	Actual 13-14	Budget 13-14	Actual 12-13	Budget 12-13
INCOME					
Investment Income (Automatically Reinvested in Fund)					
Interest Income/Wells Fargo	$ 100	$ 107	$ 100	$ 109	$ 100
Dividends/CUIT	$ 5,000	$ 8,660	$ 5,000	$ 6,084	$ 5,000
Sub-Total	**$ 5,100**	**$ 8,767**	**$ 5,100**	**$ 6,193**	**$ 5,100**
Designated Funds (Note 1)					
Previously Designated Funds	$ 14,000	$ 14,000	$ 14,000	$ 14,000	$ 14,000
This Year Designated Funds	$ 7,000	$ 7,000	$ 7,000	$ 13,000	$ 7,000
Sub-Total	**$ 21,000**	**$ 21,000**	**$ 21,000**	**$ 27,000**	**$ 21,000**
Scholarship Donations Income					
Donations Accompanying Dues	$ 2,000	$ 1,550	$ 2,000	$ 2,110	$ 1,500
Donations from Appeal	$ 6,000	$ 9,145	$ 6,000	$ 5,945	$ 6,000
Donations from Convention	$ 500	$ 1,250	$ 500	$ 950	$ -
Donations from Regional Meetings	$ 1,000	$ 1,000	$ 1,000	$ 238	$ 1,000
Sub-Total	**$ 9,500**	**$ 12,945**	**$ 9,500**	**$ 9,243**	**$ 8,500**
TOTAL INCOME	**$ 35,600**	**$ 42,712**	**$ 35,600**	**$ 42,436**	**$ 34,600**
EXPENSES					
Service Charges					
Money Market Fees/Wells Fargo	$ 1,200	$ 1,084	$ 1,200	$ 1,058	$ 500
Sub-total	**$ 1,200**	**$ 1,084**	**$ 1,200**	**$ 1,058**	**$ 500**
Postage					
General Postage	$ 25	$ -	$ 25	$ 4	$ 50
Appeal Postage	$ 950	$ 247	$ 700	$ 884	$ 700
Sub-total	**$ 975**	**$ 247**	**$ 725**	**$ 888**	**$ 750**
Printing					
General Printing	$ 100	$ -	$ 150	$ -	$ 150
Appeal Printing	$ 500	$ -	$ 200	$ 428	$ 200
Misc. Expenses				$ 80	
Sub-total	**$ 600**	**$ -**	**$ 350**	**$ 508**	**$ 350**
Scholarships					
Current Awards (Note 2)	$ 21,000	$ 17,959	$ 21,000	$ 24,098	$ 21,000
Sub-total	**$ 21,000**	**$ 17,959**	**$ 21,000**	**$ 24,098**	**$ 21,000**
TOTAL EXPENSES	**$ 23,775**	**$ 19,290**	**$ 23,275**	**$ 26,552**	**$ 22,600**

Scholarship Unit Summary *(by fiscal year)*

	Budget 14-15	Actual 13-14	Budget 13-14	Actual 12-13	Budget 12-13
EXCESS/DEFICIT	**$ 11,825**	**$ 23,423**	**$ 12,325**	**$ 15,884**	**$ 12,000**
Additional Designated Funds (Note 1)					
Funds per 2011 Board Resolution					
5% of rolling quarter CUIT Investment (12/31/12); Return from endowment				$ 23,630	
Approved Future Awards (Note 2)				$ 21,000	
Excess available for Sch. Fund expenses				$ 2,630	

Note 1: These are future funds to give out and transfers within Scholarship accounts, as such they are not included in the annual Scholarship budget. Income and expenses in FY 13-14 become income and expenses for FY 14-15.

Note 2: Assumes 3 awards at $7,000 each; one third year, one second year and one first year.

Officer's Report

Report of the Executive Coordinator

Rev. Roger H. Keeler, PhD, JCD

I begin my first report to you by expressing heartfelt thanks for your letters, notes, messages and telephone calls of welcome and encouragement. I feel especially blessed by the warmth you have shown me, and truly privileged to be invited to your service.

I would like to thank our out-going President, Fr. Philip Brown, *pss*, for the myriad ways in which he has eased me into Washington. His wonderful sense of ritual and continuity was expressed when he walked with me to the office that warm August Monday morning and introduced me to Colleen Crawford and Mary DeBroeck. He has faithfully been there whenever I have been in need and, for that, I am grateful.

The Office of the Executive Coordinator is in good hands with Colleen and Mary! I have been continually astonished at their knowledge, experience, and grasp of every detail. I am truly happy – and eager – to collaborate with them in their work. They have shown saintly patience and singular graciousness as they get me "house broken"!

On the day I arrived in the OEC, Colleen presented me with a stack of binders containing minutes and reports, protocols and plans, handbooks and workbooks, budgets and auditor's findings. "Here," she said with a sigh, "is just about everything you'll need to know about how things work. You might want to start with the Board of Governor's Minutes. It's this one." She deposited the large black-covered binder on my desk with a smile. "It has just about everything that's happened since 2008."

I have read – and am still reading! – all of that, trying to absorb the story of the CLSA so well preserved between those covers. I often find myself feeling somewhat like the young Jonas, the Receiver of Memory, in Lois Lowry's masterful tale *The Giver*, feeling at once overwhelmed – yet wondrously drawn – into the world revealed by the kind, gracious Giver. In my case the Giver's voice is heard through the pages of those books. At other times the Giver's voice is heard through many: you have offered your insights and recollections, suggestions and counsel. I have tried to absorb what you have given and, with time, I hope good fruit will be born of it.

I have been truly blessed in being able to begin my ministry of stewardship with relative ease and freedom from the anxiety that so often mars new beginnings. Why?

Because of Sr. Sharon Euart, RSM. Sr. Sharon has shown yeoman service in her five and a half year tenure as Executive Coordinator of the Society. I read her first Convention Report penned in 2008 and was dismayed to learn how she needed to "begin from ground zero." So much needed to be done! Staffing, computers, payroll, website management ... the list is taxing, almost overwhelming. Yet she established her five-point plan and stuck with it. The result is a Society on fine administrative footing, in a solid financial position, engaged in myriad initiatives, and with tack set to the wind. A tremendous debt of gratitude is owed to her by all of us.

So, as I assume the helm that was ably steered by Colleen and Mary, with Sr. Sharon's keen eye for navigation, through the months of transition, I do so with a desire to continue on that same tack, while keeping before me the Preamble of our *Constitution*:

> We, the members of the Canon Law Society of America, ever eager to fulfill our role in the Church through the proper use of canon law, hereby proclaim our desire to promote the use of every method of serving God's people that comes under the concept of law. Mindful that Church laws ought to be pastoral in character and made only to serve the people of God, we accept our responsibility as Christians trained in canon law to continue research and study and to assist any members of Christ's Body singularly or collectively, laity or clergy, who will welcome our deliberations, research and common opinion of this Society.

As we read these words anew, we whisper the words of Pope Saint John Paul II found in *Sacrae Disciplinae Leges*, turning them into a prayer asking that "we may be buoyed up by the hope that a zealous Church discipline will flourish anew, and from it the salvation of souls will be ever more fervently promoted." May God grant us joy and peace, wisdom and patience, enthusiasm and renewed vision. Amen!

Committee Reports

Constitutional Standing Committees 2013-2014

Committee: Nominations
Constituted: Constitution, Article X
Charge: The mandate of the Committee is:

1. To submit to the active members, at least one month prior to the date of election, the names of nominees as provided for in Article IX of the Constitutions; (and)
2. To formulate and recommend to the Board of Governors plans for maintaining and increasing the membership of the Society.

This is a standing committee of the Society. Its current composition is as follows:

Members: Rev. Lawrence Jurcak, *chair* (2014)
Rev. John Vaughan, *ex officio* (2014)
Rev. Lawrence DiNardo (2015)
Ms. Margaret Romano-Hogan (2016)

ANNUAL REPORT

This Committee meets annually to form nominations for the offices to be elected at the national convention in October. The Nominations Committee met in Washington, D.C. on February 18 - 19, 2014 at the Hecker Center.

During the afternoon of February 18, lists of possible candidates for various offices were compiled from recommendations to the committee from the membership at large, those suggested by the Board of Governors, and those identified by members of the committee. Attention was paid to selecting candidates who would offer sound leadership to the Board of Governors while representing diverse constituencies and regions.

The following day, committee members began contacting prospective candidates. After securing candidates for each of the required offices, which took much longer than expected, the following slate of candidates was forwarded to the Board of Governors for presentation to the membership at the 2014 convention in Saint Louis, Missouri.

For Vice-President/President-Elect:
Rev. Manuel Viera, OFM, JCL (Tucson)
Dr. Gerald T. Jorgensen, JCL (Dubuque)

For Consultor:

Ms. Anne E. Bryant, JCL (Houston)
Ms. Patricia M. Dugan, JD, JCL (Philadelphia)
Rev. Peter B. Mangum, JCL (Shreveport)
Rev. David J. Klein, JCL (Camden)

For Secretary:

Miss Mary Gen Blittschau, JCL (Evansville)
Sister Marilyn R. Vassallo, CSJ (Albany)

We think it is a slate of members, generous in accepting the nomination, with experience in the Society and in practical Church positions. The Committee thanks those individuals who have been willing to consider service to the Society as elected officers. The Committee also thanks those who were contacted for consideration, but for varied reasons were unable to accept nomination at this time.

The Nominees' *Curricula Vitae* and Photographs were compiled by the Executive Coordinator's Office. That office publishes the Convention Program and Report Booklet – which includes the information pertaining to the candidates.

The Committee will meet during the Saint Louis Convention as necessary in preparation for the election which takes place during the Business Meeting.

The Committee believes that the on-going development of individuals for leadership in the Society is a reality that needs to be addressed by the Board of Governors.

Respectfully submitted
Rev. Lawrence Jurcak, Chair

Committee: Resolutions
Constituted: Constitution, Article X
Mandate:

1. To solicit, develop and draft proposed resolutions which will express the concerns of the Canon Law Society of America;
2. To consult with the membership at large and, in particular with the Board of Governors the standing and ad hoc committees of the Society, and the organizers of the convention;
3. To formulate resolutions on given points in response to requests of the members of the Society;
4. To compose differences in the formulation of similar proposals and to revise all the proposals so the meaning of each is clear; (and)
5. To encourage resolutions which authentically express in a positive way the activities and concerns of the Society.

Members: Ms. Susan Mulheron (2014)
Rev. Langes Silva (2015)

Rev. Jamin David (2016)

ANNUAL REPORT

The Resolutions Committee will hear and process resolutions during the 2014 convention.

Committee: Resource and Asset Management
Constituted: Constitution, Article X, as last amended in 2008 and 2013
Old Committee Structure: Committees on Budget, Investment and Scholarship Fund.
Charge: The functions of the Committee on Resource and Asset Management shall be:

1. To develop a comprehensive budge for all the activities of the Society and report on the funding available for projects;
2. To submit the proposed budget for the coming fiscal year to the Board of governors for approval at its springs meeting;
3. To conserve, invest and disburse the monies of the Scholarship Fund in accord with the criteria established by the Society; (and)
4. To advise the Treasurer on all matters pertaining to the Society's investments. (Article X, 7)

Membership: The Committee of Resource and Asset Management shall consist of the Vice-President, the Treasurer, and a senior consultor and two additional members appointed by the President. The Treasurer shall act as Chair of this committee. (Article X, 2)

Members: Rev. Tom Cronkleton, *chair; treasurer* (2016)
Msgr. Charles Antonicelli (2014)
Msgr. Michael Souckar, *ex officio* (2014)
Sr. Margaret A. Stallmeyer, CDP (Advisor)
Most Rev. Joseph R. Binzer (Advisor)

ANNUAL REPORT

The Resource and Asset Management Committee in mid-January discussed via email the upcoming interim when the Executive Coordinator position would become vacant and prepared a several recommendation concerning compensation for the Board of Governors to be presented at their January meeting

The Committee met electronically the morning of February 28, 2014. We reviewed the Proposed 2014-2015 Budget Materials prepared by Sister Sharon Euart and Colleen Crawford. After reviewing the materials and making some changes, the decision was made to forward the Proposed Budget to the Board of

Governors for their approval. Upon review of the quarterly rolling average of the Scholarship CUIT fund as of December 31, 2013, we determined the average to be $521,542.03. Five percent (5%) of this is $26,077.10. We determined that up to $21,000.00 should be made available for scholarships and the remainder to help finance the expense of the scholarship unit.

Respectfully submitted,
Rev. Thomas E. Cronkleton, Jr., Chair

Please see the Report of the Treasurer on page 369. The proposed budget for fiscal year 2014-2015 may be found on page 390.

Committee: Professional Responsibility
Constituted: Constitution, Article X, as last amended in 1995, and the Code of Professional Responsibilities, canon 9c(1), d(1)
Charge: The mandate of the Committee is:

1. Regarding complaints:
   a) To receive complaints of any party aggrieved with respect to provisions of the *Code of Professional Responsibility* originally adopted by the CLSA in October, 1983, and its can. 9d(i);
   b) To make an initial finding that the complaint is not frivolous but is serious in character; (and)
   c) By majority vote to refer the matter to the hearing officers.
2. To issue advisory opinions and decisions on the application of the *Code of Professional Responsibility*; (and)
3. To advise on all other questions concerning the professional responsibility of canonists (can. 9d(i) of the PR Code).

Members:
Rev. James Conn, SJ, *chair* (2014)
Dcn. Gerald Jorgensen, *ex officio* (2014)
Ms. Catherine Gilligan, *ex officio* (2014)
Rev. Paul Hartmann, *hearing officer* (2014)
Msgr. Frederick Easton, *hearing officer* (2015)
Msgr. John Alesandro, *hearing officer* (2016)

ANNUAL REPORT

Inasmuch as no cases have been brought to the attention of the Professional Responsibility Committee this quarter, there is no activity to report.

Respectfully submitted,
Rev. James Conn, SJ, Chair

On-Going Committee Reports 2013-2014

Committee: Church Governance
Constituted: 2009
Mandate: It is the function of the Committee on Church Governance:

1. To initiate as needed any projects pertinent to the study of canon law pertaining to Church structures and governance or the implementation thereof, including but not limited to the following: (a) diocesan and parish temporalities; (b) consultative bodies; (c) diocesan and parish structures; (d) power of governance; (e) comparative law issues; (f) Eastern canon law and institutions
2. To oversee projects referred to the committee by the BOG;
3. To oversee its subcommittees working on projects concerning Church governance; (and)
4. To collaborate with national organizations and other groups dealing with issues of Church governance.

Members: Ms. Barbara Bettwy, *chair* (2016)
Rev. J. Patrick Reynolds (2015)
Msgr. William King (2016)
Rev. Francis Marini (2016)
Sr. Nancy Reynolds, SP (2016)

ANNUAL REPORT

The committee has spent the year constructing, conducting and analyzing the Survey of Diocesan Finance Councils which was mandated by a resolution passed at the 2012 Convention.

In January, some of the committee members met with Dr. Charles Zech, the Director of the Institute for Church Management at Villanova University. Dr. Zech is an expert in the area of church financial matters. He volunteered his services as a consultant on this project and was extremely helpful. The committee is indebted to him for his invaluable service. The committee spent the next few months designing the survey instrument with Dr. Zech's assistance.

In May a letter was sent to all Bishops and Eparchs in the United States from the President of the CLSA and the Committee chair informing them of the survey, its purpose and its methodology. Bishops and Eparchs were assured that they would receive the final report of the results. In order to keep the survey results anonymous, it was decided to conduct the survey on-line using SurveyMonkey. The committee also determined that it would attempt to fulfill the resolution's goal of evaluating the effectiveness of diocesan finance councils by conducting two different surveys.

In June, the first survey was sent to all Diocesan Financial Officers (DFO). To do this the committee had already arranged with Mr. Patrick Markey, the Executive Director of the Diocesan Fiscal Management Conference (DFMC), to send the survey out to all DFOs through the DFMC membership e-mail list. The committee also wishes to express its gratitude to Mr. Markey for his tremendous assistance with this project. In addition to completing the DFO Survey, the DFO was asked to send another survey to two members of his/her Diocesan Finance Council (DFC).

Again, in an attempt to ensure anonymity, the two members of the DFC received the link to the Members Survey (also through SurveyMonkey) directly from their DFO. The Member Survey differed from the DFO Survey in that it is shorter and asked more questions dealing with the effectiveness and functioning of the DFC.

The surveys were closed on SurveyMonkey the first week of July. A total of 121 diocesan financial officers responded to the DFO Survey or 62% of all dioceses and eparchies. We also received 70 Member Survey returns. By the end of July the committee began to prepare its report for the 2014 Annual Convention.

One of the questions asked in both surveys concerned suggestions for ways in which the CLSA could be of assistance to diocesan finance councils. The committee will look carefully at these suggestions to determine future projects of the Church Governance Committee.

Respectfully submitted,
Barbara A. Bettwy, JCL, Chair

Committee: Clergy
Constituted: 2008
Mandate: The mandate of the Committee is:

1. To initiate as needed any projects pertinent to the study of canon law pertaining to the life and ministry of bishops, priests and deacons or the implementation thereof, including, but not limited to, the following:
    a. canonical issues related to the sexual abuse of minors
    b. clergy personnel issues and resources
    c. advocacy for clergy in penal cases
2. To oversee projects referred to the committee by the BOG;
3. To oversee its subcommittees working on projects concerning clergy; (and)
4. To collaborate with national organizations and other groups dealing with clergy issues.

Members: Rev. James I. Donlon, *chair* (2015)
Rev. Tomas Marin (2014)
Sr. Maureen A. McPartland, OP (2015)
Rev. Msgr. Steven J. Raica (2015)

Rev. Kenneth A. Riley (2015)

ANNUAL REPORT

The Committee congratulates and extends our prayerful best wishes to our colleague on the Clergy Committee, Steve Raica, as he prepares to be ordained Bishop of Gaylord.

Respectfully submitted,
Rev. James Donlon, Chair

Committee: Convention Planning Committee
Constituted: 1971
Previous Committee Structure: Committees on Convention Planning (constitutional) and Convention Liturgies
Mandate: It is the function of the Committee on Convention Planning:

1. To receive from the Board of Governors the approved general theme of the next convention as well as any suggestions from the Committee on Research &Discussion for the development of the theme;
2. To recommend to the BOG, in accord with the general theme, topics for major addresses, seminars or other presentations at a future convention, as well as a list of potential speakers and the honoraria for such speakers;
3. Following BOG approval, to arrange for the speakers, addresses and seminars for the annual convention;
4. To plan all convention liturgies and prayer services;
5. To review the evaluations of the most recent Convention and assist the Convention Chairperson in planning future arrangements, as needed.

Membership: A chair and three active members of the Society, appointed by the President, each with staggered three year terms, the Executive Coordinator *ex officio*, and the Past President *ex officio.*

Members: Rev. Michael Joyce, CM, *chair*
Rev. Paul Counce
Sr. Sharon Euart, RSM
Rev. John Vaughn, *ex officio*

ANNUAL REPORT

The undersigned chair met with the Board of Governors by conference call on January 28, 2014. The Board of Governors approved the program and speakers presented by the Convention Planning Committee for the 2015 Annual Convention which is themed *Church Structures Fifty Years after Vatican II: Present and Future.* Several changes in speakers have occurred since that meeting. There was an error in the report. Msgr. Roch Page has agreed to present the seminar on how to evaluate first instance decisions in the second instance.

The chair had presented Msgr. John Johnson as the proposed speaker for the seminar. The committee now proposes the following changes for approval:

- Dr. Brian Reynolds, Chancellor of the Archdiocese of Louisville, to replace Dr. Barbara Ann Cusack as co-presenter with Bishop Charles Thompson on models of shared responsibility since Vatican Council II; and

- The committee still needs to find a replacement for Rev. Mark Spalding on fiscal irresponsibility and its impact on the *communio* of marriage.

William Daniels has had to decline the invitation to give the seminar on jurisprudence for the ground of *contra bonum coniugum* at this year's convention in St. Louis for family reasons. The committee then recommended that the Reverend Augustine Mendoņca be approached to give the seminar. The chair was in correspondence with Father Mendoņca despite health problems on Father Mendoņca's part. Finally, he had to decline the invitation for those reasons. At the recommendation of Father Bruce Miller, the committee asked the Reverend Peter Akpoghiran of the Archdiocese of New Orleans to give a seminar on Witnesses in Marriage Nullity Cases. Father Akpoghiran graciously accepted the invitation.

Repectfully submitted,
Rev. Michael Joyce, CM, Chair

Proposed Program for the 2015 CLSA Convention
Prepared by the Convention Planning Committee
January 17, 2014

Convention Theme: Church Structures

Keynote Address

Topic: *Reflections on Church Structures and the Norms that Support Them: Promoting and Sustaining Communio*
Archbishop Joseph Tobin, C.Ss.R., Archbishop of Indianapolis

Major Addresses

1. The Impact of the Teachings of Vatican Council II on Marriage in the Twenty-First Century
Rev. Anthony Kerwin

2. Global Perspectives on the Local Church and the Universal Communio
Archbishop Bernard Hebda, Coadjutor Archbishop of Newark

Seminars

1. *The Current Process for the Revision of Canon Law*
Rev. Cuong Pham (Pontifical Council for Legislative Texts)

2. *The Use of Electronic Media in Church Structures*
   Dr. Michael Nobel (Saint Paul University)

3. *Recent Developments in the Law on Temporal Goods*
   Rev. John Renken (Saint Paul University)

4. *Models of Shared Responsibility Since Vatican Council II*
   Bishop Charles Thompson (Bishop of Evansville) and Dr. Brian Reynolds (Archdiocese of Louisville)

5. *Diocesan Review Boards as Structures of Communio*
   Sr. Sharon Euart, R.S.M. (Resource Center for Religious Institutes)

6. *Communio in the Presbyterate*
   Rev. Ronald Knott (St. Meinrad Seminary)

7. *How to Evaluate First Instance Decisions in the Second Instance*
   Msgr. John Johnson (Diocese of Columbus)

8. *The Ground of Error Determining the Will*
   Dr. Lynda Robitaille (Archdiocese of Vancouver)

9. *Tribunal Management*
   Ms. Kelly O'Donnell (Diocese of Shreveport) and Rev. Thomas Cronkleton (Diocese of Cheyenne)

10. *Case Instruction*
    Rev. James Donlon (Diocese of Albany)

11. *Fiscal Irresponsibility and Its Impact on the Communio of Marriage*
    Presenter undetermined

12. *Parish Membership and Territoriality*
    Rev. Lawrence DiNardo (Diocese of Pittsburgh)

Committee:	General Convention Chair
Mandate:	To assist with the coordinating, planning, and implementation of the yearly Convention of the Canon Law Society of America.
Member:	Reverend Monsignor Victor F. Finelli, J.C.L.

ANNUAL REPORT

2014: St. Louis, Missouri

Welcome to St. Louis! What a wonderful place to visit for a few days during our 76th Annual Convention. The lobby of our hotel, as you have seen, is worth the visit in and of itself. Our rooms have recently been renovated at this historic Union Station Hotel. Don't forget to enjoy your free wi-fi hookup! Although our Convention Mass is not at the Saint Louis Cathedral Basilica, hopefully you'll get a chance to visit this magnificent place of worship. Many restaurants are within a fifteen minute walk. Of course a real "must see" is the Arch of St. Louis in Jefferson Memorial Park. Don't forget to ride to the top of the arch ... you won't want to miss it! Here's hoping that our convention, in this great city, is a good one ... I have every reason to believe it will be!

2015: Pittsburg, Pennsylvania

Planning is under way for the 77th Annual Convention. To date I have not personally visited this site but it has been visited by Rita Joyce, our past President. More details will follow. The dates for this convention will be October 12-15, 2015.

2016: Houston, Texas

I traveled to Houston in August of 2013 to begin the planning for the 78th Annual Convention which will be held from October 10-13, 2016. We will be gathering at the Houston Marriott Westchase. Houston is a wonderful town of fine eateries ranging from Tex-Mex, wonderful steakhouses, and of course many bar-b-que establishments. The hospitality of the people in the city was excellent. Houston will be yet another great location for us to visit.

2017: Indianapolis, Indiana

Work has already begun for our 79th Annual Convention which will be held in Indianapolis, Indiana, from October 16-19, 2017. We will be residing at the Westin Hotel in Indianapolis. I have not personally visited this location, but I thank Father John Vaughan, our past President, who made the initial contact for this venue.

I am thankful to Colleen Crawford of the Office of the Executive Coordinator and to NIX Associates for their assistance in planning this year's Convention. It is a real corporate work with everyone sharing the load. In the end, it is our goal to make these days truly a benefit to your canonical ministry, in whatever capacity that may be. Personally, it's an absolute pleasure to assist in this endeavor and to work with these fine, dedicated people.

Respectfully submitted,
Rev. Msgr. Victor F. Finelli, Chair

Committee: Institutes of Consecrated Life and Societies of Apostolic Life
Constituted: 2010
Mandate: The mandate of the Committee is:

1. To initiate as needed any projects pertinent to the study of canon law pertaining to the life and ministry

of Institutes of Consecrated and Apostolic Life or the implementation thereof, including but not limited to the following:

a) Sponsorship;
b) Mergers and restructuring institutes;
c) Governance;
d) Membership;
e) New forms of consecrated life.

2. To oversee projects referred to the committee by the Board of Governors;
3. To oversee its subcommittees working on projects concerning Consecrated and Apostolic Life;
4. To collaborate with national organizations and other groups dealing with issues of Consecrated and Apostolic Life.

Members: Rev. Manuel Viera, OFM, *chair* (2015)
Sr. Amy Hereford, CSJ (2015)
Sr. Catherine Darcy, RSM (2015)
Sr. Lynn McKenzie, OSB (2016)
Sr. Karla Felix-Rivera, VDMF (2016)

ANNUAL REPORT

The Committee members that were present at the Sacramento Convention met (Manuel Viera, OFM, Amy Herford, CSJ and outgoing member Kevin Niehoff, OP). There have not been any meetings or contacts since the convention.

During the meeting the committee voiced the necessity of having at least one presentation dealing with some aspect of consecrated life during every convention. Some possible topics that were raised were: Sponsorship of Ministries – Civil and Canonical Ramifications; Renunciation of Goods; Basic Issues of Consecrated Life for Non-Religious; Hermits and Consecrated Virgins.

The possibility of sharing documents and files through the society's webpage was discussed. Not much has taken place within this area.

Several names for future membership were raised, and these names were presented to the President. It is our hope to meet at the 2014 Convention and discuss different proposals for the year of Consecrated Life.

Respectfully submitted,
Rev. Manuel Viera, OFM, Chair

Committee: Laity
Constituted: 2009
Mandate: The mandate of this committee is:

1. To initiate as needed any projects pertinent to the study of canon law pertaining to the life and ministry of lay persons or the implementation thereof, including, but not limited to, the following:
    a. Lay ecclesial ministry;
    b. Collaboration with clergy;
    c. Rights of the lay family.
2. To oversee projects referred to the committee by the BOG;
3. To oversee its subcommittees working on projects concerning the laity, (and)
4. To collaborate with national organizations and other groups dealing with the role of the laity in the Church.

Members: Dr. Marie T. Hilliard, *chair* (2015)
Msgr. Steven Callahan (2014)
Mr. Timothy Cavanaugh (2015)
Ms. Anna Marie Chamblee (2014)
Ms. Amy Tadlock (2016)

ANNUAL REPORT

A. Three COL members who were available to travel met on July 14-15, 2014 for a working meeting in Minneapolis, MN. Another COL member was available to attend by conference call, but logistics prevented this from occurring. A second meeting of COL for this fiscal year will occur at the CLSA Convention in October 2014. During this past budget year a total of two planning conference calls and two in-person planning meetings have occurred. A report follows.

B. In October 2014 it was decided that the project focus (approved by the Publications Advisory Board) would be narrowed to marriage preparation issues when one or both persons are from a non-dominant culture from those dominant in the United States. The format will be a quick reference guide, in perhaps a Q/A format (similar to *Our Sunday Visitor* publications; but the Publications' Advisory Board cautioned that the publication is to be CLSA's) of issues that need to be addressed in marriage preparation of such couples. The project would be done in collaboration with the Publications Advisory Board, and perhaps the Sacramental Law Committee. The COL determined that the expertise for such a document exists in the COL, since the focus will be on the issue of a valid marriage, not legal issues related to immigration. However, early in the drafting, review by other experts is being sought.

C. Status of proposed project was reviewed on April 8, 2014, with a report to the total Committee, also with assigned data collection among members for discussion at the April 28, 2014 conference call meeting.

D. At the July 2014 COL meeting in Minneapolis the following progress/plans were completed:

I. Review of existing diocesan/canonical literature was completed:

a. Decision coram De Lanversin, July 17, 1996 (Abana, Nigeria), *RRT Dec.* 88 [1996] 520-531; trans. in *Studia canonica,* "Jurisprudence II: Culture and Conditioned Consent" 36 [2002] 517-540.

b. Decision coram De Lanversin, June 27, 1997 (Calcutta, India), *RRT Dec.* 89 [1997] 548-558; trans. in *Studia canonica,* "Jurisprudence I: Culture and Conditioned Consent"36 [2002] 497-516.

c. L.H. Duquin, "Cohabitation: What the Church Teaches," *Our Sunday Visitor* (April 21, 2008).

d. Eid v. Thompson, U.S. 3rd Circuit Court of Appeals (Jan. 10, 2014). Court decision on those seeking marriage for permanent residency status.

e. V.M. Parachin, "Marriage Preparation: Nine Questions to Ask Before You Say 'I Do,'" *Church* 31 (Winter 1993).

f. Lynda Robitaille, "Exclusion of *Bonum Coniugum*: Interpreting and Assessing Evidence," *Proceedings: 68 Annual Convention of CLSA*. (9-12 October 2006, Fort Worth, Texas).

g. R.A. Ruhnke, "Pastoral Issues of Marrying & Tips for Pastoral Ministers," *Marriage Preparation Resources* (San Antonio, TX, 2010).

h. M. Tarver, "The Effects of Pornography Addiction on Marital Consent," *Studia canonica* 44:2 (2010), 343–367.

USCCB: An Analysis of Diocesan Marriage Preparation Policies: http://www.usccb.org/issues-and-action/marriage-and-family/marriage/marriage-preparation/mpanalysis.cfm.

II. Additional research sought: Lynda Robitaille, "Marriage Preparation from the Perspective of the Chancery and the Tribunal," *Studies in Church Law (*Jan-Dec 2009).

III. Review of existing diocesan resources was completed:

a. Chicago (Latino); Rapid City (1st Nation/Native American); Fort Worth (Vietnamese), and Brownsville (Filipino and sponsor/mentor couples).

b. Possible further beneficial resources to be sought: Miami, Alexandria, Los Angeles, Milwaukee.

c. COL met with the Archdiocese of Minneapolis Office of Marriage, Family and Life, and received input on the importance of including in the document:

i. The need to identify who are the primary educators: e.g., priest, sponsor/mentor couples.

ii. Root causes of difficulties, e.g., machismo; unawareness of differences and an inability to balance them.
iii. Managing expectations.

IV. Resource development for Appendix to publication specific to non-dominant cultures (Resources to be developed by COL, or from experts identified by COL, with submission/progress report at October 2014 meeting of COL):

a. African (A.M. Chamblee); Filipino (A. Tadlock); 1st Nation/Native American (A.M. Chamblee); India (A.M. Chamblee); Latino (M. Hilliard; Hmong (A. Tadlock); Vietnamese (A.M. Chamblee - already developed and to be sent to COL).
b. An example would be how Hmong brides expect to be "kidnapped" by groom's family (not constituting coercion).
c. **COL requests input from the BOG on additional cultures that may be relevant to this document, e.g., Middle East (especially for marriages in which one party is non-baptized).**

V. Preliminary format of document:

a. Introduction: Goal not to alter decision to marry but increased awareness of how differences impact the relationship; theology of the Sacrament of Marriage; what is marriage consent (re: c. 1055)?; primordial sacrament tied to culture as no other sacrament; issues framed positively (presumption that couples want what Church envisions); importance of seeking counsel (A. Tadlock drafter).
b. Types of Marriage Preparation and when does it begin.
   i. Just adapting to language of couple is insufficient.
   ii. COL recommends sponsor/mentor couples: presumption that couples have "feet in both cultural worlds" - dominant/non-dominant; sponsor/mentor couples reflective of culture/s of couple (may involve two non-dominant cultures) and well trained (e.g., Brownsville).
   iii. Begins long before engagement: importance of the family of origin.
   iv. Addressing catechesis of the Faithful (e.g., San Antonio).
   v. Format would include exploring issues with couple together and each person separately.
c. Content Themes: No more than 12 points per theme (Assigned).

i. Partnership whole life. E.g.: "Describe what 'faithfulness' means to you?" "What would justify you ending your marriage?" (A. Tadlock).
ii. Spirituality. E.g., "How will God be a part of this marriage?" "Are you comfortable praying together?" (M. Hilliard).
iii. Intimacy. E.g., "What are your expectations of each other sexually?" "What are you expectations once children come?" (A.M. Chamblee).
iv. Children. E.g., "Have your discussed the number of children, and how responsible parenthood (number of children) will be addressed" "How will you educate your children?" "How will you handle issues of discipline?" (A.M. Chamblee).
v. Domestic life. E.g., "For what reasons, other than love, are you marrying?" "Where will you live, family of origins expectations?" "How do you envision the division of labor/addressing of finances in your home?"(M. Hilliard).
vi. Family expectations. E.g., "What role did your family play in the choice of your spouse?" "What concerns do your families have concerning this marriage/spouse?" "What does your culture/ future spouse say is your role in marriage?" "How do you balance differing cultural expectations?" (A.M. Chamblee).
vii. Conflicts. E.g., "How do you as a couple make decision/resolve conflict?" "What happens when you disagree?" "In the years to come, what is your future spouse's perception of your role in your marriage?" (A. Tadlock).

d. "Red flags," e.g.:
i. Avoiding scandal as reason for marriage (cohabitation; pregnancy).
ii. Pornography as culturally accepted.
iii. Male dominance.
iv. Evidence of conditions attached to consent (citizenship; employment; standard of living; military benefits, etc.).
v. Evidence of simulation, i.e. a positive act of the will against: fidelity; permanence; children; the sacrament; the *bonum coniugum* – true choice against the good of the spouses for one's own good/benefit (can be implicit due to cultural norms).

vi. Evidence of an incapacity to exercise discretionary judgment (c. 1095.2) or to assume the essential obligations of marriage (c. 1095.3). The "goods" of marriage cannot be intended when one cannot conceive them as such, and appreciate (discretionary capacity), and actualize them (assume the essential obligations), due to cultural norms.

e. Addressing suspicion of "Red Flags:" Any suspicion of issues impacting the consent of marriage, document, placed in a sealed envelope at parish level, in event annulment sought later.

f. Culturally-specific Appendices.

VI. COL has had contact with Rev. Bruce Miller of the Sacramental Law Committee to keep that Committee apprised of COL's progress.

On-site meeting planned for October 2014, as a working meeting, to report back on aforementioned tasks. Proposed Budget for July 1, 2014 – June 30, 2015 submitted to the Board of Governors.

Respectfully submitted,
Marie Therese Hilliard, Chair

Committee: Publications Advisory Board
Constituted: 2007; revised in 2008
Mandate: The mandate of the Committee is:

1. To advise the Board of Governors about all aspects of current, periodic and proposed CLSA publication projects, including financial, literary, educational and marketing issues.
2. To monitor the progress of all CLSA publication projects.
3. To implement the procedures for peer review of CLSA publications.
4. To make the final recommendation to the Board of Governors regarding specific publications.
5. To review the coordination and management of the CLSA's publications activity on the part of the Office of the Executive Coordinator.
6. To provide a written report to the CLSA membership at the annual convention.

Members:
Sr. Sharon Euart, RSM, *chair* (term began 7/1/14)
Rev. Patrick Cogan (2017)
Rev. Patrick Cooney, OSB (2015)
Msgr. Thomas Green (2015)

Rev. Paul Hartmann (2018)
Chorbishop John Faris (*ex officio*)
Msgr. John Alesandro, chair (term ended 6/30/14)
Very Rev. Lawrence DiNardo (term ended 6/30/14)

ANNUAL REPORT

Meetings

During the past year, the members of PAB followed their usual pattern of meetings. They met in person at the October 2013 Convention in Sacramento, California, and at the CLSA office in Washington, D.C., on June 30-July 1, 2014. Msgr. Alesandro also participated by conference call in the BOG meetings in January and April, 2014, to offer progress reports on publications. The members also communicated by conference call and e-mail throughout the year. A subcommittee of PAB met after the Penal Law Workshop in April to discuss follow-up publications.

Publications Budget

The actual revenue and expenditures for CLSA publications for FY 2014, as of May, are below the budgeted estimates, but the bottom line is still in the black; the decrease in sales income balances with the decrease in book production. The members discussed the idea of reviewing standing orders for publications by libraries and tribunals, even for publications such as *Roman Replies & Advisory Opinions*. It might be advisable to market such standing orders if they have ceased.

The expenditures for PAB itself have been in line with the approved budget for FY2014. The assumptions and estimate for FY2015 for both publications in general and for PAB itself seem to be accurate.

PAB remains concerned that there were no new CLSA publications during the past year, with the exception of *CLSA Proceedings* and *2013 Roman Replies and CLSA Advisory Opinions* both of which are primarily member services. The PAB has identified several ways it and the Society might address this dearth of publications. A few of the possibilities are included elsewhere in this report. Besides being a source of income to the Society, English-language canon law publications are immensely important to our membership. Over the past six years many of our new international members commented that the access to English-language canonical resources played a significant role in their decision to join the Society. It is important for the future of the Society that we look at ways to address this concern. The PAB welcomes your insights and suggestions.

Inventory

PAB continues to monitor and manage the inventory, reducing it where there is little likelihood of additional sales of any significance, in order to consolidate the volumes into fewer pallets and thereby reduce monthly storage expenses at *BrightKey*. This is an ongoing task, which involves collaboration with the Office of the Executive Coordinator and the staff of *BrightKey*, the company that provides fulfillment services (sales, handling and shipping) on behalf of the CLSA. For example, due to the large number of volumes in the inventory and the low number of annual sales, the PAB decided to offer 50 complimentary copies of two publications related to religious life, *Sponsorship in the US Context: Theory and Praxis* and *Consecrated Life* to the three religious conferences in the United States: the Leadership Conference of Women Religious, Conference of Major Superiors of Men and Council of Major Superiors of Women Religious. In addition, 50 copies of *Sponsorship in the US Context* were also sent to the Catholic Health Association, Resource Center for Religious Institutes, and Association of Catholic Colleges and Universities. The letters offering the book were mailed in July.

Another purpose for examining the inventory is to determine publications that are being depleted in order to decide whether to print additional volumes. One of the steady sales each year is the most recent, soft-cover translation of the Latin Code. Approximately, two-years worth of volumes remain in inventory. Over the next year a decision must be made about reprinting. Impacting this decision will be the timing of any changes in Book VI by the Holy See.

Webinars

Three webinars have been held since February 2014: Jay Conzemius on "Sacramental Record-Keeping"; Sr. Victoria Vondenberger, RSM on the "Defender of the Bond"; and Msgr. Fred Easton on "Preliminary Investigation and the Extrajudicial Process." No webinars were scheduled for July and August. The evaluations have been very positive. The number of live participants has been high and, for some webinars, the number viewing the archived webinars exceeded the number of live participants. The main challenge currently is finding presenters who are willing to make a 40-45 minute presentation. PAB discussed the introduction of a video component which is being researched by the CLSA Office staff. PAB has identified several potential topics and presenters for future webinars and welcomes suggestions from members and volunteers to be presenters to make possible future programs. The OEC staff provides an orientation for presenters on the technique of webinars and is available to assist with the preparation of power point slides.

Penal Law Workshop

The Penal Law Workshop, sponsored by the PAB and the Executive Coordinator's Office and held at Bethany Center, in Lutz, Florida, March 31-April 2, 2014 was very successful on all accounts. Fifty-three members registered for the workshop, including the presenters; forty-seven were present for the workshop. The workshop brought in revenue of approximately $23,000; expenditures were approximately $19,000. The evaluations were generally quite positive; the only real concern was the fact that a great deal of content was offered in a limited time frame, something the presenters recognized in designing the agenda. The participants appreciated the workshop format, its focus on a single topic, the practical materials, and the opportunity to share ideas among the attendees and the presenters. PAB has discussed how to incorporate the presentations, notes, summaries and materials into a CLSA publication.

Discussion of the CLSA *Handbook on Church Finance*, of which there are approximately nine volumes remaining in inventory and which continues to have annual sales, led to a proposal that Temporalities be the subject of a special workshop (similar to those held in 2011 on Special Faculties and this year on Penal Law). An outcome of the workshop would be a successor publication to the *Handbook*, benefiting from the presentations and the input of the participants. The PAB Chair has written to the CLSA President requesting authorization to initiate planning for such a workshop in the early Fall.

CLSA Research Database

PAB continues to move forward with the CLSA electronic database. Though there have been difficulties with the availability of our volunteer computer expert, the Rev. Mark Barr, due to illness and additional parish responsibilities, Msgr. Alesandro is working with local computer experts to analyze the software program hosted by *Rimuhosting*, the firm that maintains the files for the database demo. PAB members, Revs. Paul Hartmann and Patrick Cooney, are investigating the information available from *Rimuhosting* to identify the language in which the software is written and determine how to go about using it. When *CLD* is completely uploaded, Msgr. Alesandro has identified volunteers to assist in this project. They include Aldean Hendrickson, New Ulm; Mark Gantley, Hawaii; and Cathy Gilligan, Little Rock. John Renken is serving as Research Documents Coordinator, and Chad Glendinning will assist him in regard to the addition of documents once the database is active.

Roman Replies and Advisory Opinions

The Index on the CLSA website continues to be a valuable research tool for canonists. It is maintained by the Office of the Executive Coordinator, including uploading the titles of new advisory opinions. This method refers the reader to both the original volume of *RR&AO* and to the printed *Collections*, both of which contain the entire article. The entire text of all advisory opinions will eventually be available in the *CLSA Research Database* for all those who hold a subscription. *Roman Replies and Advisory Opinions* was published again this year in time for the St. Louis Convention. Once again, we urge all members to submit both replies (which will be sanitized) and advisory opinions, so that we might continue to maintain this important annual publication.

The Publications Advisory Board is grateful to Msgr. John Alesandro for his long service to the PAB and to the Society. Msgr. Alesandro chaired the Publications Task Force in the mid-2000s, which recommended the establishment of the PAB. He served as the first chair for two terms. He will continue as an advisor to the PAB and oversee the continued development of the *CLSA Research Database*. We are grateful for his continued service to the PAB.

Respectfully submitted,
Sister Sharon Euart, RSM, Chair

Committee: Research and Development
Constituted: 2008
Mandate: The mandate of the Committee is:

1. To initiate or cooperate in all CLSA research projects such as seminars, symposia and special studies;
2. To design and implement Think Tanks that will allow for diverse views on issues of ecclesial life having canonical implications;
3. To develop and recommend themes for the annual conventions for submission to the BOG for approval and subsequent referral to the Convention Planning Committee for implementation;
4. To maintain close communication with all the committees
5. To interact with the Publications Advisory Board in order to assess the current and contemplated publications of the CLSA and offer suggestions and guidance for publication planning.

Members: Chorbishop John D. Faris, *chair* (2014)
Dr. Michael Nobel (2015)
Rev. Msgr. F. Stephen Pedone (2015)
Sr. Rose McDermott, SSJ (2015)
Ms. Rita Joyce (2016)
Michael Souckar, *ex officio* (2014)

ANNUAL REPORT

The Committee had three conference calls for the purpose of elaborating a plan to implement the 2009 resolution passed by the general membership regarding possible changes to the *Code of Canon Law* and other legal texts. A report was submitted to the Board of Governors.

The Committee submitted several drafts of the 2015 Convention Theme to the Executive Coordinators office and the BOG, but the texts were not found to be satisfactory. We are grateful to Sr. Sharon Euart for her re-write.

The group will have another conference call in September to discuss implementation of the *Future Initiatives Project.*

Respectfully submitted,
Chorbishop John Faris, Chair

Committee: Sacramental Law
Constituted: 2009
Mandate:

1. To initiate as needed any projects pertinent to the study of canon law pertaining to the sacramental life of the Church or the implementation thereof;
2. To oversee projects referred to the committee by the BOG;

3. To oversee its subcommittees working on projects concerning the sacramental life of the Church;
4. To offer suggestions to the BOG for marriage topics for pre-convention workshops;
5. To collaborate with national organizations and other groups dealing with the sacramental life of the Church.

Members: Rev. Bruce Miller, *chair* (2015)
Mr. JD Flynn (2014)
Ms. Amy Jill Strickland (2014)
Dr. Chad Glenndinning (2015)
Mr. Jay Conzemius (2016)

ANNUAL REPORT

- The terms of J.D. Flynn and Amy Jill Strickland expire this year.
- On Wednesday, February 5, 2014, our newest member, Jay Conzemius of the Diocese of Pittsburgh, was the first CLSA webinar presenter. His topic was sacramental recordkeeping, an issue which has been recommended for many years by this committee as the subject for a webinar. Jay's presentation on this topic at the 2013 Sacramento Convention was extremely well received, and he is a great asset to this Committee.
- As for marriage topics for future pre-convention workshops, it was recommended that a workshop be offered on how to **instruct** a solid case in first instance. Another workshop could focus on how to **write** an effective first instance decision, and it is suggested that Roch Page be approached on this topic. That being said, given the length of the workshops, multiple presenters may be more attractive to participants.
- For future webinars, the committee suggests that the PAB and the BOG consider the question of faculties/the drafting of *pagella*.
- A conversation between the SLC Chair and Marie Hilliard, Chair of the CLSA Committee on the Laity, in late January yielded several topics for consideration that the COL had determined were the prerogative of another committee:
    - o "Revision of the *Tribunal Handboo*k on *Dignitas Connubii*
    - o "Support Eastern Church Laity re Marriage
    - o "Issues re *Omnium in mentem*
    - o "Webinar Addressing Use of Expert: What Should be Requested of Expert and Interpretation of Opinions"

The SLC finds these topics worthy of further consideration. The SLC awaits further direction from the BOG that was sought in April 2014.

Respectfully submitted,
Rev. Bruce Miller, Chair

Committee: National Penal Tribunal Study Commission
Constituted: 2014
Mandate:

Following upon a resolution of the Canon Law Society of America approved at its annual business meeting on October 16, 2013, the President of the Society offered to the Most Reverend Joseph Kurtz, President of the United States Catholic Conference of Bishops the assistance of the Society to study and make recommendations including but not limited to structure, personnel, education, and finances of a regional/ national tribunal to achieve the expeditious resolution of causes and controversies concerning ecclesiastical delicts. In a letter dated March 7, 2014 to the Rev. Philip Brown, SS, the CLSA President, Archbishop Kurtz expressed openness to receiving from the CLSA a more detailed study of such a structure for addressing penal cases which would also include a realistic assessment of the human and financial resources which would be necessary to achieve the goal. Therefore, by June 9, 2014 this CLSA Study Commission was established and the members were appointed by the President of CLSA.

Members: Msgr. Frederick Easton, *co-chair*
Msgr. John A. Alesandro, *co-chair*
Very Rev. Lawrence A. DiNardo
Very Rev. Mark O'Connell
Msgr. Michael Padazinski

ANNUAL REPORT

The first meeting of this Study Commission took place by way of a telephone conference call on June 19, 2014 with all members involved.

It became immediately clear to the members that some form of survey of the bishops of the USCCB would be in order, in order to better determine the needs for such a tribunal which would then help the Commission to make suggestions about structure, financial and human resources for a regional and/or national penal tribunal. Since Archbishop Kurtz had stated that further correspondence regarding the work of this Study Commission should be directed to the Most Reverend Timothy P. Broglio, Archbishop for the Military Services, USA, and Chairman of the USCCB Committee on Canonical Affairs and Church Governance, it was decided that the co-chairs would author a letter of inquiry to Archbishop Broglio about the feasibility and the protocol of achieving such a survey.

Following the conference call, Msgrs. Easton and Alesandro prepared and sent a letter to Archbishop Broglio on or about July 14, 2014. As this report is being presented, there has been no response from Archbishop Broglio. However, some of the members have already presented to the co-chairs some suggested survey questions.

Through some networking, Msgr. Easton became aware that the Ecclesiastical Province of the Netherlands has established interdiocesan tribunals of first and second instance for penal cases and have received the *nihil obstat* from the Supreme Tribunal of the Apostolic Signatura. Copies of the decrees of erection of these two tribunals have been received.

It is the goal of the Study Commission to be able to give some report of our work to Archbishop Broglio before the fall meeting of the USCCB.

Respectfully submitted,
Rev. Msgr. Fred C. Easton, Chair

VARIA

SEVENTY-SIXTH ANNUAL BUSINESS MEETING
St. Louis, Missouri
October 15, 2014

MINUTES

Call to Order and Opening Prayer

Reverend Phillip Brown, President, called to order the Seventy-Sixth Annual Business Meeting of the Canon Law Society of America (CLSA), on October 15, 2014 at 11:00 a.m., at the Union Station Hotel in St. Louis, Missouri. He presided over the meeting as Chair.

The Chair then led the assembly in an opening prayer.

Following the opening prayer, it was announced that Brother Patrick Shea would serve as Parliamentarian for the Business Meeting and that *Robert's Rules of Order* would resolve matters not provided for in the CLSA's *Constitution* or *Bylaws*.

The Chair then gave instructions on the voting procedures to be observed for the election of Vice-President/President-Elect, Secretary, and Consultors during the Business Meeting. The procedures were adopted as described by the Chair.

The Chair then reviewed the procedures for addressing the assembly, and the CLSA's practices for presenting resolutions. The procedures and practices were adopted as presented by the Chair.

The Chair then entertained a motion that Associate Members present at the meeting have the opportunity to address the assembly, as called for in Article 5.3 of the CLSA's *Constitution*. The motion was seconded and approved unanimously by the assembly.

The Chair then called upon the Secretary, Ms. Zabrina Decker, to read the Minutes of the Seventy-Fifth Business Meeting of the CLSA, unless there was a proposal to accept the Minutes as published in the 2013 CLSA *Proceedings*. A motion to accept the Minutes was presented. The motion was approved by the assembly by unanimous acclamation.

Election of Officers and Consultors

The Chair called upon Rev. Lawrence Jurcak, Chair of the Nominations Committee, to present the slate of nominees for Officers and Consultors. Rev. Jurcak announced the candidates for Officers and Consultors. No additional nominations were added to the slate, as is provided for in Article 9.5 of the CLSA's *Constitution*.

The Chair then read the provisions of the CLSA's *Bylaws* regarding elections. The active members of the CLSA were instructed to cast their votes. The tellers collected the ballots and retired to a separate room to count them. Later in the meeting, Rev. Jurcak returned to the Business Meeting and informed the Chair of the election results. The Chair then announced that:

For the Office of Vice-President/President-Elect:

210 valid ballots were cast, with 106 votes needed for election. There were no invalid ballots. There were 2 abstentions. The votes cast were:

Rev. Dr. Gerald Jorgensen: 98

Reverend Manuel Viera: 110

The Chair declared an election with the Reverend Manuel Viera selected as Vice-President/President-Elect. The election was received with applause.

For the Office of Secretary:

210 valid ballots were cast, with 106 votes needed for election. There were no invalid ballots. There were 6 abstentions. The votes cast were:

Ms. Mary Gen Blittschau: 117

Sister Marilyn R. Vassallo: 87

The Chair declared an election with Mary Gen Blittschau selected as Secretary. The election was received with applause.

For the Office of Consultor:

210 valid ballots were cast, with 106 votes needed for election. There were no invalid ballots. There were 2 abstentions. The votes cast were:

Ms. Anne E. Bryant: 93

Ms. Patricia M. Dugan: 119

Very Reverend David J. Klein: 82

Reverend Peter B. Mangum: 108

The Chair declared an election with Ms. Patricia Dugan and the Reverend Peter Mangum selected as Consultors. The election was received with applause.

Reports

PRESIDENT'S REPORT

The Chair referred the assembly to pages 19-24 of the *2014 Annual Reports Booklet,* distributed at convention registration, for the full text of the President's

Report. Since the membership had the opportunity to read the Report in advance of the Business Meeting, he called for any questions or observations on the Report. There were none.

The President thanked the members of the Executive Coordinator's Office and the former EC, Sister Sharon Euart. He also thanked the Past President, Rev. John Vaughan, and the president- elect, Msgr. Michael Souckar. Rev. Brown thanked the chairs and members of the committees. He noted that there has been increasing collaboration with, and support from, our Anglophone societies.

There has been meaningful progress on the goals of the society in the past year.

All committee chair appointments were completed by January of 2014.

A major task was to fill the position of Executive Coordinator. An interim plan was put into place in January of 2014, which focused on Colleen Crawford's expertise, Sister Sharon Euart's willingness to assist as a consultor to the Office, and Rev. Phil Brown's availability. The plan was a success. The society then hired Father Roger Keeler and he was able to take the position on August 1.

Rev. Phil Brown then reviewed the highlights of his presidential year. All can be found in the Presidential Report. Highlights include:

- National Penal Law Tribunal Study
- The institution of an annual spring seminar to be conducted by the Publications Advisory Board
- An examination of the title of Executive Coordinator vs. Executive Director. The Canon Law Society is a civil organization and the title director is well understood in civil law. The BOG will decide at their January meeting if a resolution is to be proposed at convention in 2015. This topic was first discussed when Sister Euart was Executive Coordinator and the discussion continues now that Rev. Keeler has the position.
- Further collaboration with Anglophone societies. The Presidents meet informally at the conventions of their sister societies. There may be more formal ways to advance collaboration. Some possibilities include joint membership and a possible international federation of canon law societies. The BOG has established an internal task force to examine this question.

Rev. Brown indicated that it has been an honor to serve as president. He pledged on-going service to the Canon Law Society.

EXECUTIVE COORDINATOR'S REPORT

The Chair then invited Reverend Roger H. Keeler, CLSA Executive Coordinator, to the podium to present the Executive Coordinator's Report. Reverend Keeler referred to his written report, found on pages 59-60 of the *2014 Annual Reports Booklet.*

He is very happy to be of service to the society.

TREASURER'S REPORT

The Chair next invited Reverend Thomas E. Cronkleton, Treasurer, to the podium to provide the Treasurer's Report. The written report was found on pages 25-57 of the *2014 Annual Reports Booklet.*

Reverend Cronkleton thanked Sister Sharon Euart and Colleen Crawford for their assistance. He also thanked Rev. Roger Keeler.

The society operates out of four units. The financial auditor of the Society has indicated that the Society is in excellent financial condition. It is anticipated that the Society will have a "break-even" budget for the next fiscal year.

General Operations

Fiscal year 2013-2014 showed a net gain in General Operations. The office of the EC was open for approximately 5 months and that realized savings for the Society. The committees did very well in containing their expenses. The Society will need to use more of the realized net assets to balance the budget over the next few years so there may be a need to increase dues.

Publications

This unit experienced a minor loss this year. Projects did not make it to completion. The concept of publications is dramatically changing from print media to electronic. The PAB has been concentrating on this through the CLD database available by the end of 2015. The BOG authorized up to $27,000 to bring this CLD project to completion.

Conventions

The money is self-contained.

Scholarship

Scholarship money is segregated. The Society has moved $50,000 into a doctoral scholarship account according to a resolution passed at the 2013 convention.

Sister Nancy Reynolds from Louisville, Kentucky inquired as to how interest income is budgeted when the Society does not know how the markets will do in any given quarter or year. Rev. Tom Cronkleton responded that previous performance is taken into consideration. There is the element of interest and dividends. Investments are in the CUIT balanced fund with 60 percent in equities and 40 percent in bonds. Rev. Phil Brown indicated that the use of a rolling average was suggested at the past presidents meeting. This is based on total value of investments. He will be taking this to the BOG for consideration.

Resolutions

The Chair read the applicable CLSA *Bylaws* that govern proposing resolutions from the floor and asked if there were any such resolutions to be presented. There being none, he called upon the Reverend Langes Silva of the Resolutions Committee and the Reverend Jamin David, time-keeper, to approach the podium and present the resolution previously submitted to the Resolutions Committee. There were no resolutions previously submitted.

One resolution was presented at the convention.

The full text of the resolution was projected onto screens in the hall. In addition, printed copies of the resolution were accessible to those in attendance.

Resolution 1. The Resolution Committee moved the resolution.

PROPOSED BY: Rev. James A. Coriden

TITLE: A Task Force on Matrimonial Procedures

STATEMENT OF RATIONALE:

WHEREAS the Holy See has created a Special Commission to make recommendations to facilitate and expedite the process for deciding on the validity or invalidity of marriage; and

WHEREAS the circumstances and expectations indicate that the commission will make its recommendations in the near future; and

WHEREAS the CLSA has both vital interest in and considerable experience with matrimonial adjudication procedure; therefore

BE IT RESOLVED that the BOG appoint a special task force to reflect upon and make recommendations concerning possible changes in the process for discerning the validity or invalidity of marriage; such recommendations shall be made in a timely manner and communicated directly to the Special Commission.

COST: $6,000.00

COST SUPPLIED BY: General Funds of the CLSA

Rev. James Coriden spoke to the resolution in that there is some urgency attached to this resolution in that we do not know what changes may be enacted by the Roman Synod. He has been asked what kind of people should be on this commission. He does not know. He hopes the BOG will choose good members.

Many interventions then followed. There was concern and discussion regarding the involvement of the members of the society and exhortations to the BOG to consider the ideas of all members as they are expressed.

Having heard the many interventions, the Chair, Rev. Phil Brown, called the question on the resolution. The original resolution as worded passed with majority vote of the membership.

Old Business

The Chair then opened the floor to discuss any Old Business of interest to the assembly.

James Coriden called attention to the 2009 resolution passed for the Research and Development Committee regarding possible changes to the Code and other legal texts. The report states that the BOG has a report from the committee. He hopes it will be shared with membership.

Barbara Anne Cusack of Milwaukee, Wisconsin thanked the Governance committee for submission of their survey of finance councils.

New Business

The Chair opened the floor to discuss any New Business of interest to the assembly. There was none.

VARIA

Greetings by Officials of Canon Law Societies

The Chair then invited visiting officials of other Canon Law Societies to the podium to address the assembly.

Monsignor Gordon Read, President of the Canon Law Society of Great Britain and Ireland (CLSGB&I), brought the greetings and good wishes of the CLSGB&I. He thanked the CLSA for its hospitality, welcome and cordiality. This is his second visit. The society is considering revamping their website and putting their newsletter and abstracts in on-line form with links to the text. The conference is scheduled in Scotland in 2015 and in Galway in 2016.

Sister Maria Casey, President of the Canon Law Society of Australia and New Zealand (CLSANZ), thanked the membership for the invitation and reception she has received. She heartily endorses cooperation among the societies. The CLSANZ annual convention for 2015 will be hosted August 31-September 3, west of Melbourne. The focus will be all forms of consecration and consecrated life. In 2016, it will be the 50th anniversary of the society and the conference will take place from September 5-8. The website has the applications for membership. Sister Maria extended cordial greetings to all.

Dr. Robert Lariviere, President of the Canadian Canon Law Society (CCLS), shared warm greetings of the CCLS. The 50th anniversary convention of the Canadian Society will be held next year in Ottawa. Communio is alive and well in the membership of our societies.

Adjournment

There being no further business, the Chair entertained a motion to adjourn the meeting. The motion was brought and seconded, and passed unanimously.

At 12:45 p.m., Reverend Phil Brown thanked many and formally closed the Seventy-Sixth Business Meeting of the Canon Law Society of America.

Respectfully Submitted,
Ms. Zabrina R. Decker
Secretary

Varia

Convention Homily

Very Rev. Phillip J. Brown, pss, JD, JCD

Warning: Walk not according to the Flesh, but according to the Spirit. *The New Jerome Biblical Commentary* introduces Joseph Fitzmyer's commentary on the passage from Galatians that we just heard under this heading. Then come these comforting words: "The Christian in union with Christ and endowed with the Spirit still struggles with the 'flesh.'" "Whew!"– I thought it was just me!

But of course Paul doesn't just mean the lustful desires of the flesh – When Paul refers to "the flesh," he means all human opposition to God: Everything in us that resists and sets itself in opposition to God. Flesh is not *just* flesh in Paul, it is also spirit: Everything carnal *and* spiritual that opposes God; everything intellectual and affective that turns away from the ways of God. So even Christians – especially Christians – must be on alert for all that resists within us, all that sets itself in opposition to God. We need to make room for the Spirit, not just spiritually, but in our affections and our carnal desires, in the way we think, in the way we reason. Only as perfected by God's grace, only through a deeply spiritual way of thinking, through an attentively cultivated spiritual life, can we reason rightly.

Oh you lawyers, you scholars of the law! "You impose on people burdens hard to carry, but you yourselves do not lift one finger to touch them." In his monumental two-volume commentary on the Gospel of Luke, Fitzmyer says of this passage: "It echoes the first woe against the Pharisees, castigating the lawyers for minute legalistic interpretations of the Mosaic Law and the 'traditions of the elders.' Their interpretations created a mass of regulations incumbent on all the people."

As we who work in the field of canon law know, laws have to be interpreted. The principles embedded in the text of a law do not apply themselves to actual situations, to the circumstances of real, live human beings that come before a tribunal for judgment; real, live human beings wounded by their circumstances and who are hurting. Principles embedded in laws have to be interpreted and applied *by* human beings using good judgment; jurists seeking to do justice tempered by mercy. Anything less than that devolves into the kind of legalism and cynicism Jesus condemned before the Scribes and the Pharisees and the scholars of the law.

Justice doesn't mean detachment from the real effects of legal rulings in peoples' lives. Mercy doesn't mean disregarding the real meaning of laws for the sake of being "pastoral." Wouldn't it be nice if it were that easy, if there were automatic solutions – or no need for solutions – to justify results? Wouldn't it be nice if we could feed a summary of facts and the citation of a few laws into a computer, which could calculate a just and merciful solution, and be done with it? Wouldn't it be nice if we didn't have to expend much effort to do justice and know what is truly merciful?

But it's not that easy, is it? There is no such computer. It requires real *human* judgment, hard thinking, profound and sincere prayer – not absolute mathematical precision, but moral certainty. Decisions that you can live with because you have wrestled mightily with facts and laws. Because of this effort, even this suffering, you do justice to facts and law. You show mercy that is meaningful to human beings. There are no automatic answers. We have only our minds and their power to reason; our hearts and their capacity for sympathy, for empathy, for love.

Disregard for the text of the law will not do it, nor will overlooking detailed regulations or the depth and complexity of well-considered jurisprudence in favor of a well-meaning, but superficial, "pastoral sense." The pastoral sense proper to the law has to be deep and discerning; one that is willing to grapple with the complexities of the law and of human situations, to discover how pristine principles really ought to apply in individual cases.

Fitzmyer goes on to say in his commentary on Luke in the *JBC*, "It should be noted that Luke does not repudiate the supererogatory practice of the legalists in his community." Now there's a great word you don't hear very often: Supererogatory! What the heck does that mean? I had to look it up. Webster's unabridged Dictionary says that "supererogation" means "the act or process or an instance of performing more than is required by duty or obligation." It goes on, interestingly, to say, "specifically the performance beyond what is considered by the Roman Catholic Church to be necessary for salvation of good deeds of the kind believed to have been done by the saints or to be capable of being done by men."

When is the last time you thought of canon law, of canonical work in marriage tribunal or chancery practice, as a good deed? Or as good deeds done for others that redound to your own salvation, beyond what is minimally necessary?

So Luke does not repudiate the supererogatory practice of the legalists in his community as far as Fitzmyer is concerned. He saw nothing objectionable in a Pharisaic lifestyle *per se*. The commitment to an expanded legal system was something necessary in a complex world. Rather, what he objects to is the neglect of central commands that the Pharisees themselves recognized as essential. All the additions of an expanded legal system, all the interpretation, all the minutiae, are for the sake of understanding and fulfilling the central commands of the law.

Interpretation and the minutiae are supposed to clarify central commands and how they ought to affect real situations. It is only when interpretation and minutiae obscure what is central and pervert its meaning in real-life application, especially when interpreted and applied in self-serving ways, or ways that are merely exculpatory to those given the authority to interpret and apply the law, that the practices and the lifestyle of the Pharisees, Scribes, and scholars of the law are to be condemned. Complex, incomprehensible, facile, and obscurantist interpretations are too easily employed by the clever to avoid hard decision-making, and accountability for the administration of justice and the outpouring of mercy. The innocent and the simple are baffled by decisions they can't understand and that don't feel right, but they lack the expertise and cleverness to explain why. Procedural complexity too easily serves as a dodge for real, hard decision-making that does justice, dispenses mercy, and stands accountable, through clear and comprehensible sentences that truly explain in a satisfying way why a decision was arrived at, why that decision had to be arrived at.

Those who see through it all too often lack the human authority or the raw power to be anything other than frustrated by perversions of justice and disregard of mercy. But when those tools of legal interpretation and human reason are used to clarify what is complex, and demonstrate how all the minutiae of the law relate to central commands, to central principles of justice that lead the way to just and merciful results, truly that is a thing of majesty: the majesty of the law, the majesty of justice, and the healing power of mercy.

The complexity of the law, the complexity of canon law and the kind of expertise they require, is a two-lane road: One lane, the pathway to justice tempered by mercy; the other, the roadway of legalism and cynicism, to frustration and hopelessness, even despair, and disregard for the true well-being of those subject to the law. This second lane is a means of evading responsibility and accountability through facile, incomprehensible, ultimately unsatisfying reasoning that in the end does more to defeat justice and impede mercy than serve true needs.

"You impose on people burdens hard to carry, but you yourselves do not lift one finger to touch them."

Once again Fitzmyer tells us:

> Jesus' words do not mean that they [the lawyers] impose burdens on others but do not keep them themselves; they do keep them themselves, but their preoccupation with minutiae and their failure to concentrate on justice and the love of God renders the service of God burdensome. The service of God

> should not be burdensome. The Gospel is not a burdensome thing. "My yoke is easy, and my burden light," says the Lord. The lawyer's job is not finished when he points out to the weak that they have sinned and must repent; he must raise his finger to lighten the load, and bring his followers to a lightsome comprehension of God's law as an expression of God's love for his people.

What this says to me is that we must not be content to provide people with a process and then walk away from them. What it says to me is that as Church we must not make decisions that affect peoples' lives and then walk away from them. What it says to me that is that we must walk *with* them *in* the process, and *through* the process and *after* the process. We have to hang in there with people, through thick and thin, always – never giving up on them; never leaving them alone.

We must not pervert the process, but we can never think that the process is enough. We must not leave people alone. We need to be with them; we need to walk with them; sometimes we need to carry them. We need to lift burdens hard to carry from their shoulders, to lighten the load, and bring them to a lightsome comprehension of God's law as an expression of God's love for his people.

We must never walk away from those we are called to serve, and we must invite those who *have* walked away to return, to come back, so that through the power of God's grace, through the power of the sacraments, healing and wholeness have a chance to restore individuals, to restore communities, and to restore true communion, so that the very face of God will be manifest to the world in a people made holy through God's grace, through justice tempered by mercy, through good deeds done by trained professionals dedicated to the hard work of doing justice tempered by mercy grounded in truth and dispensed in love.

VARIA

ROLE OF LAW AWARD CITATION
Very Rev. Phillip J. Brown, pss, JD, JCD

This year's Role of Law Award recipient was born in 1939 in a rural diocese far from the ecclesiastical and governmental centers of power, but he eventually spent most of his ecclesiastical career in the nation's capital. He was ordained a priest in 1964 for his home diocese and proceeded immediately to earn his JCL at the Pontifical Gregorian University in Rome. He earned a JCD from Saint Paul University in Ottawa in 1968.

Back in his diocese, in addition to serving as a diocesan priest in parochial assignments, this man was responsible for the permanent diaconate formation program and also served as Promoter of Justice and Defender of the Bond. He served as Spiritual Director at the diocesan seminary for a time, where he also taught courses in catechesis.

This individual served for a time as Dean of a canon law faculty – not at the Catholic University of America, but in the nation's capital where he has spent most of his career – Ottawa, Canada. Here, at Saint Paul University, he became adjunct professor of canon law in 1977, Associate Professor in 1983, and Ordinary Professor of Canon Law in 1987, accepting the role of Dean of the Faculty of Canon Law from 1996 to 2003. He has been a member of the Faculty of *études supérieurs* and postdoctoral studies at the University of Ottawa from 1985 to the present, and he has served the Saint Paul Faculty as Emeritus Professor since 2005 and assistant professor since 2007. He continues to teach regularly in the summer program of the School of Canon Law at the Catholic University of America in *our* nation's capital, and he has also taught in the Faculty of Canon Law at Leuven, Belgium where he held the W. Onclin Chair in 2001 and 2007.

This canonist was a member of the *Institut des communications sociales* of the University of St. Paul from 1983-1985, a member of the delegation of the Holy See to the meeting of the International Commission of Telecommunications under the Organization of American States in 1990, and a member of the Administrative Council of the University of St. Paul University from 1994-1996. He served as President of the Canadian Canon Law Society from 2004-2006, and Judicial Vicar of the Ottawa Regional Tribunal from 2005-2007. He was a member of the *Ad Hoc* Committee of the Conference of Catholic Bishops of Canada for the revision of the Protocol "*De la souffrance à l'espérance*" ("From Suffering to Hope") regarding the sexual abuse of minors by Catholic clergy in

2001, and a member of the *Ad Hoc* Committee for the revision of Book VI of the *Code of Canon Law* regarding penal law from 2011-2012.

Currently, this canonist is the Judicial Vicar of the Appeal Tribunal of Canada. He has written five books, over thirty-five articles on canon law, and has contributed to fourteen volumes of articles by various authors. He has had – and continues to have – a truly distinguished career as a canonist, a professor of canon law and scholar, and as an educational administrator. He received the *Mention de Mérite Jean Thorn* from the Canadian Canon Law Society in 1997 and was made Prelate of Honor by His Holiness St. Pope John Paul II in 1999. He has been a member of the Canon Law Society of America since 1980, modeling joint membership in our two Societies. That close, collaborative relationship has done so much to enhance the professionalism and competence in the field of canon law in the United States and Canada.

Tonight's award recipient is much beloved by his former and current students and his colleagues in the ministry of canon law, and truly needs no introduction; but even this brief résumé of his many ministerial and professional accomplishments is an indication of how much he merits to be recognized and honored by the Canon Law Society of America with its Role of Law Award. I could not be more pleased, more delighted, to announce the recipient of the 2014 Canon Law Society of America Role of Law Award, my friend and colleague, the good friend of so many of us, and our shared friend with Canada and the canon law community throughout the world, our highly respected and beloved colleague Msgr. Roch Pagé. Roch, would you please join me on the stage to receive your award and grace us with a few remarks upon your receipt of this distinguished honor.

VARIA

ROLE OF LAW AWARD RESPONSE
Rev. Msgr. Roch Pagé, JCD, PhD

Thank you very much, Phil, for your kind presentation.

When our president called last January to inform me about the decision of the Board of Governors to honor me with the Role of Law Award this year, I was stunned and told him: "I am speechless". Phil replied: "I am glad to be probably the first one to find you speechless." I thanked him for the compliment.

I wish to sincerely thank the Board of Governors and the CLSA membership for this honor. When I read the characteristics the chosen person should demonstrate during his or her life and legal practice, I cannot but regret to have neglected the advice of my spiritual directors, inviting me to strongly work on the acquisition of an eventual humility. I am sure they are now as proud as I am, even the two who passed away; hopefully not by my fault.

I consider the present honor a great privilege, especially when I think of the group of previous recipients. It is the last of a long list of privileges I have been granted so far in my life as a canonist.

The first privilege was to study canon law in Rome during the Second Vatican Council. About five years before the beginning of my studies, Pope John XXIII announced the revision of the *Code of Canon Law* as a natural consequence of the Church being re-visited by the Council. This also meant that the law which I was to study would be a rather uncertain law with regard to its future application. I used to say that I studied canon law on loose sheets of paper rather than on a firmly bound *Code* – which made me realize that it is not bad for a canonist to feel sometimes insecure.

At the same time, the Council led me to rethink, among other things, my theology of the Church and of the sacraments, which inspired me throughout my teaching years. Moreover, after getting a sense of how the law – civil and canonical – is approached and applied in Rome, it was very good to "land" in Canada for my doctoral thesis and benefit from two different ecclesiastical cultures. It is probably around that time that, in a discussion about the interpretation of a law, I realized it is possible to pass between the paint and the wall.

After seven years as spiritual director of our diocesan seminary, I was permitted by my bishop to return to Saint Paul as a teacher. Instructed to go to Ottawa for only one year, I had to renew the request for a few more years, which prevented me from speaking in terms of career longevity. That is why I am used to saying that I spent thirty-five "one year" stints as a permanent teacher at St. Paul.

After four years in Ottawa, I realized that there was no future there for someone from Chicoutimi who had never spoken English. I decided then to grant myself another privilege and, in the image of Abraham, I left Canada for an unknown country to learn English... I went to Texas. (I do not understand why y'all are laughing.) I went to San Antonio on the advice of an Oblate who had been there for more than twenty years. I thought he was a friend of mine, but after I returned from Texas, he overheard a conversation in English between a student and me. This supposed "friend" who joined us said to the student: "You know what? Since he is back from Texas, Pagé speaks Spanish and he thinks he speaks English."

A final privilege that I wish to share with you – and thank God for – is that after about five years of retirement from regular teaching at Saint Paul, I accepted the request of the Conference of Bishops to become Judicial Vicar of the Canadian Appeal Tribunal. After having taught procedural law for thirty-five years, it is something quite special to be in a position to apply it. Recently, I have accepted the invitation of the Dean of our Faculty to teach procedural law next semester. Let me tell you, I will certainly add some nuances to my usual commentaries on different norms.

After more than forty years of teaching and canonical practice, how could I not be moved, probably like most of you, by the subject matter of the present extraordinary Synod of Bishops in Rome, especially by the question of divorced and remarried Catholics?

I know that it is a difficult issue. Therefore, I will not suggest any solution, but allow me to try to express my own questions or at least, the state of the question as I see it.

As we know from our experience, in whichever field we apply the law, more often than not canonists find themselves specializing in impasse. This is not restricted to those individuals who work in tribunals, even if the problems of married persons constitute their daily lot. Chancellors too, have a large part to play in the resolution of impasses caused by the application of law; just as professors and consultants do in matters of interpretation.

I think the question of divorced and remarried people is to be considered from the very beginning, that is to say: what do we seek to accomplish when we prepare Catholic Christians for marriage? Is it to render them able to live their marriage as **the sacrament of the love** which Christ unfailingly holds for His Church, or as **the sacrament of the bond** which permanently unites Christ to her?

If the theology of marriage clearly favors the first aspect, the couple's problems begin when love no longer exists between them, and they conclude that they have no reason to continue living together. It is at that point that they need to come to terms with the reality: they have committed themselves to be the human setting in which not only **the love of Christ** for his Church is lived out, **but also the bond** which is the logical consequence of that love; and so, they remain permanently responsible for being a sign of the latter, **the bond**, without being a sign of the former, **the love**. It must be admitted that in the Church it is possible to be a sign of the bond without the existence of the love; but it is not possible to be a sign of the love of Christ in a marriage if one is not at the same time a sign of the bond which unites Christ to his Church. This is the avenue canon law has taken in determining that it is consent, rather than love, that makes marriage; even if the *bonum conjugum* has emerged of late as one of the ends of marriage.

Canon law has been blamed many times for the difficulties encountered by married people, including Catholics who have divorced and remarried civilly or otherwise. Such reproaches cannot be extended to canonists themselves, unless it be that they try too hard to regulate, on a juridical level, situations whose resolution could at times be better sought on a theological or pastoral level. To what extent have we not been responsible in this way, for delays to offer real solutions to the problems of those who have experienced the breakdown of their marriage? I mean that we must not forget that marriage, once again, is not only the sacrament of bond but also the sacrament of love. And then, the problem and its solution might be of a theological nature, without forgetting that the juridical dimension would have to be taken into account at one stage or another since it is this dimension which is the basis of the contract.

Speaking of the theological dimension of marriage, we should not forget a theological solution. I am reminded of the solution used by a number of Orthodox Churches and already mentioned by Pope Francis. It should lead us to consider a question: did the Church stretch to its limit the power to forgive, a power which was handed over to her by Christ? We possess a good **spirituality** of forgiveness, but do we possess an equally good **theology** of forgiveness? Would it not be possible to grant pardon to those members of the faithful who made a mistake in marrying or in entering a sacramental marriage? Or to those guilty of a grave offense against their commitment to be a sign in the community of the love of Christ for His Church?

My fear is that the present Synod has created too high expectations. **My hope** is simply that the Synodal Fathers will face the true questions and accordingly examine the true, possible solutions.

Thank you very much for your kindness.

Varia

U.S. Tribunal Statistics
2013

Since 1975, the CLSA has published Tribunal Statistics annually in *Proceedings*. These statistics are provided voluntarily by participating tribunal offices in the United States. This year's statistical report was compiled by means similar to last year's report. Tribunals were asked to submit a copy of the report sent annually to the Apostolic Signatura, as well as some basic financial information. Submissions came by mail to the Office of the Executive Coordinator or by online entry via clsa.org. This change, implemented three years ago, has resulted in a more accurate comparison of statistics among U.S. tribunals.

Participation in the survey increased in comparison to last year. This year, the CLSA received information from 165 tribunals, compared to 163 last year. Included again in this year's report is the number of decisions found contrary to nullity from each reporting tribunal, with the percentage of negative decisions out of the total calculated. Following the same gradual trend as indicated in the past several years, the number of cases introduced and decisions made in American tribunals continues to decline, while expenses continue to rise.

The tribunals of the Archdioceses of Baltimore, Galveston-Houston, Los Angeles, Philadelphia, San Francisco, Santa Fe; and the Dioceses of Amarillo, Arlington, Burlington, Covington, Fort Worth, Helena, Juneau, Kalamazoo, Las Vegas, Pittsburgh, Winona, the Eparchy of St. Maron of Brooklyn, The Archeparchy for Ukranians in Pittsburgh, the Ukrainian Diocese of St. Josaphat in Parma and the Holy Protection of Mary, Byzantine Catholic Eparchy of Phoenix did not participate in the survey.

Number of Tribunals Represented	
2009	131
2010	135
2011	130
2012	164
2013	165

Documentary Cases Introduced

Year	2009	2010	2011	2012	2013
Cases	12239	4147	3774	3692	3592

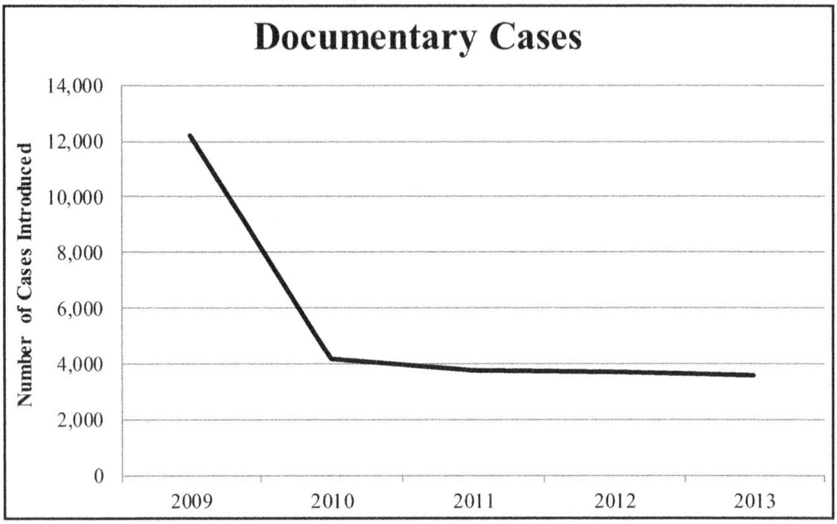

Fees and Expenses

Year	2009	2010	2011	2012	2013
Fees Received	$4,980,461	$5,193,872	$4,569,371	$4,824,170	$4,925,213
Dioc. Subsidy	$26,104,591	$26,477,648	$25,211,816	$45,148,059	$28,397,617
Total Expenses	$31,123,946	$31,612,970	$30,372,513	$30,073,434	$32,233,606

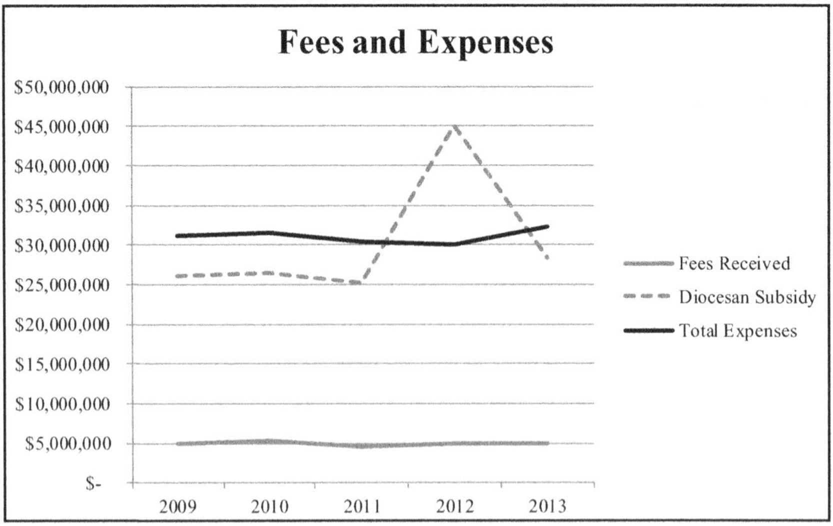

Formal Cases					
Year	**2009**	**2010**	**2011**	**2012**	**2013**
Decisions	17106	14360	14314	14781	14045
Introduced	19039	16787	15589	16191	16462
Abated	1846	1284	1515	1593	1463

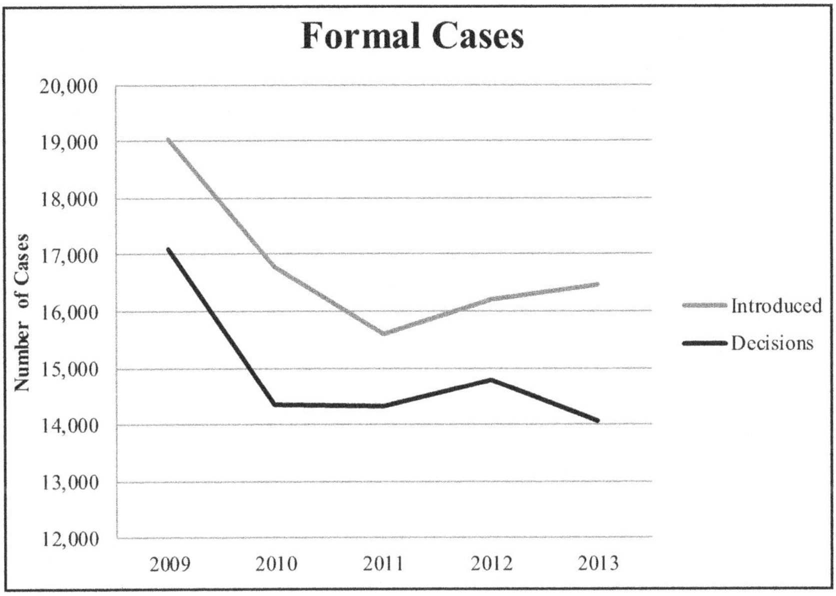

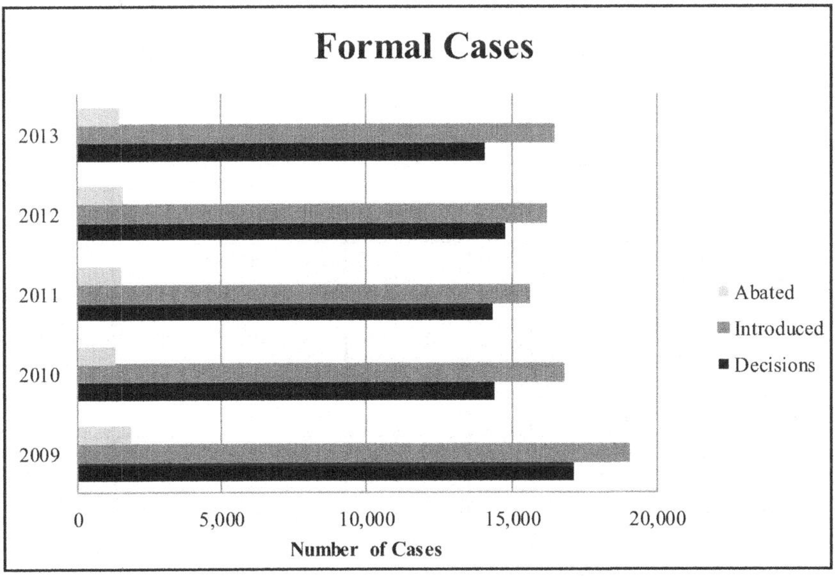

First Instance Statistics 2013												
(Arch)Diocese	Documentary Cases Closed	Formal Cases Held Over	Formal Cases Introduced	Sentences in Favor of Nullity	Sentences Contrary to Nullity	Total formal decisions (affirmative & negative)	% of Total Decisions Found Contrary to Nullity	Peremption/Renunciation	Total	Total Fees Received	Amount of Diocesan Subsidy	Total Annual Expenses
Albany	0	47	97	52	2	54	4%	7	61			
Alexandria	8	52	50	48	2	50	4%	4	54	$14,525.00	$181,435.00	$195,960.00
Allentown	0	143	157	77	0	77	0%	0	77	$37,200.00	$227,000.00	$264,200.00
Altoona-Johnstown	3	15	86	60	0	60	0%	5	65		$73,000.00	$60,000.00
Anchorage	0	39	32	36	0	36	0%	4	40	$9,076.50	$86,797.95	$95,874.45
Atlanta	0	491	301	380	80	460	17%	38	498			
Austin	19	290	173	185	10	195	5%	15	210	$61,163.00	$233,532.00	$294,695.00
Baker	16	31	23	19	1	20	5%	7	27	$5,750.00	$88,453.00	$94,203.00
Baton Rouge	17	138	144	97	0	97	0%	12	109	$39,740.00	$226,815.22	$266,815.22
Beaumont	5	150	77	56	1	57	2%	14	57	$19,521.00	$157,640.00	$177,161.00
Belleville	8	100	53	40	0	40	0%	6	46	$9,980.00	$50,506.00	$60,486.00
Biloxi	0	125	35	42	0	42	0%	10	52	$4,025.00	$142,500.00	$145,135.00
Birmingham	0	68	91	37	0	37	0%	10	47	$24,730.00	$169,560.00	$192,055.00
Bismarck	0	36	41	22	1	23	4%	4	27	$14,280.00	$170,083.00	$184,363.00
Boise	13	190	159	107	0	107	0%	9	116	$25,523.00	$164,688.00	$190,211.00
Boston	4	173	156	111	0	111	0%	7	118			
Bridgeport	0	44	57	41	2	43	5%	3	46			
Brooklyn	6	114	116	89	2	91	2%	9	100	$115,013.00	$124,500.00	$225,400.00
Brownsville	237	70	67	56	0	56	0%	8	64	$36,350.00	$25,100.00	$61,450.00
Buffalo	91	35	87	92	0	92	0%	0	92	$63,983.00	$192,713.00	$256,696.00
Camden	2	75	47	39	1	40	3%	9	49	$30,130.00	$169,303.00	$199,433.00
Charleston	18	91	80	86	3	89	3%	10	99	$119,577.80	$211,424.26	$331,002.06
Charlotte	21	97	131	131	2	133	2%	6	142	$63,805.00	$409,316.78	$415,678.69
Cheyenne	5	68	45	61	1	62	2%	4	66	$31,175.00	$95,362.00	$126,537.00
Chicago	24	130	367	287	5	292	2%	11	303	$265,062.93	$967,835.69	$1,232,898.62
Cincinnati	0	174	221	188	13	201	6%	0	201	$73,050.00	$402,217.00	$474,391.08
Cleveland	216	236	275	201	7	208	3%	11	219	$131,178.00	$557,544.00	$688,721.00

First Instance Statistics 2013												
(Arch)Diocese	Documentary Cases Closed	Formal Cases Held Over	Formal Cases Introduced	Sentences in Favor of Nullity	Sentences Contrary to Nullity	Total formal decisions (affirmative & negative)	% of Total Decisions Found Contrary to Nullity	Peremption/Renunciation	Total	Total Fees Received	Amount of Diocesan Subsidy	Total Annual Expenses
Colorado Springs	4	38	28	18	8	26	31%	1	26			
Columbus	13	117	168	137	6	143	4%	13	156	$0.00	$416,471.00	$534,053.00
Corpus Christi	0	81	119	51	0	51	0%	2	51	$38,069.00	$145,702.00	$183,771.00
Crookston	18	31	31	27	1	28	4%	6	34	$0.00	$148,238.00	$148,238.00
Dallas	24	244	257	179	1	180	1%	106	286	$43,100.00	$440,444.00	$483,544.00
Davenport	8	99	64	55	3	58	5%	13	71	$33,415.00	$109,221.00	$142,636.00
Denver	0	413	135	180	6	186	3%	17	203			
Des Moines	39	48	79	52	1	53	2%	2	55	$36,350.00	$57,590.00	$93,940.00
Detroit	12	98	355	259	5	264	2%	26	290	$21,250.00	$659,741.98	$7,275.00
Dodge City	0	15	33	28	0	28	0%	5	33	$3,605.00	$86,596.68	$90,201.68
Dubuque	1	152	125	111	0	111	0%	13	124	$54,301.00	$194,570.00	$248,871.00
Duluth	0	18	26	11	1	12	8%	2	14	$3,144.00		
El Paso	0	119	64	73	6	79	8%	7	86			
Erie	3	52	132	100	1	101	1%	1	102	$38,300.00	$332,826.00	$371,126.00
Evansville	2	4	52	48	0	48	0%	5	53	$16,207.00	$216,808.00	$233,015.00
Fairbanks	0	19	10	11	0	11	0%	6	17	$1,550.00		
Fall River	0	84	51	31	0	31	0%	12	43			
Fargo	45	66	38	62	4	66	6%	7	73	$3,875.00	$214,433.38	$219,065.24
Fort Wayne-South Bend	70	48	108	35	17	52	33%	10	62	$5,133.00	$374,047.00	$379,180.00
Fresno	209	158	179	159	5	164	3%	16	159	$95,811.95	$64,574.44	$160,386.35
Gallup	0	31	13	16	5	21	24%	9	30	$1,900.00		$28,380.00
Gary	1	181	57	53	0	53	0%	5	53	$21,735.00	$202,301.00	$224,036.00
Gaylord	3	42	39	27	1	28	4%	1	29	$0.00	$85,176.00	$85,176.00
Grand Island	44	68	47	37	0	37	0%	2	39	$6,375.00	$189,190.89	$195,565.89
Grand Rapids	85	139	129	106	1	107	1%	9	116	$0.00	$112,110.00	$112,110.22
Great Falls-Billings	23	19	22	12	0	12	0%	11	23	$1,050.00	$107,273.04	$108,323.04

First Instance Statistics 2013												
(Arch)Diocese	Documentary Cases Closed	Formal Cases Held Over	Formal Cases Introduced	Sentences in Favor of Nullity	Sentences Contrary to Nullity	Total formal decisions (affirmative & negative)	% of Total Decisions Found Contrary to Nullity	Peremption/Renunciation	Total	Total Fees Received	Amount of Diocesan Subsidy	Total Annual Expenses
Green Bay	0	52	102	99	3	102	3%	0	102	$32,155.00	$114,128.00	$146,283.00
Greensburg	0	33	66	72	0	72	0%	0	72			
Harrisburg	0	311	174	149	8	157	5%	16	173	$91,461.94	$371,079.94	$462,541.88
Hartford	1	82	76	57	11	68	16%	12	80			
Honolulu	0	20	31	31	0	31	0%	2	31	$16,501.00	$131,367.00	$147,868.00
Houma-Thibodaux	0	29	41	29	3	32	9%	1	33	$12,710.00	$55,450.00	$68,160.00
Indianapolis	32	139	108	101	0	101	0%	9	110	$32,741.25	$0.00	$0.00
Jackson	5	22	41	23	0	23	0%	12	35	$0.00	$95,602.00	$95,602.00
Jefferson City	11	109	103	69	1	70	1%	5	75	$0.00	$161,836.00	$161,836.00
Joliet	6	60	175	171	0	171	0%	22	199	$67,217.50	$462,200.00	$542,200.00
Kansas City - St. Joseph	0	127	90	77	0	77	0%	2	79			
Kansas City in Kansas	119	366	274	225	7	232	3%	18	250	$76,990.00	$217,866.00	$294,856.00
La Crosse	1	56	120	112	3	115	3%	9	124	$45,583.00	$105,561.00	$170,850.00
Lafayette in Indiana	69	71	80	56	7	63	11%	7	70			
Lafayette in Louisiana	0	173	136	112	17	129	13%	2	135	$46,950.00	$117,940.00	$8,453.00
Lake Charles	7	57	69	35	6	41	15%	1	42	$17,325.00	$121,919.98	$139,244.98
Lansing	12	108	130	148	1	149	1%	17	166	$26,320.17	$386,297.46	$412,617.63
Laredo	52	21	27	11	0	11	0%	4	15	$6,425.00	$81,330.28	$53,254.13
Las Cruces	0	90	59	46	0	46	0%	11	46	$18,674.00	$71,995.30	$90,669.30
Lexington	6	28	63	63	0	63	0%	6	72	$0.00	$203,922.00	$203,922.00
Lincoln	3	63	52	49	1	50	2%	8	58		84%	
Little Rock	29	73	179	149	0	149	0%	15	164	$24,700.00	$149,876.00	$174,576.00
Los Angeles, Eparchy of Our Lady of Lebanon of	18	15	19	23	0	23	0%	1	24	$12,850.00	$3,150.00	$16,000.00

First Instance Statistics 2013

(Arch)Diocese	Documentary Cases Closed	Formal Cases Held Over	Formal Cases Introduced	Sentences in Favor of Nullity	Sentences Contrary to Nullity	Total formal decisions (affirmative & negative)	% of Total Decisions Found Contrary to Nullity	Peremption/Renunciation	Total	Total Fees Received	Amount of Diocesan Subsidy	Total Annual Expenses
Louisville	7	13	119	117	0	117	0%	1	117	$25,715	$285,338	$270,101
Lubbock	42	72	61	45	0	45	0%	3	48	$17,305.92	$9,015.00	$73,611.71
Madison	0	78	62	18	23	41	56%	12	53	$19,655.00	$233,677.00	$253,332.00
Manchester	70	169	82	85	0	85	0%	5	90	$30,907.00	$8,793.00	$39,700.00
Marquette	26	0	24	27	0	27	0%	0	27	$5,880.00	$29,473.00	$35,353.00
Memphis	12	41	82	35	2	37	5%	5	42	$1,400.00	$134,590.00	$135,990.00
Metuchen	4	102	80	61	0	61	0%	9	70	$45,965.00	$329,352.27	$375,317.27
Miami	4	165	234	183	8	191	4%	17	208			
Military Services	5	184	99	82	1	83	1%	0	83	$48,190.00	$124,771.06	$173,325.73
Milwaukee	1	217	208	173	0	173	0%	21	193	$61,247.50	$591,439.74	$530,192.24
Mobile	0	111	127	44	10	54	19%	5	59	$15,144.00	$290,856.00	$306,000.00
Monterey	0	44	20	18	1	19	5%	5	24	$15,300.00	$81,120.00	$96,420.00
Nashville	19	96	115	56	18	74	24%	3	77		$403,589.00	$403,589.00
New Orleans	17	213	116	119	12	131	9%	0	137	$53,080.00	$396,943.00	$450,023.00
New Ulm	2	29	30	13	0	13	0%	3	16	$500.00	$110,326.30	$110,826.30
New York	3	204	245	186	39	225	17%	5	230	$232,000.00	$1,061,900.00	$1,293,900.00
Newark	0	114	104	102	1	103	1%	35	138	$67,555.00	$360,478.00	$428,033.00
Newton, Eparchy of	10	3	12	9	0	9	0%	0	12			
Norwich	0	48	36	39	2	41	5%	0	41	$8,585.00	$343,972.92	$352,557.92
Oakland	0	227	77	59	2	61	3%	11	72	$73,413.00	$609,706.00	$683,119.00
Ogdensburg	0	35	42	30	1	31	3%	14	45	$12,428.57	$48,674.46	$61,103.03
Oklahoma City	118	145	212	173	14	187	7%	13	200		$155,580.00	$155,580.00
Omaha	0	222	170	99	8	107	7%	9	116	$33,113.00	$322,088.42	$355,201.42
Orange	20	86	180	0	0	0	0%	0	169	$141,558.99	$778,619.74	$920,178.73
Orlando	0	170	265	312	47	359	13%	8	359	$144,454.61	$330,812.01	$536,870.12
Owensboro	15	105	61	67	0	67	0%	6	73	$9,539.00	$236,726.00	$246,265.00
Palm Beach	24	55	67	65	2	67	3%	2	68			

First Instance Statistics 2013												
(Arch)Diocese	Documentary Cases Closed	Formal Cases Held Over	Formal Cases Introduced	Sentences in Favor of Nullity	Sentences Contrary to Nullity	Total formal decisions (affirmative & negative)	% of Total Decisions Found Contrary to Nullity	Peremption/Renunciation	Total	Total Fees Received	Amount of Diocesan Subsidy	Total Annual Expenses
Parma, Byz. Eparchy	0	4	3	4	0	4	0%	0	4			
Passaic, Byz.-Ruthenian Eparchy	0	17	6	6	0	6	0%	1	6	$4,800.00	$18,000.00	$24,000.00
Paterson	0	131	71	30	8	38	21%	12	38	$47,235.00	$255,120.00	$302,355.00
Pensacola-Tallahassee	0	27	73	46	3	49	6%	5	54	$7,150.00	$62,890.00	$70,040.00
Peoria	7	91	124	95	1	96	1%	4	100	$71,250.00	$321,615.00	$382,914.00
Philadelphia, Archeparchy for Ukrainians	2	0	5	4	1	5	20%	0	5	$1,450.00	$0.00	$2,686.03
Phoenix	11	385	138	63	29	92	32%	6	98			
Portland in Maine	0	89	127			0	0%	0	126	$35,000.00	$281,395.00	$316,395.00
Portland in Oregon	20	142	140	138	0	138	0%	7	145	$44,769.00	$0.00	$29,123.60
Providence	0	67	67	41	8	49	16%	2	51	$57,300.00	$259,178.00	$316,478.00
Pueblo	5	29	26	23	0	23	0%	4	23	$3,390.00	$139,601.00	$142.99
Raleigh	139	113	104	107	1	108	1%	8	116	$34,190.00	$220,824.00	$266,263.00
Rapid City	9	33	27	7		7	0%	2	9	$2,535.00	$54,347.31	$56,882.31
Reno	54	42	30	17	2	19	11%	2	21	$9,145.00	$157,167.85	$166,312.85
Richmond	0	96	169	139	13	152	9%	7	159			
Rochester	0	43	59	45	7	52	13%	6	58	$28,609.00	$223,815.00	$252,424.00
Rockford	114	69	172	199	3	202	1%	14	216			
Rockville Centre	4	406	236	205	1	206	0%	44	250			
Sacramento	9	250	93	67	24	91	26%	57	148			
Saginaw	65	41	72	81	2	83	2%	1	84	$2,625.00	$124,971.35	$127,596.35
Salina	0	58	61	49	0	49	0%	9	68	$17,590.00	$57,525.00	$75,115.00
Salt Lake City	32	10	65	63	2	65	3%	6	63	$13,495.00	$100,090.00	$113,585.00
San Angelo	0	37	61	50	0	50	0%	2	52	$8,593.00	$197,574.86	$206,167.86

First Instance Statistics 2013												
(Arch)Diocese	Documentary Cases Closed	Formal Cases Held Over	Formal Cases Introduced	Sentences in Favor of Nullity	Sentences Contrary to Nullity	Total formal decisions (affirmative & negative)	% of Total Decisions Found Contrary to Nullity	Peremption/Renunciation	Total	Total Fees Received	Amount of Diocesan Subsidy	Total Annual Expenses
San Antonio	12	113	281	248	11	259	4%	4	263	$125,150.00	$234,757.00	$259,907.00
San Bernardino	5	143	145	96	11	107	10%	11	118	$56,855.00	$282,536.00	$339,391.00
San Diego	5	218	192	136	5	141	4%	12	153	$47,740.00	$299,798.00	$347,538.00
San Jose	132	104	97	93	2	95	2%	3	95	$65,513.87	$358,800.07	$424,313.94
Santa Rosa	0	13	38	36	2	38	5%	0	38	$17,346.00	$67,747.00	$85,092.00
Savannah	9	20	60	42	0	42	0%	14	56	$18,462.76	$216,404.00	$174,195.81
Scranton	0	56	110	108	2	110	2%	3	113	$79,434.50	$278,618.51	$358,053.01
Seattle	32	216	173	177	0	177	0%	5	182	$61,892.00	$430,583.00	$553,113.00
Shreveport	5	49	34	39	4	43	9%	6	41	$1,250.00	$187,943.00	$108,346.45
Sioux City	1	55	63	65	0	65	0%	3	68	$23,354.00	$165,001.43	$188,355.43
Sioux Falls	0	29	82	68	0	68	0%	7	75	$21,179.00	$111,165.60	$120,465.90
Spokane	3	20	51	63		63	0%	0	63	$11,925.00	$34,128.00	$46,053.00
Springfield, Cape Girardeau	45	76	141	93	12	105	11%	14	119	$13,155.00	$199,758.68	$217,017.00
Springfield, Illinois	88	128	111	107	1	108	1%	3	111	$63,593.00	$214,742.44	$278,335.44
Springfield, Massachusetts	50	76	74	80	0	80	0%	10	90	$25,405.00	$163,516.00	$188,921.00
St. Augustine	22	155	88	25	2	27	7%	7	34	$58,290.00	$163,633.96	$241,950.91
St. Cloud	0	98	75	49	0	49	0%	3	45	$34,467.00	$141,954.00	$165,245.00
St. Louis	12	274	216	187	1	188	1%	30	218	$127,677.00	$323,370.00	$451,047.00
St. Paul and Minneapolis	0	300	102	64	26	90	29%	5	95	$74,385.00	$855,424.00	$929,809.00
St. Petersburg	0	26	215	158	44	202	22%	5	207			
Stamford, Ukrainian Eparchy of	0					0	0%	0		$600.00	$250.00	$400.00
Steubenville	4	27	39	43	4	47	9%	2	49	$10,600.00	$74,693.10	$85,293.10
Stockton	0	88	38	50	1	51	2%	4	55	$47,707.00	$110,082.00	$157,789.00
Superior	0	29	32	43	0	43	0%	0	43	$6,227.50	$97,185.48	$130,412.98

First Instance Statistics 2013												
(Arch)Diocese	Documentary Cases Closed	Formal Cases Held Over	Formal Cases Introduced	Sentences in Favor of Nullity	Sentences Contrary to Nullity	Total formal decisions (affirmative & negative)	% of Total Decisions Found Contrary to Nullity	Peremption/Renunciation	Total	Total Fees Received	Amount of Diocesan Subsidy	Total Annual Expenses
Syracuse	0	34	95	108	0	108	0%	1	109	$67,750.00	$35,372.00	$103,722.00
Toledo	119	72	177	151	0	151	0%	12	163	$39,605.00	$200,394.36	$239,999.36
Trenton	6	152	95	88	0	88	0%	3	91	$73,430.00	$322,785.00	$396,215.00
Tucson	8	161	47	48	1	49	2%	47	96	$31,285.00	$91,903.00	$123,188.00
Tulsa	90	33	53	58	0	58	0%	11	69	-		$70,057.00
Tyler	0	42	70	43	7	50	14%	12	62	$7,415.00	$54,203.00	$107,745.00
Venice	93	116	70	49	28	77	36%	54	131			
Victoria	4	14	42	43	1	44	2%	2	46	40%	60%	
Washington, DC	6	58	282	124	25	149	17%	43	192			
Wheeling-Charleston	45	99	72	31	13	44	30%	1	45			
Wichita	150	355	178	180	7	187	4%	20	207	$28,000.00	$48,000.00	$76,000.00
Wilmington	4	72	56	37	0	37	0%	0	37	$36,250.00	$176,202.00	$202,453.00
Worcester	0	25	55	34	0	34	0%	0	34	$15,175.00	$151,082.00	$166,257.00
Yakima	7	50	27	28	1	29	3%	1	30	$16,705.00	$149,396.00	$156,843.59
Youngstown	66	82	83	51	1	52	2%	4	56	$16,713.53	$268,071.70	$273,817.56

Second Instance Statistics 2013						
(Arch)Diocese	Second Instance Pending at Beginning of Year	Introduced	Closed	Decree Confirmation	Sentence in Favor of Nullity	Sentence Contrary to Nullity
Boise	1	117	118	118		
Boston	14	177	180	173	4	2
Bridgeport	7	31	25	20	0	4
Camden	21	37	38	29	1	8
Cleveland	10	317	317	0	312	4
Columbus	19	51	52	50	50	1
Davenport	0	42	42	42	0	0
Denver	0	101	91	90	1	0
Des Moines	0	52	52	40	40	0
Detroit	46	462	434	432	0	2
Dubuque	24	170	170	168	2	0
Evansville	0	52	52	52	0	0
Fargo	0	6	3	3	0	0
Fort Wayne-South Bend	8	58	54	35	5	14
Fresno	5	94	89	89	0	0
Gary	0	53	53	53	53	0
Grand Rapids	57	155	190	189	1	0
Green Bay		155	155			
Hartford	1	61	56	53	2	1
Indianapolis	43	40	61	56	56	4
Kansas City in Kansas	7	190	186	186	185	1
Lafayette in Indiana	12	97	101		101	0
Lafayette in Louisiana	3	39	38			
Lake Charles	21	35	47	35	35	12
Lexington	10	44	52		51	0
Louisville	20	127	119	119	119	0
Memphis	5	81	82	82	0	0
Metuchen	7	39	41	41	41	0
Miami	17	698	636	621	1	13
Milwaukee	14	272	277	277	0	0
Mobile	50	95	113	110	2	1

Second Instance Statistics 2013						
(Arch)Diocese	Second Instance Pending at Beginning of Year	Introduced	Closed	Decree Confirmation	Sentence in Favor of Nullity	Sentence Contrary to Nullity
Nashville	5	47	36	0	0	0
New Orleans	44	326	355	317	3	32
Newark	3	170	168	168	0	0
Newton, Eparchy of	0	16	15	10		
Norwich	1	19	19	19	0	0
Orange	25	407	396	395	144	0
Owensboro	12	55	48	47	1	0
Paterson	8	39	29	27	1	1
Philadelphia, Archeparchy for Ukrainians	0	1	1	1	1	0
Phoenix	53	180	155	144	3	7
Portland in Maine	3	182	185			
Portland in Oregon	30	226	247	247	0	0
Richmond	22	275	273	271	271	2
Saginaw	0	102	100	98	2	0
San Bernardino	0	81	57	57	0	1
San Diego	38	234	258	255	0	2
San Jose	16	91	91	91	91	0
Seattle	19	243	246	242	2	2
Sioux City	0	32	28	28	0	0
Springfield, Massachusetts	11	129	129	128	1	0
St. Cloud	13	27	27	27	27	0
St. Louis	123	461	532	525	3	3
St. Paul and Minneapolis	192	304	242	224	11	7
Steubenville	2	50	48	0	48	0
Stockton	28	174	189	189	0	0
Toledo	29	154	158	156	2	0
Trenton	0	43	43	43	0	0
Washington, DC	4	209	187	156	8	10
Wheeling-Charleston	2	82	73	65	7	1
Youngstown	5	102	91	142	91	0

VARIA

CONTRIBUTORS

Rev. Peter O. Akpoghiran, JCD, Judicial Vicar and Chancellor, Archdiocese of New Orleans, Louisiana

Dr. Anne Asselin, JCD, Dean, Faculty of Canon Law, Saint Paul University, Ottawa, Ontario, Canada

Dr. Diane Barr, JD, JCD, PhD, Chancellor, Archdiocese of Baltimore, Maryland

Very Rev. Phillip J. Brown, SS, JD, JCD, Rector, Theological College, The Catholic University of America, Washington, DC; President, Canon Law Society of America

Rev. Thomas T. Brundage, JCL, Judicial Vicar, Archdiocese of Anchorage, Alaska

Dr. Margaret Chalmers, JCD, PhD, JD, Chancellor, Personal Ordinariate of the Chair of Saint Peter, Greenville, South Carolina

Rev. James J. Conn, SJ, JD, JCD, Professor of the Practice of Canon Law, Boston College, Massachusetts

Chorbishop John Faris, JCOD, Adjunct Professor, The Catholic University of America, Washington, DC

Most Rev. Brian Farrell, LC, STD, Secretary, Pontifical Council for Promoting Christian Unity, Vatican City, Europe

Mr. James-Daniel Flynn, JCL, Special Assistant to the Bishop, Diocese of Lincoln, Nebraska

Sr. Amy Hereford, JD, JCD, Religious Law and Consultation, Private Practice, St. Louis, Missouri

Rev. Michael Joyce, CM, JCD, Local Superior, Perryville, Missouri

Rev. Francis J. Marini, JD, JCOD, Judicial Vicar, Tribunal of the Eparchy of Saint Maron of Brooklyn, New York

Most Rev. David Motiuk, Bishop, JCOD, Eparch of Edmonton, Alberta, Canada

Most Rev. Kevin Vann, JCD, Bishop, Diocese of Orange, California

Rev. Manuel Viera, OFM, JCL, Judicial Vicar, Diocese of Tucson, Arizona

Prof. Dr. Myriam Wijlens, STL, JCD, Full Professor of Canon Law, University of Erfurt, Germany; Honorary Professor of Ecumenism and Canon Law, University of Durham, Great Britain

Sr. Patricia Wittberg, SC, PhD, Professor of Sociology, Indiana University, Indiana

Varia

Participants

Peter Akpoghiran
New Orleans, LA
Ellie Alcala
Los Angeles, CA
John Alesandro
Rockville Centre, NY
Margaret Lola Alokan
Millen, GA
Anna Amato
Palermo, Italy
Krystyna Amborski
San Francisco, CA
Thomas Anslow
Los Angeles, CA
William Anton
Lubbock, Texas
Charles Antonicelli
Washington, DC
Gary Applegate
Kansas City, KS
Christopher Armstrong
Washington, DC
Das Arockia
Lexington, KY
Joseph Arsenault
Kansas City, KS
Anne Asselin
Ottawa, ON
Joseph Augustine
Romney, WV
Alberto Avella
Grants, NM
Diane Barr
Baltimore, MD
Andrew Bartell
Sioux Falls, SD
Virginia Bartolac
Kansas City, KS
Mary Ann Bartolac
Kansas City, KS
James Bartoloma
Camden, NJ
Carlotta Bartone
Rosemont, PA
Ronald Barusefski
Bayonne, NJ
Ricardo Bass
Harrison Twp., MI
Anthony Bawyn
Seattle, WA
John Bell
Allen, TX
Joseph Bellerive
Eustis, FL
Iden Bello
Laredo, TX
Charles Benoit
Saint Benedict, LA
Paul Berghout
Arlington, VA
Matthew Bergschneider
Rockford, IL
Diego Berrio
Chicago, IL
Barbara Bettwy
Erie, PA
Mary Gen Blittschau
Evansville, IN
Michael Boccaccio
Bridgeport, CT
Celeste Boda
Owensboro, KY
Frank Bollich
Austin, TX
James Bonke
Indianapolis, IN
Janelle Boyum
New Ulm, MN
Michael Bradley
Chicago, IL
James Bradley
London, UK
Barry Brinkman
Salina, KS
Timothy Broglio
Washington, DC
Phillip Brown
Washington, DC
Robert Brown
Atlanta, GA
Thomas Brundage
Anchorage, AL
Anne Bryant
Houston, TX
Michael Burchfield
Fresno, CA
Kurt Burnette
Woodland Park, NJ
Jeffrey Cabral
Fall River, MA
Steven Callahan
San Diego, CA
Giovanni Capucci
Denver, CO
Michael Cariglio
Youngstown, OH
John Caronan
Orange, CA
Maria Casey
Croydon, Australia
Anthony Celino
El Paso, Texas
Martin Celuch
Youngstown, OH

Deborah Cerullo
Providence, RI
Charles Chaffman
San Antonio, TX
Margaret Chalmers
Greenville, SC
Anna Marie Chamblee
Fort Worth, TX
J. Michael Clark
Owensboro, KY
Paul Clark
Harrisburg, PA
Cherry Clark
Baltimore, MD
John Cody
Columbus, OH
Patrick Cogan
Sterling, VA
James Conn
Boston, MA
Jay Conzemius
Pittsburgh, PA
Patrick Cooney
St. Meinrad, IN
James Coriden
Washington, DC
Paul Counce
Baton Rouge, LA
Cheryl Criss
Peoria, IL
Thomas Cronkleton
Cheyenne, WY
Barry Cuba
College Station, TX
Barbara Anne Cusack
Milwaukee, WI
Jamin David
Baton Rouge, LA
Zabrina Decker
Milwaukee, WI
David Deibel
Monterey, CA
Jesus Del Angel Leon
Fresno, CA

Vicente DeLa Cruz
Houma, LA
Robert DeLand
Saginaw, MI
Louis DeNinno
Pittsburgh, PA
John Dermond
Trenton, NJ
Georges de Laire
Manchester, NH
Francis Dolan
Chicago, IL
John Donovan
Syracuse, NY
Jerald Doyle
Bridgeport, CT
Patricia Dugan
Philadelphia, PA
Brian Dunn
Antigonish, NS
Frederick Easton
Bloomington, IN
Mary Edlund
Dallas, TX
Heather Eichholz
Owensboro, KY
Peter Eke
Gaylord, MI
Jace Eskind
Lake Charles, LA
Sharon Euart
Washington, DC
Ramil Fajardo
Chicago, IL
John Faris
Utica, NY
Brian Farrell
Dublin, Ireland
Adrian Farrelly
Brisbane, Australia
Thomas Feeney
Corpus Christi, TX
Karla Felix-Rivera
Long Beach, CA

James Ferguson
Alexandria, LA
Christopher Ferrer
Austin, TX
Victor Finelli
Allentown, PA
Daniel Firmin
Savannah, GA
Robert Flummerfelt
Las Vegas, NV
James-Daniel Flynn
Lincoln, NE
Shannon Fossett
Portland, ME
John J. Foster
Washington, DC
Thomas Fransiscus
Reno, NV
Matthew H. Frisoni
Albany, NY
Matthew Furgiuele
Gaylord, MI
Engelberto Gammad
San Jose, CA
Mark Gantley
Honolulu, HI
Stephen Garbitelli
Denver, CO
Elpidio Geneta
Princeton, WV
John Giel
Orlando, FL
Karen Giffin
Seattle, WA
M. Margaret Gillett
Dallas, TX
Catherine Gilligan
Little Rock, AR
Garry Giroux
Brasher Falls, NY
Donald Goetz
Louisville, KY
Paul Golden
Denver, CO

James Goodwin
Fargo, ND
Robert Graffio
San Francisco, CA
Thomas Green
Washington, DC
John Griffiths
Chicago, IL
Janice Grochowsky
Dodge City, KS
David Gross
Grand Rapids, MI
Ralph Gross
Milwaukee, WI
Luis Guzman
Orlando, FL
Paul Hachey
Atlanta, GA
Kathleen Hahn
Grand Island, NE
Edward Hankiewicz
Grand Rapids, MI
Paul B. Hartmann
Milwaukee, WI
Mary Hauck
Indianapolis, IN
Robert Hayes
San Jose, CA
Denis Heames
Saginaw, MI
Jelisei Heikkila
Helsinki, Finland
Amy Hereford
St. Louis, MO
John Hergenrother
Chicago, IL
Anthony Hewitt
Fort Myers, FL
Patrick Hill
Los Angeles, CA
Marie Hilliard
Philadelphia, PA
Christina Hip-Flores
Camden, NJ

Viet Peter Ho
Orange, CA
Thuan Hoang
San Francisco, CA
Christopher House
Springfield, IL
John Huels
Ottawa, ON
Francisca Igweilo
Denver, CO
James Innocenzi
Trenton, NJ
Eileen Jaramillo
Lansing, MI
Lynn Jarrell
Louisville, KY
John Johnson
Columbus, OH
Gerald Jorgensen
Dubuque, IA
Rita Joyce
Pittsburgh, PA
Michael Joyce
Perryville, MO
Lawrence Jurcak
Parma Heights, OH
Thomas Kadera
Wheatland, WY
Christopher Kadrmas
Bismarck, ND
Robert Kaslyn
Washington, DC
Connie Kassahn
Cheyenne, WY
Nicholas
Kastenholz
St. Louis, MO
Roger Keeler
Washington, DC
Elaine Kerscher
Joliet, IL
Rita Killackey
Kansas City, MO
Adela Maria Kim
Peoria, IL

R. Anne Kirby
Sioux City, IA
Wayne Kirkpatrick
Toronto, ON
David Klein
Camden, NJ
Joseph Klos
Buffalo, NY
Frederick Klotter
Louisville, KY
Dr. Lee Kneipp
Alexandria, LA
Daniela Knepper
Muskego, WI
Jose Kochuparambil
Lubbock, TX
K.S. Kopacz
Fargo, ND
Heidi Krupp
Montrose, MI
Francis Kub
Chicago, IL
Thomas Kunz
Pittsburgh, PA
Robert Lariviere
Ottawa, ON
Daniel Laurita
Athens, AL
Laura LeFave
Dallas, TX
William Leser
Northridge, CA
Andres Ligot
San Jose, CA
Judene Lillie
New Orleans, LA
John List
Lexington, KY
Douglas Loecke
Dubuque, IA
Paul Luniw
Terryville, CT
Vinh Luu
New Orleans, LA

Gregory Luyet
Little Rock, AR
Sandra Makowski
Charleston, SC
Edward Malesic
Harrisburg, PA
Michele Mangan
San Jose, CA
Salvatore Manganello
Buffalo, NY
Peter Mangum
Shreveport, LA
Wilfredo Manrique
San Jose, CA
Kurt Martens
Washington, DC
Peggy Martin
Denver, CO
Sunny Mathew
New York, NY
Joseph Matt
Independence, MO
Reynaldo Matunog
Los Angeles, CA
Valerie Maxineau
Charleston, SC
Herbert J. May
Lake Charles, LA
Robert McBride
Newark, NJ
Jeremiah McCarthy
Columbus, GA
Rose McDermott
Trenton, NJ
Wendy McGrath
Manchester, NH
Fergal McGuinness
Santa Rosa, CA
Linda McKinney
Fort Worth, TX
Maureen McPartland
Dubuque, IA
Mark Mealey
Arlington, VA

Ken Mikulcik
Owensboro, KY
C. Thomas Miles
Charleston, SC
Bruce Miller
Alexandria, LA
Richard Millette
Houston, TX
Christopher Moore
Baltimore, MD
Francis Morrisey
Ottawa, ON
David Motiuk
Edmonton, AB
Robert Nalley
Gaylord, MI
Luis Navarro
Stockton, CA
Dennis Nesser
Dunbar, WV
Joseph Newton
Indianapolis, IN
Truc Nguyen
Los Angeles, CA
Kevin Niehoff
Grand Rapids, MI
Michael Nolan
Wichita, KS
Anthony Norcio
Annapolis, MD
Aaron Nord
St. Louis, MO
Robin Nordyke
Springfield, MO
Nwazi Nyirenda
Austin, TX
Mary Judith O'Brien
Saginaw, MI
Mark O'Connell
Boston, MA
Kelly O'Donnell
Shreveport, LA
Stephen Ogheneovo
Warri, Nigeria

Kathryn Olsen
Oklahoma City, OK
Timothy Olson
Fargo, ND
Sinclair Oubre
Port Arthur, TX
C. Michael Padazinski
San Francisco, CA
Roch Pagé
Ottawa, ON
William Palladino
Boston, MA
Duaine Pamment
Laingsburg, MI
Peggy Paoli
Orange, CA
Thomas Paprocki
Springfield, IL
John Payne
New Orleans, LA
F. Stephen Pedone
Worcester, MA
Lori Peery
Bigfoot, TX
Anthony Pileggi
Kansas City, MO
Robert Pine
Austin, TX
Rafael Pisso-Rivera
Silver Spring, MD
Peter Polando
Youngstown, OH
Jaimes Ponce
Colorado Springs, CO
Stanley Pondo
Indianapolis, IN
Andrea Ponzone
Boston, MA
John Porter
Grand Rapids, MI
Frank Pugliese
San Diego, CA
George Puthusseril
Miami Shores, FL

Daniel Quinan
Eagan, MN
Gerry Quinn
St. Louis, MO
Kevin Quirk
Wheeling, WV
Angel Quitalig
San Francisco, CA
Steven Raica
Gaylord, MI
Marco Rajkovich
Lexington, KY
Margaret Ramsden
Orange, CA
Michael Ravenkamp
San Diego, CA
Gordon Read
Brentwood, England
Ann Rehrauer
Green Bay, WI
Richard Reidy
Worcester, MA
Charles Renati
San Francisco, CA
John Renken
Ottawa, ON
Nancy Reynolds
Louisville, KY
J. Patrick Reynolds
Owensboro, KY
William Reynolds
Newton, IA
Mark Richards
Sacramento, CA
Joseph Richards
Crookston, MN
Thomas Richstatter
St. Meinrad, IN
George Rigazzi
Oklahoma City, OK
Kenneth Riley
Kansas City, MO
J. Michael Ritty
Feura Bush, NY

Giovanni Rizzo
Newark, NJ
Lynda Robitaille
Vancouver, BC
Manuel Rodriguez
Brooklyn, NY
Carolyn Roeber
Seattle, WA
Marie Roldan
San Jose, CA
Meg Romano-Hogan
Fort Worth, TX
Eloise Rosenblatt
San Jose, CA
Patricia Ruiz
Fresno, CA
Marvin Samiano
Honolulu, HI
Mary Santi
Seattle, WA
John Santone
Notre Dame, IN
Alessio Sarais
Rome, Italy
Edward Schaefer
St. Rose, IL
Joseph Scheib
Pittsburgh, PA
Gerald Scherkenbach
St Paul, MN
J. Gerard Schreck
Savannah, GA
Gilbert Seitz
Baltimore, MD
John Sekellick
Passaic, NJ
Donetta Shaw
Kansas City, MO
Patrick Shea
Cleveland, OH
Langes Silva
Salt Lake City, UT
Robert Sinatra
Camden, NJ

Joseph Sinchak
Mobile, AL
Jaroslaw Skrzypek
New Madrid, MO
Daniel Smilanic
Chicago, IL
Mark Smith
Jefferson City, MO
Nathaniel Sokol
Lansing, MI
Richard Soseman
Rome, Italy
Michael Souckar
Coral Springs, FL
Anthony St. Louis-Sanchez
Colorado Springs, CO
Ronald Stake
Chicago, IL
Susan Stankis
Orange, CA
Sahaya Stanly F
Grand Rapids, MI
Jeffrey Steenson
Houston, TX
Peter Sullivan
Albany, NY
David Szatkowski
Nesbit, MS
Amy Tadlock
St. Paul, MN
Michael Taylor
Somersworth, NH
Nancy Thompson
Indianapolis, IN
Charles Thompson
Evansville, IN
Matthew Thundathil
Miami Shores, FL
Gregory Trawick
Cadiz, KY
Ann Tully
Indianapolis, IN

Robert Turner
Pomeroy, WA
Irene Valles
Las Cruces, NM
Kevin Vann
Orange, CA
Marilyn Vassallo
Watervliet, NY
John Vaughan
Madisonville, KY
Carlos Venegas
Denver, CO
Manuel Viera
Tucson, AZ
Michael Vigil
Santa Fe, NM
Mauro Visigalli
Rome, Italy
Victoria Vondenberger
Cincinnati, OH
Justin Wachs
Sioux Falls, SD
Richard Wahl
Houston, TX
James Walsh
Matamoras, PA
A. David
Warriner
New Orleans, LA
Rick Wells
St. Petersburg, FL
Emmett Wells
St. Paul, MN
Daniel Welter
Chicago, IL
Paul Wienhoff
Belleville, IL
Myriam Wijlens
Erfurt, Germany
Thomas Wisniewski
Darby, PA
Patricia Wittberg
Indianapolis, IN
Joseph Wolf
Davenport, IA
Geri Woodward
New Orleans, LA
Jamie Workman
Arlington, VA
Dennis Yurochko
Pittsburgh, PA

Made in the USA
Monee, IL
04 November 2026

67381624R10262